ESSAYS ON CHINESE PHILOSOPHY AND CULTURE

by T'ang Chun-i

唐君毅全集 卷十九

英文論著彙編

臺灣 學生書局 印行

Student Book Co., Ltd.

ESSAYS ON CHINESE PHILOSOPHY AND CULTURE

by T'ang Chun-i

1

The Development of Ideas of
Spiritual Value in Chinese Philosophy

Before I talk about the ideas of spiritual value in Chinese philosophy, I will define what I call spiritual value.

By the word "spirit" I mean any self-conscious subject and its activities which are initiated by self-conscious ideas. Any value which has the following characteristics is called spiritual: (1) created or realized "by the spirit"; (2) presented or revealed to the spirit, that is, "for the spirit"; (3) self-consciously recognized as such in (1) and (2), and then the value can be predicated on the spirit, that is, "of the spirit."

According to (1) of the above definition, we can differentiate spiritual values from the values of outer natural objects and from the values of the satisfaction of our natural instincts. Outer natural objects usually have the value of utility, for they are instrumental in the realization or attainment of spiritual aims or purposes. Sometimes, outer natural objects may have some aesthetic values which are presented to our enjoying spirit, too. However, at least at the moment when we say these values are created or originated or manifested by outer Nature and belong to outer Nature they are not spiritual values. It is generally agreed, too, that, when our instinctive desires are satisfied in instinctive ways, there is the realization of natural values which need not be taken as spiritual.

According to (2) of the definition, we can differentiate spiritual values from a certain kind of social values which come from the effects of a certain action (or actions) of a person (or persons) on other persons and the whole historical society. As the chain of effects of human action may stretch and extend to an indefinite number of persons, areas of society, and even ages in history, the social values of a human action cannot all be presented and known by any personal spiritual subject except God. These values are always realized outside

1

the self-consciousness of the person who performs the action. Therefore, the existential status of these values should be said to be in the historical society as a whole and not within any particular personal spirit.

According to (3) of the definition, we may differentiate a genuine spiritual value from a certain quasi-spiritual value, which is created by a certain spirit and then presented to that same spirit but is not self-consciously recognized as such. For example, the imagery of a dream may be merely symbols of a spiritual idea we have had before. Thus, it is created by our spirit and presented to our spirit. However, when we are dreaming, the aesthetic value of the imagery seems to belong to the imagery itself and is not self-consciously recognized as created "by the spirit," "for the spirit," and "of the spirit." This is not a genuine spiritual value. So, any value of human activity, though originally created by the spirit and presented to the spirit, if its origin is forgotten and taken as belonging to the world outside the spirit, is only a quasi-spiritual value, which is alienated from the originating spirit itself.

From the above, we may say that the first group of spiritual values are the values of moral and religious activities. Generally speaking, in moral and religious activities, one is self-consciously commanding himself how to act, to meditate, or to pray. All such activities are initiated, at least to some degree, by one's spiritual subject in the very beginning, and their values, such as goodness, peace of mind, holiness, and so on, are more or less taken as created or realized by the spiritual subject and presented for the spiritual subject, and can be taken as inhering in, and then predicated of, the same spiritual subject.

The second kind of spiritual values consists of those of the artistic and intellectual activities of man. It is doubtless that there are values of beauty and truth realized by, and presented to, the spiritual subject through one's spiritual activities, such as speculative thinking, experimental observation, and creative imagination. Yet, the truth-value or beauty-value is not only capable of describing the spiritual activities of man but also can be predicated of aesthetic objects or the objective realities as outside of the spirit of men. It is much more difficult to say that moral goodness and peace of mind exist in themselves outside the spirit or personality of man, even when we believe in a Platonic metaphysics of value. Thus, the spiritual values of artistic and intellectual activities are differentiated from the moral and religious values, and they may not have the same degree of spirituality.

The third kind of spiritual values consists of natural values and social values, defined above as non-spiritual, which are transformed into spiritual values. These transformations are achieved usually by highly exalted spiritual activities. For example, the utility or beauty of natural objects is generally taken as having originated from the objects themselves. If we, as some poets, religious men, and metaphysicians have done, take man and Nature as created by some absolute spirit, such as God or Brahman, or as the manifestation of some absolute spirit, then all the utilitarian aesthetic values of natural objects may be taken as having originated from the same spiritual substance of man, in which case the values of natural objects can be taken as transformed into spiritual values.

On the question as to how social value also can be transformed into spiritual value, the crucial point is that any social value of one's action which is taken as outside the personal spirit can also be taken as inside the spirit by the more fully developed moral consciousness of the subject. For example, a discovery in the theoretical study of a scientist may benefit mankind in the indefinite future and generate infinite social values which are beyond the expectation of the theoretical consciousness of the scientist. Yet, if the moral consciousness of the scientist is fully developed into infinite love of mankind, such as the love of Jesus or the *jen*[b] (humanity, love, benevolence) of Confucius (551–479 B.C.), then he understands that all the social values generated from his inventive action are by principle such as can satisfy his love of mankind, although all the details of all the effects of his action could never be foretold by him. If the satisfaction of this love is purely spiritual and has spiritual value, then the actual realization of any social value of his present discovery any time in the future is at the same time a realization of the spiritual value of his present love of mankind. The realizations of these two kinds of values are co-extensive and equivalent in domain, at least in his present lofty moral consciousness. Therefore, for this consciousness, all social values which are not taken as external values become internalized, immanently present to the spiritual subject, and thus transformed into spiritual values. Needless to say, outside such a lofty moral consciousness, the social value is just a social value, just as, outside the consciousness of poets, religious men, and metaphysicians, as mentioned above, natural value is merely a natural value.

II. SPIRITUAL VALUES IN CONFUCIAN MORAL TEACHINGS AND THE KEY CONCEPT OF "SEARCHING IN ONESELF"

The Confucian school and the Taoist school are the main currents of thought of native Chinese philosophy. They and Buddhism have usually been mentioned together and called "*san-chiao*,"[c] three teachings or three religions. Generally speaking, these three teachings all intend to deepen spiritual experience, cultivate the spiritual life of man, and have much social-cultural influence on the Chinese historical society. Hence, if we wish to know the main ideas of spiritual value in Chinese philosophy, we have to study them in the Confucian and Taoist and Buddhist philosophies.

It is held by some writers that there are no really spiritual values in Confucianism. It is said that in the body of Confucianism dealing with the virtues of men in definite relations only social values can be realized. Some contend that when Confucius talked about the importance of the cultivation of these virtues he always said this is a way for preserving the social solidarity of the nation or the peace of the world or for training the people to be contented with their circumstances and not to offend their superiors. These values are therefore alleged to be only socio-political and not spiritual values as defined

4

above. Others contend that when Confucius talked about the values of the virtues he was considering the values as a means to the achieving of harmony and order in human relations, which were taken as a part of the harmony and order of the natural universe. Yet, the harmony and order of the natural universe may have a natural value only and not necessarily a spiritual value.[1]

The views which efface the ideas of spiritual value from the Confucian ethical system are not without some justification. Actually, many Confucians in the course of Chinese history, such as those of the Yung-k'ang school[d] and Yung-chia school[e] of the Sung Dynasty (960–1279), and Yen Yüan[f] (1635–1704) and Tai Chen[g] (1723–1777) of the Ch'ing Dynasty (1644–1912), laid their emphasis on the exposition of the social utilitarian value of ethical actions. Many Confucians in the Han Dynasty (206 B.C.–A.D. 220) emphasized the natural value of ethical action.

But, from our point of view, the values of the virtues in Confucian ethics should be considered essentially spiritual values. The central idea of virtue peculiar to Confucius, Mencius (371–289 B.C. ?), and the Neo-Confucianism of the Sung-Ming period (960–1644) is to consider the virtues as the inner essence of one's personality, and their values as intrinsic to one's moral consciousness and tinged with a certain religious meaning, and thus as definitely spiritual values. The key concept in this interpretation is the concept of "searching in oneself," which is a teaching handed down from Confucius himself and developed by all later Confucians. I shall explain its meaning from three aspects.

(1) In the first aspect, "searching in oneself" means that in all ethical relations one has to do his duty to others, but not require others to do their duties to him, reciprocally, though the others should do their duties of their own accord. In order to explain this we have to know that there are three ways to develop one's spiritual life to the fullest extent, and all three may be called in a certain sense "backward ways."

The first way is to get real freedom from all the instinctive and irrational desires in human life. The extreme of this is what Schopenhauer called the denial or mortification of the will. This way is practiced, more or less, by all ascetics and mystics, as a negative step in the very beginning of spiritual cultivation for the higher positive spiritual development.

The second way searches for some kind of higher or highest Idea or Existence in the very beginning of spiritual cultivation which is supernatural and transcendent, such as the Idea of the Good in Plato and the self-existent God in the otherworldly religions. We may call this the way of leaving the mundane world behind, in our process of spiritual ascent.

The third way is to live in definite ethical relations with others in the actual world, practicing the morality of doing one's duty to others but not asking them to do their duties, reciprocally, as taught in Confucianism. This way of

[1] Many writers, such as Ch'en Tu-hsiu[h] (1879–1942) in the period of the New Culture movement at the beginning of the Republic of China, took the utilitarian point of view to interpret the ethical value of Confucian teachings, and some missionaries and naturalism-biased Chinese scholars usually interpret the ethical values of Confucian teachings as just natural values in contrast with the supernatural or spiritual values.

life may be called the way of thinking or acting morally just for oneself, which is opposite to the "forward way of asking others to do something morally for me," as in the common attitude of our daily life. It is a "backward" way of life and is as difficult to put into practice as the other two ways.

The difficulties of this third way arise from the fact that when one does his duty to others he naturally supposes that others are moral beings like himself. According to the universal principle of reason, man naturally expects others to do their duties in response to his action. Thus, he naturally thinks he has the right to demand that others do their duties. Actually, social justice and legislation are based upon the reciprocity of rights and duties. One who does his duty without asking others to do theirs is the same as one who has only duty-consciousness without right-consciousness and lives beyond the idea of social justice. In duty-consciousness, one does what his conscience commands him to do, and never goes beyond his conscience to see what happens in other consciences, and so the value realized is completely internal to his conscience and is therefore a purely spiritual moral value. If I have this kind of duty-consciousness in full degree, then, the less others do their duty to me, the more I shall do my duty to others. That is to say, the more my expectation from others is disappointed, the more intensified is my self-expectation from myself. The value of social justice, which is offended and lost because others do not do their duty, is recompensed and satisfied by the moral values of my fulfillment, which is purely spiritual and belongs to my inward life. Yet, this kind of duty-consciousness is the most difficult for human beings, because we have to do to others more than they deserve. What we do to others is the same as the grace of deity conferred on man though man may not be aware of it or respond to it with a sense of thanksgiving. It is significant that Christians translate the word "grace" with the Chinese word "*en*"[b] in the term "*en-i*,"[1] which means that one does his duty without reciprocation, and so confers something which is absolutely beyond what others deserve. Therefore, we may say that in the first meaning of "searching in oneself" in Confucianism a deification of human life is implied and has religious and spiritual meanings.

(2) The second meaning of "searching in oneself" is that one ought to cultivate his virtues and abilities without asking praise from others. This is also very difficult to practice due to the fact that men, motivated by the universal principle of reason, naturally want others to appreciate or approve what they themselves have appreciated or approved. This desire may not be morally bad, if it is accompanied by a moral feeling of respect when we request it from others and accompanied by our gratitude when we receive it from others. But, leaving the desire for praise itself alone and as unconditionally right, then we may simply take the praise of others as personal gratification. When we are anxious to receive this kind of gratification, many modes of moral evils, such as ambition, or the will to power to control the will of others, or disloyalty to one's original ideals in flattering others and then receiving praise in return, can be generated in different circumstances. When I ask the praise of others, I

6

am taking my virtues, and abilities and their expressions in actions and speech
as a means, and they then have only instrumental or utilitarian value, which
is non-spiritual social value or quasi-spiritual value as defined in Section I,
above.[2]

If our ordinary outward desire of gaining others' praise is diminished, we
may live a life which is directed by our moral conscience itself. We can then
eradicate the roots of our desire to control the will of others; we will never be
disloyal to the moral ideal in order to please men, and, at the same time, never
have any complaint or grudge against others or Heaven. This is the meaning
of the Confucian saying: "There is no one that knows me. . . . I do not murmur
against Heaven. I do not grumble against men. . . . But it is Heaven that knows
me."[3] This is a kind of deified human life.

(3) The third meaning of "searching in oneself" is that all the moral principles, moral ideals, and moral values of our actions and intentions can be
discovered by self-reflection. This is strongly implied in the teaching of Confucius, and is explicitly stated and elaborated in the teaching of Mencius and
many later Confucians, as in the thesis that "human nature is good.".

The thesis that "human nature is good" has had various interpretations in
the various schools of Confucianism. In the teaching of Mencius, the first
exponent of this thesis, the doctrine does not say that all men's actions or intentions are actually good enough. It says simply that there are good tendencies or
good beginnings in human nature and, most important, that, when we have
good intentions or do good actions, there is usually an accompanying feeling
of self-satisfaction or self-joy or self-peace.[4] This may be said to be deep self-
praise when I find my intention or action is really good. This deep self-praise
is usually concealed when we are eager to ask for praise from others or when
we lack deep self-reflection. Yet, when we withdraw the desire to ask others for
praise and have deep reflection, then everybody can find the deep self-praise
which accompanies all good intentions or good actions. However, this deep
self-praise is a result of my deepest self-evaluation, which immediately follows
my intention or action. This self-evaluation reveals to me what is good as good
and what is not good as not good, and from the former I feel self-satisfaction,
self-joy, and self-peace, but from the latter I feel disquieted, unjoyful, and dissatisfied. As my mind feels self-peace or self-joy or self-satisfaction in the good
only, so my human nature is disclosed as essentially good. I shall take this as
the orthodox doctrine of the thesis that "human nature is good," which was
morally expounded in Mencius' teaching, was metaphysically explained
by Chu Hsi's[j] (1130–1200) theory of Li^k (Principle, Reason, or Law), and culminated in the teaching of $liang$-$chih^l$ (almost the same as conscience) in Wang
Shou-jen's (Wang Yang-ming,[m] 1472–1529) philosophy.

If we take human nature as essentially good, moral ideals and moral prin-

---

[2] Cf. my essay, *Tsai ching-shen sheng-huo fa-chan chung chih hui-yü i-shih*[am] ("A Phenomenological
Study of the Consciousness of Praise and Defamation in the Development of Spiritual Life"), *Jen-sheng*,[an] X,
No. 1 (1954).

[3] Cf. Legge's translation: *Confucian Analects* XXXVII.

[4] The Chinese words are *"chih-te"*[ao] for self-satisfaction, *"yüeh"*[ap] for self-joy, *"an"*[aq] for self-peace.

ciples are nothing other than the norms or standards awakened within or originating in the nature of our mind and immanently presented to our moral self-consciousness for self-evaluation. Consequently, our moral training and moral cultivation have no other purpose than to preserve and extend what is judged or evaluated as good, and all the achievements of moral life and the formation of a moral personality express no more than the desire to conform to these immanent norms or standards, to realize what originates from the nature of the mind, and to know to the maximum what is implicitly contained in the nature of the mind.

However, in the development of our moral life, any phase of our ordinary life which is taken by common sense as non-moral or immoral can be evaluated as either good or evil. So, every phase of our life has moral meaning, can be moralized by a certain cultivation, and then has moral value, which can be presented immediately to our self-reflection, as defined above, and become a purely internal value. It is not difficult to see that if we resolve to have all the phases of our life moralized, then our self-evaluations and self-reflections may arise successfully and co-extensively with the extensions of all phases of life, including those phases of our life which are considered by common sense as merely directing to, or dealing with, the so-called external environment.

Hence, self-evaluation and self-reflection should not be taken as subjective and self-closed, but should also be taken as objective and self-open to all the other social and natural objects of the universe as our whole environment. Here the "investigation of things" as taught by Confucianism has not only intellectual value but also moral value, and then we may have the wisdom that all the objects in the universe can be taken as the occasions for the realization of spiritual moral values, and that all may be lighted and permeated by spiritual and moral values as well. This is the vision of the moral man, who realizes his good nature, develops his moral life to the fullest extent, attains unity of the inner world and the outer world, and achieves the grandeur and beauty of personality as expounded in the *Doctrine of the Mean*[5] and the *Book of Mencius*.

III. (1) HUMAN NATURE AS GOOD, (2) HEAVEN, (3) MIND, AND (4) THE UNIVERSAL ATTAINABILITY OF SAGEHOOD

If we compare the thesis that human nature is good with the idea of original sin in Christianity or the *karma* theory and the *avidyā* theory of Buddhism, there are many pros and cons worthy of discussion. Yet, if we acknowledge the existence of original sin or impure *karma* in the depth of our mind, we may still believe that human nature is essentially good. We may hold that original sin and impure *karma* are not derived from real human nature, but that the feeling of unrest that arises when we are told we have original sin or impure *karma* originates from our real human nature. This nature, as revealed in unrest, is the same as the nature revealed in our unpeacefulness in our evils,

---

[5] Cf. the *Doctrine of the Mean* XXV.

and is absolutely good. In the feeling of unrest, of course, I may find at the same time that I am so weak as to try to set myself free from the bondage of original sin or impure *karma*, and I may pray to some transcendent being, such as God, Brahman, or Amida Buddha, to save me. In this type of religious consciousness, we think our nature is not good enough. Yet, the very confession of our weakness and our praying come from our nature, too. Our very confession may not be weak, and our praying must be good in itself. If it is objected that the very confession and words of prayer do not come from our human nature, but are the result of human nature as affected by a transcendent being or receiving grace from above, then we reply that our capacity for being (and our unconscious willingness to be) affected and receiving grace are additional evidences that human nature is essentially good. If we deny this, then how is it possible that men can be saved? The thesis that human nature is good does not fundamentally oppose the ultimate teachings of Christianity or Brahmanism or Buddhism, which believe either that man is the image of God, or that man is Brahman, or that the Buddha is a sentient being awakened to the fullest extent. Therefore, the thesis that human nature is good cannot be denied, even if we concede the existence of original sin or impure *karma,* because we can reassert our nature as good again in the very self-reflection of our unrest or unpeacefulness in our evils and our very unwillingness to be bound by them. However, the Confucian thesis that human nature is good is still different from many religious points of view which take the evil origin of human actions much more seriously and believe that only a transcendent being can save man from evil. The crucial point is that men who hold the latter point of view always look at human nature as a mere potentiality and insist that the principle of its actuality resides in some transcendent being. Yet, from the thesis that human nature is good the principle of actualization is seen to be immanent in human nature.[6]

What we have said above does not imply that Confucian thought lacks the idea of a transcendent reality, such as God, the Mind of Heaven, or the Universal Mind. In fact, many Confucians have these ideas. The real difference between the Confucian point of view and the above religious point of view is that, in the latter, the idea of a transcendent being, such as God, Brahman, etc., is more easily brought to light by contrasting it with our sin or impure *karma* or bondage; while, in the former, the idea of the Mind of Heaven, the Universal Mind, God, or Heaven is usually brought to light by the positive development of our moral life to the fullest extent, with the knowledge that the transcendent being is at the same time immanent in our moral life. How is it possible to have these ideas brought to light by the positive development of our moral lives? The answer was suggested in the teaching of Mencius and culminated in the Neo-Confucians of the Sung-Ming period, who had a deep understanding of the thesis that human nature is good.

Briefly, the central theme of this trend of thought is that when we develop

---

[6] For example, in Aristotelian-Thomian metaphysical and religious thought, human nature is usually taken as a potentiality in contrast with God, which is pure actuality.

our moral life to the fullest extent, as a sage does, the essence of our good nature is wholly actualized in, presented to, and known by, our self-consciousness. The essence of our good nature may be said to be *jen*, which is love, beginning with filial piety, and flowing out as universal love to all the men with whom I have definite ethical relations, to all the people under Heaven, and to all natural things. So, the moral consciousness of *jen*, in its fullest extent, is all-embracing love, which pervades, permeates, and fills heaven and earth as a whole. So, Mencius said: "The virtuous man transforms all experiences he passes through and abides in holiness or deity-nature. His virtues are confluent with heaven above and with earth below."[7] Chang Tsai (Chang Heng-ch'ü,[n] 1020–1077), Ch'eng Hao (Ch'eng Ming-tao,[o] 1032–1085), Ch'eng I (Ch'eng I-ch'uan,[p] 1033–1107), and Chu Hsi had the same idea, namely, that the man who realizes *jen* considers Heaven, Earth, and the ten thousand things as one body. Lu Chiu yüan (Lu Hsiang-shan,[q] 1139–1193) said: "The universe is my mind and my mind is the universe." Wang Shou-jen said: "Pervading Heaven and Earth is just this spiritual light—my spiritual light—which is not separated by, or separated from, Heaven, Earth, deities, and the ten thousand things."[8] But is this mind only my own? In the mind which identifies itself with the universe, where is the dividing point between what is mine and what is not mine? When selfish ideas and motives are transformed into universal and all-pervading love, where is the borderline or the boundary between our mind and the universe? Why can I not take this type of mind as belonging to me and also to Heaven? Why can I not take this type of mind both as created and presented by myself and as revealed and descended to me from Heaven? Is its belonging-to-me incompatible with its belonging-to-Heaven? If I take this kind of mind as mine and not of Heaven, does this not simply contradict the very nature of this kind of mind, which has no borderline to differentiate itself from what is not itself and which is felt as a universal and all-pervading mind? Therefore, when I have this kind of mind and know its nature truly, I shall never take this mind merely as my own; I shall know that this kind of mind is conferred by Heaven as much as it is mine and I shall know Heaven (which was originally synonymous with the word "God" in the Chinese Classics). As this kind of mind is the mind of one who develops his moral life to the fullest extent, and whose *jen* is wholly actualized as a sage, so the sage is said to be the same as Heaven, and human nature is therefore sometimes called Heaven-nature, and the human mind is called the mind of Heaven in some Confucian literature. So, Mencius said: "To have our mind preserved and Nature nourished is the way to serve Heaven" and "The man who has passed through the stage of completing his virtues and sheds forth his spiritual light brilliantly, and then can transform the world, is called a sage. The sage, unfathomable by intellect, is called holy or divine."[9]

Yet, the highest teaching of Confucianism is not merely the realization that

[7] This is my own translation of the *Book of Mencius* VIB.13.
[8] Wang Shou-jen: *Ch'uan-hsi lu*[ar] ("Records of Instructions for Practice"), III.
[9] My free translation of the *Book of Mencius* VIIB. 25, from 5 to 9, and condensed into two sentences.

the sage is the same as Heaven, but the realization of the universal attainability of sagehood for all men and what is implied by it. The universal attainability of sagehood is a logical consequence of the belief that human nature is good. The sage is the man who has fully realized his nature. If all men have the same good human nature, surely all can realize their nature and attain sagehood. Furthermore, the universal attainability of sagehood is itself an immanent belief of the mind of the sage. Since the mind of the sage is full of love and unselfishness in the fullest extent, he could not have any idea that he is the only sage, because this is selfish and contradictory to the very nature of his mind. He must love to see, expect, and hope that everyone else shall be a sage. Therefore, the universal attainability of sagehood is a belief immanently involved in the mind of the sage. If I believe there is a sage, or if I can be a sage, then I have to think of the idea of the sage through the mind of the sage, and thus the universal attainability of sagehood is also involved in my idea. Yet, according to the thesis that human nature is good, I must believe there is a sage and that I can be one, because sagehood is nothing more than my own nature, *jen*, wholly realized. So, I must believe in the universal attainability of sagehood.[10]

According to the idea of the universal attainability of sagehood, an actual sage can be born at any time and any place in the world, and no one sage of any particular place or particular time has the privilege to be the only sage. As all sages have the same fundamental virtue, *jen*, or universal love, so all sages go in the same way, and are of the same spirit of mind, and live with the same principle or the same Tao.[r][11] This idea led the Chinese people to believe that there can be sages in different religions of different peoples.[12] This is one reason there were no religious wars or large-scale religious persecutions in Chinese history. So, this idea has its religious value.

Furthermore, when we know there is a single spirit, or a single mind, or a single principle, or a single Tao in the world of sages, we have to know one thing more. This is: "I can know all this in my here-and-now mind." This is to say that I can comprehend what is universal and all-pervading in the world of sages in my here-and-now mind. So, the world of sages is as much immanent in my here-and-now spiritual world as it is transcendent to my here-and-now

[10] Cf. on the spiritual aspect of forgiving, chap. 12, sec. 9, of my book: *Chung-kuo jen-wen ching-shen chih fa-chan*[a] ("The Development of the Chinese Humanistic Spirit").

[11] About the universal attainability of sagehood, we may cite the saying of Mencius and Lu Chiu-yüan. Mencius said: "Those regions (of Shun and King Wen,[af] reigned 1171–1122 B.C.) were distant from one another more than a thousand *li*[au] (about a third of a mile) and the age of one sage was later than that of the other by more than a thousand years. But . . . the principles of the earlier sage and the later sage are the same." (Legge's translation, *Book of Mencius* IVA.1.) Lu Chiu-yüan said: "The universe is my mind and my mind is the universe. If in the Eastern Sea there were to appear a sage, he would have this same mind and this principle (*Li*). If in the Western Sea, there were to appear a sage, he would have this same mind and same principle. If in the Southern or Northern Seas, there were to appear sages, they, too, would have this same mind and this same principle. If a hundred or a thousand generations ago, or a hundred or a thousand generations hence, sages were to appear, they (likewise) would have this same mind and this same principle." Fung Yu-lan,[av] *A History of Chinese Philosophy*, Derk Bodde, trans. (Princeton: Princeton University Press, 1953), Vol. II, p. 537.

[12] In the *Lieh Tzu*,[aw] supposedly written by a Taoist philosopher of the pre-Ch'in period, there is a paragraph about the sage of the West which was originally taken as an argument to convince Chinese people that the Buddha is a Western sage. Yet, when Jesuits came to China during the Ming Dynasty, this sentence was reinterpreted by Matteo Ricci in his book, *T'ien-chu shih-i*,[ax] as the prophecy of Jesus Christ as a Western sage.

actual existence. When I am awakened to this idea, then all that is remote, such as the highest ideals or holy virtues of sages, is nearest to my here-and-now mind, and all the values of the highest ideals and holy virtues belong to my mind as much as they do to the minds of sages themselves. This is perhaps the highest idea of human spiritual life expounded by the thinkers of the late Ming (1368–1644) after Wang Shou-jen. It is too subtle to explain all its meanings here.[13]

IV. SPIRITUAL VALUES IN TAOISM

The Taoist ideas about spiritual life were usually expounded as in contrast with the life of worldly man. Such names as "real man," "Heavenly man," "spirit-man" or "divine man," "perfect man," and "sage man" were used by Taoist philosophers to differentiate their ideal man from the worldly man.

The Taoist philosophers, who looked aloof at everything here, felt some fatigue in worldly affairs and sought spiritual quiescence and tranquillity, and then, withdrawing their minds from worldly things, were men who had a transcendent mentality. The Taoist philosophers usually thought and spoke about their ideals of human life *negatively*, unlike the Confucians, who usually thought and spoke *positively*. Lao Tzu[s] (6th century B.C.) taught men to be weak, soft, quiet, and foolish, instead of strong, hard, active, and wise. Chuang Tzu[t] (399–295 B.C. ?) taught man not to seek reputation, honor, or social success, to forget himself and be indifferent to worldly gain and loss, happiness and misery, and life and death. They taught people to live a way of life which is neither driven by instinctive desires nor motivated by calculation, forgetting worldly benefits. So, the value of their ideal life is quite beyond the category of the satisfaction of natural desires and utilitarian value as defined in Section I, above. But what is the spiritual value of this kind of life, which seems purely negative and from which we can derive nothing?

The answer is twofold. First, the Taoist ideal of life has its positive side. Second, this positive value of life can be realized by living in a negative way. I shall begin with the latter point.

The reason the positive value of life can be realized by living in a negative way is very simple. If our ordinary way of living is considered of no value or of disvalue, then not living in this way is a positive value. For example, if the toil of the whole day is considered to be disvalue, is not rest itself a positive value? The important thing is that the negating of disvalue should be presented to the spiritual subject. If the negating of disvalue is presented to a spiritual subject, the value of the negating itself is positively presented to the spiritual subject, immanently exists in the subject, and becomes positive spiritual value. So, when I am not seeking worldly wealth, reputation, and honor, which are considered to be of disvalue, the very quiescence and tranquillity in my non-

---

[13] The sayings of Wang Lung-ch'i[ay] (1498–1583), Lo Chin-ch'i[az] (1515–1588), Lo Nien-an[ba] (1504–1564), and Liu Ch'i-shan, [bb] (1578–1645) are available in *Ming-jü hsiieh-an*[bc] ("Writings of Ming Confucians"), edited and written by Huang Tsung-hsi.

seeking can be presented to my spiritual self as full of positive value (just as rest after a day of toil can be presented as of positive value).

If we understand this clearly, then we know there are as many kinds of values experienced by the men who want to transcend worldly things as by men who cling to worldly things. The sense of tranquillity and quiescence of the men who transcend worldly things successfully seems homogeneously extended. Yet, under this homogeneous extension, the heterogeneous worldly things are transcended co-extensively. So, the spiritual content of the life of the man who transcends worldly things is as full as the life of the worldly man, the difference being that all worldly things are transcended and superseded in his mind. From this point we may proceed to the reason many Eastern and Western mystics who see the transcendent world as Divine Nothing estimate the value of the Divine Nothing as higher than everything, full of everything that has been superseded, and as a Divine All-Being.

The problem of all mystics, who want to transcend worldly things, is that the deep quiescence or tranquillity of the spirit is not easily preserved, and the Divine Nothing is not easily revealed. So, it may be easily concluded that, without faith in a transcendent savior who descends from above to help us ascend to the transcendent world, we can never raise ourselves. However, in Oriental religious and metaphysical thought there is an idea which is most important: that it is not necessary for us to have faith in a transcendent savior to help us transcend the mundane world. Instead, we may have wisdom to see that worldly things are themselves sunk down and have no power to disturb our tranquillity and quiescence of mind and that the world is itself a place where something like the Divine Nothing reveals itself. This is the wisdom of Nothing in Taoist philosophy.

This wisdom is very simple in essence. It is the realization that any worldly thing begins in or comes from "where it is not," or "Nothing," through a process of transformation or change, and ends at or goes back to "where it is not." Then, "beginning and ending in Nothing" is the general nature of all things and the Great Way, or Tao, where all things pass through. This idea is based primarily on our everyday experience. Everybody agrees, at least from the point of view of phenomena, that the future is what has not "yet been" and is now nothing, and that the present, which was the future and becomes the past, may be said to come from Nothing and go to Nothing. If we know deeply that everything comes from the Nothing and goes back to Nothing, then all things may be taken as involved in a Great Nothing,[14] or as floating out from the Great Nothing, only to sink into it again. Then not anything can really constitute bondage or disturb our spirit. When its very nature of "shall-be-sinking" is really presented to me in the immediate present, it is already nothing and has no effect as a disturbance or bondage for me even now.

---

[14]Taoist philosophers used the word "wu,"[bd] which has not actually the same sense of "nothing." "Wu" means nothing or non-being in phemomena but may not mean nothing or non-being in reality. We use the phrase "Great Nothing" here as the translation of the word "wu" to indicate that it is like nothing in the phenomenal world, yet it may be something in reality.

The two great founders of Taoist philosophy, Lao Tzu and Chuang Tzu, both present the wisdom of Nothing in metaphysics as the theoretical basis for the development of the spiritual life of tranquillity and quiescence so as to achieve an actual transcendence over worldly things. This is the negative side of their teachings. On the positive side, there are differences in their teachings on the spiritual life. When Lao Tzu thought about the relation of worldly things to the "Nothing," he usually thought that worldly things were involved and contained in the Nothing. The ideal spiritual life, corresponding to this metaphysical vision, is identified in our mind or spirit with the Nothing and is free from all the limitations of finite particular worldly things. Thus we can comprehend and embrace all things without partiality. When this kind of mind is used in political philosophy, it is the mind of a sage-king, which has no special reaction to any particular thing, but is glad to see all things and actions of all people well done, and embraces all people as his children. This kind of mind is mild, kind, soft, as broad as Heaven or the Void, always wishing for all things to go their own way, and tolerating them, following them, and never interfering with them. This is the first aspect of Lao Tzu's teaching, which has cultivated the virtue of tolerance and broad-mindedness in the Chinese people, and has provided Chinese government with the political ideals of non-interference with people, concession to the will of the people, and so on.

In the second aspect of Lao Tzu's teaching, the mind, which is identified with Nothing and is as broad as Heaven or the Void, may simply contemplate the "coming and going," "birth and death," and "prosperity and decay" of all things without affection or mercy. It is the mind of a spectator of the universe. It is neither morally bad, nor morally good, and maintains ethical neutrality. The metaphysical truth is thus presented to this mind with a kind of intellectual value.

In the third aspect of Lao Tzu's teaching, the mind, which knows that what is prosperous shall decay, that what is strong shall become weak, and that what is born shall die, can generalize all these into a principle: Everything moves in a curve which represents the natural law of all things. According to this principle, when a thing reaches the top of the curve it is destined to fall. Therefore, if we do not want to be a victim of this natural law, the only way is never to progress to the top of the curve, or, when we do approach the top, to go back to the beginning of the curve again, for then the top of the curve will always be in our purview, but we shall never arrive there, and so we shall never fall. So, Lao Tzu taught us to go backward, to learn the way of the child or the female, and to be humble and modest, in order to preserve our vitality and other powers to prevent falling down. This is the utilitarian aspect of Lao Tzu's philosophy, which is neither morally good nor morally bad and may not include any spiritual value to be realized by this kind of mind.

In contrast with Lao Tzu, when Chuang Tzu thought about the things of the world, he did not hold that all things are contained in the Great Nothing, but paid more attention to the great process of incessant change or transformation of all things in the Infinite Heaven. In this process, all definite forms and

14

colors of things come into being and pass away. So, this process can also be taken as a great change or transformation of a Great Ether or Air, which is itself formless and colorless, being combined with non-being. Since Chuang Tzu paid more attention to the process of transformation in the universe, his view of human life placed more emphasis on the spiritual transformation of human life itself. If one wants to be a real man or a man of Heaven, free from one's past habits or ordinary self, one ought to live a life of spiritual flight, or spiritual wandering, through the process of the infinite transformations in the universe. He should also take all things as equals when they are presented and enjoyed by one's spirit, yet without judging them as good or bad from one's partial, personal point of view. In its flight or wandering in the universe, one's spirit sees everything with empathy and takes the myriad forms as the forms of things which it encounters, yet without attachment to any one, and lets the forms successfully be taken and then left. When the form of anything is left, then nothing remains and nothing needs to be remembered. When the form of anything is being taken, it is absolutely new, just as the world which is present to the new-born child or new-born animal is preceded by nothing, and, as we may not expect anything from it, is followed by nothing. It is immediately presented and enjoyed, as if it were floating in an infinite Void or Heaven as its background. This is the way of life of the real man, the man of Heaven, or the spirit-man of Chuang Tzu. Therefore, the word "spirit" (*shen*[u]), which originally meant an invisible spirit which existed objectively, was used by Chuang Tzu as the name of the spiritual mood or activity of the spirit-man which extends his spirit beyond the limitation of the universe. He used *"shen-yü"*[v] (literally, spirit-meeting) as the term for the way of the ideal man when he encounters anything immediately with empathy for the moment, without attachment.[15]

From the above, we may conclude that the spirit of Chuang Tzu's way of life is more aesthetic than Lao Tzu's way of life, which comprehends all things from above, but is, rather, a universal way of all things in heaven and earth, and so can appreciate with empathy the beauties of all things or the "beauty of heaven and earth," as he called it.[16] Yet, this kind of beauty does not consist simply in the forms of things. As every form exists in the process of "transformation of ether or air," so the most beautiful forms should never be clear-cut and should be permeated by the flow of ether and become ethereal forms. As the forms pass through the ether and return, they create rhythms. Ethereal rhythm (*ch'i-yün*[w]) is a key term of Chinese aesthetics; it has the Infinite Void or Heaven as its background. It permeates the whole universe charged with life.[17]

---

[15] The whole paragraph is my elaboration of Chuang Tzu's idea of spiritual life. It would require much space to cite all the documents concerned with comments which are omitted.

[16] Cf. *Chuang Tzu* XXII.

[17] This is just a way of deducing an idea of Chinese aesthetics from the philosophy of Chuang Tzu. Historically speaking, the idea of Chinese aesthetics has its origin in the philosophy of Confucianism, too. But, as we know that almost all the later Chinese artists liked to read Chuang Tzu, we have more reason to suppose that the philosophy of Chuang Tzu influenced the aesthetic ideas of later artists prominently.

V. BUDDHIST IDEAS AS A SUPPLEMENT TO
CHINESE PHILOSOPHY

From the Chinese point of view, the Buddhist theory of the non-permanence of everything is very similar to the Taoist idea that everything is in a process of change, as coming from Nothing and returning to Nothing. Yet, impermanence in Buddhism is based on the principle of *yüan-sheng*,[x] sometimes translated as causal or dependent origination, meaning that everything is a combination of conditions. (It was never consciously posited by Lao Tzu or Chuang Tzu.) The meaning of *yüan-sheng* is simple in itself. It leads our thinking from the assertion that "a thing is generated by its conditions and has no 'self' concealed in it to sustain its existence" to the assertion that "the self-nature or self-essence of a thing is emptiness," that is, that there is no such self-nature.

To show that *śūnyatā* is the nature of everything, according to the theory of *yüan-sheng*, the Buddhists argue that, if we know a thing is generated by its conditions, then there is absolutely nothing which exists as such, before or after all conditions have met together. Since all the conditions which come together can be separated, nothing has any permanence, and what is existing can also be non-existing. Therefore, the existing thing has no self-nature or self-essence to sustain its existence, and the possibility of its non-existence is the very nature of its existence. (This is *śūnyatā*.) Yet, when we really know this starting point and other, further theories of *śūnyatā*, we have to see directly and intuitively the *śūnyatā* of all things. This requires strict training in spiritual concentration, spiritual quiescence, and spiritual wisdom. When we understand *śūnyatā*, then all things of the world become clear to us. Then all is enlightened by non-being, and non-being is enlightened by being. This is, of course, an awakening which is beyond the self-consciousness of the layman and the speculation of philosophers.

The idea of *yüan-sheng* in Buddhism, especially in the Mādhyamika school, never requires us to know merely the conditions of a thing. On the contrary, its main purpose is to direct our consciousness to *depart* negatively from the false idea of self-nature or self-essence, and to look to the conditions of a thing. As every existing condition has its various conditions, too, so the idea of *yüan-sheng* directs our consciousness to depart from the thing as a center, to extend its light to the conditions, to the conditions of conditions, and to go beyond the thing itself. Then the self-nature or self-essence of anything can be cancelled and the *śūnyatā* of all things may be revealed.

In the cultivation of spiritual life, the value of the teaching of *śūnyatā* is tremendous. Since all the bonds of our spiritual life and the infinite evils of human life come from clinging to the apparent realities of worldly things, these teachings remove the roots of all bonds and evils. Infinite merits can be achieved and infinite virtues or spiritual values can then be realized by us. This is the ideal of Buddhahood.

Buddhist demonstrations of the *śūnyatā* of all things are based upon the conditional relations of things, which are acknowledged as actually existing in the intellect of common sense and science. Therefore, all these demonstrations can logically be carried out as in the Mādhyamika school of Buddhism.

Another point to be discussed is the idea of the *ālaya* (storehouse) consciousness and its seeds as expounded by the Yogācāra school of Buddhism. These ideas come from our spiritual light reaching into the unconscious nether world. From the teachings of the Yogācāra school, we can understand the world of *ālaya* and its seeds through indirect and mediate reasoning only, though they can be consciously known directly and immediately by deep contemplation of the *bodhisattva* or the Buddha. In the teachings of this school, many layers and aspects of the world of unconsciousness are elucidated and analyzed, and so are many ways of *yoga* for the self-transformation of the whole personality in order to attain the vision of the *bodhisattva* or the Buddha. These were all new teachings of spiritual cultivation for the Chinese people.

The ultimate purpose of Buddhism is to teach man to attain Buddhahood and to see the *śūnyatā* of all things, which is super-intellectual. This is different from Taoist philosophy, which usually uses metaphorical symbolism or aesthetic imagination to attain the super-intellectual. The combination of the spirit of the teaching of Buddhism, mainly the Mādhyamika school, and the spirit of Taoist philosophers is the way of Ch'an^y (Zen), which may be taken as the free use of intellectual ideas to cancel other ideas and let the vision of *śūnyatā* of Ch'an experience be expressed by symbolic language and actions.

VI. NEW ORIENTATION OF VALUE-CONSCIOUSNESS IN THE NEO-CONFUCIANISM OF THE SUNG-MING PERIOD

It is generally agreed that the Neo-Confucians of the Sung and Ming dynasties were men of an introvert type. They propounded the values of quiescence, serenity, reverence, self-reflection, and self-examination. They even adopted static sitting as a way to spiritual cultivation. All this seems quite different from the pre-Ch'in (220–206 B.C.) Confucians, who were more active in social, political, and cultural activities. So, the Confucians of the Ch'ing (1644–1912) criticized the Confucians of the Sung and Ming dynasties as Buddhists or Taoists in disguise. This is an exaggeration. Almost all the Confucians of the Sung and Ming dynasties most sincerely opposed many teachings of the Buddhists and Taoists. Their ideas of the ethical relations and of the sacrificial ceremonies for ancestors, sages, and worthies and their many other historical, cultural, political, and economic ideas are all of Confucian origin. So, we have to explain why they laid more emphasis on the self-reflective or quietistic way of spiritual cultivation through the influence of Buddhism and Taoism, plus the development of Confucianism itself.

Compared with the earlier Confucians, the Neo-Confucians were more conscientious about the inner obstructions to the development of spiritual life. These obstructions, such as the evil elements of *karma* and *ālaya,* had not been taken seriously by earlier Confucians. It is usually the case that the higher in spiritual life one wants to ascend, the more inner obstructions one finds. The more self-reflective one is, the more faults or potential inner motive of faults one finds deep in his mind. The Neo-Confucians called these inner obstructions insincere ideas, e.g., selfish desires, habitual materialistic tendencies, obstinate opinions, variegated temperaments, and the manipulative or calculating mind, which are all deeply rooted and always concealed in our minds. Only deep inner meditation or self-reflection can illuminate and reveal the way to eradicate the roots of these obstructions. In order to eradicate these ideas, which are all purely negative to the development of spiritual life, we have to avoid absolutely doing certain things and let the negative things be arrested, appeased, and transformed, and thus our spiritual life may be purified. In these cases, all our ways of life must be quiet and static, at least in appearance.

Secondly, the Neo-Confucians were more metaphysical and religious than the earlier Confucians, and consequently they usually had a sense of life, both moral and super-moral. The ideas of Heaven, God, the Reason of Heaven, and the Mind of Heaven, as mentioned before, were always discussed by them. They always talked of man from the point of view of Heaven and had a belief in the eternal Tao. These were somewhat similar to Taoist thought. Ch'eng Hao said that "the achievements of the sage-emperors, such as Yao[z] and Shun,[aa] may be like a floating cloud in an infinite void,"[18] since the eternal Tao of the universe has no addition by "the achievements of Yao or Shun, the sage-emperors," nor is there any loss by all the evils done by Chieh[ab] or Chou,[ac] the worst kings. When a pupil of Lu Chiu-yüan regretted that Chu Hsi (an opponent of his master) did not know the Tao rightly, Lu reproached his pupil and regretted that he had made no improvement and said, "The Tao shall neither be added nor subtracted whether there are Lu Hsiang-shan (Lu Chiu-yüan) and Chu Yüan-hui[ad] (another name of Chu Hsi)."[19] All these sayings took the standpoint of Heaven and originated from a metaphysical and religious faith in the eternal existence of Tao, or a spiritual mood which is, at least in a sense, beyond the distinction of the good and evil of conduct and the right and wrong ideas of man. In the philosophy of Wang Shou-jen, liang-chih (conscience) is sometimes said to be beyond good and evil. This is based upon the fact that, in the practice of liang-chih, when evil is wholly undone, no evil is left, and, when good is done, no good is left. So, in the practice of liang-chih we can pass beyond good and evil, and the nature of liang-chih is neither good nor evil, and this is called the chief good of liang-chih. Here we find Wang's view to be moral thought combined with the super-moral idea, and this may be said to be a combination of the moral ideas of earlier Confucians and the super-moral ideas of the Buddhists and Taoists.

However, the Tao and the liang-chih of the Neo-Confucians are still essentially moral concepts. "To see man from the point of view of Heaven" is itself a phase of moral life, according to the Neo-Confucians. When Wang Shou-jen said that "liang-chih is neither good nor evil, and this is called the chief good,"

---

[18] Erh-Ch'eng ch'üan-shu[be] ("The Complete Works of the Ch'eng Brothers"), chap. 4.
[19] Hsiang-shan ch'üan-chi[bf] ("The Collected Works of Lu Hsiang-shan"), chap. 8.

18

it is still beyond mere evil and ordinary good, but never beyond the chief good. So, the super-moral ideas of the Neo-Confucians should be taken as the expressions of their highest moral experience, though, in the profundity and depth of this moral experience, they may exceed all the earlier Confucians in certain respects.

VII. SPIRITUAL, SOCIAL, AND NATURAL VALUES DURING THE PAST THREE CENTURIES

In the development of Chinese thought there has been a great change since the end of the Ming Dynasty. During this period, generally speaking, the trends of thought have moved from depth of thought to extent of thought, from inward reflection to comprehensive understanding, from meditation on the spiritual and moral life to a consideration of natural and social life, and from the gaining of material for thought from personal experience to the gaining of material for thought from historical documents and relics. At the end of the Ming Dynasty, great scholars, such as Wang Fu-chih[ae] (1619–1692), Ku Yen-wu[af] (1613–1682), and Huang Tsung-hsi[ag] (1610–1695), even though they were erudite and usually based their ideas upon documentary evidence, all held a lofty idea of culture and had high personal characters, to which their knowledge was subordinated, and the spiritual and moral values of all social, political, and cultural life was expounded by them. From the school of Yen Yüan and Li Kung[ah] (1659–1733), a new current of thought began to flourish, which laid more emphasis on the social utilitarian values. Even the values of music and of the moral virtues were considered by them according to a utilitarian standard. From the middle of the Ch'ing Dynasty, in the thought of Tai Chen and Chiao Hsün[ai] (1768–1820), much attention was paid to the satisfaction of men's natural feelings and desires. The moral values of benevolence and social justice were interpreted to be the results of men's mutual consideration of the satisfaction of natural feelings and desires. So, the ideas of moral value, social utilitarian value, and natural values were combined into one homogeneous system. The most important current of thought late in the Ch'ing Dynasty was the thought of the Kung-yang[aj] school, which gradually laid more emphasis on the political and economic problems of the time (and found its justification in the commentaries on the Classics). These currents of thought finally joined with the thoughts of social construction from the West and resulted in the thought of K'ang Yu-wei[ak] (1858–1927). In recent decades, the spirit of searching the documentary evidence of the scholars of the Ch'ing Dynasty has become gradually connected with the Western scientific spirit and transformed into the popular high estimation of all things of scientific value. The two watchwords of the so-called new cultural movement at the beginning of the Republic of China were democracy and science, which were taken to have a very high social utilitarian value and truth value. Other spiritual values were generally neglected. When Marxism attracted the minds of the young generation, a communist party was organized and now has gained political power on the mainland of China. The communists' sense of value has further narrowed down to the political and social sphere. Only the technical value of science has been emphasized by them.

From the above, it is clear that the direction of the development of Chinese thought, from the end of the Ming Dynasty to recent years, has gradually left the spirit of Neo-Confucianism, which paid more attention to the spiritual values of human life, and now pays more attention to the importance of the social, utilitarian, technical, and natural values of human life. Since the nineteenth century, the value-consciousness of Westerners has gradually concentrated on the social, utilitarian, and technical sphere and on the values of satisfaction of natural desire. Here is a meeting of the value-consciousnesses of East and West, which represents a *Zeitgeist*. On its good side, this *"Zeitgeist"* may be taken as an extensive development of human value-consciousness for the preparation of the spiritual ground of the coming age, which should pay more intensive attention to the importance of spiritual values. But when and how the various kinds of natural value, social values, and spiritual values can be integrated into a great harmony in the new age is a complicated problem which is quite beyond the sphere of this essay.

QUESTION: You talk about spiritual life in Taoist philosophy and you identify the wisdom of Lao Tzu with the wisdom of Nothing in metaphysics as the theoretical basis for the development of spiritual life. It seems to me that the Tao of Lao Tzu is a metaphysical being, the primordial mover of the universe or the Godhead. How can the wisdom of Lao Tzu be identified with the wisdom of Nothing?

ANSWER: The wisdom of Lao Tzu is not identified simply with the wisdom of Nothing. I did not use the word "identified." Surely, the Tao of Lao Tzu may be interpreted as a metaphysical being or primordial mover of the universe, perhaps something like the Godhead. However, in this paper, I had to stress the Nothingness side of Lao Tzu's Tao. One reason for this is that the Tao of Lao Tzu as a metaphysical being is said to be revealed to us through the transiency of natural things. The transiency of things is explained as their coming from Nothing and sinking into Nothing. The other reason is that the meditation on Tao as metaphysical must begin with the thought of worldly things themselves as nothing. "Nothing" is a mediation between the thought of worldly things and meditation on Tao. When we want to ascend to Tao, we must transcend worldly things and encounter Nothing first, and the very transcending is itself a "nothing-ing" activity initiating from the Tao. This is explicitly stated in Lao Tzu's thought also. When we talk about Lao Tzu's idea of spiritual value as a higher value transcending worldly values, as my paper does, the wisdom of Nothing in Lao Tzu must be stressed.

b 仁
c 三教
d 永康
e 永嘉
f 顏元
g 戴震
h 恩
i 恩義
j 朱熹
k 理
l 良知
m 王守仁,陽明
n 張載,橫渠
o 程顥,明道
p 程頤,伊川
q 陸九淵,象山
r 道
s 老子
t 莊子

u 神
v 神遇
w 氣韻生
x 緣生
y 禪
z 堯
aa 舜
ab 桀
ac 紂
ad 朱元晦
ae 王夫之
af 顧炎武
ag 黃宗羲
ah 李璟
ai 焦循
aj 公羊
ak 康有為
al 陳獨秀
am 在精神生活發展中之毀譽意識

an 人生
ao 自得
ap 悅
aq 安
ar 傳習錄
as 中國人文精神之進展
at 文
au 里
av 馮友蘭
aw 列子
ax 天主實義
ay 王龍溪
az 羅近溪
ba 羅念菴
bb 劉蕺山
bc 明儒學案
bd 無
be 二程全書
bf 象山全集

2
The Individual and the World in Chinese Methodology

I SHALL LIMIT this paper to the four important typical ways of thinking about the individual and the world in Chinese epistemology:

1. To think of the individual as objectively existing as a part of the world.

2. To think of the world as a part of, or the content of, or identical with, the being of the individual subject.

3. To think that both the individual and world must be transcended, and that there is then in reality neither individual nor world.

4. To think that both the individual subject and the objective world are to be asserted positively as existing, yet neither is asserted as a part of, or the content of, or identical with, the other; nor are they asserted as mutually exclusive, because their mutual transcendence and mutual immanence are both accepted.

I. The individual known as objectively existing and as a part of the world through class names, pointing, spatio-temporal location, and relational thinking

First, the way of thinking of the individual as objectively existing and as part of the world is that way of thinking which *starts* from the world as the objective side of our knowledge (through the temporary forgetting of the individual as a unique knowing or acting subject and the conscious—though not self-conscious—activity of the objectivation of the subject as one of the individual things in the world) and *ends* in the assertion that I, as an individual, and all other individual things co-exist as parts of the world. The problem here—how I as an individual person can be objectively known or conceptually determined as an individual—is included in the general problem as to how any individual thing is objectively known or conceptually determined

21

as an individual. Since individual things are usually thought of objectively by general concepts or class terms, which are universal in meaning, the problems as to how the individuality of a particular individual can be conceptually determined and how the individual can be thought of objectively have been complicated and delicate problems from Plato to the present in Western thought. However, Chinese philosophers have not taken the problem so seriously as has the West, though they are not lacking in answers to the problem. These answers are represented by the Moists,[b] the Logicians,[c] Hsün Tzu[d] (313-238 B.C.), and the Yin-Yang[e] school in classical Chinese thought.

(a) Moists think of the individual objectively merely as a member of a class. They stress the idea of class (lei[f]) earlier than Mencius[g] (372-289 B.C.) and Hsün Tzu. Mo Tzu[h] (468-376 B.C.) teaches universal love as based upon the idea that all human beings are of the same kind. He teaches also that one should love the father of another man as he does his own. Thus, Mo Tzu takes my father merely as one member of the class of fathers. So, when Moism is developed into a theory of epistemology and logic in Mo Pien,[i] an individual thing is called an individual or an actuality (shih[j]). A shih may have its proper name and class names such as species name and genus name. As a proper name is arbitrarily given to a shih, conceptual knowledge of a shih requires the use of a class name. However, Mo Pien did not discuss the problem as to how an individual can be conceptually determined by the class name, which expresses the universal concept only. In Mo Pien's thought, the use of a class name to denote an individual is a practical matter. If a genus name is not enough to express the peculiarities of an individual, then a species name or sub-species name is required to differentiate one individual from another of the same kind. As the process of using class names with more specified meanings goes on, there is no problem as to how the individual can be conceptually determined and expressed by a class name. Consequently, this problem is not raised and discussed by Moists. However, it has to be raised and discussed, because the process of using names with more specified meanings cannot go on indefinitely, since there is no infirm species or lowest subordinative class-name to use; and, even if there were, it would still be a class name, and we could know the individual only as a member of the class.

(b) Another way to know the individual as existing objectively is represented by Kung-sun Lung[k] (498-? B.C.) of the logician school of Pre-Ch'in (Ch'in, 221-206 B.C.) philosophy. This is the way of knowing an individual by pointing to it. Kung-sun Lung is famous for his insistence on the difference of meanings between species name and genus name. Thus, "White horse is not horse" is his slogan. If genus name is different from species name because it has a wider denotation, it is implied that the lowest class-name still can denote more than one individual, and so, individuality cannot be expressed by any class-name as such. Thus, the individual can be pointed out or indicated only by names and not conceptually determined by them. These are the topics of his two other treatises, "Chih-wu lun"[l] (On Pointing and Things) and "Ming-shih lun"[m] (On Name and Actuality), which are less mentioned than his theory of the difference of species and genus as expounded in his treatise "Pai-ma lun"[n] (On White Horse). It is quite clear that Kung-sun Lung thinks that the actuality (*shih*) of an individual thing can be pointed to only by names and that the differences between species name and genus name are based upon their different functions in pointing.[1] We use names for pointing out the individual thing, and the individual thing is shown and known to us in the very act of pointing.

It is one thing to use a universal name to point to an individual thing, and another for a person to be understood by others, as when we use a certain universal name to point to a certain individual. If the individuality of an individual is not capable of being determined in some other way, where can one get the guarantee that one shall not be misunderstood? Thus, the third way of knowing the individual, as propounded by Hsün Tzu, needs consideration.

. (c) The third way of knowing the individual as existing objectively is that of determining an individual in a spatio-temporal system. When Hsün Tzu discusses how an actuality or an individual thing is determined in his chapter of the *Cheng-ming*[o] (Rectification of Names), he disagrees with the view that an individual is determined by its appearances or attributes, which are usually expressed by universal names. Two things may have the same appearances or attributes but be in different places. Thus, they have to be called two distinct actualities, two individual things. On the other hand, in the process of becoming, "one [individual] thing may have different appearances or attributes [at different times] but must still be called one individual."[2] An actuality, or an individual, is determined by its location in the spatio-temporal system, with emphasis laid on the different spatial locations of different individual things. However, when we differentiate the different things according to their different locations in space and time, we presuppose that the space-time system is already differentiated in its structure prior to the things in it. Here the epistemological problem is: if there are not things related differently to one another in

---

[1] He begins his treatise "On Pointing and Things" with the statement that nothing is incapable of being pointed to, but that the pointing (with the names we use for pointing understood) is not being pointed to. *Kung-sun Lung*, 3.

[2] *Hsün Tzu*, 22, "Rectification of Names." For detailed discussion on Hsün Tzu's theory of names, see my paper "Hsün Tzu cheng-ming yü ming-hsüeh san tsung"[ax] (Hsün Tzu's Rectification of Names and Three Schools of Logicians in Pre-Ch'in Philosophy), *New Asia Journal*,[ay] V, No. 2 (August, 1963), 1-22.

24

space-time, how can space-time, which is simply extended in spatio-temporal dimensions and is thought to be homogeneous everywhere, be differentiated by itself into different locations? If we cannot find any other answer to this problem, we can look for the principle of individuality only in the different things as differently related to each other.

(d) As things which are similar in appearances or attributes and subsumed under a class name do not usually have the same relations, such as causal relations, with other things, so any two individuals can be differentiated according to their different relations with different things. The Yin-Yang school is representative of this way of thinking: the fourth way of knowing the individual, that of relational thinking, the way of knowing the individual in its many-sided relations with other things. This way, expounded first by the Yin-Yang school, was adopted by many Confucianists after the Han Dynasty (206 B.C.–A.D. 220).

The meanings of *yin*[p] and *yang*[q] are subtle and complicated.[3] Originally, *"yin"* meant what is concealed and unknown to us, and *"yang"* meant what is manifested and known to us. They were originally concepts of attributes of things based on their status relative to other things, and were not originally concepts of substance or force. According to their derivative meanings, anything which is in front of or before other things is called *yang*, and that which is in back of or after other things is called *yin*. Consequently, what is progressive or active or generative is *yang*, and what is retrogressive or passive or degenerative is *yin*. All these meanings are relative. Therefore, according to the Yin-Yang school, everything takes the role of *yin* or *yang* relatively to other things, and anything of the same class can be differently determined as having different relations of *yin* and *yang* to these other things. Even if we limit the meaning of *"yang"* to "active" and *"yin"* to "passive," it is not difficult to determine the things to which a certain individual thing is peculiarly related, actively and passively, and then to differentiate it from the other individual things of the same class, in order that the uniqueness of a certain individual can be expressed through this kind of relational thinking without confusion.

The way of relational thinking of the Yin-Yang school was originally a way of thinking of an individual thing as existing objectively in the natural world. Yet, it is exactly like the Confucian way of thinking of the status of the individual person through his ethical relations in the human world. When an individual person is seen as existing objectively in the human world, his action

---

[3] For the original meaning and the derivative meanings of the words *"yin"* and *"yang,"* consult my book *Che-hsüeh kai-lun*[az] (A Treatise of Philosophy) (Hong Kong: Mencius Educational Foundation, 1961), Vol. II, Part III, chap. 5, sec. 3, and chap. 9, sec. 1.

and personality are regulated and determined by his reciprocal relations with other persons. As there are no two individual persons who have the same ethical relations to the other persons around them, so the unique status of an individual person in the human world can be cognized and conceptually determined through knowledge of his peculiar ethical relations to others.

II. THE INDIVIDUAL AS A SELF-CONSCIOUS MORAL SUBJECT AND THE WORLD AS SEEN BY SUCH A SUBJECT

I myself as a subject am a self-conscious subject. When I am self-conscious, what I am conscious of can be known as the content of my consciousness, and comprehended by my self-consciousness, which therefore transcends the world, and can then include it as a part of itself. If we say that only the self-consciousness which immediately reveals itself to me exists, this is extreme individualism or solipsism; and, if we say that there are different worlds belonging to the different self-consciousnesses of different individuals, this is pluralistic idealism or pluralistic spiritualism, and is a kind of individualism, too.

But, how can we know that self-consciousness is itself an individual reality belonging to me exclusively or belonging to each person separately? It is quite possible that self-consciousness, revealed immediately as a self-conscious subject, is simply a subject without being an individual, or a part of, or an expression of, a universal self-conscious subject, which is the only reality, as objective idealism or absolute idealism contends. Nevertheless, we still have reason to call the self-conscious subject an individual, because the self-conscious subject, since it transcends the world, can differentiate itself from the world. Hence, it is a unique being and capable of being defined negatively as different from everything else in the world and from the world as a whole, and can be called an individual, because any individual thing in the ordinary sense is usually defined as that which is different from everything else. Although we may not be able to define the self-conscious subject positively as an individual in the ordinary sense, we should leave open the question as to whether it is a part of or an expression of a universal self-conscious subject. If it is legitimate to call the self-conscious subject an individual, then any thought which thinks the world-being as the content of, or a part of, or identical with, the subject is a process of thinking of the world subjectively.[3a]

[3a] As for individualism, we have Yang Chu[a] (400-? B.C.) in the Pre-Ch'in period, who insists on the theory of one self (*wei-wo*[bb]), and who is as influential as the Moist school was in the Mencius age. However, we know nothing clear about all his arguments for individualism. He does not expound any solipsism or subjective idealism in the epistemological sense.

There is no eminent philosophy of pure Chinese origin—other than Buddhist Vijnāna-vāda idealism, which comes from India—which argues for a subjective idealism or for individualism by taking the self-conscious subject as a purely knowing subject and taking the world simply as the object known. However, there is a very important trend of Chinese thought which takes the self-conscious subject as both acting and knowing, and thereupon thinks of the world-being as subjectively included or comprehended as a part of, or the content of, or identical with, the subject.

This trend of thought may be called a kind of ethical idealism. Mencius, Lu Hsiang-shan[r] (1139-1192), and Wang Yang-ming[s] (1472-1528) are the leading philosophers involved. All of them emphasize the self-consciousness of the subject as a moral subject, which is not purely a knowing subject but a subject which knows its moral ideal, acts in conformity with it, and then knows itself self-consciously as a subject of both knowing and acting. There is here the thesis that "the universe (the ten thousand things) is perfectible in myself"[4] and "The universe is my mind, and my mind is the universe"[5] and "Pervading Heaven and Earth, there is just this spiritual light . . . my spiritual light is the master of Heaven, Earth, and deities . . . leaving my spiritual light, there is no Heaven, Earth, deities, or ten thousand things."[6]

It would be quite misleading, however, to interpret this thesis from the point of view of epistemological idealism or ordinary mysticism. Chinese philosophers who have held this thesis have never stated in a strict sense their epistemological arguments for this kind of idealism, nor have they said that the meanings of their thesis are mysterious as beyond the reason of man.

In ethical idealism, we take those things which ought to be as our ideal. This ideal determines what we ought to do to realize the ideal, and then the realization of the ideal is itself a moral ideal and moral action. The way of thinking in ethical idealism begins, in its first step, with seeing the things of the world as what they ought to be as our ideal prescribes, and then they are seen as full of possibilities or potentialities. It then proceeds, in the next step, to seeing things through our moral ideal and moral action. Henceforth, things are seen as gradually transforming themselves and tending to be what they ought to be; and their possibilities, when realized by our moral action, are found as of the nature of what they ought to be and of the ideal; while, on the contrary, what they are in actual fact is thought of as not so in reality. Therefore, if the moral subject has a moral ideal and moral action which are so high and lofty as to

---

[4] *Mencius*, VIIA.4.

[5] *Hsiang-shan ch'üan-chi*[bc] (Complete Works of Lu Hsiang-shan) (Shanghai: Chung Hua Co., 1935), Vol. 36, p. 37.

[6] *Yang-ming ch'üan-shu*[bd] (Complete Works of Wang Yang-ming) (Shanghai: Chung Hua Co., 1935), Vol. III, p. 26.

realize the universal *jen* (the utmost goodness in the world) through the self-consciousness of our good nature, or our original mind,[t] or *liang-chih*[u]—as held by Mencius, Lu Hsiang-shan, and Wang Yang-ming—then all things in the world will be seen through this high and lofty ideal and action of the moral subject, and all things and the whole world will be seen as acted upon by the subject's moral action and as tending to realize its moral ideal, and will be thought of as of the same nature as the moral mind. Consequently, it is quite natural for Mencius to think that the ten thousand things are perfectible by me as a moral subject, for Lu Hsiang-shan to think that the universe is my mind, and for Wang Yang-ming to think of *liang-chih* as the spiritual light of Heaven, Earth, deities, and the ten thousand things.

The expression "see the world through the ideal and action of the moral subject" states a way of thinking by a fully self-conscious moral subject as a moral individual. It is not a way of thinking of the world as an object opposite to the subject. It is a way of thinking which begins by withdrawing the light in the ordinary outward-knowing process back to our inner self; and then throws the light out again, along the very line of the extending of our moral ideal and our moral action; and knows the world as mediated by that very ideal and action, and as the realm for the embodiment of that ideal and action. Here, the seeing "eye" of the moral subject is immanent in the extending of the ideal and moral action, being acted upon by the action and transformed by the action. As the world is itself transformed to conform to the ideal, the "eye" will see the world as absorbed into the action and the ideal of the subject, and will experience it as one in being with the subject. When the subject is self-conscious and knows itself as transcending the world as experienced, the "eye" will see the subject as above the world, and the world will be seen as just a part of, or the content of, the subject as an absolute individual or an absolute I. This is the reason Liu Ch'i-shan[v] (1578-1645), a great Neo-Confucianist in the late Ming Dynasty (1368-1644), gives so high a place to the idea of *tu*[w] and *tu-chih*[x]—the awareness of the solitary individual in absolute morality.[7]

III. THE INDIVIDUAL AND THE WORLD AS TRANSCENDED IN VACUITY AND RECEPTIVITY OF MIND AND IN ENLIGHTENMENT AND SPIRITUALITY

The third typical way of thinking of the individual and the world in Chinese philosophy is to think that both the individual and the world have to be tran-

---

[7] Liu Ch'i-shan's discussion on the ideas of *tu* and *tu-chih* is available in the last volume of *Ming-ju hsüeh-an*[be] (Anthology and Critical Accounts of the Neo-Confucians of the Ming Dynasty), edited and written by Huang Tsung-hsi[bf] (1610-1695). For a contemporary exposition, see Mou Tsung-san's[bg] article "Liu Ch'i-shan chih ch'eng-i-chih-hsüeh"[bh] (Theory of Authenticity of Will of Liu Ch'i-shan), *Tzu-yu hsüeh-jen*[bi] (Free Thinker), I, No. 3 (October, 1956), 9-24.

scended, such that there is in reality neither world nor the I as an indivdual. This is the same type of thinking as that of Western and Indian mystics and philosophers who think of "before the day of creation," but with different emphasis about the way in which the world and the I, or the self as an individual, are to be transcended.

Chuang Tzu[y] (369-? B.C.), one of the two most important Taoistic philosophers, is representative of this way. He has a spiritual vision which is beyond the sense of self as an individual and of the world as opposite to the self. "Forgetting of myself," "loss of myself," "forgetting the world under Heaven," and "out of the world under Heaven" are pertinent sayings of his. When Chuang Tzu talked about the "upward wandering with the creator [and] downward having friends who are beyond death and life and of no beginning and ending,"[8] he was using a metaphor for the expression of his spiritual vision. His spiritual vision originates from his profound wisdom, aesthetic enjoyment, and inner spiritual cultivation, rather than from his primary belief in the existence of a mystic state.

Chuang Tzu has three ideas about the mind which are closely related to the experience of forgetting the world and the self as an individual. The first idea concerns the nature of mind as *hsü*[z] and *ling*.[aa] "*Hsü*" means to be vacuous and receptive. Confucius and Lao Tzu spoke of *hsü* mainly as a moral teaching. Chuang Tzu, followed by Hsün Tzu and the Neo-Confucianists, takes *hsü* as one fundamental nature of the mind and connects it with the word *"ling,"* which means knowing freely, spontaneously, and without attachment. When the nature of the mind is seen as both vacuous and receptive, the sense of ego or of self as an individual differentiating itself from other things is uprooted in the depth of the mind.

The mind can be receptive without being a positive receiver. When the mind is vacuous and receptive, all things of the world can be received by it, and then pass through it without meeting any barrier. This self-forgetting can be cultivated and continued in principle. Here, the most important thing is that the mind will be revealed to itself as both vacuous and receptive simultaneously. When it knows, it is receptive. But, if it is not simultaneously vacuous, then what is received is attached to the mind, and the mind is in turn attached to things. This is the ordinary way of knowing with attachment. On the contrary, if the mind is revealed to itself as both receptive and vacuous simultaneously, it can know things without attachment.

Secondly, Chuang Tzu uses the idea of *ming*,[ab] which means the lasting actual state of the mind when its nature, as purely vacuous and receptive, is fully realized in its knowing. Literally, *"ming"* means "light." As a state of

---

[8] *Chuang Tzu*, 33.

mind, it is enlightenment of mind. When Western religious thought talks about enlightenment of mind, it usually means that the mind is enlightened by something above. It is not so in Chinese thought. All Taoists, Confucianists, and Buddhists use the word *"ming"* as self-enlightenment or enlightenment without self. For Chuang Tzu, enlightenment is a state of mind which is purely transparent, and this transparency of mind, which comes from that nature of the mind as both purely vacuous and purely receptive, is fully realized in its knowing. Ordinarily, we know things through concepts and names. When the concepts and names are applied to the things coming to our attention, we meet the things halfway. Here the mind is not purely receptive. The only remedy for such ordinary thinking is to transcend and withdraw our ordinary concepts and names and let the vacuity of mind be realized. Then the mind becomes purely receptive, and is willing to welcome things wholeheartedly, and all the things are thus transparent to us. Here we have enlightenment and also self-forgetting. Nevertheless, the enlightenment of the mind is difficult to achieve, because before things come to attention we already have habits from the past, ready concepts or subconsciousness. These are waiting for our use, and, when things come to us, they pour out like fluids and fill the vacuity of mind and sentence it to death, as it were. Chuang Tzu said that the death of the mind is the greatest lamentation.[9]

According to some philosophies and some religious thought, as, e.g., in Buddhism, we must engage in practice of inner meditation and concentration of mind to enlighten what is dark in our foreconsciousness and subconsciousness. It is not clear whether Chuang Tzu has the same point of view. In Chuang Tzu's philosophy, besides the dialectic thinking used for canceling our presupposed judgments, ready concepts, and names and habits of the past, there is a third important idea about the mind, the idea of *shen*[ac] as the function of mind which is complementary to the idea of *ming*. Meeting things with *shen* is Chuang Tzu's way for attainment of the state of self-forgetting and enlightenment. This is quite different from the way of quiet meditation or serious concentration of mind as generally understood. The word *"shen"* originally meant deity or spirituality. *Shen* is usually connected with—sometimes synonymous with—the word *"ling,"* as explained above. Chuang Tzu uses it to indicate a function of the mind which is not a definite psychological process such as willing, feeling, perceiving, imagining, conceiving, or reasoning, but one which is pervading, and meets the things in their changing processes with intuitive and sympathetic understanding but without attachment. *Shen* is a function of the mind when the mind is permeated with fully living life. *Shen* is always characterized by freedom and spontaneity and is never contracted

---

[9] *Chuang Tzu*, 2.

and reflexive. When *shen* is extended and meets things with intuitive and sympathetic understanding, we have self-forgetting immediately, and we transcend any things which fill our mind. Thus, vacuity of mind can be realized, and enlightenment can be attained through the very extending of *shen*.

In view of Chuang Tzu's three ideas of the mind, it is quite clear that self-forgetting is possible of achievement. When such self-forgetting is achieved, the sense of the self as an individual is gone—and, since the world is correlated with the individual self, the sense of the world can thus be forgotten also.

As self-forgetting and world-forgetting are both stressed by Chuang Tzu, we call his way that of transcending the sense of both the individual self and the world as dualistically related, and as thinking that there is, in reality, neither world nor individual. We may interpret this as the way of experiencing the two as one. Chuang Tzu says, "I am living with Heaven and Earth; I am one with the ten thousand things."[10] However, experiencing the two as one is not necessarily to be thought of or talked about. If it is thought of or talked about, the very thinking or talking has to be transcended again. Here we have paradoxical thinking and talking. This is because, when the mind is vacuous, receptive, and knowing without attachment, and enlightenment and spirituality of the mind are realized, the concept "one" cannot be used. It, too, has to be enlightened through and passed by the extending of spirituality, and so the sense of the world and the individual as one has to be transcended, too. Therefore, according to this type of thinking, there is neither world nor individual. The state of mind of this type of thinking is thus neither subjective nor objective. Instead, it resides in the center of subject and object, and, hanging *in vacuo*, escapes from the duality of these two.[11]

When Lin-chi I-hsüan[ad] (785-867?), the Ch'an master, talks about his way of teaching disciples, he says: "Sometimes I cancel the [idea of] 'person' [as subjective], but not [the idea of] 'world' [as objective]; sometimes I cancel the [idea of] 'world' [as objective] but not the [idea of] 'person' [as subjective]; sometimes, I cancel both the 'person' and the 'world'; and sometimes I cancel neither the 'person' nor the 'world.' "[12] His first way of teaching corresponds to the first way of thinking described above, with the difference that the latter positively asserts the individual person as existing in the objective world. His second way of teaching corresponds to the second way of thinking mentioned above, with the difference that the latter asserts positively the being of the objective world as identical with, or part of, or the content of, the being of the

---

[10] *Ibid.*

[11] The second chapter of the *Chuang Tzu* begins with talking about "loss of reason," which can be rightly explained as getting out of the duality of subject and object.

[12] *Chih-wu lun*[bj] (Records of the Pointing of the Moon), edited by Chu Ju-chih[bk] (Taipei: Far East Book Co., 1959), Vol. 14, p. 5.

individual as subject. His third way of teaching is more like the third way of thinking, as discussed in this section; it is a synthesis of the earlier two, and rightly represents the spirit of Ch'an. Therefore, the way of thinking of Ch'an also belongs to this type. His fourth way of teaching is the negative of the third way in its logical form, and is actually the same in the spirit of negativity. "I cancel neither the person nor the world" is not the same as "I assert positively both the existence of the subjective person as an individual and the objective world." This will be discussed in the next section.

IV. THE INDIVIDUAL AND THE WORLD KNOWN AS MUTUALLY TRANSCENDENT AND IMMANENT THROUGH KNOWLEDGE OF VIRTUOUS NATURE AND SENSE-KNOWLEDGE

The fourth way of thinking of the individual and the world—that both exist —is a general tendency of Chinese thought. Even those thinkers who have been classified above as belonging to the other three types never deny this explicitly. However, only the Confucianists take the co-existence of individual and world seriously, and only in Confucianism do we get the philosophical basis of this way of thinking, a view of the mind which is more synthetic than in the other three views.

This fourth view takes the mind as both receptive cognitively and active and creative morally, and insists that, when its nature is realized authentically, enlightenment (*ming*) and spirituality (*shen*) can be included. This view originated with Mencius and was developed in *The Doctrine of the Mean* (*Chung yung*[ae]) and the Commentaries on *The Book of Changes* (*I ching*[af]), which can be supposed to be later than Mencius, and was further developed by Neo-Confucianism in the Sung and Ming dynasties (960-1644). It is sometimes neglected by some Confucian thinkers who are more practically oriented.

In this trend of thought, when the mind knows cognitively and becomes intelligent or wise, it should also be as vacuous as it can be. When the mind is vacuous, it is purely receptive and can become transparent and enlightened. In this respect there is no fundamental difference between Confucianism and Taoism. Yet, on the other side, the mind has its activity and creativity, and it can be self-conscious of itself as an acting subject or a creative subject. When the mind knows the objective world cognitively and has no reflection of itself, or thinks of its knowing subject or itself as a thing existing in the world objectively, then we have the first type of thinking, which neglects the subject as an individual which is incapable of being objectified as one among the other things in the world. When the mind is self-conscious of itself as a knowing and acting subject, and thinks of the world-being as identical with its own being or as the content or a part of itself, we have the second way of thinking, which neglects the independent and transcendent existence of the objective world. The first way of thinking may lead man to lose the sense of individual dignity and go astray in the myriad things of the world. The second way of thinking may lead man to assert his self as an absolute and in that case may engender the sense of pride, which is contrary to the moral sense of man. The third way of thinking considers the mind as vacuous, and then self-pride is eradicated. The shortcoming of the third way is its neglect of the mind of the individual self as a subject which is active and creative and self-conscious of itself as such. As it is active and creative, it is not simply vacuous as non-being, but is being and existence also. As it is self-conscious of itself, it can know itself as being an existing self-conscious individual self. On the other side, as the mind is receptive and can know things other than itself, the things also can be self-consciously known as existing. As it is possible also for the mind to forget itself as self-conscious, it is not necessary for it to see things existing merely as a part of, or the content of, or identical with, its being, and it is quite possible for the mind in its self-forgetting to assert the existence of the world and to see it as independent existence.

When the existence of the mind of the individual self and the existence of the things of the world are both asserted, we have the fourth way of thinking of the individual and the world. In this fourth way, Confucianists have the idea of enlightenment and spirituality, which are connected with the mind as active and creative more than with the mind as vacuous and receptive.

According to Mencius, the mind is active and creative, because it has moral nature, which is essentially good, with an inner light. When man fully realizes his good nature and has sageliness, which is unfathomable by knowledge, he has spirituality or holiness.[13] As Mencius' thought is developed into the thought of *The Doctrine of the Mean* and the Commentaries on *The Book of Changes*, ideas about enlightenment and spirituality become more important. In the former, the virtue of human nature is called *"ch'eng,"*[ag] which means "creating and accomplishing oneself and all the things of the world."[14] *Ch'eng* is *Tao*, the principle of the world as well as of man. The highest *ch'eng*, as it is realized by the sage, is a way of everlastingly creating and accomplishing, which is the same as everlastingly creating and accomplishing Heaven and Earth. When *ch'eng* is realized and is expressed, there is light or enlightenment, and from enlightenment one can also realize *ch'eng*.[15] Therefore, the "everlastingly

---

[13] *Mencius*, VII.

[14] The word *"ch'eng"* is sometimes translated as sincerity. This is quite misleading and does not conform to the text of the *Chung yung*. It is better to define it as "creating and accomplishing oneself and all the things of the world" than to follow a literal translation.

[15] *Chung yung*, 21. (Shanghai: Commercial Press edition, 1937), p. 12.

creating and accomplishing" is not only a process of continuous activity; it is also a process illuminated by light and transparent from beginning to end; it is the same as the way of the deity, which is a way of spirituality.

In *The Doctrine of the Mean,* one's inner self and outer things are harmonized in the idea of *ch'eng* as a universal principle. This is rightly called the way of thinking whereby both the individual and the world exist in one ultimate harmony,[ah] with light illuminated through it. The inner self as subjective and outer things as objective are then mutually reflected, as mutually creating, mutually accomplishing, and interdependent in a common spiritual enlightenment. In the Commentaries on *The Book of Changes,* the principle of Heaven is called *"ch'ien,"*[ai] which is a principle of knowing and creating, and the principle of Earth is called *"k'un,"*[aj] which is a principle of realization and accomplishment.[16] These two principles are embodied in man as his human nature, in which intelligence or wisdom, and *jen,*[ak] generating love, originated. Here intelligence or wisdom is receptive in knowing, and, at the same time, knowing is an act and is creative also. Generating love is creative, and, at the same time, is receptive to what is loved. The mind as receptive may be called its *yin* aspect, and as creative may be called its *yang* aspect.[17] As *yin* and *yang* are two principles or two aspects of the one ultimate *Tao,* and are mutually rooted in each other, therefore the creative aspect and the receptive aspect of mind are mutually rooted in its nature, and the mind, as knowing and acting, or as intelligence or wisdom and generating love (*jen*), are mutually implied in their meanings.

In the Commentaries on *The Book of Changes,* the idea of enlightenment (*ming*) and the idea of spirituality (*shen*) are also emphasized. *Ch'ien,* a universal principle of knowing and creating, is also characterized as a "great enlightenment from beginning to end,"[18] and spirituality is taken as "pervading all things of the world" and "without particular direction."[19] Here enlightenment is not merely a static state of mind; it also resides in a dynamic process of changing life; and spirituality is not only meeting things with intuitive and sympathetic understanding and without attachment, but also "pervading in creating and accomplishing all things according to their particularities without

---

[16] The best exposition of *ch'ien* as principle of knowing and creating and of *k'un* as principle of realization and accomplishment is available in the *Yü-tan-chih-chüan*[bl] (Looking around the Altar with Straightforward Illustrations) of Lo Chin-ch'i[bm] (1515-1588). See my essay "Lo Chin-ch'i chih li-hsüeh"[bn] (On the Philosophy of Lo Chin-ch'i), Special issue for one hundred issues of *Min-chu p'ing-lun*[bo] (Democratic Review), V, No. 6 (March, 1954), 2-10.

[17] See my book *Che-hsüeh kai-lun*[bp] (A Treatise on Philosophy), Vol. II, Part II, chap. 19, sec. 6.

[18] See "Ch'ien wen-yen"[bq] (Commentaries on *ch'ien* as a Principle of Heaven), in *The Book of Changes.*

[19] Commentaries on *The Book of Changes.*

remainder."[20] As spirituality and enlightenment exist in man, what should be sought is the "preservation of them in silence and the realization of them in virtuous action."[21] Thus, the "human nature of oneself is realized" and "Heaven's decree is attained or fulfilled."[22] This is a way of thinking which puts emphasis on both oneself as an individual subject and other individual things of the world as objects, and all of them are seen as organically related in one ultimate harmony, a universal principle of man or of human nature and of all things in the world, and the co-existence of the world and the individual was thus established in classical Confucianism.

Its development in the Neo-Confucianism of the Sung and Ming dynasties consists in the clearer elucidation of the thoughts of classical Confucianism with some new interpretations. One new idea agreed to by almost all Neo-Confucianists of the Ch'eng-Chu[al] school is the idea of "one principle (or one reason) participated in by different things," which is a metaphysical idea for the synthesis of the one and the many, identity and difference, and the universal and the particular individual. It is also closely related to a new theory of mind and knowledge. As Chang Tsai[am] (1020-1077) and the Ch'eng brothers classify man's kinds of knowledge into sense-knowledge and knowledge of virtuous nature, the latter is always taken as universal, self-identical, and one, and the former is always taken as particular and as differentiated according to the many sensed objects.

As knowledge of virtuous nature can be expressed through sense-knowledge, we have an example of "one principle participated in by different things." According to Chang Tsai and the Ch'eng brothers, "knowledge of virtuous nature"[an] is quite different from "sense-knowledge."[ao] One of the differences is that we can have knowledge of virtuous nature which comprises spirituality and enlightenment,[23] but we cannot attain to spirituality and enlightenment through sense-knowledge alone. The reason knowledge of virtue can comprise enlightenment and spirituality is based upon the fact that knowledge of virtuous nature is not merely knowledge which takes virtuous nature as its object.

. Knowledge of virtuous nature is knowledge through the very virtuous practice of the moral mind. More adequately, it is not knowledge about anything else; it is only self-knowledge of the moral mind as such, or of the moral

---

[20] *Ibid.*

[21] *Ibid.*

[22] *Ibid.*

[23] The ideas of *shen* (spirituality) and *ming* (enlightenment) are two very profound ideas of Neo-Confucianism which are closely related to the knowledge of virtuous nature, but are usually neglected by contemporary scholars of Confucianism. I have given some hints on the significance of these two ideals in Confucianism in Chapter 4 of my book, *Chung-kuo wen-hua chih ching-shen chia-chih*[br] (The Spiritual Worth of Chinese Culture) (Hong Kong: Cheng Chung, 1953). Further study of their meanings in Neo-Confucian thought is needed.

mind self-conscious of itself as such, or the moral mind as transparent to itself as such, and this is self-enlightenment. As the self-conscious moral mind is active, creative, and pervading all things in the world, it knows no limits in its creative and active extending, and it acts like deity and comprises spirituality. However, sense-knowledge is directed to the sense-object, which is opaque by itself, but can, so to speak, absorb the light radiated from our minds. Therefore, when isolated from the knowledge of the virtuous mind, it does not comprise self-enlightenment, and thus we can never attain spirituality through it alone.

Sense-knowledge is distinctly different in kind from self-knowledge of virtuous nature or spiritual enlightenment, but they are not necessarily separated in existence and can co-exist. In fact, they ought to co-exist, and the knowledge of virtuous nature can fully exist only through sense-knowledge. This is because the virtuous nature ought to be realized in moral action, and moral action is purposive in creating and accomplishing objective things, which can be known only through the senses. So far as our knowledge of virtuous nature is realized and expressed in the outer world through sense-knowledge about outer things, the knowledge of virtuous nature is taken as one, and sense-knowledge about outer things varies according to the differences of things. We thus have an actual exemplification of "one principle expressed [and participated in] by different things." Since knowledge about outer things is the necessary condition for the expression of our knowledge of virtuous nature, it ought to be sought and stressed even from the point of view of the knowledge of virtuous nature. Since things known by sense-knowledge are all individuals, "investigation of individual things one by one" is included in the teaching of the "investigation of things" as expounded by Ch'eng I[ap] (1033-1107) and Chu Hsi[aq] (1130-1200).

Furthermore, since these two kinds of knowledge are related and are differentiated only by their directions as outer-oriented and inner-oriented, what is known through them as "I as self-conscious moral subject" and "individual things of the world" should both be posited as really existing. Here we have four points of view about the mutual transcendence and immanence between the world and individual self.

First, when I am known by myself mainly through my sense-knowledge as an individual existence, I then co-exist with other outer things and persons in one objective world, and I as one individual and all other individuals are immanent in one objective world.

Second, if all outer things, including my body and other persons and things known as outer things, are taken as nothing but those known only through my sense and immanent in my world of sense, and if I am convinced also that I have knowledge of virtuous nature, which belongs to a higher level above my knowledge of outer things, then I, as an individual self-conscious moral subject, can be taken as transcendent to all things of the world as outer, and, similarly, can be looked upon as transcendent to the whole outer world.

Third, from a higher point of view, I know also that I am not the only individual self-conscious moral subject, and that other individual persons whom I know through sense as existing in the outer world are each actually having their knowledge of virtuous nature, and each is an individual self-conscious moral subject as well as I am; and I as an individual am known by others through their sense and by being seen by them as existing in their outer worlds also; therefore, I have to acknowledge their transcendence to me and that I am immanent in their sense of the outer world. Thus, I am immanent in the outer worlds of others, which are transcendent to me.

Fourth, from a still higher point of view, we should have the self-conviction that I know all that has just been said. I know that each person has the same self-conscious moral mind and knowledge of virtuous nature. I know also that I have to act toward them with respect and love. I know all of these through the reasoning of my moral mind (also the rational mind), which is based on the knowledge of my virtuous nature. Consequently, nothing is transcendent to this reasoning of my moral mind, which is based on the knowledge of my virtuous nature. Thus, the reasoning of my moral mind is without doubt mine. However, this reasoning leads me to the acknowledgment of others as having the same moral mind, the same outer world, and the same reasoning as mine. It is, then, a transcendental reasoning which leads me to transcend the "very reasoning as only mine," and such reasoning should be taken as self-transcending reasoning and not only as belonging to me but also as revealed to me. Thus it may be taken as heavenly reasoning, or the heavenly principle, as participated in by me and flowing in my mind. As heavenly, the reasoning or principle is universal and of the world as well as mine. It is revealed to me and participated in by me as an individual, as well as revealed to, and participated in by, any different individual who is a self-conscious mind or moral subject, as I am. Hence, we have an ultimate belief in "one principle" or "one reason" participated in by different individuals, which is closely related to the ideas about the nature of moral mind, the knowledge of virtuous nature, and sense-knowledge.

In conclusion, though the world and the individual are either immanent or transcendent to each other from the different points of view of different levels of thinking, they are ultimately included as moments of one idea of an ultimate harmony of mind and Heaven, or one vision of the ultimate harmony of the individual and the world which expresses "one principle expressed by (or participated in by) different things," as in the Ch'eng-Chu school.

As the fourth way of thinking about the individual and the world is not denied explicitly by other schools of Chinese thought, the relation of the individual subject and the objective world is usually thought of by Chinese thinkers as in one ultimate harmony.

The Chinese translations of the words "subject" and "object" of Indian and Western philosophy are *"chu"*[ar] and *"pin,"*[as] or *"jen"*[at] and *"ching,"*[au] or *"chien"*[av] and *"hsiang."*[aw] Originally *"chu"* means host, and *"pin"* means guest; *"jen"* means man, and *"ching"* means environment or things in vision; *"chien"* means seeing, and *"hsiang"* means what is seen and taking the role of assisting in the seeing. The three pairs of words are reciprocally complementary as in a harmonious whole or a harmonious experience. Taking the subject as host, the object is the guest who is invited and loved by the host (this symbolizes the object's immanence in the subject), and also respected and sent out by the host (this symbolizes the object's transcendence to the subject). On the other hand, the world can be seen also by the poets and philosophers as host, and then the man (or I as an individual) is guest of the world and is entertained by the hospitality of the world. It is quite clear that there is no dualism between host and guest. This metaphor is the best symbol for Chinese thought about the relation of the subjective individual and the objective world as mutually immanent and transcendent in an ultimate harmony.

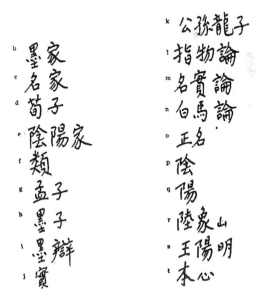

u	良知	at	人
v	劉蕺山	au	境
w	獨	av	見
x	獨知	aw	相
y	莊子	ax	荀子正名與名學三宗
z	虛靈	ay	新亞學報
aa	明	az	哲學概論
ab	神	ba	楊朱
ac	臨濟義玄	bb	為我
ad	中庸	bc	象山全集
ae	易經	bd	陽明全書
af	誠	be	明儒學案
ag	太和	bf	黃宗羲
ah	乾	bg	牟宗三
ai	坤	bh	劉蕺山誠意之學
aj	仁	bi	自由學人
ak	程朱學派	bj	指月錄
al	張載	bk	瞿汝稷
am	德性之知	bl	壇直詮
an	見聞之知	bm	羅近溪
ao	程頤	bn	羅近溪之理學
ap	朱熹	bo	民主評論
aq	主賓	bp	哲學概論
ar		bq	乾文言
as		br	中國文化之精神價值

3

COSMOLOGIES IN ANCIENT CHINESE PHILOSOPHY*

1. Cosmologies in Western Philosophy and Science

My discussion in previous chapters was limited to the origin of Chinese culture and its fundamental spirit exhibited in the process of historical development. In what follows, I am going to discuss the spirit of Chinese culture in specific areas such as philosophy of nature, theory of human nature, ideals of moral life, the world of daily living, the world of ideal personalities, and the spirit of art and religion. The center of discussion will be a comparison between Chinese and Western philosophy and culture. Therefore, before discussing Chinese cosmologies, I am going to present the cosmologies in the West as a preparation for comparison. Nevertheless, the main task of this chapter is not a special treatise on the natural sciences and philosophies of China and the West. Instead, my focus is on the differences between ideas of nature, their values and fundamental spirit. I hope my readers understand this point first.

In discussing cosmologies in Western thought, what I am now after is the spirit of transcendence together with the spirit of pure theoretical analysis. In Science and the Modern World, Whitehead rightly pointed out that the origins of the natural sci-

---

*T'ang Chün-i, "Chung-kuo hsien che chih tzu-jan yü-chou-kuan." Chapter V of Chung-kuo wen-hua chih ching-shen chia-shih [The Spiritual Values of Chinese Culture] (Taipei: Cheng Chung, 1953), pp. 56-88. Translated by Joseph S. Wu.

39

ences in the West were in the notion of Fate in Greek tragedies,
the concept of Law in the Roman legal tradition, and the idea of
a Created Order in Christianity. The concept of Fate in Greek
thought implies the idea of some transcendent power controlling the happenings of the human world. The notion of Law in
the Roman legal tradition is also a kind of necessary ruling
force governing the world. The God of Christianity is conceived
as having existed prior to the world which He created. All these
exemplify the idea of transcendence. The basic spirit of the
rationalism in Western science is its early belief in the governance of all things in the world by an objective, universal, and
necessary Order or Reason. Whitehead, again, in Adventures
of Ideas, presented four main doctrines in the West concerning
natural law. The first theory maintains that Law is immanent
in things. The second one holds that Law is imposed by a higher
power. The third position holds that Law is but description of
observed order of succession. The fourth advocates that Law
is only conventional interpretation. The last two positions are
theories of modern subjectivists, the third being represented
by Hume and Mach, and the fourth by Poincare. They are in
fact the products of modern epistemology, which is the result
of reflection upon the empirical data and terminologies of established scientific knowledge. With the exception of medieval
nominalism, there had not been in the West a single theory
close to these two positions. The Law of Nature in these two
theories, being a subjective product, could hardly have been the
foundation of the adventure of the "upward and forward search
for Law of Nature" of the natural scientists and philosophers
of the West. The foundation of such a spirit lies in the belief
that law is immanent in nature or that law is imposed by a
deity. The scientists of early modern Europe, such as Newton,
Descartes, and Leibniz, believed that law of nature is imposed
by God. Aristotle and the Stoics, on the other hand, believed
that law is immanent in nature. What has permeated both
the ancient and early modern theories of nature is the concept
of a mathematical order. This is why E. A. Burtt in his The
Metaphysical Foundations of Modern Science maintains that the

rise of modern physics originated in the belief that mathematics
orders all things in nature, that all laws of nature can be demonstrated by mathematics, and that the essential nature of things
can be explained in terms of mathematical concepts. This kind
of thought has its remote origin in the Greeks, particularly in
the thought of Pythagoras and the cosmology of Plato's Timaeus.
Both men viewed mathematical order as the fundamental principle of all things in nature. Aristotle assigned a less valuable
status to mathematics, probably because in his concept of nature
he emphasized the classification of fixed species. The fixation
of species is based on the notion that formal and final causes
can direct the development of things in nature. The emphasis
on formal and final causes, as a matter of fact, had its origin
in Plato, who maintained that the universals had transcendent
existences over the particulars.

From what has been discussed, we can well observe that the
remote origin of Western science was a union of the spirit of
theoretical analysis and the spirit of transcendence. The resulting spirit of such a union, as exemplified in an upward movement, has become a transcendence of the concrete perceptual
world, a recognition of the existence of universals such as general forms, general relations, a mathematical order, and categories of existences and knowledge. In extending toward the
external world, such a spirit goes beyond perceptual phenomena
and affirms the existence of substance, and the concept of matter is thus formed. This was first affirmed by the Greek philosophers of Miletus. Even the One of Parmenides of the Eleatic
School, according to J. Burnett's Greek Philosophy, was also a
concept of material substance. When Western philosophers applied the spirit of analysis to the concept of substance, it resulted in the concepts of atoms and elements, which referred
to entities invisible but having all sorts of forms. These notions
were the product of the process of transcending the empirical
world, the employment of analysis, and the affirmation of ultimate realities. Therefore these notions represent substantiality
rather than mere abstractions. Democritus affirmed the existence of atoms through observing the interpenetration of ob-

jects, yet he believed that atoms were impenetrable. Anaxagoras maintained that everything was composed of elements which were changeless and indestructible. This revealed the analytic and transcendent spirit of the Greeks, who went beyond the obvious empirical level and searched after what was implicit and nonempirical. It also appeared that the notions of atoms and elements were the objectification and externalization of the Greek concept of individuals. The Greek atomists viewed atoms as impenetrable entities; this was probably the reason why the earlier Chinese translation of the term "atoms" was mo po [impenetrable]. Consequently, the relations among atoms could only be external relations, impact upon one another being the major relation. In Empedocles' theory, elements such as earth, air, fire, and water did not have motion initiated from within. Their change was due to the two mythical forces, Love and Hate. In Anaxagoras' theory, elements did not spontaneously unite with one another to form objects. Their motion was due to an external force called Nous. All this was the progenitor of mechanism in physical science and the idea of an imposed order in modern thought. It was also the source of early modern naturalistic materialism and individualism, the former holding that natural objects were external to one another, and the latter maintaining the individual was an unanalyzable unit. Both the Greek and early modern atomists and pluralists, in order to interpret change, had to postulate a pure space in which the motion and change of the atoms took place, and in which things were formed. There were those like the Eleatic philosophers and Descartes who did not recognize the existence of pure space, but assumed that everywhere in nature it was full of ether. These two alternative modes of thinking, a sharp either-or dichotomy between substantiality and void, lasted until twentieth century physics, when there emerged concepts of electromagmatic fields and the notion that matter can be transformed into energy.

Modern cosmologies have shown progress over those of the Greeks, because the methodology used by the Greeks was limited to observation and reason, while the moderns developed the

method of experimentation by which we invade the depth of
nature and force it to answer our questions (to paraphrase the
words of Bacon). Thus the theories of atoms of the Greeks and
in early modern times are superceded, and there is no more
belief in any impenetrable atoms or electrons. Atoms and electrons are to be conceived as centers of energy. This new belief is the result of the progress of experimental method in
natural science. It is discovered through the impact between
various forms of radia, electric currents released by experimental tools and equipment and the atoms. We can even say
that it is the result of the impacts between the insights and
theoretical analysis of Western men and the atoms. The exhibited spirit of transcendence in modern science is superior
to what was in the Greeks. For in modern science the approach
to natural objects in the empirical world departs from the obvious and leads to the subtleties of the microcosmos and the
infinity of the macrocosmos. In search of the macrocosmos,
scientists approach the laws of astronomy, the solar system,
the world of nebulas, and even the laws governing the change
and motion of all the heavenly bodies of the universe. Indeed
modern astronomy has far exceeded the Greek contribution.
But we have to realize that the interest in an approach to the
infinity of the universe has its origin in the medieval belief that
God's glory is exhibited in the creation of the world. Owing to
this belief, men seek to see the glory of God through His creation. Thus men have to transcend the limited empirical world
and approach the distant heavenly bodies of the infinity of the
universe with the aid of rational analysis. (Both Copernicus
and Kepler held that the ultimate goal of astronomy was to understand the cosmic order under the governance of God and
thus understand His greatness.) From such a spirit of transcending the immediate and the limited, the concept of infinite
space and time is formed.

After the development of the concept of infinite space and
time (which had its origin in the concept of an infinity Deity),
the main approach to the heavenly bodies of the infinite space
is astronomy. The spirit of modern astronomy seems to have

cooperated very well with the spirit of the practical life of modern Western men, whose efforts have been in exploration, immigration, and voyage which aim at enlarging the boundaries of their activities on earth. On the other hand, the interest in the approach to infinite time has generated the search for the beginning of the earth, the beginning of life, and the beginning of the human race. Consequently new scientific theories, like the theory of the origin of species, evolution of man, and evolution of the universe, came into being. As a result of new scientific theories, Aristotle's concept of fixed species is superceded. From the emergence of lives to the emergence of all beings in the universe, the theory of evolution exhibits an ascending order of growth. It is fundamentally the same spirit exhibited in Plato's hierarchy of forms and Aristotle's order of form-matter relation. The basic difference is that the evolutionary theory presupposes a process view of the universe while that of Plato and Aristotle was a static view. Process view being implied in the theory of evolution, Western men, in addition to a search for an understanding of the past, seek to know the development of the future. Consequently modern men, being fascinated by the future, begin to conceive ideals and plans for the future. Therefore we may well judge that the spirit of evolution is immanent in the actual life of Western men who struggle forward, crave for creativity, and seek to transcend reality in order to demonstrate their elan vitae of life.

In Greek astronomy, it was held that heavenly bodies were endowed with divine nature and moved in accordance with a perfect order of harmony. This led to the notion that the movement of planets exhibited truth and beauty. According to the mythology of the Greeks, Plato's allegories, and Christian mythology, man's golden age had already passed. The Christian doctrine held that man's paradise was found only when Adam was born. All these concepts are in opposition to modern thought. From Kepler's discovery in astronomy (the movement of heavenly bodies is oval rather than a circle) to Newton's law of gravitation (which was a synthesis of Galileo and Kepler), the notion of force, which was conceived as operating only on earth, is now shifted to the middle of the infinite space, as relations among the heavenly bodies. All the centrifugal force, centripetal force, and forces of attraction and repulsion are considered opposite to one another and struggling against one another. The result of such struggles and oppositions is the track of the movement of the heavenly bodies. The basic presupposition of this cosmology is that every heavenly body is an absolute and self-sufficient unit. Thence the beauty of the mathematical order as exhibited in the harmony of the movement of heavenly bodies is to be conceived as the result of oppositions and struggles among the heavenly bodies. Likewise, according to the discoveries of biology and anthropology, the relation among animals as well as the origin and development of man are not as beautiful and harmonious as we usually see in nature. Instead, they are full of struggles and conflicts. The drives of an organism, according to the theories of Spencer and Darwin, are aiming toward a balance between internal and external forces, in order that it may lead to adaption and survival. Schopenhauer and his followers maintained that all living beings were manifestations of a blind impulse, which he called "the will to live." Because of this, each living organism knows only loving itself and its offsprings. Through the search for the infinity of the universe and the origin of man in modern astronomy and biological science, Western men have put the myriad things of the universe in a tension as a result of the conflicts and struggles among forces. Such a tension is also a very basic feature of the life style and social institutions of modern Western men. The more radical variation of such a cosmology, like that of Hegel and Marx, naturally maintains that the world is formed through the union of two opposing forces. In Hegel we can still see a transcendent idea which is the synthesis of a pair of contradictories. But in Marx the natural world is but composed of contradictories and struggles, which are exemplified in society and historical development.

What has been discussed is the kind of cosmology before the emergence of relativity and quantum physics. Such a cosmology has provided a background for relativity and new physics. Certainly such a cosmology can be termed representative of Western culture. However, the fundamental principles of the cosmology underlying relativity and new physics are very close to those of the cosmology in Chinese philosophy, although it employs the kind of mathematics which is typically a product of the West. Because of this, I have not discussed this new cosmology in the contemporary West. It will receive attention in my presentation of Chinese cosmology, and the similarities between the two (Chinese and contemporary Western) will be demonstrated.

2. Chinese Cosmologies: Law as Immanent Rather than Transcendent

Unlike cosmologies in the West, Chinese cosmologies were not substantiated by the experiments and systematic theories of science, which were not well-developed in Chinese culture. Nevertheless, Chinese cosmologies have unique characteristics which are representative of Chinese culture and wisdom. The culture background of such cosmologies is the earlier ancient Chinese tradition together with the spirit of Confucianism and Taoism which developed later. This kind of background, no doubt, is very much different from that of the scientific culture in the West. According to Whitehead's interpretation, the inevitableness of fate in Greek thought and the idea of necessity in the notion of law in the Roman tradition gave birth to the concept of law of nature as absolute, necessary, and external to natural objects and events. On the other hand, from the beginning in Ancient Chinese religious thought there were the ideas that "Destiny of Heaven [t'ien ming] is impermanent," and "Destiny of Heaven is not final." Therefore, for the ancient Chinese the law of nature was neither absolute nor necessary. Furthermore, China never had the concept of transcendence, as does Christianity; nor did she have Pythagorean and Platonic philosophy, which affirmed a transcendent mathematical world. Consequently, the concept of law of nature in ancient China was not something imposed by a higher power from outside or from above. On the contrary, it was believed that law of nature is immanent in all natural objects and events. In the text of the I Ching [Book of Changes] and the philosophies of early Confucianism and Taoism, there was already developed a concept of natural law as immanent in the processes of myriad things and events. However, such a law is not one of necessity or inevitableness. This theory of law of nature is not a conclusion reached by pure intellect. It is the result growing out of immediate experience, direct contact with events and objects. It is substantiated by the spirit of art and morality of both Confucianism and Taoism. According to this cosmology, the logos of myriad things constitute their nature, which is manifested through their functions and development. In the processes of events and things, there are beginnings, completions, roots, and ends, wherein lies the order. Wherever there is order, there is law. Such an order and law are exhibited through the evolution and change of things and events. Therefore, in our immediate experience, order and law are manifested facts which are immanent in the processes of things and events, and thus constitute their nature. There has been in Europe a theory which maintained that there were only discrete sense-data in our immediate experience. This was the philosophy of Hume and his followers, who doubted the existence of causality as immanent in nature and maintained that what we experienced was limited to data in temporal succession and spatial contiguity. For Hume the necessary connection in causality was imposed upon natural objects by our expectation or habit. Kant, advancing one step further, held that causality was an a priori category, a product of pure reason. As a matter of fact, the theory which held that our immediate experience was but a collection of discrete sense-data was the product of pure analysis. In our immediate experience, continuity immanent within the processes of things and objects is directly felt by us. Hence we can conclude that causality as well as order of things and events is in our immediate experience. Recent philosophers like Bradley, Bergson, James, Whitehead, and my friend Professor Tsung-san

Mou have criticized Hume and, indirectly, given support to
Chinese cosmology.

There is a need of further explanation here. My point is that
the concept of law and order as external to things and events
was a result of the discovery of universals (which were law and
order) shared by more than one particular object or event. The
law or order discovered usually went beyond one particular and
governed other particulars. Although it went beyond one particular, it could be exhibited in some particulars and not in some
other particulars. Consequently, the concept of law or order as
external and transcendent was formed. This theory was not
necessarily groundless. But we have to note that externality
and internality are not necessarily exclusive of each other. The
immanent nature of law and order can be explained in terms of
our experience of knowing. In knowing the law or order of one
thing without comparing it with other things, we can still have
the cognizance of the law and order under which that particular
thing is governed. My point is that any knowledge of a law or
order in one thing can be prior to the knowledge of it (law or
order) as a universal, as law and order commonly shared by
some other things. I have no objection to the concept that law
and order are universals or united sets of universals. But our
cognition of the universals in a particular can be had through
our experience of that particular alone. When we observe the
change and motion in the process of the growth of an organism,
we can have a knowledge of its developmental order. In the
growing process of an organism, when a form (or relation)
changes from A to B to C and then to D, each change is not an
independent unit disconnected from another; neither is it a
mere temporal succession of sense-data. It is a continuous and
integral process. Likewise, our stream of ideas is also continuous and integral. In the process of our consciousness,
when it changes from idea A to idea B, we are aware that there
was an A before B. When it comes to C, we are aware that
there were an A and B before C. At that time, A, the form itself, appears as a universal to us. When it changes from C to
D, we are aware that there were C and B before D, and then B

appears to us as a universal. With our cognition working in this way, we can acquire knowledge of universals, law and order immanent in things and events. Hence we can have a judgment about how it developed (from what point to what point) and what order and law it has exhibited. It follows that our knowledge of universals is an emerging product amid the changing process where events and phenomena take place. Therefore, through a particular alone, we can know the law and order of that particular object or event, and we can even know that such a law and order is immanent in the developmental process of this particular, or its phenomenal manifestation.

3. The Life Principle in Chinese Cosmologies

Universals are not a priori. The basis of the existence of anything is its "life essence" which constitutes the nature of the object — The nature of anything is exhibited in its modes of interaction with other things. Nature or "life essence" is a principle of "freedom and evolution," but not a "necessity" principle.*

I have maintained that law or order is immanent in natural objects or events. This means that law or order of a natural object or event is its nature rather than a universal "possessed" or "shared" by this object or event with other objects or events. A universal is something that is above the particulars, and it "covers" the particulars in a transcendent manner. This was a discovery of Western men long ago. But, according to Chinese cosmologies, universals are posterior; they are products

---

*The concept li (理) in Chinese has very rich meanings. It is sometimes translated as "universal," sometimes as "order," sometimes as "essence," sometimes as "principle," depending on particular contexts. The phrase kan-t'ung (感通) virtually has no exact English equivalent; my translation of it as "interaction" is only a very rough approximation. — Tr.

emerging from experience. If we take universals as prior to
particulars, we will be easily led to the conclusion that forms
are externals to natural objects and events and are imposed
upon them. However, if we take the order exhibited in a particular object or event as something which comes first, epis-
temologically we come to grasp the event or object by its perceptual phenomena first, and then we come to cognize its inner
essence or order. Ontologically we should say that there must
first be the essence or order, then comes the phenomena, and
then the cognizance of the order or essence. The order from
which the event evolves is the life principle of nature. This
life principle is the foundation of the formation and development
of every event. Therefore it is the most general principle in
the universe. It is also a basic principle underlying the rise
of any event. Since it is the principle followed and shared by
all things, it is the Tao of myriad things or the Tao of nature.
It is also what the I Ching called the principle of ch'ien and
k'un through which all existences are evolved and completed.
It is also the principle of jen in the universe. This principle
of life, or principle of jen, being immanent in everything, makes
the rise and growth of every natural object or event possible
and necessary. This is also the principle which makes the
natural world continue to exist. Nevertheless, this life principle, making the rise of events possible and necessary, does
not make the forms of an object or event necessary. The rise
of an event or object is a result of the interacting process
among some prior events or objects. The modes of interaction
between one object and other objects are not determined by the
object itself. What forms will be assumed by the object is not
determined by the object itself either. This is to say, although
the principle of life as exhibited in an object gives rise to the
forms of the object, such forms can be changed or modified
through the interaction between the object and other objects.
Therefore the nature of an object implies its changeability or
modifiability through interaction with other objects. The more
adaptable a thing is, the richer its life principle will be. Therefore we can observe in Chinese philosophy that the nature of an

object or event is not a principle of necessity, but one of freedom and evolution. The saying "What is endowed by Heaven is
called nature" does not imply any fate which governs all the
motion and conduct of men and things. On the contrary, Heaven
endows every man with an ability to free himself from the control of his own mechanical habits and external forces, and thus
he is able to create along with the change of his environment.
An object or event needs interaction with other objects in order
that its freedom in the process of creative evolution can be
fully manifested. Furthermore the more interaction with other
objects and events, the greater creativity an object or event
will attain. From this we can see that this principle of life and
freedom does not depend on the ability of the single object or
event; nor does it depend on its will. Rather, it depends on the
growing vital life force endowed by nature, which lies in its
power to interact with other objects and events. The power or
ability of an object or event becomes dominant and manifest
through its creative growth, which is a result of its interaction
with others. Its power can grow stronger through its conscious
desire for more interaction, and its increasing freedom from
the control of its own past mechanical habits and physical forces
of the external world. But this is beyond the capacity of ordinary natural beings. Man seems to be the only being which is
capable of this.

4. The Hsü [Nothingness]-Shih [Substantiveness] Principle
in Chinese Cosmologies

Chinese philosophers view individual existence as
nothingness [hsü] prehending somethingness [shih],
so that growth and development are possible.
Therefore there has never been a concept of material substance. The basic principle governing all
existences is "interaction leading to harmony" rather
than to "contradiction" or "struggle."

What has been discussed above includes three fundamental

themes. First, the law of nature in Chinese cosmologies is
law of immanence, in contradistinction to law of transcendence
in the West. Second, Chinese thinkers conceived the law of
nature as a constituent of the essence of things, and such an
essence is exhibited in the capacity for adaptation and creation
through interaction with the changing environment. Therefore
it is an immanent principle of freedom and principle of evolution. This is in sharp distinction from the notion of necessity
in the law of nature in the West. Third, for Chinese philosophers the nature of an object lies in its capacity [the Chinese
original implies the meaning of tolerance] for interaction with
other objects. This is very different from the Western view
that the essence of a material object is energy or force. These
three themes constitute the core of all Chinese cosmologies and
can be directly affirmed in our experience with nature, where
we observe directly the interaction among individual beings and
the growing process of myriad lives. Such a thesis was implied in Chinese religious thought, where it was believed that
"even the sky is high and the earth low; the Lord is everywhere
and nowhere." It was also implied in Confucianism, which
viewed nature through humanity and human-heartedness. It was
also implied in Taoism, which viewed the universe with the
feeling of freedom and the principle of the equality of all beings.
The most important implication in this kind of cosmology is
the concept of "nothingness within somethingness." The nature
of every object is exhibited in its capacity for interaction with
other objects. This means that it is its nature that can prehend
other objects. Its ability to prehend lies in its nothingness.
When an object interacts with other objects, events and phenomena arise. According to the principle of continual growth
and reconstruction, an object is not determinately controlled
by its past habits. Nor is it determined by any external mechanical force. At the same time, there is no transcendent
form [like final cause or teleology in the West — Tr.] to direct
or define the rising event. All these are based on the concept
of "nothingness with somethingness." Because of this, there
has never been in ancient China any theory like atomism, which

held that there were indestructible and permanent atoms. In both India and the West there were theories of atoms. Later Indian thought had transformed the concept of atom into the shapeless and sizeless unit, which lasted until the rise of Buddhism. In China, nevertheless, there have never been such theories. The Hung Fan spoke of the five elements: metal, wood, water, fire, and earth, which were but elements in daily life. They were defined in the following manner: "Metal means that which goes with leather. Wood means that which can be straight or crooked. Fire means that which is flaming up. Water means that which is wet and flowing downward. Earth means that which fits farming." All these were defined in terms of their functions manifested in the interacting process with other objects. The eight trigrams in the I Ching — ch'ien, k'un, k'an, li, tui, ken, chen, and sun — all indicated the qualities or virtues of heaven, earth, water, fire, mountain, lake, wind, and thunder. Ch'ien means firmness and k'un means gentleness. K'an and li are predicated by "dangerous" and "dependence." Ken and tui are characterized by "standstill" and "pleasure." Sun and chen have the virtue of penetration and movement. The function of an object as manifested in its interaction with other objects is its capacity for prehending other objects and the power of generating new events and phenomena. Therefore, in the philosophical context of the five elements and the eight trigrams, there has never been any idea which suggested some pure material substance underlying objects and events. It is very obvious that this kind of thought is different from the Indian or Western theories which held that the original stuff of the universe consisted in earth, water, wind, and fire, although they bear superficial resemblances.

In the West the concept of material substance from the very beginning implies some substratum underlying the world of sense perception. This has been discussed thoroughly in Spaulding's New Rationalism, Cassirer's Substance and Function, and Burnett's Greek Philosophy. In the Greek tradition, since the time of Empedocles, there has been the notion that matter could not move itself and its motion was due to its being

acted upon by external forces or due to the impact between material objects. Therefore, in modern natural science the concept of material substance is the mass which fills space, and it
is represented by density as divided by volume. It can also be
represented by its force (which operates upon other objects)
as divided by the distance it travels. It is quite clear that the
fundamental nature of material substance is inertness and resistance. The dialectical materialists held that matter itself
is in motion or movement. But they never interpreted its nature
in terms of its capacity for interaction and prehension, so that
its motion is blind rather than exhibiting the principle of creation and transformation. Nevertheless, owing to the revolution in physics, it has been discovered that the mass of an object can be transformed into energy and such energy can be
dissipated into other objects. Hence the concept of material
substance as an absolute and self-sufficient substratum is
seriously challenged. In Leibniz's philosophy, however, we already found that a monad is a center of forces and that it mir-
rors the whole universe from its own viewpoint. After the rise
of new physics and relativity, we notice that Bertrand Russell
held that events or phenomena themselves constitute the reality
of the universe, and that atoms and elements are but logical
constructs. But this theory may be criticized for explaining
away the reality of nature. Whitehead alone is able to develop
Leibniz's theory, and he holds that events are the only constituents of reality and later changes "event" to "actual entities." The formation or growth of each actual entity implies
the prehension of other actual entities and the prehension of
new forms (Whitehead calls them "eternal objects"). This
means that the rise of any new object or event, and the exhi-
bition of the principle of creative evolution, lies in the interaction among existing events or objects and the prehension and
actualization of new forms. The actualization of new forms and
the interaction among objects and events is the process of
value-realization, which is the manifestation of virtues of new
and existing events or objects. Now, in Western scientific
thought, the concept of inert pure material substance is almost

abandoned, and the replacement is a concept of life process in which all existences show interprehension because of the complimentary nature of "somethingness" and "nothingness." Nevertheless, when we look back in the history of Chinese philosophy, the I Ching already had these ideas. This is probably why Whitehead confessed in his preface to Process and Reality that his philosophy of organism is different from traditional Western thought, and is close to the philosophy of organism; is different from traditional Western thought, and is closer to the philosophy of the Orient. Here in our comparative study his statement is confirmed.

Owing to the complexity of the philosophy of the I Ching and the diversity of its commentaries, we shall discuss only some general notions and omit the minute details. First of all, let me point out that the concept of interaction among existences, the interprehensive nature of "nothingness" and "somethingness," and the principle of creative evolution as a result of interaction and interprehension, can be found almost everywhere in the text. Earth, as we observe from its surface, is hard and firm pure material substance. Heavenly bodies such as the sun, the moon, and the stars were conceived by ancient Greeks as only some light without material substrata, and were conceived by some as the dwellings of deities. Nevertheless, according to the I Ching, the function of ti [earth] is k'un and the virtue of k'un is "receptive" or "yielding." Therefore it is symbolized by ☷. T'ien [sky or heaven], according to the I Ching, performs its function of penetrating into earth in order to germinate the seeds and thus make them grow on earth. Therefore the attribute of t'ien is ch'ien, which means heaven and strength. This interpretation implies that t'ien, in its interacting process with earth, recognizes earth's reality as having nothingness (the potential to prehend) in its apparent substantive nature and makes full use of it. It is quite clear that in the philosophy of the I Ching the reality or nature of any object does not lie in its self-sufficiency but in its nothingness as capacity for prehension and interaction with other objects. Therefore, the trigrams (as well as the hexagrams) are constructed with simple and unen-

closed lines. This is very different from the symbolization of
objects with geometrical figures constructed by the ancient
Greeks like Pythagoras, Plato, and the atomists. Originally,
the eight elements symbolized by the trigrams are pairs of
apparent opposites which compliment and perfect each other.
For example, sky [t'ien] is high and earth [ti] is low; they are
opposite but complimentary. What is rising up toward the sky
from the earth is called mountain, and what seems to have
collapsed due to the force of sky is called a lake. That which
is flowing downward is water, and that which is flaming upward
is fire. Thunder indicates something moving from inside toward
the outside, while wind signifies that which comes in from outside. Therefore we can say that what the eight trigram signify are
the relations among the eight elements, interactions between
apparent opposites like the upper and the lower, the inner and
the outer. The way in which the trigrams characterize the attributes of an element focuses on how (creatively, receptively,
actively, passively, etc.) it interacts with other elements. T'ien
[sky or heaven], evolving unfailingly, expresses its power to
penetrate into earth. Therefore its virtue is characterized as
"the strongest" and "the firmest." Ti [earth], submitting itself to the action of t'ien, gives rise to various existences according to seasons, and its virtue is therefore characterized
as "the softest" and "the most receptive." The three lines of
a trigram are used to indicate the stages of the beginning, the
middle, and the end. The symbol for ch'ien [t'ien] is ☰, and
that for k'un [ti] is ☷. The Lake, being collapsed-down and
movable, appears soft in its surface and is symbolized by ☱.
The Mountain, being static and uprising, appears very hard and
firm and is symbolized by ☶. Water, flowing downward, exhibits its strength in the midstream and is symbolized by ☵.
Fire is flaming up but without substance inside, and is therefore symbolized as ☲. Thunder rises from the ground and extends itself outward toward all different directions and is therefore symbolized by ☳. Wind, being soft in its inner essence,
appears furious and strong, and the more upward the stronger
it becomes and is therefore symbolized by ☴. From all these

we can observe that the attributes of the eight elements as symbolized by the trigrams are but "firmness," "receptive-ness," "motion," and "rest." These attributes are revealed through the interaction of things and through interprehension of "nothingness" and somethingness." The I Ching employs tri-grams to symbolize the attributes of natural things. They may also be used to symbolize things in interaction and their at-tributes in order to show that all things in the world manifest the relation of mutual implication between "nothingness" and "somethingness." This is why through the combination of the trigrams there have been produced the sixty-four hexagrams. The sixty-four hexagrams symbolically characterize that all existences interact with one another through their virtues or power, so that they give rise to new events or objects. The process of each event, in fact, is the formation of novel events or objects through the interaction among events or objects. The fundamental principle of giving birth to new events or new ob-jects lies in the occasion that the firm matches the receptive and the moving matches the rest, so that there is interprehen-sion between "somethingness" and "nothingness." This is why the concept chung ho [comprehensive and dynamic harmony] is an ultimate value. If the interaction between the two objects fails to attain any harmony, these two objects have to readjust themselves by turning to other objects for new interaction so that their virtues can be changed or improved. After some change or improvement of virtues, the two objects can interact again in order to lead toward the complimentariness of their virtues so as to attain harmony and to give birth to new objects or events. As based on this theory, there are only temporary conflicts and struggles among the myriad things in the universe but no such things as perpetual conflicts and permanent strug-gles. The path leading from conflicts to harmony is not a sim-ple synthesis resulting from one opposite element conquering the other. It lies in the two interacting objects' conscious ex-pansion of their interactive perspectives through their own ex-ploration of a broader path, so that they can form two broader evolutionary processes and these two processes interact with

each other again. Because of this, conflicts can finally lead to
harmony, so that disasters can lead to good fortune and dead
ends can lead to open vistas. Only because of this, all existences can continue to be born and to grow, and the universe
thus can perpetuate its existence. What has been discussed is
only a sketchy summary of the teaching of the I Ching, a work
which is indeed comprehensive and profound and which has in-
vested the Chinese mind with its everlasting metaphysical insights.

5. Space and Time in Chinese Cosmologies

In Chinese Cosmologies there is no opposition between matter and energy, matter and space, or space
and time. Space and time are interpreted in terms of
position and succession. There has never been a notion
of time and space without the existence of any object.

According to the teaching of the I Ching, every object interacts and interprehends with other objects so that new existences
are born and developed. This is why, in the I Ching as well as
in later Chinese cosmologies, there has never been any opposition between matter and energy or matter and space as there
was in the West. Since the reality of any object is its nothingness within somethingness, the nature of an object lies in its
capacity for interaction and interprehension. There are many
theories of matter in the West. It has been held, as was discussed in previous sections, that material substance was the
underlying support of the world of sense-perception, its nature
being inertness and filling up space. Plato and the Platonists
held that matter was the principle of limitation. Aristotle had
a concept of pure or formless matter. For Fichte, matter was
a resistance to the will, being the ground of "nonego" waiting
to be conquered by the "ego." Hegel interpreted matter in
terms of mutual externalization of diversified objectifications
of reason. All these theories failed to establish the positive
nature of matter. To say that matter is inert and fills space
and to say that matter resists our will is not different from

saying that it renders the force operating upon it (by us) dissipated and thus prehended. To say that a material substance is formalized matter means forms can be prehended into matter. The notion of mutual externalization can in our theory mean that each object forms a distinct prehensive unit or center. The limiting nature of matter is exhibited in the selection or rejection of the prehensive process. Therefore, according to our theory, the so-called "filling up space," "pure inertness," "pure matter," and "the externalizing and limiting nature" are but reflected results of the fact that an object has its active prehensive nature yet its prehension is unable to cover the scope as we hope or expect. Apart from our hope or expectation of what its prehension should be, there is no such thing as inertness or resistance. The prehensive nature of an object is its Yin aspect. The essence of matter is its Yin nature. This Yin or prehensive nature lies in its nothingness, which not only takes external forces as somethingness but also renders them recessed. As to the so-called energy or force of an object, it is exhibited in its capacity to move other objects and interact with them. When one object x makes another object y move, this means that x shows power to y and at the same time x loses its own power — according to new physics the loss of power or energy is the same as the loss of mass. The externalization of the power of an object is what we call shih [somethingness or substrativeness]. This externalized power depends on the power's being prehended by other objects and thus being dissipated and transformed into nothingness. A natural object's possession of power and mass which is the capacity for prehension is demonstrated in the successive growing process in which its change interacts and correlates with the change of other objects. Therefore mass and energy are mere abstract notions. What there is in nature is an evolutionary process of "opening" and "closing."* Opening

---

*These two terms are only very rough approximations. The Chinese originals are k'ai-ch'i and sou-nien, which virtually defy English translation. — Tr.

yields the way to closing, and closing, to opening. When one
object opens and the other closes, this means that the latter
prehends the former and the former had empathy in the latter.
Hence nature is not conceived as a process of mere mutual
transformation between mass and energy but understood as a
giant evolutionary process which is composed of intertrans-
formations among diversified evolutionary processes. It is not
a prehension between mass and energy but an interprehension
among different evolutionary processes. Some moves toward
"closing," and some moves toward "opening." Hence it is an
intertransformation between nothingness and somethingness,
growth and decline. This is the alternation between Yin and
Yang, and the Tao which permeats the interprehensive and
interactive process of the two. This clearly reveals that the
notion of the unity of mass and energy can be implied within
the Yin-Yang philosophy.

In Western thought there is the concept of matter as something fulfilling space, and something that can have a certain
shape or form. Therefore there has been the concept of space
which is separate from matter. An object's motion which is
the expression of its power or energy takes place in time. The
space an object occupies is limited, and its magnitude and the
time it takes to move are also limited. Even when we think of
the totality of the objects with their motions, there still seem
possible that there exist independent space and time. Consequently, there come the notions of infinite space and infinite
time. In the West, time and space are considered to be two
separate things. There develops the interest of investigating
things that are infinitely great or small, in the past, in the
present or in the future within the infinite space and time.
This was already discussed in some previous section. But in
Chinese thought, first, time and space are not considered two
things. Therefore, yü (宇) and chou (宙) are together to form
one single term. So are shih (世) and chieh (界). Shou-wen
[an ancient Chinese etymological dictionary] interprets yü and
chou saying: "Yü, the extended cover of a boat or a carriage.
The lower part is yü and the upper chou." Thus yü and chou

from the beginning have not been implied to be two separate
things. Second, in Chinese thought an object is not conceived
merely as something occupying specific space and time; therefore an abstract concept of infinite space and time has never
existed in Chinese philosophy. The I Ching speaks of wei [po-
sition or location] rather than space, speaks of hsü [successive
order or occurring order] instead of time. Every object has
its position, and its rise and development are in accordance with
occurring or successive order. When position changes, successive order follows change. When successive order changes,
position will change correspondingly. When both succession
and position change, the object itself and other objects involved
(in the interaction with the object in question) also change.
Therefore, events or objects are not separate from their position and succession. Take, for example, the fact that the
distinction between east and west, north and south, is based on
the position of the sun. The four seasons — spring, summer,
autumn, and winter — are based on the regularity of the successive order of natural phenomena. Of course we do not deny
the fact that a specific object has its position and occurrence
order. Nevertheless, the position of the object is determined
by its relation with other objects or events. From the viewpoint that nature is a huge network of interprehensive processes, we may say that although an object is located here, what
it interacts with is there. So it is very difficult to say that this
object is definitely here. As to the time of the rise of an event
or object, it is determined by its contemporaneous events. Although we may determine that an event is rising now, it succeeds previous events which took place before it and, at the
same time, it opens up the process for the events which develop after it. This means that its rise is a result of the prehension of past events and, as it completes itself, it becomes
available for prehension by the events which grow after it.
Therefore its time cannot be determined simply as now. Although we can define the position (or location) and successive
order of an object, we cannot make the judgment that it occupies exclusively some definite time and definite space. There-

fore we can say that what Whitehead criticized as "simple location" has never existed in Chinese thought, either in the I Ching or in other philosophical systems. Or, we can say that "simple location" had already been superceded or abandoned long since. The position of the sun is not limited to one location in the sky; it also includes everywhere the sunshine can reach. The birth of a plant is not to be defined in terms of some specific time, for its birth has rested on the ongoing evolutionary process of the universe and, at the same time, its birth is involved in the future evolutionary process which it opens up. The "where" (or location) of any object lies in its field of activities, where its function takes place. Sunshine traverses a vast space in order to reach the earth. Such a vast space is not to be conceived as empty space. At least it is filled with sunshine. In a certain sense such a vast space is occupied by the sun. What has existed in the past, by its function and capacity for interaction and prehension, contributes something to the future. This means the past also exists in the future. Therefore, according to this theory, the so-called infinite space and time as independent from existing objects or events cannot be established on any experiential ground. The so-called space existing among myriad things is but a vast field for the interactivities of these things. The space as viewed by an object (which is usually conceived as having a definite position) is no more than a perspective for its interaction with other objects or a perspective for prehension. The time existing among objects or events is but the "occassion" or "opportunity" for their successive interaction. The future time of an object is no more than a perspective or possible scope for its prehension. It is quite clear that what has been conceived as empty space and time is but a field full of life activities of ch'ien and k'un, full of evolutionary processes which constitute the universe. There is no need to construct, as was done by Newton and Kepler, an image of infinite space and time, objectified as a huge container to embrace the myriad objects of the universe. Consequently, Chinese philosophers did not have clear-cut concept of time as one-dimensional space or three-dimensional space and time.

Chuang Tzu once said: "That which has real existence but has no location is called yü; and that which has continuous growth but has no birth and death is called chou." The distinction between the two is but a distinction between contemporaneity and successiveness. If we take space and time as means of measurement, we can easily fall into the trap of thinking of their infinite extension, since our measuring activities, in principle, can be extended repeatedly and infinitely.

When Chinese philosophers spoke of yü and chou, they spoke of it in terms of position and succession as immediately related — Chou means past, present, and future, and yü means the upper, the lower, and the four directions. If we speak of the universe [yü-chou] in terms of succession and position immediately related, the immediate situation is the limit or the harmonizing ground of the interconnected network of the upper, the lower, the four directions, the past, the present, and the future. When we stand on the ground of such a spot to view the universe, it is indeed full of evolutionary processes which are constituents of other objects and events. At the same time, our own life is an evolutionary process itself, and it is in constant interaction with other processes which seem to be external to our life. Consequently it is impossible for us to get rid of the world or give up things "outside" us and thus cut off our interaction with them. If we realize this, we do not need to explore the extreme of going into "nothingness" to affirm the existence of an infinite empty space. Nor do we need to go back through history to explore the time when nothing existed. The infinity of space and time can be conceived as the unfailing process of evolution in which there are infinite varieties of interaction among the myriad beings. When an object interacts with other objects, it can go beyond (or transcend) its original position and original successive order so that it transcends its finitude and participates in infinity. Infinity in the positive sense is inconceivable. This was already explained thoroughly by Kant. But infinity as exhibited in the negative sense can become manifested and acquire a positive meaning when limitation or finitude is transcended. Therefore, any interaction among objects is transcendence of a limitation and is an affirmation of infinity. According to Chinese philosophy, the interaction among objects exhibits the meeting of objects with different position and succession in order to attain harmony. Therefore Chinese philosophers do not speak of infinity but speak of harmony. For them, where there is harmony, there is implied infinity.

We have explained that ancient Chinese philosophers did not attempt to abstract from reality the concepts of space and time which, again, through objectification, form the notion of spatial and temporal infinity. Chinese philosophers look at things and events as inseparable from their succession and position. When an object or event changes, its position and succession change correspondingly. Owing to our observation of events or objects which seemed to have come back after apparent perishing, and owing to our observation of the rise of events and objects of the same kind based on the same order, we tend to imagine that whatever "goes" will "come back." We then further imagine that the reappearance of the event or object implies the reappearance of the same position and succession. Therefore, according to the cyclical Yin-Yang theory, any object or event which perishes can be born again according to the same principle (the principle which gave rise to it before). Therefore, it seems that the "bygone" may always "come back." Owing to this belief, ancient Chinese philosophers see space and time (where myriad things have their lodging) not as boundlessly infinite, but as "going round and round" then "coming back." [These phrases defy exact translation and should be understood metaphorically — Tr.] Therefore the I Ching holds that "between heaven and earth, there is nothing that goes without coming back." Thus ancient Chinese philosophers, observing the coming and going of the heavenly bodies (the sun, the moon and the stars), the rising and withering of grass and trees, see the unceasing nature of the evolutionary process and the perpetual immanence of harmony among heaven and earth, and thus experience infinity through the infinite comings and goings of myriad things. Consequently, in ancient Chinese astronomy, there were theories like hun-t'ien (渾天), kai-t'ien

(蓋天), and hsüan-yeh (宣夜) (Cf. Tai-p'ing yü-lan 太平
御覽 , the section on Sky) interpreting the unceasing nature of the evolution of heavenly bodies and its unfailing function
in nourishing and sheltering all the beings. Because of these,
there has never been any theory similar to the concept of levels
of heaven as found in the Greek thinkers like Pythagoras and
philosophers after him. There has neither been a notion of infinite extension of heavenly bodies. The reason Chinese astronomy is underdeveloped (e.g., the lack of theories like the sun
as the center of the universe, and the theory of nebular, etc)
is probably due to the fact that our imagination by which we
explore the heavenly bodies usually comes back with the return
of the sun, the moon, and the stars. As to the lack of interests
in exploring the origin of species, the formation of the earth,
or the beginning of the universe, it is probably due to the lack
of an objectification of infinite time as independent from myriad
existences and a lack of the desire for a thorough knowledge of
it. This is why Chinese philosophy has never developed along
the line of scientific philosophy such as the evolution of the universe and the origin of species.

Let us turn to some astronomy in ancient Chinese thought.
Chou-yin is known for astronomy. His description of space
constituted his theory of eighty-one (9×9) possible continents
arranged in a circular manner. It is a kind of circular or
cyclical theory of space. Ch'ü Yüan's T'ien-wen [Heavenly
Questions] had the name of "nine Heavens," but it did not imply
levels or hierarchies. They were classified in accordance with
the four corners, the four directions, and the center, the last
being earth (based on the commentary of Wang I). Yang Hsiung
also had a theory of "Nine Heavens," but it was based on the
functions of t'ien, not implying hierarchies or levels. In English the term "sky" indicates what is immediately above us,
while "heaven" refers to where it is much more distant from
us, or a synonym of firmanent. But in Chinese the word t'ien
includes the meanings of both English terms. In the history of
Chinese thought, the interest in the formation of the universe
started in the period of the Warring States and was developed

in the Ch'in and Han dynasties. However, when we investigate
such an interest as developed in the wei books* and Huai Nan-
tzu and other Han writers, their theories were developed only
up to the concept of "the original force of the very beginning."
They never tried to explore the origin of the evolutionary process of either the human species or myriad things or the universe. The orthodox Confucian philosophers were mostly indifferent to these topics. Hsün Tzu once said: "The beginning
of the universe is here and now." This kind of saying has cut
off the topic at its root. As to theories such as the cycles of
virtues in the Yin-Yang philosophy, Mencius's "five hundred
years cycle theory of the rise of sage kings," and Shao Kang-
chieh's theory of historical cycle, they did not emphasize the
linear progress of human society and history or the development of the universe. They focused primarily on the cycles of
cosmic evolution. From this, we can see that Chinese philosophers never viewed the universe apart from the position of
man; nor did they try to postulate an infinite network of space
and time which embraces the myriad beings of the universe or
to regress infinitely into the ancient period. The standpoint of
Chinese philosophy is that that which is at far distance is related to here, and that which is in the ancient is related to the
present. Since they hold that "the going away implies the coming back," they then believe that that which has been in the past
will recur in the future, and that which has taken place far away
may also happen close by. So they are more interested in the
interaction and growth of myriad things rather than in bound-
lessness and infinity of the universe. They like to see the
"cycles of the stars, alternation of the sun and the moon, and
the succession of the four reasons" (Hsün Tzu). "Going too
far away results in a return, the evolution of destiny is like a
ring" (Hsieh Kuan Tzu). "Oppositions like beginning and ending
reveal no clue, and no one knows what they lead to" (Chuang

---

*Most of these are treatises in cosmology. In contrast with
the orthodox classics, which are called ching, the term wei may
imply unorthodoxy. — Tr.

Tzu). In a word, they are interested in the kind of infinity
which is immediately presented in experience. Thus the I Ching
says:

> When the sun goes, the moon comes, and when the
> moon sets the sun rises. In the succession between
> the sun and the moon there comes light. When the
> cold season goes the hot comes, and when the hot goes,
> the cold comes. Successive alternation between the
> two therein makes the year complete. That which
> goes is recessed, and that which comes is dominant.
> Through the interaction between the recess and the
> dominant, Heaven benefits the myriad things.

Again, it says: "The endless alternation between 'going' and
'coming' is called 'open.' Once when it is open, it will last."
The Chung Yung [Doctrine of the Mean] says: "That which
lasts will perpetuate." The infinity [limitlessness] of objects
is exhibited in their interaction and continuous growth. Thus
the infinity of space and time is also revealed. This is the
viewpoint held by Chinese philosophers, and their sayings and
statements can be found in many passages in classical writings.

6. The Unity and Inseparability of "Li," "Hsiang," and "Shu" in Chinese Cosmologies*

Chinese cosmologies since the time of I Ching have three
unique characteristics. First, the concepts of matter and en-

---

*These three terms, li, (理) hsiang, (象) and shu (數)
have very rich meanings in the Chinese original and defy exact
English translation. Li can mean "reason," "essence," "principle," "form," "pattern," "order," "rationality," etc. Hsiang
can mean "resemblance," "image," "manifestation," "phenomena," "appearance," "perception," "perceptual data," etc. Shu
can mean "number," "mathematics," "mathematical order,"

ergy are assimilated into the fundamental principles of Yin and
Yang. Second, space and time are interpreted in terms of position and succession. As a result of this, there has never been
developed a notion of infinity of space and time, the emphasis
being on the interaction and interprehension among the myriad
things as we experience them. The third characteristic is the
unity of li, hsiang, and shu. Such a unity of these three notions
in ancient Chinese thought is a product of direct experience
rather than a result of abstract rational analysis. A commentator on the Li Chi [Book of Rites] says: "The rise of an object
gives birth to perceptual data [hsiang], then growth, then
mathematical order [shu] become manifest." The I-Wei [Ap-
pendixes to the I Ching] says, "I [change] gives rise to nothingness, then from nothingness to somethingness where there are
forms [li] which seem to have shape. Again, change takes
place and phenomena [hsiang] rise, then comes number [shu]."
["Then comes number" implies becoming countable — Tr.]
This, together with the idea of the unity of shu, li, and hsiang
in the I Ching, forms a fundamental notion in ancient Chinese
mathematical thought. The ancient Chinese paid attention to
only numbers as formed in series like one, two, three, and
four. The foundation of numbers is the evolutionary processes
of myriad things. The growth of an object is based on its principles of development. When something rises, there must be
some concrete image [perceptual data] which becomes manifest. This concrete image, on the one hand, exemplifies the
life principle of the object; on the other hand, it exhibits new
relations [i.e., interactions] between the object and other objects. It also signifies that it will give rise to further images
in accordance with the life principle. A concrete image

"an account," "fate," "destiny," etc. Therefore the translator
is unable to furnish a uniform English translation for each
term throughout the section. The English approximation will
be chosen according to the translator's intuition of the meaning
in a given context. When he feels that an English translation
is impossible, he will leave it untranslated. — Tr.

[hsiang] signifies the virtue, the nature, and the essence
[principle] of the object. Therefore, such an image is not
a mere subjective product or mere superficial appearance
of an object. It is an image inseparable from the principle
or essence of the object. Again, when an image rises, there
must be a movement of the Yang. This means that its reality can be affirmed. From the first image to the rise
of the second image, there must be a transition in which the
first image changes from being dominant to being recessive.
Therein is a completion of the Yin. In this process, the individuality [or "special content"] of the first image passes
from its visible form to formlessness. This also means that
the individuality of the first image is transcended. From the
viewpoint of the observer, at this moment, there is a completion
of the affirmation of this image. The completion of such an
affirmation, in itself, is the objectification of an affirming act.
This is the objectification of a contentless "this is this." It is
also the formation of the contentless concept "one." When the
second image emerges and is near to its completion, we, as
observers, will form another "one" different from the previous
"one." Nevertheless, in our awareness as a whole, we can
affirm the two "ones" together and form the concept "two."
But this "two" in its existential aspect has developed from the
image of the first "one" which gives rise to the image of the
second "one." As a knower or observer, we can be at first
aware of the first "one" and the second "one," then through reflection, we began to be aware of these two "ones" which belong to the "whole one" in our awareness. From this it follows
that three, four, five, six, etc., can be established in accordance
with the life principle which governs the emergence of images.
This also means that numbers like one, two, three, four, cannot be separated from the wholeness or oneness of the life
principle which governs the growth or emergence of objects
or events. Number one, in particular, can prehend or embrace
other numbers, yet its prehension or embrace can be in various
ways, such as one prehending two, two prehending four; or one
prehending three, three prehending nine, etc.

Nevertheless, the number of numbers which are objects of
intuitive knowledge, and which are established upon the images
which are in turn the product of the rise and growth of things,
cannot exceed its proper limit. According to ancient Chinese
culture, they do not exceed ten, and this has been substantiated
by the Ho T'u and the Lo Shu. (We are not going to discuss why
ten is the limit here.) The reason is that in ancient Chinese
philosophy, number is formed from li and hsiang and is not
separate from the two. Therefore the union of numbers exhibits
the union of hsiang [images], and exemplifies the function of li
[principle or reason]. Therefore, no matter whether it is
serial [ordinal] number of coordinating [cardinal] number, the
change of number exhibits the change of phenomena [hsiang],
and the change of phenomena exhibits the change of essence
[li]. This is the most fundamental presupposition of Chinese
mathematics throughout its history. Because of this, there has
never been developed the kind of mathematics that was developed in the West, which is the objectification of pure reason. It
follows from this that Chinese philosophers or mathematicians
are not interested in concepts like infinity, imaginary numbers,
progression numbers, negative numbers, and irrational numbers, which are concepts transcending intuition and are thus
remote from concreteness and unity of human experience.

It is an undeniable fact that Chinese mathematics is under-
developed if it is compared to that of the West. But its basic
presupposition that li, hsiang, and shu form an inseparable
unity is philosophically significant. Western scientists and
philosophers, owing to the success of the construction of abstract mathematical concepts, tend to think that what is analyzable in mathematics is also analyzable in reality, that what
is constant in mathematical analysis is also constant in reality.
They also tend to think that mathematical quantity is the most
fundamental property of myriad things. Differences among objects lie in the differences in mathematical quantity as immanent in the objects. They also tend to think that what is
mathematically equivalent can be conceived as of equal value.
They do not realize that addition and subtraction in mathematics

are not the same as increase and decrease in reality. Any increase or decrease in reality very often not only causes some change in the quantity of the objects involved in interaction, it also causes qualitative change in their modes of prehension and interaction. The correspondence between mathematical operation and change in reality can be found only under the circumstance that the objects involved are external to each other, or that they have very little capacity for interaction with each other. Among the higher levels of existences, the change of quantity often alters modes of interaction and thus produces qualitative differences. The value of an object is exhibited in its capacity for promoting the growth, development, or realization of human or other kinds of beings. Therefore, value is found in the sum total of relations between the object and the subject rather than in a mathematical formula. Therefore mere quantitative increase does not necessarily entail increase of value. Likewise, equivalence in mathematical quantity does not necessarily mean equality of value. Nevertheless, if we trust too much or overemphasize abstract mathematical concepts, mathematical increase will often produce the illusion of of value-increase. Because of the basic presupposition of the inseparability of li, hsiang, and shu, the position held here maintains that our judgment of value should be based on whether the object or idea under evaluation can promote our growth or development, whether it can help in actualizing our goal, rather than based on any mathematical calculation. When li functions, hsiang emerges. When hsiang rises, shu will be developed. The purpose of shu is to know hsiang and to understand li, in order to see into the nature of things (how they grow in accordance with their li), and thus leads to the realization of the values of beauty and goodness. It is this purpose of Chinese mathematics which is fundamentally different from that of the West, the latter being the objectification of pure reason and the instrument for measuring the quantities of things.

The most striking feature of Chinese cosmologies lies in viewing nature as embracing values such as goodness and beauty. This was found in the I Ching and inherited by all later Chinese philosophers. This is probably the greatest difference between traditional Chinese and traditional Western thought. We already discussed that under the interpretation of physical and social sciences in the West, nature and society were conceived as constituted of conflicts and struggles among animals, among human individuals, and among social classes. Nevertheless, in the book of the I Ching, we learn that all conflicts and contradictories in nature and society can be transformed into harmony. In the modern West, the cosmology which views nature as indifferent had its origin in medieval thought in which physical nature or the material world was downgraded. We can even say that it had its remote origin in Greek philosophy where, on the one hand, Pythagoras, Plato, and the Neo-Platonists held that the material world was an inferior world and that matter was a principle of limitation; on the other hand, the materialists held that physical nature was mechanical and devoid of values. This mode of thought was probably due to the fact that Western men have viewed nature in terms of forms and mathematical quantities. This is why modern scientists in the West viewed natural objects only through forms and mathematical quantities, without any willingness to seek or to recognize values in nature. This has led to Bertrand Russell's claim that man had to hold a morally neutral position toward nature. Whitehead, a great exception among Western philosophers, pointed out that the greatest defect of Western culture was its view of nature as value-neutral or devoid from value. Darwin and Marx, who influenced modern Western social theory tremendously, instead of viewing nature as implying values, interpreted nature as full of disvalues. This has developed into the kind of scientific thought which holds that nature and society are full of contradictories, conflicts, and struggles. Such a theory undermines values and thus jeopardizes the ideals of human life.

What I want to maintain, first of all, is that conflicts and struggles in nature and society are only a part of the phenomena. Therefore we cannot hold such a theory as a settled or undisputed truth. After Darwin's theory of "survival through competition," Wallace published The World of Life, maintaining that pleasure constituted the essence of the world of living beings. Kropotkin held that cooperation was the principal of survival. The view of matter in contemporary physics has departed from the theory which interpreted the existence and motion of physical nature in terms of conflicting forces. Instead, recent physics maintains "field interaction," "the least action principle," and "four dimensional natural curvilinear motion." As to whether society is full of conflicts among individuals and struggles among classes, there is no one single answer, for it seems that both the affirmative side and the negative side are justifiable. This means that according to our scientific theories and facts discovered, there is still no final conclusion. An alternative approach is one from the religious viewpoint. If we adopt the notion of an absolute and transcendent God from Christian theology, we have to accept that what God has created is good. Nevertheless, matter and God maintain too far a distance to be congenial to each other. Furthermore, according to Christian doctrine of transcendent God, myriad things in nature were created for man. It is very difficult to see any intrinsic value in nature. If we hold the viewpoint of pantheism, there is difficulty also, for it is difficult to conceive of an omnipotent and benevolent God who was unable to create things in nature with intrinsic value of their own. If we look at nature from the viewpoint of art and literature, it will be difficult for us to deny the existence of the beauty of harmony in nature. Philosophers like Kant, Hegel, and Schelling all recognized beauty in nature. As to viewing nature through the spirit of morality and philosophy, we should not explain away the value as exhibited in the natural world. Thus our line of thought is led to what the I Ching has taught. Now I am going to discuss this thesis.

What I mean by "viewing nature through the spirit of moral-

ity" is through the spirit of Chinese morality. The fundamental
spirit of Chinese morality is the belief in the jen of human nature. It is also the jen [human-heartedness] of the way of
heaven. According to the interpretation of Chinese philosophers, jen in human nature is essentially an absolute negation
of self-centered interests. Such an implication of jen is exemplified in the well-known saying of the Li Chi: "Goods are
not to be wasted, yet they are not to be possessed. Efforts are
to be exercised, but not exercised for oneself." This saying
is representative but not thorough enough. True and absolute
negation of self-interests implies the spirit of not taking one's
own virtue as exclusively one's own. Therefore a man of jen
will not only affirm his own possession of such a virtue but
also recognize other individuals and other objects as having the
same virtue. When one individual is full of, and permeated by,
jen, naturally he will look at other individuals as equally capable of jen and thus look at them as men of jen. He will also
look at all living beings and even inorganic objects as having
the same virtue. The jen in a human being is exhibited in his
feeling which is the capacity for interaction with myriad things
as a way of self-realization and realization of others. When
we observe a natural being, in its process of growth and development, interacting with other beings as leading to its self-
realization and realization of others, shall we not call this the
manifestation of jen? Here let us discuss the four cardinal
virtues, jen, i [righteousness], li [rites, proprieties, rituals,
courtesy, etc], chih [wisdom or knowledge] as manifested in
the human world. Jen is the spiritual and empathetic interaction
among men and is the feeling of one with others. This is the
beginning of all other virtues. Li is the spiritual affirmation
and respect for others. I is the rectification of the relation
between oneself and others. Chih is the cognizance of the reason and order manifested in the completion of self-realization
and the realization of others. The basic fact that myriad things,
through their functions, interact with one another, penetrate one
another, and prehend (used very much like Whitehead's) one another, constitute the life-beginning of everything. It is the orig-

inating function [yüan] of myriad things and is their jen.
Through such an interacting process, there comes growth and
development; it is the prosperity [heng] of things and is properly called their li. Each finite object, through interaction,
gets what it needs; this leads to its self-realization and realization of others. This is called the benefiting (or furthering)
function [li — as different from the li which means proprieties]
of things. It is also their i. The new-born lives [also objects],
accomplish self-realization, and the life-principle is thus manifested. It is what the I Ching called "Through the development
of the Way of ch'ien, everything fulfills its nature and destiny,"
and this is properly called the perseverance [cheng] and mature
wisdom [chih] of things. [The term thing in Chinese original
naturally implies also "lives" — Tr.] To say that things are
not aware of their own manifested nature and virtues is not too
far off the track. But, if we grant that things (including lives)
exhibit jen, i, li, and chih in the life process, yet we still maintain that their virtues exclusively belong to man, then this will
be dogmatic and groundless. If man views all beings in accordance with his cardinal virtue of absolute unselfishness,
jen, and at the same time does not regard jen as exclusively
his, because of the overwhelming virtue of jen he will view all
beings in their processes of growth and development as manifestations of such virtues as jen, i, li, chih; as possessing yüan,
heng, li, and cheng. Even though such virtues are not attributed
to individual natural objects, they would be attributed to the
character of heaven and earth. In fact, in viewing nature, man
seldom pays attention to individual objects. Instead, he views
nature or the universe as one great process of evolution or
growth. When one finite being perishes, it becomes a condition
for the birth and growth of other beings. The apparent death
of a being does not imply that it is a complete extinguishment
and nothing is left. Hence we can say that ends lead to beginnings and death gives way to birth.

As to the notion of competition or conflict, it is not to be explained away. But conflicts and competitions are aiming toward
survival or existence. The concept of craving for survival or

existence, from the viewpoint of Chinese philosophy, is not to
be conceived as merely the preservation of one's own physical
body. Nor do Chinese philosophers view the craving for survival or existence as evil or morally neutral. The craving for
survival or existence lies in the craving for development and
creation. The existence of even a natural object depends on the
fact that it has jen. It is interesting to see that Chinese people
call a seed "jen." The seed of peach is called "t'ao jen" or
"the jen of peach," and the seed of apricot, "hsin jen" or "the
jen of apricot." If we realize that jen is the basis of the urge
for existence of all beings, we shall recognize that conflicts
and competitions are also based on jen. The theory maintaining
that there are struggles and contradictories everywhere in nature is not wholly mistaken. Nevertheless the survival or the
existence of the individual object is prior to its fight with other
individual objects. Its survival or existence is due to its jen.
This means that there must be an internal order (namely unity
and harmony) within the life of the individual object, otherwise
its fight with other individual objects is totally impossible. If
we recognize this, we can understand that the contradictories
and struggles in nature are only on the superficial or surface
level of nature, or that it is only a facet of the main process
of growth and development of all beings. It is not to be conceived as the essence of nature. According to the I Ching, the
apparent conflicts, hindrances, and struggles in nature can
lead to a larger perspective of interaction in order to attain a
greater harmony through coexistence and mutual adaptation.
Theoretically, all the conflicts and contradictories in nature
can be resolved. However, it is difficult for us to view Tao or
nature as a whole from such a one-sided theory based on conflicts and struggles. It is not mistaken to say that there is an
aspect of "darkness" (perishing principle) and "killing" (violence principle) in nature. But the fundamental principle lies
in "light" (life-giving principle) and "birth" (love principle).
Because of this, all beings can grow and develop and the universe thus perpetuates its existence. If "darkness" and "killing" were the fundamental principles, there would be more than

just fights among the individual lives and objects. There would also be fights among the internal parts within an individual life or object. It follows from this that there would not be any individual object which could survive, and the universe would have ceased to exist. Nevertheless the fact shows that the universe does exist and myriad things grow and develop. This is the fundamental premise for us to argue that the basic principle is life and jen. This also demonstrates that nature is not morally neutral or devoid of values.

The origin of the theory which holds the immanence of value in nature is found in the I Ching, and it is recognized by almost all later Confucian philosophers. The Li Chi says: "The sharp and freezing force which starts in the southwest and develops in the northwest is the force of 'dignity' and 'rigidity,' and is called the force of i. The warm and tolerant force which starts in the northeast and develops in the southeast is the force of 'exuberant virtue,' and is called the force of jen." Again, the Yüeh Chi [a chapter of the Li Chi — Tr.] says: "Spring gives birth and summer helps grow, it is jen. Autumn reaps and winter stores, it is i." The Han scholar Chia Kuei, in his commentary on the Tso Chuan, says: "To develop interest and utility is the virtue of earth, and that which enriches life is the virtue of heaven." Tung Chung-shu very often mentioned jen and i as the virtues of heaven and earth. Sung philosophers have even more penetrating interpretations, which cannot be detailed here. Unfortunately, contemporary scholars took this kind of philosophy as a variation of the naturalism of the West without knowing that the basic weakness of the naturalism of the West lies in the separation of value from nature. As a matter of fact, the kind of philosophy in which the Western transcendent spirit is embodied usually rejects naturalism. Chinese philosophers maintain that virtues and values are in nature, and their theoretical foundation lies in the spirit of Chinese morality which does not conceive jen in a narrow or exclusive way (not as exclusively possessed by human beings). Therefore, in Chinese philosophy jen is objectified in the universe. This theory in natural philosophy is an integral part of Chinese in-

tellectual and cultural history in which we find that the concept
of Deity and t'ien in ancient China did not imply the notion of
transcendence. Such a religious thought holds that "the Lord
is nowhere and everywhere" and "the Tao of Heaven is immanent in myriad things on earth." This kind of thought is close
to the idealism in the West. Therefore it is not satisfied with
the idea that values are exclusively possessed by man, and it
holds that all beings possess certain virtues of a moral God as
comprehended by the human mind.

8. A Comparison of the Cosmologies of Confucianism, Taoism, Legalism, and the Yin-Yang School

Our discussions of Chinese cosmologies have been primarily
restricted to those implied in the I Ching, Confucianism, and
the Yin-Yang School and have not been extended to other schools
such as Taoism. The central themes in Mohism and Legalism
were politics and society. The Mohists often spoke of the Will
of Heaven, but what they emphasized was the virtue of Heaven
as exhibited in the fact that Heaven nourishes myriad things
without discrimination. As to Legalism, the cosmology implied
in Han Fei Tzu's "Chieh Lao" and "Yu Lao" was taken from
Taoism. The cosmology of Taoism was indeed different from
those of Confucianism and the Yin-Yang School. Their differences, however, did not lie in their fundamental spirit but in
their distinctive selected emphasis. If we compare these
schools with Western cosmologies, we shall find that they
shared many common themes. Confucians and Yin-Yang philosophers spoke of Yin and Yang as implying both substance
and energy, and the Taoists certainly shared this. Confucianism
and the Yin-Yang School did not entertain the notion of "infinity
of empty space and time"; neither did Taoism. In the first
essay in the Chuang Tzu, there was a question raised: "Blue,
blue, is it the real color of the sky? Or does it mean infinite
distance?" There was, however, no attempt to answer such a
question. Again, both Confucianism and the Yin-Yang School
never had the notion of the separation of mathematical order

from natural phenomena; nor did Taoism. Among all cosmologies, the cosmology of the Yin-Yang School particularly emphasized the order immanent in the process of growth and development of things. This is why it stressed the importance of the principle of the five agents [metal, wood, water, fire, and earth]. Probably due to the concept of the fixed order of the five agents, there was a tendency toward determinism. But this kind of determinism differed from that of the West, for the order of the five agents was considered immanent in the process of the development of things and was not imposed upon them by a deity or any external force. Nevertheless it is a form of determinism, and it became the foundation of some sciences in Chinese culture, such as astronomy, phonology, astrology, and medicine. The tendency toward determinism marks an important difference between the Yin-Yang School and Confucianism. In speaking of life and history, Yin-Yang philosophers often emphasized the governance of destiny. Confucian philosophers, on the other hand, emphasized "knowing destiny," "waiting for destiny," then, "establishing one's own destiny," and "maximum fulfillment of one's own destiny." In original Taoism, the focus was not on "establishing one's own destiny"; nor was it on historical order or actualization of principles as exhibited in the developmental process of things. The Taoists were more interested in birth and death, succession and replacement, among myriad things. Hence the Taoists were more interested in the two ends rather than the mid-process, or the virtues like yüan, keng, li, and cheng, or the stages of the five agents. Chuang Tzu, in his essay "The Evidence of Virtue Complete," says: "Death and life, existence and perishing, prosperity and decline, wealth and poverty, the good and the evil are the change of events and the operation of destiny. It is impossible to know their beginnings, for they simply succeed one another like the alternation of day and night...its division is its completion, and its completion, destruction." Again, in the chapter "Autumn Floods," he says: "Tidings appear high and low, clear and obscure. In life there is something being born; in death there is something ended. Oppositions

such as beginning and end do not give us any clues, and there is
no way to know their whereabouts." Lao Tzu once said: "Reversion is the motion of Tao." "Being and non-being give birth
to each other." All these ideas can be found in the I Ching. But
the basic difference is that the Taoists only spoke of the relativity of two opposed ends and paid little attention to the inter-
mediate process. Hence,-in the Taoist philosophy, the significance of the process of growth and development has not been
given due attention. In the cosmology of Taoism, we only see
alternations of affirmation and negation, compliments of being
and non-being, or substance and emptiness. All these are the
phenomena of the operation of the destiny of myriad things. As
to the order of such an operational process, Chuang Tzu showed
very little interest in it. Nor did he say that such an operation
was determined by any external force. He seemed quite satisfied with merely knowing that it is "change of event" and "operation of destiny." If we can transcend our finiteness to view
the "change of events" and "operation of destiny" of myriad
things, we can see that all beings are from nothingness and go
back to nothingness. The nothingness is the foundation of all
existences. Therefore it was stated as "going back to nothingness." "Something comes out and something goes in. In the
process of 'in and out' we do not see any door, for it is the door
of Heaven. The door of Heaven is nothingness." The Yin-Yang
principle of Lao Tzu and Chuang Tzu is the central passageway
of all existences. Heaven and earth give birth to all existences,
and such a life-giving virtue is the character of nature. Nevertheless, Heaven and earth do not have sympathy for myriad
things. When Heaven and earth are described as "having great
jen," this in fact means "lack of jen." This is why there are
such sayings as "Heaven and earth do not have jen" and "The
greatest jen is no jen." The significance of this theory lies in
its emphasis on the nothingness of nature so that the indeter-
minateness of things can be observed. Also, through the impermanent factor amid the change and development of everything, we can see that all things are capable of sharing the
great virtue of Heaven and earth without hindering one another.

Therefore we can say that Chuang Tzu's cosmology is all-embracing and broad-minded, for it exhibits the beauty of myriad things through their tolerance, self-realization, and the process of a self-enjoying journey. But the main weakness of this philosopher lies in that he knew only nothingness as the foundation of all existences without knowing that everything can make use of its own nothingness to prehend the somethingness of others in order to accomplish its growth and development. This means that Chuang Tzu did not know that the use of nothingness lies in the prehension of somethingness such that self-realization and self-fulfillment are made possible. Neither did he know that the succession of myriad beings is the process of nature which implies gradual enrichment, growth, and substantiation. Thus Chuang Tzu failed to appreciate the virtues of firmness [ch'ien] and gentleness [k'un] of Heaven and Earth [the main theme of the I Ching — Tr.]. It follows from this that Chuang Tzu failed to understand the world of life, society, and history, which are the result of succession and development. Therefore, I can say that in Chuang Tzu's philosophy the Tao of Heaven and Earth is only capable of beauty but not of goodness. It has only the birth-giving virtue but not the virtue of nourishing and cultivating the growth and development of things. In Chuang Tzu's philosophy, although Heaven and Earth give birth to myriad things, the life principle is not immanent in each of them to enable its growth. Confucian philosophers, on the contrary, spoke of Heaven as having the virtue of nourishing life and cultivating growth. After the birth of myriad things, such a virtue is immanent in them so that everything can continue to grow without retardation. Consequently everything (or life) is endowed with such a virtue. Hence the Tao of Confucian philosophy can be characterized as Goodness.

The inactive aspect of Taoism emphasized the principle that "everything comes from nothing and goes back to nothing." Consequently the Taoists value the Tao of Yin rather than the Tao of Yang, and value closeness rather than openness. The influence of this kind of thought has resulted in individualism. The more educated man practices a life of solitary nobility with

tranquility and simplicity. The less educated man becomes
egocentric and selfish. As to those who are shallow and narrow-
minded, they would hold the premise that "all things negate
one another in order to lead to nothingness" and jump to the
conclusion that Heaven and Earth are really cruel (lack of jen).
For them, birth-giving is only for the sake of perishing or killing, and all lives are but straw dogs. [Last statement is from
Lao Tzu — Tr.] Consequently, some of Lao Tzu's sayings and
the book of Yin Fu Ching interpret Tao in terms of the killing
or perishing principle. Han Fei Tzu views human nature as
implying selfishness. The coldness and the lack of tolerance in
Han Fei Tzu's thought is derived from Lao Tzu, whose inactive
position views nature as an executor in the sense that it "swal-
lows what it has given birth to." For this kind of philosophy,
the void and quietude of nature fit properly as the storage of the
dead body of myriad things. Consequently, Han Fei Tzu advised
emperors to stay in nothingness and tranquility, rule the people
with the legalist strategy, and determine whether they should
live, die, be given reward, or taken by force. If we focus our
attention on the cruel aspect of the universe and the evil aspect
of human nature, we may discover what Western men called
"the world of devils." However, the Tao of Yin and the killing
(or perishing) principle alone do not constitute the foundation
of the existence of this world. This has been discussed with
some thoroughness. Therefore the orthodox Taoism developed
in later Chinese philosophy did not develop such a one-sided
theme. On the other hand, the Legalist thought based on Yin
Fu Ching became least valued by later thinkers. According to
Confucian philosophy, the Yang has to be developed and the Ying in-
hibited. The Confucian philosophers also talk about the nothingness
of a thing. But this only means its function to prehend in order to
lead to somethingness or substantiation. Philosophers in the Confucian tradition look at nature as a "lively successive process of
enriching growth and development," the universe as "a great enterprise [meaning activity — Tr.] with the cardinal virtue of continual refinement and renewal." Therefore, after the Chin dynasty,
the Confucian cosmology then was inherited by later Chinese philosophers. From this we can see the basic spirit of Chinese culture.

4

The T'ien Ming[a] *[Heavenly Ordinance] in Pre-Ch'in*[c] *China*[1]

I. INTRODUCTION

IN GENERAL, Chinese philosophy emphasizes the unity or non-duality of Heaven and man. Thus, Chinese philosophical terms like "mind," "nature," "emotion," "desire," and "ambition" all undoubtedly refer to the realm of man; but, at the same time, it is asserted that they have their source in Heaven. On the other hand, terms like "God" (ti[d]), "cosmic energy" ($ch'i$[e]), "yin"[f] and $yang$,"[g] "Heaven and Earth," "being" ($t'ai-chi$[h]) and "non-being" ($wu-chi$[i]), "$yüan$"[j] (the unfolding of the originating power of the Tao[k]), and Nothingness (wu[l]) all evidently refer to the realm of Heaven, but they also have their functions or manifestations in man. There are also some terms in Chinese philosophy that express something Heaven and man have in common, such as "li"[m] (the operational principle of Tao), "Tao," "te"[n] (capacity), and "$hsing$"[o] (action). The term "$ming$"[p] represents the interrelationship or mutual relatedness of Heaven and man. Therefore, if we wish to understand the meaning of the unity or non-duality of Heaven and man, the easiest and most direct approach will be to give a careful elaboration of the precise meaning of the term "$ming$" as it was used by the ancient Chinese schools.

Now, since *ming* as such is to be perceived in the interrelationship of Heaven and man, we can say that it exists neither externally in Heaven only, nor internally in man only; it exists, rather, in the mutuality of Heaven and man, i.e., in their mutual influence and response, their mutual giving and receiving. Past commentators on the term "*ming*" have always fallen into

---

[1] [This article has been translated from the Chinese by Mr. Gi-Ming Shien.[e1] It was originally published in *Hsin-ya-hsueh-pao* (*The New Asia Journal*), II, No. 2 (February, 1957), 1–33.]

one or the other of two extremes—regarding it either externally in Heaven only, or internally in man only. And others who have tried to apprehend the true meaning of the term as used by the ancient Chinese philosophers have been unable to avoid guesswork or dogmatic conclusions. Consequently, they have been unable to reach a precise and comprehensive view of it. The only way to understand the true meaning of the term is to follow the historical development of the doctrine in the schools of various periods in antiquity. We must isolate them and discuss them separately, so that we may determine their precise differences. In this way a clue to the doctrine of *ming* may be apprehended, and its ultimate meaning determined. This article will illustrate my view on the subject.

The doctrine of *ming* first appeared in the pre-Ch'in period [Ch'in, 221–206 B.C.], as may be seen, for example, in Confucius' doctrine of "understanding *ming*," Mo Tzu's⁹ "against *ming*," Mencius' "establishing *ming*," Chuang Tzu's⁷ "resting in *ming*," Lao Tzu's⁸ "returning to *ming*," Hsün Tzu's⁷ "controlling *ming*," Tsou Yen's⁹ "playing host to the cycle [of *ming*]" and his "omen of receiving the Heavenly *ming*"; in the *Doctrine of the Mean*'s⁷ "What Heaven has conferred (*ming*) is called the nature," and "The superior man is quiet and calm waiting upon the Heavenly *ming*"; and in what is said in the *Great Commentary*ʷ of the *Book of Changes*,ˣ "By exhausting the principles to the end and by exploring the law of their nature to the deepest core, they arrived at an awareness of *ming*." The doctrines of *ming* indicated in these references are quite different from each other, but, despite their differences, they have a common remote source in the religious doctrine of the Heavenly *ming* in the *Book of Odes*ʸ and the *Book of Governmental Documents*ᶻ [usually called the *Book of History*].

Later, the scholars of the Han Dynastyᵃᵃ (206 B.C.–A.D. 220) followed Tsou Yen's theory of *ming,* and so they were particularly interested in upholding the theory that "Kings receive the mandate (*ming*) from Heaven," and the idea of the "mandate of fortune." In accordance with this tendency, theories like "the mandate of life" [the length of one's life], "the mandate of suffering" [the good man suffers misfortune], and "the mandate of correspondence" [the fortune of men corresponds with their good or bad deeds] arose. Then the theory that human nature is connected with the cosmic energy (*ch'i*), as well as the quality of *yin* and *yang* and the five cosmic agents, flourished. The scholars of this period were interested chiefly in discussing human nature in terms of what Heaven has conferred on men. Still later, in the *Lieh Tzu*,ᵃᵇ a forgery of the Wei Dynastyᵃᶜ (220–265) or the Chin Dynastyᵃᵈ (265–420), there is an argument between "strength" and "destiny" (*ming*). And, in the Sung Dynasty[aa] (960–1279), Chang Heng-ch'ü[ab] regarded Heaven as the substanceless cosmic energy (*hsü-ch'i*[ac]), and he regarded *ming* as the "ceaselessness" of Heaven [i.e., its creative power]; therefore, he defined *ming* as an "operation in the cosmic energy" and, consequently, understood the *ming* of men to be what men received from this "operation in the cosmic energy." This theory of *ming* is somewhat different from that of the scholars of the Han Dynasty. The school of Ch'eng [I,[ad] 1013–1107] and Chu [Hsi,[ae] 1130–1200] (of the Sung) spoke of Heaven in terms of *li* (the operational principle of Tao). They believed that Heaven sends down its *ming* to men and endows them with the *li* (principle), thus completing human nature; and this is what is called *ming*. This theory of *ming*, again, is different from that of Chang Heng-ch'ü. The school of Lu [Chiu-yüan,[af] 1139–1193] and Wang [Yang-ming,[ag] 1473–1529] believed that the mind itself is the universe, and that the "natural awareness of the good" [another name for the original nature] represents the transcendental intelligence of Heaven and Earth. The development of this theory culminates in the view of Wang Lung-ch'i[ah] and Lo Chin-ch'i,[ai] that [original] human nature itself is *ming*. Later, Wang Ch'uan-shan[aj] followed Chang Heng-ch'ü's view of *ming* as an "operation in the cosmic energy" and, consequently, arrived at the theory that "human nature generates, and, therefore, *ming* descends daily." In the Ch'ing Dynasty[ak] (1644–1911), the problem of human nature and *ming* was brought up again by Yen Hsi-chai,[al] Tai Tung-yüan,[am] and Chiao Hsün[an]; their different views added further complications to the problem. In the same period, scholars like Ch'ien Ta-chin[ao] and Yüan Yüan[ap] devoted themselves to examining the evidence on the precise meaning of the terms *"hsing"*[aq] (human nature) and *"ming"* in the ancient classics, and thus passed judgment on the former scholars' views on the subject. These studies culminated in the modern scholar Fu Szu-nien's[ar] *An Examination of the Evidence on Hsing and Ming in the Ancient Teachings.*[as]

To discuss each one of these theories of *ming* would be too great a task, and we have not even mentioned the Buddhist theory of "the root of *ming*," the Taoist idea of "the parallel cultivation of *hsing* (nature) and *ming*," or "the *ming* of fortune" of the schools of astrology and physiognomy. In this essay, however, we shall concentrate upon the main Chinese schools of antiquity; if we can grasp the essence of their teachings on *ming*, the theories of the various pre-Ch'in schools on the subject will be easier to understand, and their similarities with and differences from the views of later Chinese scholars will, by comparison, be made clear.

To understand the pre-Ch'in doctrine of *ming*, we must first acquire a general knowledge of the meaning of the Heavenly *ming* in the *Book of*

Odes and the *Book of Governmental Documents*. For this purpose, we shall quote relevant texts from the pre-Ch'in schools, on the one hand, and from the *Odes* and *Documents*, on the other, and examine the meaning of *ming* in all these texts. We will discuss the views of the Han and Sung scholars separately. It will not be necessary to quote a great many texts; however, our investigation of the meaning of the texts we quote must be thorough. We may occasionally add some words to the quotations in order to express their implied meaning, but this is only reasonable. After the original meaning of *ming* in the ancient classics has been clarified, the theories of the Han and Sung scholars will fall into their proper places. To what extent later scholars have entered into the realm of the ancient doctrine of the Heavenly *ming* will then be easier to understand. It is for this purpose that I have written this article.

II. The Doctrine of "Ming" in the "Book of Odes" and the "Book of Governmental Documents"

There is a comprehensive collection of texts relating to *ming* in the pre-Confucian period in *The Ancient Teaching on the Hsing and Ming*,[ax] by Yüan Yüan, and *An Examination of the Evidence on Hsing and Ming in the Ancient Teachings*, by Fu Szu-nien. The purpose of these books, however, was only to oppose the Sung scholars' views on *hsing* and *ming*.

In Yüan Yüan's book there is the passage, "The teachings on *hsing* and *ming* in the Yin[ay] [1751–1112 B.C.] and Chou[az] [1111–256 B.C.] dynasties are mostly related to human affairs, and so they are empirical and easy to follow," while "the teachings on *hsing* and *ming* in the Chin and T'ang[ba] [618–907] dynasties are always related to the mind, and so they are easily interpreted in a distorted way." In his book, though he does not directly attack the Sung scholars' theories on *hsing* and *ming*, he nonetheless frequently attacks Li Hsi-chih's[bb] views on them, seemingly ignoring the school of *Li* (reason) of the Sung and Ming[bc] period [1368–1644]; but he thus obviously opposes the doctrines of the Sung scholars as well.

Fu Szu-nien, in his book, regards Hsün Tzu as the orthodox representative of the Confucian school, thus indirectly attacking the Sung scholars' view that such a position belongs to Confucius and Mencius alone. Yüan Yüan, basing himself on texts in the *Odes* and *Documents*, thought that the term *"ming,"* in its ancient meaning, indicated the mandate of fortune, while the term *"hsing"* (human nature) meant simply what one is born with. He said, further, that Mencius does not disagree with this meaning of the word *"hsing"* as what one is born with. Fu Szu-nien also supports this view of the ancient meaning of *hsing,* and tries to prove this point by compiling statistics from the ancient books and classics. By this same method of statistics he also attempts to prove that the word *"ming,"* in antiquity, meant simply "commandment." However, that the "Heavenly *ming"* originally indicated a commandment from Heaven, and *hsing* originally meant what one is born with —these are self-evident facts which may be known without his statistics. With regard to the argument that *ming* is identical with the "mandate of fortune," this, similarly, is implied in the teaching on *ming* in the *Odes* and *Documents;* but the explicit advocacy of this view comes quite late and is the view of the Han scholars, rather than the original meaning of *ming* in the *Odes* and *Documents.* Their arguments about these terms, therefore, are trivial and unimportant.

Our own purpose in discussing the Heavenly *ming* in ancient Chinese thought is to point out the particular features in which it differs from the religious Heavenly ordinance of other peoples, and also to show how it is the great root and source from which all the later pre-Ch'in schools derived their ideas on the Heavenly *ming.* As for the relatively trivial points mentioned above, we shall not discuss them here.

1.

The first notable feature of the view of the Heavenly *ming* at the beginning of the Chou Dynasty, as revealed in the *Odes* and *Documents,* is the fact that "the Heavenly *ming* is not unchangeable." This idea is common knowledge, and is obvious to those who read the Classics. The Chou people probably grasped this idea from the fact that the Yin Dynasty (1751–1112 B.C.) ultimately fell, even though its people devoted themselves piously to the service of the spirits; and they used this fact to caution the future kings of the Chou Dynasty. It is said of the *Documents:*[2]

[a]   There is no mistake about the decree of Heaven (*ming*).

[b]   Heaven's appointment is not constant.

[c]   Oh! God dwelling in the great heavens has changed his decree (*ming*) in favour of his eldest son and this great dynasty of Yin.

[d]   The great Heaven has changed the *ming* of the great state of Yin.

---

[2] [James Legge, trans., The Chinese Classics, Vol. II. *The Shoo King or the Book of Historical Documents.* 2d ed., with minor text corrections and a Concordance Table (Hong Kong: Hong Kong University Press, 1960).]

And in the *Odes:*[3]

[a]   The Heavenly *ming* is not constant [or unchangeable].

[b]   Heaven gave birth to the multitudes of the people, but the Heavenly *ming* [it confers] is not to be depended on.

That "the Heavenly *ming* is not unchangeable" indicates that Heaven never absolutely predetermines who will be king; it may give a new mandate to another man and command him to be king. It is said in the *Odes:*

[a]   Although Chou was an old country, the favouring appointment lighted on it recently.

[b]   The favouring appointment was from Heaven, giving the throne to our king Wen.[bd]

The idea of the Heavenly ordinance in the above quotations is obviously different from Hebrew religious ideas. In the Hebrew view, God, Jehovah, by his commandment predetermines Israel to be the chosen people, and he also predetermines all the future kings. This view similarly differs from that of the oracle at the temple in Athens, according to which a man's destiny is determined by the prediction of the oracle and is totally unavoidable.

2.

In ancient Chinese religious thought there is another idea closely connected with the view that the Heavenly mandate is not unchangeable and that man's future is not predetermined. According to this idea, on the one hand the mandate of Heaven comes to a man only after his cultivation of virtue, and not before; and on the other hand the mandate of Heaven implies an advising of the people, so that by further cultivation of their virtue they may determine their own future. This is the reason that, in the *Odes* and *Documents,* King Wen's receiving the Heavenly *ming* is repeatedly mentioned, while the receiving of the *ming* by both Wen and Wu,[be] and by the Duke of Chou,[bf] is only occasionally mentioned. The reason the Heavenly *ming* came to King Wen is set forth in the *Documents:*

King Wen . . . was able to illustrate his virtue and be careful in the use of punishment. He did not dare to show any contempt to the widower and widows. He employed the employable and revered the reverend; he was terrible to those who needed to be awed:—so getting distinction among the people. . . . The fame of him ascended up to the High God, and God approved. Heaven gave a great charge to King Wen, to exterminate the great dynasty of Yin, and receive its great appointment (*ming*).

[3] [James Legge, trans., The Chinese Classics, Vol. IV. *The She King* (Hong Kong: Hong Kong University Press, 1960).]

And the reason King Wen received *ming,* according to "The Great Odes of the Kingdom," was because "god cherishes the illustrious virtue of King Wen" [and so the Heavenly *ming* came to him]. From this it is obvious that King Wen first cultivated his virtue, and then, the influence of his virtuous conduct reaching to God, God conferred *ming* upon him. This view of the Heavenly mandate is therefore different from the view of the Old Testament that God first had a will, and then conferred the mandate on Abraham and the future kings. It is also different from later Christianity, according to which God first has a predetermined plan for the world, and then, in order to realize this plan and wishing people to do good and cultivate virtue, transforms himself and comes to the world as the God-man, Jesus.

It is conspicuous that in the view of the Heavenly mandate in the Old and New Testaments the commandment of God comes first and man's cultivation of virtue comes afterward. Since God's commandment comes first, man's future can be determined by God, and the word "commandment" thus somehow implies predetermination. In ancient Chinese thought, on the contrary, the Heavenly mandate comes after man's cultivation of virtue, and the future of men is thus not determined by God. Moreover, after a man receives the Heavenly mandate, there is still something (i.e., cultivation of virtue) for him to do which can be done only by himself. The "acceptance of the Heavenly *ming,*" in its true meaning, is therefore the starting point of something to be done, rather than a terminal point of something already accomplished. It does not necessarily follow that upon the man who "receives the Heavenly *ming*" God will definitely bestow wealth and high rank, and make him the actual king; and this is why Yüan Yüan's statement that the original meaning of *ming* is the mandate of fortune is incorrect. If Yüan Yüan's view were correct, and "receiving the Heavenly *ming*" means that Heaven gives a man wealth and rank and makes him king, then the *Odes* and *Documents* ought to ascribe the "receiving the Heavenly *ming*" to King Wu, the Duke of Chou, and King Ch'eng[bg] only, and not to King Wen, who received the Heavenly *ming* as a result of his virtuous conduct.

Further, in Greek, Hebrew, and Arabic thought there was never the custom of placing a man in the company of God and sacrificing to him together with God; in China, however, the Chou people placed Hou-chi[bh] [the ancestor of King Wen] in the company of God and sacrificed to the two together, and they likewise placed King Wen in the company of God and sacrificed to both at the Hall of Distinction. Such a custom, it is true, has its root in the traditions of the Yin Dynasty; but, on the other hand, early Chou culture rather emphasized the aspect of human virtue, for it is because the influence of a man's virtue reaches to Heaven that Heaven commits the mandate to him. And, after such a man receives the Heavenly mandate, there is still something more for him to do [to cultivate his virtue further]— it is such a man who is qualified to be placed in the company of God and sacrificed to with God.

3.

We have seen, in our discussion above, that the phrase "receiving the Heavenly *ming*" has a twofold meaning: on the one hand, the conferring of the Heavenly mandate follows a man's cultivation of virtue; and, on the other hand, after a man accepts *ming*, he ought continuously to cultivate his virtue—and his reward will come. Heaven's conferring its mandate and man's receiving it, as set forth in the *Odes* and *Documents*, both emphasize the continuity and unceasingness of *ming*. This is because, the mandate of Heaven following men's cultivation of virtue, men must be mindful of the Heavenly *ming* and continue to cultivate their virtue even after they have received *ming*; the more fully men cultivate their virtue, the more fully will Heaven confer its mandate on them. Thus *ming* is continuous and unceasing in this world. This is why the *Odes* and *Documents* frequently mention the necessity for cultivating one's virtue in order to preserve *ming*. Some quotations from these texts will substantiate this view. [In the *Documents:*]

[a] I must diffuse the elegant institution of my predecessors and augment the appointment which they received from Heaven.

[b] I do not presume to know and say "the dynasty of Hsia was to enjoy the favouring decree of Heaven for so many years," nor do I presume to know and say "it could not continue longer." The fact was simply that, for want of the virtue of reverence, the decree in its favour prematurely fell to the ground. Similarly, I do not presume to know and say, "the dynasty of Yin was to enjoy the favouring decree of Heaven for so many years," nor do I presume to know and say, "it could not continue longer." The fact simply was that, for want of the virtue of reverence, the decree in its favour prematurely fell to the ground.

[c] To assist in his prayers to Heaven for its long-abiding decree (*ming*).

[d] Think you of the distant future and we shall have the decree in favour of Chou made sure.

These quotations indicate that, in order to preserve *ming* unceasingly, men must exert effort to cultivate their virtue.

There are passages in the *Odes,* too, that refer directly to the unceasingness of *ming* on the part of Heaven itself, as, for example, "The ordinances of Heaven, how profound are they and unceasing!"

From these passages we may see just why "the Heavenly *ming* is not unchangeable." It is because, if men cannot preserve their own *ming* by cultivating their virtue, Heaven, to realize its unceasing *ming,* cannot but confer it upon another virtuous man. Thus, the doctrine that "the Heavenly *ming* is not unchangeable" is secondary; the primary doctrine is the continuity of the Heavenly *ming* in this world. This is why the Heavenly *ming* may be taken from one king or dynasty and given to another, as it was, for example, when the Yin Dynasty overthrew and succeeded the Hsia⁵¹ [2183–1752 B.C.], and later the Chou succeeded the Yin. Heaven constantly loves the people and therefore looks on all parts of the world to find a dwelling place for its mandate, which it confers unceasingly, whether upon a single king or upon a succession of kings.

In the doctrine of *ming* discussed above there are three distinct implications. First, in ancient Chinese thought Heaven is seen as omnipresent and impartial, favoring no particular man or nation. This view culminates in the later Taoist and Confucian idea that Heaven's overspreading and sustaining of the world are not partial, and that the dwelling place of God in this world is not unchangeable.

Second, the Heavenly mandate is conferred on a man only after his cultivation of virtue. This view later developed into the primary emphasis—in Chinese religious, moral, and political thought—upon exerting human effort to the utmost, rather than upon prayer. The teaching that, once one has received *ming* he must further cultivate his virtue was followed by later Confucians in their view that the way to serve the Heavenly *ming* was to illustrate one's illustrious virtue and to stand in awe of the Heavenly *ming*. And the implications of the teaching that the mandate will be conferred on one that has virtue, and that cultivation of one's virtue is the way to serve Heaven, are extended in the *Great Commentary* of the *Book of Changes,* where it is said, "The Great Man acts in advance of Heaven and Heaven does not contradict him," and "When the Great Man follows Heaven, he adapts himself to the time of Heaven."⁴ These teachings, finally, are the source of such later ideas as: man is one of the three primal powers of the universe (together with Heaven and Earth); man is one with the transforming forces of Heaven and Earth; there is mutual influence and response between Heaven and man; and there is mutual identification between Heaven and man.

---

⁴ Richard Wilhelm, trans., *The I ching; or Book of Changes.* The Richard Wilhelm translation rendered into English by Cary F. Baynes. Foreword by C. G. Jung (New York: Pantheon Books, 1950).

Third, to preserve the Heavenly *ming,* men ought to cultivate virtue; and the Heavenly *ming* is unceasing. These are the source of the later Chinese idea that the Tao of men ought to follow the Tao of Heaven, i.e., the eternal Tao, which unceasingly gives birth to all things. This idea culminates in the search for the continuity of human history and culture.

These three implications of the ancient doctrine of the Heavenly *ming* may be summarized as follows: first, "the omnipresence of the Heavenly *ming*"; second, "the common root of the Heavenly *ming* and human virtue"; and, third, "the unceasingness of the Heavenly *ming.*" The full implications of these three ideas were not realized in as great detail in the *Odes* and *Documents* as they were in the thought of later Confucians; and [partly for this reason, no doubt] the ideas have not been grasped by previous scholars. If, however, we base our view upon the doctrine of the Heavenly *ming* in the *Odes* and *Documents,* and compare it with analogous ideas in the religious thought of other ancient peoples, clarifying the similarities and differences between them, then there can be little doubt that the view of the Heavenly *ming* in ancient Chinese thought is, indeed, as we have described it here.

III. THE VIEW OF THE HEAVENLY "MING" IN THE SPRING AND AUTUMN PERIOD[bi] (721–481 B.C.)

Our discussion so far has referred only to the view of the Heavenly *ming* held in the first part of the Chou Dynasty. The development of this idea during the next several centuries, to the time of Confucius, may be found in the *Tso Chuan*[bk] and *Kuo Yü.*[bl] We may summarize the views of these two books under four headings.

1. *Expansion of the Early Chou idea that "the determination of the* ming *is in accordance with one's virtue."*

In the *Tso Chuan* (Duke Hsiang,[bm] 29th year), Pi Ch'en[bn] of Cheng[bo] says, "That the virtuous succeed the unvirtuous is a matter of the Heavenly *ming.* How could we avoid Tzu Ch'an?"[bp] (—meaning that Tzu Ch'an, being a virtuous man, must attain power in the State of Cheng).

In the *Odes* and *Documents* the idea that the receiving of the Heavenly *ming* is in accordance with one's virtue refers only to the mandate of a king. Here, however, the idea is evidently extended even to the minister of a state. Further development of this idea culminates in the Han scholars' theory of "the *ming* of correspondence": the fact that a person has wealth and prestige or poverty and low status is determined by and in correspondence with his virtue.

2. *Development of the theory that* ming *is in correspondence with one's virtue; and that it implies predetermination.*

In the *Tso Chuan*,[5] Wang-sun Man,[bq] replying to the Viscount of Ch'u[br] [when the Viscount asked about the size and weight of the tripods], says,

Heaven blesses intelligent virtue:—on that its favour rests. King Ch'eng fixed the tripods in Chia-ju[bs] and divined that the dynasty should extend through thirty reigns, over seven hundred years. Though the virtue of Chou is decayed, the decree of Heaven is not yet changed. The weight of the tripods may not yet be inquired about.

Now, in the "Announcement to Chou" in the *Documents* it is said that, if a king cannot devote himself to virtue, his mandate will be terminated by Heaven. In this passage, however, it is said that, though the virtue of the Chou Dynasty has declined, its mandate still has not been changed. It would seem, then, that there is no connection between one's virtue and *ming*. This contradicts, too, the statement in the *Odes* and *Documents* that "the Heavenly *ming* is not unchangeable." My own view of the matter is that this idea of predetermination is derived from the popular religious thought of antiquity. Yet, if we examine the passage carefully, we see that the statement of the oracle, that the dynasty would last thirty generations and seven hundred years, indicates no more than that the virtuous deeds accumulated by King Wen, King Wu, and the Duke of Chou, and their influence on future generations, are sufficient for their dynasty to last that long. Thus, though "there is a final end of Heavenly blessing to the virtuous man," still it will take thirty generations and seven hundred years for the *ming* of the Chou Dynasty to be changed. This view of predetermination reappeared later in the Chinese schools of divination, according to which, in addition to predetermination by a man's star or destiny, there is the influence of the virtuous deeds accumulated by a man's ancestors. From this discussion we can see that the development of the early Chou idea of *ming*—that the destiny of a man corresponds with his virtuous deeds—will naturally end in a theory of predetermination.

This kind of predetermination, however, is based upon the virtuous deeds accumulated by one's ancestors, rather than upon the absolute free will of God, as in the Old Testament. Still, this idea of the Heavenly *ming* does imply a sort of predetermination, and it is precisely this idea that Mo Tzu opposes in his essay "Against *Ming*"; and it is also the remote source, later, of the *Lieh Tzu's* view of *ming*.

---

[5] [James Legge, The Chinese Classics, Vol. V. *The Ch'un Ts'ew with the Tso Chuen*. 2d ed., with minor text corrections and a Concordance Table (Hong Kong: Hong Kong University Press, 1960).]

3. *The twofold extension of the meaning of* ming: *as "the length of one's life," and as "duty."*

In the *Tso Chuan* (Duke Wen, 13th year) it is said:

Duke Wen consulted the tortoise-shell about changing his capital to I. The officer [of divination] said: "The removal will be advantageous to the people but not to their ruler." The viscount said: "If it be advantageous to the people, that will be advantageous to me. When Heaven produced the people, it appointed for them rulers for their profit. Since the people are to get advantage [from the removal], I shall share in it." His attendants said, "If your life may so be prolonged, why should you not decide not to remove?" He said: "My appointment is for the nourishing of the people; my death sooner or later has a [fixed] time. If the people are to be benefited let us remove, and nothing could be more fortunate." The capital was accordingly removed to I, and in the fifth month Duke Wen died. The superior man may say that he knew his *ming*.

According to this passage, the officer of Duke Wen of Chu advises him, in order to extend his *ming* or life [here *ming* means "life"], to follow what was revealed by divination and not move his present capital; and immediately after the move to the new capital the historian tells us of the Duke's death. Thus the *ming* in this passage seems connected with what was later called the "mandate of age." However, the term "mandate of age," as one of the three definitions of the word *"ming,"* appeared only quite late, in the Han Dynasty; in ancient China, the one word "age" served to express this meaning. Moreover, the word "life" (*sheng*[bt]) means the life of a man, while "mandate" (*ming*) means the mandate derived from Heaven; these two words are not identical. Thus, there were no such terms, in the early Chou Dynasty, as *sheng-ming* or *hsing* (human nature) *-ming*.

Here, however, a question arises, for in the chapter *"Ku-ming"*[bu] of the *Documents* it is said that the length of King Wen's life corresponds to the duration of the Heavenly *ming* he received; this would seem to indicate that *ming* means "mandate of age." Further, in the chapter *"Hung-fan"*[bv] of the *Documents,* there is a passage referring to the Five Blessings, and one of them is "accomplishing to the end the mandate"; here "accomplishing to the end" is connected with *ming,* and *ming* would thus seem to refer to "the mandate of age." Moreover, in the passage from the *Tso Chuan* quoted above, the officers of Chu advised their ruler not to change the capital, so as to prolong his life, and, after the change was made, the Duke soon died. Here *ming* in the mind of the officers has two meanings: on the one hand, the maintenance of the government of their ruler, a government he possesses because of *ming;* and, on the other, the lifetime of the ruler himself. Both of these they wish prolonged, though the emphasis of the passage is definitely on the latter meaning. This latter meaning is probably the original source for all those—from Chuang Tzu on—who connect "life" with *ming* and express them together in one term.

If, however, we examine the reply of Duke Wen to his officers: "When Heaven produced the people, it appointed for them rulers for their profit. Since the people are to get advantage [from the removal], I shall share in it [etc.]." We see that Duke Wen evidently did not think of *ming* as the "mandate of age," but, rather, in its ancient meaning as the duty of cheerfully maintaining his government, cherishing and embracing his people by protecting the helpless, etc. Further, in the judgment of Duke Wen at the end of this passage—"The superior man may say that he knew *ming*"—what is the meaning of *ming?* It evidently refers to Duke Wen's understanding that the duty of a ruler is to nourish the people as Heaven commanded him, rather than simply his understanding that the time of his death is determined by the "mandate of age." To nourish and take care of the people is the responsibility of a ruler, and it represents his "duty" as well. Thus the term *"ming"* as used by the superior man, as well as by Duke Wen himself, refers to a ruler's understanding of what he ought to do in view of his "duty." Duke Wen, for the sake of his people, understands *ming* and does not regret his own death; this is precisely the virtuous conduct that was later called "sacrificing oneself for the sake of duty." Thus, when the superior man here attributes to Duke Wen the "understanding of *ming*," his idea of *ming* represents an advance over the idea of *ming* in the early Chou Dynasty. The latter stops short at saying, "If a ruler has virtue, he will receive the Heavenly mandate. After he receives it, he ought to cultivate his virtue even more; and thus he will be able to maintain his kingdom and enjoy his government for a period of so many years." But what the superior man meant by "understanding *ming*" was, rather, abandoning the desire for long life and preferring the accomplishment of a ruler's duty; this idea of *ming* clearly is an advance over the Early Chou idea. The latter idea is henceforth abandoned, to be replaced by the new idea of how to serve the Heavenly *ming*. And the meaning of the phrase "understanding *ming*" here is almost the same as the later "understanding *ming*" of the Confucian school.

4. Ming as the [revealed] rules of personal behavior and demeanor.

It is said in the *Tso Chuan:*

The people received the central harmony between Heaven and Earth, to which they owe their existence. Thereupon, there are the [revealed] rules to govern their personal behavior and demeanor, and it is through them that the *ming* of men is defined and fixed. The superior keeping observance of them, blessing comes; the inferior ignoring them, disaster results. Thus the superior diligently devote themselves to the practice of the *li* . . . while the way to practice the *li* resides in devotedness, which in turn resides in respect of the spirits. Now he ignores his own *ming* [i.e., he is lax in the rules]; he probably will not return home again.

We may compare the first few sentences of this passage with a passage in the *Odes*: "Heaven gives birth to the people. If there is a thing, there is a rule for it; thereupon the nature of the people will naturally incline to virtue." At first sight, both of these passages seem very similar to Mencius' "Heaven gave me my original mind" and the *Doctrine of the Mean*'s "What Heaven has conferred is called the nature"; but there is still some difference between them. In the passage just quoted from the *Odes,* it is not definitely stated whether the virtue desired by the people is internal, inherent in their very natures, or external, the virtue of following the good sayings and virtuous conduct [of a good man]. Further, what does "rule" mean in this passage? It may refer simply to external ethical rules. And in the passage from the *Tso Chuan* it is not made clear whether or not the "rules" spoken of, as well as the *ming* they define, spring from within. Since *ming* is defined and fixed by the "rules," the inner content of *ming* also ought to be defined by them. As for the "rules" themselves, they have their origin in Heaven and Earth, i.e., in "the central harmony between Heaven and Earth."

If what we have said here is true, then *"ming"* in the passage from the *Tso Chuan* and the "rule" in the passage from the *Odes* are very close in meaning to *"ming"* and "rule" in the *Odes* and *Documents* discussed in the previous section. Thus, the statement of K'ung Ying-ta,[bw] in his commentary on the *Tso Chuan,* that *"ming"* here means "didactic commandment," has probably caught the original meaning.

Let us return now from these interpretations of the passage from the *Tso Chuan* to the passage itself. In it, Liu K'ang-kung[bx] [whose words the passage quotes] connects the *ming* of Heaven and Earth with the rules of human life, and thus explicitly connects the natural life of a man with the duty commanded him by Heaven. Now, since "human nature" in ancient China is identical with "life," Liu K'ang-kung in this passage is the first man to connect human nature with the Heavenly *ming.* Further development of this idea in Confucius, Mo Tzu, etc., culminates in the ideas [on the Heavenly *ming*] of Mencius and the *Doctrine of the Mean.* These we shall discuss in what follows:

IV. Confucius' Doctrine of Understanding Ming

It is common knowledge that the true meaning of Confucius' statements on *ming* has always been something of a problem. The *Analects*[6] says:

[a] At fifty, I knew the *ming* of Heaven. (*Analects*[br] II. 4.)

[b] Confucius said, "There are three things of which the superior man stands in awe. He stands in awe of the ordinances (*ming*) of Heaven. He stands in awe of great men. He stands in awe of the words of sages." (*Analects* XVI. 8.)

[c] If the Tao is realized in the world, it is a matter of *ming;* if the Tao is not realized in the world, it is also a matter of *ming*. (*Analects* XIV. 38.)

[d] The Master said, "Without understanding the *ming*, it is impossible to be a superior man. Without an acquaintance with the rules of propriety, it is impossible for the character to be established. Without knowing the force of words, it is impossible to know men." (*Analects* XIV. 3.)

From these passages it is clear that Confucius emphasizes devotion to and standing in awe of the Heavenly *ming,* rather than regarding it as an external predetermination. However, other passages in the *Analects* seem to have a different emphasis.

Po-niu[bt] being ill, the master went to ask for him. He took hold of his hand through the window, and said, "It is killing him. It is the appointment (*ming*) of Heaven, alas! That such a man should have such a sickness! That such a man should have such a sickness! (VI. 8.)

And Confucius' disciple Tzu Hsia[ct] said, "As for one's wealth and honor, they are appointed by Heaven. As for one's life and death, they are a matter of *ming"* (XII. 5). In these two passages, Confucius and Tzu Hsia both seemed grieved over a *ming* that is externally predetermined. It was on the basis of these passages that Mo Tzu said, "The Confucians think that there is an ultimate determination of men's long life or premature death, poverty or wealth, order or disorder [in the world] by *ming*, which can neither be decreased nor increased." And Fu Szu-nien says, "The *Analects* clearly contain the idea of the predetermination of *ming*. It is just on this point that Mo Tzu attacks it." Besides these interpretations of Confucius' view of the *ming,* there is also the Han scholars' idea of Confucius as the uncrowned king who

---

6 [James Legge, trans., The Chinese Classics, Vol. I. *Confucian Analects,* the *Great Learning, Doctrine of the Mean* (Hong Kong: Hong Kong University Press, 1960).]

received *ming* from Heaven, and the view of the Sung scholars, who express *ming* in terms of *li* [the operative principle of Tao].

Because of these different interpretations of Confucius' view of *ming,* its real meaning becomes more difficult to grasp. But let us, for a moment, put aside Confucius' emotional words on the death of Po-niu, as well as Tzu Hsia's saying and the views of later scholars, and try to examine Confucius' view of *ming* objectively. If we do so, we shall discover that he holds no such view as the predetermination of *ming;* nor does he hold, as do the *Doctrine of the Mean* and the Han Confucians, that "[the man of] great virtue is certain to receive the mandate from Heaven." Confucius' idea of *ming* is similarly different from those expressed in the *Odes, Documents,* and *Tso Chuan.*

The reason we cannot say that Confucius' view of *ming* was entirely similar to that in the *Odes,* the *Documents,* or the theories of the Han Confucians is simply that there are no such ideas in the *Analects* as man's "receiving *ming*" or Heaven's "bestowing *ming*" [Han Confucian ideas]; nor did Confucius teach the people to practice the [revealed] unchangeable codes and the path commanded by Heaven [as did the *Odes* and *Documents*]. Confucius, rather, taught his disciples human-heartedness and love of parents, things directly connected with the routine affairs of daily life. His teachings were intended to bring about self-examination and realization of what one's heart finds peace in. Those, therefore, who think Confucius' doctrine of *ming* stops short at that of the *Odes* and *Documents* are mistaken.

Here, however, a question arises. If Confucius' teaching emphasizes self-examination and realization of what one's heart finds peace in, how can we explain what Confucius said about "standing in awe of the Heavenly *ming*" and "understanding *ming*"? To answer this question we must turn to the *Tso Chuan* and the *Kuo Yü* (Duke Wen, 15th year): "The superior man does not maltreat the young or those of inferior status, because he stands in awe of Heaven." We may see from this passage that in ancient Chinese religious thought there was already the idea that Heaven is sympathetic to the people and loves them in the highest measure; thus, to practice human-heartedness —and dare not to maltreat the young and inferior—is the way to devote oneself to and stand in awe of the Heavenly *ming*. This idea is taken up by Han Ying,[cb] who followed the teachings of Mencius to explain Confucius' doctrine of "understanding *ming*." In his book, *Additional Treatise on the Book of Odes,*[cc] he said:

Confucius said, "If one does not understand the *ming*, one cannot be a superior man." The meaning of this is: All that are born of Heaven have a heart of human-heartedness, righteousness, propriety, wisdom, obedience, and goodness. If one does not understand what Heaven conferred on him at birth, then he will lack this heart of human-heartedness, righteousness, propriety, wisdom, obedience, and goodness; and such a one is called an inferior man. Therefore it is said, "If one does not understand the *ming,* one cannot be a superior man.". . .

"Heaven gives birth to the people. If there is a thing, there is a rule for it." This means that man by his natural endowment tends to model himself after Heaven. If one does not know how to model himself after Heaven, how can he be a superior man?

We must acknowledge, thus, that "self-examination" and "realization of what one's heart finds peace in," on the one hand, and "standing in awe of the Heavenly *ming,*" on the other, really mean the same thing, though they seem different.

But here another problem arises. If what we have just said is true, it seems to contradict Confucius' statement, "If the Tao is realized in the world, it is a matter of *ming;* if the Tao is not realized in the world, it is also a matter of *ming.*" If Heaven really loves the people, it is correct to say that the realization of the Tao is a matter of *ming,* but incorrect to say that the failure to realize the Tao in the world is also a matter of *ming.* If this failure is a matter of the Heavenly *ming,* then it would seem that Heaven does not love the people. And, if a man ought to devote himself to and stand in awe of the Heavenly *ming,* ought he not then also devote himself to and stand in awe of the failure to realize the Tao in the world [for that is also the Heavenly *ming*]? And why did Confucius travel throughout the world attempting to realize his Tao? Did he fail to stand in awe of *ming?* Again, when Po-niu was ill, Confucius said, "It is killing him. It is the *ming* of Heaven"—here *ming* seems to be the "mandate of life and death," which comes from without, not from within. And in Confucius' grief over Po-niu, did he fail to stand in awe of the Heavenly *ming?* But, if this is so, why did Confucius make such statements as "stand in awe of the Heavenly *ming,*" "without understanding *ming,* it is impossible to be a superior man," and "at fifty, I knew the *ming* of Heaven"?

I have repeatedly pondered these problems, and I have hesitated, in the past, between two points of view with regard to them: (1) Confucius' view of the Heavenly *ming* still follows the old idea that *ming* is a revelation from Heaven: in other words, that it is a direct commandment of the ethical rules that men have to follow; or (2) The Heavenly *ming* of Confucius resides only in what one's heart feels at peace in, and thus is a commanding of oneself. Finally, however, I realized that both of these points of view are incorrect. If Confucius held the first view, that *ming* is the commandment of ethical rules that men have to follow, this is simply the common view held ever since the time of the *Odes* and *Documents,* and even Mo Tzu could grasp its meaning and use it to complete his treatise on "The Purpose of Heaven." This view is easy to understand and is so elementary that Confucius ought not to have said he understood it only at the age of fifty. If, on the other hand, Confucius held the second view, that *ming* resides in what one's heart feels at peace in, a commanding of oneself, then we shall have difficulty explaining the stages of Confucius' life before he reached the age of fifty. "At fifteen, I had my mind bent on learning. At thirty, I stood firm. At forty, I had no doubts" (*Analects* II. 4).

In these stages he had already practiced such things as self-cultivation, self-commandment, self-examination, inner penetration, ardent realization, and realization of what the heart feels at peace in; and, again, he ought not to say that he understood *ming* only at the age of fifty.

From Confucius' serious statements—that he understood the Heavenly *ming* at the age of fifty; that, "if one does not understand *ming,* one cannot be a superior man"; and that one should "stand in awe of the Heavenly *ming*"—we may know that Confucius' understanding of *ming* comes as a result of the accumulation of learning and from his virtuous conduct; and these, in turn, developed from his traveling throughout the world, being frequently confronted with the fact that his Tao was not to be realized in the world, and his apprehension of the fact that, whether or not his Tao was realized, he had to accept willingly whatever happened. This was the way to "devote oneself to and stand in awe of the Heavenly *ming*." This great development in Confucius' thought, resulting in a view which is different from the purely traditional one, is at the same time not simply limited to "realization of what one's heart feels at peace in." All the doubts I have expressed here are the result of my ignorance of this new view of the Heavenly *ming* of Confucius, a view rooted in the unity of duty and *ming* [*ming* understood here as realization of goodness]. If we wish to understand the true meaning of the *ming* in Confucius' thought, we must, first of all, understand this point.

In the *Book of Mencius* (VA.8),[7] it is said:

Wan Chang[cd] asked Mencius, saying, Some say that Confucius, when he was in Wei, lived with the ulcer doctor, and when he was in Ch'i,[ce] with the attendant, Chi Huan[cf];— was it so? Mencius replied, No; it was not so. Those are the inventions of men fond of strange things.

When he was in Wei, he lived with Yen Ch'ou-yu.[cg] The wives of the officer Mi[ch] and Tzu-lu[ci] were sisters, and Mi told Tzu-lu, If Confucius will lodge with me, he may attain to the dignity of a high noble of Wei. Tzu-lu informed Confucius of this, and he said, That is as ordered (*ming*) by Heaven. Confucius went into office according to

[7] [James Legge, trans., The Chinese Classics, Vol. II. *The Work of Mencius* (Hong Kong: Hong Kong University Press, 1960).]

propriety, and retired from it according to righteousness [or duty]. In regard to his obtaining office or not obtaining it, he said, That is as ordered (*ming*). But if he had lodged with the attendant Chi Huan, that would neither have been according to righeousness (duty), nor any ordering (*ming*) of Heaven.

From Mencius' words in this passage we know that Confucius speaks of *ming* together with "duty"; this is in accord with what Confucius said in the *Analects:* "If one does not understand *ming,* one cannot be a superior man." The reason Confucius does not want the ulcer doctor, or Chi Huan, to be his host is because this is not the way of duty; therefore, he absolutely will not do it. And, when the officer Mi told Tzu-lu that if Confucius were to stay with him the prime-ministership of Wu would be available for him, Confucius replied, "That is as ordered (*ming*)"; Mencius comments on this that, if there is no duty, there is no *ming,* either. In Mencius' view, thus, where duty is, there *ming* is also. The term *"ming"* here is clearly far from meaning predetermination by the Heavenly *ming,* as in the divination concerning the duration of the Chou Dynasty mentioned earlier. This *ming* is, rather, to be found where duty is. Where duty is, there also lies a man's mandate to himself; and this is where the Heavenly *ming* is. Thus we see that what Confucius meant by the Heavenly *ming* is in accord with the "rules" enjoined by Heaven for man to follow, as set forth in the *Odes* and *Documents.* These "rules" are identical with the duty which men ought to realize as self-commanded; the two, therefore, mean the same thing.

Similarly, the seeming contradiction between two aspects of Confucius' teaching—on the one hand, "standing in awe of the Heavenly *ming,*" and, on the other, "self-examination," "realization of what one's heart feels at peace in," and "cultivating virtue in accord with one's intrinsic human-heartedness"—the seeming contradiction between these does not exist in actuality, for they are two aspects of one thing; their meaning is the same.

The problem that arises now is, since the "Heavenly *ming*" and "duty" are identical with their inner content, why did Confucius, in addition to teaching "self-examination," mention "standing in awe of the Heavenly *ming*"? And why did he say that the failure to realize the Tao is also a matter of the Heavenly *ming?* On the assumption that, "if there is no duty, there is no *ming,* either," and "where duty is, there *ming* is also," it is clear that, if the realization of the Tao in the world is one's "duty" and Heaven's allowing one to realize the Tao is *"ming,"* there is an accord between "duty" and *"ming."* However, at a time when the Tao cannot be realized in the world, one's duty lies in the realization of the Tao, while the *ming* lies in the failure of this realization; there is a conflict here between one's duty and the Heavenly *ming.* If in such a situation one still desires to realize one's duty in the world, it will have to be precisely against *ming;* and in that case one's duty is not the realization of the Heavenly *ming.* Mo Tzu saw this contradiction and thought that it could not be resolved; he therefore advocated realizing one's duty in spite of the Heavenly *ming* [which he saw as predestination]. And, indeed, if one accepts such a superficial definition of *ming,* he will naturally arrive at Mo Tzu's position.

For Confucius, however, at a time when *ming* [i.e., objective circumstances] tends to the non-realization of the Tao, while one's duty is to realize the Tao in the world, he continues to say that one ought to "understand ming" and "stand in awe of the Heavenly *ming."* Why does he still make such statements? Does he contradict himself?

To answer these questions we must realize that, in Confucius' teaching, the duty of a man is to realize the Tao in the world, and when outward circumstances are such that he cannot achieve this aim he must simply accept this fact, "understand" it, and "stand in awe" of it; for this, too, is his "duty." If a man cannot accept this, and wishes to act unjustly in order to realize the Tao, and blames Heaven and men, he is not doing his duty. On this point, we see a great advance in the teachings of Confucius and Mencius over those of Mo Tzu.

But how is it that, if desiring to realize the Tao is one's duty, to accept voluntarily the fact that the Tao cannot be realized is also one's duty? The answer to this question rests upon the basic teaching of Confucius and Mencius, that one's desire to realize the Tao is a matter of self-examination [to discover the goodness of one's nature] and exerting to the utmost one's human-heartedness. This being so, it is by no means certain that one will be able to realize one's Tao in the world; and this is the source of an important teaching of Confucius. The *Analects* says:

[a]   There were four things from which the Master was entirely free. He had no foregone conclusions, no arbitrary predeterminations, no obstinacy, and no egoism. (*Analects* IX. 4.)

[b]   "I have no course for which I am predetermined, and no course against which I am predetermined." (*Ibid.,* XVIII. 8.)

[c]   "When called to office, to undertake its duties; when not so called, to lie retired." (*Ibid.,* VII. 10.)

According to these passages, when one seeks to realize the Tao, he must be prepared to accept either of the two consequences: that his Tao will be realized, or that it will not. Thus, when a man is called to office and his Tao is realized, this is his duty; but it is just as much his duty, if his Tao cannot be realized, to accept this fact willingly and simply embrace the Tao for oneself. If, on the other hand, at a time when the Tao cannot be realized, one seeks to realize it in an unjust way, blaming Heaven and other men, he goes contrary to the fact that the realization of the Tao is a matter of self-examination, which is prepared to face either victory or defeat in the world; and, thus falling into injustice, he opposes the Tao. Accepting the fact that the Tao cannot be realized—this, too, is one's duty.

This acceptance of the unrealizability of the Tao is, on the one hand, a duty, and, on the other, it is that "understanding of *ming*" that Confucius teaches. "Understanding *ming*," of course, does not mean merely an understanding of the Tao's unrealizability; one cannot respect or "stand in awe" of such *ming*. To grasp the true meaning of "understanding *ming*" and "standing in awe of the Heavenly *ming*" in the teaching of Confucius, we must approach it through an exalted sense of duty. This I shall now attempt to demonstrate.

When a determined and human-hearted man desiring to realize the Tao in the world meets with disastrous circumstances, he is faced also with the personal problem of life and death. Still, however, he will not do anything unjust, or blame Heaven and men, for his entire spirit is directed to the accomplishment of his just purpose, and to the examination of goodness within himself. At this moment, both the dangerous situation without and the problem of his own life or death are but circumstances that give encouragement and exaltation to his own spirit, making him feel no regret, despite the danger; he perceives nothing but his duty—and he has no time to blame Heaven and men but simply feels satisfaction in the realization of his own goal. This virtue proceeds from the good will of Heaven, which assists him in adhering to his duty in spite of circumstances. Therefore, the determined and human-hearted man does not feel that his purpose and his human-heartedness are possessions of his own; they are rooted, rather, in Heaven. In his sublime state of mind at the moment, he is in union with Heaven: his task of self-examination and realization of his purpose, for which he commands and looks to himself, is absolutely identical with the entire situation sent to him by Heaven. His unceasing exalted spirit, encouraged and nourished by duty, is one with his unceasing duty commanded by Heaven, a duty that increases daily, continuously shining forth and flourishing in his heart. In such a state of mind, where his duty is, there, too, is his *ming;* there is no way to avoid his duty, and, similarly, no way to avoid *ming*. The two become one in their absolute goodness.

The unceasing exalted spirit, encouraged and nourished by duty, and the unceasing Heavenly *ming,* shining forth and flourishing in one's heart—their source is inexhaustible and infinitely rich, and thus a feeling of "devotion to" and "standing in awe of" them naturally arises. Here the expressions "devotion to" and "standing in awe of" refer to the Heavenly *ming*, but they are really the same as devotion to one's purpose and standing in awe of the goodness of one's nature. The reason Confucius refers these qualities only to the Heavenly *ming* is that, while the motive of a determined and human-hearted man wishing to realize his Tao in the world springs from within, it is, however, directed outwardly. Later, in the school of *Li* in the Sung and Ming dynasties, which emphasized personal conduct and the self-awakening of one's nature, this "devotion" and "awe" became "self-devotion" and "self-awing." This is a further development of Confucius' thought, but there is no contradiction between the teaching of Confucius and that of the Sung school, for both are rooted in the actual feelings of man's spirit.

If a man wants to realize his Tao in the world, it is his duty to accept all the difficult circumstances he encounters, even the facing of the problem of his own life or death, for these are what Heaven has commanded for him. In Confucius' teaching, if a man really wishes to be a superior man, or a determined and human-hearted man, then all his attempts to realize the Tao in the world, and all the circumstances he encounters in these attempts, are equally part of his duty; and they are likewise the place where *ming* is. If he is used by a king, then he will realize the Tao in the world and share his goodness with the world; in this case, his duty lies in acting. On the other hand, if he is not used by a king, then he simply embraces the Tao for himself and retires from the world; in this case, his duty lies in not acting at this particular time. For a superior man, thus, circumstances do not matter; for him, there is no distinction between "success" and "failure"; or, rather, both "success" and "failure" are for him "success" [for he has done his duty]. Therefore, if a superior man does not succeed, there is no man for him to hate, no Heaven to be blamed. All circumstances, both fortunate and unfortunate—wealth and high rank and poverty and low status, life and death, gain and loss, self-interest and self-harm, success and failure—all converge in one reality: the accomplishment of his purpose and his human-heartedness. At the same time, all of these are, for a superior man, manifestations of the Heavenly *ming*, and therefore he ought to devote himself to them and stand in awe of them. This state of mind, of course, is difficult to attain, so that Confucius could say that only his disciple Yen Yüan[1] had reached it. "When called to office, to undertake its duties; when not so called, to lie retired;— it is only I and you [Yen Yüan] who have attained to this" (*Analects* VII. 10).

With this teaching of Confucius in mind, let us recall Confucius' grief over the illness of Po-niu: "It is killing him. It is the appointment of Heaven, alas!" Here Confucius naturally has a feeling of regret, but he still does not blame the Heavenly *ming*. The real meaning of this passage is simply that Confucius expects the same thing for his disciples that he expects for himself, namely, that even at the time of one's death one ought to practice his duty to the full; and "respect" for and "awe" of the Heavenly *ming* lie therein. Thus, Tzu-lu fixed the silk cord of his cap at the very moment of his death, and Tseng-tzu[cx] changed his mat just before his death [both following the *li* appropriate to the time]. In Confucius' lament over Po-niu, then, how do we know that he did not expect the same sort of behavior from Po-niu? And the statement of Tzu Hsia—"As for one's wealth and honor, they are appointed by Heaven. As for one's life and death, they are a matter of *ming*" —may be explained in the same way.

If our understanding of this teaching is correct, then it is wrong to adopt the view of the modern Chinese scholars who, following Mo Tzu, believe that Confucius and his school subscribe to the theory of *ming* as predetermination.

To be continued.

[a] 天 [b] 唐 [c] 先帝 [d] 帝 [e] 氣 [f] 陰 [g] 陽 [h] 太 [i] 無 [j] 元 [k] 道 [l] 無 [m] 理 [n] 德 [o] 行 [p] 命

命君 泰

毅

極 極

[q] 墨 [r] 莊 [s] 老 [t] 荀 [u] 騶 [v] 中 [w] 傳 [x] 易經 [y] 詩經 [z] 書經 [aa] 漢 [ab] 列子 [ac] 魏 [ad] 晉 [ae] 宋 [af] 張橫渠

子 子 子 衍 庸

經 經 經

[ag] 虛 [ah] 程 [ai] 朱 [aj] 陸 [ak] 王陽 [al] 王龍 [am] 羅近 [an] 王船 [ao] 清 [ap] 顏習 [aq] 戴東 [ar] 焦循 [as] 錢大 [at] 阮元 [au] 性 [av] 傅斯年

氣 頤 熹 九 陽 溯明溪 龍 溪 近 山 船 清 齋 習 原 東 循 昕

斯 年

[aw] 性命古訓辨證
[ax] 性命古訓
[ay] 殷
[az] 周
[ba] 晉 唐
[bb] 李習之
[bc] 明
[bd] 文 王
[be] 文 武
[bf] 周 公
[bg] 成 王
[bh] 后 稷
[bi] 夏
[bj] 春秋時代

[bk] 左傳
[bl] 國語
[bm] 襄公
[bn] 褅諦
[bo] 鄭
[bp] 子産
[bq] 王孫滿
[br] 楚子
[bs] 郊廟
[bt] 生
[bu] 顧命
[bv] 洪範
[bw] 孔穎達
[bx] 劉康公

[by] 五十而知天命
[bz] 伯牛
[ca] 子夏
[cb] 韓嬰
[cc] 韓詩外傳
[cd] 萬章
[ce] 齊
[cf] 齊環
[cg] 顏讎由
[ch] 彌子
[ci] 子路
[cj] 顏淵
[ck] 曾子
[cl] 鮮繼明

5

The T'ien Ming

[Heavenly Ordinance]

In Pre-Ch'in China —II

V. Mo Tzu's "Against Ming"

IF CONFUCIUS' doctrine of "understanding *ming*" is interpreted as above, it will be clear that Mo Tzu's attack on the Confucian idea
of *ming* cannot apply to the idea of Confucius himself, or to that of his true
followers. In the chapter "Kung-meng"^{"°"} of the *Mo Tzu,* there is this passage:

It is the way of the Confucians to regard that there is a destiny (*ming*) that determines either long life or premature death, poverty or wealth, order or disorder,
security or danger; and what is thus determined cannot be changed, cannot be taken
from nor added to. If superiors follow this teaching, they will not devote themselves
to the government; if inferiors follow it, they will be idle in their work. Thus it is
sufficient to cause a great loss to the world.

According to the Confucian doctrine of "understanding *ming*," external
circumstances such as success and failure, poverty and wealth, and life and
death are conditions that can promote the advancement of virtue. Therefore
one ought not to sacrifice the Tao for the sake of wealth or high rank, or
covet life and thereby lead an unworthy existence. This is all the Confucians
ever said; where, then, do we find the idea attributed by Mo Tzu to Confucianism that poverty and wealth, order and disorder, security and danger
can be neither increased nor decreased? If this is a Confucian idea, why did
Confucius travel throughout the world to realize his Tao? It is obvious that
Mo Tzu is attacking an imaginary Confucianism, a product of his own mind.

It is clear, too, that the *ming* Mo Tzu attacks is not the Confucian *ming.*
Mo Tzu understood *ming* to mean predetermination, as exemplified by the
divination as to the duration of a dynasty; but this idea is clearly contrary to
the Confucian teaching of exerting one's strength to the utmost and desiring
to change the world by the Tao. The reason Mo Tzu attacks this kind of

ming is because it is opposed to his chief teaching, which is to honor one's ethical duty and forcefully realize it in the world. In his essay "Against *ming,*" he therefore repeatedly says such things as, "If the theory of pre-determination is upheld, the people will be idle in their affairs"; and "If the people assert that there is a predetermination by *ming,* they will not follow the governmental instructions and will not devote themselves to routine tasks." Such an idea of *ming* has its root in the religious superstitions of antiquity, though it may be derived, too, by extension from the view of the Heavenly *ming* in the *Odes* and *Documents* in the early Chou. Since Mo Tzu emphasizes the purpose of Heaven, it is therefore necessary for him to point out that there is no predetermined *ming,* lest the people confuse the "purpose of Heaven" with "predetermination by Heaven."

Although Mo Tzu, in his discussion of Confucianism, did not have a true idea of it, he was in direct contact with the traditional religious spirit as transmitted by the *Odes* and *Documents* in his attacking the idea of pre-determination. The most important aspect of Mo Tzu's thought is not to be found, as modern Chinese scholars assert, in his revival of the faith in Heaven of traditional religious thought, something that was opposed by both Confucius and Lao Tzu; nor in his further development of the traditional religious faith retained by the common people. These points are obvious and superficial. The most important part of his teaching lies, rather, in his asserting the existence of the purpose of Heaven, while at the same time attacking the Heavenly *ming.* In the religious thought of other peoples, if there is concern about the Heavenly purpose, there will likewise be concern about the manifestation of this purpose in the form of a commandment regulating man's future. Thus, the Heavenly purpose cannot be conceived apart from the Heavenly commandment.

Mo Tzu, however, talks only of the Heavenly purpose and not of the Heavenly commandment, for, according to him, Heaven's purpose lies in universal love. Mo Tzu nowhere mentions any way in which Heaven tries to realize this purpose, or any commandment that it makes to do so, or any man or people chosen to be its representative in the world to realize this pur-pose. We may see, thus, that Mo Tzu's Heaven is the same as that of the *Odes* and *Documents,* a Heaven whose function is only to look on all parts of the world and examine men's conduct to see whether it be in agreement with Heaven's purpose, and to impose rewards or punishments accordingly. Rewards and punishments are imposed only after men's deeds have reached Heaven; this is the implication, too, of the view in the *Odes* and *Documents* that *ming* is not unchangeable and that Heaven has no chosen man or peo-ple as its representative, but gives its mandate to a man only after he has cultivated virtue, and likewise sends blessing to good men and calamity to evil men following their good or bad deeds. This kind of Heaven first quietly observes men, and only later acts on its observations.

The *Odes* and *Documents* further indicate that to retain the mandate a man must mindfully and diligently continue to cultivate his virtue; this, too, is the source of one of Mo Tzu's teachings, that one must continue to devote himself to his tasks. Thus, though Mo Tzu attacks the Heavenly *ming,* he does not oppose the chief implications of the *ming* in the *Odes* and *Documents;* what he opposes is simply the idea of predetermination. He advocates the theory of Heaven's purpose solely to show the superiority of Heaven and establish the idea of Heaven's power to reward good and punish evil; but reward and punishment only follow good and evil deeds. Furthermore, Heaven never uses its *ming* to limit a man's personal conduct or the extent of his endeavor; in these, therefore, man is prior to Heaven, Heaven's function being merely to reward good and punish evil so as to encourage further good and to uproot evil. Thus, the relationship between Heaven and man, though on one level it is that of superior and inferior, on another is that of parallel powers. This is why Mo Tzu can, on the one hand, honor the Heavenly purpose, and, on the other, emphasize human tasks. Mo Tzu attacks the Heavenly *ming* because Heaven has no power to determine man's future; Heaven is "illustrious above, awe-inspiring below"—but always remains in its proper place. Man, therefore, is able to follow the Heavenly purpose and exert his own effort to the utmost in undertaking human tasks, earnestly striving thereby to do good in the world and uproot evil. The merit of Mo Tzu lies in his making a clear distinction between Heaven and man and clarifying the function of each and the relationship between them.

VI. MENCIUS' DOCTRINE OF ESTABLISHING MING

Mo Tzu attacked *ming* because he believed there was no such thing as predestination limiting human endeavor from without. Confucius' "understanding *ming*" means understanding the fact that the uncontrollable external circumstances we encounter cannot be an obstacle to our devotion to the Tao or self-realization. Mencius' doctrine of "establishing *ming*" is a development of Confucius' doctrine of "understanding *ming*," though Mencius emphasizes more advanced preparation for cultivating one's virtue. This I shall point out in what follows.

If a man encounters a disaster, or perhaps even a matter of life and death, if his duty is clear, he will die for it if necessary; if there is no way to avoid the disastrous consequences of the situation, he will accept them and accord with them. This is the teaching of both Confucius and Mencius; it is one's duty as well as the Heavenly *ming* that one accept the situation. But how can a man encounter such a misfortune and not blame Heaven or men, but willingly and devotedly accept it as the Heavenly *ming?* To reach such a state of mind, one must clearly be prepared in advance, or one will lack the necessary courage. Without such preparation, too, the desire to pursue one's duty and *ming* cannot take firm root in the depths of one's life. This preparation—from its beginning in daily self-cultivation to its fulfillment in the sacrifice of oneself for the Tao when duty requires it—is the way to establish *ming.* This establishment of *ming* depends solely on one's own efforts—there is no determination of it from without. On this, Confucius and Mencius agree with Mo Tzu; for, though Mencius uses the phrase "establishing *ming*," his *"ming"* is quite different from Mo Tzu's, and in fact he means by the phrase something quite similar to what Mo Tzu meant by "against *ming*." But the teaching of Mo Tzu fails to come up to that of Confucius and Mencius, because, though Mo Tzu rightly attacks the *ming* of predetermination, he is unable to cope with a situation in which the Tao cannot be realized. If the purpose of Heaven cannot be realized, will not that purpose then be blocked, and the very heart of Heaven fail? Mo Tzu could probably give no answer to this question. In the teachings of Confucius and Mencius, however, if the Tao cannot be realized in the world, it can still be realized within oneself. Outward success being impossible, one can, if duty requires it, sacrifice oneself for the Tao, or realize one's purpose in retirement from the world, in neither case blaming Heaven or men—such actions are themselves a realization of the Tao, and the Heavenly *ming* is to be found in them. Such, for Confucius, is "understanding *ming*"; for Mencius, "establishing *ming*." In neither teaching is there any interruption or end of *ming,* for the important thing is not the outward realization of the Tao, but our willingness to take up the task of the Tao. If we do this, the Tao of man is established, and thereby also the Tao of Heaven, and thus, likewise, the *ming* of Heaven and of man. Mo Tzu, though he believes in the Heavenly purpose and the fact that human effort is not to be limited by any predeterminism, does not know how to cope with any limitation of human effort when it occurs. Confucius and Mencius, on the other hand, overcome such limitation by means of the Tao; for, while human effort is limited, the Tao is unlimited [and may be realized equally in the outward success and the outward failure of men]. Confucius' "understanding *ming*" and Mencius' "establishing *ming*" may thus be seen to be much deeper and richer than Mo Tzu's "against *ming*."

Confucius' view of *ming* is developed further by Mencius. The merit of

Mencius' view is that he points out a clearly defined method for "establishing *ming*." He brings together the "Heavenly *ming*" and his teaching on "understanding [original] human nature through the utmost devotion of one's heart." He said,

> He who has exhausted all his heart knows his nature. Knowing his nature, he knows Heaven.
>
> To preserve one's heart, and nourish one's nature, is the way to serve Heaven.
>
> When neither a premature death nor long life causes a man any double-mindedness, but he waits in the cultivation of his personal character for whatever issue;—this is the way in which he establishes his Heaven-ordained being (*ming*). . . .
>
> Therefore, he who has the true idea of what is Heaven's appointment will not stand beneath a precipitous wall.
>
> Death sustained in the discharge of one's duties may correctly be ascribed to the appointment of Heaven [or the correctness of *ming*].
>
> Death under handcuffs and fetters cannot correctly be so ascribed. (VIIA. 1–2.)

This passage points out two things: on the one hand, the way to understand Heaven is through understanding one's own [original] nature, which, in turn, is known through the exhaustion or utmost devotion of one's heart; on the other hand, the way to serve Heaven is to preserve one's heart within and nourish one's own [original] nature. The first meaning of "Heaven" here is similar to the Heaven in the *Odes, Documents,* and *Tso Chuan,* which is sympathetic to and loves the people and cherishes virtuous men; and it is not far from the Heaven of Mo Tzu, the source of justice and universal love. The Heaven of Mencius is not opposed to the Heaven of traditional Chinese thought; neither Confucius nor Mencius, indeed, doubted the existence of such a Heaven. Confucius, however, placed more emphasis upon the self-discovery of the good and standing firm in one's determination to do the good. Mencius accepted these goals, though he regarded them as rooted in one's heart or nature and therefore emphasized "understanding human nature through the utmost devotion of one's heart" and "preserving one's heart within and nourishing one's nature." To follow these teachings is, for Mencius, the way to know and serve Heaven, and, at the same time, the way to establish *ming*. Mencius' Heaven is known through one's own nature and is thus different from the Heaven of Mo Tzu, who investigated the relationship between Heaven and man from the outside, and concluded, from the fact that Heaven embraces all things and gives food to all, that its purpose is universal love.

Mencius' teaching differs from Mo Tzu's also on the manner of serving Heaven. According to Mo Tzu, man must model himself on the actions of Heaven; he thus emphasizes the external actions of universal love and non-differentiation as the way to serve Heaven. Mencius, however, taught the knowing of Heaven by "understanding human nature through the utmost devotion of one's heart," and serving Heaven by "preserving one's heart within and nourishing one's nature"—here, knowing Heaven is directly rooted in one's own heart or nature. And the reason Heaven may be known through one's own nature is simply that one's nature is bestowed by Heaven, and the most direct way of knowing Heaven is through what it has given us and made a part of us. Similarly, the way to serve Heaven is through preserving and nourishing the heart or nature that Heaven has given us. The universal love, justice, etc., that Mo Tzu ascribes to Heaven may be substantiated by the human-heartedness, justice, etc., that Heaven has given us and that are part of our nature.

Whether *ming* is correct or incorrect may not be judged by external circumstances; from this point of view there is no *ming* that is not correct. The correctness or incorrectness of *ming* resides, rather, in the way we receive it. If one's death is in accord with the Tao, *ming* is correct; if one's death is not in accord with the Tao—if one, for example, "stands beneath a precipitous wall" or is "under handcuffs and fetters"—then *ming* is incorrect. Anything, whether fortunate or unfortunate, that happens to a man in accord with the Tao is correct. "That which is done without man's doing it is from Heaven. That which happens without man's causing it is from the *ming* [of Heaven]." (VA.6.) All things sent by Heaven and *ming* converge to assist a man in his devotion to the Tao. They are what Heaven has commanded and thus are correct. One should therefore regard them as part of himself and willingly accept them; thereupon, they become correct. Consequently, there will be no such distinctions among the different kinds of *ming* as the Han scholars made: the *ming* of life, the *ming* of correspondence, and the *ming* of suffering. Mencius' idea of *ming* may thus be defined as follows: What I command to myself is what Heaven intended to command to me; thus, the Heavenly *ming* is established through me.

A problem arises here. We said that, according to Mencius, whether *ming* is correct or not depends entirely on the way one "understands one's nature through the utmost devotion of one's heart" and "preserves one's heart within and nourishes one's nature." But this seems to contradict the fact that Mencius sometimes speaks of "human nature" and *"ming"* as quite distinct [whereas the implication here is that they are one]. For example:

Mencius said, "When we get by our seeking and lose by our neglecting—in that case, seeking is of use to getting, and the things sought for are those which are in ourselves. When the seeking is according to the proper course and the getting is only as appointed (*ming*)—in that case, the seeking is of no use to getting, and the things sought are without ourselves." (VIIA.3.)

Mencius said, "For the mouth to desire sweet tastes, the eyes to desire beautiful colours, the ears to desire pleasant sounds, the nose to desire fragrant odours, and the four limbs to desire ease and rest—these things are natural, but there is the appointment of Heaven (*ming*) in connection with them, and the superior man does not say of his pursuit of them, 'It is my nature.'

"The exercise of love between father and son, the observance of righteousness between sovereign and minister, the rules of ceremony between guest and host, the display of knowledge in recognizing the talented, and the fulfilling of the heavenly course by the sage—these are the appointment (*ming*) of Heaven. But there is an adaptation of our nature for them. The superior man does not say, in reference to them, 'It is the appointment (*ming*) of Heaven.'" (VIIB.24.)

In these passages "nature" and *"ming"* are contrasted. To see why this is so we must find out in what sense "nature" and *"ming"* are to be taken here. In the first passage, Mencius seems to mean by *"ming"* the limitation imposed by external circumstances; while, in the second passage, *ming* seems to imply an external judgment of circumstances and to involve ethical duty. *Ming* as referring to external circumstances is something upon which Confucius, Mencius, and Mo Tzu would probably all agree. Mo Tzu, however, sees such circumstances as a limitation imposed by predetermination and thus opposed to duty, and he advocates practice of one's duty in defiance of *ming*. For Confucius and Mencius, on the other hand, the limitations imposed by external circumstances cannot themselves be regarded as *ming*. Instead, they reveal to us our duty with regard to them, as if suggesting a course of conduct: whether we should stay in the world or retire from it, whether we ought to bring the Tao to men or embrace it for ourselves, whether we ought to save ourselves or die in accomplishing our duty—it is these actions by means of which we respond to the circumstances that really contain *ming*.

From this point of view, any circumstances we encounter may reveal to us what we ought to do; it is up to us to handle the circumstances in accord with our duty. It is obvious, therefore, that the Heavenly *ming* is manifested everywhere, in everything, and that there is no *ming* that is incorrect. Looking now again, in this light, at the first quotation above, we see that it is not circumstances as such that determine whether or not we will get something, but, rather, that, if we cannot get it in the given circumstances, we ought not to try getting it in an unvirtuous way, opposing the Tao. Moreover, the very limitations imposed upon us by the circumstances represent a

Heavenly commandment to us, telling us there is something we should not do; if we satisfy ourselves with these limitations, then, we have done our duty in accord with the Heavenly *ming*.

On the one hand, "preserving one's heart within and nourishing one's nature," and then practicing one's duty and realizing the Tao in the world; and, on the other hand, accepting the Heavenly *ming* and establishing it—these are still two things, the one springing from within, the other determined from without. To distinguish them more fully, we may say that the first emphasizes positive action—doing something to prepare for accepting and establishing *ming*; while the second emphasizes non-action—external limitations revealing that there is something one ought not do if one seeks to realize his duty. In the state of action, one establishes *ming* by cultivating oneself and waiting upon *ming*; in the state of refraining from action, the result of one's self-cultivation is seen in the way one accepts all circumstances —good or bad, satisfactory or unsatisfactory—and acts toward them in accordance with the correctness of *ming*. In Mencius' philosophy of human nature, the duty of the "greater part" of our mental function [i.e., our original nature] lies in developing, expanding, nourishing, and being mindful of our nature; while the duty of the "lesser part" of our mental function—the desires of eye and ear, and the desire for wealth and rank—lies in their being regulated and controlled. When a man seeks to satisfy the desires of his "lesser part" and fails to do so, this is called "perceiving one's duty by *ming*," which means that in the limitations of circumstances we perceive our duty; in other words, through the manifestation of our "greater part" [the original nature] we immediately perceive that our original nature is not to be found in our "lesser part"—the source of our desire for wealth and rank, and for the pleasures of eye and ear. This is why Mencius said,

For the mouth to desire sweet tastes, the eyes to desire beautiful colours, the ears to desire pleasant sounds, the nose to desire fragrant odours, and the four limbs to desire ease and rest—these things are natural, but there is the appointment of Heaven (*ming*) in connection with them, and the superior man does not say of his pursuit of them, "It is my nature."

If we really seek to expand, develop, retain, and nourish our "greater part," we will succeed—this is called "perceiving one's *ming* by duty." Thus, between father and son, there should be human-heartedness; between minister and ruler, righteousness; between guest and host, courtesy; etc. In this way we perceive the correctness of Heaven's mandate to us. No matter whom I meet, good or evil men, I must treat each properly in accordance with the Tao; and my encountering them is as if I were given a command to apply human-heartedness, justice, and propriety to them—and it is just as if Heaven had given me this command itself. On the other hand, the reason I practice these virtues is not simply to follow *ming* externally revealed in these circumstances, but to realize and develop my own nature. And this is why Mencius said,

The exercise of love between father and son, the observance of righteousness between sovereign and minister, the rules of ceremony between guest and host, the display of knowledge in recognizing the talented, and the fulfilling of the heavenly course by the sage—these are the appointment (*ming*) of Heaven. But there is an adaptation of our nature for them. The superior man does not say, in reference to them, "It is the appointment of Heaven."

From our discussion we have clarified the distinction between "human nature" and *"ming";* and we have seen that the teaching of Mencius is founded on his doctrine of human nature, and that the doctrines of "understanding and establishing *ming"* are included in his teaching on "preserving one's heart within and nourishing one's nature."

VII. CHUANG TZU'S DOCTRINE OF "RESTING IN MING"

Chuang Tzu's idea of *ming* is different from both that of Mo Tzu and that of Confucius and Mencius. Chuang Tzu uses the word *"ming"* together with "human nature" (*hsing*) to form a single term, not separating them as do the other schools. In Chapter VIII, for example, he speaks of the "evidence of *hsing-ming"*[en]; and, in Chapters XII and XIX he connects the term *"hsing-ch'ing*[eo] [the nature and its evidence] with *ming*. But the *hsing* and *ming* in these passages are still somewhat distinct; in them there is not yet the view that the nature is derived from the Heavenly *ming*. And in the "Inner" chapters of the *Chuang Tzu, hsing* and *ming* do not occur together at all. Still, expressions in the "Outer" chapters such as "to realize the evidence of *ming*" (chap. XIX), "do not eliminate *ming* by acquired human experiences" (chap. XVII), "to understand *ming*" (chap. XXI), "to return to *ming*" (chap. XXV)—these all have their origin in passages from the "Inner" chapters such as "resting in *ming*," "attaining complete accord with *ming*," and "following the direction of *ming*."

In Chapter IV of the "Inner" book, Chuang Tzu quotes Confucius as follows:

In all things under Heaven there are two great cautionary considerations: the one is the requirement implanted by *ming,* the other is the conviction of what is right [duty]. The love of a son for his parents is the implanted requirement, and can never be separated from his heart; the service of his ruler by a minister is what is right, and from its obligation there is no escaping anywhere between heaven and earth. . . . Therefore, a son finds his rest in serving his parents without reference to or choice of place; and this is the height cf filial duty. In the same way, a subject finds his rest in serving his ruler, without reference to or choice of the business; and this is the full discharge of loyalty. When men are simply obeying [the dictates of] their hearts, the considerations of grief and joy are not readily set before them. They know that there is no alternative to their acting as they do, and rest in it as what is appointed; and this is the highest achievement of virtue (*te*). He who is in a position of a minister or a son has indeed to do what he cannot but do. Occupied with the details of the business [at hand], and forgetful of his own person, what leisure has he to think of his pleasure in living or his dislike of death? . . . The best thing you can do is to put yourself in complete accord with *ming*, and this is the most difficult thing to do.[8]

In this passage, Chuang Tzu first separates *ming* and "duty," but then says that devoting oneself to duty has to do also with "putting oneself in complete accord with *ming*"; thus, "duty" and *ming* are not two separate things. Therefore, Chuang Tzu's *ming* is the same as that of the Confucian school, where *ming* is identical with "duty." Here Chuang Tzu regards the "height of filial duty" as consisting in "serving one's parents without reference to or choice of place," and the "full discharge of loyalty" to a ruler as consisting in serving him "without reference to or choice of the business"; whereupon, "what leisure has he to think of his pleasure in living or his dislike of death?" This is the very implication of Confucius' doctrine of "understanding *ming*"; thus we see that Chuang Tzu's doctrine of "resting in *ming*" has its origin in Confucianism. Further, in Chapter V, Chuang Tzu quotes Confucius' statement:

Death and life, preservation and ruin, failure and success, poverty and wealth, superiority and inferiority, blame and praise, hunger and thirst, cold and heat: these are the changes of circumstances, the operation of our appointed lot (*ming*). . . . They are not sufficient therefore to disturb the harmony [of the nature], and are not allowed to enter into the treasury of intelligence. (*Ibid.*, pp. 231–232.)

In this passage, Chuang Tzu contrasts the "harmony" and "spiritual treasury" of our nature, on the one hand, and with the "operation of *ming*," on the other; the passage implies, therefore, that whatever circumstances may be produced by the operation of *ming* from without, they will not cause either grief or pleasure in our inner harmony or spiritual treasury. This is precisely the meaning of another statement of Confucius:

The superior man does what is proper to the station in which he is; he does not desire to go beyond this. In a position of wealth and honour, he does what is proper to a person of wealth and honour. In a poor and low position, he does what is proper to a poor and low position. Situated among barbarous tribes, he does what is proper to a situation among barbarous tribes. In a position of sorrow and difficulty, he does

---

[8] [James Legge, trans., *Texts of Taoism*, Vol. XXXIX, Sacred Books of the East (Oxford: Clarendon Press, 1891), pp. 212–214.]

what is proper to a position of sorrow and difficulty. The superior man can find himself in no situation in which he is not himself. (*Doctrine of the Mean* XIV.)

In the end, however, there is a difference between Chuang Tzu's "resting in *ming*" and Confucius' "understanding *ming*." Confucius' doctrine emphasizes a man's inner devotion to loyalty or filial piety; Chuang Tzu goes a step further in saying that, through this inner devotion, grief and pleasure will become indifferent to a man. A man who can preserve his spiritual glory and his inner harmony, according to Chuang Tzu, ought to be so united with variable circumstances and the operation of *ming* that he will be in accord with all circumstances. From this premise proceed his ideas of "enjoying one's heart in accordance with things as they are" and "non-differentiation of things leading to a state of untroubled ease." The highest implication of Chuang Tzu's "resting in *ming*" may be seen in the fact that Chuang Tzu is able, beyond the ethical realm, to possess the same state of mind as that possessed by a filial son or a devoted minister; like them, he is indifferent to circumstances in pursuing his duty, even to death, but he is thus under *all* circumstances he encounters, not just those involving ethical relationships. Such a view is quite absent in Confucius' "understanding *ming*," in Mencius' "establishing *ming*," and in Mo Tzu's "against *ming*." It is unique to Chuang Tzu. This I shall clarify in what follows.

Let us begin with a quotation from Chapter VI of the *Chuang Tzu:*

Tzu-yü^{ᶜᵖ} and Tzu-sang^{ᶜᵠ} were friends. [Once,] when it had rained continuously for ten days, Tzu-yü said, "I fear that Tzu-sang may be in distress." So he wrapped up some rice and went to give it to him to eat. When he came to Tzu-sang's door, there issued from it sounds between singing and wailing; a lute was struck and there came the words, "O Father! O Mother! O Heaven! O Men!" The voice could not sustain itself, and the line was hurriedly pronounced. Tzu-yü entered and said, "Why are you singing, Sir, this line of poetry in such a way?" The other replied, "I was thinking, and thinking in vain, how it was that I was brought to such extremity. Would my parents have wished me to be so poor? Heaven overspreads all without any partial feeling, and so does Earth sustain all;—would Heaven and Earth make me;—so poor with any unkindly feeling? I was trying to find out who had done it, and I could not do so. But here I am in this extremity!—it is what was appointed for me." [Or: it is simply a matter of *ming*.]

Underlying this tragic scene there is a very deep metaphysical and religious emotion. Tzu-sang is nearly dead of hunger and illness, but, unlike those determined and human-hearted men who sacrifice themselves for the good [Confucians], he has reached a stage of hunger and illness that is quite beyond a man's duty. Still, he blames neither Heaven nor men, and in his moment of extreme hunger and illness can still think about the love of parents and the impartial overspreading and sustaining of Heaven and Earth. If one speaks here of "resting in *ming*," the *"ming"* indicated is obviously not

118

that which the *Odes* and *Documents* speak of accepting, nor is it that union of "duty" and *ming* spoken of by Confucius and Mencius. Chuang Tzu's *ming* is simply resting in and completely surrendering oneself to the inevitable circumstances of human life, and regarding them as the *ming* of one's parents and of Heaven and Earth. This point is again clearly pointed out by Chuang Tzu in Chapter VI:

Whether a parent tells a son to go East, West, South, or North, he simply follows the command. The Yin and Yang are more to a man than his parents are. If they are hastening my death, and I do not quietly submit to them, I shall be obstinate and rebellious. There is the great Mass [of Nature]—I find the support of my body in it; my life is spent in toil on it; my old age seeks ease on it; at death I find rest on it—what has made my life a good will make my death also a good.

Here now is a great founder, casting his metal. If the metal were to leap up [in the pot], and say, "I must be made into a [sword like the] Mo-yehᵉʳ [a famous sword]," the great founder would be sure to regard it as uncanny. So, again, when a form is being fashioned in the mould of the womb, if it were to say, "I must become a man; I must become a man," the Creator would be sure to regard it as uncanny. When we once understand that heaven and earth are a great melting-pot, and the Creator a great founder, where can we have to go to that shall not be right for us?

This passage describes one who does not blame Heaven and applies the attitude one ought to have toward one's parents to Heaven and Earth and to the *yin* and *yang*. One thus finds satisfaction in all the limiting circumstances one encounters in life, unconditionally accepting all inevitable situations, looking on them with indifference, and finding rest in them.

For a man who is thus able to rest in *ming,* accepting all inevitable situations: "Death and life are great considerations, but they could work no change in him. Though Heaven and Earth were to be overturned and fall, they would occasion him no loss" (chap. V). Such a state results in "a man working together and being one with creative transformation" (chap. VI); for such a one, "I and Heaven and Earth are born together, and I and all things in the universe are in a state of unity" (chap. II); he "expands himself in the midst of the cosmic force and, sharing with *ming* the task of transforming things, he at the same time holds fast to the center of Tao" (chap. V). A man who thus works together with creative transformation will feel that *ming* is at the same time in Heaven and in himself.

In the "Outer" book of the *Chuang Tzu,* the teaching of "resting in the Heavenly *ming*" emphasizes voluntary acceptance of all circumstances one encounters—failure and success, gain and loss, life and death, etc. In Chapter XVIII, for example, it is said that Chuang Tzu did not weep over his wife's death, regarding such an action as an indication that one does not understand *ming.* And in Chapter XVII we find,

When he knows that his strait is determined (*ming*) for him, and that the employment of him by a ruler depends on the character of the time, and then meeting with great distress is yet not afraid;—that is the courage of the sagely man. . . . You will see what there is determined for me in my lot (*ming*).

And in Chapter XVI,

If the conditions of the times had allowed them to act in the world on a great scale, they would have brought back the state of unity without any trace being perceived [of how they did so]. When those conditions shut them up entirely from such action, they struck their roots deeper [in themselves], were perfectly still and waited.

Further, in the "Outer" book, Chuang Tzu particularly emphasizes the contrast between posterior human experience and *ming* [Heavenly constitution]. Thus it is said in Chapter XVII, "do not by the Human [doing] extinguish the Heavenly [constitution] (*ming*)." The point is referred to again in Chapter XIX:

I began [to learn the art] at the very earliest time; as I grew up, it became my nature to practise it; and my success in it is now as sure as fate (*ming*). . . . I was born among these hills and lived contented among them;—that was why I say that I have trod this water from my earliest time. I grew up by it, and have been happy treading it;—that is why I said that to tread it had become natural to me. I know not how I do it, and yet I do it;—that is why I say that my success is as sure as fate.

And in Chapter XIII he says, "Regulate it by the spontaneous *ming*."

From these passages we may see that when Chuang Tzu says, "Human experiences extinguish the heavenly constitution," he means that a man who indulges in and limits himself to past experiences and habits cannot expand his heart so as to follow whatever circumstances he encounters just as they occur. On the other hand, if a man can do this, he is what is called "as innocent as a calf just born, not knowing any [posterior] habits or experiences." What one encounters is nothing but the renewed transformations of all things. Thus "do not by human experiences extinguish the heavenly constitution" is really the same thing as "enjoying oneself together with Heaven" and "being one with and penetrated by Heaven day and night." Here "Heaven" and *"ming"* are to be distinguished thus: the term "Heaven" emphasizes objective circumstances, the whole situation presented to one by spontaneous happenings; while *"ming"* emphasizes the subjective aspect, one's personal encountering of external circumstances.

In chapters VIII and XII, as we saw above, Chuang Tzu spoke of the unity between *hsing* (human nature) and *ming*. This is because the *ming* of the external circumstances we encounter, and the *ming* we receive as our nature—these two, though seeming to be different, yet, when they come together, are really one. To be more specific: When our heavenly constitution (*ming*) is free from Human habits and experiences, our nature is unbounded and one with the cosmic transformation—our nature, liberated [from human habits], unfolds itself in union with the creative transformation. In this case, how could our own nature be separated from the *ming* we encounter? Human nature and *ming* are complementary, not separate. Pursuing this point further, we see that the continuity of life within ourselves is the same as the continuity of the *ming* before us; we may call this continuity of life within ourselves the "ceaselessness and non-interruption of *ming*." Further, it is not only the circumstances we encounter that pertain to *ming*; for my present life encounters my immediately future life and carries on my immediately past life. Past and future life, in respect to my life at this moment, may also be called the *ming* of what I encounter.

Thus, to have a life is the same as to have a *ming*. In Chapter XVIII, Chuang Tzu speaks with the bones of a corpse, telling him that he will talk to "the spirit in charge of *ming*" and have him give new life to the corpse. Here "the spirit in charge of *ming*" is in charge of nothing else but the life of a man; therefore, "life" is identical with "*ming*," and this spirit is directly in charge of human life, or human nature. Thus we may see that *hsing* (human nature)—which is the same as "life" in ancient China—and *ming* really represent two aspects of one and the same thing.

VIII. Lao Tzu's "Return to Ming" and Hsün Tzu's "Controlling Ming"

As for the doctrine of *ming* in other pre-Ch'in schools, we have yet to examine Lao Tzu's "return to *ming*," Hsün Tzu's "controlling *ming*," the idea of "attaining to *ming*" in the *Great Commentary* of the *Book of Changes,* and the idea of *ming* as the root of all things in the *Li Chi of the Elder Tai*" and that of the Younger Tai. Too, in the "Record on Music" in the *Li Chi* and the *Great Commentary* of the *Changes,* "*hsing*" and "*ming*" are again used together as a single term. We shall discuss each of these ideas separately.

The phrase "return to *ming*," as it appears in the *Tso Chuan,* refers simply to a minister's returning the instructions given him by a ruler; it has no philosophical implication at all. It is only later, in Chapter XXV of the *Chuang Tzu,* that the same phrase comes to have a philosophical meaning. Whether Chuang Tzu or Lao Tzu was the first to speak of "return to *ming*" in a philosophical sense will not concern us here. It is obvious, however, that the phrase does not have the same meaning in their two philosophies; if "return to *ming*" is important for Chuang Tzu, it is even more so for Lao Tzu.

In Chapter XXV, the *Chuang Tzu* says,

The sage reaches a state of comprehensive apprehension spontaneously and effortlessly. Embracing all things as one body, through the spontaneity of his nature, he returns to the *ming* and is in a state of transcendental freedom and unboundedness, modeling himself only after the way of Heaven. And it is in consequence of this that men style him [a sage].

"*Ming*" here has the same meaning it does for Chuang Tzu in Chapter XXVII, where he said, "Do not by human [habits] extinguish Heaven, or by posterior experiences extinguish *ming* [heavenly constitution]." To get rid of "posterior experiences" and return to the *ming* as we originally received it—this is the meaning of "return to *ming*." It thus implies not indulging oneself in "posterior experiences," but enjoying oneself in accord with whatever one encounters, in this way expanding oneself and becoming one with the transformations of things; thus one "embraces all [Heaven, man, and all things] as one body." Such a view is also implied in Chuang Tzu's teaching on "resting in *ming* and being in complete accord with the transformations of things and with whatever one encounters."

Lao Tzu says of the Tao, in Chapter LI of the *Tao-te ching*," "None commands it and it always [proceeds] spontaneously." And, in Chapter XVI, he defines the state of returning to *ming:* "All things strive and increase, but they must return to their origin. This return is called tranquillity. Tranquillity is called return to *ming*. Return to *ming* is called the unchangeable. Knowing the unchangeable is called intelligence."

The Tao, according to Lao Tzu, is the originating principle of all things. In this passage, however, he says that all things must return to their origin, whereupon there is tranquillity, which is called return to *ming*. Thus we see that Lao Tzu regards the root of the *ming* of all things to reside in the Tao, while there is nothing further to command the Tao. Again, "There exists a completing thing prior to the manifestation of nature" (chap. XXV). The return to *ming* thus results from the things' returning to their origin and then being in a state of tranquillity. This emphasizes the inner condensation and concentration of things that allow them to return to the Tao, the origin whence they sprang. This point is diametrically opposed to Chuang Tzu's view. For him, "understanding *ming*" and "resting in *ming*" emphasize liberation from physical limitations, allowing one to be in complete accord with the transformation of things externally; once one reaches this stage, his spirit will expand in the four directions and overflow the entire world. In Lao Tzu's "return to *ming*," on the other hand, *ming* is something like a life-root existing tranquilly within a thing; it probably refers to the potential motivating force of the very life of sentient beings, the energy of life itself, rooted and originating in itself.

Lao Tzu indicates the process of "return to *ming*" in various passages of the *Tao-te ching:* "reduce selfishness and lessen desires" (chap. XIX); "pay careful attention to the immaterial breath and nourish it without violence" (chap. X); "purify the people's minds, while enlarging their inner intelligence" (chap. III); "weaken ambition and make character strong" (chap. III); "moderate brightness and become one with all existing things" (chap. IV); "possess abundant virtue" (chap. LV); "be like an infant" (chaps. X and LV); "observe plainness, lay hold of simplicity" (chap. XIX); reach "the mother's gate" (chap. VI); "take nourishment from the mother" (chap. XX); etc. The way of return indicated in these passages proceeds from the tangible world back to the intangible metaphysical world, which is something like the "completing thing prior to the manifestation of nature" described in Chapter XXV. Lao Tzu's "return to *ming*" thus proceeds from quite another kind of thought from that to be seen in Chuang Tzu's teaching of "resting in *ming*," Confucius' "understanding *ming*," Mencius' "establishing *ming*," or Mo Tzu's "against *ming*."

Quite naturally the development of Lao Tzu's thought—particularly his idea that "the deep and firm living root is the way to achieve long life and constant seeing" (chap. LIX)—will end in an otherworldliness. The later Taoist idea of parallel cultivation of *hsing* (nature) and *ming* is likewise directed to the cultivation of the root of one's life, which has to do with the infinite potentiality of a man's life. This was probably a further development of Lao Tzu's view of *ming*.

As for Hsün Tzu's view of *ming*, in his chapter on the "Rectification of Names" he says, "timely occurrences are *ming*." Such a *ming* is quite different from any of the traditional religious, moral, or metaphysical views of it, such as those we have discussed above. *Ming*, for Hsün Tzu, is nothing but empirical facts. The *ming* in the *Odes* and *Documents* was mainly religious, though with a moral aspect, too; these books emphasized "receiving *ming*" from Heaven, and Heaven's "conferring *ming*." The *ming* attacked by Mo Tzu was one of religious predetermination. The *ming* of Confucius and Mencius was based on men's duty, and thus the emphasis was on "understanding" and "establishing" *ming*. Chuang Tzu's and Lao Tzu's views of *ming* were bound up with the Tao of Heaven, and thus their emphasis was metaphysical. Hsün Tzu, however, defines *ming* simply as "timely occurrences," which is correctly interpreted by the commentator

Yang Ching[eu] as "what one encounters or suffers at a particular time." Hsün Tzu's view of *ming* excludes all the ideas of previous thinkers summarized above. It is concerned solely with the practical relationships between men and the circumstances they encounter. The Han philosopher Wang Ch'ung's[ev] later definition of *ming* as "what a man encounters" is identical with Hsün Tzu's definition and is a product of the same kind of thinking.

Hsün Tzu's view of Heaven is one directed to the ordinary course of it. As for the attitude men ought to adopt toward Heaven, Hsün Tzu said [in his chapter, "Discourse on Heaven"], "Rather than follow Heaven and praise it, what about controlling the Heavenly *ming* and utilizing it?" And in the same chapter he said, "Heaven gives the course of the four seasons, Earth gives its products, while men have the way to govern them." What Hsün Tzu meant by "men have the way to govern them" was that, in accordance with the seasons of Heaven, we should control and arrange all things for the sake of human beings, and thus men will be a power equal with Heaven and Earth and will control and utilize the Heavenly *ming*. Men will always encounter something, and so there will always be something for them to manage or arrange. Therefore, men are always in a situation to control and utilize the Heavenly *ming*. What Hsün Tzu meant by "controlling the Heavenly *ming*" is something like the modern idea of controlling circumstances or destiny. Hsün Tzu's view of *ming*, therefore, is completely different from the other views discussed above.

IX. The Doctrine of the Heavenly Ming in Late Chou Dynasty Confucianism

There is still another view of the Heavenly *ming* in pre-Ch'in thought: that of certain late Chou Confucians. Texts in which this view is set forth are the *Great Commentary* of the *Book of Changes;* "Ming as the Root" in the *Li of the Elder Tai;* and, from the *Li Chi,* the chapters "Record of Music," "Doctrine of the Mean," and "Li Yün." Now, it is not necessarily true that all these sources have precisely the same viewpoint, but they do have much in common: for one thing, they put the terms *"hsing"* (nature) and *"ming"* together as one expression; and, for another, they regard the Heavenly *ming* as flourishing amid Heaven, Earth, and all things, and hold that all things derive their nature from it. Their *"ming,"* therefore, is in the realm of cosmology, and also in that of religion and ethics in the modern sense.

It is said in the *Book of Changes,* "The way of the creative works through

124

change and transformation, so that each thing receives its true nature and *ming*."[9] And: "That which lets now the dark (*yin*), now the light (*yang*) appear, is Tao. As continuer, it is good. As completer, it is the nature [of all things]."[10] Again: the way of men resides in "exhausting the principle [of duty or justice] to the end, and by exploring the law of their nature to the deepest core, they arrived at an understanding of *ming*."[11] Thus men and things receive their proper nature as a result of the changes and transformations of cosmic forces, which, in turn, result from the mutual influence of the *yin* and *yang* and the unfolding of the originating power of the creative and receptive. And in the harmony among these influences— the *yin* and *yang,* the creative and receptive—we see the Ultimate Harmonious One (*T'ai-chi*). Thus, the *Great Commentary* says, "There is in the *Changes* the Ultimate Harmonious One. This generates the two primary forces (*yin* and *yang*). The two primary forces generate the four images. The four images generate the eight trigrams."[12] This indicates that the transformation of things takes place through the mutual influence between the firm and yielding, movement and stillness, *yin* and *yang,* the creative and receptive; and in this way all things complete their own *hsing-ming*. Thus, the source of the *hsing-ming* of all things is in the Ultimate Harmonious One, in the creative and the receptive, and in the *yin* and the *yang*. But man is the only being that can explore and exhaust the principle to the end, and the law of Nature to the deepest core, and reach the source of human nature and, finally, *ming*. According to the *Great Commentary*, therefore, man forms one of the three primal powers of the universe, together with Heaven and Earth.

In the chapter "Li Yün"[*] of the *Li Chi* it is said, "And therefore it must have a fundamental connection with Heaven. This uses a variety of ways in sending down the intimations of its will (*ming*)—to the altars of the land, to the ancestral temples, to the altars of the hills and streams and to the Five Sacrifices of the House. In this passage it seems even more certain that there is such a thing as *ming* sent down from above and bestowing its essence on all things; and this is in agreement with the ideas of the *Great Commentary*. In the same chapter of the *Li Chi,* the phrase "Ultimate One" is mentioned; this is the same as the "Ultimate Harmonious One" of the *Great Commentary*. Both terms are seen as the source of Heaven and Earth and the *yin* and *yang*.

---

[9] [Wilhelm, *op. cit.*, Vol. II, p. 4.]
[10] [Wilhelm, *op. cit.*, Vol. I, pp. 319–320.]
[11] [Wilhelm, *op. cit.*, Vol. I, p. 281.]
[12] [Wilhelm, *op. cit.*, Vol. I, p. 342.]

Then there is the passage in the *Li of the Elder Tai:* "What we receive as apportioned by the Tao is *ming;* this, manifested as one, is the nature." This indicates that the individual nature and life of all things result from a single root, the apportionment of the Tao; and our receiving this is called *ming.* This *ming* therefore exists uninterruptedly in our nature and life, and is the beginning and end of all things. This agrees with the statement just quoted from the "Li Yün." All the views of *ming* here discussed, then, are in substantial agreement with each other. In all of them, *ming* is a cosmological phenomenon, something bestowed from above downward, apportioning itself among all things and received by men and by things as their nature.

This is quite different from Confucius' idea of *ming* as bound up with men's duty, through which we apprehend the *ming* of the Heavenly Tao. It is different, too, from Chuang Tzu's theory of "according with the path of transformation, and thus resting in the timely situation and willingly accepting it." And it is different from Lao Tzu's "return to *ming*" by "ruling men and serving Heaven, which reside in self-restraint and desirelessness." Nor can we say that the "Ultimate One," or "Ultimate Harmonious One," and *ming* as set forth in this trend of thought have the same meaning as "Heaven" and the "Heavenly *ming*" in the thought of the early Chou Dynasty; for then the conferring of *ming* was in accordance with men's virtue, whereas the Ultimate Harmonious One bestows *ming* on all things and gives them life, each thing receiving its nature and having its virtue thereby.

However, though this kind of thought differs from all that we have discussed in previous sections, it is still a development of Confucius' and Mencius' ideas on the Heavenly *ming* and human nature, and did not, as some scholars think, originate in Taoist thought. Confucius emphasized ethics and man's duty, culminating in the doctrines of understanding and establishing *ming.* In all circumstances we encounter—life or death, success or failure—we may perceive our duty and be immediately aware of the shining forth and flourishing of the Heavenly *ming* before us; and we thus see the correctness of the Heavenly *ming* revealed to us. Following these ideas, forgetting oneself and expanding our idea of the correctness of the Heavenly *ming,* regarding this correctness as a virtue of the universe in general rather than one's own possession, we shall see that the Heavenly *ming* flourishes everywhere and at every moment in outward circumstances. And we perceive, in this way, that the transformation and flourishing of all things are themselves the continuity of the goodness of the Heavenly *ming,* and at the same time a result of the mutual influence among things. In this mutual influence, there is now movement and now rest, now firmness and now yielding, now *yin* and now *yang*—and in the midst of these we see the Ultimate One, the Tao, which is the source, both of the continuous transformation and flourishing of things and of the goodness of things. Thus, if we trace back the ethical goodness of the Tao of man, we shall find that it has its source in all these mutual influences and responses, which, in turn, are rooted in the Ultimate Harmonious One. If we understand this, we shall realize that Heaven and Earth and all things are united and share in one common transformation. We may then obliterate the seeming differences among things and see the whole process of mutual influence and of the succession of all things in the universe as but a result of change, which, in turn, is a result of the mutual influence of the *yin* and *yang* of the Ultimate Harmonious One.

The things produced by this mutual influence are distinct from one another; as it is said in the *Great Commentary,* "they receive their respective proper natures." But, if we trace the origin of all things, we see that there is but one Tao or Ultimate Harmonious One that underlies things and apportions *ming* to them. The man who can exhaust principles to the end and explore the law of his nature to its core ends in a state of absolute good and justice; in accord with the virtue of the Tao of *yin* and *yang,* Heaven and Earth, he arrives at the highest realm of the Heavenly *ming,* which is the source of his nature and *ming.* From this is derived the idea of the *Great Commentary* as well as the *Doctrine of the Mean,* that the great man is in accord with the virtue of Heaven and Earth, and, if a man can exhaust his own nature to the end, he can do the same to the natures of other men and things, and thus, according to the *Doctrine of the Mean,* he can assist the transforming and nourishing power of Heaven and Earth. This is why the *Doctrine of the Mean* compares the purity of the virtue of King Wen with the unceasing creative power of Heaven.

In the *Great Commentary,* the *Doctrine of the Mean,* and the "Li Yün," *hsing-ming* is regarded as what Heaven has conferred on men as well as on things, whereupon each receives it as his respective nature. Thus, the Han and Sung scholars for the most part agree that "the endowment of the nature and the receiving of *ming* belong to the same category" [in the words of Wang Ch'ung], *ming* being thought of as men's endowment. Cheng K'ang-ch'eng[cx] and Chu Hsi both followed this view in their commentaries on the Classics. The *Great Commentary,* the *Doctrine of the Mean,* and the *Li Chi* speak of Heaven in terms of the Ultimate One or the Ultimate Harmonious One, and thus emphasize the fact that the Heavenly *ming* is sent from above to the world. This idea leads to the revival of the ancient doctrine of the Heavenly mandate and the receiving of this mandate by kings; it is an attempt to re-establish the idea of God held at the beginning of the Chou Dynasty. Such is the view of the scholars of the Han Dynasty.

^{cm} 公孟篇
^{cn} 性命
^{co} 性情
^{cp} 子輿
^{cq} 子桑
^{cr} 鎮鄒

^{cs} 大戴禮記
^{ct} 道德經
^{cu} 楊倞
^{cv} 王充
^{cw} 禮運
^{cx} 鄭康成

The spirit and development of neo-Confucianism

The ideal of human life as a life of sagehood is the core of Confucian thought. In neo-Confucianism the stress is on the self-perfectibility of man, and the central concern of neo-Confucianist thinkers has accordingly been with the question of how man can cultivate his own potentiality to be a sage. The different answers they give are in the form of teachings about the 'way', these teachings incorporating different philosophical views of mind, human nature, and the universe. The author outlines the views of successive neo-Confucianists and their versions of the 'way', seeing their teachings as developments towards the doctrine presented by Wang Yang-ming (b. 1472), whose thought can be seen in particular as a synthesis of the views of Chu Tzu and Lu Shiang-shan.

I. INTRODUCTION

The year 1972 is the five-hundredth anniversary of the birth of Wang Yang-ming. Wang's teaching is generally considered to belong to the school of Lu Shiang-shan and to be opposed to that of Chu Tzu. This view is less than adequate. In two recent articles[1] I have traced the origins of Chu Tzu's and Lu Shiang-shan's thought to their different answers to the common problem of how to acquire sagehood, answers which incorporate different concepts of the human mind and of human nature. There I insisted that Wang's thought actually developed from the teaching of Chu Tzu, but that it ended in certain agreements with that of Lu. In the present article I shall take the self-cultivation of sagehood to be the central spirit of neo-Confucianism as contrasted with preceding Confucianism. I shall take the problems of this self-cultivation as a continuous thread in order to point out the development of neo-Confucianism through the key ideas in its exponents' thoughts about the problems. And I shall end with a brief summary of my former two articles.

II. The Creative Ideas of Ancient Confucianism, the Idea of the Sage in Han-Confucianism, and its Transition to Neo-Confucianism

All the main Confucian ideals of life and culture and the central Confucian view of the universe were originally propounded by Confucius, Mencius, and Hsün Tzu, or occur in the commentaries on the *Book of Changes* and in chapters in the *Book of Rites*. Thus, Confucius himself taught the idea of *jên*, or humanity, and other virtues, and man's duty to revere the decree of Heaven; the ideas of man's difference from the animal, of human nature as essentially good, of the spiritual stages towards sagehood, of man as *tien-ming*, or cosmic citizen, and of the life of the sage as also a holy life and confluent with the life of universe, were all taught by Mencius; the ideal of a cultural society or kingdom, the social-cultural-political responsibilities of different classes of men, and the ways for transforming man's evil nature to fit the needs of society and to be worthy, or a sage, were propounded by Hsün Tzu; the metaphysical ideas of the cosmos as the expression of eternal *tao* in creative change and as permeated with cosmic spirituality, are explained in the commentaries on the *Book of Changes*; the spirit of rites, music, and other human cultures, as identical with the spirit of Heaven and Earth, is explicated in chapters of the *Book of Rites*; and finally the identity of Heaven's decree and human nature, the realization of them in the authentic or real manner of human life, and the adoration of the sagehood of Confucius as conforming to the creativity of Heaven, were systematically expounded in the *Chung Yung*, one chapter of the *Book of Rites*. Thus practically the whole of the central core of Confucianism was laid down by the Confucianists two thousand years ago. There is no question that these ancient Confucianists were the most original and creative contributors to the tradition.

The ancient Confucianists were idealistic philosophers in Plato's sense. They aspired to be sages themselves, admired the sage-kings of the past, and wished to teach the princes to be sage-kings. Very lofty ideals certainly, indeed so much so as to appear unattainable in practice. Confucian scholars of the later Han dynasties were accordingly more realistic in their political and ethical thinking. They did not deny the existence of the ancient sages, but were content to revere and worship them in a religious spirit. The people of the Han dynasties had faith in God or gods. In the apocryphal classics, forgeries by

Han's scholars, Confucius as a sage is sometimes worshipped as an incarnation of a god descended from Heaven. This thought was rejected by rationalistic Confucian scholars and Confucius did not emerge as an incarnation of God, like Jesus Christ. Nevertheless Confucius, as a sage, and all the sages of the past were still generally considered to have been born in Heaven and to have descended from above, because no ordinary men could compete with their supreme virtues and talents.

The religious ideas of 'heaven' and 'the sage' held by Confucian scholars in the Han dynasties had very important practical significances in Chinese history. The idea of Heaven as identified with one God, the great-grandfather of all men, as in Tung Chung-shu's thought, greatly helped to establish the sense of the unity of Heaven as a model of the unity of the imperial kingdom on earth, as also the sense of God's way of sovereignty in Heaven as something to be followed by the imperial emperor. The idea that gods in Heaven, sometimes taken as five in number, with five kinds of divine virtue, reigned in rotation over definite periods of time justified the Confucian idea of political evolution and revolution, and the division of political powers among different officials. As gods have different divine virtues and powers, so different officials need different kinds of moral virtues and different talents or abilities in order to fulfil their different functions in government, and an individual man need not become a sage, that is, possessed of all virtues, talents, or abilities. Thus human nature, as generally considered by Confucianists of the Han dynasties, is not the same for all men, as Mencius or Hsün Tzu thought, but is classifiable into many kinds according to men's born abilities and dispositions for virtue. The realistic understanding of differences in human nature, and of their different functions in the whole human community, became the important thing for Confucian scholars of the Han dynasties. A scholar of these times did not need to ask how he could become a sage like the Confucius he worshipped, because he may not have been born with abilities and dispositions corresponding to those of Confucius.

However, after the Han dynasties, some thinkers from the Wei-Chin dynasties believed it possible for man to become a sage through the Taoistic contemplation of life and the universe. Buddhism brought from India the new gospel of man's ability to become a sage like Buddha. From the Wei-Chin to the so-called five dynasties the main current of Chinese philosophical thought was Buddhism. Confucian scholars continued to write many commentaries on the Confucian classics, but without making any philosophical innovations. It was the neo-Confucianism of the Sung-Ming dynasties which raised again the problem of the cultivation of sagehood.

III. The Spirit of Neo-Confucianism Compared with the Confucianism of the Han Dynasties and Ancient Confucianism

In contrast to the Confucianists of the Han dynasties, we should say that neo-Confucianists, generally speaking, do not believe that sagehood is beyond the ordinary man; they believe that an ordinary man can become a sage from within, and ascend from below, to acquire virtues of a divine status. This is because the differences in man's natural dispositions are not taken by them to be differences of essential human nature, which, being pure, good, and the same for all men, is the real ground for man's development through inner spiritual cultivation; and also because they generally consider the differences in men's abilities or talents to do things in the external world to bear no essential relation with man's development to sagehood. Hence, actually to become, and not just to worship, a sage became the aim of Confucian scholars or students at the very beginning of neo-Confucianism, as finally, for Wang Yang-ming and his school, it became that of all laymen in their different professions in the human community. Hence the saying that 'those who fill the street are all sages (in potentiality)'.[2] This is rightly conceived as a revival of the Confucian faith in man, as it had been propounded by Mencius and Hsün Tzu, and was implicit in Confucius's teaching — a faith which had been lost to Confucianism since the Han dynasties.

Yet this revival of Confucian faith was no mere repetition of earlier Confucian thought. The ideal of human life as a life of sagehood, the central core of Confucian thought as it had been provided by ancient Confucianism, remained generally accepted by neo-Confucianists. However, in regard to the 'way', or *tao*, for one's spiritual cultivation, there were many problems that had not been discussed by the ancients. The Confucian thinkers of the Han dynasties had pointed out that man has a temperamental nature which may be partial and not good. The neo-Confucianists, though denying that man's temperamental nature is his essential human nature, could not deny its existence. For them, in order to realize the goodness of this essential human nature, man must confront his temperamental nature, which, being partial and biased, may hinder his advance to sagehood. And there are also other obstacles, such as emotions, selfish desires, personal habits, subjective opinions, unconscious inclinations, and so on, which one has to confront on the way. All these negative factors stand, literally, in the way of man's realization of his positive ideal of sagehood. The ancient Confucianists, however, did not take these factors seriously. I would maintain that the central spirit of neo-Confucianism, on the other hand, is acceptance of the need to face all the negative factors and to find a way which is the negation of these negations of the possibility of realizing the positive ideal. In the following sections I shall support the above thesis by means of illustrations of the main teachings of the greatest neo-Confucianists on the ways in which man can acquire sagehood, in relation to their most important philosophical ideas about man's nature and mind, and the universe.

IV. Shao K'ang-chieh's Ideas of Contemplation of Things and the Sage as Man of Men

I begin with Shao K'ang-chieh, Chou Lien-ch'i, and Chang Heng-ch'u, as thinkers of the first period of neo-Confucianism. In the first period, Heaven still tends to come first and man second. Man, however, is able to improve his position and to identify himself with Heaven by acquiring the virtues of the sage through a proper spiritual cultivation.

I take Shao K'ang-chieh first in this period because he is senior in age to the other two. Shao has not been recognized as an orthodox Confucianist, because his attitude to life is too artistic and self-indulgent, like a Taoist, and his interest in the esoteric knowledge of numeralogy is also unorthodox. Yet he is an avowed Confucianist, and his ideas about the contemplation of things may also be taken as the first stage of development in the growth of neo-Confucianism.

I wish to explain only one, central idea of Shao's, in his book on the contemplation of things. This is the idea that man's emancipation from his subjective viewpoint, whereby he sees things through his own emotions, and his acquiring a way of contemplating things as they are objectively are the way to realize his essential human nature. Here it is the subjective emotions that are taken as the obstacles to progress to sagehood. The positive contemplation of things objectively includes also the contemplation of man as a thing in the natural world. Man differs from other things because, with his free activity of mind, he can know the beings of other things and then, as it were, absorb or comprise their beings in his own being. Hence man is defined as 'a thing of all things'. Here, man as a thing is taken as originally standing on the same level with other things, and then as ascending above other things as a thing of all things. Shao also takes the sage, as a man, to stand originally on the same level with ordinary men. The sage, however, is a man who has universal wisdom and universal sympathy with other men's minds. The mind of the sage, then, is 'a mind of all minds', and hence the sage is defined by Shao as 'a man of all men' above the ordinary man. Having universal wisdom and sympathy, the sage may also be considered as having a universal mind co-extensive with all the minds of all men without any self-limitations. Thus his knowledge, speech, and actions all represent the doings of Heaven, and his virtue is actually identified with that of Heaven. This type of thought, without going into details, is clearly quite different from the Confucianism of the Han dynasties in which the sage is regarded not as man-made and to have ascended from below, but as Heaven-born and to have descended from above.

V. Chou Lien-ch'i's Idea of Heaven as the Ultimate Original Source of Things and the Establishment of the Way of Man's Becoming a Sage as Man's Ultimate Goal

Chou Lien-ch'i, considered an orthodox Confucian, differs from Shao. In Chou's teaching the extensive contemplation of things, man, and sagehood is not considered essential for spiritual development. Man's own intensive aspiration to sagehood is considered to be the basic requirement. This intensive aspiration is called 'chih' or the 'resolute aim of man'. Chou said that 'the sage aims to be Heaven, the worthy aims to be the sage, and the scholar aims to be the worthy'.[3] The ladder for man's ascent to Heaven is the steadfast resolve of his inner mind. In Chou's thoughts we find an inner world of moral or spiritual cultivation with height and depth. He did not, in his metaphysics, conceive of Heaven as a mere totality of infinite things in a horizontal sense, but as the ultimate, real, and original source of the creation of infinite things successively, in a vertical sense. This original source, being creative, was called 'kan-yüan', and being ultimate and infinite, 'tai-chi', or the 'infinite-ultimate'. As a universal and eternal 'way' for the creation of things it was called 'tao'. And *tao* as the reality of the infinite creation is called 'chen'. Man, as a creature, has his original source within his mind, which is his nature, and the sage is the man who reveals and realizes his nature from within, through his creative wisdom and action in response to the outside world. Thereafter, the sage also realizes the ways of *jên-chi*, or 'man's ultimate', corresponding to the 'infinite-ultimate' of Heaven, and acquires the very same virtues as real, universal, and eternal, which Heaven has as the original source of all creation. Chou may not deny that Heaven's manifest virtue is greater, in creating infinite things, than the virtue of the sage whose life is short and creations limited. Yet the question of virtue is not to be considered in relation to its outer manifestation, and the quantity of the products of a virtue is not a standard for estimating the value or essence of that virtue. As we said before, the sage is not defined by neo-Confucianism as a man superior to other men by virtue of his talents or abilities; so Heaven, or God, despite having infinite creative power to create infinite things, is not necessarily superior to the sage, who has qualitatively the same virtue. This idea is also common to all later neo-Confucianists, and must be borne in mind, otherwise all their pronouncements about the identity in virtue of man and Heaven will have no meaning and should be taken to express an impossible ideal.

Chou saw clearly that the inner nature of man originates from the ultimate source of Heaven with its *tao* of creativity, and took this as the metaphysical ground for man's capacity for sagehood. Yet he also recognized that there are obstacles in the way of man's actually becoming a sage. In his view, however, it was not only the subjective emotions that man must emancipate himself from, as Shao Kang-chieh thought. Rather it was the desires that form the background of emotions, and which come from a partiality in the orientation of the mind and disturb its tranquility, that he considered to be the real obstacles to man's realizing his true nature in an upright, i.e. not partial or biassed, response to things, and to lead man astray and make him evil. Thus he taught of being 'without desires to keep the tranquility', and of there being tough-minded evil connected with tough-minded good, and soft-minded evil connected with soft-minded good.[4] The mind has to be 'void' when it is quiet, so that it can be enlightened and transparent. It must respond to things uprightly when it is active, so that it can be impartial and universal.[5] Voidness of the mind is the prior condition for the realization of its nature in its response as impartial and universal, so that the heavenly virtues of the sages, such as universal love, universal justice, universal righteousness, and so on, can be cultivated.

Chou was always considered the first founder of neo-Confucianism, and was admired by almost all the later Confucianists. All his writings are very short, yet rich in meaning. I cannot discuss all of them, but the above rough outline of his thought of the 'way' is enough to justify our talking of him as the orthodox representative of the spirit of neo-Confucianism.

VI. Chang Hêng-ch'ü's Idea of the Universe as a Comprehensive Harmony and of Man's Becoming a Sage as Filial Piety to the *Tao* of Heaven and Earth

Compared with Chou Lien-chi, Chang Hêng-ch'ü is a more systematic and articulate thinker. Here I shall mention only the central thought of his metaphysics in connection with his ideas about the 'way' of spiritual cultivation. This central thought is of the universe as 'tai-ho', or 'comprehensive harmony', from both the horizontal and the vertical point of view. In this metaphysics the discrete things of the universe only *appear* to be discrete. In reality they are composed of 'chi', which is the 'being' of things and has voidness within itself, an inner space which extends an invitation to other beings and through which it lets itself be transformed or recreated into a new being.[6] Hence the principle, or *tao*, of transformation and creativity subsists in *chi* itself. *Chi*'s voidness and its extending an invitation to other beings is called its 'shen' or 'function of spirituality'. *Chi*'s function of spirituality is then the principle of unity of different beings and of different things. Seen through their 'spirituality', all the discrete things of the universe made of *chi* are mutually immanent, and the universe has to be thought of as a comprehensive harmony which is full of spirituality in one great process of the transformation and creativity of things into a unitary whole. This harmony as it originates from the mutual immanence of things has a horizontal aspect, while as a whole above discrete things, it has a vertical aspect.

From the above metaphysics, man's perception of external things is nothing but a function of his spirituality as one who invites other beings or things to come to the voidness of his mind. Yet the voidness of man's mind is not finite, for it can allow the perceived object to be forgotten and superseded, and it then transcends the limitation of perception and enlarges itself infinitely, extending its invitation for all the things or persons of the universe to be known with wisdom and sympathized with love, and so on. Hence man's spiritual virtues, when fully developed, are the spiritual virtues of the sage, which are identical with the spiritual virtues of the universe as a comprehensive harmony.

In the process of the development of his spiritual virtue, man, as a child of the universe, gradually creates his new virtues, realizing his nature and also extending his filial piety to the 'principle of creativity' of the universe, or 'kan', the 'principle of Heaven', as his father, and 'principle of realization' of the universe, or 'kun', the 'principle of earth', as his mother, in order to continue the life of the universe as a great family, with 'all men as brothers' and 'all things as companies'. This is the world of man as seen through the eyes of the developing sage.

Chang's philosophy is something more than just a beautiful picture. He too knew of the obstacles to be encountered on the 'way'. Although man has a nature that is directed towards the universal principles of the universe, which he called the nature of Heaven and Earth, as ground for his possibility of becoming a sage, he also has a 'nature of chi-chih', a 'temperamental nature', or 'material nature', which is directed only to particular things in the world, and may be self-limited and self-closed to these particular things, and from this stem men's selfish desires and evil as obstacles to sagehood.

The self-limitation or self-closedness of man is a solidification of his being, as if it lacked voidness. The solidification of his being is also its materialization. Chang did not deny this tendency to solidification of man's being in his material nature, which makes him become self-limited and self-closed, then selfish and evil. Man who aspires to go the way to sagehood must come face-to-face with this nature of his and transform it. To do this is to open the closed, to transcend the limitation, or to make the solid fluid; it is to increase the spiritual voidness in his mind, to enlarge his mind so as to comprehend the things of the universe and the realization of his nature as the nature of Heaven and Earth. As it is possible for man to do all this, his material nature can in principle be transformed without residue, which is also proof that his material nature is not his real or essential nature, but just a natural obstacle to one who, while aspiring to realize his essential nature as a potential sage, is at a stage where this is still only his potentiality. At this stage he is in inner conflict. His life in itself is not harmonious, nor is it in harmony with the universe. And here he may also doubt that the universe really is a comprehensive harmony. Yet when he becomes a sage, all the obstacles and conflicts are gone, the universe as a real harmony is verified in his very life. Chang's metaphysics is therefore in fact the description of the world of the sage, though it still seems that he thought of his metaphysics as primary and his idea of the sage as secondary, as if the former was not simply a description of the life of the latter. But whatever inadequacy we may find in *his* exposition of the relation of man to universe was avoided in the further development of neo-Confucianism.

VII. CHENG MING-TAO'S IDEA OF MAN'S MIND WITH ITS NATURE AND UNIVERSE AS WITHOUT DUALITY AND HIS WAY OF SPIRITUAL CULTIVATION FOR BECOMING A SAGE

Cheng Ming-tao's thought, as a further development of Chang Hêng-chu's, began from seeing the universe as the outer side of man, and man's mind, with its nature, as the inner side, and the two sides of man as counterparts of one whole. Heaven is not thought of as primary and man as secondary, and the metaphysics of Heaven was actually taken as the description of the sage's world, this description being nothing else than the revelation of the reality of Heaven.

Cheng Ming-tao wrote very little, though his sayings were recorded by disciples. Here I shall refer only to one of his short letters to Chang Hêng-chu,[7] concerning the problem of how to make mind and nature as peaceful and constant as a sage. In this essay, Cheng said that the sage's mind is itself wide open and universal, without partiality, and that when it encounters things it responds spontaneously and concurrently with 'that with which the thing should be responded to'. Thus the sage delights because the thing should be delighted in, or is angry because it calls for anger, and when the thing is gone nothing is left. The sage's mind and its nature are then open, universal and without partiality, and at the same time always peaceful and constant. Now in Cheng Ming-tao's thought, the thing is no more than the object of the sage's response, and whether his response is delight, anger, or something else, is determined by 'that with which the thing should be responded to'. The thing as such is objective, though the actual response is subjective. The objective and subjective are two sides of the mind of the sage which arise simultaneously and then sink into silence, again simultaneously. Thus the mind of the sage is always responsive and always peaceful and constant.

Yet Cheng Ming-tao, too, fully recognized the difficulties or obstacles in the way of becoming a sage. He said, in the same letter, that the ordinary man usually has two attitudes, involving respectively a subjective and an objective bias. When he confronts things as objective, he usually turns his consciousness outward, using his intellect to grasp and attach to them and so losing it in the objective things. This is called 'yung-chih', or 'using intellect'. When thinking about his subjective response, on the other hand, he usually turns his consciousness backward to possess his response, and becomes self-centered and self-closed in his already existing response. This is called 'tsu-szu', or 'selfish'. The ordinary man is either using his intellect to grasp and attach himself to things, or he is self-possessed and becomes selfish, and is constantly running first in the one and then in the other of these two opposite ways.

Both ways lead man away from the proper middle way of the sage's mind, which is open, without self-possession, and responds immediately and spontaneously to things in the right way, and without attachment.

Cheng Ming-tao's views on how to become a sage are congenial and intimate to man's present experience. This is a way which every man can go immediately, if he wants. It does not depend on any established system of truths about the universe, which is seen simply as the outer side of man, and as unified with his mind and its nature as his inner side. Through man's right response the universe and man's mind, with its nature, can be seen as an undifferentiated and integral whole without separation or duality. Hence the sense of communion of feeling of all men and of all things in the universe as 'i-t'i', or 'one body', can be generated as the ground of all virtues. Cheng Ming-tao has also many sayings, full of metaphysical significance, on what the reality of the universe which is revealed as 'one body' consists of, but this I shall not discuss here. I would maintain, however, that all these sayings have to be understood as the description of the world of the mind of the sage, and not only as a metaphysics of this world as a reality immanent in the mind of the sage.

VIII. CHENG I-CHUAN'S IDEAS ABOUT THE PRACTICE OF REVERENCE AND INVESTIGATION OF THINGS AND THE SEARCH FOR *LI* AS TWO PARALLEL WAYS FOR MORAL PRACTICE

Taking many of his elder brother's ideas about man and the universe for granted, Cheng I-chuan knew, as a teacher, even more of the obstacles and hindrances to the realization of sagehood. For example, he saw that 'selfishness' and 'using intellect to grasp things', mentioned by Cheng Ming-tao, are actually the 'habitual ways' in which ordinary man takes both things and himself. Man's actions are controlled by habit, which is formed by his whole past life, and also stems from unconscious desires and animal instincts, which are included in the concept of 'temperamental nature', as Chang Hêng-chu and the Cheng brothers all agree. The habits and temperamental nature of man are burdens and irritations in the background of his present immediate experience. His striving for sagehood in this present experience is like sailing in an ocean full of waves. The neo-Confucianists were always heroic in not praying for salvation from a transcendent God, but there were still these more immediate difficulties to face, without self-deception, on the way. In talking more than did his brother about the moral practices for remedying moral sickness Cheng I-chuan went one step further in the development of neo-Confucianism.

The ways of moral practice, as Cheng I-chuan taught them, are divided according to the inner side and the outer side of man. In the inner side, the idea of reverence, already proposed by Cheng Ming-tao, was stressed still more by Cheng I-chuan, and replaced Chou Lien-chi's teaching of tranquility. The idea of reverence is subtle. It is not necessarily a reverence for any definite object, such as man or a god, but a reverence that subsists whether one is doing things or doing nothing. In either case, one can acquire a spiritual state of reverence which is not merely a state of tranquility. The mental state of tranquility may be thought of as static and flat. The mental state of reverence, as living and always growing, Cheng I-chuan thought of as dynamic and like a round sphere of mental light surrounding things and the mind itself, making the mind self-enlightened and open, both in knowing and in doing things with concentration and without self-closure. It can also be explained as a state of constant wakefulness where the mind is neither crowded by selfish desires nor sunk into the things which it is concentrated in knowing and doing. The predominance in the mind of such a state of reverence is called 'chu-ching'. *Chu-ching* is a way in which the mind keeps itself awake, and therefore existing, and it goes by the name of 'han-yang', which may be translated as 'self-immersion and self-nourishment' of the mind.

Another teaching of Cheng I-chuan's is the investigation of things with a view to knowing their *li*, for the realization of our knowledge of them. The idea of *li*, or Heaven-*li*, was also proposed by Cheng Ming-tao, but he usually meant by it a universal principle of the universe, where Cheng I-chuan usually took it to mean principles of particular or individual things. 'Li' is a word without a definite translation. It may be rendered in English as 'principle', 'law', 'form', 'essence', 'pattern', 'rule', 'regulation', or 'maxim'. In connection with 'mind', it may also be translated as 'reason'. *Li* may be universal or particular, or the property of a unique or individual thing. It may also be what things actually are, shall be, or ought to be. The word's etymology is from the regulation of fields and the polish of jade, and it later came to mean the line of jade. The line of jade is the smoothness one can feel by passing one's hand from one part to another of a piece of jade after it has been polished. *Li* may be synonymous with *tao*, which originally means 'way' or 'road'. The line of jade can be thought of as the way or road of jade, and the way or road can be thought of as the line on Earth. Because the line in jade is smaller, and the way or road is larger, so *tao* is the *li* of larger things, and *li* may be the *tao* of smaller things. As the line of jade may be seen once for all as an object, so *li* is more objective, while the way or road is what man has gone through, and is therefore more subjective. Yet *tao*, when objectively thought, is *li*, and *li*, subjectively considered as what man thinks and acts through, is *tao*. So although there are differences in these two terms, they are nevertheless mutually implicated in each other, and can be used synonymously. However, *li* or *tao*, as the line or way of men's thinking and acting, has a more important meaning in Chinese thought. The *li*, if translated as 'objective principle', or 'natural law', is also to be taken as the way or road of man's thinking about specific things, and not merely as objective Platonic ideas before the subjective mind. The *human* law, rule, regulation, or personal maxim is the right way for man's action. Every *thing* may also be taken as formed according to its process of formation, so man can *think* through a process in order to know the form, and the form here is then nothing else than that course which man's thinking takes. When the essence or pattern of a thing is taken as man's thinking of it, or acting with regard to it, then it is also precisely the way or road man has to pass through to complete his knowledge and action. It is a pity there is no English word corresponding to 'li' or 'tao' meaning just that which 'man's thinking and acting can pass through', like the line, way, or road, and with the same richness of meaning.

As *tao* or *li* means the way man's thinking or acting can take, then any *tao* or *li* which man cannot take, or which leads only to an impasse, is not a real *tao* or *li*. The error or falsehood of an idea or proposition is found where thinking is unable to continue. When ideas are self-contradictory, or fail to correspond with the facts, thinking reaches an impasse. Similarly the evil or wrong in our action is found where an action is unable to continue because it conflicts with other things or with the ideals of the mind. The action which is morally good and right is the action which can really be carried on indefinitely from the present to the future, from oneself to other men, and from the human world to the natural world, and to heaven, without meeting any impasse. Here we have the criterion of 'real' *tao* or *li*. Real *tao* or *li* is the way man should go, and also the only way man *can* really pass along and through. The 'ought to be' of man is what, in the end, he 'shall be' and 'actually can be'. So the Chinese philosopher always uses the same word, 'li' or 'tao', for the universal way of human life, including all acting and thinking. As one's universal way of acting and thinking, *tao* or *li* is one's reason, so the word 'li' may be translated as 'reason' when it is thought as something immanent in one's actual thinking and acting. And as such *li* is also called 'human nature'. Man has an innate capacity to think and act with his reason as an embodiment of *li*. Cheng I-chuan's saying that '(human) nature is *li*' was admired by Chu Tzu as putting what no one before him had said so definitely.

Although *li* may be a universal, a particular, or simply a property of an individual thing, when Cheng I-chuan talked about *li* he was more concerned with the *li* of particular and individual things in ordinary life than with the universal principle of the universe as a whole. Here Cheng I-chuan paid more serious attention to the fact that our ordinary life takes place in concrete situations composed of particular things. So man has to search for and grasp the forms, patterns, principles, and laws of these things as their *li*'s, and the rules, regulations, maxims, and laws, as the *li*'s of his own thinking and acting which are necessary for his having true knowledge of these things, and for his right and good action in terms of the proper response to these things. In doing so, man realizes his human nature as reason or *li*, which means that he then has virtues. When the virtues are genuine and perfect then man can be a sage. There is no short-cut to sagehood by merely thinking the spiritual mentality of the sage or the metaphysical universal principle of the universe, and neglecting knowledge of particular things in everyday life. This is because, lacking this knowledge, he will not know what the proper response to things is. He will have made a cleavage between the outside part and the inside part of himself as man, and he can never attain to sagehood, for the sage is a man of the world as well as of Heaven, a man who realizes his human nature in every concrete situation of his life.

The two parallel 'ways' of Cheng I-chuan's teaching, the insistence on reverence as a subjective way for moral practice, and the investigation of things in a search for their *li*'s and the *li*'s of our responses, as an objective way, are of equal importance The practice of reverence, in opposition to man's private desires, habits, and his temperamental nature, for the purification and constant wakefulness of mind, is certainly a difficult matter. So also is the investigation of things, in view of their multitude; indeed one might even say that due to their great, even infinite number, the investigation of all things is an impossible requirement for sagehood.

However, this does not necessarily follow from Cheng I-chuan's view. If man's investigation of things in his search for their *li*'s was merely a quest for theoretical knowledge of objective things themselves, as for the scientist, then it surely would be an endless enterprise. But if it is for the purpose of knowing the *li*'s of our right and good responses to things in concrete life-situations, it is not a hopeless matter. The things a man encounters in concrete situations are limited, and the *li*'s of right and good response that he should know may be even less. For example, the colours I see in a situation may be many, yet the right and good attitude in seeing them may be just one. The people I meet in a room may be many, but my respect for them may be one. The problem of our moral action in regard to things only arises where a number of different actions or responses seem right and good, and then to help our choice and define what is really right and good in the very situation, we have to study the things in the situation and to know what they really are. This, too, is not a hopeless matter. Even in a situation where two possible actions conflict and both are equally right and good, one can still refrain from doing either. In an extreme situation, one may even commit suicide in order to preserve his reverence for both. To commit suicide in such a case is right and good, according to Confucian teaching. Cheng I-chuan also said that the scholar should see only the right and good and nothing about his living or dying. Whether an action or response is right and good or not, the standard is in man himself. In a particular situation, there must be a particular right or particular good, which can be searched out. Hence the investigation of things with a view to finding their *li* is what man *can* and *should* do.

In the thought of the Cheng brothers, problems about the ways for cultivating sagehood were not discussed objectively on the basis of a general metaphysical or cosmological idea of the universe and man. Their teachings were addressed to their disciples as individuals. Each individual had to think for himself how to relate his mind to his nature and things, including other men. When the Chengs died, scholars of this school came to hold different ideas about such questions as the meaning of reverence, the meanings of *jên*, the real difference between the mind of the sage and that of ordinary people, whether a state of reverence or of tranquility should be cultivated first, what is contemplated in a state of tranquility, what the relation of nature or *li* is to mind, and whether mind is merely a function, and its nature, or *li*, its reality or substance, or whether mind is itself the reality or substance. Some of these questions were raised by disciples of the Cheng brothers, but their masters gave ambiguous or unsatisfactory answers. Some of them were not discussed by the Cheng brothers at all. Discussions of them by the scholars of the whole Cheng school were very subtle and the scene became rather confusing, especially since all the problems centered on something so elusive as the inner mind. But about a hundred years later there came two great thinkers, Chu Tzu and Lu Shiang-shan, to dissolve the confusion, each with a metaphysics of mind as the foundation of the practical attainment of sagehood. Since the thought of Lu Shiang-shan is the more simple and somewhat like the elder Cheng's, I shall deal with him first, though Lu is in fact younger than Chu by about ten years.

IX. Lu Shiang-shan's Idea of Original Mind and Man's Self-Establishment

The most important contribution of Lu's thinking is that he revived Mencius's idea of 'pen-hsin', or 'original mind'. Lu taught that the original mind and its nature as *li* are identical in being and that it is good in an absolute sense as the origin of all moral virtues. Cheng I-chuan, and some scholars of his school, thought that although the 'nature' of mind, as its substance or reality, was good, the conscious mind, as merely an expression or function of that nature, may be morally neutral. They did not take 'nature' here to mean the very nature of original mind. In Lu's thought, the original mind is not always expressed wholly and fully. This is so with the mind of ordinary man. But it *can* be wholly and fully expressed, and this is so with the mind of the sage. There are only differences of degree in expression of the original mind between the ordinary man's and the sage's mind. Therefore when the ordinary man is fully self-conscious of his original mind as the root of his present mind, which is true equally for him and the sage, he can find his way to sagehood even without studying the sayings of sages, or thinking of the sage as only an ideal. Man, as he stands in the universe, can attain to sagehood with his own resources. Yet Lu knew as well as other neo-Confucianists of the need to overcome impediments to the original mind's full expression. Man is dependent upon external things for his existence in the universe. So his mind is always directed and attached to things, and can entertain selfish desires for them. When it does that, it is bent down towards those things and man is no longer able to stand up in the universe, his mind now being separated from its root, namely the original mind. And again, although the mind, as that which thinks, can acquire real knowledge of things, it can also inject its thought with prior conceptions, thus constructing opinions about real things which do not amount to real knowledge. Even real knowledge of certain things when used out of context constitutes wrong opinion. So a man who attaches himself to his knowledge as if it were a constant possession, unaffected by context or occasion, is always transforming it into wrong opinion.

Lu Shiang-shan is remarkable among neo-Confucianists for his view that opinions are more detrimental than selfish desires to man's mind, because opinions are a systematic net formed by the mind as its own snare. Selfish desire is bad, in his view, but desire as such is not bad, and sympathy with men's desires and their fulfilment is good. Opinions, on the other hand, are bad; though knowledge itself is not bad and thinking liberated from opinion is good. When one is liberated from one's opinions and selfish desires, one's mind is without attachment either to things or to one's knowledge, and one's knowing and thinking then become a pervasive light shining upon the whole world of one's knowledge or thought. This light is coextensive with one's world or universe, and the universe then becomes the embodiment of the light of mind; hence Lu's dictum: 'the universe is my mind, my mind is the universe.'[8] In such a state of mind, a man will take all that should be done in the universe as all that he should do for himself. If he acts from a sense of responsibility, he will have no sense of self-possession, and this is the properly spiritual state of sagehood accessible to anyone who can liberate himself from the bondage of his mind and stand up in the universe as an independent man.

X. Chu Tzu's Thoughts about Mind and Moral Practice as a further Development of Cheng I-chuan's Thoughts

Chu Tzu was considered the most systematic thinker and versatile scholar among neo-Confucianists of the Sung dynasty. However, what his main contribution to neo-Confucianism is and how his thought differs from that of Lu Shiang-shan are controversial questions. I myself, after many years of hesitation,[9] would now say that his main contribution is in his thought about mind. Chu Tzu was for a'long time perplexed at the confusing ideas of mind held by scholars of Cheng's school in his youth. And even just a few days before he died, ill as he was, he was correcting sentences in his commentaries on the chapter of 'making the (moral) will real' in *The Great Learning*. Throughout his life he anxiously sought the right way to sagehood through an understanding of mind, and changed his views on mind many times. But his conclusive and central idea seems to have been that mind has its substance or reality in itself and its functions in its response to things.

The substance or reality of mind itself comprises, for Chu, all its *li*'s as its inner nature. When no *li* or nature is expressed, the substance or reality of mind itself is just a pure consciousness, void, serene, transparent, and luminous. But when mind is affected by things inner or outer, it functions through its knowing, feeling, willing, and acting in response to them, and therein *realizes* its nature or *li*. The mind's response as an actual occurrence is composed of *chi*, or substance, just as any actual thing. When *li* or nature is not realized, it is prior to *chi*. It is then not something that 'is', but merely what 'ought to be', i.e. a 'way' the mind's actual responses must take in the process of becoming.

Mind as a pure consciousness which is void, serene, transparent, and luminous is the possession of every man. However, since it can be clouded and concealed by selfish desires and man's temperamental nature, the corresponding way for its recovery and purification is called the 'chen-yang', or 'self-preservation and self-nourishment', of mind, i.e. the maintenance of the state of reverence taught by the Chengs. Yet for Chu Tzu the state of reverence is'not just an outcome of man's own practice, it is the mind's real and original state. Its reality as void, serene, transparent, and luminous is always flowing and growing silently. Since the state of reverence itself, however, is the same as that taught by Cheng I-chuan, Chu Tzu may be thought simply to have made explicit what was implied in the teaching of the Chengs. But in fact he has gone a step further.

The reality of mind, or pure consciousness, as void, serene, transparent, and luminous, was also in Chu Tzu's view a pure subject of its functions and never an object. When affected by things, the mind functions by knowing, feeling, or willing in regard to them, and then it is directed beyond itself. Hence, to want to know the mind as an object, and to direct our knowing backwards upon its origin, is to become involved in an endless circle, and one that is 'selfish' in a very subtle sense. One reason why Chu Tzu opposed Lu Shiang-shan's teaching is that Chu thought Lu's teaching about 'the self-consciousness of the original mind' to be enjoining man to know and grasp his mind as an object. Here Chu may have misunderstood Lu to some extent. Still, he saw clearly that man may direct his knowing backwards to its origin and think of his mind as an object, thus becoming selfish in this subtle sense, and this is a profound insight into a potential error of the mind's ways. The right way of seeing the mind as it is is not to know it as an object, but simply to let it reveal itself in its self-preservation and self-nourishment.

Of course, we have a word 'mind' to express or denote the existence of mind; we can therefore refer to its existence by this word, and the word itself may be an object. But what it expresses is only a subject. The particular functions of mind may also be thought of as inner objects, in the self-reflection of consciousness, but the consciousness which reflects is not an object. Inferring from the word and the particular functions of mind as objects to the conclusion that mind or consciousness is itself an object is just an extension of our habit of grasping external things. It is an illegitimate procedure.

The knowing mind, when not turning in upon itself, is directed to things in order to acquire knowledge of them. The investigation of things with a view to finding their *li*'s is no artificial matter, but necessary to a mind whose nature is to address itself to things. Besides Cheng I-chuan's teaching of the practice of reverence, then, Chu also accepted his teaching of the investigation of things, but found, in two directions, a wider significance in 'investigation of things'. In one direction, Chu Tzu did not think of the investigation of things so much in terms of uncovering the principles of particular things. For him there is a general scheme of all things in the universe, and this can be investigated and known as their universal principle or *li*. Thus Chu Tzu has his metaphysics or cosmology of nature.[10] In this, even man's mind can be seen objectively as a combination of *li* and *chi*, and since he can know the most general scheme of objective nature, as its *li*, his mind may pass through the general scheme or *li* to comprehend the natural universe as a whole. The mind extends to the whole universe. On the basis of this knowledge of nature man can then realize the dignity of his mind.

In the other direction, Chu Tzu found a further significance in the investigation of things in relation to inner spiritual cultivation. According to Cheng I-chuan, the purpose of the investigation of things is to know the *li*'s of things themselves, and then also the *li*'s which man should follow to make his response to them right and good. But how is it possible for the response to follow the *li*? Why do many people know the *li* yet fail to follow it? Here Chu Tzu had to go a step further. Following the book of *The Great Learning*, he took the response of man to outward things to originate from will and feeling. If we want our response to be right and good, we have to take the *li* which we know and should follow as a standard for making our will good, and then the will can be directed to the good alone. That is, we must first have a will which actually likes good and dislikes evil. Liking good and disliking evil are feelings accompanying the will directed to the good when the mind knows the *li* and takes it as a standard. Through liking good and disliking evil, the positive good is posited, and the negative evil is negated; and then our will is directed only to the good, and becomes itself a really good will. This teaching of *The Great Learning*, known as 'making the (moral) will real', Chu Tzu adopted as the next step of moral cultivation after man's realization of his knowledge about the *li* which he should follow.

However, merely 'making the will real' is not enough. The will springs from the mind. If the direction of the mind is partial and wrong, the will may not be directed only to the good. Here *The Great Learning* has a teaching about how to correct the direction of mind, called the 'rectification of mind'. In it, the causes of partiality of mind are discussed. It is said that our natural feelings or emotions such as anger, delight, or fear, which attach to things, have particular directions and the mind's own activity may limit it to a particular direction and make it partial or biased. Therefore 'rectification of mind' is meant to put the mind in its right place and point it in the right direction as master of its feelings or emotions, so that the will, springing from mind, will then be directed only to the good, and have that moral feeling which is its liking good and disliking evil, as noted above. And then from this will, which conforms to the *li* which man knows and should follow, will naturally be generated, by our mind and body, the right and good response to outside things, which in turn means that the *li* which is the inner nature of our mind is also realized. Through one's body one is connected with other men, of one's family, country and the whole world under Heaven. In *The Great Learning* there are also teachings about how to train the body, regulate the family, govern the country, and maintain peace and justice in the world. All these Chu Tzu adopted as connected with the doctrine of the investigation of things and the realization of knowledge as the first two steps in *The Great Learning*.

Although these two steps also came into the teaching of Cheng I-chuan, the latter did not connect them specifically with 'making the will real' and 'rectification of mind', or 'practice of reverence', as ways of inner cultivation. Chu Tzu in effect bridged the two sides of Cheng I-chuan's thought. When Chu talked about reverence as inner cultivation, he knew that the mind should not grasp *itself*, and that the knowing function of mind is naturally directed towards things, as we have explained. And when he talked about the investigation of things and the realization of knowledge, he knew also that they are connected with inner cultivation. Thus the two sides of Cheng I-chuan's teaching can be seen as mutually implicated and connected. It is clear that Chu Tzu's thought centered on the 'mind' with its 'li'. So, on the one hand, the investigation of things is a search for the *li* which man has to follow as an inner standard for 'making the will real' and 'rectification of mind', while, on the other, 'rectification of mind' or 'practice of reverence' is necessary for the realization of the *li* which is our inner nature. That is, while, on the one hand, the *li* of objective things, as it is known through the realization of the mind's knowing function, is also immanent in this very function, so that when the *li* is known from outside things we can say that it has also been revealed from the mind inside,[11] so, on the other hand, when man practices the 'rectification of mind' or 'reverence' to purify his mind and preserve it as a void, serene, transparent, luminous reality, it is precisely in order to keep open the door of mind, and to let the *li*, as its nature, be the more easily revealed and realized. Hence the two ways of Cheng I-chuan mutually help one another to make the *li* known or be revealed to and followed by the mind in its knowledge and actions; which then makes the mind reasonable, and brings man to the 'way' which leads to sagehood.

When mind is not knowing or acting, it is still a mind and remains in a state of reverence; and Chu Tzu explained the *Chung Yung*'s teaching of 'ch'en tu', or 'self-care in solitude', as differentiated into two kinds of inner reflection. One is when a certain idea motivates one's action and one has to examine whether it tends to be, or is, good or evil, right or wrong, and then likes or dislikes it accordingly. This corresponds to the way of 'making the (moral) will real' in the *Great Learning*. The other is when there is no idea motivating action, and there is therefore nothing to occasion either like or dislike. Here too the mind should be in a state of self-care, to prevent evil or wrong ideas arising unconsciously.[12]

Chu Tzu's thought about the mind and moral cultivation is subtle, profound, and generally sound. However, he took *li* merely to reside *within* the mind, and thus to be distinguished from it. And he further distinguished between mind's reality, or substance, as static or tranquil, and its function as dynamic or effective. In Chu Tzu's cosmology, too, the 'mind', as a synthesis of *li* and *chi*, is in an ambiguous position. How to unite the dualities of *li* and *chi*, of mind as reality, or substance, and as function, and of mind and its *li*, remained outstanding problems. For although Chu explained how 'investigation of things', 'realization of knowledge', 'making the moral will real', 'practice of reverence' and 'rectification of mind' were related to one another, these still remained distinct ways of moral cultivation. A unitary way was still to be found. So Chu Tzu's teaching is not so simple as Lu Shiang-shan's who saw that the mind with its *li*, or nature, is simple, that the mind, whether static or dynamic, is the same moral mind, and that there is only one way for moral cultivation, i.e. knowing the original mind and encouraging its self-enlightenment. The differences between Chu Tzu's teaching and that of Lu had also to be unified. This was the achievement of Wang Yang-ming.

XI. Wang Yang-ming's Realization of Liang-chih or Conscientious Consciousness as both a Function and the Substance or Reality of Mind — a Synthesis of Chu Tzu's Dualism and Lu Shiang-shan's Teaching of Original Mind

Wang Yang-ming has generally been taken to belong to Lu's school. This is not quite right. Of course Wang admired Lu, and his thought is an attempt to unify the dualities in Chu Tzu's teaching. It was also his view that the mind of the sage and that of the ordinary man do not differ in kind, but only in degree of enlightenment. All this is close to Lu. Yet Wang's learning began with his study of Chu Tzu, and all his problems and key ideas stem from Chu. Wang admired Lu as a successor of Mencius, but he was a greater admirer of Yen Tzu, whom Chu Tzu also admired. Wang said that he was grateful to Chu Tzu as to his parents or Heaven. Whenever he found that he differed from Chu Tzu, he was most anxious to find sayings in Chu that minimized the difference, and he edited a book of Chu's sayings, entitled *The Conclusive Thesis of Chu Tzu's Late Age*, which was taken to represent his own thought. Which all shows that Wang's learning originated from Chu Tzu even though its conclusions were closer to those of Lu Shiang-shan. So I take his teaching to be a synthesis of Chu Tzu and Lu Shiang-shan.[13]

From his study of Chu Tzu, Wang evolved a development of the former's theory of the investigation of things. According to Chu, the investigation of things and search for their *li* culminate in knowing the *li* of our response to objective things. But this response is something man can investigate directly. So Wang thought that the word 'thing' in the *Great Learning* should be understood to refer to that ('thing') which man does to the so-called objective thing, where the 'thing' he does can include the so-called objective thing as an ingredient. For example, where the doing in question is seeing something, that doing includes colours as its ingredients; similarly hearing can include sounds as its ingredients. The moral problem is connected with the doing as a whole. There are moral problems about the ways of seeing and hearing, for they can be right or wrong, and good or evil, but not about the colours or sounds themselves. The right and good way of our doing is the *li* which we have to know in order to make the thing which we are doing right and good. This is the only *li* which has to be known when we want to be a moral being or a sage. Hence Wang interpreted the realization of knowledge as realization of knowledge about the *li* of our doing, or of our response to so-called objective things. This constituted an important break with Chu's view, even though it was a development of Chu's rather than of Lu Shiang-shan's teaching.

According to Wang, then, our universe is a universe which we act upon and respond to, and we know it only through our acts and responses. My own universe of things and men, therefore, extends no further than the range of my affections and responses. It is a kind of idealism, though not a theoretical idealism supported by metaphysical or epistemological arguments. Rather, it is simply a vision of man as capable of immediate knowledge of the universe through his own actions and responses.

As the *li* connected with morality, or with the ideal of sagehood, is the *li* of our doing or response, and our doing or response is in the self and known by the mind, then all the *li*'s have to be reached and known in the mind. There is no *li* of doing or response outside the mind and belonging to so-called objective things alone. For example, the *li* of filial piety is in our minds when we act with regard to our parents, not in the parents themselves. The same is true of all *li*'s. The *li* in our mind is at the same time the mind's *being* conscious and the *li* that we are conscious of. Yet when the *li* is conscious, mind or consciousness are also *in* the *li*, as well as the *li* being in that very mind or consciousness. Here the identity of mind and *li* can be directly confirmed and intuited if man reflects upon the relation of *li* and mind or consciousness as they really are.

If we agree that the *li* is in our mind as consciousness, and the mind as consciousness of *li* is also in the very *li*, we still have to ask how the consciousness of *li* functions in relation to the other parts of the mind as a whole. That the *li* is what should be followed is the common teaching of neo-Confucianism. Yet Chu Tzu granted that the *li* may not actually be followed. In that case, the *li* is transcendent or only subsists in the substance or reality of mind as its nature, and is not actually expressed in the mind. However, if the *li* which 'should be' is taken as transcendent, then the consciousness of its transcendence is a transcendental consciousness, and the *li* which 'should be' is not transcendental to *this* consciousness, but immanent in it; and so the *li* should not be taken as merely transcendent, as Chu Tzu thought. Of course, the *li* may very well not be expressed in the mind, and when that is so it can be taken as only subsisting in the reality or substance of mind as unexpressed and unrealized. But in this sense the 'consciousness of the very *li*' is also unexpressed. The expression of *li* and the expression of the consciousness of *li* are always simultaneous, never separate. Thus there is an existential identity of *li* and the mind as consciousness of *li*, which should be referred to by one term. Wang calls it 'liang-chih', which may be translated 'conscientious consciousness of mind', and its content is the moral *li* which should be and actually is followed when it is realized. In the teaching of Wang Yang-ming, every man has *liang-chih* because he has a consciousness of some *li*'s which should be followed, and thus has some knowledge of what should be, whether he actually tries to bring it about or not. We need not know all of what ought to be, or all *li*'s. They will be revealed gradually in the process of our lives. We are ordinary men not because we have no knowledge of what ought to be, but because we do not act fully upon the knowledge we have. We are not responsible for the 'should be's' we do not know. Our responsibility consists in responding to any 'should be' that is immediately expressed, revealed, and known. This is quite enough for our immediate moral practice. Therefore to say that the *li* is one thing and practice another, as Chu Tzu, Lu Shiang-shan, and others taught, does not do justice to our moral consciousness. Moreover, the very inadequacy of the notion is a hindrance to our efficiency in moral practice. We have to understand that this consciousness of *li*, or *liang-chih*, is originally both knowing *and* feeling. The fact is that when *liang-chih* knows the right or good, a feeling of liking it arises simultaneously, as does, when *liang-chih* knows the wrong or evil, a feeling of disliking it. Chu Tzu did say that liking or disliking is connected with our knowledge of good or evil, but he still thought the realization of knowledge to be only the first step in moral practice, and disliking evil and liking good to be the next step. This is an inadequate understanding of the consciousness of *li*, or *liang-chih*, as moral consciousness. The adequate understanding is that the feeling of liking good comes no later than knowing good, and feeling of disliking evil comes no later than knowing evil. The knowledge of *liang-chih* includes the feeling of like or dislike; and the will to do or undo subsists in the feeling. So *liang-chih*'s knowledge and its action are taken as one thing and not two. 'Realization of knowledge' and 'making the (moral) will real', as taught by the book of *The Great Learning*, and which Chu Tzu interpreted as two steps or two ways of moral practices, Wang conceived as but one single step, or one way. In Chu Tzu's thought the rectification of mind is yet another step, or way, of moral practice. For Wang, however, the consciousness of *li* as *liang-chih* is the very being of the moral mind. When a man realizes his *liang-chih* as liking and doing good, and disliking and undoing evil, then his mind is already on the right way and in the right place. So the 'rectification of mind' is included in the realization of *liang-chih*. Furthermore, when whatever is good for my body-behaviour, my family, my country, and the whole world, is done, and whatever is evil for all these is undone, then my body is trained, my family regulated, my country governed, and the world's justice and peace attained. So all the teachings of *The Great Learning* which Chu Tzu interpreted as separate are included in one teaching of the 'realization of *liang-chih*'.

The above concerns realization of *liang-chih* when there are things for the mind to like or dislike. But what about the mind when it has nothing special to like or dislike, when it is in a quiet, tranquil, and static state, and all mental activity is unexpressed? Now Wang Yang-ming certainly agreed that there is such a state of mind, and indeed that one must have it in order to keep the mind, as Chu Tzu said, void, serene, transparent and luminous. And Wang Yang-ming also agreed with Chu that even in such a state the mind is not just idle, but still exercises self-care against the possibility of evil or wrong ideas being motivated from the depths of unconsciousness. But Wang did not agree with Chu that because nothing is known in this state, then it is a state of 'no knowing'. He asked: If it is a state of 'no knowing', then who is exercising self-care? The mind's, or *liang-chih's*, knowing must always exist, whether there are things or ideas to be known or not. The state in which things or ideas are known and that in which nothing is known are in fact mutually implicated. When ideas or things come to consciousness, then the *liang-chih* must know immediately whether they are good or evil, right or wrong, and therefore whether liking or disliking, and willing to do or willing to undo, is the appropriate expression of its activities for its self-realization. Through its self-realization its own activities are carried on and fulfilled. When evils are removed and good attained the mind as *liang-chih* reaches a state beyond good and evil. It returns to the state in which it was prior to its expressive activity. But because *liang-chih's* activities themselves originate from a state prior to their being expressed and have to return to that state, there can be no separation of the state in which its activities are expressed from that in which they are not.

Moreover, when *liang-chih* is not prompted by evil or good, but is in a 'pre-expressive' state, it continues to safeguard itself for its own self-realization. Nor is it really without expression in this state. For the state of self-care is a state of knowing which is also a state of bliss and liberation from any limitations of mind, and this is itself an expression of *liang-chih*, even though it has no particular object in view.

From the above two paragraphs, it is clear that, contrary to Chu Tzu's view, we must say that the mind as *liang-chih* never exists either as a merely static substance or reality without expression of its function, nor as a merely dynamic function without expression of its substance or reality. When the mind does not express itself in ordinary activity, its function of knowing is still expressed in its substance or reality, and when it does express itself in ordinary activity, the latter expresses the state of rest in which the mind's reality or substance, though unexpressed, still remains. So the mind as *liang-chih* is always both dynamic and static, always creating or acting and always tranquil or at rest. It is a pure knowing or conscientious consciousness, and can never be posited as an objective being. It can only be enjoyed subjectively as a kind of transparent spiritual light always in process of self-creation out of a state of 'self-rest'.

In Wang Yang-ming the dualities of *li* and mind, of the substance, or reality, and function of mind, of the external investigation of things and the internal ways of spiritual cultivation, were all unified into one integral doctrine of the realization of *liang chih*. His doctrines of the unity of mind and *li* and of mind as both static and dynamic are precisely those of Lu Shiang-shan, though, as we have said, many of Wang's key ideas and problems stem from Chu Tzu. His idea of *liang chih* as conscientious consciousness is also very similar to Lu's idea of original mind as a unity of *li* and mind, though *liang chih* is always concerned with particular things, and must realize itself in its response to things in concrete situations. Wang's 'liang chih' is more intimate to our immediate experience than Lu's 'original mind', which is always spoken of as identical with the universe as a whole. There is an analogy between the practice of realization for *liang chih* and Cheng I-chuan and Chu Tzu's investigation of things, in that both involve consideration of individual cases on their own merits.

Because *liang-chih* concerns present concrete situations, it is possible to know the existence of *liang-chih* in any present situation, given immediate self-reflection. The realization of *liang-chih* is a way to sagehood because every man has it in himself to be a sage. We could even say that in the depth of every man's heart there lies hidden a sage waiting to be revealed when the closed door of the mind is opened. Because it taught that every man can be a sage, Wang's teaching flourished in the late Ming period and its influence was felt throughout the whole Chinese community. Many of Wang's disciples developed his thought to a very high level. But his teaching was also perverted because people assumed that, being potential sages, they were as good as sages already, and therefore in no need of spiritual cultivation or moral practice in confronting actual or possible hindrances to spirituality and morality. This, of course, was not Wang's teaching, but merely a degeneration of the spirit of his doctrine of 'becoming a sage through the self-transformation of one's life'. When this degeneration reached its lowpoint in late Ming, there was a movement by great thinkers to revise Wang's teaching, and also an anti-Wang movement which ended in a movement opposed to the neo-Confucianism of the Sung-Ming dynasties as a whole.[14] Hence the main currents of thought from the Ching dynasty to present-day China are not in line with the development of neo-Confucianism. It is regrettable that the spiritual depth and moral grandeur of the neo-Confucianists, and the significance of their thought, have so often been forgotten or misunderstood, and still await revival and new understanding.

NOTES

1. Tang Chun-i, 'An Evaluation of the Similarities and Differences between Chu Tzu and Lu Shiang-shan's Thoughts as Seen from their Origin', *New Asia Journal*, Vol. VIII (1967), No. 1; and 'The Learning of Wang Yang-ming and a Re-evaluation of Similarities and Differences between Chu Tzu and Lu Shiang-shan's Thoughts', *New Asia Journal*, Vol. VIII (1967), No. 2, and Vol. IX (1969), No. 1.

2. Wing-tsit Chan (Trans.), *Instructions for Practical Living (Ch'uan hsi lu)*, Columbia University Press, New York 1963. See pp. 193, 194, 239 and 240.

3. *T'ung shu*, Ch. 10.

4. Ibid., Ch. 7.

5. Ibid., Ch. 20.

6. Cf. my 'On Chang Hêng-chu's Theory of Mind and its Metaphysical Basis', *Philosophy East and West*, Vol. VI (1956), Nos. 1 and 2. I discuss the meaning of 'chi' for the benefit of Western readers.

7. *Ming-tao-wen-chi* (Essays of Cheng Ming-tao) Vol. III.

8. *Shiang-shan-chuan-chi* (Complete Works of Lu Shiang-shan), Vol. 36.

9. Cf. Sec. 5 of my 'An Evaluation of the Similarities and Differences...', op. cit.

10. In this respect he accepted Chou Lien-chi's ideas about the origin of the universe as infinite-ultimate, Chang Hêng-chu's ideas about *chi* as the real being of things, and Shao Kang-chieh and the Han dynasties' scholars' ideas about number, *ying* and *yang*, the five activities, and the eight diagrams. Chu Tzu used all these ideas to construct his metaphysics of objective nature.

11. Cf. Ch. 2, Sec.4 of my 'The Learning of Wang Yang-ming and a Re-evaluation ...', op. cit.

12. This is the innermost practice of the moral mind in man's solitude. It is also the most serious experience in the mind's inner life at the transition between consciousness and unconsciousness, and also between consciousness's *function* of knowing and the knowing itself. This doctrine of Chu Tzu's should actually be included in the doctrine of 'rectification of mind' in the *Great Learning*.

13. Cf. Ch. 3, Sec. 1 of my 'The Learning of Wang Yang-ming and a Re-evaluation. ...', op. cit.

14. Cf. Ch. 15 of my *The Development of the Ideas of Human Nature in Chinese Philosophy*, New Asia College, Hong Kong, and my 'The Development of the Concept of the Moral Mind from Wang Yang-ming to Wang Chi', in *Self and Society in Ming Dynasty Thought*, Columbia University Press, New York 1970.

7
Chang Tsai's Theory of Mind and Its Metaphysical Basis *

I. The Place of Chang Tsai's[2] Thought in The Philosophy of the Sung (A.D. 960–1279) and Ming (A.D. 1368–1644) Periods.

CHINESE PHILOSOPHY DURING the Sung and Ming periods is generally divided into two schools, that of Ch'êng-and-Chu and that of Lu-and-Wang. Yet, the school of Chang Tsai is really a school by itself. The central concept of Ch'êng-and-Chu is reason, that of Lu-and-Wang, mind, and that of Chang Tsai, ether (ch'i[3]). It is generally accepted that the philosophy of the Sung and Ming periods started with Chou Tun-i, whose major work is the T'ung Shu. Now, the T'ung Shu deals mainly with the ways of spiritual cultivation in order to become a sage or a worthy. As for Chou's "Explanation of the Diagram of the Supreme Ultimate," it would seem too simple except for Chu Hsi's commentary. The Chêng-mêng[4] of Chang Tsai, on the other hand, is a book that seeks consciously to establish a system of philosophy of its own, and thus establishes a theoretical foundation for spiritual cultivation. Ch'êng I critically referred to the book as exhibiting much effort and strain, which meant at that time the lack of mellowed maturity. In our day, however, we can see that the philosophy of Chang Tsai is worked out with much care and detail, though it might not have reached the high level of Ch'êng Hao, Chu Hsi, or Wang Shou-jên. He defined unequivocally such vague terms in traditional Chinese thought as Heaven and man, human nature and the Heavenly decree, spirituality (shên[5]) and transformation (hua[6]), the mind and the nature, the void[7] and the ether, the searching for spirituality and the knowledge of transforma-

---

*Originally published under the title 唐君毅張橫渠之心性論及其形上學之根據 in 東方文化 (Journal of Oriental Studies), I, No. 1 (January, 1954). Original translation of Sections 1–3 by Sung Lei, Sections 4–7 by Louis Shiao. Complete revised translation by Y. P. Mei.
[1] Chün-i T'ang 唐君毅.
[2] Chang Tsai 張載, an alternate name is Chang Hêng-ch'ü 張橫 (1020–1077).
[3] ch'i 氣.   [4] chêng-mêng 正蒙.
[5] shên 神.   [6] hua 化.   [7] void 虛 (hsü).

tion, complete development of the nature and full realization of the decree, etc. In this respect, only Chu Hsi among the philosophers of this period may be considered Chang's equal.

The philosophy of Chang Tsai proceeds from the existence of the objective universe to the problems of human life, aiming at the overthrow of the prevalent idealism of Buddhism, especially Ch'an Buddhist thought. And yet, his idea about the mind is not without similarity to that of the Ch'an thinkers. Chang Tsai may therefore be taken as the philosophical turning point from Buddhism to Confucianism. The scholars of the two schools of Ch'êng-and-Chu and Lu-and-Wang differ from Chang, in that they are not much interested in discussing nature and the universe. The only exception is Chu Hsi, who, in his theory of the mind, inherited a number of the problems and conceptions of Chang Tsai, pursued them further, and elevated the position of the human mind in the universe. At the time the philosophy of Lu-and-Wang flourished at the end of the Ming Dynasty there came forth one great thinker who reverted to Chang Tsai. That was Wang Fu-chih.[8] Wang Fu-chih, on the one hand, was interested in the problems of philosophy of the Sung and Ming periods, and, on the other hand, placed much emphasis on the value of history. In this latter emphasis he was joined by Ku Yen-wu and Huang Tsung-hsi, all of whom are the scholars responsible for the intellectual reorientation taking place at the juncture between the Ming and the Ch'ing dynasties. In view of Wang Fu-chih's enthusiasm for Chang Tsai, the value of the philosophy of Chang Tsai throughout the philosophy of the Sung and Ming periods becomes evident. Though Chang was a careful and exact thinker, his language is terse and archaic, frequently expressing his ideas in brief sentences. As a result, he is often misunderstood. If we merely take some of his sayings and try to explain them, we shall often miss his central point. It is for this reason that in this article I shall attempt an over-all discussion of his theory of the human mind, which has been so often misunderstood, together with its metaphysical basis. I think we can grasp the spirit of his thought as a whole if we can truly understand his theory about the human mind. Moreover, one step further from the theory of the human mind of Chang Tsai we have the philosophy of human nature and the reason (*li*) of Ch'êng-and-Chu, and the philosophy of the original mind and intuitive knowledge (*liang-chih*) of Lu-and-Wang. In Chang Tsai's doctrine of the mind, emphasis is placed on its void character, and this void is derived from the Supreme Void,[9] whereas the concept of reason is made secondary. The Ch'êng-

---

[8] Wang Fu-chih 王夫之; an alternate name is Wang Ch'uan-shan 王船山 (1619–1692).
[9] Supreme Void 太虛 (*T'ai-hsü*).

and-Chu school substituted reason for void and assumed nature as the manifestation of the cosmic reason. Chang says that apart from oneself there is a universe with which one ought to enter into a union. While Ch'êng Hao says, "Every activity of the universe is an activity of myself," and "The universe and oneself are not two, and there is no point of talking about their union," Lu Chiu-yüan says, "The universe is my mind and my mind is the universe." And finally, Wang Shou-jên says that man's intuitive knowledge (*liang-chih*) is the cosmic reason, and that the *liang-chih* of one single man is the *liang-chih* of the universe and of all things. If Chang Tsai had not established for the mind an objective cosmic basis, these philosophers after him would not have been able to elevate the human mind to the same high level as the heavenly mind. And, if one did not comprehend what Chang Tsai called the void of the mind, one would not be able to grasp what the Ch'êng-and-Chu school called reason, or what the Lu-and-Wang school referred to as the original mind that is one with the cosmos and all things.

II. Chang Tsai's Theory of Mind as Compared to that of the Ch'an Buddhists

Chu Hsi particularly admired Chang Tsai's saying, "The mind comprises nature and feeling." And he is fond of quoting Chang thus, "From the Supreme Void, there comes the name of Heaven; from the ether and its transformation,[10] there comes the name of the *tao;* when the void and the ether come together, there is nature, and, when nature and consciousness come together, there is the mind." These utterances are all difficult to understand, and we shall deal with them later. As an introduction to Chang Tsai's doctrine of the mind, let us first note the following saying of his:

From phenomena[11] the mind is discerned; preoccupied with the phenomena the mind will be lost. The mind that becomes merely a storehouse for phenomena will be nothing but phenomena. How, then, can it be called the mind?

"Phenomena" here means the appearances of things perceived by the mind and the impressions and ideas left on the mind due to its perceptions. Generally, the mind is known first through the impressions and ideas left by the mind's perceiving its objects. Western introspective psychology, for instance, tries to understand the mind by the impressions and ideas in the

---

[10] Ether and its transformation 氣化 *(ch'i-hua)*.

[11] Phenomena 象 *(hsiang)*.

mind. Empiricists like Berkeley, Hume, and Mill take the mind as simply a collection of innumerable impressions and ideas. But, in traditional Chinese thought, it is the activity of the mind that is emphasized. Even when Chinese thinkers deal with the problems of mental perception, the emphasis is not placed on the impressions and ideas left in the mind so much as on the ability of the mind to produce these impressions and ideas of objects and to make them pass away, which might be attributed to the apprehensive function of the void of the mind. This notion has been discussed most by such ancient philosophers as Chuang Tzǔ, Hsün Tzǔ, and Kuan Tzǔ. The theory of "experiencing nothingness" of the philosophers of the Wei (220– 264) and Chin (265–419) periods, Wang Pi [12] and Ho Yen,[13] is just another expression of the void character of the mind. In traditional Chinese thought, mind is seldom taken as a collection of numerous ideas and impressions, for ideas and impressions come and go constantly in the mind. When they are there, they are there; when they are gone, they are gone. Since the comings and goings replace and cancel each other, we cannot really locate these impressions and ideas in our minds, and let them be taken as the determinant of its nature, nor can we take the mind as a collection of impressions and ideas of objects. As for the perception of the mind, one can call it only the function of pure consciousness, which is capable of producing any phenomenon, impression, or idea, and yet, it is also capable of transcending all these and producing others. Hence, the nature of the mind is void. This way of thinking, I believe, is the basic conception in traditional Chinese thought toward an understanding of the mind. The Indian Vijñānavāda school of Buddhism also holds the theory that "the mind is a collection." But this is not the popular Buddhist school with the Chinese. Though in the end the Vijñānavāda school also teaches the changeability and inconstancy of the mind as a collection which is devoid of any self-nature and which is illusory and not real, its first step is always "the mind is a collection." According to this theory, the human mind is a collection of innumerable actual or potential ideas. But the fundamental theory of the Ch'an school, a school founded by Chinese themselves, teaches that one should not try to understand the mind by the appearances, impressions, and ideas left on the mind. They insist that the mind is not to retain or hold on to any impression, appearance, or idea, so that our mind might really become manifest and our original nature revealed. For this reason, though the Ch'an school is not a realism that assumes things as being outside one's mind, yet it is not an idealism that takes things as mental ideas inside one's mind. It

---

[12] Wang Pi 王弼 , (226–249).
[13] Ho Yen 何晏 , (d. 249).

imposes on the mind a kind of bondage and restriction to say that there are things outside the mind, and it is also a bondage to the mind for one to say that things are located in the mind. Therefore, the Ch'ans sometimes "snatch away the environment but not the man," sometimes "snatch away the man but not the environment," and sometimes "snatch away both the man and the environment." One who sees the mind by the phenomena of things and ideas sees it only in terms of its objects and its states, and fails really to understand the mind and to know the apprehensive function of the void of the mind. And yet, the Ch'ans cannot permit one to insist on the character of the apprehensive function of the void of the mind either, for to permit such an insistence would be to permit an instance of holding-on. When detained and held on to, the void character of the mind is no longer void. Therefore, sometimes the Ch'ans would "snatch away neither the mind nor the environment." The Ch'ans devote themselves especially to the attainment of "non-abiding."[14] Their Sixth Patriarch, Hui Nêng,[15] came to this apprehension when he heard the following saying from the *Vajracchedikā-prajñāpāramitā-sūtra,* "The mind is born when it dwells on nothing." When nothing is dwelt upon, "no idea refers to its preceding condition." This is "non-abiding." When the mind is not contaminated by anything from the environment, this is "non-ideation." When self-ideation leaves its environment behind, this is "non-appearance." The book by Hui Nêng says, "Non-ideation is the origin, non-appearance is the frame, non-abiding is the essence." The non-abiding doctrine of the Ch'ans relegates the past to the past, the present to the present, and the future to the future, and no succeeding idea is attached to its preceding idea. As each moment is cut off from the next moment, the opposition of the external and the internal, or the subjective and the objective, naturally disappears, and Buddha-hood is attained through sudden enlightenment. If a person will make a resolution and disjoin the relation of past, present, and future, he will at that very moment be able to make manifest his mind, his nature will be revealed, and he will gain deliverance. The main objective of the Ch'ans lies in "deliverance," and all they say has to do with one's spiritual cultivation rather than with ontological substance. What they have said is to be blotted away as soon as it is said, and nothing in what they say is meant to make clear anything in particular. Actually it is not what we call philosophy. Yet, from the standpoint of philosophy, we can say that the basic spirit of the Ch'an school comes from a deep apprehension of the void nature of the mind—the mind that can produce any phenomena or impressions

[14] Non-abiding 無住 *(wu-chu).*
[15] Hui Nêng 慧能 (638–713).

and ideas and yet can transcend them all. This concept of the Ch'ans comes from traditional Chinese thought, and, in turn, the philosophy of the Sung and Ming periods develops itself from Ch'an. For this reason, the Sung and Ming philosophers agreed in taking the void and intuitive nature of the mind seriously.

Now, let us go back to the quotation from Chang Tsai which we gave at the beginning of Section II. What Chang means is this: though we know at first the existence of our mind because of the phenomena, that is, the objects and their impressions and ideas, yet our mind, if it holds on to the phenomena and allows itself to be submerged in them, will lose its void and intuitive nature. The mind that preserves the phenomena will become phenomena and will no longer be mind. All this comes from traditional Chinese thought on understanding the mind, and accords with the spirit of Ch'an.

Nevertheless, on the whole, Chang Tsai's theory of mind is different from that of the Ch'ans on three points: first, the Ch'ans make no reference to the objective and cosmic origin of the void and intuitive mind; second, the Ch'ans have nothing to say about the virtue and value content of the mind; and, third, the Ch'ans are silent on the practice of social ethics through the complete realization of the mind and its nature. In the eyes of Chang Tsai, the key to all these three points may be found in the Ch'ans' lack of interest in the objective and cosmic origin of the mind and its intuitive and void character. Hence, this will be the central point of our discussion in this essay. It is because they are interested in seeking the immediate enlightenment of the mind that the Ch'ans fail to pay much attention to the cosmic origin of the human mind. When emphasis is laid on the enlightenment of the mind, it is not necessary to ask what is the origin of the mind, for, when we raise such a question, we are already assuming the mind to be a thing, and to seek a firm grasp of it. Here we run into the Ch'an taboo from the outset. Furthermore, the Ch'ans have inherited the Buddhist theory already worked out by the various sects that the mind is existent from the very beginning, even before one is borne by his parents. This is an idealist cosmology. Chang Tsai, of course, does not subscribe to this idealistic cosmology, but holds that the mind, or the nature of the mind, has its origin in an objective universe. This is the metaphysics of the Great Harmony[16] (*Magnum Harmonicum*) involving the identity of the ether and the void. On the one hand, he says that the human mind ought to "seek existence in the void," and, on the other hand, he says that the void of the mind depends upon the *"Tao* of the Universe, according to which there is no existence but what

---

[16] Great Harmony 太和 *(T'ai-ho)*.

is found in the void." It is because he does not think that the mind can be kept separate from the body that Chang seeks to find an origin of the mind in the objective universe. Since the body cannot have existed from the very beginning, neither can the mind. Our body is given us by our parents, and nourished by the things in the universe. Just as the body owes its existence to an external universe, so should the nature of the mind. From the standpoint of origination, all things in the objective universe constitute the Great Harmony of the undifferentiated ether-void. Considered from its aspect as the Supreme Void, the Great Harmony is Heaven; from its aspect as ether-transformation, it is *Tao*. As man is produced by this Great Harmony of undifferentiated ether-void, he is naturally endowed with the *Tao* of the Supreme Void and ether-transformation as his nature. The nature of man reveals itself when in contact with things, and this is called consciousness. As to mind, it is the combination of this consciousness with the nature that can perceive from its void and intuitive character. When man becomes conscious of a thing, he expresses in accordance with the ether that is in him his attitude toward the thing. This is the man's emotion and will toward things. Hence, Chang Tsai says (as quoted at the beginning of Section II), "From the Supreme Void, there comes the name of Heaven; from the ether and its transformation, there comes the name of the *Tao;* when the void and the ether come together, there is nature, and, when nature and consciousness come together, there is mind." And he also says, "The mind comprises nature and feeling."

III. The Meaning of Ether Stated in Modern Terms

It is not easy for people to understand properly Chang Tsai's theory that the origin and nature of the mind lie in the existence of the objective universe. Often it is taken as a sort of materialism like that of the West. Not only this, but, in addition, his explanation of the Great Harmony of the universe and the nature of man in terms of the void and ether-transformation puts him especially under the difficulty of the independence between the void and the ether and makes his view seem like dualism. Yet, in truth, Chang Tsai's theory of the Great Harmony of the undifferentiated void-ether is, after all, just ether. What he calls void, though it looks like something lying outside ether-transformation, is actually inside the ether.

If we want to have a true grasp of what he is trying to say, we must know what ether means in traditional Chinese thought. The conception of ether *(ch'i)* is a peculiar conception in Chinese thought. In olden days, Chinese came to know its meaning by experience, and, in our time, it is usually taken as a kind of matter. For example, Fung Yu-lan and others take ether as the same as Aristotle's matter in Western philosophy. Actually this is wrong. In the usage of past Chinese philosophers, the word ether *(ch'i)* could mean either something spiritual, as in ambition *(ch'i-chih)* or something vital, as animation *(shêng-ch'i)*, or something material, as geo-gaseity *(ti-ch'i)*. And these three kinds of ether are usually treated by Chinese thinkers as belonging together, so that the ether that denotes something material may at the same time denote something spiritual or vital. Ether in traditional Chinese thought is completely unlike matter as understood by Western science or philosophy. In Plato's and Aristotle's thought, matter is usually contrasted with the forms of things. Everything has its form, but form alone does not constitute a thing. That to which form adheres or that which gives form its actuality is matter. But in Chinese thought, whether the term "ether" denotes something spiritual, material, or vital, it is a conception prior to form and matter. Ether does not have a definite determination as form does, nor does it have the resistant corporeality of matter. From the ancient apocryphal treatises of the Six Classics to the Yin-Yang followers and the Confucianists of the later periods, it is generally agreed that the material universe has ether first and form next. When the form is set, tending toward a definite direction, and making it difficult for any other thing to penetrate, then we have matter. Before the appearance of quantum theory and theory of relativity, modern scientists of the West used to be of the opinion that the fundamental character of physical matter was inertia and impenetrability. Chinese philosophers have never adopted such a view, for they hold that the idea of matter is subsequent to form and ether. And, when dealing with the problems of nature and the universe, it is a very common Chinese assumption that *matter comes from form, and form comes from ether*. It is also improper to take Aristotle's primary matter to explain ether in Chinese philosophy, because Aristotle's primary matter is a potentiality absolutely without any form. This is evidently a remaining substratum after the form has been subtracted by logical analysis, whereas ether in Chinese thought, though formless, can assume any form. It is not restricted by any definite form, but is inclusive of all forms. Therefore, ether may be said to be a formlessness surpassing forms and yet containing forms; and it is not absolutely without form. And, whether we are considering the primary matter of Aristotle or the matter of Western science before modern physical quantum theory and relativity theory, matter in the West was not active but passive, waiting for some external force to set it in action, while in Chinese thought ether is invariably active, or, in other words, there may be said to be force within it. It is not an absolute formlessness or a sub-formal matter or potentiality, but a real existence that is capable of motion or quietude, and of assuming a definite form while also capable of transcending one form to assume another form. The characteristic of this existence lies in the process in which it assumes definite forms successively and successively transcends them. When it assumes a definite form, it becomes a definite thing, and this means the condensation of the ether, or the ether in its masculinity. When it transcends this given form and causes it to disintegrate, this means the dispersion of the ether, or the ether in its femininity. The capability of ether to act so is force. To understand clearly the formlessness of ether, we have to take a synthetic conception of these three ideas, forming, transcending, and force. To understand the actuality of ether, we also have to take a synthetic conception of existence and process. Therefore, ether may be defined as an existential process, within which there is the mutation of forms, or as an existence within which there is the process of the mutation of forms. On this theory, ether may be regarded as a primary metaphysical principle for the explanation of the universe. This is my explanation stated in modern terms of the concept of ether in traditional Chinese thought according to its generally accepted meaning.

IV. CHANG TSAI'S THEORY OF IDENTIFICATION OF THE "ETHER" WITH THE "VOID"

This traditional conception of ether in Chinese thought, as discussed above, was accepted by Chang Tsai. Therefore, he always tied up the idea of transformation to the idea of ether and spoke of ether-transformation. Chang represented an advancement over the scholars of the Ch'in (221–206 B.C.) and Han periods (206 B.C.–A.D. 220) in the discussion of ether, in that he emphasized the void nature of the ether and insisted upon it. He said: "Empty and void is the ether." Though the scholars of the Ch'in and Han periods knew that the ether had neither any fixed form nor any fixed matter, they rarely discussed the ether in terms of the void. The authors of the apocryphal treatises on the Six Classics were in the habit of talking about the original ether as the origin of the universe. The Taoists, on the other hand, emphasized void and non-being and occasionally took non-being as the origin of all things, and thus suffered from a one-sided emphasis on the void and non-being. Chang objected to all these contrasts between being and non-being and between void and con-cretion. Besides, according to him, the "void" as advocated by the Buddhists still implies an opposition to "being." What Chang wanted to do was to achieve a synthesis of the "ether" of the scholars of the Ch'in and Han periods with the "non-being" or "void" of the Taoists and Buddhists. The result of this synthesis is a return to the conception contained in the ancient text of "The Commentary on the *Book of Changes*" as presented in a new expression.

This new explanation, if we analyze it, may be said to contain two aspects: the vertical and the horizontal.

The vertical aspect: Beginning with the fact that all things constituted of form and matter (as stated above, not in the sense of Aristotelian form and matter) are incessantly coming to be, on the one hand, and being dis-solved to become other things, on the other hand, Chang concludes that all things are in an "incessant process of appearing and disappearing." When they appear, the Taoists call it being and the Buddhists call it gen-eration. When they disappear, the Taoists refer to it as non-being and the Buddhists refer to it as extinction. But this contrast of being with non-being and generation with extinction, in Chang's view, is applicable only to the existence of form and matter but not to the ether itself from which both form and matter are derived. Here we must advance from the conception of form and matter to the conception of ether. But how can we achieve such an advance? It is to be realized that since all form and matter pass from generation into extinction and from being into non-being, the existence of form and matter is at the same time their non-existence. And that which truly exists in the universe is only the existential process from existence to non-existence and from non-existence to existence. And this is just the cyclic movement of the ether. This conception of the cyclic movement of the ether comprehends in a synthesis the two contrasting conceptions of being and non-being and void and concretion. If we take the standpoint of the cyclic movement of the ether and observe the generation or being and extinction or non-being of things, we shall not consider generation or being as merely being or generation, but as being containing non-being and generation containing extinction; nor shall we consider extinction or non-being as merely extinction or non-being, but as non-being containing being or extinction containing generation. This is to say, the generation or coming-to-be of things is concretion and yet concretion containing with-in itself void, while extinction or non-being of things is void and yet void containing within itself the seeds of concretion. The passing from being to non-being is not really entering into non-being but entering into the realm of the invisible, and similarly the coming from non-being to being is but emerging from the realm of the invisible to that of the visible. To substitute the visible and the invisible for being and non-being is to achieve a synthesis of being and non-being as well as one of void and concretion. It is from such a cosmological point of view that Chang defined his Great Harmony as "the constant unity of being and non-being."

He said:

If one should assume that the ether is created out of the void, then one would be beset by the difficulty of the discrepancy between reality and its activity,[17] as void is infinite while the ether is finite.

Those who uphold the idea of *nirvāṇa*[18] (i.e., extinction) proceed along a single-track path without any provision for return, while those who insist on the idea of generation and being are dazzled by the existence of things and overlook their transformations. Though these two schools are widely apart, both fail equally as far as following the right way is concerned.

The void and the ether are identical.

The Supreme Void without form is the substance of the ether.

Chang Tsai further upheld the knowledge of the cause of the visible and invisible in place of the knowledge of the cause of being and non-being. He said:

When it (the ether) condenses one cannot but call it being. But when it disperses, one must not call it non-being. Therefore, when the sages had carefully observed Heaven and earth, they only said they knew the cause of the visible and invisible and did not say they knew the cause of being and non-being.

When form is there we know the cause of the invisible; when form is not there we know the origin of the visible.

The above quotations are from the chapter on "The Great Harmony."

The cause of the visible and invisible is also the reason things appear and disappear, disappear and appear. And this reason rests in the fact that the ether is void while it is concrete and concrete while it is void, i.e., the ether is not just concrete but contains also the void in its very nature.

The second aspect of the explanation that Chang Tsai offers for his theory of the inseparability of the ether and the void may be called the horizontal aspect. Everything is generated through intercourse between other things, and this thing is, in turn, in intercourse with other things to generate still other things. Hence, the ether is both many and one, both diffused and united. The ether, therefore, is not just a concrete thing, but has in it the limpid and void nature. This view goes back directly to "The Commentary

[17] Reality and its activity 體 用 *(t'i-yung)*.
[18] *Nirvāṇa* (or extinction) 寂 滅 *(chi-nieh)*.

on the *Book of Changes*," in which all explanations about the generation
of things are given in terms of the intercourse between other things. The
generation of things through the intercourse of other things is like the birth
of the child through the intercourse between its parents. But the intercourse
of things is also the mutual prehension[19] of things. And from the fact that
one thing can prehend another we can see that the thing must have the
void within itself in order to be able to absorb the other. And this void
must be within the thing or within the ether out of which the thing is
generated, but never outside. Here, if we accept the ordinary view about
form and matter, every form would be a concrete thing, and what is beyond would be all void, void and form thus becoming mutually exclusive,
as Newtonian physics teaches, namely, matter exists in an infinite vacuum.
This view is just what Chang firmly rejects. Thus he says: "If one should
hold that phenomena were the things visible in the Supreme Void, things
and the void would be independent of each other. Then, form would be
just form, and nature would be just nature, and form, nature, Heaven, and
man would all be separate existences unrelated to one another, and one
would fall into the difficulty of the Buddhists, who consider the mountains,
rivers, and the earth itself as illusory." Therefore, the void of a thing must
be understood as lying within the thing and, in fact, lying within its generating ether, which contains the void in itself. And the void of the ether
of a thing may be perceived in the process of the generation and transformation brought about through the constant intercourse of the thing with
other things. When a thing enters into intercourse with other things, it
transcends its own corporeal existence and extends itself into what is beyond
itself. This is just what we have said about the function of the ether. The
function of the ether of a thing is to enable the thing to transcend its own
corporeal existence and prehend in the other thing so as to have intercourse
with it. It is the ether of man, for example, that makes him transcend his
own corporeal existence and extend itself so as to reach the corporeal existence of the woman and prehend her in his spirit in order to have intercourse
with her. The function of ether, therefore, is the function that enables the
ether with its inner void to prehend within itself concrete existence. We
must, then, deeply realize this theme of ours: Whenever a thing is in intercourse with another, it is always that the thing by means of its void contains
the other and prehends it. Opinions similar to this have been held by
Western contemporary philosophers, such as Bradley and Whitehead. Bradley compares the wolf's devouring of a lamb to man's relation of prehension

---

[19] Prehension 涵攝 *(han-sheh)*.

with other things, which he calls "feeling." Whitehead extended this view to cover all the existential relations among things and called them "prehension." In his book *Process and Reality,* he declares that this view of his is not in accord with the traditional thought of the West, but comes close to Chinese philosophy. He is indeed right. Chinese traditional thought about nature, from the *Book of Changes* down, has consistently maintained that the mutual relation and influence among things is a relation of intercourse and prehension. But Chang Tsai was the first to point out clearly and definitely that what makes the intercourse and prehension between things possible is the intrinsic void of the ether, and that it is this void nature of the ether that is the basis of the intercourse and prehension among things. There is constant generation and concretion of things in the universe because the ether of all things in the universe is fundamentally void. Hence, Chang said: "The *Tao* of Heaven and earth consists in nothing other than taking the completely void as the concrete." Again, "The virtue of Heaven and earth is but the void." It is by the void, according to him, that things can diffuse their ether and extend themselves to other objects, and thus the "one" becomes manifest in the "many." And this activity of extension by virtue of the void is called by Chang spirit (*shên*[5]), and by *"shên"* here he means "to extend." [The word *"shên"* in Chinese has a double meaning. The one is "to extend" and the other is "spirit."—Tr. note.] By the intercourse and prehension among things through this void-extension, there is transformation of these things and generation of new things, which activity Chang Tsai calls transformation (*hua*[6]). "Extension" causes the intercourse and union of two things or diffused ether. "Transformation" causes the dissolution of two things or diffused ether in the generation of a new thing. *Shên* becomes manifest where the process runs from contraction to extension, from quietude to motion, from submergence to emergence, and from defeat to victory. And *hua* becomes manifest where the process runs in the reverse direction. Extension and transformation, transformation and extension, and all things in the universe are generated without end.

Therefore, Chang Tsai said:

(1) The Great Harmony that is the *Tao* contains in it the principle of interaction between emerging and submerging, ascending and descending, and motion and quietude, which sets going the process of stress and strain, victory and defeat, and contraction and extension. . . . As it is diffused and spread it becomes visible ether; as it illumines and penetrates it becomes invisible spirituality. Unless one knows the ceaseless and modulating activity of the sunbeams, one is not in a position to know the Great Harmony.

(2) A thing cannot exist in isolation. Unless it was made manifest through the processes of identification and differentiation, extension and contraction, and beginning and ending, a thing would not be a thing. An activity is produced when it has its beginning and end, but there is activity only when there is interaction in the nature of identification and differentiation and mutual supplementation between things. Unless there is activity, a thing would not be a thing.

(3) Where there is unity, there is spirituality; where there is duality, there is transformation.

If there is duality, there will be interaction; since originally it is all one, there will be unity.

Spirituality, or *shên*, is the virtue of Heaven; transformation, or *hua*, is the way of Heaven. Its virtue is its substance; its way is its function. And both become one in the ether.

All the phenomena and appearances in the universe are but so many dregs of the process of spirituality-transformation.

The conclusion from the above quotations is this: Things are brought into being through the extension and contraction of the ether that has become diffused due to its void nature.

Each so-called thing is but a process of beginning and ending, extension and contraction. It is generated through the intercourse of preceding things, and therefore, unless there is transformation of preceding things, a thing will not be brought into existence. Now that this thing is here, it is in turn in intercourse with other things and engaged in activity. And were it not for the spirituality, i.e., extension, character in the thing, it could not have produced any activity. Since the generation of a thing depends on the transformation of preceding things, there must be a difference between the thing generated and the preceding things. On the other hand, since this thing is a successor and continuation of the preceding things, there must also be a degree of unity between them. The fact that this thing and other things are in intercourse producing activity indicates that there is a difference between them, and, yet, at the point of their intercourse there must also be a unity between them. The difference between one thing and another means that it has what the other lacks and vice versa. Since everything has certain qualities and lacks others, things come into intercourse. And it is by this intercourse that things have their activities. Therefore, a thing could not have any activity if there were no "interaction" in the nature of identification, differentiation, and mutual supplementation," and a thing without activity would not be a thing. All the above is meant to make it clear that the activity-thing (event) finds its place only in the process of the invisible transformation of the Great Harmony that consists of the undifferentiated cosmic void-ether and that is by no means an immutable matter. Neither is the ether itself then an immutable matter. For this reason Chang Tsai said that "unless one knows the ceaseless and shuffling activity of the sun-beams, one is not in a position to know the Great Harmony." This is a very apt description of the interacting prehension of the ether, due to its void nature.

It is to be noticed that this cosmological view of Chang Tsai is drastically different from that of Western materialism and naturalism for still another reason. The latter contend that the universe itself is amoral, or, in Bertrand Russell's words, ethically neutral. Chinese traditional thought, from "The Commentary on the *Book of Changes*" down to the Confucianists of the Han, and even the Sung and Ming, to the contrary, is convinced that the universe is filled with moral values, sometimes expressed in terms of originating growth,[20] prosperous development,[21] advantages,[22] and correct firmness,[23] and sometimes in terms of human-heartedness, righteousness, decorum, and wisdom. Here again, Chinese thought is very similar to Whitehead's view that the existential process of the universe is a process for the realization of values, for the cosmological view handed down from "The Commentary on the *Book of Changes*" holds that the whole existential process in the universe is a process of generation and evolution through intercourse. And the generation and evolution of a thing are themselves activities of positive values, and exhibit a moral character. Hence, this natural universe is still a universe filled with moral values, no matter whether the human mind has achieved self-consciousness or not and whether the human spirit has any part in it or not. According to Chang, the void nature of the ether is the basis for the objective existence of values, since he insists that all intercourse is made possible by the void nature of the ether. That is why he said, "Heaven and earth take the void for their virtue, for the supremely good is the void." The whole process of the generation and evolution of things engendered by intercourse of the ether due to its void-concretion nature is the process of ether-transformation, and may also be said to be spiritual[5] transformation.[6] It follows from the above that the sum-total of the world of objective existence is also the sum-total of the world of value-laden existence. This value might also be referred to as righteousness from the angle of the constant differentiation and comple-

---

[20] Originating growth 元 *(yüan)*.

[21] Prosperous development 亨 *(hêng)*.

[22] Advantage 利 *(li)*.

[23] Correct firmness 貞 *(chên)*.

tion of things, for righteousness means the attainment of completion by one and all. This value might be referred to as human-heartedness from the angle of the constant generation and intercourse of things, for human-heartedness means the sharing of the same feeling by me and others. The differentiated completion of things is an indication of the multiple extension of the ether, whereas the intercourse and formal or material dissolution of things for the generation of new things is an indication of the dissolution of the ether or of the multiple transformation of the ether. Chang Tsai said: "When human-heartedness permeates itself in all transformations, it transcends all individual corporeality; when righteousness submerges itself in spirituality, i.e., extension, it transcends all restrictions." Inasmuch as the cosmos possesses the way and virtue of Heaven, e.g., extension (spirituality) and transformation, human-heartedness, and righteousness, it follows that man should examine spirituality and know transformation and serve Heaven and earth, and venerate them as we do our parents so as to be in harmony with heavenly virtue and thereby achieve sagehood.

V. The Meaning of the Nature of the Mind

The reason that a mere man with his body no taller than six feet is in a position to serve Heaven and earth and be in harmony with heavenly virtues does not lie in the human mind as such, but in the nature that makes it possible for the mind to have consciousness. This nature of man is bestowed on man by the objective universe, or Heaven, and this nature is intrinsically in our body. Our share of the ether from the objective universe is indeed very little, considered merely from our six-foot body. And if the ether that Chang talks about were just matter, then the attitude between me and the world external to me could be only one of opposition or utilization so that each might maintain its own material body, since the matter endowed upon me is not the matter endowed upon others. And consequently it would be very difficult to speak of intuitive knowledge about the external world and moral values, as well as veneration toward the cosmos or harmony with heavenly virtue, thereby achieving sagehood. But the ether, according to Chang, is not matter, but possesses the void nature by which it can have intercourse and prehension with other things. Therefore, although a man's share of the cosmic ether is very little, the void nature of this ether enables him to transcend the material limit set by that same ether. The cosmic ether that man has received has been endowed by Heaven, and so Chang said, "The Decree lies within the ether." At the same time, the nature of man transcends the material limit of the body as formed by the ether, and so Chang said, "The nature penetrates beyond the ether." But Chang Tsai also said, "Actually, the ether itself has neither interior nor exterior, and we are using a figure of speech when we speak of the 'within' and the 'beyond.'" Since the nature of the ether in man can transcend the limit of the body, by this nature man can reach to infinite extension within which to direct his consciousness and emotions toward other objects. Take this for example: Here below is my bodily existence, and there above are the sun and the moon and the stars in the sky. Considered spacially, of course, they are in different spaces and separate existences. But we can become conscious of these heavenly bodies. Why? We may say that this is caused by the radiation energy of these bodies that is infused into our sense perception, but we may also say it is caused by the power of our perception and consciousness that reaches out to the heavenly bodies. But how can our perceiving power reach those bodies in the heavens? If we answer and say that our perceiving power originates in our sense organs, then we must admit, on the one hand, that our perceiving power can transcend the space that our body occupies, and, on the other hand, that this perceiving power is generated through the expenditure of the form-matter of our body or through the self-dissolution of our material body. In short, this power of sense perception is a kind of ether. And it is this ether of ours that reaches out into the heavenly bodies, when our power of sense perception reaches them. It is improper to say, therefore, that our bodily ether—the ether that is produced by the self-transcendence and self-dissolution of the material body—exists in isolation from the external world, although our body and the celestial bodies are in different spaces and separate existences. The fact that the form-matter of our body can transmute and dissolve itself so as to send forth the ether of the power of sense perception is proof that the form-matter of our body is in the first place nothing but the ether. The ether is related to external things, is not in isolation, and in it the internal and external are unified. The fact that we meet things and perceive them everywhere and that perception is not restricted to any specific object or space is direct proof that the ether that is in us is in complete communication with the ether of the universe and all things. And, finally, the fact that we come into contact with things and perceive them, and also act toward them from the attitudes and emotions excited in us, is proof of the infusion of our ether into the ether of objects.

Having understood the truth that when we perceive an object or when we act toward it our ether is in communication with the universe and all things, we can affirm that this doctrine of Chang Tsai and typical materialistic views are fundamentally opposed to each other—the views of material-ism that observe the form-matter existence of our body and the other things and conclude: "I am nothing more than myself, and things themselves in the universe are outside myself, and, therefore, I am absolutely unable to know them immediately, and all that I can do is to react to the stimuli received from them; or, I am but myself, and my nature is just to conserve and maintain the matter of this body of mine"—such materialistic views overlook the fact that I and my body as such are fundamentally derived from the ether. The form-matter of my body is not a constant thing but is always in a process of transformation and intercourse with other things. The proc-ess of transformation means the process of transmutation of the thing, and intercourse with other things means penetration into them. Hence, the na-ture by which I am constituted to be I is actually my power of transcending myself and taking unto myself things and persons that used to be other than I. And the form-matter that has become the form-matter of my body is also that which is constantly being formed by the condensation of cosmic ether and constantly being dissolved and diffused back into the cosmic ether. Therefore, I can never hold that there is an I or my body existing separately from other things in the universe; neither can I say that my nature is merely to conserve and maintain my material body. On the contrary, I should say that my nature is to enter into intercourse with all things in the universe, and by the void nature of the mind it is to perceive all, prehend all, regard-ing other persons and things as myself, and it is universally to bestow our emotions and wills to all things with which we have intercourse. For this reason, when Chang Tsai discusses nature, he discusses nature together with feeling and spirituality (extension). He said:

"Feeling is the spirituality of nature, and nature is the concretion of feeling."

"When it makes things marvelous it is called spirituality, when it gives things their concretion it is called nature."

"Nothing is excluded from concretion, and concretion is called the nature of things."

The reason nature can give all things their concretion is not that there is such a thing as nature besides the ether, but that the void of the ether gives concretion to all things and excludes none. This void of the ether is the basis for man's having intercourse with all things, for his extending his ether into them, and expressing to them his inclinations.

Therefore, Chang Tsai said:

At the extreme the nature merges with the void.

That which cannot be entirely without feeling is nature.

When we have understood that the nature according to Chang Tsai is to be regarded as the ether in us transcending our material body and having intercourse with all things in the universe because of its void nature, then we see why he said that human nature is good and that the nature has in itself the qualities of humanheartedness and righteousness, for all the virtues of human-heartedness and righteousness come out of the denial, abnegation, and transcendence of oneself. That human nature at the extreme can "merge with the void" means self-oblivion. And humanheartedness and righteousness are but self-oblivion and communication with others, regarding others as oneself and giving completion to others together with oneself. Thus the goodness of human nature is justified and established, and our moral conduct becomes metaphysically and cosmologically based. And we should henceforth magnify and extend our mind so that we might feel "All men are my brothers and all things are my kin," and that we might wish "Establishment is to establish all, wisdom is to render everyone wise, love is to love universally, and completion is not just to make oneself complete.

Such would be the fullest realization of one's mind and thereby of one's nature, and even the decree of Heaven. And such a man is in a position to be the human-hearted son of society and the filial son of Heaven and earth, and thereby to have come into harmony with heavenly virtue and achieve sagehood.

VI. THE NATURE OF THE UNIVERSE AND THE NATURE OF THE ETHER-MATTER[24]

The most difficult part in Chang Tsai's theory of mind and nature comes in his distinction between the nature of the universe and the nature of the ether-matter. The former is said to be completely good, while the latter sometimes inclines man to evil. Therefore, if one wants to be in harmony with heavenly virtue and strive to be a sage, the most important part of his cultivation lies in transforming the ether-matter in him. The transformation of the ether-matter is to make manifest the nature of the universe that is in him. This is apparently a dualistic theory of human nature. But Chang Tsai's metaphysical view seems to be, as explained above, a monism of the Great Harmony of the undifferentiated void-ether. Since the way of Heaven is completely good, how is it that man should also possess a nature of ether-matter that inclines him toward evil? There is evidently a contradiction here, but how real is it? This we feel called upon to explain.

In speaking of the nature of the universe and the nature of the ether-matter, Chang Tsai does not place the two natures in opposition to each

---

[24] Ether-matter 氣質 (ch'i-chih).

other on the same level of existence. Fundamentally, the nature of man is just the nature of the universe. And this nature is in direct communication with the ether or the way of the universe. The nature of the ether-matter is generated when the nature of the universe is concealed by ether-matter, and is therefore the nature that appears after the ether of the universe has by condensation become the material body of man. The emphasis in the nature of the "ether-matter" is laid on the part of "matter" and not on the part of "ether." Hence, Chang Tsai said, "Upon the formation of the body, there appears the nature of the ether-matter." This is to say, from the standpoint of the original ether from which man derives his form, man has no such thing as a nature of the so-called ether-matter. The nature of the universe is based on an objective cosmos. The nature of the ether-matter of individual man or other individual things, however, can be stated only in terms of the individual form-matter that has been produced, for this nature is groundless in terms of the Great Harmony of the undifferentiated void-ether, of the objective universe. In those same terms, the evil that comes out of the ether-matter in man is also groundless. But how does man happen to have a nature of the ether-matter to incline him to evil upon his generation, since man is generated from the Great Harmony of the undifferentiated void-ether? This is because the ether which is in itself formless can undergo condensation and appear in various forms. And, when it appears as form-matter, the ether may be said to be particularized or individualized. It is because of this particularization or individualization that material bodies (including men and things) are set opposite to one another, and by this opposition they become obstructions to one another. All evils of man are the result of his selfishness and self-insistence that in turn are due to opposition and obstruction. Having acquired his body of form-matter, man has also acquired the inclination to be in mutual opposition and obstruction to other men and things, and out of such an inclination come all his selfish passions. This inclination is the nature that arises in man after he has acquired his body, and this is the nature of the ether-matter in man, the nature that is the origin of all evil in man. This so-called nature, therefore, of the ether-matter is the secondary nature that prevails when the ether has become form-matter and has lost its limpid and spiritual void. Therefore, Chang Tsai said:

> The ether originates from the void and, therefore, it is at first clear and formless. When it becomes agitated for generation, it undergoes the process of condensation and becomes visible. Becoming visible means being placed in opposition (against other visible things); being placed in opposition means acting contrarily to one another; and contrariety results in enmity. But enmity will have to resolve itself

in harmony. Therefore, both love and hate originate from the Supreme Void and will ultimately result in desires and passions.

The theory that contends that the human nature received from the universe is good but that when man's ether becomes form-matter there appears the ether-matter that inclines man to be bad does not envisage in man simultaneously two equal natures, but, rather, considers them as in a sequence. From the standpoint of the beginning, man has only the nature of the universe; and from the standpoint of the end man has come to have the nature of the ether-matter. But how can it be that a good beginning should have a bad end? Since the view from the end demonstrates clearly that man has a nature of the ether-matter to incline him to evil, that on the basis of his body man stands in mutual opposition and obstruction with other men and things, and that man generates feelings of love and hate all on the basis of selfishness, why not let us judge the beginning by the end and say that human nature is originally bad and that even the Great Harmony of the undifferentiated void-ether, of the objective universe contains in it an element of evil? But, according to the Confucian tradition of Chinese thought on the problem of good and evil in man and the universe, one may proceed from the good of the beginning to the evil of the end but may not proceed from the evil of the end to infer the evil content of the beginning or to attribute the evil of the end to the beginning. For example, if we call nature the beginning and passion the end, then we cannot attribute the evil of passion to nature. Similarly, if we call the universe and the way of Heaven the beginning and man and man's nature the end, then we cannot attribute the evil in man and man's nature to Heaven and what Heaven has endowed in man. There is a parallel in the West. According to Christianity, God is the creator of man, and yet the sin of man cannot be attributed to God himself or God's creation, for the evil of man can be regarded only as a part of man. This is exactly Chang's view. As for the reason why the evil, caused by the nature of the ether-matter in man, cannot be attributed to Heaven, this is because it is simply impossible for evil to exist from the standpoint of Heaven, for from this standpoint there is no form-matter existence in this universe (including man) that will not eventually be dissolved and return to the Supreme Void or the Great Harmony. For this reason the mutual opposition and obstruction among things are only temporary. The nature of the ether-matter in man can be said to exist only when man's form-matter exists. There is the nature of the ether-matter in man, not in Heaven. Hence, there is evil in man, not in Heaven. Heaven not only does not have the nature of the ether-matter, but has the nature that makes all things that have evolved from the ether into form-matter be eventually dissolved and return to the Supreme Void and the Great Harmony. Heaven not only does not have any evil, but has the nature that deprives man of his form-matter to which evil adheres. Hence, in the universe as a whole or in the Great Harmony of the undifferentiated ether-void evil has no roots. Whatever is generated from the universe is generated through the intercourse of prior things by virtue of the void. That is, this generation results from the process of self-transcendence and ether-transformation of things from their form-matter existence. It may also be said that things are generated through the spiritual way and the virtue of the goodness of Heaven. Therefore, the nature by which things are generated can be said to be good only because this very nature is also the decree that Heaven gives for its coming into existence. And the evil can be admitted only with respect to the state of things after they have acquired their form-matter existence, but never attributed to the objective universe from which they have derived their existence.

To sum up, the nature of man in its origin is the nature of the universe, which is completely good, for the universe or the origin of the objective universe, the Great Harmony of the undifferentiated void-ether, is supremely good without evil. It is for this reason that man's heart cannot be truly at rest in remaining selfish, self-assuming, and mean even though the nature of the ether-matter in man inclines him to be such. And when man cannot be truly satisfied in being always motivated from his bodily considerations, he must transcend the holding-ons and the passions of his form-matter existence and make manifest the nature of the universe that is in him with its capacity for being void, in order to extend his mind and fully develop his mind and to help others as well as himself to be perfect and thereby to become a sage. The reason man is not to be selfish and self-insisting but should be motivated by human-heartedness and righteousness and become a sage is also that the nature of the ether-matter in man is not his true nature. One cannot realize his true self if he confines himself within the shell of his material body. The one way out is, therefore, to extend his mind fully, to nurture the human-heartedness and righteousness in his nature completely, and to employ his material body for the assistance of others as well as himself, in order to find the heavenly way that is capable of "gladdening all hearts" and "facilitating all wishes," so that one's true nature may be realized. And this way of realizing oneself is, according to Chang Tsai, to pursue the way to the extreme and to extend the nature to the full, and then the nature will be in harmony with the virtue of Heaven. Thus, the ether-matter that is received by the decree of Heaven will be changed in conformity with the way. In Chang's own language, this is "To establish the decree," i.e., to make human destiny conform to heavenly decree. Referring to Heaven, Chang Tsai says, "Spirituality is Heaven's virtue, and transformation Heaven's way"; while referring to man, he says, "Nature is Heaven's virtue, and decree Heaven's rule." (Heaven's way differs from Heaven's rule in that the former is used mostly in connection with the universe, the latter with man. On this point, Chang Tsai is quite different from the Ch'êng-and-Chu school.) When the nature of man and the decree of Heaven are in tune, man can truly be said to be the filial son of Heaven and earth, and to have arrived at a state in which Heaven and man are unified and man becomes a sage. When one reaches the state of the sage, the nature of ether-matter is identified with the nature of the universe. Therefore, Chang said, "The nature of the ether-matter is sometimes rejected by the superior man." Hence, the nature of the ether-matter that can incline a man to evil is not rooted in the origin of the universe, nor can it adhere to the life of the sage and the superior man. It has but a temporary existence during the period after a man's birth and before his mind is fully extended and the nature of the universe in him has come to its realization.

VII. Conclusion

Chang Tsai's theory on the nature of the mind as discussed in this paper may be summed up under five points as follows:

(1) The human mind as a knower is void and intuitive and is not a collection of ideas and impressions, and, therefore, one should not discuss the mind in terms of impressions and ideas.

(2) The reason the human mind can be void and intuitive is that it has its origin in an objective universe, i.e., in the Great Harmony, in which the ether and the void are undifferentiated and being and non-being are one, or in the way of Heaven that is both void and concrete and by which the process of ether-transformation is in operation.

(3) The process of ether-transformation or the process of the extension and reversion of the objective universe embodies in itself the heavenly way or heavenly virtue that are similar to the moral nature or the virtues of human-heartedness and righteousness among men. Therefore, man should strive to extend his mind fully so as to come into harmony with the heavenly way and heavenly virtue.

(4) The reason man can come into harmony with the heavenly way and heavenly virtue is that by the void of the ether (this is actually human

nature) he can prehend all things in the universe, though his share of the ether of the universe is very little. Therefore, human nature contains the qualities of human-heartedness and righteousness, and human nature is good.

(5) Man has the nature of the ether-matter, but it is not on the same level as the nature of the universe. The nature of the ether-matter has no basis either in the origin of the universe or in the personality of a sage, and, therefore, is not truly the nature of man. The man who wishes to realize his true nature, however, must apply himself to the discipline by which the ether-matter is transformed and made more limpid and better able to enter into intercourse with other things—whereof Chang Tsai has set down a whole system of cultivation of moral virtues. But this paper cannot concern itself with that.

8

The Development of the Concept of Moral Mind from Wang Yang-ming to Wang Chi

CHU HSI'S SYSTEM OF MORAL MIND AS ONE SOURCE OF WANG YANG-MING'S TEACHING

日月 In this essay, I shall discuss some important features of Wang Yang-ming's idea of moral mind, and how Wang-chi's ideas of moral mind were developed from the problems concerning moral cultivation which Wang Yang-ming left unresolved. However, I have to begin by tracing the problem of moral mind in Neo-Confucianism back to Chu Hsi and Lu Hsiang-shan and I shall try to explain, in a more definite way, what Yang-ming's idea of moral mind is, and how it synthesized and went beyond the thought of Chu and Lu.

Generally speaking, all the ideas of Neo-Confucianists about mind are closely related to the moral aspects of mind or moral cultivation; so we may consider all their ideas of mind as ideas of moral mind.

In the Sung dynasty, the ideas of moral mind of all the previous Neo-Confucianists converged and culminated in Chu Hsi's thought. In his thought, the mind is analyzed and explicated from three points of view. From the first point of view, which may be called a psychological point of view, the mind is taken as the spirituality of *ch'i*,ᵃ or the transparency and sensitiveness of *ch'i*. As *ch'i* animates our bodily life, the mind governs our whole life as its master. The mind which receives the impressions from its perceptions of external things and bodily life is affected thereby and responds to them with its different faculties, such as feelings, emotions, will, volitional ideas, and deliberations. All of them show the abilities of mind to form the actions and knowledge of man. From this point of view, the different faculties of the mind are known through its functional relation to the principles of Heaven, our body, and other things (including other people and natural things) as external objects in the so-called objective world.

From the second point of view, which may be called an ontological or metaphysical point of view, the mind contains the principles of Heaven (or *t'ien li* [b]), which are universal principles, as its inner nature. Thus the nature of mind has a cosmic significance, because the universal principles of Heaven prevailing in all things are permanent, immutable, and divine. In this sense, the nature of mind has its absolute dignity which transcends all things in the natural world. However, the principles of Heaven as mind's nature are not necessarily self-consciously known or realized and then expressed. That aspect of mind which contains the principles of Heaven, yet unexpressed, is described as *wei fa*, [c] which means that part of mind which is "still not" or "not yet" expressed. The unexpressed part of mind was considered by Chu Hsi to be static or quiet. In contrast, the other part of mind, described as the "expressed" part, denotes that in which its nature is expressed when it is affected by and responds to things of the ordinary empirical world, through its feelings, wills, desires, deliberations, volitional ideas, and so on, as mentioned above. This part of mind, as it is actually responsive to the things of the world through its faculties or functions, is described as active and affective. The technical term for it in Chinese is the *i-fa* [d] part or aspect of mind. As the unexpressed part of mind is found in inner intentions, feelings, etc., it is known only by oneself in solitude. When it is expressed in outer action, it may be known by other beings also. The inner part of mind is its transcendental or metaphysical part, because it is closely related to the principles of Heaven, or *li*, [e] and the outer part of mind is its empirical or physical aspect, because it is closely related to the *ch'i*. I shall not further discuss their relations to *li* and *ch'i* here.

From the third point of view, which may be called the axiological or purely moral point of view, the mind may be classified into two or three kinds, according to its level in the realization of moral values. The first kind of mind is called the mind of Tao. [f] Tao means the principles of Heaven or the nature of mind as actually expressed and realized in the mind's faculties or functions as feelings, will, and so on. This is a mind which is purely good. If a man has his mind of Tao fully realized to its utmost, he is a sage (*sheng*),[g] and if a man has his mind of Tao gradually transforming his other kinds of mind, he is a man of worth (*hsien*).[h] The second kind of mind is called the human mind (*jen-hsin*).[i] It means a kind of mind which just keeps its natural spirituality, natural transparency, and natural sensitiveness with its natural desires and instincts. Such a mind is cognitive, and responsive to ordinary things in a natural way. It is by itself neutral in moral value. However, when the natural desires or instincts of man conform to or are governed by and become the self-conscious embodiment of the principles of Heaven as our nature, then this mind is morally good. On the other hand, if these natural desires go uncurbed and depart from the principles of Heaven as our nature, then such desires become selfish or sensual desires. The human mind which is stained by such desires is a selfish mind too. Then it is evil. In Chu Hsi's thought, the human mind by itself stands in the middle. It may ascend to the level of expressing the principles of Heaven as its nature and transform itself into the mind of Tao which is morally good. It may also descend to the level of selfish desires, and degenerate into the mind of an animal or a mind even worse than that of an animal.

From each of the above three points of view, Chu Hsi discussed mind in an analytical way, and the mind as a whole was differentiated into many different faculties or functions, inner and outer parts, and kinds and levels of existence that differed according to their moral value.

As Chu Hsi made many distinctions in regard to one's mind, he also made many distinctions in regard to the ways of moral cultivation or the moral task of man. In Chu Hsi's thought about the ways of moral cultivation, if one intends to transform his mind which is full of selfish desires, and then to elevate his human mind into the mind of Tao, he must have different ways of moral cultivation corresponding to the inner mind—the unexpressed part—and the outer mind—the expressed part.

Corresponding to the unexpressed part, one should have a way of moral cultivation which is designated by the technical term *han-*

yang [j] or *ts'un-yang*.[k] It roughly means the self-nourishment and self-preservation of mind in its static and quiet state. In this state of mind, though static and quiet, there is an inner activity which is self-circled, or self-conscious in its self-nourishment or self-preservation. So Chu Hsi called this way of moral cultivation the mind in its static function. In this way of moral cultivation, the mind in its static function is a pure consciousness which can reveal the principles of Heaven as its nature, as if it shed light on its nature and let its nature be revealed or made conscious of itself. This way of moral cultivation is the fundamental way of moral cultivation Chu Hsi expounded.

However, the mind should also have other ways of moral cultivation, corresponding to the expressed part of mind. On its expressed side, the mind, as perceiving and knowing the world and things, should have a way of moral cultivation which is called the investigation of things for the attainment of right knowledge about things. In the investigation of things, we have to know or to search for the principles of what things are to be and what actions should be done.

Corresponding to our selfish desires, and all our volitional ideas, deliberations, feelings, emotions, and wills, which are selfish and evil, we should have a way of moral cultivation which Chu Hsi calls *ko-chih*,[1] that is self-conquest or self-governing.

Corresponding to the feelings, ideas, wills, and so on, which appear to be neutral in their moral value, we should have a way of moral cultivation which Chu Hsi calls *sheng-ch'a*,[m] meaning self-observation, self-reflection, or self-examination. Through this way of moral cultivation we learn that what appears to be neutral in moral value, when self-observed or self-reflected, is actually either good or evil. When it is found to be evil, we have to conquer it; and when it is found to be good, we have to preserve and strengthen it in order to make all our feelings, will, and ideas perfectly good. In short, this is a way of moral cultivation which makes our will pure, sincere, or authentic.

Corresponding to the initial expression of our mind in our feelings, will, ideas, and so on, we should have a way of moral cultivation which Chu Hsi calls the way of *shen-tu*,[n] which means self-prudence or self-care of mind in its solitude and in the inception of activity from its unexpressed state to its expression. The self-prudence or self-care, when it is serious, is like self-fear, or self-dread, or the self trembling on a cliff. Here our mind may either ascend to the principles of Heaven, being conscious of them as our nature and thus expressing them in all good actions, or descend into the pit of selfish desires and commit the worst deeds.

On the basis of the foregoing, Chu Hsi's thought about moral mind and moral cultivation can be taken as the most comprehensive system, encompassing the whole field of morality, in the Neo-Confucianism of the Sung dynasty. Chu Hsi also interpreted the teachings on moral cultivation of *The Great Learning* in this way. He interpreted the investigation of things and the attainment of knowledge in *The Great Learning* as searching for the principles of things for the purpose of attaining knowledge. He interpreted the making of the moral will authentic as the result of *ko chih* and *sheng-ch'a*. He interpreted the rectification of mind (*cheng-hsin* °) as corresponding to his way of moral cultivation in the *han-yang*. Chu Hsi also interpreted the *shen-tu*, (the "self-carefulness in solitude") of *The Great Learning* through the thought of *The Mean*, placing it in a position between *han-yang* and *sheng-ch'a*, or between the *cheng-shin* and *ch'eng-yi* ᵖ of *The Great Learning*.

LU HSIANG-SHAN'S CONCEPT OF ORIGINAL MIND AS A BASIS FOR WANG YANG-MING'S "REALIZATION OF *LIANG-CHIH*"

In comparison with Chu Hsi's complicated system of morality, Lu Hsiang-shan's thought, although very simple and straightforward, is more penetrating and essential.

As to the first point of view from which Chu Hsi analyzed the mind's functions, Lu Hsiang-shan took no interest in it. In one dialogue of Lu Hsiang-shan, when Li Pa-ming, one of his disciples, asked about the distinction between mind, nature, feeling, and ability, Lu Hsiang-shan reproached him severely. He said that his disciple merely asked trivial questions and had never plunged into the sources and roots of learning. He also said that Li only wanted to define and to explain the terms etymologically, which is unnecessary for becoming a sage.[1]

As to the second point of view of Chu Hsi, which divided the mind into two parts, an inner-unexpressed and outer-expressed, Lu Hsiang-shan mentioned no distinction between the inner part and the outer part of mind. He said that the universe is our mind and our mind is the universe, and that all the things of the universe are rightly things in the domain of one's own sense of responsibility, and things in the domain of one's own sense of responsibility are rightly things of the universe also. The mind which is undifferentiated from the universe is a metaphysical mind or a cosmic mind, but it exists as a whole in one's individual and empirical self as well. Thus any distinction between the "unexpressed" and the "expressed" part of mind is of no importance. Lu Hsiang-shan's original mind contains not merely the principles of Heaven as its content, or substance, but also is existentially identical with the principles of Heaven. This is the reason why it is also a cosmic mind or metaphysical mind. As the mind is existentially identical with the principles of Heaven, which are also its nature, where there is any expression of the original mind there is the mind expressed simultaneously with the principles of Heaven as its nature. The original mind never just preserves its nature internally nor is it self-contained; it is always open and manifests its principles or nature without any reservation in its expressions.

In contrast to Chu Hsi's third point of view, which distinguished mind as of two or three kinds on different levels, Lu Hsiang-shan strenuously criticized the theory of mind which classified it as the mind of Tao and that of human selfish desires. He said that his theory originated in Taoistic thought and had been adopted into the chapter of the "Records on Music" in the *Record of Rites*. Chu Hsi in his dialogues and letters sometimes acknowledged Lu Hsiang-shan's criticism of this traditional theory. Nevertheless, Chu Hsi continued to follow this theory in the "Records on Music" and went further by making a distinction of the human mind into two kinds: one is the human mind by itself which is morally neutral; the other is the human mind stained by selfish desires which is evil, as has been explained above.

From Chu Hsi's conceptual analysis, there are not only two, but actually three kinds of mind. Hence his theory of mind is even more complicated than the theory of the "Records on Music." However, Lu Hsiang-shan insisted that there is only one original mind, which, as undifferentiated from the universe, is unlimited or infinite in its essence. But as an ordinary man may not know that he has such an original mind, so great, sublime, and lofty, the ordinary man's mind may be self-limited or narrowed down, and sunk in his private ideas or opinions, or in his egoistic sensual desires which only run after sense objects.

However, though the original mind may be sunk in these base things, it can still emancipate and liberate itself from this self-limitation. Thus it has a self-consciousness, self-illumination, or self-awakening. Therefore, from Lu Hsiang-shan's point of view, the original mind can either be unconscious of itself and descending, or self-conscious and self-awakened and ascending. Whether the mind is descending or ascending, it is the same one mind. The descending or ascending of the mind is determined by the mind itself. The mind has its self-determination and its self-mastering, and then has its self-establishment based on its moral self-cultivation; the foundation of moral cultivation is nothing other than the self-awakening of the original mind. In this sense, the original mind is absolutely free even in its descending actions because it can arise or reawaken again and nothing outside can be an obstacle or hindrance to the original mind, if it resolves to reawaken itself.

Lu Hsiang-shan, unlike Chu Hsi, who made distinctions in the mind from different points of view, has a simple and essential idea of the original mind which is existentially identical with the principles of Heaven. This original mind of Lu Hsian-shan is not merely a contemplative or knowing mind in the theoretical sense, it is also a practical and active mind. Therefore there is actually no distinction between his theory of moral mind and his theory of moral cultivation. The original mind of Lu Hsiang-shan has the power of self-awakening. It needs no other way of moral cultivation to assist its self-awakening. And we may say that any other way of moral cultivation, such as self-nourishment, self-preservation, self-care in solitude, self-examination, self-conquest, self-governing, and so on, which we find in Chu Hsi, are all only different modes or moments of man's self-awakening. Even the investigation of things and the search for the principles of things, which Chu Hsi emphasized, may be reinterpreted by Lu Hsiang-shan from his point of view. As all things are within the universe and the original mind is undifferentiated from the universe, the task of investigating things never goes outside the domain of the original mind's self-knowledge or self-consciousness and is just a task for its self-awakening.

The different ways of moral cultivation as taught by Chu Hsi were all united into one teaching of self-awakening of mind as taught by Lu Hsiang-shan. The original mind is what is greatest in the universe and man. "To establish first this greatest" is a teaching of Mencius and is often quoted by Lu Hsiang-shan. Some people criticized Lu Hsiang-shan's teaching as being too simple and said, "Besides the phrase 'to establish this greatest,' Lu Hsiang-shan has no other teaching." When Lu Hsiang-shan heard this criticism, he said, "It is quite true, quite true." We have to say "quite true" also.

WANG YANG-MING'S "REALIZATION OF LIANG-CHIH" AS A SYNTHESIS OF CHU HSI'S AND LU HSIANG-SHAN'S MORAL MIND AND MORAL CULTIVATION

As to Wang Yang-ming's thought, it is ordinarily understood that Wang is a follower of Lu Hsiang-shan, and we always talk about the "Lu-Wang school" in contrast to the "Ch'eng-Chu school." Actually, however, Wang Yang-ming also took over Chu Hsi's problems of moral cultivation. After his industrious study of such problems as the meaning of ko-wu,[q] which Chu Hsi interpreted as the investigation of things, and also the relation of han-yang or ts'un-yang (self-preservation or self-nourishment) and sheng-cha (self-reflection or self-examination) as taught by Chu Hsi, he had a self-enlightenment about the way of being a sage which is similar to Lu Hsiang-shan's teaching about the awakening of the original mind. Therefore, from a historical point of view, Wang Yang-ming's thought may be taken as a synthesis of Chu Hsi's and Lu Hsiang-shan's thoughts. This is why I have had to explain the ideas of moral mind of Chu Hsi and Lu Hsiang-shan in the first two sections of this essay.

The central idea of Wang Yang-ming's thought is *liang-chih*,[r] which is a word difficult to translate. *Liang* means, etymologically, "innate" or "original." *Chih* means knowledge or consciousness, or awareness, as a noun; and means to know, to be conscious, or to be aware, as a verb. As a noun, *chih* is a concept of substance or essence. As a verb, *chih* combined with *liang* to form one word, *liang-chih*, may mean the innate knowledge or original knowing, original consciousness, or original awareness. I prefer to translate the word *liang-chih* as the original knowing or original consciousness. Yet, as the word *liang* has also its derivative meaning of "good," and what is good is also moral; we may also translate the word *liang-chih* as original-good-consciousness or original-good-knowing. Furthermore, *liang-chih* as a good consciousness is always knowing and sensitive to the value of goodness, and its contrary, evil; thus it is even better to translate *liang-chih* as original-good-conscientious or original-good conscientious-knowing. But as the romanized term *liang-chih* is simpler to use, I shall adopt this in the following discussion.

In Wang Yang-ming's thought, *liang-chih* was taken as a substance or essence of mind, and his thought about the ontological and moral status of *liang-chih* in the universe was very similar to Lu Hsiang-shan's thought about the status of original mind in the universe; therefore the meanings of these two terms are also very close to each other. However, the word *mind* is usually used as a noun to denote a substance, and the word *chih* is usually used to denote also a function or activity of mind. When Wang Yang-ming said that *liang-chih* is the substance of mind[s 3] and that "the self-illumination and self-consciousness of the principles of Heaven is *liang-chih*,"[t 4] his intention seems to have been to replace Lu Hsiang-shan's idea of original mind by *liang-chih* as existentially identical with the principles of Heaven. As the word *mind* is just a name for substance, and the word *chih* is a name for function, when we say that *liang-chih* is a substance of mind, it implies that the function of the mind is identical with the substance of mind. Hence the most essential point of Wang Yang-ming's thought is to see the mind's substance functionally and then also to see the mind's function substantially; thus the substance and function of mind, or of *liang-chih*, can be taken as existentially identical in its being. This theory, like Chu Hsi's, uses the words of substance and function differently, and each has its logical meaning. Yet it differs from Chu Hsi's, as substance and function are thought to be existentially identical. This theory emphasizes the self-consciousness of *liang-chih* as the original substance of mind, as Lu Hsiang-shan emphasizes the self-awakening of the original mind as the substance of the so-called ordinary mind. But Lu Hsiang-shan never called his original mind *liang-chih* or original knowing, and never stated clearly that he saw the substance of mind through its function. Wang Yang-ming inherited Chu Hsi's distinction of substance and function in their logical meanings, but rejected Chu Hsi's distinction of substance and function in their existential. meanings. He also inherited Lu Hsiang-shan's idea of original mind, but supplemented Lu's thought with the idea of seeing the substance of original mind through its function as knowing, and called it *liang-chih*. It is certainly a theory which synthesized Chu's and Lu's ideas of mind, as well as distinguishing itself from both of them. Chu Hsi, speaking metaphorically, said that the principles of Heaven, as the content and nature of our mind, are self-radiating, illustrious, and bright. This compares the principles with the sun shining. Lu Hsiang-shan, who took the original mind as existentially identical with the principles of Heaven, usually compared mind as a whole with the sun which shines through the whole universe. This seems to mean that, as light radiated from the sun also shines back on itself, so the awakening of the mind as it originates from the original mind makes the original mind itself self-awakened. In Wang Yang-ming's dialogues, he too compared *liang-chih* to the sun.[5] The sun functions in its enlightening as *liang-chih* functions in its knowing. Yet, in Wang-ming's thought, it seems not merely that the light radiated from the sun is shining back to the sun, but that the sun, when radiating the light, is itself immanent in its own light. If this is so, then in using the metaphor of sun and light, he means that while there is light, there is a sun; so where there is *liang-chih's* knowing as its function, there is also *liang-chih's* substance in its knowing. As the sun, immanent in its light, pervades the whole universe, the substance of *liang-chih's* substance, as immanent in its function of knowing the whole universe, pervades the universe also.

As the distinctions among the three theories of Wang Yang-ming's *liang-chih*, Lu Hsiang-shan's original mind, and Chu Hsi's mind as containing the principles of Heaven may not be easily understood by everyone, it may be better to think of their ideas through the metaphor of sun and light.

Because Wang Yang-ming's thought that the substance and function of *liang-chih* are mutually seen through each other and existentially identical, in *liang-chih*, when it is unexpressed, there is an expression of the transcendental, because it is always knowing; and when it is expressed, there is the unexpressed immanent, because it is still *liang-chih* itself as the original substance of mind. The original substance of mind, as Wang Yang-ming said, is the principle of Heaven. Principles are always within the mind or *liang-chih*, and thus are always unexpressed principles within. Surely *liang-chih*, in its expression, is active, yet it is always at rest with its unexpressed principles within. Therefore, it never gets in motion, and is always static. As *liang-chih* is static, it is quiet (*chi*),ᵘ but as *liang-chih* is active, it is affective (*kan*).ᵛ Therefore, the unexpressed and the expressed, the static and the active, and the quiet and the affective, which are related concepts in Chu Hsi's system and show different parts of mind, are now just relative adjectives to qualify one absolute *liang-chih*, and all are existentially identical in their meaning.

Liang-chih is the substance of mind seen as a knowing function. *Liang-chih* as the substance of mind is always existing; therefore, as a knowing function, it is always knowing even with nothing to know. It is just like the sun always shining even with nothing to shine on. When *liang-chih* has nothing to know and is still knowing, this is called its expression in the unexpressed. In this state, the moral cultivation of *liang-chih* is nothing other than the self-continuity of its knowing, or its self-awakening, and thus its self-consciousness of its own existence. This corresponds to what Chu Hsi called the way of moral cultivation through self-preservation or self-nourishment. Wang Yang-ming used these terms also to indicate the state of *liang-chih* when it is always knowing, yet has nothing to know.

However, *liang-chih* usually has something to know, as the sun usually has something to shine on. In this state, *liang-chih* has its objects to be known. Yet the direct objects of *liang-chih* are not the things ordinary people call external objects. The direct objects of *liang-chih* are our volitional ideas, or *i-nien*,ʷ which are intended for handling affairs or doing things concerning the so-called external objects. Thus the so-called external objects are merely indirectly related to *liang-chih*, or are merely the constituent elements of our affairs, or things which are intended by our ideas. So the word *chih* (knowing) in Wang Yang-ming is to be taken as quite different from ordinary knowing. It is not a purely intellectual activity, the purpose of which is to get theoretical knowledge about external objects through our psychological functions such as sensing, perceiving, imagining, abstracting, conceiving, and understanding. It is also a different knowing from Chu Hsi's knowing which knows both the principles of the external objects theoretically and the principles of our actions practically. Wang Yang-ming's *liang-chih* knows immediately the good or evil of ideas in one's solitude with an inner certainty and without any reflection. *Liang-chih* never errs in its knowing. If it errs, it is not the voice of *liang-chih*; but what knows that one errs is *liang-chih*. Nevertheless, *liang-chih* may know only partially about the principles of Heaven as its nature; its nature is gradually self-revealed in a continuous process, as I have said before.

The most important point of Wang Yang-ming's thought about *liang-chih* is that when *liang-chih* knows, it is through an immediate feeling of the good and evil of our volitional ideas as these ideas are confronted and felt by *liang-chih*. Here *liang-chih* favors what is good and resists what is evil, and then likes the former and dislikes the latter. *Liang-chih* knows simultaneously with its feeling and its feeling continues itself and extends into its action. This action is an action which avoids what is evil and does what is good. This is why Wang Yang-ming insisted that knowledge and action are one.

Liang-chih, when it knows the good and evil of its volitional ideas, which are the motives of our ordinary feelings, will, desires, deliberations, and so on, actually practices the same thing Chu Hsi called self-examination. As *liang-chih* is avoiding what is evil, it does the same thing as the mastery of oneself that Chu Hsi called self-conquest and self-governing. When it both knows and feels what is good or evil and does what is good and avoids what is evil, *liang-chih*, as a function, is *fully* realized and its substance is embodied, incarnated in its function and realized therein also; then all our volitional ideas become good and are the expressions of our moral will. Thus the realization of *liang-chih* is at the same time the making of our moral will, pure, sincere, genuine, and authentic.

Furthermore, as *liang-chih* is always knowing and is essentially liking what is good and disliking what is evil, even when it is unexpressed and there is nothing to be known, its self-continuation or self-preservation is still in a state of self-restraint (*chieh*),[x] self-care (*shen*),[y] self-fear (*k'ung*),[z] and self-dread (*chü*)[aa] for avoiding evil; and also in a state of self-orientation and self-establishment of one's moral will (*i-chih*)[ab] for doing good. This is the state of *liang-chih*'s self-expression in the unexpressed, which rightly corresponds to the way of moral cultivation: self-care in solitude, as Chu Hsi taught.

The only way of moral cultivation which Wang Yang-ming seems not to give intensive attention to is the way of investigating things, or *ko-wu*, which Chu Hsi taught. Yet Wang Yang-ming also had his interpretation of *ko-wu*, which can include Chu Hsi's theory of *ko-wu* on a higher level of thought. In Wang Yang-ming's thought, when *liang-chih* is realized and what is evil is avoided, then all our volitional ideas are good and at the same time perfectly right, and any affairs or things originating from the right ideas are rectified and put in their right place by a right way. This is Wang Yang-ming's interpretation of the word *ko-wu*, which seems to be too subjective and has no such objective meaning as is contained in Chu Hsi's idea of *ko-wu*. However, Wang Yang-ming never denies that men should have knowledge of objective things, or so-called external objects. Yet this kind of knowledge originates from our senses and is called sense knowledge (*wen-chien chih chih*).[ac] It is not the knowing of *liang-chih* or the knowledge of our virtuous nature which originates from ourselves. Surely it is not enough for one to have merely the knowing of *liang-chih*, or the knowledge of virtuous nature in a narrow sense. Nevertheless, as our volitional ideas are related to our affairs or things concerned with objective things or so-called external objects, we can never have *liang-chih* without including some knowledge about objective things within the whole domain of its knowing.

When man is motivated by his *liang-chih* and is oriented toward something good, he must and should know the ways to accomplish those good things and then carry out these ways through objective things. In this case, the world of objective things should be observed, researched, and known from the moral obligations of *liang-chih* too. Thus the theory of *ko-wu*, according to Wang Yang-ming's thought, may actually include the way of *ko-wu* according to Chu Hsi's thought, as an aspect of or a moment in the process of realization of *liang-chih*. As the knowing of objective things is a moment of our doing something with them and our doing something is preconceived in our volitional idea as its content, the volitional ideas exist on a higher level than the knowing and doing. *Liang-chih* which knows the good and evil of the ideas exists on a still higher level, or on the highest level, and can include ideas known by itself as within itself also. Therefore, the realization of *liang-chih*, which stretches through ideas, affairs, and down to objective things, can definitely include also the investigation of objective things, such as Chu Hsi taught, on a higher level of thought. Although Wang Yang-ming may not put so much emphasis on knowing objective things as Chu Hsi did, and we may not be able to deduce all the implications clearly from his teaching, we still may insist that his teaching of the realization of *liang-chih* can include what Chu Hsi taught in principle.

In Wang Yang-ming's thought, objective things are not so objective or external to our mind as Chu Hsi and common sense suppose. Here the crucial point we have to understand is that our ideas are always to be carried out through the objective things, and our *liang-chih*'s substance is immanent in its function as knowing. From Chu Hsi's point of view, there are externally existing objective things, such as other persons and things in the natural world, which are outside our mind. These outside things are assumed to have their independent principles or *li* for their being, although metaphysically speaking these principles are also principles of our being. For Chu Hsi all principles, whether without or within, have to be searched out by our "investigation of things." This is a teaching for our empirical and ordinary consciousness. However, it is quite inadequate to a higher state of man's moral, metaphysical, or ontological self-consciousness, as Wang Yang-ming expressed it in his very profound and simple sayings. In such a self-consciousness, when we know or act morally toward objective things, we have to see these things as immanent in our moral consciousness at the same time that they are confronted as objects. Here not only is the principle of moral knowledge and action ours, but even what the actions and knowledge are directed toward as objects are inseparable from our action and knowledge, and are ours also. In Wang Yang-ming's thought, as *liang-chih's* substance is expressed and immanent in its function as knowing, therefore, where *liang-chih's* knowing is, its substance is also. Whatever is knowing, or enlightened by *liang-chih's* knowing or light, is penetrated by *liang-chih's* light and being enlightened. Thus Wang Yang-ming said that there is no substance of eyesight, and the substance of eyesight is in the color; there is no substance of mind and the substance of mind is in its affections and responses and judgments of the right or wrong of the myriad things in Heaven and Earth. These statements mean nothing other than that *liang-chih's* substance is in its knowing, which is the essence of its affections, responses, and judgments; its substance is in all the things in the universe, and all the things in the universe are within the domain of *liang-chih*. This is why Wang Yang-ming said that *liang-chih* is the spirit of the creative and transforming universe, and that nothing is outside the domain of *liang-chih*. This is an idealism which is very like Lu Hsiang-shan's idealism. Yet Lu Hsiang-shan's thought is based on the "self-awakening of the original mind," while the idea of Wang Yang-ming is based on his seeing the substance of *liang-chih* through its function as knowing and residing in what is known.

According to Wang Yang-ming's thought, all ways of moral cultivation, such as self-preservation, self-examination, self-conquest, rectification of the mind, making the will authentic, and the investigation of things which Chu Hsi taught, are aspects or moments of one process of the realization of *liang-chih*; thus all are expressions of *liang-chih's* substance in its function. Therefore, Wang Yang-ming also views the psychological functions or faculties which Chu Hsi analyzed into different kinds as simply different expressions of *liang-chih's* nature, or *liang-chih's* substance in its functions.

Wang Yang-ming frequently states that the nature, mind, will, ability, and knowing are the same thing, seen from different aspects, existentially identical and ontologically one. Now as Wang Yang-ming acknowledged also the differences of meaning in these psychological terms, he distinguished his attitude from that of Lu Hsiang-shan, who refused to discuss the meanings of these terms in answer to his disciple's question. However, as Wang Yang-ming thought these different functions were existentially one, he still belongs to the camp of Lu Hsiang-shan, who saw the original mind as one.

As to the distinction between the mind of Tao and the human mind, Wang Yang-ming had a view which seems to be a synthesis of Lu Hsiang-shan and Chu Hsi. Wang Yang-ming said that there is only one mind or one *liang-chih* in man, and that the mind which realizes the principles of Heaven as our nature is good, rational, and the mind of Tao, while the mind which does not do so is irrational and evil, a human mind with selfish desires.[6] This latter point is slightly different from Lu Hsiang-shan's thought, which insists that there is no distinction between the mind of Tao and the human mind. Wang Yang-ming still distinguished between the mind of Tao and the human mind of private opinion or selfish desires as originating from two contradictory directions of the same mind, and his thought is somewhat closer to Chu Hsi's idea of the human mind as standing midway between the mind of Tao and the human mind with selfish desires, and serving as a neutral medium for the mutual transformation of these two opposite kinds of mind.

WANG CHI'S INTERPRETATIONS OF *LIANG-CHIH* AS BEYOND IDEAS OF GOOD AND EVIL AND HIS TEACHING ABOUT "LEARNING PRIOR TO HEAVEN"

After Wang Yang-ming's death, his disciples were divided into different schools. The two most important of them were the Chiang-yu school and the Che-chung school.[ad] Yet all the thinkers of these two schools faced one important problem in the teaching of Wang Yang-ming. That is: how can sagehood really be attained by the realization of *liang-chih*?

According to Wang Yang-ming's teaching, there are volitional ideas, either good or evil, coming and going in our mind. The moral task of realization of *liang-chih* is to know them and evaluate them, and to do what is good and avoid what is evil. However, as the volitional ideas come and go indefinitely, we can never have the guarantee that all the evil volitional ideas will never come back; thus we have no self-confidence that we can attain sagehood. Again, the very coming and going of good and evil ideas is proof of our lack of moral stability or moral integration in the general sense. Furthermore, good and evil ideas, as known and evaluated by *liang-chih*, usually go ahead of *liang-chih*'s knowing. It seems that we have good and evil ideas first and then *liang-chih* follows their traces and knows them. It seems also that *liang-chih* is destined to remain a step behind these ideas, and thus always to be running after them. If this is so, how can it really master them, and how can its like and dislike of them necessarily be powerful enough to preserve or eradicate them absolutely? This is surely a very serious problem.

In dealing with this problem the thinkers of the Chiang-yu school, Ni Shuang-chiang [ae] and Lo Nien-an,[af] took "back to tranquillity" (*kuei-chi*)[ag] as their slogan. By the phrase "back to tranquillity" is meant a moral task which is temporarily separated from all affections, and thus stops all volitional ideas, and then abides in an inner state of tranquillity to meditate on the substance of *liang-chih*, which is quiet and transcendental. Here both Ni and Lo had very profound insights and experienced a deep spiritual enlightenment, which I shall not discuss here. I mention them only as a stepping stone to the discussion of Wang Chi's [ah] idea of moral mind.

Wang Chi disagreed with the Chiang-yu school's idea of substance and function as two distinct parts of *liang-chih*. He was more congenial than Ni and Lo to Wang Yang-ming's thought about the identity of substance and function. Nevertheless, Wang Chi saw also that the coming and going of good and evil ideas in our mind are disturbances of our moral mind, and therefore "passing beyond good and evil ideas" also became a central thought of Wang Chi.

From the historical point of view, Wang Yang-ming had already thought that the principle of Heaven is the substance of mind or *liang-chih* at rest with itself; therefore, in a sense, it may be taken as static and beyond the distinction of good and evil. This thought does not mean that one need not act according to the principles of Heaven, as the nature of *liang-chih*, or that the realization of *liang-chih* is not good; it only means that the principle as static and as the origin of our ordinary good is above ordinary good and it means also that when good is done for the realization of principle one should not still keep the idea of good as something reserved in one's mind. Wang Yang-ming compared the very idea of good kept in mind as bits of gold in our eyes which, though precious, obstruct the seeing power of our eyes. In our common sense, we all agree that a man who is really good does not think of himself as good. A man who always thinks of himself as good is a man of pride, which is not good. This proves that the utmost or supreme good of man may consist in the self-forgetting and self-transcending of the idea of his goodness. This proves also that the ideas of supreme good and of "beyond good and evil" are not incompatible ideas on a more profound level.

From this point of view, in talking about the nature or substance of *liang-chih* as the origin of our ordinary moral good, Wang Yang-ming took it both as supreme good and as beyond the distinction of good and evil. At the same time, in talking about the function of *liang-chih*, Wang Yang-ming never ceased to say that the function of *liang-chih* is to know the good and evil of our volitional ideas, to like and do what is good, and to dislike and avoid what is evil, and that the distinction of good and evil must be clearly known by *liang-chih* without any obscurity and confusion. In Wang Chi's thought, "passing beyond the distinction of good and evil" rightly became a thoroughgoing teaching for moral cultivation.

Concerning the problem of "Beyond the distinction of good and evil," there is a famous discussion of Wang Yang-ming, Wang Chi, and Ch'ien Te-hung,[ai] another disciple of Wang Yang-ming. The record of this discussion is called "The Record of Confirmation of Tao in T'ien-ch'üan." [aj] T'ien-ch'üan is a place name which literally means "the source originated from Heaven," and thus symbolically shows the importance of this discussion. However, the record by Wang Chi and that by Ch'ien Te-hung of this discussion were slightly different. The version in the *Ch'uan hsi-lu* [ak] was based on Wang Chi's record. A hundred years later Huang Tsung-hsi, who edited the *Ming-ju hsüeh-an*, also used the record of Wang Chi in the section on the latter's thought (*Lung-hsi hsüeh-an* [al]). Yet, in one of his other essays, he doubted that what was recorded by Wang

Chi was genuinely Wang Yang-ming's teaching. All these documents are of the utmost importance for our understanding of the development of thought in Wang Yang-ming's school. At one point in this famous discussion, both Wang Chi and Ch'ien Te-hung asked questions about the essence of their master's teaching of the realization of *liang-chih*, which were summarized in four sentences. My translation differs slightly from the translations of others, and my reasons for translating the four sentences this way will become apparent in the discussion that follows.

> Beyond the distinction of good and evil is the original substance of mind.
> There is either good or evil in the arising of volitional ideas.
> To know the good and evil of the volitional ideas is the "function" of *liang-chih*.
> Doing what is good and avoiding what is evil is to make things righteous.

According to our interpretation of Wang Yang-ming's thought in the last section, it is beyond question that these four sentences summarized most important features of Yang-ming's teaching. The first sentence represents Wang Yang-ming's ontological or metaphysical idea of *liang-chih* as a transcendental being. It means nothing other than that the substance of mind as the origin of our ordinary good is beyond distinctions of good and evil and is the supreme good, as I have said above.

The second sentence is a descriptive statement about our ordinary experience and consciousness of the moral value and lack of value, or good and evil, arising in our volitional ideas. Here the word *i* [am] does not mean moral will, which does only what is good and avoids what is evil. The moral will is purely good and not evil; therefore here the word *i* means simply "thoughts" (*i-nien*), which come and go in our ordinary consciousness and are only our volitional ideas, which may be either good or evil.

The third sentence says that the *liang-chih* which confronts the good or evil ideas knows them and evaluates them. Here *liang-chih* definitely has a higher level of existence and is master of the ideas. It is the substance of mind of the first sentence, where the emphasis is put on the substance of *liang-chih*, so the word "substance [of mind]" is used. In the third sentence the emphasis is put on the function of *liang-chih*. As the word *chih* means "knowing," which is the function of mind, the word *liang-chih* itself is used. The first sentence is an ontological statement which is intended to show that *liang-chih*, as the substance of mind, is beyond good and evil and transcends them. The third sentence says that *liang-chih* has its function in knowing ordinary good or evil ideas, and is immanent in its function. Thus it is also close to us in our moral practice.

The fourth sentence refers to things directly related to moral practice. Strictly speaking, doing what is good and avoiding what is evil and thus making things righteous is just the continuation of knowing good and evil in the process of realizing *liang-chih*, as I have explained before. Thus to make things righteous is nothing other than the last step in realizing *liang-chih*. Here one may ask, "What happens after the last step in realizing *liang-chih*?" or "What happens once the thing is already made righteous?" Wang Yang-ming did not answer this explicitly in his four sentences. However, according to the explanation of Wang Yang-ming's teaching in the preceding section, Wang Yang-ming would say that when *liang-chih* is realized and things are made righteous, no idea of good should be reserved in the mind and we should again go beyond the distinction of good and evil. This means that we have to return to the thought of the first sentence. Thus the meaning of the "four sentences" as a whole is just a description of the circular process of moral practice which begins from the realm beyond the distinction of good and evil, then proceeds to know the distinction of good and evil, and to do good and avoid evil, and ends in a state of mind again beyond the distinction of good and evil. This is rightly a very concise summary of Wang Yang-ming's teaching.

However, both Wang Chi and Ch'ien Te-hung had questions about the teaching of the four sentences. Both their questions were raised from points of view which are more logical than the teaching of the four sentences as such. Ch'ien Te-hung asked: If there are good and evil in our volitional ideas, and we have the knowledge and actions to do good and also avoid evil, then how can the substance of mind be beyond the distinction of good and evil? Thus it seems that there are good and evil in the substance of mind also. On the other hand, Wang Chi supposed that if the substance of mind is beyond the distinction of good and evil, then *liang-chih's* knowing of volitional ideas and all things should also be beyond the distinction of good and evil. It is recorded by Wang Chi that, after these two questions were raised by the two disciples, Wang Yang-ming said he had two ways of teaching: one for men born with high or sharp intelligence (*li-ken*),[an] and the other for men born with ordinary intelligence (*tun-ken*),[ao] and that what Wang Chi said was implied by the first sentence was for the sharp minds, and what Ch'ien Te-hung spoke of as implied in the other three sentences was for ordinary men. Yet, according to Ch'ien Te-hung's record in his biography of Wang Yang-ming, Wang Yang-ming did not say that he had two kinds of teaching; he said only that there are few people who are of sharp intelligence and that the two disciples' understanding of his teaching should supplement each other, and he said also that his disciples should never forget the four sentences as a whole. As the records of Wang Chi and Ch'ien Te-hung are slightly different, we need to know which one is closer to the actual situation at T'ien-ch'üan. I assume that Ch'ien Te-hung was a more faithful disciple of Wang Yang-ming, while Wang Chi, who was a more brilliant student, may have interpreted his master's saying according to his own predispositions. I think that Huang Tsung-hsi is quite right in saying that Wang Yang-ming never said anywhere that he had two kinds of teaching, because the teaching of the four sentences, if understood as I have explained it above, is both sufficient and necessary for the summarization of Wang Yang-ming's teaching. I think also that the criticism implied by the questions of his disciples about the moral practice of moral mind is actually irrelevant, because the four sentences understood as a whole are descriptive statements and not a deductive system. I suppose that in this discussion, Wang Yang-ming merely said that each of his two disciples had understood only one side of his teaching, and that later Wang Chi interpreted the two sides of his master's teaching as two kinds of teaching. Therefore, when Wang Yang-ming died, the idea of "beyond the distinction of good and evil" was further developed by Wang Chi and became his central teaching.

In the discussion at T'ien-ch'üan, as stated above, Wang Chi just supposed that, if *liang-chih* is beyond the distinction of good and evil, our volitional ideas and knowing of *liang-chih* should be likewise. However, in his dialogues and letters we also find his theory of the abolition of volitional ideas. This is plainly a further thought naturally arising in his mind. His reason for the abolition of ideas seems to be that, as volitional ideas are actually either good or evil, if we want to go beyond the distinction of good and evil, we have to go beyond the volitional ideas themselves, and then abolish volitional ideas altogether. The belief in the abolition of volitional ideas was originally held by Yang Chien [ap] (1140–1226), the disciple of Lu Hsiang-shan in the Sung dynasty, and was adopted by Wang Chi as a disciple of Wang Yang-ming. However, Wang Chi not only took the abolition of volitional ideas (*i*) as a way for the realization of *liang-chih*, but also distinguished *liang-chih* from both volitional ideas (*i*) and ordinary consciousness (*shih*),[aq] and even thought, to transcend ordinary consciousness as well. This idea is not difficult to understand, if we know that our volitional ideas reside in our ordinary consciousness. The difference between the knowing of *liang-chih* and ordinary consciousness consists in there being a duality of subject and object in our ordinary consciousness, while there is no such duality in the knowing of *liang-chih*. The difference between *liang-chih* and volitional ideas consists in that volitional ideas come and go, appear and perish, and are transitory, while *liang-chih* is permanent. As volitional ideas appear and perish, they are rightly the origin of the birth and death of our life and mind. As consciousness has its subjective and objective sides, this is the basis of its inner world in contrast to the outer world, and the origin of the breaking of the identity of self and the world. So all consciousness and volitional ideas have to be abolished or transcended. Thus, in our moral consciousness, if there are still subjective good and evil ideas coming and going in opposition to the outer objective world, this is the stage of "consciousness and volitional ideas." In this stage even good ideas are limited to what we are conscious of and thus are not identical with the universe as a whole nor with the transcendental being of our moral mind itself. Therefore, Wang Chi said that we should have a moral task which transforms the conscious ideas into the moral mind or *liang-chih* itself, if we really take the moral life of the sage as our ideal. In the moral life of the sage there are surely many expressions of his which are expressions of the principles of Heaven. However, any sage's self-expression is natural and spontaneous, as it should be in accord with his present situation. So there is nothing added to the principles of Heaven as the unexpressed substance of his mind, nor is there anything remaining after the expression has passed; thus, though all his expressions are good, he also has no conscious idea about the goodness of his activity in the life of the sage, as there are no conscious ideas left after the expression of *liang-chih*. Here *liang-chih* is superconsciousness as Nothing (*wu*),[ar] and also as transcendental being, always unexpressed as well as always expressed, and supremely good as well as beyond good and evil. Therefore, when talking about *liang-chih* in this highest sense, Wang Chi in his terminology even cut off the word *liang*, which implies goodness. *Liang-chih* to Wang Chi is identical with *chih* or "pure knowing." This pure knowing passes beyond good and evil. This pure knowing itself is both being (*yu*)[as] and Nothing (*wu*). This pure knowing is like a vacant valley which echoes a sound, but in which nothing remains after the echo. It is like the void space through which a bird passes and leaves no trace. Thus, from our *liang-chih* as pure knowing, there may arise all kinds of good expressions in response to things which we confront, yet, when any good expression has passed, nothing remains, as in the vacant alley or void space. This is rightly the moral life of the sage, which passes through the ideas of ordinary good to realize the utmost or supreme good which is beyond good and evil.

On the basis of the foregoing, Wang Chi distinguished between two kinds of moral task in becoming a sage. One he called learning how to make the will authentic. He called this learning "the learning posterior to Heaven" because it is posterior to the arising of volitional ideas. Where we have an idea, there we have a world before us, and we have Heaven. Thus the learning posterior to an idea is posterior to Heaven. In my opinion, this kind of learning is actually similar to the teaching of Wang Yang-ming. The other kind of moral task for becoming a sage, which Wang Chi preferred, he called "the learning anterior to Heaven." This is actually the learning prior to the arising of ideas. As here ideas do not arise, no world or Heaven is before our mind. Yet the mind as pure knowing is still there, the mind which is Nothing as well as being, unexpressed as well as always expressing, beyond the distinction of good and evil, and the supreme good. Here the mind or *liang-chih* as pure knowing, though confronting nothing to be known, exists in its own right and is wholly righteous in itself. So this kind of learning is called by Wang Chi "learning how to put the mind in its right position," and it is in this that Wang Chi's thought went beyond Wang Yang-ming's thoughts about *liang-chih* as pure knowing, which is both Nothing and being, both unexpressed and expressed.

The word *cheng-hsin* [at] is usually translated as "rectification of mind." But in Wang Chi's so-called learning of *cheng-hsin*, there is nothing to be rectified, and it is perhaps better to translate his *cheng-hsin* as "putting the mind in its right position." Even this, however, is not adequate, because in Wang Chi's thought there is no action of "putting" beside the mind's knowing of itself. The only thing we can do is to let our mind stand as it is in its right position, which is actually no position, since the mind is universal being, as well as universal Nothing.

Wang Chi further attempted to synthesize the teachings of Buddhism and Taoism with Confucianism. In Wang Yang-ming's thought, there is already the germ of such a synthesis. Wang Chi, however, stated plainly that the meaning of *liang-chih* covers Buddhism and Taoism as generally understood, but that Confucianism is positivistic, while Buddhism and Taoism are negativistic. Now, in Wang Chi's thought, *liang-chih* as Nothing is negativistic, and as being is positivistic; it is not difficult to understand why Wang Chi took *liang-chih* to cover the essentials of the three teachings.

After Wang Chi there was still further development of the idea of *liang-chih* in the schools of Yang-ming's disciples, ending with the thinkers of the Tung-lin school and Liu Tsung-chou,[au] who criticized severely Wang Chi's idea of "Beyond good and evil" and his thought about the synthesis of the three teachings. They also have a profound idea of moral mind, but this is beyond the scope of this essay.

CONCLUDING REMARKS

Above I have said that Wang Yang-ming accepted the problem which Chu Hsi left, replaced Lu Hsiang-shan's idea of original mind with his *liang-chih*, and actually had a theory of mind which is a synthesis of the thought of Lu Hsiang-shan and that of Chu Hsi. Wang Chi took up the problem where Wang Yang-ming had left it and went beyond his master, even, in a sense, beyond Confucianism. While Wang Chi is usually considered close to Yang Chien, the disciple of Lu Hsiang-shan, he is also close to Lu Hsiang-shan himself. In the thought of Lu Hsiang-shan, one should have a self-awakening of the original mind. This requires a sudden jump in the moral task. Lu Hsiang-shan's concept of mind is simpler than Wang Yang-ming's. The teachings of both Lu Hsiang-shan and Wang Chi are illuminating and brilliant in talking about the higher level of the mind. But the teachings of Chu Hsi and Wang Yang-ming are closer to ordinary life and more easily practiced. This may be taken as a rough comparison of these four thinkers as I have discussed them in this essay. Although my exposition has emphasized Wang Yang-ming and Wang Chi rather than Chu Hsi and Lu Hsiang-shan, I feel that we can never understand Wang Chi adequately except through Wang Yang-ming, nor can we ever understand Wang Yang-ming without comparing him with both Lu Hsiang-shan and Chu Hsi.

NOTES

1. *Hsiang-shan hsien-sheng ch'üan-chi* (Shanghai, 1935), 35/447.
2. *Chu Tzu yü-lei* (Taipei, 1962), 8/4817.
3. *Ch'uan-hsi lu* (Shanghai, 1917), 2/19.
4. *Ibid.*, p. 28.
5. *Ch'uan-hsi lu*, 3/19.
6. *Ch'uan-hsi lu*, 3/12.

GLOSSARY

a	氣	y	愼
b	天理	z	恐
c	未發	aa	懼
d	已發	ab	意志
e	理	ac	聞見之知
f	道心	ad	江右, 浙中
g	聖賢	ae	聶雙江
h	賢	af	羅念菴
i	人心	ag	歸寂
j	涵養	ah	王畿
k	存養	ai	錢德洪
l	克治	aj	天泉
m	省察	ak	傳習錄
n	愼獨	al	龍溪學案
o	正心	am	意
p	誠意	an	利根
q	格物	ao	鈍根
r	良知	ap	楊簡
s	良知即心之本體	aq	識
t	天理之昭明靈覺即良知	ar	無
u	寂	as	有
v	感	at	正心
w	意念	au	劉宗周
x	戒		

9

The criticisms of Wang Yang-ming's teachings as raised by his contemporaries

I. INTRODUCTION

When the teaching of *liang-chih* was expounded by Wang Yang-ming, various criticisms were put forward by his contemporaries. After Wang's death, his disciples divided into different schools, and doubts about the self-sufficiency of Wang's teachings, felt by some of his disciples, already contained some implicit criticisms. By the end of the Ming dynasty, Li Chien-lo, a second-generation follower of Wang, had made explicit his criticisms of Wang's teachings, and a debate occurred between Shu-Ching-an and Chou Hai-men, representing the Chan Kan-ch'üan and Wang schools respectively. About the same time, such scholars of the Tung-lin school as Ku Ching-yang and Kao Ching-yi also criticized Wang's teachings severely. This critical assessment culminated in Liu Chi-shan, the disciple of Shu Ching-an (of the Chan Kan-ch'üan school), who replaced the teaching of *liang-chih* with his own teaching of *chen-yi* or "to make the will authentic." Liu nevertheless claimed that the real teachings of Wang Yang-ming were identical with his own.[1]

As we can see, the whole question about the position of Wang's teachings in the development of Neo-Confucianism during the late Ming dynasty is rather complicated as well as interesting. In this article I shall try to discuss in a very general way where these explicit or implicit criticisms of Wang's teachings originated, whether they were internal or external to Wang's teachings, and what were the philosophical problems involved. The criticisms of Wang's teachings as raised by scholars of the Tung-lin school and by Liu Chi-shan, I have discussed elsewhere,[2] and I shall just mention them without further comment. My conclusion in this article will be that, although the criticisms may not be fatal to Wang's teachings, they were historically and philosophically significant in clarifying Wang's teaching and that some of the internal criticisms were especially valuable in remedying some of the defects and pushing the development of Ming Confucianism further.

II. WANG'S TEACHINGS CRITICIZED BY LU CHING-YEN

From the historical and philosophical points of view, the criticisms raised by four of Wang's contemporaries may be divided into four types. The first was presented by Lu Ching-yen, the great Confucian moral teacher in North China,

---

[1] Liu's criticisms of Wang's teachings were scattered in Liu's various writings. As a summary, see the *Complete Works of Liu Tzu*, Tao Kwang ed., vol. 5, pp. 13-24. In vol. 6, p. 13, Liu said the original meaning of Wang Yang-ming's teaching is not far from his thought.

[2] I wrote an article on Liu's doctrine of moral mind with a critique of Wang Yang-ming, which was read in the conference of "Thoughts of Ming Dynasty" held in Como, Italy, in 1971. The conference papers are expected to be published by Columbia University Press. In my article, I pointed out the most important criticisms of Wang's teaching, as raised by scholars of the Tung-ling school and by Liu.

who criticized the adequacy of the teaching of *liang-chih*. He pointed out that in Mencius, where the term *'liang-chih'* originated, it was coupled with *liang-neng*. While *liang-chih* means "moral knowledge," *liang-neng* means the "capacity for moral action." Hence, Wang's negligence of *liang-neng* was not justified.[3] Further, he claimed that in taking the realization of *liang-chih* as a way of universal moral practice, Wang was differing from Confucius, who taught his disciples differently—according to their temperaments and stages of moral practice and moral learning.[4] However, it seems to me that Lu did not realize that Wang's *liang-chih* is not merely the origin of moral knowledge but also is the origin of moral action. *Liang-chih* is the original conscientious or moral consciousness which knows and acts at the same time. Nor did Lu realize that Wang's *liang-chih*, as the original conscientious consciousness, can be expressed in the "different stages of moral practice and different degrees of learning of different men, with their different temperaments." Hence, he did not succeed in criticizing Wang's teachings from within. Huang Tsung-hsi, author of *Ming-ju-hsüeh-an*, defended Wang's point of view with vigor, judging that Lu failed to understand that *liang-chih* is a universal reality of the mind, for everyone, and not merely a special way for the moral practice of particular persons.[5] Although Lu could still rejoin that the realization of *liang-chih* is just a particular teaching of Wang Yang-ming's which Confucius did not talk about, there being many other ways of moral practice, I would agree with him on this point. Nevertheless, such a criticism can be used against all Confucianists who went beyond Confucius' sayings, including Lu himself. Even taken as an internal criticism, it is too general to be used specifically against Wang's teachings. Lu's criticism really can be taken only as an external criticism and the least important of the criticisms against Wang's teachings.

III. HUANG WAN'S CRITICISMS OF WANG'S TEACHINGS FROM THE PRAGMATIC POINT OF VIEW

The second type of criticism of Wang's teachings was represented by Huang Wan. Huang was first Wang's friend before becoming his disciple, and he defended Wang's learning and character in the court when Wang was attacked by his political enemies. Yet Huang in the end of his study became suspicious of his master's teachings and criticized the teaching of the "realization of *liang-chih*," especially as propounded by Wang's disciples.[6] It seems to me that his

[3] *Ming-ju-hsüeh-an*, Chung Hua Press ed., vol. 8, p. 4.
[4] Ibid., p. 3.
[5] Ibid., p. 1.
[6] Huang Wan wrote the *Ming-tao-pien*. It is a rare book and is still not available to me. There is a short biography of him in vol. 13 of *Ming-ju-hsüeh-an*. In Jung Chao-tsu's *History of the Thought of the Ming Dynasty*, reprinted by (Taiwan: Kai Ming Book

208

criticisms stem from his awareness of the bad influences which arose from Wang's teachings. Indeed there were such pernicious influences, and they worsened in the later period of the Ming. As the root is responsible for the fruit, Wang's reachings, and indeed the whole tradition of Sung and Ming Neo-Confucianism, came under the attack of Ch'ing scholars. Huang Wan may be considered the first representative who criticized Wang's teachings in terms of its influences.

Huang's criticisms were not purely external criticisms of Wang's teachings, for he understood Wang to a certain degree. His main difference from Wang may be seen in Huang's interpretation of the sentence "*chih-chih* (realization of knowledge) *tsai ke-wu* (investigation of things)." For Wang, this sentence means that *ke-wu* is the same thing as *chih-chih*. For Huang, the word *tsai* means "for the purpose of" and the word *ke* means "*fa*" or "norm."[7] Thus the whole sentence means that the purpose of the realization of knowledge is to put the norm into practice and to end in a pragmatic reconstruction of objective things. Hence, the realization of moral knowledge is not just for inner spiritual cultivation to attain sagehood (and Huang did not neglect its importance), but is also instrumental in the reconstruction of the objective things of the social, political, and natural worlds. In Huang's thought, the orientation of the inward moral mind should be turned outward, and his thought ended in a pragmatism or utilitarianism very close to the Yung-chia and Yung-k'ang schools of Sung dynasty philosophy, and the Yen-Li school of the Ch'ing dynasty. Thus, Huang not only criticized Wang Yang-ming, but extended his criticisms to Yang Tzu-hu, Lu Hsin-shan, then to Chu Tsu, the Chen brothers and even to Chou Lien-hsi, charging that all of them merely knew some way for the inner spiritual cultivation, which had no pragmatic utility. Their learnings were accused, by him, of consisting of Māhāyana Buddhism or Hināyāna Buddhism and not the original Confucianism of Confucius and Mencius.

Huang's criticisms of Wang and the Neo-Confucianist tradition foreshadowed later criticisms of them toward the end of the Ming and the Ch'ing dynasties. Yet, because he was originally Wang's disciple, his learning may be characterized as one which started within Wang's teaching but ended in going outside it to take quite a different philosophical stand. Because his criticism was based on a standpoint outside of Wang's philosophy and was directed mainly against the pernicious influences which arose from Wang's teaching but which are essentially outside of Wang's teachings, Huang Wan's criticisms were still mainly external. Furthermore, as this type of criticism was used by

Store, there is a section which introduces Huang's thoughts with quotations from the *Ming-tao-pien*, which I used for my discussion.

[7] Jung, *History of the Thought of the Ming Dynasty*, p. 171.

him to attack the other thinkers of the Neo-Confucian tradition, it is still too general to be taken as a special criticism of Wang's teachings as it is.

IV. CHAN KAN-CH'ÜAN'S TEACHINGS VERSUS WANG YANG-MING'S TEACHINGS

The third type of criticism of Wang's teachings was represented by Chan Kan-ch'üan who was a good friend of Wang Yang-ming. Their systems went the same way of moral idealism. But, while Chan talked about the importance of *liang-chih* for moral cultivation in a way which was very similar to Wang Yang-ming, Chan had different thoughts about *ke-wu* as related to *liang-chih*. Hence, his criticisms provide an internal criticism of Wang's philosophy, which is historically and philosophically important. Chan's thesis was that the *liang-chih* or the conscientious consciousness is a consciousness of *ke-wu* or an experience of the Heavenly principle of things in the universe. *"Sui-ch'ü-t'i-jen-t'ien-li"* was taken by Chan as the moral slogan, instead of "realization of *liang-chih*" as taught by Wang Yang-ming. *Tien-li* means the Heavenly principle or the moral principle of things of the universe. *T'i-jen* means both "to be acquainted with" and "to be identified with" and "to investigate," which may be translated as "to experience" to include these two meanings.[8] *Sui-ch'ü* means everywhere, or in any occasion of life. This means, as Chan explained, "whether in the occasion of knowing, or willing, or acting, or in the occasion of oneself, or family, or country, or the world under Heaven; whether in the expressed state of the Mind, or in the unexpressed state of the Mind."[9] Thus the way of *ke-wu*, for Chan, is to experience the Heavenly principle in any occasion of life. His Heavenly principle is a principle of existing in a state of spiritual equilibrium, which is not partial or biased, but is always impartial and keeps or preserves the whole and the particular principles in view.[10] Through the experiencing of the Heavenly principle, man knows the righteous way, and when keeping or preserving this very knowledge in acting, man acts rightly. This is called the "co-progression of knowledge and action" of man's moral life, "attaining and abiding in the utmost good" with a "sense of reverence" in every occasion of life. This is roughly what Chan taught.

[8] *Complete Essays of Chan*, K'ang-hsi ed., vol. 22, p. 20, Chan taught that *T'i-jen* means *T'i-t'ieh* and *Ch'a-shih*; I prefer to translate *T'i-t'ieh* as "to be acquainted with" and "to be identified with." *Ch'a-shih*, I prefer to translate as "to investigate."

[9] Consult Chan's letter to Wang Yang-ming, *Complete Essays of Chan*, vol. 7, p. 25, where Chan explained the meaning of *sui-ch'ü*, and vol. 8, p. 22 and vol. 9, p. 5, where Chan commented on the interpretation of *sui-ch'ü* as understood by his disciples.

[10] Chan always used the word *chung* or *chung-cheng* to explain the state of *t'ien-li* as the reality of mind. *Chung* means that the mind is located in the center, and *cheng* means mind's response is on the right way. This state of mind can be translated as a spiritual equilibrium which is easily understood. The idea of *chung-cheng* was explained in the article "The Way of Mind as Inherited from Confucian School," in *Complete Essays of Chan*, vol. 21, pp. 15–18; vol. 8, p. 9; vol. 17, p. 14; vol. 9, p. 21; vol. 18, pp. 17 and 23.

It is my impression that Chan's teaching is a very well-balanced system. The meaning of *"T'i-jen-t'ien-li,"* in including "to investigate the Heavenly principle," is very much like Chu Hsi's philosophy, while by including "to be identified with the principle" Chan is very much like Lu Hsiang-shan and Wang Yang-ming. Chan did not explain the Heavenly principle merely objectively or merely subjectively. It is a principle of our mind as well as a principle of things of the Heaven or the universe. It is apprehended or contained in the mind, and penetrated by mind's knowing and acting. Thus, in philosophy he is as idealistic as Wang Yang-ming. His system is well balanced; it may be taken to be self-sufficient, and we may not be able to find any flaw in it. Chan Kan-ch'üan was surely a great moral master of Neo-Confucianism of the Ming dynasty as was Wang Yang-ming. As a scholar, Chan was perhaps even more erudite and wrote many more books than Wang Yang-ming. However, his criticisms of Wang Yang-ming are a controversial matter. There were letters that Chan wrote to Wang and sayings that were scattered in his other writings which criticized Wang's teachings. He was dissatisfied with Wang's discussion about the nature or reality of mind as beyond good and evil. He claimed sometimes that Wang's teaching of the realization of *liang-chih* was taking "learning to be a sage" to be too easy and that Wang's teaching was rather biased. Yet we need not take such criticisms seriously, because Chan just asserted them occasionally, and he did not take them very seriously himself.[11] Now I shall just discuss one criticism of Chan's that is crucial to Wang's teaching.

This criticism is concerned with his interpretation of *ke-wu* as different from Wang's teaching. Chan's interpretation of *ke-wu* was along the line of Chu Hsi's. *Ke-wu* means, for him, "to investigate and to be acquainted with and then, to be identified with the principle of things," or "to experience the principles of things" as stated earlier. However, according to Wang, the word *wu* is interpreted as our motivative or volitional ideas, which includes the objective things known as its part. Henceforth, *ke-wu* means *"chen-nien-tou"* or "to rectify our motivative ideas." The rectification of motivative ideas is the same thing as the realization of *liang-chih*. Wang said that Chu Tsu's

---

[11] For Chan's other criticisms of Wang's teaching, consult: *Complete Essays of Chan,* vol. 10, p. 10, where Chan criticized Wang's way of moral cultivation as too easy; vol. 10, p. 2, vol. 23, p. 37, and vol. 23, p. 79, where Chan criticized the theory of no good and no evil; vol. 11, p. 30, where Chan criticized Wang's interpretation of *ke-wu* of the *Book of Great Learning* as not conforming to the context; vol. 11, p. 22, where he quoted Wang's saying that his teaching is just a rough teaching for beginners; volume 22, p. 21, where he criticized that Wang's teaching may have had influences; volume 23, p. 3, where Chan criticized Wang's idea about the relation of knowledge and action; volume 23, p. 50, where Chan criticized Wang's way of teaching as like the army who fights for victory with special strategy not with the general strategy; and volume 11, p. 11, where Chan criticized Wang's criticism of Chu Hsi's idea of *ching,* as not convincing.

interpretation of *ke-wu* as "to investigate the principle of objective things" is to search for our moral cultivation to be a sage outside of the very moral mind and thus leading man to go outside himself.[12] Wang is also suspicious about Chan's teaching: "to experience the Heavenly principle in every occasion of life" is to search the way of cultivation of the moral outside oneself. Yet Chan wrote several letters to Wang to point out the four shortcomings of Wang's interpretation of *ke-wu* and to explain the five merits of his interpretation of *ke-wu*,[13] and asserted once to his disciple that Wang's "rectification of motivative ideas," without "other ways of moral cultivation for experiencing the Heavenly principle in every occasion of life," is merely subjective matter, and itself may be based on personal opinion which has not conformed to the Heavenly principle.[14] However, I shall not talk about the details of his criticisms in his letters to Wang and of his talks to his disciples. I just wish to point out that the difference between Wang and Chan did not merely come from their different interpretations of the term *ke-wu* in the context of the *Book of Great Learning*, but from their different philosophical backgrounds. In Wang's thought, moral cultivation is an inner matter, so the investigation of principles of objective things could never be the proper way for moral cultivation. Yet Chan had a philosophy which sees the objective things of the universe as existing in the very mind, hence, to know the principles of things is not to search for the way of moral practice outside one's mind. It is rightly what the man, as a moral being, should do for his mind. Wang taught also that the mind is pervasive in the things of the universe and that nothing is outside the mind. Therefore, when Chan's interpretation was blamed (by Wang) as searching for the way outside, Chan rejoined that, in his thought,

12 *Complete Essays of Chan*, vol. 7, p. 24. Chan said in his letter to Yang Shao-mei that his difference with Wang is concerned with the idea of mind, and that in Wang's thought the mind is just located in the body, therefore, his to "experience the heaven principle of things" is searching for principle outside mind. Wang did not realize that there is no duality of inside and outside for the mind, which is identified with the myriad things of the universe, in his thought.
13 Consult *Complete Essays of Chan*, volume 7, pp. 25–28, for Chan's letter to Wang Yang-ming. This is the most important letter which pointed out the four shortcomings of Wang's teaching about *ke-wu* and the five merits of Chan's teaching about *ke-wu;* and volume 7, p. 20, where Chan maintained that the mind inwardly-oriented and outwardly-oriented are both diverted ways of moral cultivation and not the right way.
14 Consult Chan's letter to Wang Nei-hsüeh in *Complete Essays of Chan*, volume 7, p. 22, where Chan criticized Wang's teaching of rectification of motivative ideas as the only way of moral cultivation as too narrow and biased; and vol. 23, p. 26, where Chan said that if the realization of *liang-chih* is accompanied with other ways of moral cultivation as extensive learning, accurate inquiry, careful thinking, clear discrimination, earnest practice, he shall have no objection to Wang's teaching; vol. 20, p. 21, where Chan said that Wang's teaching about *liang-chih* originated from Mencius. Yet he did not pay attention to the word *"ta"* of Mencius which means the extension of *liang-chih* through further ways of moral practice, and if it supplemented Wang's teaching with a further way, Wang's teaching would be better.

the principle of the things of the universe is also within the mind, and that it is Wang himself who separated the inside mind and the outside things and limited the way of moral cultivation to the inward rectification of motivative ideas within the mind, without experiencing the Heavenly principle by other ways in every occasion of life where the things of the universe are encountered. Chan did not claim explicitly that Wang's teaching, which emphasized the "inward rectification of the motivative ideas" in contrast to the "outward knowledge of principle of things," is also contradictory to Wang's thought that nothing is outside the mind. Yet this is implied in Chan's criticism. As this is the case, then the fault seems to be on Wang's side, and Chan's criticism of Wang is forceful and convincing.

When Chan raised his questions to Wang through several letters, Wang did not answer. Wang explained once to his student Ch'ien Hsü-shan why he did not answer.[16] Wang said that if he and Chan could live together for several months, perhaps, they could agree with each other. It is no good just to have a verbal controversy through letters. Ch'ien Hsü-shan recorded the story and regretted very much that the two great masters, both of whom he admired, did not meet. Hence the differences between Wang and Chan remained like a *kung-an* of Ch'an Buddhism, which is unsettled but worthy of our study. In the following, I shall try to defend Wang's standpoint through Chan's criticism and see what is the contribution of Wang's teaching to the ways of moral cultivation, which can compete with or be superior to Chan's teaching.

In the first place, I have to admit that the thoughts of Chan and Wang were on the same line of moral idealism and that they had many points in common. Yet the difference between them, if emphasized, is a great difference in philosophy. Chan is a very broad-minded man and his teachings form a well-balanced system. It seems to me that Chan has too many commonplace sayings and his whole teaching seems to have no definite focus. "To experience Heavenly principle everywhere" is still too broad in meaning. It may not be able to lead man to begin his moral cultivation from a definite starting point. However, Wang's teaching of the "rectification of our motivative idea" as the way of *ke-wu* and also the way of realization of *liang-chih* may be said to point out a definite starting point for moral cultivation. Surely, the motivative ideas are reflected and rectified inwardly, and Wang's teaching may be criticized as establishing "the inward" in opposition to "the outward." It seems also to be contradictory to the idealism of both Wang and Chan, which sees the outer world as existing also inside the very mind. However, the very idealism of both Chan and Wang had to be established through an inwardly oriented reflexive thinking, at least in the beginning of their thought, in contrast to the ordinary thinking of man, which is merely outwardly oriented and attached to things that are regarded as just objective and external to the mind. The idealism of both Wang and Chan is never the philosophy of ordinary thinking. The objective things encountered in the occasions of our life can be looked upon as also existing inside the mind only through reflective thinking about "the thing encountered as also a thing apprehended and contained in the mind, and then as existing also inside the mind." Otherwise, in his ordinary thinking, man's mind is just outwardly oriented and takes the things seen as merely objective and external to his mind. Yet the very thinking of man as reflexive is inwardly oriented, at least in its beginning. Henceforth, all men's idealism must arise from a certain inward orientation of mind, and Chan's idealism is no exception. This orientation of mind is called inward, because it is reflexive and is differentiated from the outward orientation of the mind in ordinary thinking. Of course, when the idealism is established and the world is known as also existing inside the mind, there shall be no duality of the outside and inside or of the inward and outward. Then the mind and the world would be taken as an identical whole. This is the point where Chan and Wang both agreed. Yet, it seems that Chan just took the identical whole of mind and world as an already given state, in the very beginning of men's thought, and had forgotten that the sense of this identical whole has to be established by reflexive thinking, which is inward oriented. The inward orientation of mind is the foundation of the very sense of the identity of mind and world. Hence, Chan seems to be wrong when he claimed that Wang's teaching is inwardly oriented. He had no reason to complain that Wang's emphasis on an inwardly oriented way of moral cultivation is contradictory to the thesis that there is nothing outside the mind. In the entire philosophical pilgrimage, perhaps we have to say that in the beginning stage there is an outward orientation of the mind in ordinary thinking, which sees the things of the world as just external and even sees the moral principle and the practice of it as external too. In the middle stage, there is the inward orientation of the mind in extraordinary thinking, which sees the things of the world as also internal and the moral principle and the practice of it as internal too. Passing through the extraordinary thinking, there is no duality of inward and outward in the last stage. So there is no self-contradiction in Wang's teaching, when Wang taught men starting from the middle stage, and ended in the last stage.

In the second place, I have to say that to experience the Heavenly principle in any occasion of life, as taught by Chan, may not be contradictory to Wang's teaching. According to Wang, *liang-chih* has a natural light as a conscient consciousness. As man exists as an occasion of life, and things are encountered in the occasion, his *liang-chih* can know by its natural light the Heavenly principle or moral principle for his responsive action. For example, when a man's father is encountered in certain occasions of life, a man can know filial piety as a moral principle for his action. Here, the father as a thing and the filial piety as a moral principle are all in man's universe and also are immanent in his mind. Chan could say also that it is an example of "to experience the principle in man's occasion of life," and that without the actual occasion of life and the father as an actual thing encountered there could be no principle actually known or experienced. Thus, "looking at the occasion and the thing," is necessary for knowledge or experience of the moral principle. As our life is going on, our encounter with things is always changing; the moral principles are known and experienced successfully in the different occasion of things. Man always had to look at what his present occasion of life actually is and to know and to experience its moral principle within his mind. I do not see that Wang could quarrel with Chan on this point. Wang understood quite well that the natural light of *liang-chih* as conscient consciousness with its moral principle is successfully known and experienced in each actual occasion of life.[16] As the actual occasion of life is changing and each occasion is concrete, the moral principle of our action could not be just a static and abstract principle. It has to be particularized, become dynamic and concrete through the present creation of *liang-chih*.[17] For example, Wang talked about the story of Shun. Shun's father was unkind to his son. According to Shun's filial piety, Shun should tell his father about his intention to marry and receive his father's permission. Yet Shun knew quite well that if he told his father of his intention to marry, he would not be permitted to do so, and without the marriage he would have no posterities to serve in the sacrifice to his ancestors. This would be even more contrary to his sense of filial piety, and therefore Shun decided to marry and not tell his father.[18] Wang quoted this story to show that filial piety as a moral principle is not a static and abstract principle but a principle which must be practiced in the concrete occasions of life and which was particularized in its expression. It would then become a dynamic and concrete principle through the present creation of *liang-chih*. Thus, Wang could never disagree with Chan's teaching "to know and experience the moral principle in the occasions of life with things."

As to the last point, we may also say that Wang's thought of *liang-chih* is rightly for teaching man to practice the moral principles experienced or revealed in his different occasions of life. The most important thing in man's moral life is to realize the moral principle which is known in his present

[16] As to the way Wang Yang-ming's idea about *li* or principle and mind, consult my article "Spirit and Development of Neo-Confucianism," in *Inquiry*, 14 (1971): 77–83.

[17] *Complete Works of Wang Yang-ming*, vol. 1, p. 15, and vol. 2, p. 8. See my interpretation of present creation of *liang-chih* in my article "Revaluation of Wang Yang-ming's Learning and Similarities and Differences between Chu Hsi and Lu Hsiang-shan," in *New Asia Journal*, section 7, 2, no. 1 (1956): 37–43.

[18] *Complete Works of Wang Yang-ming*, vol. 3, p. 5.

concrete occasions of life. So Wang said that what is known today through my *liang-chih* must be extended as far as it can be today; if there is a new enlightenment of my *liang-chih* tomorrow, then I must extend the new enlightenment as far as I can tomorrow.[10] Wang never taught that what is revealed through the function of *liang-chih* is a totality of moral principles which are the same for every man in any occasion of life at any time. And it is also quite possible that a moral principle which is known in the present occasion of my life is based on a wrong knowledge of the actual occasion and my *liang-chih* may be obscured and perverted by selfish desires or biases. Wang knew as well as Chan that even the rectification of motivative ideas may be based on wrong personal opinion, which is not in conformity with the Heavenly principle and is not the genuine expression of *liang-chih*. Yet, according to Wang, we have to know that the very intention to correct the wrong opinion and to make the *liang-chih* more enlightened and clearer— to know the wrong as wrong—still originated from the further creation or expression of *liang-chih*. What was emphasized in Wang's teaching is that man should have a reflexive and inwardly oriented thinking, and a "self-consciousness" and "self-faith" in the existence of *liang-chih* through its successive revealment and practice of what is successfully revealed. This is what Chan did not emphasize.

From what was said earlier, we can know that the central thesis of Wang's teaching is not about the general knowledge of moral principle or the knowledge of what is good or evil but the practice of the principle and to do what is good and undo what is evil. So far Wang is not very much at variance with Chan, because Chan talked also about the co-progress of moral knowledge and action. Wang and Chan both thought that the relation of genuine moral knowledge and moral action should and could go together. Yet, in the ordinary cases, man always has moral knowledge which is not going together with or followed by moral practice. Then we have to ask, why these cases exist, and what is the way for moral cultivation to make the two always going together?

It seems to me that Chan had no serious discussion about the above problem, yet Wang had an insight that could solve the problem. This insight came rightly from a deep inwardly oriented thinking that Chan lacked.

What was Wang's insight? It was that the go-together of moral knowledge and moral practice or action is not merely something which should be, but it is also the very ontological reality of original moral mind or *liang-chih* as it is. In the reality of original moral mind, moral knowledge was originally connected with moral action through a moral feeling. *Liang-chih* feels what it knows and initiates its action and thus unites knowledge and action into one, and then there is a trinity of "moral knowing, feeling, and acting," which is

---

[10] Ibid., vol. 3, p. 13.

the very original reality of *liang-chih* as revealed in its first human expression. For example, when a child knows to love his parents, there is "his knowing, his loving, and his acting in a loving way" toward his parents at one time. This is the child's *liang-chih*, revealed in its first expression as a trinity, without self-consciousness. Thus, when the child knows further that "to love his parent" is good and that "to hate his parent" is evil, he also likes the "good" and takes action to do "good," and dislikes "his hate" as evil, and takes action to undo "evil." This is his self-conscious realization of *liang-chih* revealed in its first expression as a trinity. Even in an adult, if something morally good is encountered suddenly, his knowing it, liking it, and acting in an appropriate way toward it, always come simultaneously. Here *liang-chih* as a trinity of moral knowing, feeling, and acting is revealed. In the trinity, the three exist in reality as three moments of an integral whole, which functions as a whole.

As the reality of *liang-chih* is thought, by Wang, to be a trinity of moral knowing, feeling, and acting, therefore practice of the moral knowledge is nothing more than to realize the *liang-chih* as it is. Yet why do people not practice what they know morally? Wang said that this is because they have lost the reality of *liang-chih*; consequently, its function of knowing and acting are separated. What is the cause for this loss of reality and the separation of the function of knowing and acting? Wang said that it was owing to selfish desires which interrupted the expression of *liang-chih* as a trinity. Here Wang's explanation may not be sufficient.

One may have no doubt about the first expression of *liang-chih* as a trinity of moral knowing, feeling, and acting, as explained earlier. Yet we have to know that the past expression of *liang-chih* also can be recollected in memory and that its moral principle can be abstracted out by our present conceptual thinking and be imitated or put into practice again, in the present life by the present mind. Once more, a moral principle can be known through the observation of the moral action of other people or told by other people. In such cases, the moral principle known is not necessarily accompanied by the living conscient consciousness like the first expression of *liang-chih*. Our knowledge of the moral principle is like the pure intellectual knowledge of nonmoral principles of the universe and may have no moral feeling or moral acting immediately following the knowledge, especially when we have other present selfish desires, which interrupt.

If the separation of moral knowledge and action came from what was said above, then the way to make the two one is not to take the principle as something outside my present moral consciousness, even if it is suggested by my past moral life, or by other men's moral action, or told by other people. Because the principle is known by my present moral mind, we must conceive of it as being revealed by my *liang-chih* in its present expression, with the principle being the very nature of *liang-chih* and nothing external. Thus it is necessary to think of the principle as inside the *liang-chih* or my moral life. Furthermore, the feeling of "the existence of the principle," the feeling about "the realization of principle in the present occasion of life as good," and the feeling of "the good as good" and "liking the good" are also necessary for initiating the action. The feeling itself may be thought of also as the beginning of action or as already being an action. Thus moral knowledge and moral action are seen as one thing. When said objectively, we may say that knowledge and action as two are brought into one. Actually, there is just one thing, that is, a trinity of moral knowing, feeling, and acting. This one thing, seen as one thing, is also the expression of *liang-chih's* original reality.

In our present mind, we have some motivative ideas of the knowledge of the good, which is the knowledge about what should be or what conforms to the principle known through *liang-chih*. This is a good idea. We also have some other motivative ideas which are generated by selfish desires and which do not conform with, or rather violate, the principle as known through *liang-chih*. This is an evil idea. The feeling and action which accompany the good idea are the liking and doing; and the feeling and action which accompany the evil idea are the disliking and undoing. The *liang-chih* which functions as knowing the good idea and the evil idea—liking the former and disliking the latter, and doing the former and undoing the latter—exists at a higher level than what is known, felt, or acted on as good or evil. When *liang-chih* completes its function as knowing, feeling, and acting, and the good is done, evil is undone; we have the fulfillment of our moral life. Yet when evil is undone, we should not have a self-possession of the good, because self-possession is not good. Therefore, when good is done, the good has to be forgotten. Thus we are in a state beyond evil and good, which is also the utmost good or chief good. This is the ultimate stage of the realization of *liang-chih*, where the reality or nature of our moral mind or *liang-chih* is realized as it is. This ultimate stage is a stage of "beyond good and evil" or of "no good and no evil"; therefore, the reality or nature of mind, or *liang-chih* as an ontological reality or nature of mind, can be thought as no-good and no-evil or also as beyond good or evil. In this state of mind, there is only the *liang-chih* or original conscient consciousness, which is always impartial, serene, transparent, and void. It is a state of mind full of bliss and joy. This state of mind, as fully realized, is a state of sagehood. Wang's teaching that the ultimate state of mind and the reality or nature of mind is beyond good and evil, or no-good and no-evil, was not accepted by Chan Kan-ch'üan. Chan thought that the nature of mind must be good. Yet Chan did not speak much about this problem. Wang taught that the state beyond good and evil is a very lofty state of mind identified with Heaven. The attainment of such a state is by the inward realization of *liang-chih*. Chan criticized Wang's way of moral cultivation as too inwardly oriented, so he could not have had a sympathetic

218

understanding and a serious criticism of this aspect of Wang's teaching. The
serious criticism of this aspect was expounded by Lo Cheng-an and disciples
of Wang Yang-ming.

V. LO CHENG-AN'S ACCUSATION OF WANG'S TEACHING AS DISGUISED BUDDHISM

Lo's criticisms, as the fourth type, was concentrated on the very concept of
"mind" and "nature," and the "ultimate state of mind as transparent, void,
and beyond good and evil." This criticism is quite different from Chan's
criticism which just said that Wang's teaching about the way of *ke-wu* and
realization of *liang-chih*, as starting from the rectification of motivative idea,
is rather narrowly inwardly oriented and is not broadly open to any occasion
of life. Lo's criticism was directed to the central thought about the mind,
nature, and ideal of our moral life. It is a type of criticism going into the
inner kernel of Wang's teaching, though Lo, like Chan, raised his objections
to Wang's teachings through the discussion about the interpretation of *ke-wu*.
Generally speaking, Chan's criticism of Wang was repeated by such scholars
of the late Ming as Ku Ching-yang, Kao Ching-yi, and others. Lo's criticism
of Wang was followed by such scholars of the Ch'eng-Chu school as Feng
Chen-pai, and Ch'en Ch'ing-an,[20] from the late Ming to the Ch'ing dynasties.
Lo's *Records of Hard Search of Knowledge* was almost a bible for the scholars
of the Ch'eng-Chu school during the Ch'ing dynasty.

Lo's criticism of Wang is originally based on study of Ch'an Buddhism.
He had experienced sudden-awakening, conforming to what is experienced
by the Ch'an Buddhist. Afterward, he thought that in this state of mind
only the *miao* or "mystery" of mind as transparent and void is seen but that
is not the nature of mind as principle. He said that he had thought about this
matter for several decades, and at the age of about sixty he realized the truth
of mind and nature. In his book, he concluded that Buddhism, Lu Hsiang-
shan, Yang Tzu-hu, and Wang Yang-ming had the same way of spiritual
cultivation and that each saw something about the mind with its knowing as
transparent, void, and beyond good and evil and never saw what is the real
nature, as principle of mind, which transcends the mind as such. In one
sentence: "they know mind but not its nature."[21] In Lo's thought, the nature
of mind is profounder and deeper rooted and can be expressed and known
only through the contact of the mind with objective things and the investigation of their principles, as Chu Tsu taught. The principles of things may be

[20] As to Feng Chen-pai and Ch'en Ch'ing-an's criticisms of Wang's teaching, consult
Takehiko Okada, *Wang Yang-ming and Confucianism of Late Ming* (Tokyo: Meitoku
Press, 1971), pp. 318–399.
[21] *Records of Hard Search for Knowledge*, vol. 2, p. 10.

taken as the differentiations of the one great principle of the universe. Lo liked to use the term "one *li* with its myriad differentiations as its ramifications." Through the investigation of things, we know their principles or the differentiations of the one *li*; and when we respond to the things, then, the oneness of our mind and things can be experienced. Yet we must first conceive of the *li* or principle of things as objectively existing in the universe and as something common. In the work of the investigation of things, I must look outwardly and forwardly to the objective *li* or principles as outside my mind, then when the *li* or principles are known, I may think them inwardly and backwardly as our principles or *li*, which is also my nature. On the other hand, if I just look at my nature of mind backwardly and inwardly, I shall know, in the end, only the mystery of my mind as transparent, void, and beyond good and evil, as Wang said, yet I shall never know that this nature is deeply rooted in my mind and is the common principle of the universe. In this case I shall be destined to go beyond the moral sphere and become a disguised Buddhist without genuine moral responsibility.

The thought of Lo, in which the nature of the mind as its principle is different from the mind as such, was criticized by Huang Tsung-hsi as being contradictory to Lo's cosmological theory in which the *li*, or principle, can never exist apart from the *ch'i*, the existential process of the whole universe. If *li* cannot exist apart from *ch'i*, then the nature of the mind as principle or *li* could not exist apart from the existential process of the mind as well; hence, there can be no difference between mind and its nature from the existential point of view. Thus, Lo's criticisms of Wang's teachings fall to the ground. However, it seems to me that Huang's evaluation of Lo's criticisms is not quite fair to Lo. Admittedly, from the cosmological point of view, there can be no *li* or principle existing apart from the existential process, the *ch'i*, of the whole universe. Yet man is not the whole universe, but only a part of the universe. Thus, it is not unreasonable to take the nature or principle of mind as deep-rooted, as transcending, and as being different from the mind as such, and, in a certain sense, as existing apart from the mind.

If Huang's evaluation of Lo's criticisms of Wang was reevaluated as above, then Lo's system, upon which he based his criticisms of Wang, will be clear to us. It may be called a system of objective rationalism. The nature of mind, as rational principle, is not merely immanent in our particular mind, but it is a universal principle transcending mind and existing in the myriad things of the objective world as well, and hence is different from the meaning of mind as such. Therefore, the person who wants to realize his nature as the principle must pass beyond his mind to investigate the principle of the universe of things as the different expressions of the one great principle of the universe. Consequently, it is no wonder that he criticizes Wang's theory of *ke-wu*, or realization of *liang-chih*, as knowing only the subjective mind without knowing the objective nature, or *li*, or principle of the mind.

Nevertheless, Lo's criticisms based on his objective rationalism are still external to Wang's teachings. Faced with such a criticism, Wang Yang-ming could well rejoin that nature and mind are existentially one. Nature as principle is the very moral principle in the expression of *liang-chih* as the conscient consciousness or the original moral mind. In the process of expressing *liang-chih*, the so-called objective things and their objective principles are known by *liang-chih* as immanent in the mind, constituting also the subjective principles or nature of *liang-chih* expressed from within. Even if we say that the principle is universal and existing in other entities and that it is transcendental to our empirical mind, it-may not be transcendental to *liang-chih* as the self-transcending consciousness which goes to infinity, or the very transcendental consciousness which knows that there is the transcendent. The transcendent as known may exist immanently in the very transcendental knowing as a function which originated from our mind or *liang-chih*. Wang Yang-ming did not exactly say this, but my explanations are in accord with his teachings.

However, Lo's criticisms are important in philosophy because he called attention to a certain horizontal point of view that places the principles of our mind and of other things on an equal footing, and recovered Chu Hsi's teaching that our mind has to be outwardly and forwardly oriented to investigate the principles of things for the very purpose of realizing our nature, inwardly and backwardly. This is different from Wang's vertical point of view, which always places the mind, or *liang-chih*, as existing on a higher level, above the objective things seen through the outward and forward orientation of the mind. The horizontal and vertical points of view belong to different dimensions of philosophical thought, and one could never conquer the other in an ultimate sense. Hence, Wang's teachings were not defeated by Lo's criticisms, and Lo's type of criticism was also destined to rise again in the later criticisms of Wang Yang-ming's teachings.

Lo's criticism of Wang is also important because he raised the problem of the relationship between nature and the mind. Though Lo's discussions of the problem may not be sufficient to convince Wang Yang-ming, yet this problem has its deeper side if it is discussed along the line of development of the very teachings of Wang. Looking into the deeper side, the nature and mind also may not be thought of merely as existentially identical, a problem I shall discuss later.

VI. NIEH SHANG-CHIANG'S "BACK TO TRANQUILLITY" AND
WANG LUNG-CHI'S TWO KINDS OF LEARNING

Of the four types of criticisms mentioned earlier, the first two were merely external criticisms because they did not address themselves to the problems within Wang's teachings. The next two may be taken as internal criticisms because they were concerned with problems central to Wang's teachings and were intended to point out some intrinsic inconsistency or insufficiency in Wang's thought. Yet, their criticisms, based as they are on other traditions of Confucianism and other philosophical standpoints, and lacking an adequate understanding of Wang's position, are still external criticisms. Their criticisms made the different standpoints sharper, but they were unable to shake the standpoint of Wang Yang-ming. However, the implicit and explicit criticisms of Wang from within his own school were quite another matter. They emerged from certain doubts about the self-sufficiency of Wang's teachings.

The criticisms from within Wang's school may be taken as actual internal criticisms. From among the disciples of Wang, Ch'ien Hsü-shan and Chou Tung-kuo were the most faithful to Wang's teachings and were taken by some scholars as the real heirs of Wang Yang-ming. But I shall not talk about them here, rather, I shall concentrate on the disciples of Wang Yang-ming who doubted the self-sufficiency of his teachings. I shall mention first the scholars of the Chiang-yu school. The eminent scholars of this school, such as Nieh Shuang-chiang and Lo Nien-an, were not Wang's disciples while Wang was living, but became his avowed disciples after he died. They never questioned the ontological identity of mind or *liang-chih* and its nature, or principle, as Wang taught, but they doubted that the way for the realization of *liang-chih*, as taught by Wang, was sufficient.[22] Nieh proposed "back to tranquillity" as the way for the revelation of *liang-chih*. This stems from his suspicion of the doctrine that the *liang-chih*, as the ontological reality, is really expressed in our present expressions of mind. Wang had taught that *liang-chih* is revealed in the continuous process of our life, and also that our *liang-chih* may be obscured and perverted by our selfish desires. Yet, Wang thought that the remedy for these defects is rightly the further clearer expressions of the *liang-chih* in our mind. Nevertheless, in the continuous process of the expressions of our mind, there seems to be no stopping point. If the present expressions of mind may not be the expressions of *liang-chih* as it is, we have then no a priori guarantee that the same would not be true of the future expressions of the mind as well. This is a delicate and serious problem. In view of this, Lo Nien-an commented that Wang's learnings still have not attained the ultimate stage.[23] Therefore, Nieh proposed the teaching "back to tranquillity," approved by Lo, to supplement Wang's teaching. This contained an implicit criticism of Wang's teachings also.

The "back to tranquillity" means that "if the present expressions of mind may not be the expression of *liang-chih* as it was, then we should have to

22 *Ming-ju-hsüeh-an*, vol. 18, p. 19. Lo Nien-an said to Wang Lung-ch'i that Wang Yang-ming's learning is surely the learning to be the sage, yet still had not attained the ultimate stage.
23 Consult my article, "The Development of the Concept of Moral Mind from Wang Yang-ming to Wang Ch'i," in William T. De Bary, ed., *Self and Society in Ming Thought* (New York: Columbia University Press, 1970), pp. 108–117.

transcend such expressions and let our mind return to a state of absolute tranquillity, so that in this state our *liang-chih*, as an ontological reality, shall be revealed and its light shine forth." This is a simple explanation of Nieh's proposal, which Lo approved. I shall not go into greater detail about the depth and profundity of their thoughts and the subtle differences between them. However, in discussions with Nieh and Lo on the doctrine of "back to tranquillity," Wang Lung-ch'i of the Che-tung school criticized it as indicating a certain lack of faith in the self, concerning the existence of *liang-chih*. If we had enough self-faith, we would know that the *liang-chih*, as an ontological reality, is like the sun, always shining forth. *Liang-chih*, as an ontological reality, should not be thought of as separated from its expressions, which are its functions. Thus, we have to know *liang-chih* through its present expressions, and we need not turn around from its present expressions to go back to a state of tranquillity for revealing its hidden reality. This is not the direct way for the realization of *liang-chih*. Wang Lung-ch'i is very lofty and brilliant in his discussions with Nieh and Lo, but I shall not discuss him here. I do not consider the controversy between Nieh and Lo and Wang Lung-ch'i to be a very serious one. In the present expressions of mind, there is some expression of *liang-chih* and also expressions of the other elements of mind, such as selfish desires, various purposeless ideas, habitual tendencies, and so on. Therefore, if we dislike the present expressions of mind, then going back to tranquillity to purify our mind would be quite right and proper. Thus, Nieh and Lo were correct. In the first stage of his teachings, Wang Yang-ming had also taught his disciples to practice quiet sitting for the same purpose. On the other hand, if we are conscious that there is a certain expression of *liang-chih* in our mind even when that expression is obscured and perverted, we can still be self-conscious of it, we can like it, extend it, and take actions in conformity with it, establishing our self-faith in this existence of *liang-chih*. Hence Wang Lung-ch'i was right also.

However, I wish to say further that the very decision of liking or disliking the present expressions of the mind all originate from *liang-chih*, as Wang already had taught. Hence, either the decision to "go back to tranquillity" as Nieh and Lo thought or the decision to have full self-consciousness and self-faith in the present expressions and existence of *liang-chih*, as Wang Lung-ch'i taught, may all spring from *liang-chih* itself. In my personal opinion, this is a way to reconcile Wang Lung-ch'i's view and Nieh-Lo's views within the teachings of Wang Yang-ming.

Wang Lung-ch'i had some further thoughts about *liang-chih*. He classified the learnings for the realization of *liang-chih* into two kinds.[24] One is called "making the will authentic or sincere," the other is "putting the mind itself right in its place." The former is closer to Wang Yang-ming's usual teaching.

---

[24] As to the learning of Wang I-an, consult *Ming-ju-hsüeh-an*, vol. 32, pp. 16–25, as to the sentence quoted in volume 32, p. 19.

It means that when we know what is good and evil and when we like the good and dislike the evil, the liking and disliking should be authentic without reserve, and then the moral will become genuine or sincere to the fullest extent. "Putting the mind right in its place" means something deeper and was taken by Wang Lung-ch'i to be a higher type of learning. Here the mind itself was taken, by Wang Lung-ch'i, as a pure superconsciousness which is beyond the ordinary moral consciousness which knows good or evil and has the will to do the good or to undo the evil. For Wang Lung-ch'i, even the will to do the good or to undo the evil still belongs to the sphere of will in our ordinary moral consciousness. Yet the mind itself is just a pure superconsciousness above the sphere of will, which goes beyond any ordinary good will or evil will and also any ordinary moral will, which can do the good and undo the evil. To be conscious of the mind as a pure superconsciousness beyond good and evil and to keep its purity and superiority as a pure knowing, without any attachment to anything known as good and evil, is called "putting the mind in its right place." In this case, the mind, as pure knowing, is always void, transparent, and shines forth its light. It is also the state of the utmost good of our mind and is the reality of *liang-chih* fully realized. According to Wang Lung-ch'i, it is a state of mind which is aspired to also by Buddhists and Taoists. Thus the teaching of *liang-chih* became a teaching which Buddhism and Taoism are also based on. Since Wang Yang-ming had sometimes said that when the reality of *liang-chih* is fully realized, it is in a state of no good and no evil and is also the utmost good, and that *liang-chih*, as void or empty, is no less void or empty than what the Buddhist or Taoist talked about. Wang Lung-ch'i's thought should be taken as inherited from Wang Yang-ming. However, Wang Yang-ming did not say explicitly that there are two kinds of learning, one concerning ordinary moral will and consciousness and the other, which is above ordinary moral will and consciousness. Wang's talks with Wang Lung-ch'i and Chien Shu-shan, about his two ways of teaching, did not necessarily imply that there are two kinds of learnings. Wang Lung-ch'i claimed that there are two kinds of learnings and said that the "putting the mind in its right place" where man has no ordinary moral will and consciousness, as the higher kind of learning where Confucianism, Buddhism, and Taoism meet, was plainly a further development of Wang Yang-ming's thought and emerged from his implicit dissatisfaction or implicit criticism of Wang Yang-ming's teaching.

VII. WANG I-AN'S THOUGHT ABOUT THE WILL AS A
    DIRECTIVE PRINCIPLE OF MORAL MIND TO SUPPLEMENT
    WANG YANG-MING'S TEACHINGS

Besides the Che-tung school and the Chiang-yu school, there was the T'ai-chou school, which was the most influential of all the schools of Wang's disciples. The founder of this school was Wang Hsin-ts'ai who had taught and practiced Confucian teaching before he met Wang Yang-ming and who argued with Wang Yang-ming at their first meeting. Although Wang Hsin-ts'ai submitted himself to be Wang Yang-ming's disciple, he insisted upon his theory of *kc-wu*, which was quite different from Wang Yang-ming's. This is proof that he was still dissatisfied with some elements of Wang Yang-ming's teaching.

In the following, I shall not discuss such other thinkers of the T'ai-chou school as Lo Chin-ch'i and Li Ch'o-wu, and I shall not discuss whether they were on the same line of thought as Wang Yang-ming. Instead, I will bring up Wang I-an, who said explicitly that the teaching of *ke-wu* or the "investigation of things," and the teaching of *ch'eng-yi* or "making the will authentic," should be combined with Wang Yang-ming's teaching about the realization of *liang-chih*. Wang Yang-ming's idea of will was then reexamined and clearly defined by him, and this is actually a supplement and a further development of Wang Yang-ming's thought. Wang I-an's emphasis on the will is also a reversal of Wang Lung-ch'i's underestimation of will.

In Wang I-an's thought, the will should be regarded as a directive principle of the knowing mind. He said that the mind as knowing is void, transparent, and also responsive. Yet, the will, as immanently contained in the mind, has its definite direction.[25] His thought may be taken as being derived from Wang Yang-ming's thought about the "liking good and disliking evil," which are the moments of feeling, or will, or *liang-chih*. The "liking good" is directed to the good and the "disliking evil" is directed to the good, too. Hence both the "liking good" and the "disliking evil" have the same definite direction. Yet Wang I-an did not merely consider the will as a moment of *liang-chih*. It is the directive principle of *liang-chih* as knowing. Wang I-an knew, also as did Wang Lung-ch'i, that the mind or *liang-chih* as pure knowing may exist in a state which is void and transparent, in which nothing is known even without any motivative idea or will, either good or evil. Yet, Wang I-an said that even in this state, as the mind is responsive also, there is the self-creating of the mind, or *liang-chih* as pure knowing. The self-creating is the very intention or will immanent within the mind, or *liang-chih* as pure knowing.

For the full understanding about Wang I-an's thought of the will, we have to remember that Wang I-an had the teaching of the T'ai-chou school as his background. As I said before, Wang Hsin-ts'ai, the founder of the T'ai-chou school never adopted the theory of *ke-wu* as taught by Wang Yang-ming. *Wu*, for Wang Hsin-ts'ai, includes one's self, one's family, one's country, and the world under Heaven, as objective things. *Ke-wu* means for him to will the peace and happiness of oneself, of family, of the country, and of the world, for the realization of the utmost good. Hence, in Wang I-an's thought, the

---

[25] As to the learning of Wang T'ang-nan, consult *Ming-ju-hsüch-an*, vol. 5.

will as the directive principle of mind is immanent within the mind or *liang-chih*, on the one hand, and is also immanent in all the responsive activities of our mind and body to the objective things and to the realization of the "utmost good," on the other hand. Hence it is like a horizontal axis of our moral life from the inward mind to the outward things, and also like a vertical axis from the upward mind to the downward things.

Wang I-an's discussion of the will was intended to supplement the teachings of Wang Yang-ming. Of course, Wang Yang-ming had emphasized "making the will authentic." But as Wang did not differentiate this from "realization of *liang-chih*," there was a certain ambiguity in his understanding of the will. When Wang Yang-ming talked about "making the will authentic," the will meant a transcendental moral will, which likes good and dislikes evil, existing in a higher level above the ordinary empirical will or motivated ideas, which may be either good or evil. Yet, in Wang Yang-ming's famous "Four-sentence Teaching," where he stated that "sometimes good and sometimes evil is the movement of the will," it is plain that this will is just the ordinary empirical will or motivated ideas. This ambiguity of "will" is a serious defect in Wang's teaching, indicating that Wang did not have a profound and definite understanding of the moral will of a higher level than that of the ordinary empirical will. When Wang Lung-ch'i later taught that the will has to be transcended, in his teaching of "putting the mind in the right place," the word "will" also meant primarily the empirical will which is sometimes good and sometimes evil. For these kinds of will, Wang Lung-ch'i may be quite right in saying that they must be transcended or even banished from the mind. Still, as the moral will is on a higher level, there seems to be no reason to banish it from the mind, and it is very doubtful also that it can be transcended on the way to one's becoming a sage. If it is transcended as the ordinary will is, then the moral consciousness and the moral life may be wholly corrupted, and man will fall down to a level of moral indifference as a first step, letting immoral actions go freely, leading himself ultimately to immoral being. So, the consequences of this ambiguity in the meaning of "will" in Wang Yang-ming is very serious. It is Wang I-an who elucidated the meaning of the will and used it to denote the principle within the mind, which is directed to the good or utmost good only. It is then a pure moral will, transcendental to the ordinary empirical will, and nothing else. Wang I-an's insistence on the "will as directed to the good only" is to save the idea of the "will" and the idea of the "good" as well. When Wang Lung-ch'i taught that our will may be good or evil and has to be transcended, he also taught that the idea of good and evil has to be transcended also, stressing the state of mind which is beyond good and evil as the highest state of mind, which he considered to be the highest good. Of course, when Wang Lung-ch'i talked about the utmost good, he still did not forget the idea of good. However, the term "utmost good" may be taken as an attributive term. What is attributed to is a state of mind, which is beyond good and evil. This state of mind itself may be nothing other than a supermoral state of mind, and then can be criticized as nonmoral, and its conceived neutrality may lead men to be immoral also.

VIII. WANG T'ANG-NAN'S THOUGHTS ABOUT THE PRE-HEAVEN NATURE AND ITS RELATION TO PURE KNOWING AND "CONSTANT WILL"

Wang I-an's thoughts about the ideas of "will" and "good" are all very important, both historically and philosophically, yet his sayings were not very elaborate. The relation of his will with the other aspects of mind was left unclear. It was Wang T'ang-nan of the Chiang-yu school who presented the will as the directive principle of our present mind, originating from the nature of the mind, and connected it with the other aspects of the mind, carrying the "learning of will" of Wang I-an further. This development also opened the way for later criticisms of Wang Yang-ming.

Wang T'ang-nan,[20] very much like Wang I-an, viewed the will as always existing in our mind. But it was taken by him to be the silent, self-constant-knowing of the mind with its constant creativity. As such, the will neither rests nor moves, neither rises nor falls. What rests and falls or moves and rises successively is called *nien*. The ordinary empirical will or motivated idea, which continuously moves and rests or rises and falls in our mind, was downgraded by him to *nien*, which, as attached to definite things, is merely certain solidified or dissipated expressions of will in a lower level of the mind. Hence, there are two distinct terms to differentiate the two types of will in Wang T'ang-nan's thought, and only the will which exists above the empirical will be called "will." Thus, the ambiguity of meaning of the word "will" in Wang Yang-ming's thought was definitely removed, and the underestimation of will by Wang Lung-ch'i remedied.

Wang T'ang-nan also connected the idea of the will with the idea of nature. The meaning of nature was not thought of by him to be merely identical with the idea of mind's knowing or willing. There are some subtle differences between them. Wang T'ang-nan sometimes sighed that the "learning of nature" was lost. He thought of Nature as the source of the revealed creativity of the mind. Nature as source is thus transcendent and different from what flows from it. Lo Cheng-an's thesis of the difference of mind and nature seems to be restated now in a new form with a deeper significance. Wang T'ang-nan said sometimes that nature is the "pre-Heavenly" and could not

[20] As to the learning of Li Chien-lo, consult *Ming-ju-hsüeh-an*, vol. 31.

even be talked about. As I understand it, "nature" for Wang T'ang-nan has to be understood primarily as a name to point out that the present mind and its constant knowing and willing has its transcendental source, which is not given. The mind's knowing, as originating from its source, is the son of the pre-Heaven, and mother of what follows as post-Heaven. This means that the mind's knowing is the primary connecting link between the pre-Heavenly nature and what flows from the knowing is post-Heavenly—the will with its solidification as *nien*. Thus, the will as constant-knowing, with its constant creativity, is directly originated from and expressing its source or nature, as transcendent. Hence, nature has to be posited as transcendent on the one hand, and has to be thought of as immanently expressed in the very constant-knowing and willing of the mind on the other hand. Thus there is an identity in difference between nature and the mind's will. Nature as the source of the mind's will should not be understood merely as a totality of objective principles or as one great principle of the universe with its differentiations into secondary principles, as Lo Cheng-an thought. Nature as the source is nothing less in content than the mind, which constantly knows all objective principles. Hence, the source is not merely the source of the objective principles known, but mainly the source of the mind's constant knowing or willing as pure subjectivity. If such a source has to be thought of as a principle, or as consisting of a principle, then the "*hsü erh sheng*," or the "creativity in the vacuum" is transcendent because it is the source of the constant expressed-knowing of the mind which springs constantly from the vacuum. Yet, it is immanently expressed in the mind's expressed and constant-knowing as the expressed will of the mind. The constant creativity in constant-knowing or willing of the mind is also called the "constant creativity" of "spirituality as function of nature."

From what has been said earlier, Wang T'ang-nan criticized Wang I-an's thought as being inadequate. When Wang I-an talked about the will as master of the mind, he seems to suppose that the mind is not its own master and depends upon the will to be its master. The truth is that the nature or the very creativity in vacuum expressed in the mind's constant-knowing, which masters the *nien*, or the empirical motivated ideas, is the very will. Thus we may more adequately know the relation of the will of the mind and the nature.

In Wang I-an's thought, the will is taken as having its direction toward the utmost good. Wang T'ang-nan said also that the good is originated from the nature of mind. They all wanted to save the idea of the good and oppose Wang Lung-chi's theory of beyond good and evil. I would like to say that anyone who really understood the moral will as directive must want to save the idea of the good. It may be true that when an ideal or a good is realized, then we may pass beyond the ideal as ideal and the good as good. But the ideals and goods of man and of the universe could never be fully realized, then the "idea of an ideal" and "idea of the good" can never be transcended. As the constant creativity of the mind expressed in the will is infinite and directed to the infinite good, we can never pass beyond the infinite creativity and infinite good to attain the state of beyond good and evil. Hence, the nature of mind as the source of the will cannot be thought of as beyond good either. Therefore, the thought of Wang Yang-ming and Wang Lung-ch'i that the reality or nature of mind is beyond good and evil, though attractive, is still inadequate to the nature of mind with its will.

IX. THE GENERAL TRENDS OF THOUGHT TO SAVE THE IDEA OF
     WILL AND GOOD IN CONFUCIAN SCHOOLS OF THE LATE MING

After Wang T'ang-nan, there came a thinker Li Chien-lo,[27] a disciple of Tsou Tung-kuo of the Chiang-yu school, who criticized Wang Yang-ming's teachings frankly. He said that the only good can be our goal or the end of our moral teachings, and *chih* or knowing can never be this. Since Wang Yang-ming's *liang-chih* was called *chih*, Li proposed the teaching of *chih-hsiu* to replace Wang's teachings of the realization of *liang-chih*. In *chih-hsiu*, *chih* means "to attain and to abide in the good" while *hsiu* means "cultivation of the good virtue." The influence of his criticisms of Wang Yang-ming's teachings was very wide in the academic sphere of the Late Ming.

When Wang Yang-ming died, his school was divided into six schools, as Huang Tsung-hsi said, of which Che-tung, Chiang-yu, and T'ai-chou were the most influential. I have said earlier that there were implicit criticisms of Wang's teachings raised by Nieh Hsuang-chiang of the Chiang-yu school, Wang Lung-ch'i of the Che-tung school, and Wang Hsin-tsai of T'ai-chou school. Later, there came Wang I-an of T'ai-chou school, and Wang T'ang-nan of the Chiang-yu school, who proposed the theory of will to supplement Wang's teachings. At the end came Li Chien-lo, of the Chiang-yu school, who proposed the *chih-hsiu* to replace Wang's teachings on the realization of *liang-chih*. In the final period of the Ming dynasty, Chou Hai-men still insisted on Wang's theory that "beyond good and evil" is the utmost good, but Hsu Ching-an, a second-generation follower of the Chan Kan-ch'üan school raised ten objections to attack Chou's thought. Feng Shao-shu, another scholar of the Chan Kan-ch'üan school, said also that the central idea of Confucianism is the "idea of good" in contrast with the "beyond good" of Buddhism.[28] Hsu and Feng revived Chan Kan-ch'üan's idea of nature as good, though Chan himself did not emphasize this. During the same period, the

---

[27] *Ming-ju-hsüeh-an*, vol. 41, p. 8.
[28] *Ming-ju-hsüeh-an*, vol. 58, p. 11.

learning of the Tung-ling school was rising. One of the founders of the Tung-ling school is Ku Ching-yang, who wrote a book called *Chen-hsing pien* [An Essay on the Awakening of Nature]. In this book he concentrated his attack on Wang's theory that nature is beyond good and evil, and even said that the reason this theory was flourishing is because the theory is affiliated with "the great way of the gentleman while also satisfying the selfish desires of bad men who want to find some excuse for their actions." The excuse comes from the fact that if man's nature is beyond good and evil, and all good and evil has to be transcended in the end, then the good is not good and the evil not really evil, therefore, all the evil can be done without shame.

Next to Ku there was Kao Ching-yi of the Tung-ling school who also insisted upon the good of nature. Kao revived the "learning of nature" (as good) and the teaching of *ke-wu* along the line of Chu Hsi, without contradicting the thesis that the mind and the principle of things are not separated. A friend of Kao's was Liu Chi-shan, who was a disciple of Hsu Ching-an and who was influenced by Li Chien-lo. Liu emphasized the idea of good and the "learning of nature" as connected with the "learning to make the will authentic," the idea of *ching*, or reverence as taught by Chu Hsi and Chan Kan-ch'üan. Liu's thought may be taken as a last synthesis of Neo-Confucianism in late Ming. Because I have talked about Ku, Kao, and Liu's criticisms of Wang's teachings elsewhere, I shall not repeat my opinions here.

Compared with the criticisms of Wang's teachings by his contemporaries from other traditions of Confucianism, which I have already discussed, the criticisms of Wang by scholars of his own school, by scholars of the Chan Kan-ch'üan school, and Tung-ling school, and by Liu Chi-shan, are much deeper and are internal to Wang's teachings. Their criticisms of Wang's teachings produced certain positive results to supplement what was lacking in Wang's system and ended in Liu's grand synthesis of Neo-Confucianism in the late Ming.

10   *Liu Tsung-chou's* [b] *Doctrine of*

Moral Mind and Practice and His Critique of

Wang Yang-ming [c]

In early seventeenth-century China, at the end of the Ming dynasty, there were various criticisms of the thought of Wang Yang-ming and his school. The winds of learning had still not turned "back to Han dynasty learning" and away from "Sung-Ming learning," as many scholars of the Ch'ing dynasty would later insist. Such eminent scholars as Wang Fu-chih,[d] who revived the teachings of Chang Tsai,[e] and Ku Yen-wu,[f] who was actually a descendant of the Chu Hsi school, were just at the stage of turning "back to Sung dynasty learning." However, the most important criticism of Wang Yang-ming's thought came from developments within the Wang Yang-ming school itself.

The thought of the Tung-lin school [g] and of Liu Tsung-chou originated from the teachings of Wang Yang-ming and other thinkers of the Ming dynasty. Their criticisms of Wang Yang-ming and his school may be taken as the inner criticism of developments within the school, and as one turning point in the intellectual history of the last period of the Ming dynasty. Compared with the Tung-lin school's criticism of Wang's thought, Liu's criticism was deeper and more constructive. Nevertheless, they were all concerned with the central problem of man's inner moral life and found something ambiguous and suspect in Wang Yang-ming's thought, especially as it was developed by Wang Chi [h] of the Che-tung school [i] and by thinkers of the T'ai-chou school.[j]

Wang Chi, like thinkers of the Chiang-yu school,[k] considered *liang-chih* [l] as an ontological reality. Yet the Chiang-yu school thought of *liang-chih* itself as a substance which was a quiet and tranquil reality beyond its function, more like a metaphysical being. Wang Chi never separated the substance and function of *liang-chih*; he thought the substance and reality were wholly immanent in its function. To him, *liang-*

chih, as the function of a pure knowing which is also pure substance, transcended ordinary empirical good and evil. It was beyond good and evil, and thus absolutely good. Surely this type of thinking is subtle and profound, yet it is also most dangerous in the ordinary ethical sense. Because if the absolute good is beyond good and evil, then how is it differentiated from the no-good of ordinary life? Every man can make an excuse and persuade himself that his no-good is the absolute good and his evil is no-evil as well.

The idea of beyond good and evil was also propounded by later thinkers such as Chou Ju-teng [m] of the T'ai-chou school. In the T'ai-chou school, the idea of "natural life" or "cosmic life" was stressed, as in the thought of Wang Ken,[n] the founder of this school, and of Lo Ju-fang,[o] his eminent successor. In the T'ai-chou school, man's spiritual or moral life is rooted and embodied in the natural life. The idea of natural life as such may also be taken as beyond any ethical ideas of "good" or "evil." In this school, the realization of *liang-chih* or the practice of morality is coextensive with man's natural life or ordinary life. Thus any type of human life could be pervaded with the light of *liang-chih* and could become an embodiment of it. Therefore the scholars of the T'ai-chou school could take up any profession in the community and engage in any form of action with a sense of moral enterprise or moral heroism. The type of personality developed in this school is usually not classical, as with traditional Confucianists, but more chivalrous and romantic.

T'ai-chou teachings spread rapidly among laymen and ordinary people. The disciples of the school, who took morality as existing in any kind of life, looked upon its practice as an easy thing. They did not realize how serious it was, or how morality can be perverted by personal emotions and desires.

In opposition to them, the Tung-lin school thinkers and Liu were classical Confucianists who took the practice of morality seriously. Their central philosophical ideas of morality stressed the ideas of goodness, moral reason, and moral will in the ethical sense. These ideas were differentiated from Wang Chi's ontological ideas of *liang-chih* on the one hand, and from the T'ai-chou school's cosmological idea of life on the other hand. Tung-lin school thinkers and Liu admired man's sacrifice of the natural life for the dignity of his moral reason and moral will, with a sense of the realization of good as good. As a result of their learning and teaching, there were many more from the Tung-lin school who were martyred in their political struggles with powerful men in the government, and Liu himself committed suicide by fasting for twenty-one days when the Ming dynasty collapsed.

Their actions of self-sacrifice are the everlasting glories of Confucianism in the late Ming. Yet in the following sections I shall limit my discussion to the philosophical idea of good as the thinkers of the Tung-lin school stressed it, and to their criticism of Wang Yang-ming on this point. This discussion will serve as an introduction to Liu's ideas of moral will and to his own criticism of Wang Yang-ming, which were more profound even than the Tung-lin.

THE TUNG-LIN SCHOOL'S CRITICISM OF WANG YANG-MING AS A PREFACE TO LIU TSUNG-CHOU'S CRITICISM OF WANG YANG-MING

The ideas of good as propounded in the Tung-lin school by Ku Hsien-ch'eng [p] and Kao P'an-lung [q] were centered on the "priority of goodness" over Wang Yang-ming's "liang-chih as pure knowing." Surely Wang's liang-chih, which is an original-conscientious-consciousness that knows what is good and evil, also likes what is good and dislikes what is evil, and can do what is good and avoid what is evil. It is not merely a theoretical consciousness but a moral consciousness or moral mind. However, when Wang Yang-ming talked about the substance of this consciousness or mind, he pointed out that the substance of mind is beyond good and evil.

I have explained elsewhere what he means: that when evil is avoided, no evil remains; when good is done, one passes beyond anything good as well and one does not look upon himself as good. Therefore, the substance of mind or liang-chih as the origin of man's capacity for passing through evil and good should be seen as a pure knowing which is beyond good and evil.[1] In Wang Chi's thought, the idea of liang-chih as pure knowing, which is ontologically beyond good and evil, was developed to the extreme. It was itself both the function and substance of original mind. It was like a pure light which is also void; thus it is both being and nonbeing. It is serene and quiet, as a mirror; yet when it is active, it is responsive to things without attachment. Hence it is not attached to the goodness of the responsive action, either inner or outer. The sage, whose *liang-chih* is fully realized, responds to everything in the right way and his responsive action is always good. However, as the sage never attaches to the goodness of his action, his mind as the full realization of his *liang-chih* is in a state beyond good as well as beyond evil. He also realizes that *liang-chih* itself is beyond good and evil. All good actions, inner or outer, are just out-flowings from *liang-chih*, like reflections of the moon in the water, or the trail of a bird's flight in an empty sky.[2] It is full of light and also void; it is both being and nonbeing.

Surely Wang Chi's-development of the idea of "beyond good and evil" in Wang Yang-ming came from a very lofty ontological vision. Such a vision is attainable when man's mind reaches transcendent heights, and man should have this vision, at least in certain stages of the development of his spiritual life or moral life. However, if we say that we should have such a vision or we should have such a state of mind, we already presuppose such a state of mind as "good"—because whatever should be, or ought to be, is always looked upon as good. A state of mind which is beyond good and evil must be considered as good. Here the idea of good is predicative of the "state beyond good and evil" as its subject. The predicate "good" goes beyond even this "state" as well. Here the priority of the idea of good comes in, as it does in the criticism by the Tung-lin school of the idea of "beyond good and evil."

The writings of Tung-lin thinkers who criticize the idea of "beyond good and evil" are numerous. In connection with what has been said above, I shall quote one paragraph from Ku Hsien-ch'eng's writing:

What modern men are talking about when they speak of "beyond good and evil" . . . just means that man in his moral life should not be attached to whatever is good. . . . One says that the substance or reality of the nature of mind is itself void, luminous (full of light), transparent, serene and tranquil . . . and therefore the word good is not sufficient to describe the reality of the nature of mind. However, to my way of thinking, the good is the name of ten thousand virtues (of the mind). Voidness, luminosity, transparency, serenity, and tranquility (of mind) are each a special name of a special virtue which is good.[3]

Here Ku's criticism of the idea of "beyond good and evil" is most penetrating. It means that when we say that the reality of the nature of mind is void or luminous, and so on, and that one should realize the reality of the nature of mind as Wang Yang-ming and Wang Chi have taught it, we presuppose that one's nature and the virtues are already good. Thus if the reality of the nature of mind can be thought of as void or luminous, it has to be thought of as good as well. It is then impossible for us to escape the term "good" when we think about the reality of the nature of mind. So Ku said that good is the original color of mind itself.[4] This means that the mind always tends to be good and thus to be good is the original nature of mind or the reality of the nature of mind.

In the above paragraph by Ku, the sentence "the good is the name of ten thousand virtues, and voidness, transparency . . . are each a special name of a special virtue" is most significant. It means that there are many other virtues of mind besides voidness and transparency, and that there are other sides of the mind's nature which, when realized, become man's virtues as well.

What are the other virtues? Some are, for example, filial piety to parents, loyalty to country, duty to the community, and responsibility to the age and to historical and cultural heritage. In the same essay, Ku related a story of Wang Yang-ming, in which Wang said frankly that it was impossible for him to detach himself from his parents when he was affected by the feeling of filial piety. Ku said that this is proof that detachment of mind, and such virtues as voidness, transparency, and serenity, which originate from detachment of mind, are not the only virtues, and that there are ten thousand other virtues which are good as well. Thus the idea of good has a much wider connotation than just the ideas of voidness, transparency, and serenity of mind, and the idea of good is also logically prior to them.

The priority of the idea of good is insisted upon by the thinkers of the Tung-lin school, but from the ethical point of view. It is quite different from Wang Chi's thought, which insists from an ontological point of view on the priority of *liang-chih* as pure knowing that transcends the ideas of ordinary good and evil.

The priority of the idea of good as insisted upon by the Tung-lin school is different also from the priority of the idea of natural life or cosmic life as emphasized by the T'ai-chou school from the cosmological point of view. When thinkers of the T'ai-chou school talk about the coextensiveness of morality with the natural or cosmic life, they surely make morality more active and alive. However, when morality is submerged into the exuberance of natural life, there is a danger of its losing itself.

The sense of morality should be a sense of "being a master of the flowing of natural life" as well. Man has to "stand still on the good" amidst the flowing life in order to have a genuine ethical life. Therefore, thinkers of the Tung-lin school used the term *chih-shan*,[r] which means "to stand still on the good," to differentiate their teaching from both the T'ai-chou school and Wang Chi's teaching. The term originated with the Great Learning (*Ta-hsüeh*).[s] The importance of *chih-shan* was also propounded by Li Ts'ai (Chien-lo),[t] who saw the same defects in Wang Yang-ming's thought. However, it was through the thinkers of the Tung-lin school that it became a more popular slogan.

What does it mean, "to stand still on the good"? In the Great Learning it means to stand still on the ultimate good in special existential situations with other men, as filial piety is an ultimate good when one is in an existential situation with one's parents. Life flows from one occasion to another, yet each is special and definite. What is good for any definite occasion is also definitely good. There may not be an ultimate good in the flowing of life as a whole, yet there is ultimate good in any definite occasion of life for the realization of the reality of the nature of mind. Though the occasions are relative and temporal, this realization has its absolute and eternal significance for man's becoming a sage, and it is good. Thus the good is connected with the nature of our mind on one side, and with the objective occasions of life on the other. Hence the thought of the Wang Yang-ming school—which took the good as belonging just to the mind—should be supplemented by the Ch'eng-Chu school idea of moral reason, that the good is "whatever things should be" and belongs to things as well.[s] This way of thinking actually aims at a synthesis of the Wang Yang-ming and the Ch'eng-Chu schools.

THE IDEA OF MORAL WILL AS IMPLICITLY PRESUPPOSED IN WANG YANG-MING'S THOUGHT AND THE AMBIGUITY OF WANG'S IDEA OF WILL

In comparison with the Tung-lin school, Liu Tsung-chou opposed the "idea of beyond good and evil," and emphasized "mastering the natural life" and "standing still on the good," as Tung-lin thinkers did. Yet Liu Tsung-chou went a step further to center his criticism of Wang Yang-ming and his school on the "nature of mind revealed through the will in connection with the idea of good." In the Tung-lin school, the idea of good was sometimes taken as being prior even to the nature of mind.[6] As the good is what a man is striving to be, it is an ideal the mind knows and aspires to realize; thus it may be described as prior to the *nature* of the mind which merely knows the mind's ideal and does not aspire to realize it. Yet if the mind's nature consists not essentially in "knowing the good as ideal," but in "willing to realize the good and to be good," then "the good and to be good" must be immanent in the willing itself, and the good should not be taken as prior to the mind's nature as will. Liu Tsung-chou saw the mind's nature as essentially a good will, and his idea of good was combined with his idea of will. "To stand still on the good" was for him nothing more than the "self-sustaining of good will."

The importance of will had been proposed by Wang Tung,[u] a thinker of the T'ai-chou school, and Wang Shih-huai (T'ang-nan),[v] of the Chiang-yu school, before Liu propounded it. Wang Tung had said that "the mind as knowing is void, luminous, and sensitive," and that "the will is that which has orientation and is contained therein." [7] Wang Shih-huai said that the constant creativity of spirit in its secrecy is called the will.[8] The will is different from *nien*,[w] or volitional ideas. These sayings anticipated Liu's thought of will. We may say that Liu's idea of will has also been implicitly presupposed in Wang Yang-ming's theory of *liang-chih* as conscientious consciousness, something above our ordinary will which consists just of volitional ideas. In our ordinary will, some ideas are good or right and some are evil or wrong. Yet *liang-chih* as a conscientious consciousness knows what is good, and favors or likes and does it; it knows what is evil, and disfavors or dislikes it and avoids it. It is of course transcendental to the ordinary will, stands above its goodness or evil, and may be taken as "beyond good and evil."

However, when Wang says that *liang-chih* always favors or likes the good and disfavors or dislikes the evil, simultaneously with its knowing good and evil, and passes on to doing the good and avoiding the evil, then *liang-chih* is not merely cognitive but also affective. It is not merely a knowing, but also a feeling and a will which tends to do the good only and to avoid the evil. The avoiding of evil is also good. Thus *liang-chih* as will is an absolute good and transcends the ordinary good and evil, willing or volitional ideas. Because *liang-chih* as will is inseparable from its knowing, and its will is absolute good, its knowing is also absolute good. Therefore the idea of will as an absolute good is implicitly presupposed in Wang Yang-ming's thought. Hence Liu Tsung-chou's thought may be taken as a development of Wang Yang-ming's, which makes explicit what is implicit in Wang's thought and so completes Wang's teaching. This is the reason, I think, that Huang Tsung-hsi,[x] who admired both his master, Liu, and Wang Yang-ming, did not think there was any fundamental incompatibility between them.

However, though the idea of will, as Liu propounded it, may be taken as implicitly presupposed in Wang Yang-ming's thought, Wang still did not realize this and usually talked about the "will" in an ambiguous way. When Wang talked about ch'eng-i,[y] "making the will authentic or sincere," as a way for the realization of liang-chih, he meant only the will which is absolute good and exists on the same level as liang-chih as the substance and function of knowing. Yet in his four-sentence teaching, he said simply that there are volitional ideas which are either good or evil and are known by liang-chih as a knowing of a higher level, standing above and beyond ordinary good and evil. Liang-chih, when taken as absolute good, was not seen through the absolute goodness of its "willing to do good only and avoiding evil," and then its absolute goodness was just taken as identical with its "going beyond ordinary good and evil." Thus there was much confusion, and the development of Wang's thought was diversely interpreted as Wang Chi's ontological idea of liang-chih, which emphasized it as primarily beyond any good or evil, and Wang Ken's idea, which tended to identify it with cosmic life. They all neglected the primordial importance of the ethical idea of good, and lost the spirit of ethical idealism in Confucianism. Yet from Liu Tsung-chou's point of view, all these interpretations originated from the teaching of Wang Yang-ming himself, who, though an ethical idealist in practice, was not aware of what was missing in his own teaching and taught in an ambiguous and misleading way.

Liu's criticism of Wang's teaching of liang-chih is centered on the idea of "will as absolute good," which he saw rightly as what was missing. In the four-sentence teaching, Wang took the will or volitional idea as ordinary empirical will which may be either good or evil, but he also talked about the authenticity of the will which was assumed to be of absolute good. Here the word "will" is plainly ambiguous. So Liu said, If the will is either good or evil, then, if we make the good will authentic, it is surely a better will; but if we make the evil will authentic, it is a worse will. Then, what use is the teaching of authenticity of will? [9] On the other hand, if the will in the teaching of "the authenticity of will" is good, and without it the realization of *liang-chih* is impossible, why talk about *liang-chih* or conscientious consciousness as merely a function of knowing good and evil, and not as a function of "willing the good only"?

POSTERIORITY OF KNOWING AND THE PRIORITY
OR PRIMACY OF WILL

In Liu Tsung-chou's critique of Wang Yang-ming's thought, it is a contest for the "priority or primacy" of conscientious consciousness as "willing only the good" over "the primacy or priority" of the same consciousness as "knowing good and evil." In Wang's thought, this consciousness starts with knowing good and evil; then, second, liking the former and disliking the latter; and, third, doing the former and avoiding the latter. This seems to be a psychological order conforming to common experience. However, according to Liu, this order must be converted into one which recognizes the primacy or priority of the good will as an original function of mind which is connected with another original function of mind—feeling. The knowing function is essentially determined by the orientation of the original will and its accompanying feeling, and is posterior to the will and feeling in an ontological order.

Nevertheless, this was not considered by Liu as a theoretical problem only, but was taken as most crucial for the moral practice of becoming a sage. According to him, for example, when I take the knowing of good and evil as of primary importance and as the first step for my moral practice, ordinary good and evil ideas or wills and actions must already be there. Thus the knowing is actually posterior to such good or evil things as are done by me. My moral knowledge and choice between good and evil, even in connection with moral feelings, as favoring and liking the good and disfavoring and disliking the evil, and with moral actions of doing what is good and avoiding what is evil, are all just my activities which run after the good or evil I have already done. Even though what is good is all preserved and what is evil is all checked, I still have no guarantee that I will do no evil hereafter. Thus I shall never be a moral being with the confidence that I can be a sage, for all my moral struggles follow after evils already done. My struggles for my moral cultivation are one step behind the evils already done, and the pursuit of my moral career is just to catch the tail of those evils. Where then, is the guarantee that I shall eradicate the roots of evil and become a sage?

The problem of Wang Yang-ming's thought about moral practice, as Liu points it out, is a universal problem of human moral thought. When man finds out that he has no guarantee of not-doing-any-evil-again, he realizes the limitation to his moral career and usually prays to a transcendental being, as God, to help him. Yet man still has no guarantee that God will accept his prayer. Therefore, man seems destined to worry about his future, including the future of his moral career.

In the tradition of Neo-Confucianism this problem had been seriously considered since Ch'eng I [z] and Chu Hsi and answered in different ways by different thinkers. In Wang Yang-ming's thought the problem was also raised and answered in another way. This is self-confidence about the existence of *liang-chih* or conscientious consciousness as an eternal being. The knowing of good and evil as a function of *liang-chih* is surely posterior to the good and evil already done, as Liu Tsung-chou had asserted in his criticism of Wang. Yet the substance of *liang-chih* is prior to anything in the world; it is eternally self-existing and beyond ordinary good and evil. Therefore, when man is self-conscious about the eternity of *liang-chih*, and has such self-confidence or self-faith, he need not be afraid of whatever evil he has done and need not worry about his moral future.

If we view Wang Yang-ming's thought from this side, Liu Tsung-chou's criticism can be met and answered to some degree. Nevertheless, if we take the approach of Liu Tsung-chou, we may still ask, What is the self-confidence of *liang-chih*? We shall find that it is a persisting state of mind which is not merely a knowing but also a willing. Wang Yang-ming talked about *liang-chih* as the substance of pure knowing and not the substance of pure willing. He never asserted the primacy or priority of will as essential to the very idea of *liang-chih*. His thought is still inadequate, and must be revised and reconstructed.

From Liu's point of view, if one realizes the primacy or priority of will, then the way for moral practice to be a sage does not start from knowing the good and evil already done, complemented with the self-confidence in the existence of *liang-chih* as eternal substance. It should start with a deeper understanding that our original mind, or *liang-chih*, which is oriented only toward the good after its knowing good and evil, can be thought of ontologically from the very beginning as consciousness having a primary pure will accompanied by a primary pure feeling in the very life of pure consciousness as pure knowing itself. It is absolute good before any ordinary empirical good or evil arises and is known. Therefore, the most direct way for our moral practice to be a sage is to have a self-respect or self-reverence for such an original mind or *liang-chih* in itself. When we have such an understanding in a genuine sense, we stand in a place which is absolute good and can start our moral practice from there; then all other goods follow naturally.

ORIGINAL MIND AS PURE CONSCIOUSNESS WITH PURE KNOWING, PURE FEELING, AND PURE WILL, AS THE ORIGIN OF ALL GOODS

The original mind as a pure consciousness is a philosophical idea understood by thinkers of Wang Yang-ming's school and by Wang Yang-ming himself, as well as by Liu Tsung-chou and such others as Chu Hsi. Consciousness is not pure when it is object-oriented to get empirical impressions or ideas from objects, and is mixed with them. Consciousness is pure when it withdraws itself from outer or inner empirical objects, purifies itself from what it is mixed with, and sees itself as a pure subjectivity or a pure spiritual light. Chinese thinkers usually use the words *chüeh* aa or *ling-chüeh* ab to describe this pure consciousness. *Chüeh* may be translated as "awareness" or "sensibility" or "consciousness." In the West, when people talk about awareness or sensibility, they think of objects to become aware of or to be sensed. When consciousness is mentioned, it is usually associated with being conscious of something. However, in such Western philosophies as Kant's or Husserl's, there is the idea of pure consciousness—consciousness as pure subjectivity without connection with the object. So I use the words "pure consciousness" as a translation of the Chinese word *chüeh* when it does not imply any connection with the objects and is not mixed with impressions or ideas gotten from the objects.

In Chinese thought, when thinkers talk about mind as empty (*hsü*),[ac] luminous (*ming*),[ad] and transparent or sensitive (*ling*),[ae] the words denote pure consciousness. The meaning of "mind" is "original mind" and is identical with pure consciousness. When Wang Yang-ming and Wang Chi talk about knowing *chih*,[af] it is originally a pure consciousness as pure knowing beyond good and evil, and has no connection with objects. When Liu Tsung-chou talks about *chüeh* or *tu-chüeh*,[ag] he means also a pure consciousness as pure knowing. The word *tu* [ah] means solitary, unique, and absolute. The pure consciousness as pure knowing, in contrast to its objects, is itself solitary, unique, absolute, and transcendental. Here we have a genuine philosophy beyond ordinary empirical thought, which is agreed to in principle by many great philosophers of the West and India as well as by Chinese Taoists, Buddhists, and many Neo-Confucianists. One who does not understand the existence of such a consciousness is still outside the gate of genuine philosophy.

However, passing through the gate, one finds that there are still different kinds of philosophy and many things to say. In Liu Tsung-chou's thought, as a climax to the development of Neo-Confucianism, pure consciousness is taken not merely as a pure knowing, like a light, but also as a pure feeling and a pure willing, like the heat of light. Thus, pure consciousness has a life. This life is usually described by Liu in terms of the succession of the four seasons from spring to summer, autumn, winter, and to spring again, around a heavenly axis, to symbolize the rotation of the four feelings from delight to anger, sorrow, enjoyment or happiness, and to delight again. In the pure consciousness, there is no object of delight, anger, sorrow, or enjoyment, as there is nothing produced and passed through the four seasons.[10] What Liu has said is that there is a continuous living and creative process in pure consciousness. Sometimes he called this process "primordial change," or "change before Heaven" (*hsien-t'ien chih i*),[ai] [11] which means a transcendental inner change of the pure consciousness itself, before it has objects and a universe. Here the pure consciousness is not taken as a static entity, a pure function, or anything established once and for all. It is always in a living, creative process and has its own inner rhythmic vibration. From its vibration, consciousness springs forth, grows up, regresses, and finally withdraws to its source and becomes self-consciousness. When it springs forth, it is at the stage of spring, with a feeling of delight; when it grows, it is at the stage of summer, with a feeling of anger; when it regresses, it is in the stage of autumn, with a feeling of sorrow; and when it withdraws and becomes self-consciousness, it is winter, with a feeling of enjoyment or happiness. Thus the pure consciousness, if taken as a pure light, is not radiating its light of knowing straight from the inner world to the outer; its light is originally vibrating back and forth within itself, through a curved way, as the rotation of heaven around its axis with its rotations of four seasons or four feelings.

The life of pure consciousness in its four seasons or four feelings is always anticipating its successive stages. It is intentional and has a constant will which is always willing. The constant will keeps the orientation of the mind from stopping in one stage or being partial, and always keeps it turning around and back. Thus the process of the life of pure consciousness is spiral, when viewed from outside. Yet when viewed from inside it is intentionally oriented by "will" to one creative process, and the spiral form is the expression of the creative will in the life of pure consciousness itself. Here Liu Tsung-chou called the creative will the "master" (chu-tsai) [aj] of pure consciousness. The nature of will, as creative, is the essential nature of our minds, and this nature (hsing) [ak] is continuously revealed through the creative will as the self-governing principle of the pure consciousness in its creative process.

Liu Tsung-chou's subtle explication of the inner life of pure consciousness is also an ontological conception of the original mind as pure consciousness which is transcendental to ordinary empirical consciousness. The distinctive feature of his thought is that the original mind as pure consciousness still has its inner life. So he spoke of the inner state of tu-chih [al] or tu-chüeh, which is an absolute solitary and pure consciousness, as a sphere full of the flowing of the creative will (sheng-i), [am] or creative force (sheng-ch'i), [an] or original force (yüan-ch'i), [ao] and said that there is a self-turning of the axis of Heaven in the very solitary, absolute, and pure consciousness, in order to describe the self-turning life of the consciousness around the axis of will as rooted in Heaven. Here we may say that the idea of life which was emphasized by T'ai-chou school thinkers was also emphasized by Liu Tsung-chou. However, the "life" of the T'ai-chou school usually means cosmic or natural life which may be neither good or evil in itself. Liu's "life" is one of the pure inner consciousness or original mind which is oriented by its creative will and is essentially good.

As essentially good, Liu's pure consciousness is also different from Wang Chi's, which just took the pure consciousness as pure knowing beyond ordinary empirical good and evil.

The reason the life of pure consciousness is essentially good can be seen from the fact that in all men, as Liu explains, evil begins with partiality and solidification of the activity of consciousness. The partiality and solidification come from the fact that there is something remaining when the activity of consciousness is gone. Liu called this "remaining something" *yü-ch'i*. [ap] [12] The word *ch'i* [aq] may be translated as material force; *yü-ch'i* means a residual force left or remaining when an activity is gone. Actually, what the *yü-ch'i* denotes is the potentiality of an activity when it is gone. This is the origin of habits. Every habit, as it comes from man's past activity of consciousness, has some residual effect to compel the present consciousness to take the habitual form, called *hsi*. [ar] *Hsi* may be quite different from nature. [13] When the present consciousness takes the habitual form of its past activity, which is different from nature, it withdraws itself backward to the habitual form and solidifies in that form, becoming partial and noncreative. This is the origin of error and evil.

People usually say that evil comes from egoism or selfishness. This is a superficial way of thinking. Actually, egoism or selfishness is just a sense of the solid-being of one's ego or self. This sense is nothing other than a solidification of consciousness controlled by partial habitual form. From this, the consciousness mechanizes itself and becomes a hard-being with a kernel inside and a shell outside. Thus man develops the sense of the solid-being of his ego or self and becomes egoistic and selfish. All faults, evils, and sins, naturally follow. Therefore, if one hopes to eradicate these, one must have the wisdom which goes to the root or origin of all faults, evils, and sins. The solidification of pure consciousness controlled by the partial habitual form is this very root or origin. Yet the pure consciousness is not originally a being so controlled. The essential nature of pure consciousness is always creative and lively. Thus when we have understanding about the life of such a pure consciousness and have a self-respect or self-reverence for its life, we shall find the way for our moral practice to become a sage which starts from an origin which is absolute good and beyond all evil.

THE PRACTICE OF SELF-REVERENCE, THE
SPONTANEITY OF GOOD ACTION, AND THE
IMMANENCE OF KNOWING IN THE WILLING

To have such self-respect or self-reverence, we must withdraw from our ordinary consciousness which, as object-oriented, is mixed with the impressions that come from the objects, and must then purify it until it becomes pure consciousness. When the present consciousness withdraws itself from what it is mixed with, it becomes pure, self-creative, and meets also the coming pure-consciousness from its source. Here the present consciousness, as self-creative, also intentionally wills the coming-consciousness to be. Through the willing as the connection of the present consciousness and coming-consciousness, they are all just one pure consciousness. The source of this pure consciousness, as unseen, may be taken as ultimate mystery, and Liu used the word *mi*, [as] which means mystery, secret, hidden, or unseen, to describe it. When the present consciousness meets the coming-consciousness with a sense of intimacy or gratitude, it is self-reverence of the consciousness itself. In this self-respect or self-reverence, the mystery, as it were, shines forth its light toward the light which shines backward toward the mystery. Then the mystery is also manifested in the process.

The word self-respect (or self-reverence) is my translation of the single word *ching*, [at] which may also be translated as just respect or reverence. "Respect" or "reverence" in English usually have objects to be respected or revered. This corresponds to the original meaning of *ching*, which also has an object. However, since the Ch'eng brothers talked about "abiding in reverence" (*chu-ching*), [au] it has come to mean to cultivate a state of mind which has no other object to be respected or revered. Thus it is better to add the word "self" to make clear that this is a "respect" or "reverence" which has no other object. This is similar to "being conscious of one's own dignity." Actually, consciousness of one's own dignity and the sense of self-respect or self-reverence have one origin, or are actually the same thing. That is, man realizes that "he is essentially a self-conscious subject, and not an [external] object one [he] is being conscious of, but above all objects." Thus, a man who has a sense of self-dignity is a subject who is always self-conscious and does not have a "consciousness mixed with objects." Such a subject—*qua* subject—is nothing other than pure consciousness. Hence man's sense of self-dignity originates from this pure consciousness.

Yet the ordinary man may feel only that he has self-dignity and may not know what has been discussed above. Therefore, when he is asked where his dignity comes from, he is usually perplexed. However, when man has self-reflection enough, I believe he will realize that his dignity as man comes from the fact that he has a consciousness which is above all objects, and, when not thought of as mixed with its objects, is a pure consciousness. According to Liu's teaching, to know the existence of such a consciousness, of course, one has to withdraw his ordinary consciousness from its object-orientation—and yet after the withdrawal, what he finds is not merely a pure consciousness as pure knowing which is both being and nothing, as is Wang Chi's *liang-chih*. It is a pure consciousness which is creative in its pure feeling and pure willing as well, and full of life. Hence, man's sense of self-dignity or self-respect or self-reverence should be itself a feeling and a will to realize the nature of pure consciousness as feeling and willing.

The practice of this self-reverence or self-respect to keep one's self-dignity is called *kung-fu*. [av] What is realized through practice is the reality (*pen-t'i*), [aw] substance, or nature (*hsing*), the sources of man's dignity. The practice is the realization of the reality or substance or nature—or, in other words, the realization of the reality or substance or nature of pure consciousness. Hence, Liu Tsung-chou talked about the "identity of practice and substance" (*chi kung-fu chi pen-t'i*) [ax] just as Wang Yang-ming and Wang Chi had, though Liu's understanding about the pure consciousness is deeper and more comprehensive than theirs.

When Liu takes self-reverence (or self-respect) as the origin of all good virtues in man, his thought is very similar to Chu Hsi's. However, Chu Hsi usually took both self-reverence and "investigation of things and searching out of their reasons" as parallel ways for moral practice. In Liu's thought, the latter is included in the very practice of self-reverence; there is only one way. Wang Yang-ming's theory of the realization of *liang-chih* is actually developed from Chu Hsi's theory of the investigation of things. [14] Liu disagreed with Wang's theory of the realization of *liang-chih* as well as with the theory of Chu Hsi, in that both men thought that there are ways of moral cultivation outside of self-reverence. In Liu's theory, self-reverence is the only way to realize the pure consciousness as knowing, feeling, and willing, which is itself absolute good and the origin of all ordinary good virtues and good actions.

From self-reverence all ordinary good actions follow naturally and spontaneously, somewhat as with a man who has a high sense of personal dignity, who naturally tends to do noble and good things, and is ashamed to do base or evil things. The good things are always done with noble and good feeling and willing, and here the mind's function as knowing just subsists in the feeling and willing. This will be explained below.

MORAL PRACTICE WHICH STARTS FROM "KNOWING" OUTSIDE THE "GOOD AND EVIL KNOWN" AND ITS RELATION TO MORAL WILL SUBSISTING

In Liu's thought, the best action of man is that which originates spontaneously and naturally from good will and good feeling and not from the deliberate choice between good and evil. The choice between good and evil begins with knowing good and evil. Here Wang Yang-ming said that to know the good, favor it, and do it, and to know the evil, disfavor it, and avoid it, is the way to the realization of *liang-chih*. However, in Liu Tsung-chou's thought, the knowing process itself is outside of what is known to be good and evil. The knowing does not subsist in what is known. Thus even the knowing itself is good. If what is known includes one's evil, one is still not completely good but partly bad. Therefore, the man who just knows both good and evil, and, practicing the way of the realization of *liang-chih*, starts with the choice between good and evil, is not good enough. On the other hand, if his action or behavior is completely good, there is no such thing as a choice between good and evil and there is no "knowing outside what is known as good or evil." Here the "knowing" only subsists in good willing, good feeling, and good action, and illuminating the willing, feeling, and action from within, so the "knowing" can never be taken as something above the good willing, feeling, and action.

Here Liu detected the fundamental defect in Wang Yang-ming's thought, which stresses that *liang-chih* is originally a knowing outside the good and evil known, and said that Wang's understanding of *chih*, or knowing, does not conform to the teaching of Confucius and Mencius. For example, Mencius said that a child knows to love his parents and to respect his elders. This kind of love and respect is spontaneously and naturally expressed by the child without a sense of choice. Here the word "to know" is not something outside of or above love or respect. The knowing function of mind just subsists in the very love and respect. It is not like Wang Yang-ming's "knowing" in "knowing good and evil" [15] which is a knowing above or outside of what is known as good and evil. This is proof that Wang Yang-ming's idea of knowing is not faithful to the Confucian tradition and also neglects the knowing which subsists in the willing and feeling. Spontaneous or natural good actions, such as to love and to respect, are the direct expression of our good nature, and may be taken as directly following from this nature. Its good is intrinsic to the action and is absolute good, as it is not related to evil.

In comparison with the goodness of the creative life of pure consciousness, as we have said before, the goodness of willing and feeling in the action of love and respect is still secondary goodness. The goodness of creative life in pure consciousness with its pure knowing, pure feeling, and pure willing, is the primary and absolute good and the origin of all good actions and good virtues. In comparison with our moral goods, which come from deliberate choice between good and evil, and which start with "knowing the good and evil from outside and relative to the evil," it is still an intrinsic and absolute goodness. It is a goodness that has more intimate relation to the "origin" and it is on a higher level than that which comes from the choice between good and evil and starts from knowing good and evil.

From what has been said above, it is plain that when Wang Yang-ming talks about "knowing good and evil" as the beginning of moral practice, it is moral practice starting from the lowest level. Since in "knowing good and evil" the knowing is outside and above the good and evil known, it is quite possible that the knowing itself is purely contemplative or theoretical and is neither good nor evil. In this case, the knowing is nonmoral. If one has only nonmoral knowing and then just thinks of all moral things contemplatively and theoretically, that is also immoral and becomes the very first step in man's falling into evil. Therefore, knowing good and evil from the outside is a dangerous thing.

However, when Wang Yang-ming talked about knowing good and evil, this "knowing" was not merely contemplative or theoretical. Wang knew also that "knowing good and evil things as external objects" is dangerous. So he opposed Chu Hsi's investigation of things which might include the investigation of things good or evil as external objects. In Wang Yang-ming's thought, the knowing in "knowing good and evil" is itself a knowing originally connected with feeling and willing, as we said before, and his theory of the identity of knowledge and action actually connected "feeling" and "willing" with "knowing." He realized as well as Liu Tsung-chou that mere knowing does not concern our moral life. Thus some of Liu's criticism is not fair. However, Wang still did not say that will accompanied by feeling is the very root of knowing, and that it is primary and prior to knowing. Wang did not realize that the good which comes from a choice between good and evil is a good relative to evil, a good of the lowest order, and not absolute and intrinsic good. It is far from the goodness of the life of pure consciousness as the origin of all good actions and good virtues.

Of course, the goodness realized after the choice made between good and evil as known, is still a moral good. Spontaneous and natural actions which are absolute good, though most precious, are rare. After man has left his childhood, it is only the sage who has the heart of a child and whose good actions flow from the heart of his original nature spontaneously and naturally. However, from the stage of child to the stage of sage, man has to be neither child nor sage, and just a man with both good and evil actions. A man aspiring to become a sage must know the good and evil and choose the good. This is the ordinary way of man's moral practice. Here, Chu Hsi talked about the self-examination of one's goodness and evil, and Wang Yang-ming talked about the realization of *liang-chih*, which knows the difference of good and evil. Liu Tsung-chou did not deny this kind of moral practice as understood by Chu Hsi and Wang Yang-ming. However, Liu stressed one point even in this kind of moral practice. That is, we have to know that in the choice between good and evil, the "knowing-liking-doing-the good" and the "knowing-disliking-avoiding the evil" are not two separate things but originate from "one single will" subsisting.[16]

This will is single, because to do the good is the positive will and to avoid the evil is the negative of the negative, which is also a positive will.

When one understands this point with inner intimacy, then he will not look upon his doing this and that good, and avoiding this and that evil, as moral piecework. He will realize that when he does the good, there is a will subsisting which is intentionally tending to avoid all evils which are in opposition to good. The will, like the needle of a compass, always moves from the wrong direction, which is evil, to the right direction, which is good. Thus it is absolute good. When one knows that this will is always subsisting, and practices *shen-tu*,[ay] [17] or "taking care of the absolute good will in solitude," to make this will sincere and authentic, then through mutual enhancement of doing good and avoiding evil one can have the genuine sense of integrity and unity of personality which make him a real individual with moral grandeur, an absolute and solitary being in the universe. The ultimate stage of this individual is a sage who has no evil to avoid, and then all his good flows from his nature spontaneously and naturally as a child of Heaven. This is the way from the relative good to the absolute and original good in Liu's teaching.

LIU'S FOUR-SENTENCE TEACHING VERSUS WANG'S FOUR-SENTENCE TEACHING

In conclusion, all of Liu's criticisms of Wang Yang-ming come from his idea of pure consciousness as primarily a will which is original good in an absolute sense and is always oriented toward the absolute good in its knowing of all the ordinary goods and evils. Thus the will is originally a sincere and authentic will, and Liu took self-reverence as the most direct way for our moral practice and insisted that to "make the will sincere and authentic, when it is mixed with insincerity or inauthenticity," should be taken as the central kernel even in the teaching of the realization of *liang-chih* as Wang Yang-ming propounded it. Therefore, Liu changed the four-sentence teaching of Wang Yang-ming into the following four sentences: [18]

Sometimes good and sometimes evil, is where the mind moves.

Liking the good and disliking the evil, is where the will rests.

Knowing good and evil, is *liang-chih* or conscientious consciousness.

"Good without evil" is the ruling principle of things.

What the first sentence describes is the state of our ordinary empirical consciousness which has ordinary volitional ideas or wills, feelings, and actions, which may be either good or evil. This sentence corresponds to the second sentence of Wang Yang-ming's "Four sentences." Wang took all of these as coming from the movement of will, meaning ordinary will. Here Liu used the term "mind" to replace Wang's "will," and in his second sentence he talked about the will which likes the good and dislikes the evil as the will of mind. It is a will which is transcendental to the ordinary volitional ideas or wills, and is purely a moral will existing on a level above the ordinary wills or volitional ideas Wang talked about in his second sentence. In Liu's second sentence, as the "will" likes only the good and dislikes the evil and abides in such liking and disliking, it is the center of mind which is oriented only toward the good. It is opposed to the first sentence of Wang, which says that beyond good and evil is the substance or reality of mind, and which does not realize that there is the will as the center of mind which is oriented to the good and never goes beyond good.

Liu's third sentence has the same words as Wang's. This is proof of Liu's agreement with Wang on the existence of conscientious consciousness. However, as this sentence follows the above two sentences, its significance in Liu's four-sentence teaching is different from that in Wang's. In Liu's four-sentence teaching, the will is taken as the center of mind, and thus is also the center of mind-knowing-of-good-and-evil, which is *liang-chih*. Thus in the *liang-chih* of the third sentence of Liu, the good will is implicated.

Liu's fourth sentence, corresponding to Wang's, talks about things. Wang used the word "things" to mean all our actions or doings, and not just external things. Liu's "things" should have the same meaning. In Wang's fourth sentence, "to do good and avoid evil" is the "investigation of things." Good and evil are assumed to be already there, and good and evil are relative. In Liu's fourth sentence, " 'good without evil' is the ruling principle of things" means: "good things tend to have being and evil things tend to have no-being when they are seen through the ruling principle of our doing and actions, which is directed by will." Therefore, the ruling principle is good without evil. The ruling principle of our doings or actions and will is the very nature of our mind which is revealed and expressed in the moral will of our mind. Thus the nature of mind is good. Hence the fourth sentence indicates the ultimacy of the good of the nature and will of mind, which knows and is conscious of things. This sentence points the way to understanding the mind itself as pure consciousness, which is pure knowing, pure willing, and pure feeling as good in an original sense, and also points to the practice of self-reverence as explained before, although they are not explicitly included in Liu's words.

Generally speaking, Liu's insistence on the ultimacy of goodness is very much like the thought of thinkers in the Tung-lin school. They were in the same current of late Ming thought, which took the view that the idea of good should preside over the idea of the natural life which the T'ai-chou school stressed, as well as over the pure consciousness as pure knowing which Wang Chi had stressed. We have said that the idea of natural life is cosmological and the idea of pure consciousness as knowing which is being and nonbeing is ontological. The idea of good is ethical. Yet Liu did not merely stress the priority of good in the ethical sense; he also had ontological statements about the status of good in the original mind, and connected the "good" with the innermost part of mind which is a "will" having its source in an unseen Heaven. Thus Liu's thinking went a step further than that of thinkers of the Tung-lin school.

When the Ming dynasty fell, Liu committed suicide through fasting. He did not use poison or a knife to end his life suddenly because he did not want to destroy the integrity of his body which he had received from his parents. He had to be both loyal to the country and filial to his parents. His suicide is not like that of the many martyrs of the Tung-lin school who became martyrs through engagement in struggle and combat. This is proof that his learning and thinking were fruitful in his whole personality and worthy forever of our admiration.

THE HISTORICAL SIGNIFICANCE OF LIU'S CRITICISM
OF WANG YANG-MING IN CONTRAST TO THAT
OF OTHER SEVENTEENTH-CENTURY CRITICS

From what has been said above we may understand the depth of Liu Tsung-chou's thought, his contribution to the philosophical development of Neo-Confucianism, and the moral grandeur of his personality. Liu's life, ending in martyrdom, was a life of pure spiritual inwardness, of pure subjectivity of which we can say nothing more. More can be said, however, about the significance of Liu's criticism of Wang's teachings to the intellectual history of the late Ming dynasty or of seventeenth-century China. This can easily be seen from Liu's teaching as a Confucian scholar and moral teacher, and from the difference between his criticisms of Wang Yang-ming and those of other thinkers of his time.

It is noteworthy that Liu as a Confucian scholar and moral teacher emphasized the reading of the traditional Confucian classics and books of history much more than Wang and his direct disciples had. Liu edited a bibliography of the classics [19] and wrote an important book called Jen-p'u [az] (Manual of Man). It is a book of moral instruction just as is the Chin-ssu lu [ba] edited by Chu Hsi. Yet the contents of the two books is quite different. The Chin-ssu lu begins with Chou Tun-i's [bb] discussion of the ultimate principle of the objective universe, and follows with chapters on moral principles and maxims for moral cultivation. The Jen-p'u begins with a chapter about the reality of mind as the foundation for the establishment of "man as the ultimate" (jen-chi),[bc] and follows with chapters about methods of moral cultivation as exemplified by great historical personages. The moral behavior of these great personages originated with their "moral will," which is always intentional and directed to the concrete social and cultural situation in which men live in each historical age. Thus Liu's emphasis on the "moral will" also implied an emphasis on the knowledge of different historical ages. Here we can easily understand the transition from Liu's thought as a moral teacher to the work of his disciple Huang Tsung-hsi as a historian, a critic of past and recent history and politics.

In contrast to Liu's criticism of Wang, which is almost like a self-criticism and a further development of Wang's teaching, there is the criticism of Wang made by Ku Yen-wu, who was a follower of Chu Hsi.[20] Ku was a friend of Huang Tsung-hsi and had almost the same ideal of political reconstruction and the same high moral sense of loyalty to the Ming dynasty. But he criticized Wang's disciples severely as men given to "pure talk" about "mind and nature" without making an effort to search out the manifold aspects of knowledge, and without a sense of moral responsibility answering to the crisis of the age and the miseries of the people. Ku's criticism of Wang's disciples as not searching out the manifold aspects of knowledge is true to the line of Chu Hsi's criticism of Lu Hsiang-shan.

The other type of criticism of the Wang Yang-ming school came from Wang Fu-chih. Wang Fu-chih called himself a disciple of Chang Tsai. Like Chang, he showed a religious piety toward the natural universe as objective reality and thus respected men's natural desires as the expression of heavenly principle. He also viewed the economic and political aspects of human existence as of equal importance to the cultural and moral aspects. Moreover, he had a strong sense of the continuity of culture among the Chinese people as a historical reality. Hence he rejected the thought of Wang Yang-ming and his disciples as subjective and romantic idealism, lacking a sense of objective reality in nature and history.

There were two other schools of Chinese thought and learning in the late Ming which also differed from Wang's school. Yet whether they emerged mainly as countercurrents of thought is doubtful. One type of thought and learning was represented by Fang I-chih.[bd] Fang was a theoretically oriented man and anxious, like the modern scientist, to get theoretical knowledge about physical nature. The other type of learning was represented by Yen Yüan [be] and Li Kung.[bf] Yen and Li were practically oriented and anxious to get technical knowledge for the maintenance of man's natural and social life on earth.

Yet it is doubtful that the Yen-Li type of thought and learning arose just in opposition to Wang's learning. Yen and Li severely criticized the book learning of the Ch'eng-Chu school. By comparison their criticisms of Wang's theory of knowledge and action were rather restrained and sometimes they even made statements in favor of Lu Hsiang-shan and Wang Yang-ming.[21] It is not difficult to see that there is an ideological link between Wang's idea of moral action and the Yen-Li idea of practical action.

It is also questionable whether the type of learning represented by Fang I-chih was opposed to Wang's type of learning. Here we must recognize that Wang's teaching of *liang-chih* is not logically incompatible with a broad knowledge of culture, history, and nature. Of course, some disciples of Wang may indeed have been given to "pure talk" about "mind or human nature" and lacked a sense of objective reality, as Ku Yen-wu and Wang Fu-chih asserted. Yet the idea of *liang-chih* or mind in Wang Yang-ming can be understood as an objective mind and not merely as a subjective one. This is what Huang Tsung-hsi suggested in his preface to the *Ming-ju-hsüeh-an.*[bg] When the mind is understood as objective, all things in the universe are what the spiritual light of the mind shines upon. Then the understanding of the facts of culture, history, and nature is learning that is not apart. Thus Huang Tsung-hsi could be a scholar of great erudition and still be a disciple of Liu Tsung-chou and Wang Yang-ming. There is no reason to say that an emphasis on scientific knowledge about nature, such as we find in Fang I-chih, stands in opposition to Wang's teaching.

If we do not take the thought of the Yen-Li school and Fang I-chih as being in opposition to Wang's teaching, then there remain just three types of criticism of Wang's teaching, represented by Liu Tsung-chou, Ku Yen-wu, and Wang Fu-chih. The latter two types came from traditions of thought different from Wang Yang-ming's, and were directed mainly at abuses that arose in his school. Their criticisms were external to it and negative, and not without some misunderstandings of Wang's teaching as a whole. By contrast, Liu's criticism was internal and positive, and resulted in a development of that teaching. Huang Tsung-hsi understood this point very well and identified himself as a disciple of both Liu and Wang. As a scholar of enormous erudition, he realized perfectly well that there was no logical incompatibility between the moral idealism of Liu and Wang and a many-sided knowledge of culture, history, and nature. Hence, there are clear links from Wang to Huang's scholarship, and a definite historical continuity in the thought of the late Ming and early Ch'ing. At the same time we should not overlook the importance of Ku Yen-wu and Wang Fu-chih as alternatives to Liu and Huang in this period of Chinese intellectual history.

NOTES

1. See my earlier paper, "The Development of the Concept of Moral Mind from Wang Yang-ming to Wang Chi" in de Bary, *Self and Society*, pp. 108–13.
2. *Wang Lung-hsi yü lu* ʰʰ (Taipei: Kuang-wen Bookstore reprint, [n.d.]), 7/13.
3. *Ming-ju hsüeh-an* (Chung-hua edition), 58/12.
4. *Ibid.*, 58/13.
5. Cf. My paper, "Yang-ming hsüeh yü Chu-Lu i-t'ung chung pien" ʰⁱ (The Learning of Wang Yang-ming and an Evaluation of Similarities and Differences between Chu Tzu and Lu Hsiang-shan's Thoughts) in *Hsin-ya hsüeh-pao,* ʰʲ Vol. VIII, no. 2, pp. 114–18.
6. *MJHA*, 58/25.
7. *Ibid.*, 32/19.
8. *Ibid.*, 20/4.
9. *Liu Tzu ch'üan-shu,* ʰᵏ edition of Tao-kuang 15 (1835), 21/10.
10. *Ibid.*, 2/9, 11/8–10, 9/15, 10/28.
11. *Ibid.*, 2/13.
12. *Ibid.*, 8/19, 2/11.
13. *Ibid.*, 7/8, 19/53.
14. See the article mentioned in note 5; Vol. IX, no. 1, pp. 1–16.
15. *Liu Tzu ch'üan-shu*, 8/25.
16. *Ibid.*, 19/51, 10/24–25.
17. For examples see *ibid.*, 1/3, 8/9–11, 18/24–25.
18. *Ibid.*, 10/26.
19. Cf. Yao Ming-ta,ʰˡ *Liu Tsung-chou nien-p'u*ᵇᵐ (Shanghai: Commercial Press, 1934), p. 268.
20. See the essay on Chu and Lu by Chang Hsüeh-ch'eng ᵇⁿ in his *Wen-shih t'ung-i* ᵇᵒ (Peking: Hsin-hua Press edition, 1956).
21. Cf. Tai Wang (ed.),ᵇᵖ *Yen-shih hsüeh-chi,*ᵇᵠ (Shanghai: Commercial Press edition, 1933), pp. 31–32.

GLOSSARY

a	唐君毅	x	黃宗羲	av	工夫
b	劉宗周	y	誠意	aw	本體
c	王陽明	z	程頤	ax	即工夫即本體
d	王夫之	aa	覺	ay	慎獨
e	張載	ab	靈覺	az	人譜
f	顧炎武	ac	虛	ba	近思錄
g	東林學派	ad	明	bb	周敦頤
h	王畿	ae	靈	bc	人極
i	浙東學派	af	知	bd	方以智
j	泰州學派	ag	獨覺	be	顏元
k	江右學派	ah	獨	bf	李塨
l	良知	ai	先天之易	bg	明儒學案
m	周汝登	aj	主宰	bh	王龍溪語錄
n	王艮	ak	性	bi	陽明學與朱陸異同
o	羅汝芳	al	獨知		重辨
p	顧憲成	am	生意	bj	新亞學報
q	高攀龍	an	生氣	bk	劉子全書
r	止善	ao	元氣	bl	姚名達
s	大學	ap	餘氣	bm	劉宗周年譜
t	李材，見羅 嘉靖	aq	氣	bn	章學誠
	41年進士	ar	習	bo	文史通義
u	王棟	as	密	bp	戴望
v	王時槐，塘南	at	敬	bq	顏氏學記
w	念	au	主敬		

11

THE DEVELOPMENT OF THE CHINESE HUMANISTIC SPIRIT*

1. Humanistic, Nonhumanistic, Superhumanistic, Subhumanistic, and Antihumanistic Concepts

In one sense, all academic thoughts are human ideas, and all cultures are productions of man. Therefore, the spirit of all human cultures is always humanistic. To discuss any kind of academic thoughts is to discuss the ideas of man. Speaking in this way, however, we cannot reveal and illuminate the meaning of such terms as "humanistic thought" or "humanistic spirit" because of the lack of contradistinctions. We must then say that, in addition to humanistic thought or spirit, there are also human thoughts or spirit which are nonhumanistic, super-humanistic, subhumanistic, and even antihumanistic.

What I call "nonhumanistic thoughts" refers to those thoughts concerning objects experienced and understood by man that are other than man, e.g., nature, abstract forms, and numbers; these are the thoughts included in natural sciences and mathematics.

What I call "superhumanistic thoughts" refers to those thoughts concerning transcendent or supernatural beings which

---

*T'ang Chün-i, "Chung-kuo jen-wen ching-shen chih fa-chan." From Chapter One of Chung-kuo jen-wen ching-shen fa-chan [The Development of Chinese Humanistic Spirit] (Hong Kong: Young Son, 1958), pp. 17-44. Translated by Yuk Wong.

257

are above man and beyond empirical understanding, e.g., Tao, spirits or ghosts, immortals, God, and angels.

What I call "subhumanistic thoughts" refers to those thoughts that fail to fully affirm and respect the existence and value of human nature, human relationships, humanity, human culture, and its history.

What I call "antihumanistic thoughts" refers to those thoughts that not only neglect or overlook the existence and value of human nature, human relationships, humanity, human culture, and its history, but also deny or distort them, seeing man as being the same as natural living things or minerals that are beneath man or making man fall into the hands of demons like the Devil or Satan in Christianity or into the two lowest realms of hungry ghosts [preta] and hell in Buddhism.

From the above, we know that the so-called humanistic thoughts refer to the thoughts that are willing to thoroughly affirm and respect the existence and value of human nature, human relationships, humanity, personality, human culture and its history, never neglect them purposely, or deny or distort them lest mankind should be likened to natural objects that are beneath him.

The difference between humanistic and nonhumanistic or superhumanistic thought consists in the fact that the former springs from man and that its objects are man and things pertaining to man, whereas the objects of nonhumanistic or superhumanistic thought are nonhuman or superhuman. Just as the human, the nonhuman, and the superhuman can coexist, so can humanistic, nonhumanistic, and superhumanistic thoughts; the relation between them is one of logical compatibility. When reflecting on the existence of the nonhuman or the superhuman, such as nature and gods or spirits, however, man can, at the same time, be conscious of the fact that these thoughts also belong to man and are indeed the scientific and religious ideas of man. This leads man to wonder why his nonhumanistic and superhumanistic thoughts arise? What are the influences of these thoughts on man? And where will these thoughts lead man? When nonhumanistic thought or superhumanistic thought becomes the object of human thought, nonhumanistic or super-humanistic thought is also included in the humanistic thought of man. Therefore, in the humanistic thought of man, we should affirm and respect the value of nonhumanistic or superhumanistic thought or scholarship. Otherwise, the humanistic thought of man cannot be complete and will become subhumanistic thought. The relation between the humanistic thought of man and the non-humanistic or the superhumanistic thought of man is that the former not only implies the latter but also depends on it.

The relation between subhumanistic and humanistic thought is also that the latter implies the former. For any thought as a whole contains all its parts. This is too obvious to need explanation.

As to the relation between humanistic and antihumanistic thought, these two are contradictory and incompatible with each other from a logical point of view. If humanistic thought is true, then antihumanistic thought must be false and vice versa. Hence the necessity to deny antihumanistic thought when affirming humanistic thought. But antihumanistic thought is also human thought. In the history of ideas, the prosperity of humanism is always preceded by superhumanism, nonhumanism, subhumanism, and antihumanism. When reflecting on humanism, one must also reflect on why antihumanism arises. This reflection itself is still something that man's humanistic thought ought to include. Thus, the loftiest humanism of mankind must involve both the idea of denying antihumanism and also the thoughts which explain the rise of antihumanism.

It is not until we understand the difference and relation between humanistic, nonhumanistic, superhumanistic, sub-humanistic, and antihumanistic thought that we can discuss the development of the humanistic spirit in China. The development of humanism is partly due to the gradual deepening and broadening of man's thought about humanism itself. It is also partly due to the interaction between humanistic and non-humanistic, superhumanistic, and antihumanistic thoughts which result in relations of mutual dependence, implication, opposition, and completion among them. From the process of this development, we find that nonhumanism enlarges the domain of humanism, superhumanism exalts humanism, subhumanism is assimilated by humanism, and humanism incessantly emerges in new forms to counter antihumanism. This continuous process of the development of humanism displays the spiritual aspiration of mankind. We call this spirit humanistic.

In this essay, the discussion of the development of Chinese humanistic thought is tantamount to a discussion of the development of Chinese humanistic spirit. It is not just a general discussion of Chinese thought and Chinese culture.

2. The Origin of Chinese Humanism

The first phase of the development of Chinese humanism was the period before Confucius, which we may call the age in which the Chinese humanistic spirit was expressed concretely in Chinese culture. During this period, there was, strictly speaking, little humanistic thought [on the reflective level]. But the prototype of Chinese culture became definite at this time. It is a humanistically centered one. Later Chinese humanism developed from the Chinese mind in this period. "Humanistically centered" means neither that the religious belief of the people at that time was not strong, nor that the people did not take nature seriously. What matters is their basic attitude toward God and natural objects. Such an attitude can be fully understood when it is compared with the attitudes developed in the cultures of India and Greece. In brief, there are three attitudes that man assumes toward natural objects. The first utilizes them to enrich human life. The second admires them or employs them to express human feelings and virtues; this attitude is aesthetic or artistic. The third takes them to be objective things, wondering or marveling at them and desiring to understand them. Only the third attitude can yield objective thoughts concerning nature. It was from this that Greek science and natural philosophy arose. The thought that springs from this attitude inclines toward nature and at first tends to forget man's

own self. It is said that once when the first scientist and philosopher, Thales, looked upward to observe the celestial phenomena, he fell into a well. It is also said that another philosopher, having seen the sun in the sky, decided that he would not
mind being burnt to ashes if he could land on the sun to find out
about its structure. These are really both expressions of the
attitude that inclines toward nonhumanistic thought concerning
nature at the expense of neglecting man's own life. This is the
attitude that the ancient Chinese people lacked. They were inclined toward the first and second attitudes and achieved cultural inventions and a life of proprieties [rites] and music. The
sages of ancient China, such as Fu-hsi, Shen-nung, Yao, and
Shun, were believed to have invented cultural products and constructed moral relationships and political systems. Some two
hundred years ago, China excelled the West in the quantity and
exquisiteness of its invention and production of cultural objects
and appliances for enriching life. However, this does not prove
that Chinese culture originally stressed natural studies and had
a scientific spirit. This is where I disagree with some of my
friends. Genuine thought about nature and the pure scientific
spirit consist of understanding nature and seeking truth for
their own sakes. No wonder the Greek philosophers looked
down upon crafts, and Archimedes felt ashamed of recording
his inventions. In contrast with this, the fact that cultural
products and instruments were treasured in ancient China
shows her deficiency in pure thought about nature and objective
scientific spirit. Although the ancient Chinese had to apply their
thinking to nature when inventing things, these inventions were
regarded only as the means for human survival in nature or as
contributions to a life of rites and music. This attitude is basically humanistically centered and attached to humanistic
thought.

We cannot say that the ancient Chinese did not have a strong
belief in God, Heaven, ghosts, and spirits. The statement "King
Wen ascended and descended on the left and the right of God"
means that man can be with God after death. But, unlike Indian
religionists, the people of ancient China never thought that after

death man would undergo incessant transmigrations which would relieve or liberate him from suffering, i.e., attain moksa; nor did the ancient Chinese understand the Hebrew idea that God possesses an unfathomable will and thus deserves profound awe or reverence or the discourses of medieval Western theologians on the attributes, inward actions, and outward actions of God. In sum, the ancient Chinese lacked superhumanistic thoughts concerning the "spiritual realm after death" as an independent self-existent object to be contemplated. Never did they feel that life was illusive and unreal and that human beings were sinful in the presence of God. Therefore, the status of priests and shamans as the media between God and man was comparatively unimportant. Ancient Chinese kings performed sacrificial rites for Heaven, received the Mandate of Heaven to implement their policies, and believed that "Heaven sees through my people's eyes, and Heaven hears through my people's ears." This meant that Heavenly will was shown in man's will and that Heaven ordained people according to their moral cultivation. These thoughts fused the four concepts of Heaven, emperor, people, and human virtue and made them hard to separate from one another. It also caused the religious, political, and moral consciousness of the ancient Chinese people to become easy to fuse and hard to separate. The ancient religious thoughts of China were part of her humanism as a whole and did not themselves become a superhumanistic realm of thought.

Having understood that ancient China was deficient in both nonhumanistic or natural thought and in the superhumanistic thought of a world after death and a spiritual realm, we recognize that Chinese culture is originally humanistically centered. The concrete formation of this culture must have been during the Chou dynasty. Ancient people said: "The Hsia dynasty stressed fidelity; the Yin [Shang], substance; and the Chou, culture." From the Chou dynasty on, there was an abundance of rites and music. The ancient sages' inventions and King Yü's conquest of the flood showed that the Chinese first pursued survival on the earth and control over external objects. The value of their devices and implements lay chiefly in the practical the Chin state] mentioned Heaven; when speaking of fidelity, he mentioned sincerity; when speaking of trustiness, he mentioned his own need to be trustworthy; talking about humanity [human-heartedness], he never failed to mention the people; talking about righteousness, he never failed to mention welfare; talking about wisdom, he never failed to mention managing affairs; speaking of courage, he always mentioned self-control; speaking of education, he always mentioned the distinction between right and wrong; speaking of filial piety, he always mentioned the spirits; talking about benevolence, he never left out harmony; talking about yielding, he never left out enemies.... Reverence is the respect for propriety; fidelity, the real sincerity of propriety; trustiness, the practice of propriety; humanity, the love of propriety; righteousness, the judgment of propriety; wisdom, the carriage of propriety; education, the promulgation of propriety; filial piety, the root [beginning] of propriety; benevolence, the charitableness of propriety; yielding, the application of propriety.

In this passage, all human virtues, such as reverence, were considered to belong to proprieties in connection with Heaven, etc. This is one of the best illustrations of the direct manifestation of man's inner virtue in his cultural life. Although we cannot be sure about the time when the thinking displayed in the above passage emerged, I still believe that it is most appropriate to use it to illustrate the humanistic spirit in the prosperous era of the Chou dynasty.

3. The Humanism of Confucius and Mencius, the Subhumanism of Mo Tzu, the Superhumanism of Chuang Tzu, and the Antihumanism of the Legalists

It was the pre-Ch'in Confucianism started by Confucius that really consciously understood and explicated the meaning and value of the spirit of traditional Chinese humanism. The period from Confucius to the Ch'in dynasty may be called the age when

Chinese humanism was consciously formed. The mission of
Confucius' whole life was no other than to reconstruct the traditional humanistically centered culture. The main problem of
this period was the decline of the Chou state and the rise of the
barbarian powers, the degeneration and demoralization of the
nobles, and the gradual demand of the scholars and the common
people for higher social status. In short, the problem was the
total collapse of conventional rites and music, i.e., the internal
corruption of the Chinese cultural world, and the menace of
anti-Chinese barbarians to Chinese culture. Confucius highly
esteemed the Duke of Chou and also Kuan Chung, who advocated
respecting the king and fending off the barbarians so that the
Chinese were protected from converting to the barbarian habits
of "long hair and sinistral collar." Confucius urged the scholars, who were between the nobles and the common people in the
class structure, to assume the responsibility of rebuilding the
Chinese culture. Scholars were originally warriors who took
up weapons to protect their communities. Nevertheless, Confucius instructed the scholars to "let fidelity and trustiness be
armor, and propriety and righteousness be weapons" and to
"regard humanity as their responsibility until death" in order
to guard "this culture [of Chou]" now that "King Wen has died."
This was a unique appeal to the people for resolving the problem. Confucius' eulogies and denunciations in the Spring and
Autumn Annals were different from Jesus' saying that he would
return on the Day of Judgment. Confucius' praises and re-
proaches were a straightforward type of judgment passed on
his contemporary statesman. The Day of Judgment is superhumanistic in character, whereas Confucius' judgment is an
undertaking within the cultural realm. Opposing the hypocrit-
ical morals and laws of the Pharisees, Jesus spread the faith
of the Kingdom in Heaven. Pained by the nobles who usurped
rites and music, Confucius exclaimed: "What is a rite? Is it
merely jade and brocade? What is music? Is it solely bell and
drum?" He wanted everybody to know that the inner virtue of
humanity was the source of rites and music. Although Confucius
said "that one's substance excel one's culture means rudeness,

that one's culture excels one's substance means trivialism; it is not until being excellent in both culture and substance that he can be called a superior man," we know that Confucius valued the virtue or substance which was the source of rites and music rather than etiquette or decorum. This is demonstrated by Confucius' repeated sayings: "Crafty words and flattering countenance seldom imply humanity"; "Clever words, flattering countenance, and excessive modesty are disgraceful in the eyes of Tso Ch'iu-ming, and so are they in mine"; "Those who learn rites and music before becoming officials are common people, those who become officials before learning rites and music are the sons of nobles; if asked to select youths to become officials, I would prefer the former group"; "If one still has sufficient vitality after performing his moral duties, he can use it to learn cultural subjects"; "It is propriety to be diligent in studies and to feel no shame in asking humble questions"; "The substance of the cultures of the Yü and Hsia dynasties did not excel their patterns; the way [principles] of the cultures of the Yin and Chou dynasties did not overcome their shortcomings." In order to overcome the shortcomings of those patterns and proprieties, obviously Confucius gave particular emphasis to the "substance of pattern" or "virtues of proprieties." In brief, with respect to the two terms "man" and "proprieties" in Confucius' teachings, "man" was stressed much more than the ritual "proprieties" that man outwardly displayed. The spirit of Confucius' lectures and the core of his humanism consisted in man's necessity to become conscious of his inner virtue, which is the human essence that enables him to first become the worthy substance on which ritual proprieties depend. Thus, beneath the realm of ritual proprieties handed down by the Chou dynasty, Confucius discovered a pure "world of inner virtue" of man. Through mutual encouragement, Confucius and his disciples formed a "world of personalities." A new dimension of humanism was shaped by the thought and wisdom of Confucius, his followers, and later Confucianists concerning the problem of how virtues and personalities are developed. The significance and value of this dimension were even greater than the fact that Confucius commented on ancient characters and cultures and eulogized or blamed his contemporaries by writing the Spring and Autumn Annals.

It was Mencius who advanced the humanism of Confucius. And it was the subhumanism of Mo Tzu that stimulated the humanism of Mencius.

We say that Mo Tzu's thought is subhumanistic because, although he acknowledged the importance of the people's ecomonic life, of their political and social organizations that treasured competent elites and advocated conformation to superior men, of the morality of universal love, and of international peace totally free from aggression, Mo Tzu neglected the importance of rites and music and filial piety and brotherly love which Confucianists held dear. By advocating economy in funerals and objecting to music in opposition to Confucianism, he was unable to affirm the value of a complete human culture. Hence his subhumanism. But his stress on Heavenly will and ghosts seemed to demonstrate a superhumanism. Moism could not develop into a religion, however, for the motive behind this emphasis was still practical and utilitarian. Moreover, the fact that he regarded benefit and harm as the criteria for right and wrong or good and evil might render his ideas antihumanistic. This point need not be elaborated here.

Mencius rose to defend Confucianism in response to Mo Tzu's attack and reaffirmed the value of rites and music and family relationships which Confucianists held dear. Mencius was able to affirm the goodness of the human mind and human nature; from the demand of this mind or nature the expression of rites and music flowed out spontaneously as if unable to be stopped. In view of the fact that the prevalence of human love must proceed from the near to the distant, Mencius remarked that the whole world would be at peace if everyone loved his parents, respected his superiors, and extended this love and respect to all things in the world. Believing that human nature was endowed by Heaven, Mencius bridged the paths of Heaven and man by declaring that when we fully develop our own minds, we will be able to realize our nature and so understand Heaven. It was

not until the time of Mencius that the value of human culture
and man's inner virtue, which had been affirmed by Confucius,
obtained their a priori and purely innate foundation on human
nature. It was Mencius who first established the "world of the
human mind and human nature" in a self-conscious way.

We find the further development of pre-Ch'in humanism in
the thought of Hsün Tzu, who emphasized the system of proprieties, i.e., the classification of cultures and the construction of
the world of human culture. Confucius stressed the meaning of
rites and music; Mencius, their origin; and Hsün Tzu, the effect
of the system on how to set up the world of culture in order to
give order to the world of nature. "Heaven and earth beget superior men, and superior men manage Heaven and earth." Thus,
the natural world was governed by the cultural world. This was
an inversion of Chuang Tzu's superhumanistic thought which
"regarded Heaven as the supreme teacher," revered nature,
and belittled culture. As for the Doctrine of the Mean, the Commentaries on the Book of Changes, and the chapter "On Music"
in the Book of Rites, they all explained the meaning and value
of the superhumanistic realm in terms of the humanistic realm,
saying that sincerity was the Way of Heaven, that developing
man's sincerity to the full was tantamount to developing his nature and external objects, that Heaven and Earth possessed the
virtues of originality, pervasiveness, beneficence, and firmness,
and that the harmony and order in rites and music were the harmony and order in Heaven and Earth and all things. This shows
the development of pre-Ch'in Confucian humanism which sought
to bridge the ways of Heaven and man.

We say that the thought of Mo Tzu was "subhumanistic" and
that of Chuang Tzu was "superhumanistic." The ideas of Tsou
Yen, who spoke of the nine grand continents and Yin-Yang cos-
mogony, may be called nonhumanistic. These were not necessarily "antihumanistic." In pre-Ch'in philosophy, antihumanism
was the thought of the Legalists from Shang Yang to Han Fei.
The rise of Legalism, Moism, and Taoism, etc., was due to the
decline of the Chou dynasty culture. In view of the degeneration
of rites and music into the luxuries of lords and nobles, Mo Tzu

condemned rites and music. Seeing that proprieties and regulations fettered human feelings and that the will to achieve merit
and celebrity drove people to self-alienation, Chuang Tzu
yearned to roam with the Creator and become a Heavenly man.
For the purpose of enriching their country and strengthening
their army, Shang Yang, Han Fei, and Li Ssu were against all
Chou culture, such as the feudal system, the inheritance system, rites and music, and the virtues of humanity, righteousness, filial piety, and brotherly love that supported these systems. In addition, Legalists condemned all roving sophists who
pursued wealth and position, and also condemned Confucianism,
Moism, and Taoism. But they did not articulate any ultimate
goals that would be achieved by enriching the country and
strengthening the army. They never said that these efforts
were for the welfare of the people. They considered enriching
their country merely to be "the power to lead" and strengthening troops for invasion simply to be the "power to kill." In order to kill others' power, it was necessary to raise one's own
power, having aggravated power, it must be used to kill others'
power (as the Book of the Lord Shang advocated). Hence the necessity to make their country rich and their army strong; in
other words, to stress both husbandry and warfare. In addition,
as some articles by Han Fei remarked, "the power should be
under the unique control of the emperor," and "it is natural to
operate the system (exercise control), and it is cunning to make
use of talents." These ideas constituted a pure antihumanism,
which, in the hands of Li Ssu and the First Emperor of Ch'in,
formed an authoritarianism characterized by burning books,
burying scholars alive, controlling thoughts and opinions, and
impairing people's power and vitality. This political situation
temporarily ended the development of pre-Ch'in humanism.

4. The Han People's Historical Spirit of Understanding Changes in the Past and the Present

Oppressed by the antihumanism and the political power of the
Ch'in Legalists, pre-Ch'in humanistic, nonhumanistic, super-

humanistic, and subhumanistic thought sank to the lowest stratum of the society and naturally became intermingled. The product of the blending of the superhumanistic thought of Taoism that concerns immortal beings, the nonhumanistic thought of the Yin-Yang School, and the humanism of Confucianism began during the transition from the Ch'in to the Han dynasties and flourished with the ideas about divination during the Western Han period. This eclecticism attached itself to the Confucian classics and the personality of Confucius, who was deified in many myths which speculated on the future of the world and the origin of the universe and man. When it is suppressed, human thought cannot find its direct expression in the present; it can only make wild guesses about the future and the past. When the Han succeeded the Ch'in, the ideas which had formerly been suppressed emerged again on the surface, and the retrospective spirit, free from superstition and capable of reviving the past in the present, became the historical spirit of the Han people that sought insight into ancient and modern changes. Such was the further development of humanistic thought in the Han dynasty.

Chinese culture has always treasured history. But in the pre-Ch'in period, official historians and all books of history recorded things in a straightforward way, and so did Confucius in his Spring and Autumn Annals. The genuine spirit of history should trace the present back to the past in order to comprehend all changes. It was not until the development of Chinese humanism experienced frustration in the Ch'in dynasty and the Han people sought its continuation that this spirit truly emerged. According to the dialectical way of thinking, the frustration in the Ch'in dynasty was a turning from thesis to antithesis in the development of Chinese humanism. Acting against Ch'in, Han stood for the negation of negation, which reaffirmed the thesis and included it in its synthesis. This retrospect and return marked the true spirit of history. Ssu-ma Ch'ien's Record of History [Shih Chi] was an historical masterpiece best marking the spirit of history of the Han people. This book was intended to continue Confucius' spirit in writing the Spring and Autumn Annals. However, the historical value of Ssu-ma Ch'ien's work

really surpassed that of Confucius' Annals. The greatest value
of historical books lie in retrospecting, retelling, and revivify-
ing past events as if they had just occurred. The Shih Chi managed to revive the past world of Chinese culture and personalities in the reader's mind. But never could Confucius' Annals
do this. As far as historical value is concerned, the Record of
History outshone the Spring and Autumn Annals.

In addition to recollecting and reviving the elapsed world of
culture and personalities, the spirit of history had to shoulder
all the fruits of cultural development. According to the Book
of Changes, shouldering or carrying was the way of Earth, which
was shown by the substantiality and plainness of the Han people.
In their philosophy, e.g., Tung Chung-shu's, Heaven was revered as having a personality like man's great grandfather, and
so man should embody the mind of Heaven and model himself
after the way of Heaven. Together with various doctrines on
the correspondence of man and Heaven through transcendental
affection, Tung's philosophy displayed a high degree of the spirit
of shouldering. The Han doctrine of the transcendental affection
and correspondence between Heaven and man was not a religious consciousness that made man humble or made him,
trembling in the presence of God, confess his sin and hope for
grace. Neither was it intended to achieve a theology with an
objective understanding of the nature of God. It was only a consciousness of responsibility that considered human conduct to
be responsible for all omens and pests. Man should assume
responsibility for history and culture and even for fine weather,
timely rain, favorable wind, flowing rivers and tranquil oceans.
This Han spirit of seemingly unsurpassable folly was founded
on the same moral ground that enabled the Han people to build
on earth a substantial, magnificent, and unified country.

In the late Han the philosophy of Wang Ch'ung criticized all
Han ideas on Yin-Yang, the Five Agents, and the correspondence between Heaven and man. It also criticized those who
affirmed the ancient while condemning the modern. Wang was
a naturalist who regarded Heaven and earth as natural material
forces [ch'i] and historical legends as trivialities. But his

naturalism was solely applied to a critique of unfounded doctrines. He was by no means a scientist seeking to understand nature for its own sake. His doubt and criticism about groundless doctrines led to the establishment of a plain and reasonable naturalistic humanism, which appropriately served the purpose of wiping out all undue analogies and superstitions, unloading the unnecessary overburden unworthy of the Han people and closing the Han period of philosophy.

5. The Natural Display of Feelings Valued by the Wei and Chin Dynasties

The thought which began with the Pure Conversation of the Wei and Chin after the Han period was generally called metaphysics. It was also called naturalism because it despised prescriptive morality and valued spontaneity. But this kind of naturalism differed vastly from the naturalism that was founded on natural sciences in the modern West. The Wei-Chin naturalness referred to the natural display of human feelings like joy and woe. To stress naturalness was at first merely to accentuate that spontaneity is indispensable for a true man. Yüan Chi and Hsi K'ang denounced Emperors Yao and Shun, belittled Emperors T'ang and Wu, and exclaimed that proprieties were not established for people like themselves. This was merely because they realized that the Wei-Chin courteous abdication and gentlemen's "decorums in social intercourse" were nothing but pretences, ornaments, and artificialities; they would rather be spontaneous men behaving in accordance with their passions and volitions, which meant valuing man rather than patterns [culture]. Generally speaking, in the development of Chinese humanism, the accentuation on man or pattern varied. Duke Chou stressed pattern; Confucius stressed man slightly more than pattern; Mencius stressed man; Hsün Tzu emphasized pattern; the Han Confucianists stressed pattern somewhat more than man; and the first phase of Wei-Chin thought emphasized man. But Confucius valued man's virtue and Mencius treasured man's mind or nature on which this virtue was based. The Wei-

really surpassed that of Confucius' Annals. The greatest value
of historical books lie in retrospecting, retelling, and revivify-
ing past events as if they had just occurred. The Shih Chi managed to revive the past world of Chinese culture and personalities in the reader's mind. But never could Confucius' Annals
do this. As far as historical value is concerned, the Record of
History outshone the Spring and Autumn Annals.

In addition to recollecting and reviving the elapsed world of
culture and personalities, the spirit of history had to shoulder
all the fruits of cultural development. According to the Book
of Changes, shouldering or carrying was the way of Earth, which
was shown by the substantiality and plainness of the Han people.
In their philosophy, e.g., Tung Chung-shu's, Heaven was revered as having a personality like man's great grandfather, and
so man should embody the mind of Heaven and model himself
after the way of Heaven. Together with various doctrines on
the correspondence of man and Heaven through transcendental
affection, Tung's philosophy displayed a high degree of the spirit
of shouldering. The Han doctrine of the transcendental affection
and correspondence between Heaven and man was not a religious consciousness that made man humble or made him,
trembling in the presence of God, confess his sin and hope for
grace. Neither was it intended to achieve a theology with an
objective understanding of the nature of God. It was only a consciousness of responsibility that considered human conduct to
be responsible for all omens and pests. Man should assume
responsibility for history and culture and even for fine weather,
timely rain, favorable wind, flowing rivers and tranquil oceans.
This Han spirit of seemingly unsurpassable folly was founded
on the same moral ground that enabled the Han people to build
on earth a substantial, magnificent, and unified country.

In the late Han the philosophy of Wang Ch'ung criticized all
Han ideas on Yin-Yang, the Five Agents, and the correspondence between Heaven and man. It also criticized those who
affirmed the ancient while condemning the modern. Wang was
a naturalist who regarded Heaven and earth as natural material
forces [ch'i] and historical legends as trivialities. But his

Chin thought emphasized the spontaneous display of man's feelings, demeanor, bearing, and talk, which became the so-called
Light Conversation of those famous scholars and thinkers who
crossed the Yellow River to settle in the south. In this Pure
Conversation, there was mutual appreciation of character, gesture, and personage, with mutual praise through subtle words
and clever discourse. The Wei-Chin people could assume an
artistic attitude toward men and natural objects. Consequently,
the individuality or particularity of characters and objects were
apt to be revealed in man's mind. This rendered the period of
the Wei-Chin and the Six Dynasties an era of art and literature,
i.e., an age in which people valued spontaneity, nonartificiality,
and following their own inclinations or dispositions in their philosophy of life, society, and politics. The thought of Wang Pi,
Ho Yen, Kuo Hsiang, and Hsiang Hsiu was an explanation of the
typical spirit of this era. This spirit was diametrically opposed
to that of the Han people who were substantial, plain, magnanimous, and sincere. The Han scholars' spirit was to shoulder
or carry history, to revere Heaven and esteem sages, and to become proficient in the classics for practical application. The
whole community and culture demanded stability and solidarity.
This caused the Han people to accomplish their historic mission
of gathering the Chinese nation into a great, unified country in
the world. From the political and social viewpoints, the Wei-
Chin and the Six Dynasties period was one of conspicuous decline, for China was being torn into pieces, and eventually man's
individual consciousness superseded his national consciousness.
He demanded self-expression in order to do justice to his own
individuality with freedom from the bondage of politics as well
as from laws and proprieties. During this period, the most
eminent poets, artists, and thinkers were those comparatively
lacking in a sense of responsibility for their fatherland, or if
they had a sense of responsibility, they felt this duty was too
heavy to be undertaken. The best display of human spirit in
this era lay in becoming brisk, carefree, lucid, romantic, and
fresh after reducing or unloading the sense of responsibility.
The Han people would never have dreamt of the revelation of

this spirit in the Wei-Chin art and literature. The philosophical
writings of Wei-Chin metaphysics were clear, penetrating, condensed, and interesting; for the people's thought was relieved
of the burden of traditional culture and the great responsibility
for governing the country and pacifying the whole world. It was
not until that time that they could freely employ their wisdom
to attain a lofty realm of achievement. If we say that the Han
spirit displayed the essential quality of the earth, namely, substantiality, and that its shortcoming lay in being too stagnant
and substantial as if it were smelling the soil, then Wei-Chin
literature, art, and philosophy may be said to have been cleared
of the odor of soil before sauntering throughout nature and the
human world and to seem to "float and swim in the air like an
immortal." This signified the new development of another form
of the Chinese humanistic spirit.

6. The Rise of the Superhumanistic Thought of Buddhism

The period from the Southern and Northern dynasties to the
Sui and T'ang dynasties was the era during which Buddhism arrived in China and became the mainstream of academic thought.
Buddhism should be regarded as superhumanistic. However, its
spirit cannot necessarily be paired with the general social and
cultural spirit of the Southern and Northern dynasties and the
Sui-T'ang dynasties. Han thought was in accord with the Han
culture; and in the above section my comment on Wei-Chin
metaphysics was made in conjunction with the Wei-Chin spirit
of life, art, and literature. The period from the Southern and
Northern dynasties to the Sui-T'ang dynasties was the age when
the Chinese nation, after long partition, was reunified. On the
whole, the culture of the T'ang dynasty manifested Mencius'
utterance that "substantiality means beauty," and it shone
throughout the world. In this era most statesmen, poets, and
artists were remarkable in style, substance, and endowment.
Their spirit was not as carefree as the Wei-Chin people's.
Neither was it the same as the Buddhistic superhumanistic

spirit that seeks to go beyond the mundane world. Hence the need to detect the shortcomings of Chinese thought and culture since the Wei-Chin and the Southern and the Northern dynasties in order to explain the reason why Buddhistic superhumanistic thought was fused into Chinese philosophy.

At that time the weakness of Chinese culture consisted of having lost the religious and moral spirit that it had once possessed. Most essays expressing philosophy were written in abrupt literary style, lacking rigorous structure. Nothingness, naturalness, self-transformation, etc., as stressed in the Wei-Chin philosophy were definitely the expression of the leisurely artistic spirit. However, this kind of spirit cannot provide man with the ultimate concern for his settling down. The essence of this spirit can be fully expressed by the following extract from Wang Hsi-chih's "Preface to the Collections of the Orchid Pavilion": "Wherever delighted in what I encounter, I feel temporarily pleased and contented and remain unaware of my approaching old age. But after my pleasure vanishes with the event, I cannot help sighing over the pleasant affair.... Life and death being a great problem for man, how can I refrain from sorrow!" This spirit was good at appreciating what was seen or met. But, just for this reason, the event which elicited this appreciation vanished with what was encountered. As a result, the inconstancy of life could not but be felt, and the problem of death could not but arise. The appreciative spirit did not lead to the solution of the life-death issue. The timely arrival of Buddhism in China was to resolve this problem and to satisfy the religious demand of the Chinese. The Buddhist scriptures were versed in composition and structure. No wonder that talented men studied them humbly and concentratedly. One of the reasons why Buddhism became influential during the Southern and Northern dynasties and the Sui-T'ang dynasties was that its superhumanistic thought duly managed to rectify the bad habit of pomposity of the Southern and Northern dynasties. This habit was expressed by the saying: "The content of the voluminous writings was nothing but the description of the moon and the dew, while the material of the accumulated articles in the chest never exceeded the portrayal of the wind and the cloud." This ostentation was another corruption of art. The corruption of art of the Chou had made Confucius treasure substance, Mo Tzu oppose rites and music, and Chuang Tzu roam beyond the mundane world; eventually the antihumanism of Shang Yang, Li Ssu, and Han Fei arose. Han humanism got entangled with the words ōf the Yin-Yang School. This entanglement aroused Wang Chung's naturalism and the Wei-Chin people's anti-Confucianism, their toleration of feelings, and their emphasis on the individual. The overrefined literary style of the Wei-Chin and the Southern and the Northern dynasties needed Buddhism, which advocated superhumanism transcending oral languages and written words for the sake of attaining the tranquil realm of Nirvana, to purge the literary man's love of appearances and gratify man's spiritual aspirations to a higher realm.

The entrance of Buddhism caused the construction of innumerable temples, brought along countless new ideas on human life and the universe in China, and assisted her in cultivating the new domain of art and literature. Many a high monk acquired the status of poet and painter. This signified the integration of Buddhistic superhumanism and Chinese humanism. Consequently, Buddhists' renunciation of the mundane life and Confucianists' attachment to family life in this world combined to yield Ch'an [Zen] Buddhism, which was a further development of the T'ien-t'ai and Hua-yen Schools of Chinese Buddhism. But it was Sung-Ming Neo-Confucianism that further revived the intrinsic humanism of China.

7. The Spirit of Establishing the Human Ultimate in Sung-Ming Neo-Confucianism

It is not wrong to say that Sung-Ming Neo-Confucianism was influenced by Buddhism. But its origin was solely Confucian humanism. In some respects, it really excelled pre-Sung Confucianism in spirit and thought. Han Confucianists revered Heaven and esteemed the sages, whom they believed had descended from

Heaven and, consequently, who were unable to serve as models. Among the Neo-Confucianists' common convictions, the primary saying was that everybody could model himself after sages; while the second saying was that sages can join in virtue with Heaven because Heaven or Heaven and earth do not transcend sages. These beliefs truly revived the pre-Ch'in Confucianism of Confucius, Mencius, the Doctrine of the Mean, and the Commentaries on the Book of Changes, and they surpassed Han Confucianism. In the development of pre-Ch'in Confucianism, it was the Commentaries on the Book of Changes that first established the "Supreme Ultimate" as the ultimate of the universe. The Sung Confucianists went further, establishing the concept of the "Human Ultimate," and they gradually came to use the concept of li [reason] to explain the heavenly Supreme Ultimate. They regarded human nature as reason in man and the establishment of the Human Ultimate as the full development of one's nature and the prevalence of heavenly reason. Heaven and man, or Supreme Ultimate and Human Ultimate, having been bridged, humanity and human culture acquired their metaphysical meaning. In addition, Sung-Ming Confucianists, such as Lu Hsiang-shan and Wang Yang-ming, identified the "human mind" with the "heavenly mind," so the mind also acquired a metaphysical meaning. This philosophy penetrated the heavenly way through the human way and guaranteed the human way through the heavenly way. Hence the diffusion of the Sung-Ming Confucianists' humanism throughout the superhumanistic and nonhumanistic realms. The latter realms might be considered to be where the humanistic world was rooted. Sung-Ming Confucianists might be said to have seen a straightforward path for descent and ascent between the superhumanistic and nonhumanistic realms and the humanistic realm. Therefore, on the one hand, Sung-Ming Confucianists objected to the Buddhists' and Taoists' negligence of humanity but, on the other hand, also emphasized the elimination of human desires and the preservation of heavenly reason. This idea was rejected by the people after the Ch'ing dynasty. How could a man not become nonhuman after removing his human desires? If heavenly reason was the only thing that was preserved, where had man himself gone? But these problems were not so simple as they seemed to be. Simply speaking, "preserving heavenly reason" meant none other than that "man had to possess heavenly reason by inviting it to descend"; "eliminating human desires" implied that "the heavenly reason within man demanded the exclusion of human desires." It was not until the exclusion of human desires that man could be united with Heaven in virtue. This was by no means the same as the Han doctrine concerning the mutual correspondence and transcendental affection between man and the external Heaven; neither was this groundless speculation. This was a description of an actual event felt in the most sincere and pious moral life which involved religiosity because of its need to set up the Human Ultimate and thus enable humanity to acquire its ultimate metaphysical significance. Only from the viewpoint of this religiosity can we understand that Sung-Ming Confucianism was the further development of Confucianism which had been stimulated by Buddhist superhumanism. This development was marked by a "humanism conscious of its own capability of penetrating the superhumanistic realm." In the highest achievement of this kind of humanism, man was still valued more than the "pattern" that he displayed. Sung-Ming Confucianists could regard "the feats of Yao and Shun as no other than the clouds passing by the great vacuity [heaven or T'ai Hsü]." From the standpoint of Sung-Ming Confucianists, the emotional life treasured by the Wei-Chin people and the beauty of disposition valued by the Han-T'ang people were not sufficient to reveal the true mind or nature as man's essence. It was not until man stripped himself of all "likings and desires" in his emotional life, impurities in his inborn "disposition," "volitions and passions" mingled with true will, and "opinions" interwoven with true knowing that he could see his true mind or nature as the straightforward presentation of the heavenly mind or reason. At the age of fifty, Confucius understood the Mandate of Heaven and exclaimed: "Is it Heaven that understands me?" And Mencius made the remark that, having fully developed his mind and having understood his nature, he could understand Heaven. Both the Doctrine of the Mean and the Commentaries on the Book of Changes contained the idea that Heaven and man combined in virtue, which means the penetration of the superhumanistic realm through the humanistic. But the pre-Ch'in Confucianists' realization of the superhumanistic realm seemed to have begun from advancing man's spirit to its ultimate. The Sung-Ming Confucianists began from unceasingly sweeping away all impure slag and dirt in human life and mind and found a new road of moral cultivation "beginning with the humanistic world and leading to the heavenly mind or the reason of the superhumanistic world."

8. The Accentuation of the Culture of the Ch'ing Dynasty on Cultural Relics, Philological Studies, and the Meeting of Cultural and Natural Realms

As far as Ch'ing humanism, with its special features which differed from the preceding dynasties, is concerned, we may say that the Ch'ing people's greatest contribution to the Chinese culture was the historical investigation, etymology, phonology, collations, and compilations of quotations from lost books which they conducted in order to edit the literature handed down from ancient times. This spirit was manifest at its best in the attempt to reconstruct, according to research in relics and the Chinese language, the past cultural world and to use it as a reference for governing the country and bringing peace throughout the world in their own time. At its worst, however, this spirit mistook relics and language for culture or thought themselves and was lost in the world of things. In academic thought, the Ch'ing scholars objected to Sung-Ming Confucianism, charging that the latter overlooked man's natural desires, valued tranquillity and despised activity, stressed the understanding and enlightenment of the transcendental [a priori] mind but neglected the cultivation of empirical [a posteriori] habits, and disregarded numerous crucial issues in the actual society. From this viewpoint, scholars like Yen Yüan, Li Kung, Tai Chen, and Chiao Hsün condemned Sung-Ming Neo-Confucianism.

Judging from these two facts, Ch'ing humanism was, in comparison with previous humanisms, more capable of plunging
onto the plane of man's "reality or actuality that his sensory
experiences could directly grasp." Cultural relics and the Chinese language can be grasped directly. The problems of desires, actions, habits, and problems concerning people's daily
life are also the general issues of the realm of sensory experiences. We should know that this world is also the "boundary
between the cultural world and the natural world." At any rate,
it is extremely difficult to say whether cultural relics or matters of drinking, eating, and sex in the world of sensory experiences pertain to the cultural or the natural world. For instance,
when examining relics such as an object in the shape of a stone
ax, we can hardly tell whether it was shaped by nature or by
man. Archeologists need to understand Nature's influences of
wind, frost, water, fire, etc., on the relics handed down by their
ancestors. It is also extremely difficult to say which of man's
drinking, eating, and marriage customs sprang from natural
desires or instincts and which from cultural cultivation. Thus,
in order to understand the objects in sensory experiences, we
need, in addition to the knowledge of cultural history, rich
knowledge in nonhumanistic Nature. The Ch'ing people's humanism that accentuated the world of sensory experiences,
then, necessarily attracted people to a "humanism that stressed
the nonhumanistic natural world." The kind of thought which
specializes in studying the nonhumanistic natural world is that
of natural science. Ch'ing humanism was reasonably conducive
to valuing the natural sciences imported from the West. The
majority of the eminent Ch'ing scholars could actually treasure
such sciences as astronomy, geography, and mathematics. Since
the establishment of the Republic of China, sensible Chinese
have unanimously agreed that Chinese culture ought to absorb
Western sciences, including natural as well as cultural sciences.

9. The Reason Why Contemporary Antihumanistic Marxism-Leninism Conquered the Chinese Mainland

The development of contemporary Chinese humanism encountered an age in which the social and political cultures have been controlled by the totalitarianism of Marxism-Leninism, which is fundamentally and explicitly antihumanistic. Its materialistic view of history, which takes economics to be the determining factor of human culture, denies the "autonomy of other cultural realms" beyond economics. It regards all human cultures and thoughts as a reflection of class consciousness; such a view amounts to a denial of the truth and value of cultures and thoughts. Its one-party rule totalitarianism deprives human rights of their safeguard; in other words, it does not really "treat man as man." On the contrary, all "dignity of personality" and "value of individuality" become meaningless terms under its materialistic philosophy. Therefore, its spirit is basically antihumanistic. Since this is a commonly recognized fact, there is no need for further elaboration.

Now the question is: Why has the latest development of Chinese humanism ended in a triumph of the totalitarianism of Marxism-Leninism? There are various political, economic, military, and, of course, philosophical answers to the question. Briefly speaking, as far as academic thought is concerned, the cause lies in the frailty of the humanistic spirit in Ch'ing culture. This frailty is due to its overemphasis of relics and philological studies which are relatively unimportant, purely academic matters. It is also a defect of pattern in that the scholars' effort was confined to their studies. Although not wrong in urging people to emphasize the practical life, they erred in condemning Sung-Ming Confucianism. The accent of Ch'ing philosophy was on leading men to "do things," whereas Sung-Ming Neo-Confucianism urged everyone to "become a real man" or become an upright person. We should reject the degenerated form of this Neo-Confucianism that knew nothing other than "leisure talking of mind and nature with hands hidden in sleeves." However, all genuine first-rate Sung-Ming Neo-Confucianists valued "performing deeds" and could "perform deeds." In order to urge men to "do things," Ch'ing philosophers reproached the Sung-Ming Neo-Confucianists' learning of mind and nature promulgated for teaching people "to become real men." But actually these Ch'ing thinkers, except Yen Yüan,

only "wrote books." Their spirit for performing deeds was not
equal to that of the Sung-Ming Confucianists. As a matter of
fact, before any individual can truly "do things," the first condition is to "become a real man." After the middle period of
the Ch'ing dynasty, scholars like Tseng Kuo-fan and Lo Tse-
nan were more competent in achieving practical deeds precisely because the foundation of their learning was the spirit
of Sung Neo-Confucianism. Therefore, the philological studies
of the Ch'ing dynasty which opposed Sung-Ming Neo-Confucianism
were bound to show the kind of humanism that "concerned itself
only with the surface matters of culture and practical affairs
that lacked a deep origin and hence vitality." The influence of
this kind of humanism carried through the days of the New Culture Movement in the Republic of China, during which people
still stuck with Yen, Li, Tai, and Chiao in condemning Neo-
Confucianism. Since then, the prevailing spirit in national classics studies has never been free of the typically trivial and
piecemeal style which first came into vogue in the Ch'ing dynasty and afterward pervaded the Academia Sinica. Of course,
this spirit could not withstand Marxism-Leninism. It should be
criticized. The scientific thought and the ideas of liberty and
democracy advocated in the New Culture Movement were not
inherited from the Ch'ing dynasty but were imported from the
West and should be opposed to Marxism-Leninism. But when
people preached ideas of liberty and democracy without ground-
ing them on the ideas of culture and personality or making them
concrete in the political system, their slogans could only destroy and overthrow the existing social and political power. If
the people who promulgated science did not stress actual scientific research but merely employed scientific methods and analytic, logical techniques to criticize traditional culture and
threaten old-fashioned Chinese intellectuals, then the slogans
of science could not help develop Chinese culture and were even
degraded into a forerunner of antihumanistic Marxism-Leninism
in its conquest of China. The above may be said to have offered some reasons why Marxism-Leninism succeeded in
triumphing over the Chinese mainland.

10. The Future Development That Chinese Humanism Should Undergo

However, the Chinese nation has had several thousand years of historical experience. The development of Chinese humanism has undergone many bends and frustrations. The contemporary totalitarianism of antihumanistic Marxism-Leninism in China is similar to the totalitarianism of antihumanistic Legalism which she experienced in the past; the latter was realized through emperors, while the former was enforced by strict political organizations and under the cloak of fighting for the people or the proletariat. Having combined with modern scientific techniques, its means for controlling thought and culture have become even more effective. But human culture and academic thought have always developed amidst struggles and extreme difficulties, finding exits for escaping mazes or labyrinths. It is a common event that whenever the good way rises one foot higher the evil way mounts ten feet in response. But if the devil climbs ten feet higher, the virtuous may spring one hundred feet up in response. Both brightness and darkness are revealed through contrast, and so are the good and the evil ways. If man's eye can see darkness, it must be able to recognize light. If man recognizes evil as evil, then he even more seeks for the good. All negative things will surely be negated again. This is due to the fact that human nature is forever inclined to good or brightness. Therefore, the conquest of the Chinese mainland by antihumanistic Marxism-Leninism, despite being a catastrophe for our contemporary Chinese people, may not be a misfortune for the future development of Chinese humanism. For, because of this conquest, we have become more capable of reflecting on the intrinsic values and defects of Chinese humanism, so that we can better preserve and advance its valuable aspects and make up for its shortcomings. Moreover, the scientific spirit and the ideas of liberty and democracy imported from the West during the last century can only reveal their value even more when contrasted with the Marxist-Leninist totalitarianism that shackles scientific development with dogmas

and maltreats political objectors with concentration camps.
Thus, a still greater and further development of Chinese humanism can be envisioned. On this point, I would like to make
several suggestions for my readers' further consideration.
(Concerning items six through nine in the following, readers
may refer to my book entitled The Reconstruction of the Humanistic Spirit and other chapters in this book.)

1. Because of the fact that each period in the several thousand year development of Chinese humanism represented a new
phase not isolated from Chinese history, we believe that the
coming development may also reach a new phase without being
torn apart from past history.

2. From the fact that when the Han succeeded the Ch'in, her
philosophy was a magnificent interfusion of the thought of all
pre-Ch'in schools, we may predict that after the negation of
the antihumanistic Marxist-Leninist totalitarianism, there will
be an intermingling of all schools of thought rejected by
Marxism-Leninism. This cannot but be the case whether we
adopt the Chinese or the global point of view.

3. Traditional humanisms such as the Chou "spirit of rites
and music," Confucius' valuing "human virtue," Mencius' treasuring "human nature," Hsün Tzu's appreciating "controlling
nature through culture," the Han people's "spirit of history,"
the Wei-Chin people's "artistic style stressing the free expression of feeling," the T'ang people's "opulence in talent and
endowment," the Sung-Ming people's "accentuation on erecting
the Human Ultimate, seeing the cosmic mind through man's
mind, and witnessing heavenly reason through human reason
or human nature," the Ch'ing people's stress on "tending man's
actual daily life" may fuse with and base themselves on one another. I see no reason why these humanisms cannot be retained
in future Chinese culture. But we maintain that if the expression of feelings or talents and the arrangement of everyday life
should become truly reasonable as to display cultural values
and help cultivating virtue, they must depend on man's true understanding of his nature and his original mind. Hence the necessity to understand and to advance the learning of mind and

nature in Mencius' philosophy and Sung-Ming Neo-Confucianism. Otherwise, whatever we say about China's past and future humanisms will be no better than trees without roots or waters devoid of a source.

4. The Wei-Chin people valued laisser-aller and freedom in their thought. During this period, art, literature, and philosophy could give expression to individuality. But, politically, the Wei-Chin was still an era of decline. The Han people had managed to inherit and compromise their ancestors' ideas, and socially and politically, there was a prosperous unity. But their talent was not as resplendent, lucid, or graceful, and their thought was not as crystal clear and fresh as that of the Wei-Chin people. Thus, we know that it was extremely difficult for a nation to achieve the merits of two periods in which the typical spirit of the one valued the unity of the people, whereas the other treasured the expression of individuality. Nevertheless, the flourishing era of the T'ang dynasty possessed tremendous national power with far-reaching virtue and reputation on the one hand and produced great essayists, poets, artists, and high monks with particular styles in expressing their ideas and feelings on the other. This example is sufficient to prove that the culture of a single dynasty could accomplish the merits of the two aforesaid periods. If we truly wish to synthesize the spirit which values the unity of the people and that which stresses the expression of individuality, then we must take the T'ang culture as our model.

5. The defects of the culture of an age emerged from the fact that pattern excels substance, i.e., the virtue of man cannot hold the pattern that his virtue has fashioned. The defect of the Western Chou period began with nobles who "usurped the patterns and proprieties of rites and music" and robbed them of their veritable substance. The defect of the culture of the Wei-Chin and the Southern and Northern dynasties lay in "prizing ostentatious or high-sounding phraseologies." The defect of vulgarized forms of Ch'an [Zen] Buddhism and Sung-Ming Neo-Confucianism was "talking about mind and nature with hands hidden in sleeves." And the defect of the learning of the

Ch'ing dynasty was the "indulgence in piecemeal relics and etymological studies." The patterns of rites and music, literary phraseologies, conversations, characters, and relics are all outward displays of cultural life. Whenever such displays are overemphasized, the cultures' defects become manifest. To eliminate this weakness, nothing is more important than treasuring "substance," i.e., valuing "man" more than "pattern" (which is merely outward appearance). To speak of pattern, with the fundamental stress on man himself, is to "absorb pattern in substance." To value pattern but forget man is to "sacrifice substance for the sake of pattern." The failure to eradicate this defect by treasuring both man and substance will undoubtedly arouse superhumanism and antihumanism. Such an outcome is inevitable. We may verify it through history, Chinese or Western, ancient or modern. Therefore, Chinese humanism in the days to come should value "man" more than "pattern."

6. Superhumanistic Buddhism developed side by side with the magnificent T'ang culture. Eventually Buddhism was transformed by Chinese humanism before it stimulated the rise of Sung-Ming Neo-Confucianism which valued moral achievement with spiritual exaltation. From these we learn that a superhumanistic religion can lead the human spirit to a lofty realm. Hence we should allow all religions to play their roles in future Chinese culture, believing that they cannot only help the Chinese people in raising their spiritual level but can also be transformed by Chinese culture in such a way that they would stimulate the process of a renaissance of Neo-Confucianism and the revival of the traditional Chinese religious spirit.

7. We have said that when philological studies became highly developed in the Ch'ing dynasty, attention was turned to the study of relics, the history of the Chinese border, and prehistoric studies, and the issue in question was one in the boundary situation between the natural world and the cultural world, eventually the Chinese could not but be awakened to the value of natural science. In the sense that scientific thought is also human thought, we may say that both human studies and non-

humanistic natural scientific studies are parts of human culture. That man can inquire into nonhumanistic nature shows
that man's own thought is able to extend beyond himself. This
extension shows the grandeur of human thought itself. The application of scientific knowledge to the manufacture of devices
and the establishment of social order render it possible for the
cultural world to reign over the natural world and manifest a
splendid order. So the future development of Chinese humanism should involve studying both nonhumanistic nature and human cultures.

8. Man's creation of culture and achievement of morality and
personality depend on his being his own spiritual master. In
Chinese communities of the past, the shackles and fetters of
religious beliefs and caste systems that were imposed on people were slight. This made the past Chinese society more liberal than those of India or the West. But the large extent of
freedom permitted in the bygone society of China was not
earned by the conscious efforts of individuals, but by the intrinsic magnanimity of the Chinese culture itself. Hence this
freedom has never been concretely formed into human rights
with objective laws guarding their materialization. No wonder
the precious liberty in olden days was easily revoked by sover-
eigns and is nowadays smashed by Marxist-Leninist totalitar-
ians. Just for this reason, however, we have been reminded of
the broad-mindedness of the Chinese culture and the priceless-
ness of individual liberty enjoyed by the Chinese people in bygone days. We now know that the freedom that man subjectively
demands has to be consciously constituted to become, item by
item, human rights safeguarded by objective laws. This should
be strived for even under the totalitarian rule of Marxists-
Leninists so that the future Chinese society will become genuinely free.

9. Only when man has the moral consciousness that is deeply
concerned with the destiny of his country, nation, people, and
society will he develop a true political consciousness. Political
careers and activities are the kind of career and activity pertaining to man's objective moral practice. Being equal as moral

personalities, men should seek for political equality. The political system erected by the ideal that demands political equality is the democratic political system. Under the bygone political system of monarchy in China, everyone could become a sage — this differs from a certain sect of Christianity which denies the possibility for some predestined people to receive salvation, and from a sect of Buddhism that looks upon Icchāntika as eternally incapable of becoming a Buddha — but sovereignty was hereditary and did not tolerate authentic political equality between emperors and people. Ever since the establishment of the Republic of China, it has been universally approved that the source of sovereignty must be the people. This is not only a great modification in Chinese political thought, but also a derivative that should be developed from the implication of the traditional idea that moral personalities are equal. In advancing Chinese humanism, it is a must that this democratic ideal be materialized in a valid democratic system that embodies the Chinese humanistic spirit.

10. In sum, we admit that in order to advance Chinese humanism, we must affirm the value of man's aspirations to a "superhumanistic realm," of his scientific studies probing into "nonhumanistic nature," and of a free, democratic society that provides safeguards for human rights and equality of men. But we must further realize that superhumanistic religions, advocated with disregard of man himself, are liable to induce "antihumanism"; that scientific study, accentuated with indifference to mankind, may, by sticking to its habit of studying nonhumanistic subject matter in a detached way, tend to "treat man as nonhuman," to develop a callous attitude, and to degenerate into techniques that become tools for totalitarian rulers; that liberty and human rights, stressed with neglect of the need to become "one's own master in spirit," will merely be a "negative freedom from external bondage" which may not help to develop man's creative cultural activities or form moral personalities; and, above all, that democracy, cherished without the backing of a "moral consciousness" and the ideal of "equality of personalities," has a tendency to change democ-

racy into a political system that "divides power," or, still worse, that "distributes loot." These sayings mean that "the Way is not remote from man" and so "in pursuing the Way, we should not go far away from man."

It is not until we have developed faith in the above points and eliminated the one-sided view that teaches that "ears, eyes, mouth and nose have their particular functions and the gap between them cannot be bridged," that we can become capable of inheriting the past development of Chinese humanism, assimilating the cultures of the world, and advancing Chinese humanism to its new phase.

12

THE RELIGIOUS SPIRIT
OF CONFUCIANISM*

9. Confucianism Not a Religion in the Ordinary Sense, and the Meaning of Miracle and Myths

As the title suggests, in this part of the essay I am going to discuss in brief the religious spirit of Confucianism.

Confucianism is generally not regarded as a religion. This is correct; but people differ in their opinions why it is not. One popular view holds that the ultimate concern or root of Confucianism is man whereas that of a religion is God. Nevertheless, according to our discussion in Part I of this essay, God,

---

*T'ang Chün-i, "Tsung-chiao hsin-yang yü hsien-tai Chung-kuo wen-hua," Part II: "Ju-chia chih tsung-chiao ching-shen." Reprinted in T'ang Chün-i, Chung-kuo jen-wen ching-shen fa-chan [The Development of Chinese Humanistic Spirit] (Hong Kong: Young Son, 1958), pp. 371-399. Translated by Wong Yeu Quang.

Translator's Note: This lengthy essay of Professor T'ang's first appeared in Min-chu p'in-lun [Democratic Review], VII:22 (November 1956) and 23 (December 1956). Translator's notes — footnotes and bracketed inserts in the text — are added to provide the Western reader the minimum aid to a better understanding of Professor T'ang's ideas.

or the deity, is not necessarily the ultimate concern or root of
a religion; instead, it should be the transcendental ideal of perfection and perpetuation which demand the actualization and
emergence of value or sets of values. In our view, that Confucianism is not a religion in the ordinary sense is well justified
on the commonest ground: All religions involve myth or miracle whereas, since Confucius, the Confucianists have refrained
from discussing four things, namely, something extraordinary
or miraculous, violence, disorderliness, and deity. Nowadays
those who propagate religion do not consider myth as the important element of religion. This is in accord with our discussion of religious value from the viewpoint of the religious spirit
and is what the present essay has emphasized. We would say
that while it is not the most important element of religion, it is
present in all religions. It is common in them because it is
naturally brought about by man's nature of, or inclination toward, transcendence, which expresses itself in man's religious
demand. This demand must lead to various kinds of transcendental thought, which can further lead to the imagination or fancy
of something beyond this actual world as the source for the construction of mythical stories. The demand of man's religious
spirit is always a demand for something practically beyond human power and unattainable in this world, such as the desire
for longevity, absolute justice, and the riddance of suffering,
pain, and sinful desires. This kind of demand which man longs
to see attained to, and believes to be attainable, arises in his
nature of transcendence. Hence man must believe in the existence of some transcendent power as an aid to the attainment
of that demand. To convince people of the plausibility of such
belief, actual evidence is needed: in any religion there must be
the belief in miracle and myth in which natural law or order in
the world is or is seen broken. Beliefs of this kind must be
judged irrational and impossible by common sense and science
but possible and actual by religions. This is because the religious demand calls for the possibility of what is generally impossible. Without miracle and myth, man's mind [imagination]
cannot break down or through his conception of natural law and

natural order in the world; it cannot easily elevate itself to such
a level as to make him believe in the existence of a transcendent
power and thus cannot satisfy the religious demand. Hence,
when the demand of the religious spirit arises, it becomes difficult for man not to believe in miracle and myth. People may
perhaps say that Buddhism in its original form did not emphasize miracle and myth. However, when it had reached such a
point as to become a popular religion, it involved miracle and
myth. We all realize that the masses' zeal for and conviction
in a particular religion are always aroused through miracle,
myth, and art. This is not only because they possess curiosity,
fancy or imagination, and artistic interest, but because miracle,
myth, and art can in fact enable men to break down the conceptual limitation of natural order actually expressed in things
and events in this world; thus, through them, men can easily
receive and develop the religious belief in some transcendent
power and can come to the stage that their religious drive for
transcendence is aroused and their religious spirit is revealed.
Therefore miracle, myth, and art are constantly inseparable
from religions. If the three were absent in a religion, then its
religious spirit would lack both the transcendental thought to
counterbalance the conception of things in this world and also
its spiritual support; consequently this religious spirit cannot
avoid becoming declined to the extent that it is replaced by the
practical concern expressive in the sense of history, the scientific sense, technology, and the measures for changing nature
and society, or by moral practices.

What are commonly present in all religions are lacking in
Confucianism. This qualifies the latter to be not on a par with
the former. In the periods of Ch'in [222-206 B.C.] and Han
[206 B.C.-220 A.D.] the Confucianism in the Wei shu [Wei
Books]* was mixed with astrology and alchemy and some mythical stories were attached to Confucius. This practice was

---

*They first appeared in Former Han (206 B.C.-25 A.D.),
being commentaries on the Confucian texts in the light of Yin-
Yang and Five-Elements theory. — Tr.

later rejected by the Confucianists, and clarification was made
to separate Confucius from these stories. The Confucianists
do not believe that Confucius could have undergone rebirth after
death; nor that at birth he could have pointed to heaven and
earth — a gesture symbolic to the assertion that "I am the One
in the whole universe"; nor that there could actually have existed the Garden of Eden or the Paradise on earth; nor that
Heaven should be composed of thirty-three levels; nor that Hell
should consist of eighteen strata. This is not to say that the
objects of the beliefs rejected by the Confucianists are all logically impossible, but that in their daily experience men cannot
find evidence for the necessity of their existence. At this point
the Confucianist's attitude toward miracle and myth is akin to
the empiricist's, the rationalist's and the positivist's. In other
words, it is close to the attitude of the scientist but distant from
that of the religionist. It follows that the Confucianist spirit is
undoubtedly compatible with the scientific spirit.*

10. The Religion of the Spirit of Confucianism, Its Nonrivalry with Other Religions and Metaphysics

The Confucianist spirit shares with all superior religions
one thing, namely, the religious aspect. Hence, in the past,
Confucianism, Buddhism, and Taoism were categorized as three
religions. From now on, the Confucianist thought will appear
not only as a philosophy but also as a religion. The Confucianist religion shares with other religions this emphasis: Man
lives to find a sure place to establish himself and his "fate."**

---

*The argument here is enthymematic; the missing premise
may be reconstructed as follows: One's attitude implies one's
spirit or assumption. — Tr.

**The general theory of such establishment in Confucianism
may be stated as follows: Man's establishment is found in the
realization of his vocation as a moral agent, who sees the well-
being of the world and that of his as inseparable; his establishment of "fate" (ming) lies in righteousness or, in other words,
his "fate" is inseparable from righteousness. — Tr.

Philosophical and scientific theories cannot help man obtain
this establishment because they are [abstract objects] for his
intelligence and, moreover, they may appear in various forms
oscillating and lacking certainty. Art and literature cannot
help because the artistic state of consciousness is on and above,
is isolated from, this earthly world. Art and literature can
only absorb and sustain man in a momentary aesthetic appreciation. Nor can the political and economical deeds help because they are relative to the political and economical problems of a particular period and situation. Before the problems
are solved, there is agony or anxiety in which man cannot find
himself and his "fate" established or settled; after they are
solved, man's mind will seek to be occupied with something
else. Nor can he find himself and his "fate" settled in benefits,
wealth, fame, power and rank, his evanescent and precarious
love, and the possession of various kinds of knowledge and technique — they are all contingent, changeable, and short of the
standard of final and complete satisfaction. In self-consciousness, man may be the temporary owner of them. But their actual existence is finite, and the essence of man's mind is infinity. Man's mind is capable of transcending those finite things
and cannot confine itself merely to them and nothing else. Accordingly man can acquire the place for such establishment
only when his mind of infinity and transcendence, as much as
his life and existence, are established or settled. This establishment depends on man's possession of the following things:
religious belief or faith, the demand of the religious spirit
through which the infinity and transcendence of the mind are
manifested, religious morality, and moral deeds. This establishment can be found in most religions and the Confucianist
religion.

To talk about the Confucianist religion we have to discuss
first of all the Confucianist learning. What does he learn after
all? We can say that he learns almost everything. History,
literature, and philosophy are what he learns — the learning
to be intelligent or the learning of intelligence. But this is not
the most important. The more important part of his learning

lies in this: how to be filial as a son, to be benevolent as a father, to be a friendly companion as the elder brother to a younger brother, to be respectful as a younger brother — learning to practice the ethical principle in all kinds of human relationships. The extension of it calls for learning to run the government properly, to bring peace and harmony about to the world, and to set up political, economic, social, and legal systems for people far and near. But still more important is that the Confucianist learning progresses from full utilization of one's intelligence to complete actualization of the principles in human relations, in all systems and to the complete actualization of his "human heart" and "human nature"* so as to make himself a "real" man. This is what is called "learning to make one the man." This is what we constantly talk about and what was the "real" learning of Confucianists in the past. However, with the "real" learning can a man establish himself and his "fate"? The religionist says that it is inadequate for that purpose because it is merely the learning of human knowledge, culture, and morality. We can ask, "Where is human existence in this universe rooted?" We can also ask, "Whither does man go after death?" We can further ask, "How can man guarantee that man can practice morality to attain the cultural ideal?" Or, "Even human culture can continue and develop forever; after all, where lies man's destiny?" Or, "After man has solved his problem, how would he tackle the problem of sufferings of all living beings besides himself? How can he eliminate his and all living beings' sufferings, guilts, and sins which all grow incessantly?" To all these questions, if man cannot offer each a solution, then he is still lost in this world. The dearness and

---

*The Confucianist concept "human heart," as contrasted with the "animal heart," denotes something which consists of Kant's "practical reason" plus the British empiricist's "moral sense"; the concept "human nature" as contrasted with the "animal nature" denotes the moral "germ" or "germs" in human nature which, while uninterrupted, can spontaneously have natural growth and development into the full-fledged stage, say, that of a sage. — Tr.

love of human relationships can last no more than one hundred
years; the prosperity of learnings and culture will end in void
when the greatest destruction comes some day. Those questions
gain the serious attention of all religionists. The Confucianist
simply puts them in suspense. But this amounts to saying that
beyond the actual human world confusion and ignorance prevail.
Then, from where can we derive the place for the establishment
of man himself and his "fate" in our life? And then the so-
called establishment is but the concealment of the problems
and an enjoyment in the temporary life. This puts whoever
practices the ethical principles, sets up the systems, and develops his own "moral nature" in a position like that of the monk
who carries out his assignment by striking the monastery bell
on schedule day by day as long as he is monk. How can this
form of Confucianism, so mediocre and pragmatic,* be a match
for the profound and highly transcendental doctrines of great
religions?

On the above questions I have meditated again and again, and
I feel deeply disgusted with the mediocrity and lack of transcendence and profundity of the ordinary Confucianism. This
leads me strongly to love religion and to affirm the value and
the important role of various religions, and to hope that they
continue to exist and prosper. Nevertheless I never believe
that the establishment of myself as man and my "fate" has to
be found in a particular religion, and I never believe that people must discuss man's role in the universe from the standpoint of an affirmed or dogmatic religious thought, so that they
can find the place for that establishment. Why? Because we
can never deny this: Man's religious thought which covers
heaven and earth [everywhere], as well as all its derivatives
of equal coverage, namely, religious beliefs and the content of
thought, all still belong to man's life — existence itself — at the
time when they all become the content of his self-consciousness.

We cannot deny that man has the religious spirit, a religious
thought, which tends to transcend the practical life and his ex-

---

*"Pragmatic" is here used in a pejorative sense. — Tr.

istence itself, and demands something beyond. This line of
thought and demand, when pushed to its full effect, must lead to
something like this: The Buddhist would make all living beings
enter perfect blessedness or nirvana, freed from all sufferings;
the Christian effort would clear men of their sin deep-seated
in their hearts; Islam demands the actualization of absolute
justice; and the Taoist religion pursues longevity and eternal
life. All these are demands for the realization of various values, the emergence of them and their transcendental completion, and also longings for an eternal ideal — a group of values
which we obviously consider as what ought to emerge and can
possibly emerge. It is natural that the belief of values to emerge
should lead to the faith in the possibility of their actualization,
and in such a transcendent or supernatural existence as God,
the real Master of the universe, and the other world or the stage
of transcendence. It is natural and also explicable in terms of
metaphysics. How to effect that kind of actualization is beyond
our knowledge; besides, right at this moment there is no point
in knowing. In this respect I do not like my thought to be different from that of all religionists. But I think, on the view of
Confucianism, we can extend this line of thought a step further.
We have to say that we must give rise to a sense of self-confidence out of the self-consciousness or self-awareness of the
faith itself; we must be self-confident that the "human heart"
and "human nature" that can produce and be responsible for that
faith or belief also possesses, or is identical with, or is the
passage to, the transcendent existence or the transcendental
state of mind and source of all the grave, holy values in faith
as well. However, this means that our mind cannot extend
merely in its line of infinity and transcendence to form all kinds
of religious belief; and we must also have a great spiritual leap
back or retrospection and come to be self-aware of the beliefs;
then in the retrospection we suddenly discover that all grave
and holy values in faith are rooted in our "human heart" and
"human nature" itself. On the one hand, our self-awareness
accompanies our beliefs or faith soaring upward to transcendence, to seek infinity; on the other hand, it grasps the values

shown in our beliefs or faith, and connects their root to our "human heart" and "human nature" itself. Here, in addition to our belief in a transcendent existence or the transcendental state of mind, we must have self-confidence in our "human heart" and "human nature" itself; and consequently we must have self-confidence in our transcendental self or subject. Thus the Confucianist spirit or sense of self-confidence can accept and follow all kinds of religious spirit of man, involving no denial of them. The moment in which he is engaged in the "authentic" self-awareness is the moment in which he transcends his own religious spirit, confirming and intuitively apprehending man's spirit of self-confidence which comprehends and is on and above the religious spirit. The spirit of self-confidence is manifested in religion by the self-awareness of the transcendental and infinite spirit and by becoming confident in itself. This is the spirit of man which defies further transcendence. To transcend it is to become declined. This is to say that the final stage of the development of man's religious spirit ends in approaching the spirit of self-confidence. This spirit in Buddhism becomes Zen Buddhism; in Christianity it becomes mysticism; in Taoism it becomes Ch'üan-chen chiao [School of All Truth].* Since Confucius and Mencius, the Confucianist has emphasized the spirit of self-reflection, self-awareness, and self-confidence. This spirit will become the convergence of all religions in the long run. It can be so, not depending on that we hold problems superhuman and supramundane and above our discussion, but that men can have self-knowledge about and self-reflection on themselves: Men attempt to discuss or are capable of discussing nonhuman problems, expressing their transcendental, infinite, religious spirit — all this depends precisely upon their "human heart" and "human nature," which are possessed of infinity and transcendence. It is here alone that we can talk about the meaning of Confucianism, according to which men must affirm the religious spirit in all people, and

_____

*A Taoist religion which flourished in the Yüan Dynasty (1206-1368 A.D.). — Tr.

assert that the spirit of Confucianism can be the foundation of all kinds of religious spirit and that Confucianism can cover or comprehend all religious spirits.

The spirit of self-awareness and of self-confidence was shown in the life of Confucius, was clearly pointed out in Mencius' doctrine of innate goodness in the "human nature," and became well developed and elaborated in Neo-Confucianism of the Sung-Ming period.* The doctrines embodying this spirit assert that the "human heart" and "human nature" are identical in kind with the nature and "heart" or will of heaven; they emphasize that the virtues of heaven are also those of man. The themes of these doctrines in the hand of the Neo-Confucianist become the basis for rejecting other religions. But, for us, they constitute the basis for tolerating and nourishing all religions and enable us, in a moment or flash of an authentic self-awareness, to see in all kinds of religious life and faith that there is "real" Truth for the salvation of all mankind. The Confucianist in the future can get to know and intuitively apprehend the transcendence and infinity of our "human heart" and "human nature" through studying, appreciating, or enjoying, or even attaching himself to a certain religion; so that he can widen the path to, and enrich the measures of, cultivation that makes man sage and worthy. The Neo-Confucianists made Confucianism a rival of other religions. They may be credited for defending and distinguishing it from other doctrines. Nevertheless, when they did so they were lowering its status to the degree of relativity. Nowadays that we do not make it a rival of others amounts to ascribing no relative status to it; thus it does not matter whether we rank it above or below any religion. To say that it is below the religions is to say that its spirit of infinity and transcendence is not as clearly expressed as that in any religion; to say it is above is to say that Confucianism can enable man to establish or set up the high-level self-awareness and self-confidence, through self-knowledge of his religious spirit or self-reflection

---

*The Sung dynasty (960-1279 A.D.); the Ming dynasty (1386-1644 A.D.). — Tr.

of his religious spirit. And this rightly leads to the erection
of the peculiar status of Confucianism and widens the path to the
enrichment of Confucianism.

If what we have just said concerning the relation between the
Confucianist spirit and the religious spirit is correct, then,
when we try to publicize Confucianism, there is no necessity
in fighting against any religion; or against metaphysics, which
is closely connected with religious problems, when we have to
discuss man's position in the universe. If one can discuss the
metaphysical meaning of man's position in the universe, this
means that one can transcend himself, and in so doing, one
shows the transcendence and infinity of his thought. How can
this point invite any opposition? Nevertheless, we must, in the
final analysis, ascribe the self-awareness of the metaphysical
meaning to man. Man can be the metaphysical existence itself,
and the key to the answer to the puzzle about man's position in
the universe. No conclusive statement can be established which
asserts that man has no root in the universe and has no significance whatsoever. But this need not detain us here. With
regard to that kind of Confucianism the emphasis of which is
confined to man's actual existence alone, we can say that that
Confucianism is not the development in the line of the spirit of
Confucius, Mencius, and the Sung-Ming [Neo]-Confucianists,
which is marked by the approach to transcendence ever upward,
but is a decline into practicality and mediocrity — a level on a
par with the mediocre utilitarianism and positivism. The decline is the deviation from the right track of Confucianism, a
deviation which certainly can enable man to enjoy the temporary
gain in life or makes one feel that the fulfillment of man's obligation is something like the monk's fulfillment of his assignment by striking the monastery bell as long as he is a monk.
Life like that can hardly give man any establishment of himself
and his "fate." But when we affirm the value of metaphysics
and religion, when we begin from man's source of the spirit of
religion and metaphysics, his religious demand and thought,
etc., to seek self-knowledge and self-confidence in the infinite
and transcendental "human-heartedness" or "Thusness" and

find a root in it, the spiritual height and depth of the "human heart" and "human nature" can surely match the achievement of any religion and metaphysics.

In any religion and metaphysics, whatever suffices to provide man the place to establish himself and his "fate" may equally well be sought in our "human heart" and "human nature." Accordingly, we cannot say that there is no real place of such establishment. If there is no such establishment in our "human heart" and "human nature," then what is rooted there will become rootless: the religious spirit and faith or belief and metaphysical thought, all produced by the "human heart" and "human nature," are completely uprooted. If that is the case, how can there ever be any real establishment?

11. The Geniality and Practicality of the Confucianist Establishment of Man and His "Fate"

If we can immensely appreciate the Confucianist's "human nature"-"human heart" as the self-initiative source or root from which all religious spirits and faith or beliefs arise, then we know what the Confucianist means about the moral practice of full cultivation of the "human heart," the practice which culminates in knowing the "human nature," the practice which flows from the root of all religions along the path first uplifting and then downward. The "human nature" and knowledge of the "human heart" are what Wang Yang-ming [1472-1529] called "liang-chih"; he described it as "the basis of eternity and the universe, when the unique knowledge of it is attained inside the man who is completely alone in absolute tranquility and silence." The "human heart"-"human nature" thus known is also what is called "the Great Root" and "the Great Mean" in The Doctrine of the Mean, expressed in "how earnest is his jen; how deep is his valley; how vast is his heaven." This is the self or subject of infinity and transcendence. But, being so subject, it cannot be seen first in the following cases: its gradual riddance of restrictions; its gradual transcendence of pain, sufferings, and sin; or its endless discharge of "Great Pity" for all living beings

so as to expand infinitely its spirit or life of the body. At their
early stage, infinity and transcendence are like a bud — a bud
of "the will to create," a bud of creativity which spontaneously
permeates our "human heart" in its immediacy. This is called
"the seed of earnest jen." This "seed" appears to be something
not the least shiny, but a plain rudimentary potentiality of creation and nature. It leaves no trace to be seen and is not the
object of discursive reasoning. It is embodied directly in our
natural life and physical constitution, as the master of them,
transforming our physical constitution into a subject of morality sustained and beautified by its creativity. Man's virtue
within shines through his physical body, reveals itself in his
state of movement and that of rest, in his four limbs, and it
channels itself into human relations and events, the nation and
the universe. In this case, the Confucianism which calls for
full actualization of moral principles in human relations and
systems may appear to be mediocre; but it actually contains
something above mediocrity. In the "human heart" and "human nature" and the "seed of jen" this something above mediocrity not only transcends but also permeates man's physical
constitution; it utilizes it, bursting, it shines through the body
to another man's consciousness or spirit in human and social
relationships; what it is to the "human heart"-"human nature"
is what the spring breeze is to the young buds: it awakens the
"human heart"-"human nature" from slumber and transforms,
and nurtures the "human heart"-"human nature" and helps it
grow. Here lies the genuine and genial path to the real establishment of our actual life and also to making ourselves and
our "fate" established. But other religions, because of their
emphasis on the manifestation of transcendence and infinity of
the "human heart"-"human nature" for the sake of building up
transcendental faith, inevitably look at man's body as if it were
the bed of sins of desires and passions, or the center of sufferings, or the tool or vehicle of cultivation and discipline. This
is because they cannot offer the proper way to establish man's
body and life.

What we mean by establishment of the body and the "fate"

originally is establishment of my body here and my "fate" now, by means of our own effort. But ordinary people habitually associate this phrase with the meaning that it seems to be in pursuit of some place beyond things here and now, on top of which the "fate" is placed. Hence a transcendental faith or belief of religion seems to be the only ideal place sought. In fact, when we think of a transcendental faith of religion for the purpose of acquiring such establishment, we are suspending the body and the "fate" before the faith. If we really want to establish ourselves and the "fate," we must put the faith into practice and our faith must permeate the body and the "fate." However, if this faith is transcendent and external to us in the first place, how can it permeate them and inject reality into them? If this thing transcendent and external does not transform itself at the same time into something immanent, then (1) this body and the "fate" and (2) the object of faith are still two separate things. There is no such problem for the Confucianist who absorbs and transforms the transcendent-external faith into a self-confidence, a self-confidence that his own "human heart-"human nature" is immanent in this "fate" and the body; for the Confucianist, then, all practices and disciplines require inner cultivation and moral development to the extent that his moral self shines through his body. Only this can be the right way of establishment of the body and the "fate."

From the Confucianist emphasis that the inner moral self must directly shine through the body in order to establish itself, it follows that the shining and permeating of the "human heart" or "heart of jen" in human relations must lead to an order, from near to beyond: Whoever begins with filial piety ends in respect for the elderly; whoever begins with the regulation of the family ends in order and regulation of the nation, and further, in bringing about peace and unity of the universe, and shows compassion for birds, animals, and plants — all living beings. The permeation and shining of the "human heart" or the "heart of jen" must go through different levels of concrete human relations; therefore they are confronted with levels of hindrance as if the permeation and shining in question could be

handicapped and stopped any moment and become confined to a
particular concrete human relation. In this manner, the "human heart" or "heart of jen" is unlike the love that is rooted
in the Lord in Christianity; it is also unlike the "Great Compassion" in Buddhism: this love and "Great Compassion" flow
like a river on the plain of man and living beings. But, in fact,
the same love and pity can flow from the "heart of jen" or the
"human heart"-"human nature," and they are not produced as
a consequence of something which has become worldly, descending from the transcendent along a certain fixed path. Even
if they are so, they are not to be isolated from the Confucianist
order of practice which proceeds from being dear to your be-
loved, to compassionate relationship with people, then to love
for things in the universe. When man works, in accordance
with this order of practice, through levels of hindrance, the
flow and shine of his "human heart" or "heart of jen" will carry
with them the sense of anxiety and can emerge in the form of
concrete acts. The value of these acts depends on their quality,
not quantity. It follows that it does not matter whether one has
gone through more hindrances or less. Hence the virtues of a
filial son and of a good wife in a family are not necessarily below those of a loyal minister; the virtues of the loyal minister
are not necessarily below the virtues of those who want to see
justice done to all; nor are their virtues below those of the
Christian and the Buddhist who preach love and "Great Compassion" for all but lack the appropriate order of practice —
an order through which their love and "Great Compassion"
shine and reveal themselves like a river flowing on the plain.

We have recognized that the Confucianist emphasis on cultivation of the "human heart" and "human nature," on practice,
and on the order of practice from things near to things far, can
enable man to establish himself and his "fate"; nevertheless
we cannot halt at the level of moral practice concerning the
family, society, the nation, and man's inner moral state, regarding this level of practice as if it were the whole spiritual
life of the Confucianist. It is true that this moral practice in
the progressive manner expands our life, manifesting the flow

of our "human heart" and "human nature" and their transcendence and infinity. Yet the concrete family, society, nation, and
the whole human race are each one finite existence. The expansion of our life, the flowing of the nature and passion of our
"human heart," and so forth — all can hardly confine themselves to the finite. They must flow beyond the finite into such
specific natural objects as animal, grass, and trees. Accordingly, the mind of the Confucianist will reach another level
which is both metaphysical and religious. This is the level of
respect embedded in sacrificial worships of the universe, ancestors, historic figures, sages, and worthies.

12. The Religious Meaning and Value of the "Three Sacrificial Worships"*

It is a controversial question whether the Chinese sacrificial
worship of heaven and earth, ancestors, and sages and worthies
contains a religious element. In the Ming-Ch'ing period [the
sixteenth and the seventeenth centuries] the Roman Catholic
Church forbade the Chinese Catholics from worshiping their
ancestors and Confucius because this type of worship was considered religious activity. But the missionaries then in China
were divided in their opinions in this aspect. A number of them
like Matteo Ricci [died in 1610] maintained that it was nothing
but an expression of not forgetting the root of the race, of retrospective care of people in the past; hence it was a memorial
ceremony of gratitude, a moral practice. Since 1911 this type
of worship has been regarded again as religious; hence people
have discarded the li or rites of sacrificial worship of heaven
and consequently slighted the sacrificial worship of ancestors,
sages and worthies. This tendency has further consequences:
What Hsün Tzu [flourished 298-238 B.C.] called "the place
where the three roots of propriety lie"; the three sacrificial
worships of (1) heaven and earth, (2) ancestors, and (3) the
Teacher in the past [Confucius], worships which had been

---

*Also called "the three worships." — Tr.

greatly valued by Confucianists for centuries — all are no longer
regarded by modern scholars as the core of Confucianism. The
core for them lies in the realm of learning and knowledge, philosophy, politics, and education. Christians and believers of
other religions welcome this line of interpretation — that Confucianism contains absolutely nothing religious — for if it were
true this certainly should have revealed the inadequacy of Confucianism, the compensation of which depends on other religious
doctrines — the compensation which is understood as the necessity for the enrichment of Chinese culture. However, that the
introduction of other religious doctrines can enrich Chinese
culture is one thing; it is another thing whether Confucianism
possesses something religious and whether the pure or typical
Chinese who believe in nothing but Confucianism should have
religious rites and beliefs of life; for me, they represent two
questions the answers to which are positive.

We cannot say that the kinds of worship under discussion are
merely a Confucianist philosophy. They were facts in the life
of the Chinese people in the past. Nor can we say that they are
general moral psychology or behavior. Moral psychology and
moral behavior do not take the dead and heaven and earth as
their objects. We may feel indebted to the dead, but this does
not have to be shown in activities of sacrificial worship. We
may have owed the dead an unfulfilled promise and want to show
an act of fulfillment like the one performed by Prince Kuei
who showed that he had not forgotten the friendship between the
Duke, though dead by then, and himself, by hanging his sword of
highest value at the graveyard of the Duke.* Nevertheless this
act of fulfillment has no continuity. The kinds of worship honored by the Chinese Confucianists were performed regularly

---

*According to the Shih-chi [The Historian's Record], about
544 B.C. Prince Kuei began his visits of state to various dukedoms. When he came to Chui, the Duke of Chui liked his sword
but was ashamed to say it. Kuei read it in his face, but did not
satisfy the Duke right away, for the sword had been one of the
necessary ornaments for the prince, more especially when he

according to the season or on the particular dates of a year
and were carried on without end. Furthermore, the common
moral psychology and moral act are meant to realize and practice our self-command. And we can only call them moral psychology or moral act precisely because of man's realization
of his self-command. But man's sacrificial worship is not only
the act of carrying out his self-command that he ought to worship, but also a demand of spiritual communication with the
worshiped — a demand equipped with a particular set of rites.
The worshiped in this case is a transcendent being which is
the same as the object of religion. In meaning the rites resemble all religious rites in that they are all symbolic; they
produce no practical value. In worshiping we pray for the extension of our life and spirit to the deceased ancestors, sages,
and worthies in the past and to the whole universe; we honor
the virtues of our ancestors, sages and worthies, and heaven
and earth as models of our lives. Here obviously there are expressions of the demand of realizing value or set of values and
the transcendent harmony-completion and continuity; this explains the attitude of regarding the dead as if they were still
alive and able to come back to see the worshiper, and to respect what is ended as much as what is beginning; so that continuity becomes possible and so do the interaction and communication between (1) heaven and earth and (2) man; so that
the relation between heaven and man is harmony-completion.
It follows that in the practice of the three kinds of worship there
is obviously contained what people nowadays would call "the
religious meaning."

Those who disfavor the above view perhaps would argue that
in the three sacrificial worships there generally are the spirit
of the grateful return of what was due, as well as remembrance;

---

had to tour around different dukedoms. Later, when he returned
to Chui, the Duke had died. The prince hung the sword on the
tree at the Duke's graveyard and departed. His attendant asked
why? He replied, "I had tacitly made up my mind before to give it
to the Duke; I will not change my mind because he is dead." — Tr.

but there is no sense of request [of certain favor] from the
worshiped; no sense that the objects of the three kinds of worship are primarily actual objects which are objects of the sensation, not the absolute transcendent God; no sense that in the
three kinds of worship priests are not required as media of
communication between the worshiped and the worshiper; there
is no specific Bible through which God's intention or meaning
is revealed to man, and there is no belief about any dogma
either — in short, the religious meaning is not there. In our
view, however, the religious spirit does not necessarily need
priests and the specific Bible. For instance, the religious
spirit in mysticism does not depend on either one. The sage
and the ancestor as objects of worship were alive before, but
no more; during the entire worship they are not actual objects.
The concrete objects in the universe, heaven and earth, are
actual; but the phrase "in the universe, heaven and earth" has
a range of reference so wide as to include the deities in heaven
and earth, the most comprehensive whole of natural life or
spirit of the universe, or the Being of all things before the existence of the deities and after the existence of all things.*
This means that the phrase has implied transcendental meaning.
With the emphasis on the prayer for some favor or on the return of indebtedness, the religious spirit is a kind of interaction
and communication with the transcendent; the different emphases mean (1) that in the prayer we hope that the transcendent
objects of religion will come to us; and (2) that in response to
our indebtedness we are extending our spirit to pay sincere
respect to the transcendent — here we are expressing the spiritual process leading to the transcendent objects of religion,
paying no heed to gain whatsoever. This is enough to refute the
view that there is nothing religious in the three worships under
discussion.

What distinguishes the religious aspect of the three worships

*See my "The Chinese Religious Spirit and Transcendental
Faith" in The Spiritual Values of Chinese Culture, Ch. 14. [Au-
thor's own note; originally in parentheses as part of the text.]

from other great religions is that the objects of the three worships are multiple, not single; besides, the objects which are ancestors, sages, and worthies can increase in number. This makes the objects of worship changeable, not permanent. Each one's ancestors differ from those of another; sages and worthies in one region may differ from those of another region. All these make the objects of religion differ from people to people, place to place, and thus a universal church institution impossible. Hence, the worship of ancestor, sage, and worthy will ever be the business of each individual, not the public business of a continuous, unified catholic or universal church.

If we compare the religious sense in the worships in China with the religious sense embedded in religions of church, priests, the Bible of God's revelation, and dogmas and that in the emphasis on prayer and faith or belief in a specific number of gods or a unique God, a transcendent deity, Buddha, etc., then it seems to lack the religious tenacity and the feeling of urgency and also the feeling of transcendence which is fostered by the contrast between the transcendent and the mundane. Here what is gained or lost is difficult to say.

From one angle we see this: Religious tenacity and feeling of urgency can make man's religious feeling stronger and lead to noble deeds. But, from another angle, we can say that they can make people possessed of greater religious fanaticism and bias, and thus very unlikely possessed of religious toleration.

Rich in the feeling of transcendence fostered by the contrast between the transcendent and the mundane, man may easily have an aspiration to transcend the mundane, to form a holy religious personality; nevertheless it can hardly bring one's religious spirit into harmony with different forms of humanistic spirit. Perhaps man's religious spirit may direct him upward toward transcendence, far away from the mundane; or he may develop an arrogant attitude toward people of the mundane world; thus problems in the human world carry no weight at all for him, and his attitude becomes apathetic.

Man's belief in one or more gods, in the Bible of God's revelation, in dogmas, in the church institution of priests and so forth, may well concentrate man's religious spirit so much that the religious group, religious deeds and the societal force to change the human mind will be produced. But this kind of institutionalized religion has a stronger sense of exclusion. In the history of the West, the struggle between church and political power, religious wars, the oppression and persecution among and between different religious groups — all were caused by precisely that sense of exclusion.

Man's prayers to God or gods may take forms such as the one for divine grace in helping free man from sin. In this case, it may strengthen our sense of guilt and will to rectify. In prayer, in spiritual union with God or gods, man may feel his strength in morality and life already enhanced. This is a fact. But this enhancement may also be attained through other methods of cultivation of oneself such as the practice of Yoga and the sincerity and respect in Neo-Confucianism of the Sung dynasty [960-1279 A.D.]. The many objects for which one prays to God may include the satisfaction of one's selfish desires. When one feels sure about divine grace in his favor, one's selfish desires may assume a coat of holiness and thus acquire a hiding place which makes them the more difficult to be banished.

In the Chinese tradition, the three religious worships lay no stress on the prayer for favor, but lay particular stress on the grateful return of favor; as such, their spirit is absolutely free of selfishness. It surges upward, extending itself in spiritual communication with ancestors, sages, worthies, heaven and earth. It may not give rise to any ill consequence, and in giving expression to the transcendence and infinity of human mind, it possesses value as great as any religion. And the objects of worship include one's own ancestors, the sages and worthies worshiped in a particular place or by a particular individual; the objects of worship are not merely confined to a universal God, Buddha, or heaven and earth; this expresses an emphasis on "the relation of the particular existence or being of myself to the particular life and spirit of the worshiped." What I worship may not necessarily be the same as what someone else worships; this gives my worship a unique meaning in the sense that there is no substitute for it in terms of the worshiped and the worshiper; this makes my spirit in the practice of worship easily permeate and substantiate right away the relation between myself and what I am worshiping. In proportion to the continuation of man's natural life and cultural life, the number of ancestors, sages and worthies in the world of the worshiped increases: the expansion of this world simultaneously parallels the progress of man's natural life and cultural life and the spirit of worshiping is ever expansive, never confined to a specific God. Thus man's religious spirit itself evolves always in the process of growth, creation, and expansion. It follows that the objects of man's worship as a whole, in the process of growth and change, make man's religious spirit precisely correlated with his natural life and cultural life. In this light we see that the three worships in China have a higher value, at least in some respects, than other religions.

13. Doubts About the Religious Value of the Three Sacrificial Worships and the Answer to Them

Those who doubt the religious meaning and value of the three sacrificial worships as discussed above maintain that the worshiped ancestors, sages, and worthies were primarily men — neither gods nor Buddha. They were primarily concrete persons; hence, in worshiping our ancestors we have images of the concrete objects; for example, "On the Meaning of Worship" in the Li Chi [Book of Rites] says, "Recall his laughter; recall where his pleasure lay; recall what were his favorites"; we have the way of life of the worthies in the past, their qualities as model for us, and so forth. It follows that our worshiping mind may easily remain confined to the concrete objects in our mental pictures. But our mind is possessed of infinity and cannot remain established in them. That in worship our sincere respect can only be expressed through images of the material heaven and earth or things in it cannot enable us to attain the religious stage of pure spirit. Our worship of an infinite personified God or Buddha makes us feel that we see face to face an infinite being of pure spirit; this can enable our mind to remain established in a state or stage of pure spirit. Accordingly, although there is something religious in the three worships in China, they do not have the same value as any ordinary religion.

In our view, there are pictures in all religious ceremonies. Not only are there pictures of Buddha in the Buddhist religion, but also in Christianity there are pictures of Jesus Christ on the cross. These pictures and mythical stories and miracles are all inevitable in religion, and through them we frame images of transcendent objects and go beyond the boundary of the conception of things, events, and so forth in the concrete world. In this sense, their value is mainly negative, not positive. If people positively regard the pictures and images themselves as objects of worship, then this is materialization of religious spirit, and even idolatry. But whether people take the value of the pictures, images, etc., as positive or negative depends on their attitude. If they take it as negative, then any picture of a concrete object cannot set a limit on the mind. And we have reason to say this: the recollection involved in worship of the deeds of our parents, sages and worthies, etc., is less likely to set a limit to our mind than the religious pictures and images introduced by the mythical stories. For the images and conceptions fostered by religions are not concerned with secular facts and events or, in other words, merely with some transcendent objects isolated from the earthly world. Because of this isolation, our thinking process cannot take the pictures as stepping-stones to the bank of different conceptions. On the one hand, this may enhance the degree of intensity of our religious faith or beliefs; on the other hand, it may also confine our religious mind to, and may make the mind sink into, the objects of transcendental thought. In the three worships the deeds of our ancestors, sages, and worthies in our recollection and thought, together with images of the universe and all beings in it, had their real existence once in the actual world, in the natural order, and in historical sequence. When we think about them, we have at once placed them in the natural order and

transferred them [from our subjective consciousness] into the
realm of objective existence. Placing them in the objective existence, our mind transcends the pictures of the concrete objects. Hence the concrete objects in our conception can not only
make us transcend the world of this moment but also make our
mind free from sinking into them. And in the three worships
in China the tablets in the temples of the dead, the ancestors,
sages and worthies require only the names, no pictures, but
with the pictures standing by or off in another room. This
means that when men worship in sincerity, the names, not the
concrete images, serve as the sole focus of sincere respect.
Therefore the accusation that the three worships cannot easily
lead one to reach a stage of pure spirit is not well grounded.
The core of the issue lies in whether the mind involved in worshiping is itself one of pure spirit. If not, then all the pictures,
mythical stories, and images caused by myths trap our mind
in them, far removed from what is believed in — God and Buddha, for example, who have infinity.

Those who slight the doctrine of the three worships maintain
that the objects of worship — ancestors, sages and worthies,
and heaven and earth — are many; and man's mind is one; man's
personality is one. The development of religion is from many
gods to one; [hence] man's religious spirit can reach the highest point of concentration only before one unique God. This
concentration of spirit is necessary not only for the existence
of one unified church but also for the concentration of religious
spirit.

In our view, religious spirit not only must have one place
of concentration but also a place of expansion. The religion
of absolute faith in the uniqueness or "one" of God never in
fact exists. The one body of God in Christianity assumes three
forms; Buddha has the "threefold" body, namely, (1) the
"Dharma" or the "Ideal Body," (2) the "Reward Body," and (3)
the "Transformation Body." Buddha's "Ideal Body" and God
are the self-sufficient source of the objects of worship in both
religions. Buddha's "Reward Body" in Gautama Buddha and
God transformed into Christ are both cases that manifest this

source in nature. Buddha's "Transformation Body" and "The Holy Spirit" manifest themselves to the individuals of a particular time. This is because the transcendent and unique object of religious worship must necessarily be related to nature and must duly be revealed to the individuals because they are "many." The "principle of transcendence" and the "principle of actuality" must be united; so must the "principle of one" and the "principle of many." In the case of the three worships in China, each individual has his ancestors: this represents the "principle of many." People of various places and professions worship different sages, worthies, or originators of their professions: this represents the "principle of many." But they all worship Confucius as the sage and the "Yellow Emperor" as the first ancestor of their race: this represents the "principle of one." In short, ancestors and sages represent the "principle of many"; the universe as a whole and, inside it, the whole of reality of all beings, lives, spirit, and values represent the "principle of one." Sages and worthies lived once in this world, representing the "principle of actuality." Heaven and earth have existence before and after the existence of man; this points to the fact that the whole totality or actuality of beings, lives, spirit, values in the universe is infinite, beyond the reach of thought: This represents the "principle of transcendence." If we discuss "heaven" and "earth" separately, then "heaven" represents the Ideas of substance or reality of beings, lives, spirit, and values in the universe and is the "principle of transcendence" on and above all things and events already done or completed. "Earth" represents the totality of all actual things, events, etc., already completed and preserved, and is the "principle of actuality." If we discuss ancestors and sages separately, then (1) ancestors were the source of my actual life, representing the "principle of actuality": we worship those who were dear to us, and dearness of relationship is here what counts as important; and (2) sages and worthies are transcendent on and above us and are the common objects of deep respect to all, representing the "principle of transcendence"; and in worship, deep respect is emphasized. The actuality or reality as object of worship was once real; the transcendent permeates the actual. Thus the many are real "many"; one is the totality or reality that is revealed from "many" in their self-transcendence. This marks the difference from both (1) that Buddha changed or transformed himself into various "Bodies of Transformation" and (2) that "The Holy Ghost" universally affects all people, for these two kinds of "many" are not real "many." Buddha's "Ideal Body" appeared as the "Body of Reward," and God transformed Himself into Christ; these two divine acts can only be viewed as the supernatural reality manifesting itself in the natural reality, and thus not as men who actually once lived in the natural reality.

With regard to the religious spirit of the three worships, if there is any inadequacy, then we would say only that it places less emphasis on absolute equality and absolute justice than the spirit of Islamism; less emphasis on the indestructability of life so as to pursue immortality than the spirit of the Taoist religion; less emphasis on the universal sin in human beings than the spirit of Christianity; and much less emphasis on sufferings and agonies in the world than the spirit of Buddhism. This made it necessary that in addition to Confucianism, the Taoist religion exist in China to indoctrinate the ordinary Chinese that there were Masters of Hell below, who could give fair trials; made Islamism shine with special value in the religious world of China; and made Buddhism flourish in China; Christianity possessed of value of existence in the future of China. Furthermore, this explains why we recognize the due place of each religion. However, if we assert on the basis of what has just been said that we must believe in, besides the three worships, one of the many religions, then the assertion lacks any necessary support or reason. For we can commit ourselves to compassion, forgiveness, humanity, and so forth without demanding the actualization of the "principle of absolute justice and equality" in that "compensation of good and evil is absolutely sure and precise." On the metaphysical basis we can build up faith in the principle of "whatever is really reasonable or rational will come into being in this universe" so as to

satisfy our demand for the necessary actualization of absolute
fairness and absolute justice. We can do without longing for
eternal life and regard death as a stage in human existence; we
can utilize death to expose our whole life as a mirror [reflect-
ing good or evil] for generations to come; or we can sacrifice
ourselves for some noble ideal and make our death expressive
of supreme value as weighty as Mount Tai. On the same basis
we can also establish that all human values must be preserved
in the universe and establish faith such that man's spiritual life
after death would still soar up to meet the demand for the completion or perfection of his integrity — the demand of an incessant internal drive during his lifetime; in the final analysis,
then, we do not have to desire longevity. On account of this, we
can have different opinions concerning what Christianity calls
"the universal sin of mankind," "sin as essence of life" and
concerning how the Buddhist views the world as ocean of anxiety and pain. Therefore the assertion based on the merits of
religions that man must believe in one of them rests on no absolute ground either.

Taking into account man's life and psychology, we may say
this: Man believes in certain religion for practical reasons because quite often he has a strong sense of sin or guilt, or some
agony caused by a situation into which he has fallen helplessly
and about which he can do nothing; or he feels restless within,
and his person, body, and mind are all groping after some
seeming certainty. Here Christianity, Buddhism, or any other
religion of dogma can give him a moment's consolation and a
state of tranquility. To attain the same result by way of, say,
ordinary moral education to rid him of sin, or environmental
change to eliminate his agony, or spiritial discipline appears
like beating around the bush or even beating the wind. On the
contrary, if man can believe in a religion and entrust himself
to God or priests, it appears that he could be immediately released from sin and pain — free of any spiritual burden — and
he would easily attain a tranquil and peaceful mind. This we
never deny as it is the spiritual effect most easily produced by
the common religious transcendental faith. Accordingly, we

admit that for some people it is better to possess this kind of
faith, the function of which is not replaceable by that of ordinary
philosophy, the influences of society and culture, and Confucianism. As a matter of fact, this constitutes one of the reasons
for the necessity of the existence of ordinary religions.

In fact, some people consciously possess a grave sense of
sin and agony as the victim of circumstances; or they fall a
slave to their restless excitement. But some others do not
possess this sense; instead, they feel they are their own master.
Thus religion becomes necessary only for those with the sense
of sin, but not for those without that sense.

In this case, if we want those without that sense to believe in
religion, the only way is to point out that they are sinful or
guilty even when they do not feel the sense of sin; that there
are indefinite irritations and other vexing feelings in their
hearts even when they do not feel anxiety and agony. Or, according to Jesus Christ, all are born with "original sin," and
the only salvation is through faith in him. Or, according to the
wisdom of Buddha, all living beings are actually in the ocean
of agony and anxiety, and the only way to become emancipated
from them is through the Path of Buddha.

On our view, Christianity lays heavy emphasis on "original
sin." This doctrine appears, when compared to the mediocre
version of the doctrine that man is born with original goodness,
to be more profound and comprehensive. That doctrine of
original goodness flatters and pleases the mediocre; the Christian theory of "original sin" can spur people to reflect on and
repent of their deep-seated sin. Nevertheless, too much emphasis on "original sin" will lead to an extreme. For we can
know our sin and be repented through our sincere self-reflection
or self-examination; from this we can assert that man originally possesses a moral conscience transcendent of sin and
that there is goodness in the transcendental "human heart" and
"human nature." This is the basis on which traditional Confucianism asserts original goodness in the "human nature."
And that Confucianists demand man to be self-reflective, self-
conscious, and self-confident is simply the urge to apprehend

this "human heart" and "human nature." Here there certainly is no place for the assertion of "original sin." The [Buddhist] view of agony of living beings makes a case when they are seen as blindly gripping their individuality or individual life. But they may also have activities which transcend their individuality and involve true interaction and communication with something other than their individuality. Here we see life and creativity; here is the meaning of life. Accordingly, on the one hand, you can say that this world is one ocean of sufferings; on the other hand, you can also say that it is a place where life spreads itself, where creativity flows, a place full of the meaning of life. On the human level, whether life is suffering or not is open to two possible explanations: painful anxiety does exist in man's heart; but so does self-complacency. On a rare occasion man may come across the toughest hardship in life; it is not impossible that he may surrender this moment of the concern for his "self" to the sudden enlightenment in which the sky is purity and earth is peace and attain self-complacency. In Buddhism's view, this self-complacency is not commendable. But whether it is or not need not concern us here; what we have done is explain that not all people accept the idea of "original sin" in us and of life as the ocean of sufferings.

An important question arises right here: If man basically does not believe in "original sin," or life as the ocean of sufferings, is there any other justification to persuade people to pray to God and Buddha, to show a religious activity? Or, assuming man free from "original sin," and all living beings already freed from all sufferings, is there any justification for the existence of Christianity and Buddhism? That is, without the contrast with the hardship and sin in man's life, is religious activity possible?

According to Christianity and Buddhism, it would seem, if man is sinless or if all living beings are freed of any hardship, then man should be in the paradise and the universe should be perfect blessedness or nirvana; thus there would be no necessity of the existence of religion, as religious activity is established to face hardship and sin in man's life.

14. The Timeless, Necessary Existence of the Confucianist Religious Activity, and the Metaphysical Meaning of the Three Sacrificial Worships

But if we say that the Confucianist three worships are also religious activities, then we also have to say that they are not established to face man's pain and sin in life. We worship parents, sages, worthies, and heaven and earth, not because we know that we are sinful and treat the worships as ceremonies of expiation, nor because we know we are in agony and we pray [to ancestors, etc.] to eradicate it. Our worship simply means the ability of our spirit to transcend our own self or Ego, to reach and communicate with ancestors, sages, worthies, and heaven and earth, and it means nothing else. And this is solely an expression of the religious activities of the transcendence and infinity of our mind. We worship when we are in pain; we worship when happy. We worship when sinful; we worship when sinless. Only in this manner can worship make our religious activities independent of our individual concrete situation whether it is happy or painful, sinful or sinless: this makes our religious activities unconditional and right. Accordingly, even if our souls were to become settled in Heaven, in the world of perfect blessedness, or transformed into other bodies, we must still worship our ancestors who once existed in this world, our sages and worthies who lived once. This is the height of the religious spirit of Confucianism.

One of the heights of this spirit is that, fundamentally speaking, it is not established to satisfy man's demands. Men know themselves sinful or in agony and then turn to religion; they then turn to religion with their demands. In this case, religion looks noble, but is actually low, in the sense that it is used as means to the fulfillment of their demands. In the case of the Confucianist three worships, human demand or need (for some favor) from our ancestors, sages, worthies, heaven and earth plays no part in building them up. The meaning of these sacrificial worships is what the pre-Chin Confucianists called "the great repayment of indebtedness to our origin, back to the beginning." Ancestors were the origin of our life; my spirit of worship is to return to our ancestors. Sages and worthies are the root of culture and education that we have received; our spirit of worship is to return to them. Heaven and earth are the source of our life and the creativity of all beings; our spirit of worship is to return to them. In short, the spirit of worship is in the final analysis to return and repay indebtedness to the origin. This return to the origin means transcendence beyond the limit of the branch of the root [origin] and is itself an expression of transcendence and infinity of our mind. This theory, if expressed in terminology of metaphysics, may be rendered in this manner: Heaven and earth transforming and producing or creating all beings; the multiplication of human life; the flow of influences and effects of human education and culture — all as a whole is a process on-going and ever profusing, a process which may also be considered as downward, declining revelation. But man's self-consciousness can gather up and focus whatever is ongoing, profused, revealing, and declining and can comprehend it in the manner of sustenance and righteous firmness. And the worship spirit to return to the origin, to repay indebtedness to the origin, which issues itself from man's self-consciousness or self-awareness, directly embraces that declining process and sustains it in a reverse direction, upward and inward, to reach the primary source, to counterbalance that process. The process of decline goes from nothingness to being, from darkness to brightness, from the shapeless to the shaped, from Yin to Yang. The counterbalancing process proceeds from being to nothingness, brightness to darkness, the shaped to the shapeless, Yang to Yin. The two processes come and go in succession, relating darkness and brightness, the world of supra-experience and that of experience. The mutual sustenance and union of Yin and Yang constitute T'ai Chi and then the current and change of things and events in the human realm and the universe; proceed from openness to closeness, profusion to concentration, from origination to prosperity then to righteous firmness incessantly.

Furthermore, the meaning of the three worships may be
understood through what was said in Part I of this essay,
namely, that the root of religious spirit lies in the transcendental completion and eternity of the demand for preservation
and emergence of values. In the universe, growth of natural
things, cultivation of human culture, the achievement of the
realm of human integrity — all are activities of creating and
actualizing values. But all these existent things and the completed culture and human integrity seem to become immersed
into the worlds of history, of the past, into eternal oblivion when
they become completed. Here is the striking great melancholy.
The basic demand of religion calls for the affirmation and preservation of a transcendent absolute existence of all things of
value. This absolute existence may be God, or the Buddhist
"alaya vijinana," "amala-vijinana" or Buddha, and so forth;
hence, this world is both changeable and permanent: There may
be things destructible, but also things eternally indestructible.
In the mind of the religionist, the God or the set of deities creates the world on the one hand, and preserves it on the other
hand. Creation is the path of ch'ien, the virtue of heaven; preservation is the path of k'un, the virtue of earth. Ch'ien and k'un,
heaven and earth are the source of creation and the place of
preservation of all beings. All ordinary natural things and
events and human affairs are in a process of creation, and the
transcendent religious God and heaven and earth keep creating
and preserving them. But in God's creation, only the virtue of
heaven is seen, not that of earth; in God's preservation, only the
virtue of earth is seen, not that of heaven: two virtues do not
reveal themselves at the same time. Hence when we observe
the creation of all beings, we can feel thankful to heaven and
earth and God for what they have done; and when all beings are
passing away, though we can think that they might still be some-
where in the universe embraced by God, we may feel they are
already nothingness to us, for they cannot recur. Here we cannot help extending our regret to heaven and earth and God.
Nevertheless, in worshiping heaven and earth, sages and worthies, ancestors, etc., our mind can function both as preservation

and creation and manifest a microcosm of virtues of heaven
and earth; for when we are recalling our ancestors, sages and
worthies, their virtues appear in our minds again. This means
that the existents and values preserved in the universe, embraced by God, recur in the human world and are preserved by
us. And our preservation is a deed other than that of the universe and of God. It is issued at just this moment and freshly
created by us; thus, it is our creation. This is what is meant
by "preservation is the creative human mind." All ordinary
things and events in this world are made by creation but cannot preserve themselves. Heaven and earth, or God, can both
create and preserve. But, what they are creating is not what
they are preserving. What is preserved cannot revert to the
human world. Only man can reproduce in his mind at worship
the virtues of his ancestors, sages, and worthies and have them
preserved. In this sense, man's spirit of worship supplements
what heaven and earth and God have left incomplete or undone.
We may also say this: During worship man has the virtues of
heaven and earth sustained by the flash of light or thought in
his mind — the virtue of heaven and earth's constant creation
of all beings and the virtue of infinite dimensions, which lies
in nourishingly preserving all beings. This flash of light or
thought is itself the direct expression of the virtues of heaven
and earth. The virtue of heaven and earth and that of man find
themselves rooted in each other, mutually sustained, united into
one, greatest harmony. Then the infinity of emergence and creation of values is proportional to the infinity of their preservation. And then this makes possible the complete fulfillment and
continuation of the emergence, creation, and preservation of
values. On the one hand, this complete fulfillment and continuation transcendentally spread over the spirit of worship and, on
the other hand, are immanent in the flash of light or thought in
our mind during worship at that moment. This is what is called,
"The virtue of ghost, deity, or god is at its height, pervading
comprehensively as if on and above us, as if on our right and
left, touching all things; they cannot do without it." This is the
Confucianist religious spirit at its best in terms of spiritual

height, width, and depth. As this religious spirit is not motivated by.a concern of one's transcendence from sin and agony,
it never ceases and never ends up in prayer and worship alone;
it is motivated by a sense of return to the root, to the origin,
and reaches its height in the act of eulogy. Oh, it is second to
none!

Moreover, in addition to this religious spirit being not so
motivated, it is also rooted in not believing that man has "original sin." Should man have "original sin," then the ancestors,
sages, and worthies would have passed away with sin. When
we recall this, our respect for them will become weak. On the
Confucianist principle, we ought to recall their deeds and virtues and forget amoral aspects of their lives. This is the so-
called "In concealing their vices and exposing their good examples, the heart of the filial son and loving grandson means to
patch up the vices." The spirit in concealing and patching up
the vices of the dead makes their sinful existence transcended
[above sin] in our mind: this is our attitude of forgiveness toward the dead. In the supra-experiential world, who knows if
our attitude of forgiveness may not effect the souls of the dead
of old, and make them surge upward to the brighter and brighter
day by day? Well, we can put this question aside for the time
being; we can at least forget the vices of the dead of old. To
forget in this case is itself a spirit of forgiveness and humane
compassion. When men take this stand in seeing the world,
forgiving each other, then sin will gradually slip into oblivion
through mutual forgiveness, and each man will finally seek his
transcendence from sin and vices. This is the Confucianist
doctrine of more criticism of oneself, but less of others. The
meaning of this doctrine basically requires that one should
watch one's faults and regard every person as being potentially
capable of becoming emperors Yao and Shun [each of whom was
regarded as both a sage and ideal king in one person], every
man on the street capable of becoming Yü [another sage-king] —
the street full of sages. It follows that any religion which corresponds to this religious spirit is better fitted into the positive
worship of return of indebtedness to and respect for the virtues

of heaven and earth, ancestors, sages and worthies; but quite
unsuitable for the religion of negative salvation from sin and
pain; and the least suitable for the religion which first presupposes man sinful and then indoctrinates him.

15. The Greatest Harmony in the World of Religion

The aforesaid generally suffices to explain that the value and
the religious spirit in the three Confucianist worships in China
are at least on a par with those of any of the great religions in
the world. It makes us understand why people who believe in
Confucianism do not depend necessarily on other religions for
the compensation of their spiritual emptiness. The Confucianist
spirit not only emphasizes the actual deeds — ethical, social,
and political — but it has a highly transcendental aspect, which
is shown, in the dimension of theory and thought, in the form
of the doctrine of "human nature" and "human heart," and the
ontology of Tao; and, in the dimension of way of life, in the form
of rites or propriety of the three worships. The value of these
rites has been ignored since the practice of them as educative
devices receded to oblivion. As a consequence, people have developed two attitudes toward Confucianism. Some people rank
it low, as if it contains merely historical records of the past.
Some rank it as high, as philosophy, but forget that it is also a
way of life. Some know it as a way of life, or one rich in artistic emphasis and human enjoyment, or one emphasizing moral
cultivation; but little do they know that this artistic way of life
is one aspect of Confucianism, namely, the emphasis on music,
and that moral life is another aspect, namely, the emphasis on
propriety. The center of Confucianist propriety lies in the
rites of worships, and music is for the performance of rites.
The musical performance of these rites is taken as the passage
of communication with heaven and earth, ghosts and deities, the
passage between realms of darkness and brightness. Accordingly, this way of life implies transcendental, religious, and
metaphysical meanings. Some lowly Confucianists who have
drowned themselves in opinions base, superficial, and trivial

pride themselves in talking only about the concrete but neglect the supreme and transcendental aspect of Confucianism. Some religionists, knowingly or unknowingly, have ignored this aspect. As a result, people may either rival the religion with Confucianism, thinking that Confucianism can only be combined with science, or think that Confucianism lacks the transcendental aspect and desire to transplant a God or Buddha on the trunk of Confucianism. In fact, the spirit of Confucianism can be espoused to science; but the spirit itself is possessed of religiousness and can thus be no enemy to religions, nor the rival of religions. The Confucianist religious spirit, when coordinated with the Confucianist metaphysics and philosophy of life, is already sufficient to establish man and his "fate." The question how to harmonize and compromise Confucianism with other religions is mainly one of how the Chinese humanistic world would recognize the place for other religions. But the answer to this question does not depend on those who believe in Confucianism having also to believe in one other religion, [for] the question is simply one of affirming the different values of other religions. The answer to the question mainly lies in finding out the root that gives rise to different religious spirits in the "human heart" and "human nature." We can give due place to various religions, on the one hand, and not lose the Confucianist stand which emphasizes self-awareness of man's "human heart" and "human nature," on the other hand. Hence we do not have to lose our ground by one inch, or rely on or attach to any particular religion in order to respect religion. We know that each religion has its marked spirit, that is to say, that for people with different spiritual demands different religions function differently and correspond to their demands; thus different religions may run parallel to each other in harmony or without conflict. And keeping our ground makes this parallel and harmony possible. But if we commit ourselves to one religion and become the enemy of the other, this is to make the human world of religion full of hostile conflicts, without either harmony or reconciliation; and all relationships between any two or more religions will become one of mutual oppression and destruction, like the one between easterly and westerly winds, both quivering in painful anxiety over existence and possible destruction and then nonexistence. Under these circumstances all nonreligionists or those who have no religious belief will only be the object of competition between rival religions, the fuel of their power struggle against each other, subduing each other. This is disaster not only for us but also for all people, religious and nonreligious together. Hence to stand firm on our ground is necessary not only for the continuation of the Confucianist spirit but also for the secured existence of all people. In this sense our standing fast on our ground is tantamount to the establishment of oneself and others, the establishment of Confucianism and religions. In this sense we can say that the existence of the Confucianist spirit will provide a basis for the existence of all religions in the Chinese world; this also provides the concrete basis for making possible a gradual harmonization, reconciliation, and communication among all religions.

If we want to realize or actualize the above ideal, then it is inevitable that the importance of the Confucianist spirit must be duly recognized in Chinese society and culture. The decline of the spirit and its faltering position surrounded by all kinds of unsympathetic criticism must be changed. The changes include setting up not only theoretical strongholds but also people of noble aspiration who will actualize the Confucianist doctrine in their daily lives in the form of moral practice and participation in social, cultural, political, and educational deeds. The correlation between theory and practice lies in the establishment of a new program of propriety and music. Accordingly the propriety of the three Confucianist worships of heaven and earth, ancestors and sages, and worthies must be restored. All funeral and wedding ceremonies cannot be monopolized by the religionists. Coordinated with the propriety there must be the arts of music, literature, and architecture — all as members of the class "music" in the broad sense. The success of this program depends on those creative minds which are fully occupied with the Confucian way and also versed in arts. In the beginning, there will be only a handful of them whose spirit of

"music" and propriety drives them to cultivate themselves
morally and to initiate new societal careers. Their relations
and gatherings are unlike those of a professional union, unlike
those of the church nowadays, unlike those of a political organization, and even unlike those of an academic body. Those creative minds of noble aspiration are brought together simply by
an invisible sense of moral vocation of the teacher and that of
the student and by an aspiration to extend their influences far
and wide and to set up continuity of the past, the present, and
the future. Their efforts will finally lead to the establishment
of the humanist standard for all people on earth, the fulcrum
of world religion around which the destiny of the whole world
and the direction of Providence are shaped. People of like
aspiration, let us tread the same path to that goal!

13

CHINESE ATTITUDE TOWARDS WORLD RELIGIONS

Before I discuss the Chinese attitude towards religions, I wish to cite two sayings, one of Mencius and one of Lu-hiu Yuan, as an introduction to the subject. Mencius said : "The homes of sages may be more than a thousand miles apart, and the time of one sage may be a thousand years later than that of another, but the principles of the early sage and of the later sage are the same." Lu-kiu Yuan said : "The universe is my mind, and my mind is the universe. If in the Eastern Sea there were to appear a sage, he would have this same mind and this same principle. If in the Western Sea there were to appear a sage, he would have this same mind and this same principle. If in the Southern or Northern Seas, there were to appear sages, they, too, would have this same mind and this same principle. If a hundred or a thousand generations ago, or a hundred or a thousand generations hence, sages were to appear, they, likewise, would have this same mind and this same principle."

Mencius and Lu-kiu Yuan were both Confucians. The Confucian teaching is mainly ethical; however, it has its religious aspect. The foregoing quotations and what is implied therein can be taken as still representative of the attitude of the Confucians and even of the Taoists, of the Chinese Buddhists and of the Chinese people as a whole toward religion.

The significance of these sayings is simple : A principle that is really universal should be universally and immanently presented and realized by human minds of different ages and places. Religious principles are no exceptions. Of course, the religious principle may be revealed by a transcendent God or Heaven. But, at least in the moment of its revelation, what is transcendent must reveal its transcendence to a human mind. Its transcendence cannot transcend the human mind, though this mind becomes self-transcendent in that revelation. In this sense, what is transcendent is at the same time immanently revealed to the human mind, which is as divine as it is human. Therefore, the really universal principle in religion is not only a universal by itself but also a universal which can be universally and immanently revealed and then presented or realized by any human mind. Only during the time when it is actually presented and realized by human minds in different ages and places, can its universality be actually revealed to this world and existing in this world. The human minds in which God or Heaven and His (or its) principle are revealed, presented, and realized are called the minds of the sages. The God or Heaven and His (or its) principle may be one and the same, but the minds of the sages are as many as the sages themselves—and all men who are capable of being sages—so that one and the same truth can reveal its universality, actually, in the many and different minds.

What Mencius and Lu-kiu Yuan said and its significance as I have explained it, may not be consciously recognized by the ordinary Chinese, yet this is the very essence of the Chinese attitude towards religion.

This attitude can be illustrated socially and historically. In Chinese society, individuals are not easily persuaded to think that God is simply incarnated in a physical body at a particular time and place. Nor are most Chinese inclined to believe that there are chosen persons who are predestined to be sages or prophets, and that there are others predestined to be excluded from the Grace of God and to be ignorant of God. It appears strange to a Chinese when he is told that only one religion is revealed and that all other religions are but natural. The Chinese usually think that if the rain and sunshine of Heaven are present everywhere, if God loves all human beings equally, and if human nature is essentially the same, then there seems no reason for any people to claim the privilege of being a chosen people or to claim that the universal God has been incarnated in a particular body and has revealed His truth only to a particular people or church. The Chinese prefer to believe that "the full realization of human nature in a sage is at the same time the realization of Heaven-nature and the realization of Heaven-mind or God-mind to men"; that "all men can be sages, and sages are as divine as they are human"; and that "all religions are only different expressions of the deepest human nature and at the same time the different channels where the mandates of Heaven flourish or are the different ways (Tao) by which different people attain their sage-hood and likeness or conformity to Heaven."

The belief that different religions are different ways of attaining sagehood, all conforming to Heaven, implies that the ultimate destination of all the ways may be the same, but that no one way is itself ultimate. A "way" also implies a deeper insight : when a man has travelled the way and has arrived, he can afford to forget the way. Men need not ask others who are also going home whether "home" for all is in the same place. If we mean by "home" the same destination of human life—sagehood—then we may say that whoever is already at home should remain at home to entertain the guests coming from different directions and that he should never reproach the guests for not coming by the way he came.

The historical evidences for what I have said are plentiful. For example, there have never been religious wars and only a few religious persecutions in Chinese history. The controversies among the Buddhists, the Taoists, and the Confucians in Chinese history usually culminated in a theory of reconciliation among the three teachings or of syncretism and mutual respect, each teaching performing a different function. The metaphor of three rooms in a home, used by the Confucian Wang Lung-hi is apt and significant.

It is not an exaggeration to say that the Chinese people in the past have found genuine enjoyment in religious toleration and religious freedom. However, too much religious toleration may weaken one's religious enthusiasm and may result in the absence of religious fervor. We must confess that this, too, is the case among the Chinese.

If we agree that the Chinese are most tolerant in religion, then we shall see why the most tolerant, the most liberal, and the most broad-minded religions are most convincing to the Chinese mind and most heartily welcomed by the Chinese people.

In Chinese history, Buddhism, Islam, Judaism, Nestorianism, Catholicism, Protestantism, and, recently, Hinduism have had followers. But the religion that is most deep-rooted in the lower class Chinese remains Taoism, though it is usually neglected by contemporary Chinese intellectuals. Taoism is a religion derived from Chinese primitive religion and is a variable mixture of Taoist philosophy, Confucian teachings, and Buddhist beliefs. What appeals most to the Chinese people is its love of longevity and its syncretism, which is a vague, synthetic expression of the Chinese liberal spirit, though the spiritual level of Taoists may not be so high as that of Buddhists or Confucians.

Buddhism, especially Mahāyāna Buddhism, is a religion that is widely accepted by different classes, including the highly intellectual Chinese. The liberal spirit and broad mind of Buddhism are expressed, not by its syncretism, but within the Buddhist teaching itself. Generally speaking, in Buddhist teachings every sentient being has "*Buddha*-nature" and is capable of becoming a *Buddha*. Also, there are different and convenient ways for spiritual cultivation, adapted to different circumstances and different mentalities. Actually, there are no, or very few, dogmas in Buddhist teaching. The Chan School (or Zen Buddhism), created by the Chinese, rejected all kinds of articulate preaching and used words simply as tools for the self-awakening of the mind to its own nature. This is close to the idea of "realization of human nature" in Confucianism. Hence, the flourishing of Ch'an Buddhism in Chinese culture is not an accident.

In contrast to Taoism and Buddhism, Islam and Judaism have practically no followers outside the Muslim and Jewish groups. This fact is not due to any defect in their teachings when compared with other religions, but to the fact that it is said that Muhammad preached with the *Qur'ān* in one hand and a sword in the other. This story terrified the Chinese people, and they suspected that Islam was narrow-minded, although this is not actually the case. As to Judaism, the Biblical idea of Israel as a "chosen people" has been repulsive to the Chinese people. Yet, the historical fact that the Jews who came to China in the T'ang Dynasty (618-907) were wholly assimilated with the Chinese people is significant. It is well known that Jews are difficult to assimilate. It is not improbable that the Jews of the T'ang Dynasty were influenced by the liberal spirit of the Chinese people and that their sense of belonging to a chosen people gradually melted away.

The Chinese attitude towards Christianity is rather complicated. It seems to be something between their attitude towards Taoism and Buddhism, on one side, and their attitude towards Islam, on the other.

Christianity is admired by Chinese because it is a religion for all men and not simply the religion of a single group. According to Christianity, all men who follow the ways of Jesus Christ can be saved. In this sense, it is broad-minded. When Jesuits first came to China in the Ming Dynasty (1368-1644), their erudition in Chinese classics and their writings on the similarities between ancient Confucianism and Christianity won the hearty respect of the Chinese, and a number of Chinese became devoted converts to Christianity. Unfortunately, in the Ching Dynasty (1644-1912), the Pope of Rome ordained that Chinese Catholics be forbidden to join in the sacrificial ceremonies for their ancestors or for Confucius and other sages. The Chinese Emperor was irritated by this ruling and decreed that Catholic missionaries be forbidden to carry on their activities in China. So, the intolerance of an emperor towards the Catholics was, in fact, a reciprocal response to the intolerance of a Pope. The contact of China with the Western world was thus interrupted for almost two hundred years.

When Westerners came to China again two hundred years later, the forerunners were then not gentle churchmen but merchants and warriors. Since the Opium War China has been compelled to make many contacts with the West. As churchmen came to China at this time by the same boats as merchants and warriors, the Chinese people looked upon them, too, with suspicious eyes. They were suspected of being aggressive imperialists and covetous capitalists in disguise, or of being at least their tools.

Moreover, the majority of the Chinese who had been converted to Christianity at the end of the Ching Dynasty did not belong to the families of the nobles, and they even refused to participate in Chinese traditional and sacrificial ceremonies. At last, the so-called Boxer Rebellion broke out, and for the first time in the history of China, the Chinese practised religious persecution—towards Christianity. To most Chinese, this rebellion is considered as a criminal act. Consequently, the rights of missionaries stipulated in the treaty were interpreted as punishment imposed upon China for the evacuation of the Allied Troops of the Eight Nations from Peking.

Twenty years later (forty years ago), when the students of the Republic of China considered the penalty too severe, an anti-Christian movement broke out again, combined with an anti-imperialist and anti-capitalist movement. These movements led Chinese youth to believe in materialistic Marxism and Leninism, which are hostile to all religions as well as to the Western world. But, if one has only a little knowledge of modern China, he will not be misled by the communist occupation of Mainland China to conclude that the Chinese people are irreligious, materialistic by nature, or generally intolerant towards religions.

Outside of Mainland China, however, the influence of Christianity on the Chinese is advancing. There are many Chinese who have been converted to Christianity with inner sincerity and deep devotion. But, owing to the general poverty of the Chinese, on one hand, and Western economic and political policies, on the other, a Chinese, after being converted to Christianity, will usually seek and receive material benefits through Christian churchmen. I cannot say with confidence that Christianity is a religion deep-rooted in the culture and minds of the Chinese people.

A genuine Confucian may have a religious feeling of reverence for mystical union with Heaven or God through the realization of his moral nature, which is directly conferred from Heaven. However, it is not necessary for him to be converted to any particular institutional religion. According to the doctrine of the sameness of all humanity and the universality of Heaven, a genuine Confucian believes that there is something common to all genuine religions, that the differences among religions should be considered simply as different ways of attaining the same goal, and that one should pay reverence to all the sages of all religions. It is not necessary for us to judge which of the sages is the greatest and has attained the highest state of spirituality. Is it not more humble for us to suspend judgment and keep silent on this question, concentrating our spiritual energy on admiring their greatness and cultivating our personalities towards attaining the stature they have attained ?

The only thing that can solve the dis-union and collision of different religions is neither religious syncretism nor religious imperialism, but a reverent attitude towards all genuine religions, which are the different revelations of the same Heaven or God or Brahmā or Allah, and at the same time different expressions of the human religious spirit or human nature. This may be taken as a religious attitude towards religions themselves which will bring the world of religions into a "great harmony" and overcome all religious syncretism and imperialism.

In conclusion, we may quote a paragraph from the *Doctrine of the Mean*, which was supposed to have been written by a grandson of Confucius : "All things are nourished together without mutual injury. All ways are parallel without collision. The smaller virtuous merits flow as rivers. The greater virtuous merits fulfil the whole transformation. It is this which makes Heaven and Earth so great." .

This is the essence of Confucian thought, which is also more or less implied in Taoism and Chinese Buddhism, and which also consciously or unconsciously expresses the Chinese attitude towards the religions of the world.

14

ON THE DIRECTION OF THE DEVELOPMENT
OF POLITICAL CONSCIOUSNESS IN THE CHINESE
PEOPLE IN THE PAST ONE HUNDRED YEARS*

In our discussion on the development of political consciousness in the Chinese people in the past one hundred years, we
will focus on the upward development made in the course of the
reconstruction of the nation. If we simply study the historical
facts, the past one hundred years are tragic. But if we study
the spirit of the people during this period, we cannot but recognize that the Chinese people have never given up and that
they have been constantly struggling upward. In the history of
their struggle the Chinese people have gone astray many times;
otherwise, the country would not be what she is now. But
from mistakes corrections are made, thus eliminating the
possibility of repeating the same mistakes. This is what we
call the instructional value of history. From this view, the
Chinese people are presently undergoing a crisis in which they
seem to have nothing to support and nothing to possess. But
spiritually and ideologically, the Chinese people possess the
most substantial "have," one that no other people or nation of

---

*T'ang Chün-i, "Pai nien lai Chung-kuo min-tsu chih cheng-
chih i-chih fa-chan chih li-ts'e." Chapter VII of Chung-kuo jen-
wen ching-shen fa-chan [The Development of Chinese Humanistic Spirit] (Hong Kong: Young Son, 1958), pp. 163-184. Originally published in Tsu-kuo chou-k'an [China Weekly], XII:7
(November 1955). Translated by To Chou-Yee.

the world has had. This most substantial "have" is the historical experience gained through the continuous upward struggle
against failures in the reconstruction of their nation. This historical experience can be valuable only when it has become the
self-consciousness of the people and their future generations.
This self-consciousness is related mainly to the development
of political consciousness in the Chinese people in the past
hundred years.

To understand the direction of the development of political
consciousness in China in the past hundred years, we must study
the Chinese people and their culture as a whole, rather than
simply the fragments of the successes and failures of certain
individuals and political parties. We should view these persons
and parties only as selected illustrations of the spirit of the
Chinese people at a particular time. In so doing we will consider their successes as the successes of the whole people, their
failures as the failures of the whole people. It is necessary to
realize that the evaluation of successes and failures in terms
of individual persons and parties is a task of a different nature.
This kind of task, strictly speaking, can only be done judiciously
by historians of future generations. For judgment made on this
matter by contemporaries will unavoidably lead to subjective
and biased conclusions because the judges themselves may have
been involved in the same events and may have values and beliefs that conflict with those of the persons they are evaluating
and judging. Therefore we must eliminate our own emotional,
ideological, and political prejudices in order to have a clearer
and more objective picture of the problem. I personally have
never been involved in actual political activities; nor have I
belonged to any political party. I believe that I can discuss the
present topic rather objectively and with less inhibitions. I
hope that my readers will also try to be open-minded while
reading this essay.

In the past one hundred years there were two sources that
stimulated the development of political consciousness in the
Chinese people. Externally, there were the military, economic,
political, and cultural powers of the West that challenged tra-

ditional Chinese society and culture. Internally, there was the desire of the Chinese people to build an authentic "people's nation of China." By "China" is meant the continuation of the historical and cultural tradition. By "people" is meant the nationals, the common people, the modern citizenry. By "nation" is meant a modern country. In this discussion we shall divide the process of the development of political consciousness into nine stages to show how the goal of national reconstruction is being approached. We shall see that while under the influence and pressure of the West, the Chinese people have been retreating, accommodating; they have been simultaneously rebuilding themselves and composing themselves in order to be their own master and create their own future. Whenever they encounter obstacles and suffer defeat, they seek modifications and change in their ideals and thought, or they seek to transcend themselves. When they discover new ways in their ideals and thought, they try again to overcome the difficulties in reality. Individual persons and political parties in these nine stages of development usually can represent only the stage they were in, and not the stage following their existence. For this reason, when the political consciousness develops to a new stage, individual persons and organizations that belong to the preceding stage usually cannot avoid their downfall. As the old disappears and the new emerges the Chinese people will continue to follow the direction of upward development, progressing toward their internal goal, that is, the reconstruction of a real, Chinese nation, a nation of the people. As to the work and deeds of individual persons and organizations in each stage, whether successes or failures they are eternal and valuable. They are eternal in that they are events to be admired, praised, sympathized with, or regretted. They are valuable in that they can stimulate, enlighten, and serve as a warning for the future generations. They enable us to realize where we are and what we should do. Successes and failures are found in the history of the past hundred years and in the life of the Chinese people; they enrich the history and life of the people. Thus we may say that both successes and failures are contributions to a better future. This is why in this essay I do not emphasize the success or failure of any individual persons or organizations.

I. On the T'ai-P'ing Army and the T'ai-P'ing T'ien-Kuo, Which Was Based upon the Power of the Natural Life Impulse, the Pressure from the "God-Lucifer Clamps" That the Chinese People Have Recently Experienced, and the Internal Desire of the People to Escape from Such Pressure

The first and second stages in the development of political consciousness in the Chinese people during the past hundred years are represented by the T'ai-p'ing t'ien-kuo revolutionary movement, an anti-oppression consciousness based upon the natural life impulse of the people — mainly the Chinese people. As to the political consciousness represented by Tseng Kuo-fan and others, it is known to be a consciousness stemming from the urge to defend the traditional Chinese culture and values. The T'ai-p'ing movement was similar to all the grass roots rebellions throughout Chinese history, that is, it was a natural reaction of ordinary people against oppression and unreasonable exploitation by the ruling class. But reaction against irrationality does not necessarily lead to rationality. Also the countering against the unreasonable is not necessarily generated from reason. On the contrary, the source of rebellion is often the nonrational, natural life impulse. Mobbing, for instance, is the result of mutual imitation and influence, which is emotional rather than rational. It is true that the T'ai-p'ing army and T'ai-p'ing t'ien-kuo had their military, political, economic, and social systems, as well as religion and ideology, which were founded upon rationality. But all these, in the case of the T'ai-p'ing army and T'ai-p'ing t'ien-kuo, were but external, superficial formalities. History shows that these formalities failed to regulate the nonrational power of the movement. Included among these formalities were various elements of contradiction, which eventually led to the self-destruction of the movement. Thus we may conclude that the T'ai-p'ing movement was an impulsive reaction of the Chinese people against the oppression of foreign powers and the Manchu rulers.

The natural life impulse of man has a kind of God-Lucifer quality, for when the natural life impulse of the mass becomes a process in a political revolution it can easily associate itself with certain kinds of religious worship. There have been numerous examples in history to prove this point. And the religious form taken is usually accidental. For instance, the T'ai-p'ing movement's adoption of Christianity was due mainly to the fact that Christianity had been introduced into the provinces of Kwangtung and Kwangsi. Hung Hsiu-ch'üan simply borrowed Christian teaching and organized his "God Worshipers Society." Since the Christian concept of God was foreign combined with the natural life impulse of the people it produced a power that was devastating to traditional Chinese culture and society. During the Middle Ages in Europe, Christianity, which originated in the Hebrew culture, made an effort to compromise and harmonize with the Greek and Roman cultures. Yet a century ago in China, during the T'ai-p'ing movement, it openly challenged the several-thousand-year-old Chinese history and culture. It proclaimed the six classics as evil. It used the Christian God to chastise Confucius. This is what the rebels in China dared not do in the past. After the T'ai p'ing army's establishment of its capital in Nanking, an internal power struggle among its leaders began. Social order was disrupted and traditional morality collapsed. This confirms that the political consciousness represented by the T'ai-p'ing revolution was based merely on the natural life impulse of the mass. But we must also recognize that this period was the initial stage in the development of political consciousness in modern China. This stage, philosophically speaking, failed in its effort to abolish traditional culture and custom. It failed in its inability to achieve its own form, to stabilize what was in effect an impulsive movement. However, one must also note that traditional culture and teaching could not prevent the T'ai-p'ing movement. They were not able to channel a revolutionary trend into a different form. This means that traditional culture and teaching were not deeply rooted in the lower levels of the society. In other words, the old tradition failed to regulate and control the mass. The concept of God of T'ai-p'ing t'ien-kuo and the natural life impulse of the mass can be considered, analogically, as a God-Lucifer clamp that exerted tremendous pressure upon traditional Chinese culture and teaching. One arm of the clamp pressed to go beyond traditional Chinese culture and custom. It was exemplified by the Western concept of God in the T'ai-p'ing movement. Later it was exemplified by various non-Chinese ideas; Marxism is the example for today. The other arm of the clamp was the nonrational natural life impulse. It was raw and outside of the influence of traditional culture and teaching. Today this arm is exemplified by the power of the Chinese Communist Party. Both arms of this clamp have been working to destroy the old Chinese tradition. The future development of political consciousness of the Chinese people depends on how the people succeed in stretching apart the two arms of the God-Lucifer clamp in order to free themselves.

II. On the Preserve-Traditional-Culture-and-Values
Consciousness Represented by Tseng Kuo-fan,
Tso Tsung-t'ang, Li Hung-chang and Hu Lin-i,
and the Deficiency or Burden of Guilt of
Such Consciousness

The second stage in the development of political consciousness in the Chinese people in the past one hundred years is represented by Tseng Kuo-fan and his colleagues, who suppressed successfully the T'ai-p'ing t'ien-kuo rebellion. When the T'ai-p'ing army was first organized, the T'ai-p'ing leaders advocated the worship of the "heavenly father and heavenly brother" [Jesus] and the expulsion of the barbarian rulers. In their military, political, and economic practices, they implemented various reasonable measures, including the sharing of wealth among people, which was also a Confucian teaching. Intellectuals with social consciousness were likely to support the T'ai-p'ing movement, except perhaps its foreign God. In fact, many intellectuals joined the T'ai-p'ing movement to help with the development of the new political system. Yet scholar-officials Tseng Kuo-fan and Lo Tse-nan did not think that way. They were worried by the destructive effect of the T'ai-p'ing movement on traditional Chinese culture and ethical teachings. Consequently they decided to resist the T'ai-p'ing movement and suppress it. Making such a judgement required painful determination and profound insight. Being Chinese, Tseng, Lo, and their colleagues certainly understood that they were not obligated to be loyal to the Manchu or barbarian dynasty. But because the survival of traditional Chinese culture and ethical teachings depended on the survival of the dynasty, what they could do was to fight against the T'ai-p'ing rebellion while ignoring, at least temporarily, the traditional distinction between the Chinese and the barbarians. Hence their choice was a painful one that bore the burden of a sense of guilt. The objective value of such a choice was to save traditional culture and teachings, which are considered the soul of the Chinese people, from being destroyed. Compared with this crucial task, temporary subordination of the Chinese to the Manchu dynasty was considered bearable, though regrettable. The choice to defend traditional culture when it was being threatened by the T'ai-p'ing t'ien-kuo was the highest possible form of political attitude and consciousness. That this choice bore regret and guilt shows that the transformation of the Chinese political consciousness from the first stage to the second stage was a difficult process.

III. On the Internal Contradiction of the Theory of "Learning from the Barbarians in Order to Control Them" During the Self-Strengthening Movement, and an Analysis of This Contradiction

The third stage in the development of political consciousness in modern China occurred from the suppression of the T'ai-p'ing t'ien-kuo by Tseng Kuo-fan and Li Hung-chang to the Self-Strengthening Movement advocated by Chang Chi-tung. It seems that the Self-Strengthening Movement, which suggested that the

Chinese study western science and technology in order to reconstruct their armed forces, communications, and industry,
was the consequence of the many humiliating defeats the Chinese suffered under the constant threats of the western powers.
At that time, leading Confucian scholar-officials like Wo Jen
and Hsü Tung opposed this self-strengthening idea, but I believe that the Self-Strengthening Movement was actually led by
the spirit of Confucianism. The political consciousness of this
movement is a natural development from that of Tseng Kuo-fan
and Li Hung-chang of the second stage. The T'ai-p'ing rebellion threatened the very existence of traditional Chinese culture
and ethical teachings, whereas the foreign powers' exploitation
of China threatened the very existence of the Chinese people
and nation. This invasion by foreigners was parallel with other
similar occurrences in Chinese history. In the past, the ways
and means of dealing with foreign invaders were found in China
itself, for instance, increasing the defense along the national
border, sending troops to conquer the enemy, etc. All these
ways relied on domestic resources; hence they were control-
lable. However, the threat from the Western powers was different: these new invaders possessed what the old Chinese culture did not have and could not cope with — modern science and
technology, for example. In order to survive the threat from
the Western powers the only possible solution was to study with
the Westerner and seek the solution to the problem from Western knowledge and skills. This line of reasoning led to the
sending of Chinese students abroad to study. The policy of
"studying with the barbarians in order to control them" indicated an unusual political consciousness nowhere to be found
in the past. Inherent in this consciousness was an unlimited
suffering from humiliation as well as a severe internal contradiction that could hardly be reconciled with. For if you learn
from the Westerner, you must respect the Westerner. For according to the dictates of human nature, if you learn from a
certain person you will respect him, and if you respect him you
will not feel right trying to control him and treating him as an
enemy. If you want to control someone, you cannot respect him

at the same time. Now, if you want to control the Westerner, the Westerner should be at a distance from you; if you want to learn from the Westerner, then you have to humble yourself to him. How can you reconcile yourself with this dilemma? It was impossible. Consequently the two opposites grew farther and farther apart. On the one hand, those who learned from and subordinated themselves to the Westerner came to worship Western learning and culture while despising and abandoning traditional Chinese culture and teaching. On the other hand, those who wanted to fight the Western enemies but were not willing to learn the science and technology of the enemies to control them formed another extreme — the Boxers [I-ho-t'uan]. When the Boxers failed, the trend of learning from the West could not be stopped and the dilemma could not be resolved. In this difficult third stage, the Chinese people, in order to preserve their country and culture, in which they were deeply rooted, had to find a way to fight against the West. But at the same time they had to humble themselves to learn from the West in order to attain the science and technology necessary for their survival. What the Chinese had to do then was to bear the burden of contradiction. In doing so they had to have the courage to consciously give up a certain part of their cultural pride in order to study from the foreigner, so that the other part of their culture and country could be preserved. According to Hegelian dialectics, this was the beginning of the attempt of the Chinese people in modern times to seek to "bring the outside into themselves" in order to "become themselves."

IV. On the Reform Movement in the Late Ch'ing, and the
Traditional Political System as the Subject of
Critical Examination and Modification

The fourth stage in the development of political consciousness in modern China covers the period from the end of the Self-Strengthening Movement to the end of the Reform Movement in the late Ch'ing. This Reform Movement was modeled after the Western political system. That is to say, it was a further step

in the trend of learning from the West. Here we can find the
spirit of the Chinese people: to seek to become other than themselves in order to criticize themselves and to advance. The
Reform Movement meant to strive for national wealth and
strength, and its goal was the acquisition of science, technology,
and material construction. A new social system was to be instrumental in attaining these ends, but a new system meant
breaking away from the old, traditional system. For instance,
in order to train scientific and technological manpower, new
schools must be established and the old examination system
abolished. In order to achieve material construction, which is
basically a task of the whole society, the potentials and abilities
of the ordinary people must be cultivated and employed. If the
potentials and abilities of the ordinary people are to be emphasized, then the authoritarianism of the monarchy must be broken
and the government system changed. In Western countries, industrialization and constitutionalism always developed simultaneously. A reform movement in China at this stage was inevitable. It is obvious that the "striving for a new system that
will bring about the realization of the wealth and strength of the
nation" was the logical next step toward "establishing the goal
of achieving wealth and strength through science and technology
for the survival of the people." At this fourth stage of the development of political consciousness, the traditional political
system became the subject of critical examination, evaluation,
and modification. In two thousand years of Chinese history,
this was the first time this has ever happened.

V. On the Spirit of Martyrdom Before the Republican
Revolution, Which Was Generated from the Self-Consciousness
of Nationalism and from the Traditional Teaching of Choosing
Righteousness over Life; Its Difference from the T'ai-p'ing
T'ien-kuo Movement Was Generated from the Natural Life
Impulse of the Chinese People and Reveals an Elevation of
the People's Political Consciousness

The fifth stage in the development of political consciousness

in modern China is represented by the political consciousness
of the Republican Revolution. From a historical point of view,
the Revolution stemmed from the failure of the Hundred Days
of Reform of 1898, led by K'ang Yu-wei and Liang Ch'i-ch'ao
and supported by the Kuang-hsü Emperor. For many years
prior to the Revolution, the reformers and revolutionists had
had various quarrels on politics. Both had their reasons and
arguments. The reformers believed that it was not necessary
to abolish the monarchical system, for such a change would
destroy the order of the society. They believed that a deliberate
and carefully planned reform of the government would be adequate to achieve wealth and strength for the nation. What the
reformers admired was the Meiji Restoration of Japan. At that
time Liang Ch'i-ch'ao wrote and predicted that if China had a
revolution, endless revolutions would follow, similar to what
France had experienced after the 1789 Revolution. Unfortunately, Liang was correct. For a time, I admired very much
Liang's insight. However, if the Reform had been successful,
the long desire of the Han majority to resist the oppression of
the Manchus would still not have been satisfied. If this desire,
which began with the establishment of the Manchu dynasty in
China and reached a climax during the T'ai-p'ing movement,
was to be satisfied, revolution was necessary. Here we must
note the difference between the Republican Revolution and the
T'ai-p'ing t'ien-kuo: The revolutionaries were martyrs who
sacrificed their lives in the course of the Revolution and had a
real sense of righteousness and consciousness of nationalism,
whereas the T'ai-p'ing movement was but a mob action generated from the natural life impulse of the masses, as already
discussed. This spirit of revolution was deeply rooted in Chinese culture. Hence we should consider the success of the 1911
Revolution as the success of the spirit of the Chinese people and
of the Chinese culture. It would be absurd to say that this is
not a higher stage in the development of political consciousness
of the Chinese people.

VI. <u>On the Political Consciousness of the Chinese People
in the Early Years of the Republic, Which Was That of a
Naive Master of a New, Unstable, Uncertain and Superficial
Democratic Nation, and the Inevitable Fate of Such a Naïve
Citizenry at This Stage of Historical Development</u>

The sixth stage in the development of political consciousness
in modern China was the political consciousness developed during the period between the early years of the Republic and the
New Culture Movement. For us, the closer the time, the more
details of the events we can remember and the more confusing
everything becomes. Hence the spirit and consciousness of this
stage are comparatively more difficult to understand clearly.
Therefore we must transcend the trivialities to obtain a vision
of the whole of this stage. The major events since 1911 include
the Second Revolution, Yüan Shih-k'ai's theft of the nation, warlordism, the struggle between the constitutionists and the supporters of Yüan, the split between the north and the south, and
the restoration of Emperor Pu-i by Chang Hsün. An understanding of the meaning of these events would enable us to realize the nature of the political consciousness of the Chinese people in these early years of the Republic.

Without a doubt the formal establishment of the Republic of
China in 1911 is a milestone in the political history of China.
It is the end of a fundamental political change that began with
the <u>T'ai-p'ing t'ien-kuo</u> and continued through the Self-Strengthening Movement, the Reform Movement, and the eventual overthrow of the Ch'ing dynasty. Thus the Republican government,
which claimed equality for all ethnic groups, formally fulfilled
the demand of the Chinese for liberation from the Manchu domination. Now that the emperor was gone, documents issued by
the president explicitly stated that he was but a civil servant
of the people. Theoretically this should have been an era of
real deomocracy when ordinary people would actively participate
in the task of nation-building. But the instability of the politics
during the early years of the Republic created great hardship
for the people. Grievances and complaints abounded. For in-

stance, when the revolutionaries boasted unashamedly of
their accomplishments they annoyed and alienated the masses.
Then Yüan Shi-k'ai, the president, oppressed and persecuted
the revolutionaries; this act led to the "Second Revolution"
and Yüan's dethronement. There are two explanations for
this series of events. The simplified explanation is that the
success of the Republican Revolution was so unexpected that
the people were not prepared for it. After the revolution
the military men remained the same; the politicans remained
the same; and the peasants, who had been accustomed to
worshiping an emperor, remained the same. Nothing had
really been changed. The more profound explanation is that
the Chinese people were simply too poor; the society did
not have the necessary vocational, religious and cultural organizations to create the foundations of a democratic society. I have discussed this point in my book The Reconstruction of Humanistic Spirit [Jen-wen ching-shen chih
chung-chien]. Because real democracy was absent, an authoritarian figure was bound to reappear; the political party
was to have no social ground; legislators were to represent
their individual opinions and seek their own interests and
gradually to become political manipulators; and the warlords
were to split the country asunder. Sun Yat-sen's dream of
a democracy in which the ordinary people would be the masters and the government an efficient mechanism to serve the
people's interest was completely shattered. Being called
the masters of the Republic, the ordinary people were naïve,
ignorant, and powerless; they were confused, disillusioned,
and exploited by those who were supposed to be their ser-
vants. But no matter how little was accomplished during
this period, the Chinese people at least experienced a vague
but fresh idea that they were entitled to the rights of an
independent citizenry.

VII. <u>On the New Culture Movement That Completed the</u>
<u>Process of Self-Denial of the Traditional Political and</u>
<u>Cultural Systems and the Process of Self-Transcendence,</u>
<u>the National and Spiritual Youthfulness That Was Revealed</u>
<u>in the Movement, the Consciousness That the Sovereignty</u>
<u>of the Nation Was to Be Preserved Exhibited in the May</u>
<u>Fourth Movement, and the Trend Toward the</u>
<u>Nationalist Revolution</u>

The seventh stage in the development of political consciousness in modern China started with the New Culture Movement
and continued through the May Fourth Movement to the beginning of the Nationalist Revolution. This stage of development
aimed at the construction of an organizational power in order
to promote a revolutionary movement starting from the lower
to the higher strata of the society. This seems to be a logical
development for an unstable new nation where the majority of
the people were politically ignorant and powerless.

First let us discuss the New Culture Movement. At first this
movement did not have anything directly to do with politics. At
that time the intellectuals in China were disappointed by the
political reality; therefore they geared their interests to the
study and examination of the problem of culture, for they understood that culture was the foundation of politics and that traditional culture was contradictory to the ideal of a constitutional
democracy. They concluded that in order to change the society,
the first task was to criticize and evaluate traditional culture.
There were two slogans during the New Culture Movement,
namely, "democracy" and "science." By "science" the intellectuals meant the scientific method and scientific attitude
rather than scientific techniques, scientific knowledge, or scientific systems. On the scientific method and attitudes, they
emphasized the will to doubt, the ability to think and question
critically, and the courage to examine established values. The
subject matter for criticism was, of course, traditional Chinese
culture. The significance of the New Culture Movement was
the completion of the process of self-transcendence over or

self-denial of their traditional political system and culture by
the Chinese people. The thoughts of the leaders of this movement, such as abolishing Confucianism, doubting the traditional
account of the ancient past, eliminating traditional rites and
customs, etc., can be traced back to the writings of late C'hing
scholars, like Chang T'ai-yen, K'ang Yu-wei and Tan Ssu-tung,'
criticizing traditional culture and learning. However, if the
Ch'ing dynasty had not been overthrown, the destruction of the
traditional political system would not have been complete. Similarly, if the New Culture Revolution had not occurred, the criticism and evaluation of traditional culture and political system
could not have been thorough. We may therefore say that the
New Culture Movement was the continuation and conclusion of
the trend beginning with the T'ai-p'ing t'ien-kuo that challenged
the old tradition. The Movement itself did not contain many new
things; only fragmentary Western ideas were introduced. In
regard to the ideas found at this stage, qualitatively they were
less systematic than those translated earlier by Yen Fu and
Lin Shu; quantitatively they were incomparable with what was
to develop later after the Nationalist Revolution. The "newness"
of the New Culture Movement was not to be found in its accomplishments; it was to be found in the spirit of freshness and
youthfulness that was fostered during that period. One may ask
where the freshness and youthfulness came from. They grew
out of the courage to doubt and to challenge the old tradition.
The attitude of being critical and reflective can liberate a person's mind so that he can challenge fixed ideas and authorities.
With this attitude the people of that period manifested a kind of
youthfulness of the natural mind. This trait was definitely superior to the natural life impulse exhibited by the T'ai-p'ing
t'ien-kuo. But it was still not mature enough to become the
youthfulness of the rational mind or the youthfulness of the
moral mind. This youthfulness of the natural mind was genuine,
vivid, and lovable; it was enlightening and stimulating like the
fragrance of flowers spreading in the air. But if it did not mature into the rational and moral mind, it would not be able to
yield any fruit of creativity. Strictly speaking, the philosophy

of Hu Shih, the historiography of Ku Chieh-kang, the literary
works of Ch'ien Hsüan-t'ung, and the political theory of Ch'en
Tu-hsiu, for example, all belonged to this category, and they
were unable to produce really positive and concrete results.
In order to advance to the rational and moral mind, one must
not be content with merely doubting and criticizing negatively
the tradition and talking vaguely about the reevaluation of values. One must seek to positively reconstruct the consciousness
of values and culture and the concept of history, so that the reconstruction of society and culture can be accomplished. As
far as the New Culture Movement is concerned, its activities
were basically negative rather than positive.

The New Culture Movement has always been mentioned together with the May Fourth Movement. But the significance of
these two movements are quite different. The New Culture
Movement was a cultural movement, whereas the May Fourth
Movement was a patriotic, political movement. Such a patriotic movement is a positive, affirmative activity. However,
with the critical attitude that characterized the New Culture
Movement, whether one should be patriotic was certainly a
problem to be argued. In fact, there were people who doubted
their families and extended their doubt to their country. But
at that time what the people wanted most were democracy and
science, which aimed at the domestic problems of the country.
Patriotism and nationalism aimed at China's relations with foreign powers. It is clear that although the New Culture Movement and the May Fourth Movement occurred simultaneously,
and a person could actually be a participant in both movements,
they were not identical. My interpretation is that the political
consciousness represented by the May Fourth Movement comprised a demand for the abolition of the unequal treaties imposed upon China by imperialist powers. The Nationalist Revolution in the 1920s was a subsequent movement that tried to
accomplish what the New Culture Movement and the May Fourth
Movement had attempted to do.

VIII. On the One Party Rule After the Nationalist Revolution,
the Self-Transcendence Demonstrated by Self-Consciousness
in the Craving for Constitutionalism During the Early Years
of the Republic, and the Chinese Intellectuals' Conscious
Effort to Share Their Political Ideals with the Masses and
to Integrate Their Ideals with the Natural Life of the
Chinese People

The political consciousness of the Nationalist Revolution was
another milestone in the political history of modern China. It
was Sun Yat-sen's political ideal that led the Revolution. Sun's
theory suggests that China should transform itself gradually
through three stages: first, a military government, then a period
of tutelage, and eventually a constitutional government. Sun
realized that the Chinese people's lack of readiness for constitutionalism led to what happened in the next two decades: Yüan
Shih-k'ai's enthronement, warlordism, and Tso Kun's bribery
to be elected president and the elected legislator's fate in becoming the puppets of ambitious military men. Having wit-
nessed these, Sun was convinced that China needed another revolution and that the people must be trained to become qualified
citizens of a constitutional, democratic nation. Thus Sun's next
move was to reorganize the Nationalist Party into a revolutionary organization and to subsequently build up a military force
which would be led by the Party. Undoubtedly, he was at that
time influenced by the thought of Lenin and the Russian Revolution. However, Sun emphasized that the military stage would
end and that the second stage, the period of tutelage, would not
exceed six years, and thereafter the government should be
changed into a constitutional one. Compared with Lenin's unlimited proletarian dictatorship and Communist leadership,
Sun's plan was quite different. But for those who were attracted
by the ideal form of democratic government, Sun's suggestion
of a period of tutelage and a one-party rule of the nation was
not quite democratic, for Sun's theory implied that the Party
was superior to the people as well as to the country. But the
failure of parliamentary politics in the early years of the Re-

public left no choice for the Nationalist revolutionaries. In
order to achieve real democratic, constitutional politics, the
only plausible approach seemed to be the use of a strong party
with a military government to organize the people, and then to
proceed to a period of tutelage to train the people for constitutionalism. Therefore the political consciousness at this stage
contained an internal contradiction. Sun Yat-sen and the Nationalist Party had to bear the burden of such a contradiction.
From history we know that such a burden was not easy to bear.
But many early leaders of the Nationalist Party and numerous
young people subscribed to Sun's idea and supported him. This
fact illustrates that the development of political consciousness
in modern China advanced a step further during this stage. This
process of advancement contained a unique spirit. I call this
spirit the Chinese people's craving for constitutionalism in the
early years of the Republic and their conscious transcendence
of themselves in seeking reestablishment of their own identity.

The Nationalist Revolution that was led by Sun Yat-sen's idea
exhibited another spirit, that is, the use of a political ideal to
search for comrades and to enlighten the masses in order to
organize a revolutionary power. This spirit was also shared
by the Communists and revolutionaries in the West. But there
had never been such a case in China before. In the past the
political ideals of Chinese intellectuals were such that they
would choose a potential leader and then help him conquer the
country, or in time of peace, assist him in ruling the nation.
That is to say, a political ideal would first be attached to a political power so as to infiltrate it, and then the power would be
used as a means to actualize the ideal. This approach was certainly extraordinary, and its result could also be extraordinary.
In the case of the Nationalist Revolution, the approach was different. It began with a political ideal, which was then spread
among the masses in order to enlighten them and to find comrades, revolutionists, and supporters from among them. Such
a revolutionary movement started from the top and then moved
downward to the masses and gathered its powers at the grass-
roots level. This approach enabled the intellectuals to mix with

the ordinary people and to share their ideals with the society.
Thus the ideal became something dynamic and functional and
an integral part of the life of the people. Hence the political
consciousness of this stage was fundamentally different from
that of the T'ai-p'ing t'ien-kuo. The success of the Nationalist
Revolution definitely marked a new era in the development of
political consciousness in modern China.

IX. On the War Against the Japanese Invaders and China's
   Victory, in Which the Chinese People Temporarily
   Achieved Authentic Consciousness of Their Desire for
   Independence from Foreign Domination and for the
   Actualization of Such Independence, the Internal Instability
   of the Nationalist Government During the Period of Tutelage

The eighth stage in the development of political consciousness
in modern China extended from the establishment of the Nationalist government to the end of the war against the Japanese.
During this stage the Chinese people temporarily achieved consciousness of their desire to be independent. During the war,
Japan occupied most of China, so almost every Chinese citizen
was involved, directly or indirectly, in the War of Resistance.
That the Chinese could persist over a long and difficult period
of eight years was primarily due to their high morale and firm
determination. Although the eventual victory over the Japanese
was not accomplished solely by the Chinese people, China did
achieve victory. Hence the Chinese people overcame the humiliation that they had suffered for fifty years since their defeat
in the Sino-Japanese War of 1895. This victory was the only
victory over foreign invaders for the Chinese since their defeat
in the Opium War by England in 1842. Because of this victory,
China got rid of all the unequal treaties signed with the foreign
powers and immediately became a member of the Big Four.
No matter whether China was truly powerful or not, being
called one of the Big Four made the Chinese feel glorious.
Thus the victory over the Japanese was a monumental event
in the political consciousness of the Chinese people. On the

surface China had become an independent nation, now standing
on her own feet. But actually the nation was in turmoil and
utter chaos reigned. This is why the country was eventually
taken over by the Chinese Communists. The political turmoil
that became uncontrollable at this stage can be traced back to
the founding of the Nationalist government in 1927.

As discussed previously, the success of the Nationalist Revolution was attributable to the fact that the political ideal of the
Nationalist Party was so appealing to the masses that it managed
to produce a revolutionary force. But the political ideal of the
Nationalists failed to unite their own party leaders, and hence
an internal crisis was created. The crisis was evident first in
the split between leaders into left-wing and right-wing, and later
by the domestic war between the joint forces of Yen Hsi-shan
and Feng Yü-hsiang, and the Kwangsi clique. Gradually the
Party deserted the masses, who had supported the Revolution
and enabled it to succeed. My analysis of the Nationalist crisis
in the following paragraph may sound speculative, but actually
it is very much to the point.

Sun Yat-sen's political idea of a period of tutelage had a
built-in instability. Sun advocated that before the ideal of a
constitutional government could be realized there must first
be a military government and then a period of tutelage. The
period of tutelage would provide the necessary political education to prepare the masses for constitutionalism. Thus the period of tutelage was a backward move for later advancement;
it was a transitional period for political education of the
masses. The original purpose of the period of tutelage was not
to stabilize the power and control of the Nationalist government. One government could always be replaced by another
government. Of course, if the existing government had strength
and was popular, no one could replace it. But if a government
was defined and designed as merely a transitional mechanism,
then such a government was innately temporary. The Nationalist government was founded on the theory that it was designed
for the preparation of the people for a constitutional government; therefore it was understood as a temporary government

with a six-year term. A temporary government could not be
permanent and stable, because in the political consciousness
of the masses, such a tentative government would not exist in
the future. Therefore the unexpected and continuous prolong-
ment of the Nationalist government later became a great dis-
illusionment to the people. This was a fundamental handicap
of the Nationalist government of the tutelage period.

Another defect of the Nationalist government of the tutelage
period was the theory that the Party rules the nation and that
the Party's power is supreme. This theory was originally
Russian. Later there were those who suggested that the Nationalist Party learn party organization and loyalty to party leaders
from the fascism of Italy and the Nazism of Germany. The
motivation of these people was not necessarily evil. For since
the September 18, 1931, incident, all leaders in the society emphasized the importance of government power and solidarity in
order to fight against the Japanese invaders. This kind of suggestion was rooted in the consciousness of the need for national
defense. Developing along the Russian, Italian, and German
models, the possible result would have been making supreme
the Nationalist Party and its top leader. If the Nationalist Party
had acquired absolute power, it might have made quite significant accomplishments and changed the status of its government
from transitional into permanent. By doing this, the Nationalist
Party might have been able to provide a sense of certainty and
stability for the Party members as well as for the Chinese
people in general. But if this had been the case, there would
have been a serious violation of Sun Yat-sen's original ideal
of constitutionalism, which was shared by many party members.
For this reason, though there were attempts to strengthen the
Party and its leadership, even with no theory to support them,
these efforts failed to gain the approval of the people. The result was that these attempts of the Nationalist Party further
alienated the people, whose demand for the end of the tutelage
and for the beginning of constitutionalism grew consistently
stronger.

The period of tutelage under the Nationalist rule extended

from the original six years to twenty years. It was a period
of political contradictions. While its ideal was constitutionalism, its practice was authoritarianism. Because the government was nondemocratic and authoritarian, it was criticized by
all those who believed in the ideal of democracy. Because the
government theoretically was for democracy, it had no excuse
to offer its critics. The only thing it could do was to bear the
criticism. Compared with the Chinese Communists, who explicitly advocated the dictatorship of the proletariat, the Nationalists were weak in argument and in control. Furthermore,
the Communists succeeded in uniting the masses as well as the
intellectuals. With their support, together with the concentrated strength and steel-like organization of the Communist
Party, the Communists began to exercise great pressure on the
Nationalist government. Under the joint attack of the democratic idealists and the Communists, the Nationalists had to
announce in 1937 the formal implementation of constitutionalism. It was the original promise of the Nationalist Party, as
well as the goal of the non-Nationalist people who had democratic consciousness. But in actuality this official implementation of constitutionalism destroyed the Nationalist Party's
power to control itself and its already questionable rule of the
nation. While the Nationalist power was rapidly declining, there
was no new power other than the Communist to replace it. Thus
the Communist takeover of China was inevitable.

X. On Why the Communist Party Cannot Be Considered the
Peak of the Development of Political Consciousness in
China in the Past One Hundred Years, the Ups and Downs
That the Chinese People Experienced During the Process
of the Development of Political Consciousness, the Complete
Transcendence Revealed in This Process, the Prospects
for the Future, and the Democratic Spirit of National
Reconstruction That Stems from the Moral Mind
and the Rational Mind

Today the Communists rule mainland China. But the political

consciousness of Communism cannot be considered the highest
form in the development of modern Chinese political thought.
In my judgement, although the Nationalist government took
refuge on Taiwan less than a year after the implementation of
the Constitution, the political consciousness to which the Nationalist government in Taiwan subscribe still represents the highest level of development of political consciousness in the past
one hundred years. Thus we should not judge the level of development of political consciousness in terms of the temporary
success or failure of a government. One should judge in terms
of internal goals as well as the necessary direction of the development of Chinese political consciousness in the past one
hundred years.

Communism is not the highest development of political consciousness because it is basically a negative one. Even if one
should adopt the most sympathetic attitude toward the Communist movement, one will find that it represents only the desire of the Chinese people for independence, their consciousness of anti-imperialism, their struggle against the corruption
of the government officials and politicians and the exploitation
by the landlords and capitalists, and their effort to eliminate
the outdated, undesirable aspects of traditional culture and custom. All these are negative measures. The reason the Communists could defeat the Nationalists was mainly because of the
people's increasing dissatisfaction and frustration with the
twenty-year period of tutelage. For instance, during the Political Consultation Conference, pressures from all directions
were forced on the Nationalists to end the tutelage and to begin
the implementation of the Constitution. After the implementation of the Constitution, most of the Nationalists, probably having forgotten that constitutionalism was their original goal, felt
that they had lost their political status and power and that
simultaneously they had lost their sense of responsibility. In
the society the few who understood and trusted the democratic
political ideal and system did not have the social power and
political status to support and aid the government in the implementation of the Constitution. Thus the beginning of consti-

tutionalism was the beginning of the total collapse of the people's faith in the Nationalist Party. That is why the Communist
could take over the mainland. Clearly the Communist success
was not due to the desire of the Chinese people for the ideals
of Marxism-Leninism. The Communist success was accidental.
If one studies the various stages in the development of political
consciousness in the Chinese people in the past one hundred
years, one would understand that what the Chinese people really
wanted to establish was a "truly Chinese people's nation." By
"Chinese" is meant the continuation of their history and culture.
By "people" is meant that the nation should belong to the people, who should be the sole possessors of political power, and
the nation should be democratic; this suggests that the Chinese
people would exercise their political power and participate in
political activities in accordance with the Constitution. The
nation and the Constitution, therefore, should be above all parties and not under them. Now the Communists place Marxism-
Leninism above the sacred tablet of Confucius and totally follow
the Russian line of party dictatorship. This is a fundamental
violation of the notion of an ideal nation of the Chinese people.
How then can Communism be considered the highest development in the political consciousness of modern China?

As to the Nationalist government in Taiwan, it certainly is
guilty of the loss of the China mainland. Also, this government
committed numerous serious mistakes during the period of
tutelage, although merits have to be given to it for its leadership in the war against the Japanese invasion. Basically, the
Nationalist Party and the Nationalist government have never
changed their ideal of constitutionalism, never established their
political foundation on only a single social class, and always
wanted to continue the history and culture of China. The Nationalists have always wanted to establish a Chinese, nationalistic,
and democratic nation. This is not a wrong direction. The
period from the reorganization of the Nationalist Party to the
period of tutelage when the Party exercised its control over
the government was a political regression. This regression
was an accommodation period necessitated by the failure of the

constitutional government in the early years of the Republic.
The objective significance of this regression was to enable
Chinese intellectuals to have time to work closer with the people and to generate new political power. This has been discussed earlier. During the period of regression the political
approach of the Nationalists was quite similar to that of the
Communists, that is, the power of the Party was superior to
everything. This approach of the Nationalists drove the Chinese
people to become critical and suspicious of the Nationalist Party
and its government. Later some of the Nationalists were in -
clined toward fascism, and this was a further violation of the
original ideal of their own Party. This was certainly a complicated and confused phenomenon which developed during the political regression. Also, within the Nationalist Party there were
reformers who tried to build a class foundation for the Party.
This was another complication which developed during that time
with the influence of Communism. And later there was Wang
Ching-wei's advocacy of peace between China and Japan. He
simply neglected the supreme significance of the war against
the Japanese invasion. This was a case of dislocation of the
traditional Chinese concept of "The world is one family." All
these confusing and inconsistent ways of thought and action were
eventually rejected by the people. Finally there came the implementation of the constitutional government in 1948. Constitutionalism was directly related to the original ideal of the
founding of the Republic and therefore should be considered as
the complete transcendence of all the ups and downs in political
thought and actions in the three decades preceding. Theoretically speaking, this constitutional government should be the beginning of a truly democratic constitutionalism. Now that the
Nationalist government has retreated to Taiwan, how successful it has been in its effort to promote a constitutional government is another problem. But I am sure that the Chinese people as a whole will work hard along such a path to achieve a
truly republican government. Nothing can stop such a trend
because a truly democratic republic has been the internal goal
of various stages of the development of political consciousness

of the Chinese people in the past one hundred years. On the road toward such a goal, there are all kinds of obstacles, external as well as internal. But we can gradually do away with these obstacles by means of thinking and doing. The greatest external obstacle is, of course, the Communist Party, which practices the dictatorship of one party and one class and subscribes to only Marxism-Leninism. It is completely in violation of the spirit of "building a Chinese, nationalistic, and democratic nation." The greatest internal obstacle is the confusion and tangling of certain temperaments and concepts that are in conflict with the modern political ideal of China. These confusion and tangling of temperaments and concepts have various sources and causes which are difficult to identify and clarify one by one. When the confusion and tangling are identified and clarified, a higher level in the development of political consciousness in the Chinese people will begin, which I will call the spirit of the democratic construction of the nation based upon the rational mind and the moral mind. I will discuss this topic in another essay.

15

The Reconstruction of Confucianism
and
the Modernization of Asian Countries

1. Introduction

In this paper I shall discuss in what senses the modernization of Asian countries needs Confucianism, and also in what senses Confucianism needs certain reconstruction so as to become an adequate spiritual basis of their modernization. As generally understood, modernization means a socio-cultural ideal of, and a historical process leading to, a modern state composed of people living in freedom and equality, under a democratic government, and in a modern industrialized community formed by the use of modern scientific technology for the well-being of the people. As modernization is a socio-cultural ideal and historical process, no state or community can be said to have been definitely modernized enough. The difference in modernization is but a difference of degree, and the modernization of any state or community can only be gradually realized through a historical process of change of culture, by the concerted efforts of its people after that ideal.

The historical process of cultural change is a continuous process stretching from the past to the present and reaching out to the future. It has its developmental or progressive features as well as its permanent or conservative features. There is usually a reawakening or revival in a new form of some dormant innate spirit. As East Asian countries, unlike those African ones, do have a long history of culture in the past, their modernization cannot be accomplished without certain spiritual reawakening or revival to keep the historical continuity. In the following space I shall argue that the revival of Confucianism in a new form, i.e., a reconstruction of Confucianism, is a necessary condition for keeping such a continuity in some East Asian countries.

About fifty years ago, some Chinese scholars and young men started a cultural movement to criticize and oppose Confucianism as an obstacle and enemy of the modernization of China. It was from this movement that Chinese Communism gradually emerged. Confucianism, people then charged, hindered the progress of China as it harboured feudalism, monarchism, and patriarchism. This is not unlike the charge against Christianity by those 18th-century liberal thinkers in Europe, or the one against Hinduism and other Indian religions and philosophies by those early 19th-century innovators in India. Arguments of the same type against Confucianism, I believe, could easily be found in Japan, Vietnam, and Korea, voiced by young men who craved for modern progress. It is quite understandable psychologically that when people have their mind fixed upon some novelty, they tend to be blind to the values of their old possessions, considering them as something boring, some burden to be cast off the sooner the better.

But, needless to say, it is very doubtful if their reasons for deprecating these old possessions, reasons that spring from the aforementioned psychological background, are logically sound and tenable. When all is said, Confucianism in East Asia, just as Christianity in Europe and America and Hinduism in India, still may not be the real and irremediable obstacle and enemy to modernization. In point of fact, those Asian countries which preserve their traditional customs and faiths to a greater extent, such as Japan and India, are forging ahead more successfully along the road to modernization. On the other hand, China, whose intellectuals had little kind words to say to their own culture, has lost her mainland to Communism for upwards of a decade. After her, North Korea and North Vietnam have followed suit. Does it not prove that the unreserved anxiety for modernization, not duly balanced by a corresponding willingness to preserve the tradition, may lead people to go all the way to some other extreme? Communism, it should be pointed out, is no modernism. If anything, it is a kind of super-modernism, which through a dialectical process will become in the end a kind of. anti-modernism, anti-thetic to the modernism of Europe and America. And facts seem to indicate that Asians cannot defend themselves against this ism or doctrine with a mere aspiration for modernism but without a proper recognition of the importance of tradition.

It is very strange that some Western scholars have said that Chinese Communism is an outgrowth of the Confucian tradition, is indeed Confucianism in a new form. For all I know, the same thing may have been said of Vietnamese Communism and Korean Communism. But, if that assertion is true, why should Chinese Communism have grown out from the criticism of Confucianism as mentioned above? If Communism be just a new form of Confucianism, it would follow that these East Asian countries, China, Vietnam, Korea, and others, could never escape the clutches of Communism, unless they could successfully stem Confucianism out from their cultural heritage, or else, if the roots of Confucianism are already too deep, throw the whole heritage overboard. And the only way for these countries to be saved from Communism would be to forget their past entirely, to have a clean breast—nay, a blank one—and to be an unreserved receptacle of Western ideas. But is that possible? And is that what ought to be? Facing such questions, we are here obliged to see Confucianism as it is, and to find out the truths, pro and con, about it. If it should be found out that Communism is not Confucianism in disguise, nor is Confucianism the collective name for feudalism and other anachronistic concepts, should we not then be obliged to reconstruct Confucianism, giving it new form and new meaning in response to the challenges from opposite sides?

II. What is Confucianism?

In our talk about what Confucianism is, I wish to say first that the missionary translation of the word Confucianism is somewhat misleading. In the Chinese language, we usually use the word *Ju* for the teaching of Confucius. Originally, *Ju* means a type of man who is cultural, moral, and responsible for religious rites, and hence religious. Confucius himself as an individual is only a *Ju*, a word which, as a generic term, has its universal meaning. So a more adequate translation of Confucianism should be Juism. When Juism is translated as Confucianism, people of other countries get the impression that a Confucianist is just a worshipper or admirer of Confucius as a particular individual, and pay attention only to what Confucius himself or this or that Confucianist does in his particular age, and thus the universal meaning of Juism is neglected and missed.

Of course, each *Ju*, as particular individual, exists in a particular age of history, has to accustom himself to the social political environment of his age, and naturally possesses certain social and political ideas which belong to his age. Thus Confucius had his idea of feudal system of his age. After feudal system had collapsed and the empire of Ch'in had been founded more than 2000 years age, the later *Ju*'s or Confucianists had the social and political ideas of empire-system of their ages too. But such ideas were not directly related to the essense of Juism or Confucianism. The case is not unlike that Jesus Christ had certain ideas about Caeser and modern Christians have certain ideas about democracy, neither of which are directly related to the essence of Christianity. Therefore, we have reason to say that all the criticisms of Confucianism, such as containing feudalism, monarchism, patriachism, and other things which may be found in the dictionaries of social science, may be taken as irrelevant to the understanding of the essence of Confucianism. Just as all such criticisms are irrelevant to the understanding of essence of Christianity.

In our view, the essence of Juism or Confucianism is only a teaching which aims at developing a type of man who is cultural, moral, and religious at one and the same time This is certainly the common spirit of all *Ju*'s, who, in different periods of time, have placed their definite emphases on different aspects of culture, morality, and religiosity of the individual.

III. The Essence of Confucianism

The peculiarity of Confucian teaching in comparison with other world religions, philosophies and moral teachings is its ideal of combining these three into one to form a trinity of wisdom, faith and moral practice. Whereas Western philosophy originated from pure intellectual curiosity of the Greeks, Confucian philosophy from the beginning is to be believed and to be put into moral practice. Compared with other general moral teachings, Confucian teaching is more philosophical, though a Confucian philosophy may be either idealistic or realistic, monistic or pluralistic, empiristic or rationalistic, and so on. Compared with other world religions, Confucian faith is seen to have always human reason and feeling as its foundation, thus being more rational and more human.

Confucianism may be taken as a kind of humanism, yet it is different from that kind of humanism which rose in the Renaissance and has some anti-religious flavour. Confucian is not irreligious. Confucians in the past reverently held sacrifices to ancestral deities, Heaven or God, and men of worth who were worshipped as deities. I have called the spirit of these three sacrifices as the essence of Confucian religious thought. Nevertheless, though the Confucian has reverences for deities and God, he does not base his moral teaching merely on any supernatural or transcendental revelation descending from God or Heaven above. Confucian teaching starts from what is near to man's mind in a down-to-earth and below manner in man's foot. The Confucian teaches man to begin with filial piety to his parents and fraternal love to his brothers and sisters when he is a child; and then extend his love and respect to his neighbors, friends, country, the world under heaven, and the whole history of mankind from the past to the future; and lastly, to have love and reverence for the *Tao* of Heaven and be in spiritual communication with Heaven or God and deities through the sense of gratitude in performing the three sacrifices, thus ultimately attain the sagehood which is as holy as Heaven or God. In other words, a man is to begin his life career from the near-below and lowly, then, through the development of his reason and feelings or enlargement of his mind, ascend to and arrive at what is far above.

As can be seen in the foregoing paragraph, the philosophic core of Confucian teaching is the idea that whatever is supernatural and transcendental is immanent in what is natural. For example, filial piety and brotherly love, as the Confucian teaches, are all rooted in the child's mind when he is born in the natural world, and these affections grow out naturally also. As he has such natural affections for his near relations, the child already expresses his inner nature to transcend his personal self. This nature of self-transcending here expressed is the very human nature which, when developed, can transcend even the whole sensible world and bring him to see what is far above, if there is any. Thus if man can get any revelation from the supernatural and transcendental, the ability originates in the very human nature of self-transcending. In the Confucian point of view, man's piety to the utmost supernatural is rightly rooted within the child's natural love and respect for his parents and brothers already. In some religions, the words reverence and piety are words reserved only for our emotions toward some supernatural being or deities or the clergy. To the Confucian, on the other hand, these words can be also used on any person we really love and respect. This is the proof that the Confucian never separates the supernatural and the natural, and can always see some element of the former in the latter, and have religious feeling sentiment even in daily moral practice.

Beside the aforesaid that the Confucian teaching which aims at having man see the supernatural in the natural, have religious feeling in ordinary moral practice, and then combine morality with religiocity, there is the Confucian teaching about culture and morality. This teaching sees culture as the outer expression of morality and morality as the inner source of cultural expression: they are interdependent and mutually supplementary, nourishing and enriching each other. This is quite different from some Western philosophies which takes cultural achievements merely as the realization of some objectives of eternal truth or beauty, having no inner connection with morality which is said to be the pursuit of moral goodness alone. It also differs considerably with the idea of some Indian thinkers who see man's inner morality as nothing but the purity of soul and peace with God without any necessary relation to its cultural expressions.

IV. Problems about the Motivation for Modernization in Asian Countries

If what I have said in the last section is not far from the truth, then I shall proceed to say something to the proposition that Asian countries need Confucianism for motivation of modernization. This is to prepare us for the discussion of the central ideas of this paper, which will be put forth in the last three sections.

By motivation of modernization, I mean the psychological and spiritual motive and willingness for modernization. It is well-known that without noble and lofty ideal or purpose, no lofty and noble motive and willingness can come, and then no noble and lofty thing can be achieved. People are wont to say that modernization brings about a rich and strong state. Is such a purpose lofty and noble enough? We may also ask this question: What good does a rich and strong state amount to, if it is not for the well-being of her people? And what is the well-being of people, if the individual has no well-being and has no sense of the dignity of man? What is the well-being of an individual? What does the dignity of the individual consists in, if he is not aware of or does not feel that he has either actually or potentially a spiritual being which comes from his cultural, moral, and religious life? Finally, we want to ask: How can an individual spiritual being really be an individual, if his religious, moral, and cultural life are not integrated into a unity as a genuine Confucian aspires after. Then, why not think that modernization, which is based on the idea of dignity of the individual, is for the purpose of establishing the integrated spiritual being of the individual to realize the true dignity of man, that is: the Confucian ideal of man? Is there anything in the ideal of modernization which is not based on the dignity of the individual and is of no use, even mediately, to the establishment of the well-being or spiritual being of people? If there is, how then can the ideal of modernization be ultimately justified? If there is none whatsoever, why then should we hesitate to fix the realization of the Confucian ideal of man as the final purpose of modernization? Is it not a purpose nobler and loftier than to have a rich and strong state and so on. We all know that the higher a cataract falls down from, the more beauty, power, and consequently benefit to people it gives. Likewise, if people's motive and willingness for modernization are based on such a noble and lofty ideal, they will have more beauty, power, and benefit for the cultivation of the various fields of social culture.

It is often said that from the psychological point of view, man's motivations for doing things are many and varied, and that different ones become powerful at different situations. For the modernization of Asian countries, the peoples' motives of imitation, envy, and admiration of the more affluent West states, personal love for something new, and personal desire for modern facilities can all be powerful. Thus it is concluded that any other noble and lofty ideals and motives are not necessary.

Frankly speaking, I cannot agree with the above view. The Asians do have various motives for modernization. They may all be powerful in certain space and time. Yet, it is suspicious that any motive which is just personal is necessarily beneficial to the community as a whole and that any motive with an external goal, such as the imitation or envy or admiration of some others, is self-originative, self-enduring and lasting. In the process of modernization of Europe and the United States which began from the Seventeenth and Eighteenth Century, people's motives came from their philosophical speculation, moral sentiment, religious devotion, and literary and artistic vision, all of which stemmed from their own Western traditional culture. They did not imitate anything outside, and that is why the process of modernization of the West can be self-enduring from then on. Then, how can the modernization of Asian countries be started and continue to go, without some motives in the part of the Asian people which are self-originative from their own traditional culture?

Many people know that the modernization of Asia needs some spiritual motive which is self-originative and self-enduring, but they are nonetheless still unwilling to look for it in Asian traditional culture, because they do not acknowledge the values of this culture, denying it any power to generate anything new that can furnish the spiritual basis of modernization. This is the view of some missionaries who, regretting that the Asians did not have the real grace of God before, preached to them for their renascence the gospels of God, so that they may get from Heaven some originative powers for modernization. There were also some Asian intellectuals who introduced the theory of evolution from the West to the Asians, and asked them to see their past just as something dead, let it pass away, and from now accept the new philosophy of progress as the ideological foundation for modernization.

We cannot agree with these two types of thought either. We do not believe that man can really be born anew by cutting off his historical relations with the past. We rather believe that people without historical continuity and relation with the past would be like an individual who forgets everything and therefore has a vaccum for a memory. Such a person would be a shallow and blank existence. Our rejoinder to these two types of thought may be phrased ironically as follows: If the Asian past is absolutely unworthy, and if the universal and eternal God has never given spiritual powers to Asians in the thousands of years of their history, and the Asians are now just waiting for missionaries to preach to them how to receive God's grace, it is very doubtful if God will grant it to them at this late stage. And if the Asian people have never had any idea of progress and have never kept their progress going on, how is it possible that they can progress to the stage of being qualified to accept the philosophy of progress ?

As we insist on keeping the historical continuity of the Asians in order that our existence has depth, we must insist that there should be something self-originatively growing out from the roots of Asian culture even for an epoch-making event such modernization. This is the reason why we have pointed out that the realization of Confucian ideal of man should be taken as the final purpose of modernization. In the following sections, we shall say something further about the significance of Confucianism to modern world as well as the significance of the modern world to Confucianism and we shall propose a reconstruction of Confucianism which will be a sufficient, if not necessary, spiritual basis of modernization of Asian countries. On the topics of these sections some of my friends and I myself have written many essays and books in the sixteen years since communists occupied China. Our discussions are complicated and many-sided, which could not be reproduced in entirety here. I shall put forth just some of our main points in the following sections for consideration.

V. The Significance of Confucianism to the Modern World

There are four points about the significance of Confucianism to the modern world which I shall mention briefly:

(1) First, I wish to say that while part of its accidental and transient content such as its connections with feudalism, monarchism and patriarchism, should be ruled out. Confucianism remains clearly the most reasonable type of teaching which can harmonize the conflicts of all the religions of the world. As the world's religious teachings always start from what is revealed, and revelation, though not supported by human reason, is conceived as absolute truth and acclaimed as the unconditional faith of men, it becomes dogma. The different religions of the world have different dogmas, and they naturally conflict with each other. From these conflicts come religious provincialism which is ignorant of and despises other religions, and religious imperialism which seeks to conquer all other religions. Religious provincialism is usually related to political provincialism, and religious imperialism related to political imperialism. Thus political conflicts of mankind are much more argumented by religious conflicts. The Confucian teaching, as it starts from what is near-below and extends to what is far-above, never denies that men may have spiritual communication with the divine and have certain religious insights; on the other hand, as it does not found itself on any supernatural revelation, it has no dogma. It therefore is essentially a religious liberalism, and can be a spiritual ground for the world religions to meet together. In this meeting

place men will be emancipated from religious imperialism and provincialism, and gradually religious conflicts will subside.

(2) The Confucian ideal of man is the sage who is not descended from above, but begins as an ordinary child in this natural world. This ideal is often phrased as "standing on Earth and reaching to Heaven". It is also like a tree which has its roots penetrating deep into earth and its leaves spreading wide in the air, receiving sunshine and rain. As the above is rooted in the below, the Confucianists have strong faith in the goodness of human nature which is the origin of the dignity of man. In Western Christian theology, man is created after the image of God and is good. This is the transcendental origin of the dignity of man. But ever since the Fall, the Sinful nature of man is taken as original. Only God's grace can save him from his sin, and man's dignity has thus lost its transcendental origin. Thus a man, if not a Christian and willing consciously or unconsciously to have man's sin to be punished, has theoretically no eventual escape from self-torture and torture by others, such as those under totalitarianism from Hitler to Stalin. Therefore, keeping the faith in the goodness of man in a primordial place and seeing his sinful nature as secondary and not original, is a way to preserve the man's individual dignity and to cut off at the root ego-torture and altru-torture. Here the Confucian teaching of modern significance is all apparent.

(3) The Confucian, from his rationalism and humanism, has the least superstition about and expects no miracle from nature. In the Confucian philosophy, as a man is rooted in nature, his mind has to open to things that come from nature. This is the foundation of the spirit of science. Nevertheless, the Confucian never sees man as merely an external natural object. This is because man, through extending and enlarging his mind, can transcend the whole sentient nature and possess an inner transcendental subjectivity which can never be externalized. In the modern world, science has developed to a degree that any aspects of man, be it physiological, psychological, or sociological, can all be the object for scientific study. We have no objection to these studies in principle. However, if man himself is merely seen as a object for scientific study, how about the scientist who does such a study? If man is regarded just as an object in the external world, then he like other external objects, has no reason not to be used, controlled and manufacturable. The totalitarian states do in fact use scientific knowledge and techniques to remould men for political purposes, degrading his dignity and condemming his soul. Here we see again the need of Confucian teaching, which respects scientific study on the one hand, and holds sacred the transcendental subjectivity of man on the other. With the latter firmly held, man can never be wholly externalized as merely an object for scientific study: he should instead be always the master of science, self-conscious of his own transcendental subjectivity as above its science in order to limit the use of scientific technique to control the man himself, and thus his human dignity is preserved.

(4) The Confucian ideal of man as a moral being in his inner side and as cultural being in his outer side, has also its modern significance in its anti-pan-moralism and anti-pan-culturalism. When morality is just classified as a branch of culture and as standing on the same footing as art, science, or politics, it is a kind of what I called pan-culturalism. It means that morality has no superiority to or more importance than any other branch of culture, and any branch of culture may be encouraged to develop itself absolutely independent of any moral consideration. But this will be detrimental to the full development of human culture, because when all

moral considerations are ruled out, then the conflicts between men's different activities in different fields of culture cannot be settled, and no symphony of the whole body of human culture can be performed. On the other hand, there is pan-moralism in modern thought which sees no essential connection between inner morality and cultural cultivation. There are many types of pan-moralism in different spiritual levels. The communists' acclamation of revolutionary morality as the highest morality of man is one type of pan-moralism, which is morality perverted for a political purpose. The ideology of such a pan-moralism can strip a man of all his cultural garments and sacrifice him naked on the altar of political revolution. Such an attitude, be it admitted, is not without moral sentiment originating from within. But, nonetheless, when the naked moral-being of a revolutionary hero is worshipped above all men, the preservation of traditional human culture would be considered as of no essential importance, and barbarism among other things will come out from this very pan-moralism

Pan-culturalism and pan-moralism are both attractive forms of thought haunting modern people, and can be transformed each into the other through a dialectic process. Yet either of them has done, and will do more, evil rather than good to the modern world. Therefore, the Confucian idea of morality and culture, which never separates the two, and which sees morality as the lord and inner spring of all cultural expressions but at the same time itself must be cultivated through the cultivation of the latter, is a timely help (or antidote).

VI. The Significance of Modern Community to Confucianism

What we have said so far is about the significances of Confucianism to the modern world. We now pass to the significances of modern community and culture to the reconstruction of Confucianism. Anything about culture is necessarily significant to the Confucian, as he is most concerned with man as a moral-cultural being. However, many ideas of modern community and culture are different from Confucianism in origin. I should like to mention three points. First, modern science is not founded merely on the "openness of our mind to nature"—a quality which the traditional Confucianist does not lack. It is rather founded on the spirit of free enquiry of objective research of scientists. In free enquiry or objective research man has to forget himself as a moral being and make his mind free in forming hypothesis about any object, as if his mind is for the moment sunken into the object and objectified therein. Here the traditional Confucian spirit of openness to nature seems not to be sufficient to give impetus to the modern objective enquiry or research of the scientists. Secondly, the modern industrialized community is highly departmentalized in its structure by the division of labour. Here man must particularize in something, has his special profession, and consequently has his special social position in a corner of the complicated structure. Man's moral practice as demanded by the modern community is just to be loyal to his special profession and not feel ashamed of his special position. Here the Confucian idea of the whole man as a cultural and moral being seems inadequate to be the spiritual ground for the establishment of modern community and modern vocational morality. Thirdly, the modern ideas of human rights as related with ideas of democracy, freedom, and equality are all defined objectively in terms of the individual's social, political, legal, and economical relations with others. For example, an individual has his freedom and equal opportunity with others to choose his own profession from the various trades of the community, to participate in any social or political organization, and to elect candidates or be elected himself to fill the office of some organization. All these are human rights of the individual which, as they involve other men, are prescribed and determined by law. When any new law is in the process of being legislated, people have to ponder over its objective rationality and consistincy with other laws already in force, and not only consider it from the angle of the righteousness of the law itself. Thus the human rights as protected by modern laws are actually protected by the whole legislative system which is related to the whole political and social systems and not protected merely by our subjective moral sense of justice. Here we see that the Confucian idea of moral sense of justice has never developed enough to build such a modern systems. The Confucian's idea of freedom is man's moral freedom to do the moral good. The Confucian ideas of right and equality of men are essentially the equality of moral nature and moral right to be sages. All of these Confucian ideas are not sufficient to provide a spiritual basis of modernization. To respond to the demands of the age, a further development of Confucianism from within is called for.

VII. The Reconstruction of the Confucian Spirit as a Three Dimensional Spirit

From what we have said in the foregoing pages, we have to acknowledge that there are some new ideas and new spirits which are missing in traditional Confucianism. If we do not want to keep Confucianism backward of age, we have to look forward and plan a reconstruction of the Confucian spirit to meet the modern need. The reconstruction, however, is not to change the essence of Confucianism which as we have said, is a teaching to form a kind of man based on a philosophy that sees the supernatural in the natural and sees the moral and the cultural side of man as mutually dependent and supplementary. This essence gone, there will be no Confucianism. What we should do is just to extend and enlarge the Confucian spirit from within, and open for it a new dimension to contain the modern spirit.

By the word new dimension, I mean a spiritual dimension (of the mind) which is co-extensive in principle with the differentiation of the objective world, and is free to objectify and to particularize itself in the objective expressions of its universal rationality. If the seeing of the supernatural in the natural is the first spiritual dimension, the vertical dimension "from below to above"; the seeing of the mutual dependence of inner morality and outer cultural expression is the second dimension, the diametrical dimension "from inner to outer"; then the third dimension, co-extensive in principle with differentiations of objective world, is horizontal. In this third dimension, as man is free to objectify and particularize himself in the objective expression of his universal rationality, and as any particular profession or business or cultural activity can be an objective expression of man's rationality, so man is free to choose any special profession or business and then has his special position in the whole community. Here, if man see himself as no more and no less than a member of the community, he then may fight rationally for his social, political, legal, and economical rights as any other members of the same community. Thus he has all the senses of the modern ideas of freedom, equality, democracy, and so on. Furthermore, if he is doing some scientific inquiry or research, he can objectify and particularize his rational mind in the object according to its peculiarities and forget temporarily his moral-being for getting the fruits of objective research. Thus the modern objective spirit is contained in the third spiritual dimension of the Confucian mind, and a Confucian can adjust himself to the modern community and meet its challenges.

However, as the Confucian mind has also its two other dimension, it is free also to withdraw all its outward particular objective expressions and return to its subjective inner universality and rationality. Through such a withdrawing, man becomes self-conscious of his inner spiritual space which contains and embraces all natural and cultural things objectively existing, including the objective expressions of his own self. Thus he is able to absorb all such things which will become inner stimuli and material for the formation of his moral being, a being innerly experienced as rational—even supra-rational when the rationality is seen through self-transcending nature. Henceforth, he has his freedom and equality with all the sages of the world, and also his right as a moral being in the moral order of the whole universe. Through the awareness of the moral order of the whole universe, he can have a sense of piety or religiocity growing from his moral sense.

As a Confucian is conscious of his inner spiritual space which contains and embraces anything objective it encounters, it can be spiritually ascending above the whole objective world and can from that vantage point evaluate the structure of the world as a whole. He is therefore in a position to criticize the actuality of the modern world, and look for ways to improve it according to his ideals of value. For example, the Confucian may criticize the over-differentiation of modern community which lacks the necessary integration. He may consider that the modern man who sees and does nothing else than what his profession demands of him, leads a way of life more or less like a bee or an ant, thus degrading the human spirit. He may also think that the modern ideas of freedom, equality, and democracy are merely formal, and are, ethically neutral. In the use of his freedom, the modern man can choose anything provided that it will not interfere others' freedom. As for his idea of equality, it often will take the form of an aspiration to be equal in wealth with some others. In the democratic system of election, man may be elected president, just because he pleases most of the voters. The modern ideas of equality or freedom or democracy are purely formal, because they have no value-orientation and other content. A Confucian will think that the implementation of these modern ideas is necessary, because it opens the alternatives of man's activities and widens his view and horizon. Yet he will say that this is merely the starting point, not the destination of mankind. Standing on equal basis, men will strive to progress to a higher level of existence through self-determination.

From the Confucian point of view, the ultimate value of any human activity consists in the forming of man's moral and cultural being, all the others being but instrumental to or constitutive of this ideal. In the Asian agricultural countries of the past, where peoples were bound to the land in a hierarchical feudal system, it was impossible for all the people to be educated and to have his moral and cultural being developed. Thus, the ideal of Confucian which would have all men become sages, though a highest ideal of mankind, could never be realized. Thanks to modernization, people are gradually emancipated from their bondage to the land and the feudal system, and doors to various ways of living are opened by modern industrialization and the establishment of social and political democratic systems. Thus any individual person can stand up independently and choose a way of life existence by the exercise of his free will and self-education. But, all the same, may it not be true also that the modern industrialized community gradually becomes a new bondage for men who are falling into a new slavery in the modern social and political systems? Does the man of modern city, dislocated from his native country and separated from nature not become a being of no roots in the world? Is the dissolution of family in modern industrialized community not a most serious problem for the development of man's moral personalty? Should the idea of formal freedom and formal equality not be filled with certain value-content? Is it not true that besides the equality of individuals in the socio-political sense there should also be a hierarchical order in the moral and ethical level? Whether it is so or not, there are many problems waiting for us to solve, problems that can only be settled by our value-orientation consciousness which is based on our idea of man's being. Here the Confucian, who has been concerned with man's moral and cultural being for thousands of years, finds himself still having many things unsolved and unfinished when he evaluates the world with the third spiritual dimension of his mind, aided by the other two spiritual dimensions. He has a formidable task before him.

16

PHILOSOPHICAL CONSCIOUSNESS, SCIENTIFIC CONSCIOUSNESS, AND MORAL REASON*

Section 11. The Philosophical Consciousness That Is Related to Scientific Consciousness in General — The Consciousness of a Scientific Cosmology and That of Epistemology

We may have different ways of defining the nature of philosophy. One view would take philosophy to be a system of knowledge just like science; only it is a more comprehensive system that includes all science, or rather, it is a synthetic system of knowledge. Another view would take philosophy to be just a reflective and critical attitude. It purports to reflect on methods, postulates, axioms, and fundamental concepts that science relies on to build its knowledge in order to clarify other scientific concepts and principles and to understand the limit of each science and of scientific knowledge itself so that they will not be wrongly applied to areas where they do not apply. Still another view would take philosophy to be that which helps us to understand the universe and human life, to have wisdom to penetrate into history, culture, and concrete affairs, and to give us

---

*T'ang Chün-i, "Che-hsüeh k'e-hsüeh i-shih yü tao-te li-hsing." Chapter Five of Wen-hua i-shih yü tao-te li-hsing [Cultural Consciousness and Moral Reason], Vol. II (Hong Kong: The Union Press, 1960), pp. 46-84. Translated here are excerpts from Chapter Five. Translated by Shu-hsien Liu.

direction for our actions. Of these three, the first view takes philosophy to be an activity for pursuing knowledge, the second view takes philosophy to be an activity for understanding our knowledge, and the third view takes philosophy to be an activity that starts with knowledge in order to achieve wisdom, which is above and beyond knowledge. All these views have their justifications. I would like to elaborate on them in the following.

We may say that philosophy is a system of knowledge; most of the great philosophers past and present have claimed that their philosophy is a system of knowledge; we may also say that philosophy is a more comprehensive system of knowledge which includes systems of scientific knowledge; we do find philosophers utilizing scientific knowledge and concepts in their attempts to synthesize all knowledge. Since philosophy is capable of encompassing scientific consciousness, it has the demand to synthesize all scientific knowledge and to work out an all-inclusive system of knowledge in order to actualize its encompassing power. And yet it is factually impossible for us to work out an all-inclusive system of knowledge, because a truly all-inclusive system of knowledge would have to recapitulate all scientific knowledge and include it all in the system. But no one is capable of possessing all scientific knowledge. Moreover, even if someone did know all the scientific knowledge of the present stage, there is no limit to future scientific progress. Since we cannot expect to know the scientific knowledge to be developed in the future, it is still impossible for us to have an all-inclusive system of knowledge. The reason why there is no limit for scientific progress lies in the fact that science always seeks to know empirical objects. We must use known abstract and universal scientific principles to make judgments on empirical objects for further confirmation. Although there is verification for known principles, there is also the presence of new empirical objects. And what makes these objects new lies exactly in the fact that there emerge some kind of new principles or understanding. The seeking of such new principles or understanding leads to an increase of new scientific knowledge. Hence, the progress of scientific knowledge knows no limit. Of course,

if we cease to apply abstract and universal principles to empirical objects for further confirmation, or if there is no longer
the emergence of new empirical objects in the universe, then it
may be possible to synthesize all known universal principles
into a philosophical system of knowledge. But where there is
no longer the presence of empirical objects, or when we no
longer apply universal scientific principles to make judgments
on empirical objects for further confirmation, then these universal principles are devoid of objective reference, lack significance of truth, and are locked in the subject only. Under
such circumstances, our mind would turn into a closed mind,
and there would no longer be any scientific investigations. If,
however, various scientific investigations are continued, and
philosophy still purports to synthesize scientific knowledge,
then such synthesis will never come to an end. As there is no
limit for scientific progress, philosophy will also never accomplish its final goal. In doing this kind of synthesis, philosophical
consciousness must follow scientific progress which comes
first. Since various scientific consciousnesses have different
objects and must change accordingly, the philosophical consciousness that follows must also differentiate and change accordingly. Such philsophical consciousness has two destinies.
In the first place, wherever scientific consciousness reaches,
philosophical consciousness will also follow; such a philosophical consciousness will be differentiated according to various
departmental scientific consciousnesses and hence will lose its
independent character. In the second place, however, if philosophical consciousness still wants to maintain its own identity
under such circumstances and seek to bring about a synthesis
of scientific knowledge in order to form a system, then philosophical consciousness will not be able to follow scientific consciousness step by step and will lag somewhat behind in order
to work out a synthesis. In such a case, philosophical consciousness will not be able to catch up with science; thus it becomes
inevitable that the philosophical system that purports to synthesize all scientific knowledge cannot include all scientific progress in its program. It is in this sense that it will be impossible

to achieve an all-inclusive philosophical system of knowledge.

Although it is impossible for us to have an all-inclusive philosophical system of knowledge, it is not inappropriate for us to have such an idea. We are using the idea of an all-inclusive philosophical system of knowledge to encompass the idea of all scientific systems of knowledge. In so doing, we can give expression to our philosophical consciousness that encompasses all sciences and strive to bring about the realization of this idea in a gradual fashion. But this idea is an "idea qua ideal," it is a formal idea which lacks the content to bring about its total realization. Therefore, in order to understand the philosophical consciousness that is based on this idea, we cannot appeal to its content, i.e., scientific and empirical knowledge. We can only understand it in a negative fashion: this is a consciousness that seeks to abolish the limitations of known empirical scientific knowledge in order to expand in an infinite way its content in scientific and empirical knowledge. This is a purely transcendental, all-inclusive consciousness that manifests itself in man's theoretical activity. Although this consciousness is infinite in itself, its realization has to be brought about with all sorts of limitations. The philosophical reflection we actually engage in is no more than gradually synthesizing scientific knowledge that has been achieved. By means of this synthesis, we may build our case on general laws established by various sciences which investigate objective reality in order to construct a scientific cosmology. Philosophy in this sense is a system of knowledge that rests its case on various scientific knowledge. A system like this is subject to infinite expansion following the progress of science. It also changes according to changes in sciences; hence it does not enjoy independent stability, and it can never guarantee that what it professes is always true or possesses the whole truth.

Besides advancing theories that seek to synthesize scientific theories in order to establish a cosmological philosophy, philosophy must deal with problems which differ from specific scientific problems in that they result from a [second order] reflection of the sciences. For example, how can the apparent

conflicts among various branches of scientific knowledge be
resolved? Is it possible to apply principles and concepts pertaining to one science to other sciences as well? How should
we go about establishing a scientific system of knowledge? How
can the language of scientific systems of knowledge be unified?
In order to answer these questions, we must reflect in a critical
way on methods that are used to formulate a scientific system
of knowledge; the thinking process involved, the fundamental
concepts, postulates, or axioms of the system, and the language
that is used to express such ideas. Then we will be able to
learn how to go about establishing a scientific system of knowledge, how to make rearrangements or revisions in order to remove conflicts in scientific knowledge, and how to redefine the
limits of the application of scientific principles and concepts
or go even further to achieve unity in the use of scientific language. But, philosophical activity like this has always assumed
an attitude of withdrawal once its function is fulfilled. It has
enabled different scientific disciplines to pursue their own
course, each complementary and supplementary to the other.
This kind of reflective activity has certainly contributed to scientific progress; with the help of such critical reflection, sometimes a new scientific method is formulated or new scientific
objects are discovered, resulting in the establishment of a new
science. But philosophical activity like this cannot establish a
system of knowledge over and above science or help to acquire
knowledge concerning objective reality in a positive fashion.
The philosophical knowledge that is achieved is limited to an
understanding of scientific methods, concepts, postulates, axioms, etc. And the difference between philosophy and science
lies only in that scientists are unconsciously applying a certain
method to investigate objects, while philosophers are putting
forth a method through reflection, understanding it by comparing it with other scientific methods, and relating it to our intellectual activity as a whole, including the activity of knowing
and that of using language. Furthermore, philosophy does not
merely understand what is the case, but proves that it has to be
the case by arguing that it cannot be otherwise. And this is the

critical, reflective task of philosophy. The writings of philosophers show the process of their critical and reflective activity.
Thus the knowledge philosophy acquires is through a self-
consciousness of what has been asserted and confirmed by scientists in an unconscious fashion. It is the knowledge of how
scientific knowledge is constructed. And epistemology seeks
to understand what constitutes knowledge, what is the foundation
of knowledge, and what is its relation to our intellectual activity, knowing activity, and use of language. If the emphasis is
on one science, then what evolves will also be a special branch
of epistemology.

This kind of critical reflection on scientific knowledge is, of
course, distinct from scientific knowledge. The knowledge acquired is also not the same as the scientific cosmology resulting from a synthesis of scientific knowledge. Its aim is not the
understanding of external reality but rather of our own knowledge. Since scientific knowledge is true in terms of the objective reality to which it refers, and scientific cosmology is true
in terms of the scientific truth on which it is based, neither has
independent stability nor can guarantee its truth. Our understanding of the nature of scientific knowledge does not depend
on the external reality to which such scientific knowledge refers. Whether specific scientific knowledge can apply to objects
has no bearing on our understanding of how scientific knowledge
is constructed. Therefore, epistemology has its stability. Only
if we truly understand the nature of our knowledge can we be
assured of the truth of our epistemology which does not depend
on the truth of specific scientific knowledge. Of course, it is
possible that we do not truly understand how our knowledge is
constructed. This is because we have not been critical, reflective, and self-conscious enough. The fault lies in our lack of
critical, reflective ability and lack of depth of self-consciousness.
These can be increased if we can realize the transcendental,
encompassing nature of the mind and its intellectual activity.
And every such increase would lead toward certain epistemological truth which can guarantee itself. This epistemological
consciousness, in its transaction with our actual process of

construction of scientific knowledge, would establish a relation
of both transcending and preserving it at the same time.

Section 12. <u>Metaphysical Consciousness</u>

There are other branches of philosophy besides cosmology
and epistemology; these are metaphysics, moral philosophy,
philosophy of history, and philosophy of culture. Metaphysics
seeks to understand the ultimate reality of the universe. The
difference between metaphysical consciousness and commonsense scientific consciousness lies in that it is no longer satisfied with the kind of reality common sense comprehends; it sees
such reality as merely appearance and asserts the existence of
an ultimate reality. The metaphysical demand is originated
from a doubt of the perfection of commonsense scientific knowledge. This doubt is the expression of a spiritual demand to go
beyond our commonsense scientific knowledge. Hence metaphysical consciousness is also different from epistemological
consciousness. The latter reflects on how commonsense scientific knowledge is constructed, while the former is originated
from a doubt of the perfection of such knowledge and seeks to
transcend our activity to achieve ordinary knowledge, to stop
using our mind to reflect on how ordinary knowledge is constructed, and to go beyond the reality known by ordinary knowledge in order to search for knowledge of an ultimate reality.
The ordinary knowledge which we earn step by step is always
in a process of expansion, while the metaphysical desire seeks
to leap over the manifested reality and get into direct contact
with an ultimate reality in order to have absolute knowledge of
it which can serve as the foundation for all relative knowledge.
The metaphysical consciousness is a philosophical consciousness that is out of step with our ordinary knowledge. Hence, it
has to be originated from a doubt of the perfection of ordinary
knowledge. Of course, the doubt also comes from our reflection
on knowledge, but the reflection is not on how knowledge is constructed but rather on how much truth value it has in terms of
reality as a whole. Thus it is felt that ordinary knowledge is

true only for a class of objects or a certain aspect of things. It cannot be true for all things or for reality as a whole. Thus a feeling of dissatisfaction arises. When we reflect on the facts that various kinds of knowledge claim to be true for the same object and nevertheless different from one another and that attempts to resolve the conflicts and contradictions among them fail, then we tend to suspect that they are all wrong, even to the extent of denying the truth value of knowledge altogether. Such a feeling of dissatisfaction could drive us to metaphysical thinking, the search for knowledge of ultimate reality as a whole.

Thus, metaphysical knowledge means knowledge of ultimate reality as a whole. And metaphysical discussions center on problems such as: Is reality constituted of matter or mind? Is the ultimate substance one or many? Is the transformation of reality necessary or free? Does reality have a dominant power in God? Does substance exist at all? What is the validity of common categories of being? These questions are raised because we are seeking for knowledge of an ultimate reality that goes beyond ordinary commonsense scientific knowledge. When we reflect on these problems, of course our basis must still be common experience and knowledge. But we must make transcendental use of the content and categories of ordinary knowledge so that they may be of use in answering metaphysical questions. As is well known, the content and categories of empirical knowledge are true only in relation to the reality that is manifest to us or the phenomena confined to the specific time and space that is within our experience. But when we make transcendental use of them, they become absolutely true in relation to an ultimate reality as a whole that transcends the scope of empirical knowledge, and they thus acquire a meaning that transcends ordinary empirical knowledge. We now see that metaphysics is grounded on our spiritual demand to go beyond ordinary empirical knowledge. We do not have to discuss whether such metaphysical doctrines will fall into contradiction and fail to achieve perfection. But metaphysical consciousness, even if self-contradictory and less than perfect, is still higher than the epistemological consciousness of simple reflective knowledge; in effect, it is a necessary further step from such epistemological consciousness. The further development of the transcendent spirit that reflects and asserts our knowledge would have to push the content and categories of our knowledge beyond the knowing mind and make transcendental use of them. A kind of metaphysical knowledge results from the transcendental use of the content and categories of knowledge.

The reason why metaphysical knowledge may involve various contradictions and can never achieve perfection lies in the fact that the content and categories of empirical knowledge are re- strictive and mutually complementary. When we hold on to the content and categories of one specific kind of empirical knowl- edge, make transcendental use of them, and absolutize them in order to turn them into metaphysical knowledge, they cannot avoid conflicting with other metaphysical knowledge and become mutually destructive. When we clearly see the contradictions and imperfections involved in the kind of metaphysical knowl- edge resulting from the transcendental use of the content and categories of empirical knowledge, then we understand that these categories can only be used in an immanent fashion, and metaphysics of this kind is just impossible, as Kant has pointed out. Thus we are transcending the transcendental use of the content and categories of empirical knowledge. But what has been transcended is not the spirit of transcendence but rather the erroneous use of it. When we see that the content and cate- gories of empirical knowledge can only be used in an immanent fashion, our transcendent spirit refuses to be confined within the scope of empirical knowledge only. The idea of objective reality as a whole being beyond our subjective empirical knowl- edge emerges in our metaphysical consciousness. Thus, our transcendent spirit has already gone beyond our empirical knowledge and encompassed objective reality as a whole in a way. Although contradictions and conflicts in metaphysical knowledge force us to limit the use of the content and categories of empirical knowledge to their proper scope and although our transcendent spirit no longer uses them to define objective re- ality as a whole, it does not need to confine itself to seeking

empirical knowledge alone. The transcendent spirit, in its re-
fusal to define objective reality as a whole with concepts derived from empirical knowledge, shows that it accomplishes
something in its quest for transempirical knowledge and also
manifests its ability to encompass both objective reality as a
whole and subjective empirical knowledge. If one interprets
this to mean that the phenomenal world of subjective empirical
knowledge is none other than objective reality, then he shows
the metaphysical consciousness of a phenomenalist. If the
transcendent spirit is self-conscious of the fact that the phenomenal world is nothing but the content of subjective empirical knowledge and it cannot exist apart from the mind that has
such subjective empirical knowledge, then he has the metaphysical consciousness of a subjective idealist.

These two kinds of metaphysical consciousness result from
the fact that the mind, which can "encompass both objective reality and subjective empirical knowledge," when transcending
the idea of external objective reality, limits itself to the content of subjective empirical knowledge. A higher metaphysical
consciousness is achieved when the mind, self-conscious of its
capacity to encompass both objective reality and subjective empirical knowledge, transcends both and takes the phenomenal
world of subjective empirical knowledge to be the manifestation
of objective reality; it then regards our system of subjective
empirical knowledge as a unity and objectifies it so as to constitute the ideal "system of empirical knowledge" and further
relies on reason to detect the existence of other people's systems of empirical knowledge. In so doing, the mind has objectified itself so as to constitute the ideal of the mind and to know
the existence of other minds. Thus, different systems of empirical knowledge and different minds may be regarded as instances of the ideal system of empirical knowledge and the
ideal of the mind; these are indispensable if we are to be capable of forming such ideals and thinking rationally according to
these ideals. According to rational activity, it is necessary to
assert the equal existence of different minds and systems of
empirical knowledge for the self and others; both are regarded

as objective, and our rational activity has acquired a universal objective meaning. In such a way our metaphysical consciousness has risen to that of objective idealism. When we
follow our rational activity to assert others' minds, restrain
our own behavior, disregard others' selfishness, and demand
that the patterns of our own behavior to be rational, common
to all, and usable by all, then we have shown the virtue of righteousness toward others. When we move even further to assert
the demands made by other minds and sympathize with them,
we have shown the virtue of human-heartedness, or humanity.
Hence the consciousness of objective idealism also implies a
consciousness of moral obligation. From this consciousness,
we see the relationship between our mind and others' minds
and intuitively know that these minds are really one mind, i.e.,
the mind of Heaven. If we then realize that the phenomenal
world studied by various kinds of empirical knowledge and the
objective reality revealed are really the expression of the same
mind of Heaven, then the metaphysical consciousness of absolute idealism is achieved.

The discussion of various kinds of metaphysical consciousness in the above is, of course, not exhaustive, and it does not
mean that we have committed ourselves to the metaphysics of
absolute idealism. We may still move on from absolute idealism to transcendent realism or a synthesis of the two. But
these will be beyond the scope of our present discussion. Our
intention is to make it clear that metaphysical consciousness
is different from scientific consciousness, which assumes a
duality between the subjective mind and the objective reality:
the function of the mind is to know reality in a relative fashion
and to seek the further expansion of empirical knowledge. Metaphysical consciousness is also different from the epistemological consciousness that reflects on the construction of such
knowledge. It is, instead, the expression of the transcendent
spirit which doubts or feels dissatisfied about the truth value
of our ordinary relative knowledge and seeks to go beyond the
pursuit of such knowledge in order to aspire toward the ultimate reality. Hence the aim of metaphysics is not to acquire

knowledge but to seek wisdom. Those who emphasize knowledge stress that we know something or have a comprehension of reality. But those who emphasize wisdom stress how to destroy the obstacles to knowing, manifest the subtle function and the clear consciousness of the mind, and reveal the principles of reality in a direct fashion. In effect, it is not only idealistic metaphysics that aims at achieving wisdom; all metaphysics are similar in this regard. The beginning of metaphysical consciousness has as its aim the search for absolute knowledge of the ultimate reality. However, its meaning should not be understood primarily in a positive fashion but rather in a negative one. The value of metaphysical thinking lies in its doubt about relative knowledge; we consider the truth or falsity of relative knowledge and the contradictions and conflicts among such knowledge. In this thinking process whatever has been thought about is swept away, and we end up in an empty and yet subtle state of mind which no longer thinks about anything on the level of knowledge. Of course when we make transcendental use of universal categories of empirical knowledge in order to achieve absolute knowledge of objective reality as a whole, it seems that we may have metaphysical knowledge in a positive sense. And yet the value of such metaphysical systems still lies in their refutation of other systems of metaphysical knowledge; they are not very significant as far as positive achievement is concerned. For example, when we make transcendental use of the content or categories about the shape, motion, or materiality of things that we experience and then make the assertion that the ultimate reality of the universe is nothing but material atoms with shape and motion, such claims of knowledge of a materialist metaphysics are not very significant in themselves. Materialist philosophy, if valuable, has its value in pointing out the fact that knowledge about nonmaterial phenomena can be explained in terms of physical knowledge in order to prove that these phenomena are not ultimate reality or the fact that idealistic metaphysics is impossible in order to show that its opposite materialism must be established. Again, when we make transcendental use of categories of plurality, change in our

empirical knowledge, and make the assertion that the ultimate
reality of the universe is plural or a changing stream, positive
metaphysical knowledge such as this is also not very significant.
The value of pluralism and a philosophy of change also lies in
its refutation of monism and eternalism. Moreover, from the
dialectical point of view of Kant and Hegel, all positive metaphysical knowledge established by a transcendental use of the
content and categories of our empirical knowledge is no better
than its opposite and in turn becomes the refuted. Therefore,
various kinds of metaphysical knowledge will be mutually contradictory and conflicting. Hence, even if metaphysical thinking
is originated from a demand for positive knowledge, every
achievement of positive metaphysical knowledge is dependent
upon a refutation and transcendence of other positive metaphysical knowledge. Furthermore, whatever positive metaphysical knowledge is achieved will again be refuted. The end
of such metaphysical thinking is reached when various kinds of
positive metaphysical knowledge fall into mutual destruction.
When these are being transcended, we finally realize the impossibility of this type of metaphysics. The only thing that remains
is our transcendent and encompassing metaphysical consciousness. And the value of such metaphysical thinking lies in the
fact that, through such discipline, our transcendent and encompassing metaphysical consciousness emerges as a mind that is
empty and subtle, clear and conscious, and all-inclusive.

The metaphysical consciousness of phenomenalism and subjective idealism show that we have transcended the idea of an
independent, external, objective reality. The value of phenomenalist and subjective idealistic philosophies also lies in their
refutation of an independent, external objective reality. As to
the origin of objective and absolute idealism, its foundation lies
in our self-consciousness of the absolute mind and the absolute
principle. Only when there is such self-consciousness can we
have real contact with metaphysical reality. After the contact
with reality, we may still preserve the names of the mind and
the principle and achieve positive knowledge of them; we may
make further observation of their universal expression in the

process of our knowing activity and in the phenomenal world or objective reality faced by our knowing activity. When we reflect on these expressions, we can also construct various metaphysical systems of knowledge and even claim that all knowledge is penetrated by metaphysical consciousness and therefore can only be footnotes to metaphysics. But when we have real contact with the metaphysical reality of the mind or the principle, we realize at the same time that it is beyond the scope of knowledge. Paradoxically speaking we "know" that it is beyond our knowledge. The reason why this is so lies in the fact that knowing, in this sense, is not like scientific knowledge which purports to understand objects. It is also not like epistemological reflection that investigates how human knowledge is constructed. It is a realization achieved by transcending ordinary knowledge. And the mind in this stage is a transcendent and encompassing mind; when it is referred to as the principle, it indicates its nature as capable of transcending and encompassing. Its nature or principle is precisely manifested in the capability of the mind to transcend and encompass. Our knowledge, gained through our self-consciousness, must follow the mind's activity in order to enter it and to realize its transcending and encompassing nature. But its nature is not merely manifest in our present activities. The transcending and encompassing nature is truly transcending and encompassing. And to have knowledge about it is to know its truly transcending and encompassing nature. Thus, even if we may reflect on the expressions of the mind or the principle and construct various kinds of metaphysical systems of knowledge, the consciousness that accomplishes such metaphysical knowledge must imply the consciousness of the mind or the principle that transcends our systems of metaphysical knowledge. Therefore, after contact with the metaphysical reality of the mind or the principle, following our knowledge of the mind or principle (that has the self-consciousness of transcending all knowledge) and hoping to continue realizing this mind or principle, we must then transcend all metaphysical knowledge and make all metaphysical knowledge just a bridge that leads toward the realization of this mind or principle. If we have truly achieved such a realization, then even the bridge must be left behind for the time being. But if metaphysical knowledge does not lead toward such a realization, then it has not served the function of a bridge and hence must be discarded. At this moment, all our discussions on metaphysics are for the purpose of revealing the metaphysical reality in order to enlighten others; these discussions are used temporarily in order to answer the questions and are meaningful only within the context. Therefore our metaphysical discussions are not limited to one kind. Various, apparently different systems of metaphysical knowledge may be asserted only if they can help us to move toward the realization of this mind or principle. But, since metaphysical discussions only function as bridges, they must be transcended. If this should be the case, then such discussions also must be transcended. And systems of metaphysical knowledge are only expediencies; in fact, the metaphysician has never established a doctrine for people. It is in such a way that the metaphysical spirit that seeks to transcend ordinary knowledge in its search for positive absolute knowledge finally transcends such knowledge and realizes true metaphysical reality. Furthermore, it makes use of such knowledge to illustrate metaphysical realization and leads people to seek knowledge in order to transcend knowledge. And the total realization of the metaphysical spirit lies in the expansion of the wisdom to remove the obstacles to knowing in order to reveal the emptiness, subtlety, clearness, and consciousness of the mind and, thereby, also the reality. Hence we believe that the aim of metaphysical thinking is to cultivate wisdom, and the goal of metaphysics lies in its search for absolute knowledge of the ultimate reality and ends in the wisdom of realizing the metaphysical reality.

Section 13. <u>The Consciousness of Moral Philosophy</u>

The aim of moral philosophy is to seek to understand our duty or obligation in the world, what kind of ideals or goals of life we should have, and how we should act in order to bring

about their realization in the world. Our goal or ideal is to do
something in order to improve the present state of affairs, and
our actual behavior is to carry out such reform. Hence understanding the goals and ideals we should have and how we can
realize them by action really means the understanding of the
principles we should follow to reform the present state of affairs. Such a consciousness is different from the metaphysical
consciousness which seeks only to understand the ultimate reality that serves as the foundation for phenomenal reality. Metaphysical consciousness arises at the moment when we do not
seek to reform the present state of affairs because we are taking phenomenal reality as the object and looking for its foundation in ultimate reality. But moral problems arise from our
consideration of what goals and ideals we should have and how
we should act. When we are engaged in consideration of this
sort, we are not carrying out reform of phenomenal reality.
But the motive and aim of our consideration originates from a
demand for action. When moral philosophy reflects on the ideals
and goals man should have and how they are to be realized, it
is an extension and expansion of ordinary moral considerations;
its motive or aim also originates from a demand for action. Of
course, moral philosophical consciousness itself is not moral
action but rather a philosophical consciousness pertaining to
knowledge. Owing to its demand for action, however, this philosophical consciousness advances ideals of reforming phenomenal reality. Obviously it is different from the kind of metaphysical consciousness which implies that the universe is of
fatal necessity, beyond man's power to change, and that the human will is not free. In moral philosophy, however, we must
take the future of the world to be something that man can change
to some extent and believe that the human will also has freedom
to a certain extent. Sometimes man's consciousness of moral
obligation has indeed permeated metaphysical knowledge of reality. An instance would be the teaching of moral idealism. And
if we know the metaphysical reality of the mind or principle,
we will also know what kind of ideals and goals we should have
in our transaction with the world. Hence the establishment of

principles that govern the "ought" in moral philosophy is often
based on our knowledge of metaphysical reality. But even if our
consciousness of moral obligation permeates metaphysical reality, its intention is still the assertion of the metaphysical reality; whereas the intention of the consciousness which finds
out about what kind of ideals and goals we should have from an
understanding of metaphysical reality lies in a reform of phenomenal reality. When we use our knowledge of metaphysical
reality to establish the principle of the "ought," we must of
course recognize that the realization of this principle is an enrichment for metaphysical reality, at least it has brought about
some kind of reform of phenomenal reality. Thus, metaphysics
and moral philosophy may very well be founded on the same
principle, and yet the two kinds of consciousness are distinct
from each other. Metaphysics concerns the way of Heaven,
while moral philosophy concerns the way of man. The way of
man and the way of Heaven may be the same or different. If
they are different, then the way of man can supplement the way
of Heaven; when the way of man prevails, it will enrich the way
of Heaven. If, however, they are the same, in a sense the way
of man can still bring about an enrichment of the way of Heaven.
For example, if we say that the way of man is to realize the
mind or principle and that this mind or principle is none other
than the mind or principle of Heaven, or metaphysical reality
qua the way of Heaven, then the realization of the way of man
is a manifestation of the way of Heaven. Thus, the way of
Heaven and the way of man are the same. Although, from the
viewpoint of the way of Heaven, the realization of the mind or
principle is its self-realization, yet, from the viewpoint of
man's realization of the way, man has at least attempted to
bring about certain changes in phenomenal reality so that what
lacks the manifestation of the mind or principle can change into
what manifests this mind or principle. Thus, the manifestation
of the way of Heaven has to depend on the way of man to manifest it in phenomenal reality. If we emphasize the manifestation
of the principle or mind in phenomenal reality, then we must
say that this is due to the effort or achievement of man; in this

sense we may say that the way of man is still different from
the way of Heaven and brings about its enrichment. Hence our
metaphysical thinking lays its emphasis on the knowledge that
transcends phenomenal reality in order to return to the foundation, while moral philosophical thinking has its emphasis on the
establishment of the way of man in its attempt to reform phenomenal reality in order to build an edifice on the foundation.
From the edifice to the foundation, knowledge of phenomenal
reality is being transcended, while from the foundation to the
edifice, knowledge of phenomenal reality must be reasserted,
and phenomenal reality is understood as it is. When we follow
what ought to be done according to the understanding of the
metaphysical reality of the mind or principle, then we realize
that what is done has not been up to the par of what ought to be
done. However, they can and must be united, and the nature of
what is demands such a unity. Thus, we realize even more that
the realization of the way of man is the realization of the way
of Heaven. And we also know that the affirmation of the existence of phenomenal reality that does not agree with the mind
or principle means its negation. But such negation is brought
about by action, not by activity of knowledge. Thus we will not
only follow our activity of knowledge to study phenomenal reality but will also help it in a conscious fashion to understand
phenomenal reality. Only in such a way will we learn what there
is in phenomenal reality that does not agree with the mind or
principle and should be negated and eliminated by action. We
will also learn what does agree with the mind or principle and
should be asserted and reinforced. Thus, the "negating" activity that transcends knowledge in metaphysical consciousness is
itself transcended and turns into the "affirming" activity that
reasserts knowledge. Hence philosophy does not merely seek
to transcend scientific knowledge, but also to accomplish scientific knowledge.

Our moral philosophical thinking must prescribe the ideals
and goals for how we ought to behave and how to realize them
in order to make our behavior moral; hence it demands reforming or enriching phenomenal reality. Since our ideals and goals

for behavior must involve individual persons and things, the prescriptions made must also take into account actual individual persons and things. Because of the fact that there are differences among individual persons and things, we must also establish various kinds of moral principles accordingly. Therefore, even if the highest moral principle is a unity, we must still have many subsidiary moral principles to cope with different situations. Hence the highest moral principle is a unity, but its differentiations are many. Our moral consciousness demands that our behavior must be rational in every situation so that every behavior can be made into a principle, and each behavior is the realization of a moral principle. Thus, the plurality of our moral principles is parallel to the plurality of our moral behavior. Consequently, our moral philosophical thinking must cover most universal and also most particular principles in order to make it function to the utmost extent. But even the most particular principles can be made into laws and, hence, are also universal principles. In order to reach the utmost extent of moral philosophical thinking, we must lay out all the particular principles for moral behavior as models for us to follow, but this is of course impossible, and it also seems to be impossible to make all our behavior moral. But this question need not even arise because all the principles are principles of the "ought"; they come from our conscience in an immediate fashion under a given situation and give direction to our actions. Since they come from within, not from without, we originally have them in our mind. Therefore, we have reason to say that our conscience is the supreme moral principle which comprises all the moral principles and naturally differentiates itself into subsidiary moral principles; it can react differently to different persons and things in an immediate fashion in order to give prescriptions to our behavior. Hence it is unnecessary to lay out all moral principles as models for us to follow.

Here we must further understand the nature of the reflection on moral principles in moral philosophy; it is fundamentally introvert and self-reflexive. It reflects on the principles that are revealed in our conscience, classifies them, and finds out

about the relation between them and the principles of actual
existence. Such reflection, if it were guided by the principles
of the "ought" first revealed by the conscience to the utmost
extent, would certainly end up in actions because these principles are first present in our conscience as commands, or demands that lead toward actions. Of course, if there is absolutely no interruption between the presence of the principles of
the "ought" and actions, then the reflection of moral philosophy
would be unnecessary and impossible since there would be no
occasion for it to emerge. It is only when there is an interruption between knowledge and action, when actions do not always follow the principles that are present, that there is reflection of moral philosophy to rediscover the principles of the
"ought," to reassert them, and to remove the interruption in
order to enable the principles to penetrate in actions. Therefore, when we think about the principles of the "ought," we always
think about their original intention to lead toward actions and
move toward their realization in actions. From the viewpoint
of action, the value of moral philosophical thinking lies in the
fact that it reawakens the self-consciousness of a certain principle of the "ought" in order to deepen our understanding of it
and in the fact that it reminds us of the interpenetration of various principles of the "ought" so as to unveil an even higher
principle of the "ought" or to sense an even stronger moral
imperative, so that our knowledge will be carried out in our
actions.

If the above discussions of consciousness of moral philosophy
are not erroneous, then moral philosophical thinking must go
through the effort to achieve realization. In this regard, it is
similar to the kind of metaphysical thinking that takes the mind
or principle to be metaphysical reality. But such an effort also
means that when we think about a moral principle, we must realize that it is first present as an imperative which demands
realization through action and then recognize that it is a true
imperative. In order to make it a true imperative, we must
confront it with our past and present life, especially with the
behavior that runs counter to it, even including our faults. It is

only in such a way that the imperative becomes a true imperative that really commands us to do something. Such a confrontation will help us carry out our moral imperative to the utmost extent. In so doing, on the one hand, we will have to admit our own faults in order to eliminate them and make changes deep down in our own hearts; on the other hand, we will observe our moral imperative and do something better. The two aspects will be combined to bring about a reform of our own practical life and our actual behavior in the world. In this regard, the moral consciousness is different from the metaphysical consciousness. The latter can realize the supreme goodness of the mind or principle and its transcendence of obstructions, but the former must realize that sins and faults in real life become the obstacles to moral life and that the function of the supreme good is to eliminate and transform them and bring about its own realization. Since moral philosophical thinking must lead to realization and action, then knowledge in moral philosophy may be said to be a tool to induce people to realize moral principles of the "ought" and to act accordingly. If such knowledge fails to lead people to achieve realization and to act, then it should be rejected as sham moral knowledge. In this regard it is again similar to metaphysical knowledge that takes the mind or principle to be metaphysical reality. But the expressions of moral philosophy are those that give enlightenment to our conscience, help us recognize moral imperatives, and make us conscious of our own faults. Therefore, they must be teachings that speak to a particular occasion and apply to a particular person or item. That explains why the best moral philosophical writings in the East and the West such as The Analects, The New Testament, and The Nikāyas are all unsystematic in character. Moral practice must involve different situations. In correlation to a certain situation, there is the realization of a certain principle of the "ought." In the process of moral practice, there must be a positive commitment to the declaration of a certain moral principle in order to truly accomplish our practical actions. Therefore, after moral philosophy makes people reject empty words that fail to lead toward realization and

action, it must further lead people to positively commit themselves to expressions that can induce people toward realization
or action. The aim of metaphysical expression is to help people realize metaphysical reality, but it does not need to lead to
action and does not have to include realization in action. It can
be expressed as knowledge that refutes knowledge, expression
that rejects expression; at the very moment that various knowledge and expressions cancel one another, a sudden turning
around finds the realization of the metaphysical reality. It does
not require a positive commitment to certain expressions. Thus,
consciousness of moral philosophy and consciousness of metaphysics show their different attitudes toward expressions. Metaphysical thinking must rely on the removal of the obstacles to
knowing in order to reveal the emptiness, subtlety, clearness,
and consciousness of the mind which grasps reality. In this regard, there is similarity since the manifestation of moral principles comes about only after we have eliminated our selfish
desires and opinions, when emptiness, subtlety, clearness, and
consciousness of the mind also become the condition for the
manifestation of moral principles. But metaphysical wisdom
may be confined to the contemplation of the wholesome metaphysical mind or principle, while moral wisdom has to make
differentiations according to different situations and diverse
moral principles. It is here that we find the difference between
moral wisdom and metaphysical wisdom.

Section 14. The Consciousness of Cultural Philosophy
and Historical Philosophy

Just as moral philosophical investigation originates from our
demand to prescribe the ideals and goals we should have, know
how to realize them in order to awaken our moral conscience,
and help to accomplish moral actions, the investigation of cultural philosophy and historical philosophy emphasizes reflecting various ideals and goals of life and culture that have been
realized in different cultures and studying whether these cultures conform to the ideals of life and culture we should have

or to our moral standards. We have various kinds of ideals and goals of life and culture. We also have various cultural activities to carry them out and hence have different cultural realities which are the concrete manifestations of our ideal goals. Since some of our ideals reflect what ought to be and others what ought not, since some of them are good and some evil, cultural realities also show different values, positive and negative. We may say that all cultural realities must begin by relying on a moral consciousness to a certain extent, as we have argued. But we can still admit that the concrete manifestations of the human culture may not be able to fully realize our moral consciousness or conform to the moral standards and ideals and goals of life and culture that they should. Of course, we would then demand that our actions, the cultural activities that we are engaged in, and the culture that we create must conform to the correct moral standards and cultural ideals. But culture is not the creation of one individual. It is instead a product of the society, and our cultural activities are bound to relate to others' cultural activities. This is because our ideals and goals have universality, they can be universally recognized and pursued by all. Thus, culture may be regarded as the expression of the objective spirit. The reflection on culture is a reflection on the expression of the objective spirit. Thus when we discuss whether the cultural activities we are engaged in and the culture that we create conform to moral standards or cultural ideals, we are examining whether the expressions of the objective spirit conform to such standards and ideals. And when we seek such conformity, we are looking for the realization of the moral goals and cultural ideals of the individual and, at the same time, also for the realization of the objective spirit, moral goals, and cultural ideals of the society. The concept of the society or the objective spirit includes the individual. Cultural philosophical thinking may be regarded as the reflection of cultural realities and moral goals, or cultural ideals manifested in the society or the objective spirit. Hence the consciousness of moral philosophy that examines the individual is moving toward a philosophical consciousness that investigates the society and culture. Culture has continuity and historicity. Cultural philosophy studies various actual and possible patterns of culture in a horizontal fashion, while historical philosophy studies the evolution and transformation of culture in a vertical way. It investigates the continuity of various actual patterns of culture in different historical periods, the cultural ideals realized or which ought to be realized. In comparison with moral philosophy, which investigates moral principles that can universally apply to various individuals and analyzes and awakens man's moral conscience, the consciousness of cultural philosophy and historical philosophy is concerned with an even richer and more concrete spiritual reality.

Cultural philosophy and historical philosophy differ from ordinary cultural and historical sciences in that cultural sciences such as political science, economics, and studies of the arts always start with a certain actual cultural phenomenon. Each science only postulates the existence of meaning of the ideals that serve as the foundation of a certain cultural phenomenon and lacks self-conscious criticism of them, and each fails to recognize the relation between this cultural ideal and other cultural ideals or morality for the whole of human life in a self-conscious way. If we want to have a critique of a certain cultural ideal and to recognize its relation to other cultural ideals or morality of the whole of human life, then we have entered the scope of cultural philosophy. As for the difference between historical science and historical philosophy, historical science seems to follow only the chronological order. Its aim is to understand historical facts. It can describe cultural ideals that have been realized in historical facts, but it has not been able to transcend the idea of chronology and ascertain the meaning and value of the cultural ideals realized in the historical facts of a certain age in connection with the whole history of the nation state, the human race, or the cosmos. It fails to construct a comprehensive picture of ideals for the whole nation state or the whole human culture in order to examine where those ideals, which were realized in the historical facts of a certain age, stand in that picture. If, on the contrary, we are able to do the above, then we have entered into the scope of historical philosophy. The so-called ideals for the whole nation state or the whole human culture are merely the totality of cultural ideals manifested in cultural activities of communities of individuals in the history of different ages. Thus, we can also proceed by gradually studying the manifestations in order to find their unity. Hence the difference between cultural and historical sciences and cultural and historical philosophy rests on a difference of perspectives, not a difference of subject matter. There is also no difference in their aim to promote man's cultural activities and to create the future history of mankind. Thus, the scope of cultural activities that constitute human history is also the scope of cultural and historical philosophy; whenever there are new cultural activities, there are also new reflections of cultural and historical philosophy, just as whenever there are new behaviors, there are also new moral reflections. Moral philosophers consider it their duty to promote man's moral reflection, awaken the individual's conscience, and accomplish moral actions, while philosophers of culture and history consider it their duty to promote cultural reflection on a generation, awaken the cultural consciousness of a generation, and show us the spiritual mission of a generation. Great moral philosophers give us moral lessons that apply to different individuals in diverse situations, while great philosophers of culture and history give us cultural criticisms that apply to changing times. While moral philosophy can awaken man's conscience, its value lies in leading toward moral actions. If cultural and historical philosophy can awaken man's cultural consciousness and show him the spiritual mission of the age, then it can provide leadership to form the cultural atmosphere of the society and help mankind create new chapters of history. Therefore, both the consciousness of moral philosophy and the consciousness of cultural and historical philosophy, when developed to their utmost extent, demand that we change our attitude of knowledge for knowledge's sake to that of knowledge for action's sake. When a scientist seeks knowledge, he does not need to be engaged in action. Even an applied scientist need not actually apply science. The scientists can delimit the scope of knowledge that they want to seek, and their goal can be set at seeking only knowledge within this scope. Even epistemological and metaphysical studies in philsophy may set their goal at studying how knowledge is constructed or what metaphysical reality is; they need not be engaged in action. But the consciousness of moral philosophy and the consciousness of cultural and historical philosophy must keep pace with the historical development of man's actual moral and cultural activities. They seek to know the totality of what man has actually done and what he actually should have done. Hence philosophers of culture and history cannot be satisfied in the same way as an historical scientist, who investigates only a section of past history. They must take up the problem of history and culture for the present and the problem of morality for ourselves and for others. They have to get into contact with reality and discover what should be, what is, and what is sought. Thus, the expression of their thoughts aims at calling for others' action, and hence thought must move on toward action. Therefore, it is not necessary for the scientists, but absolutely necessary for true moral philosophers and philosophers of culture and history, to change the attitude of knowledge for knowledge's sake to that of knowledge for action's sake and to move on from knowledge to action. Philosophical consciousness, when developed to the utmost extent, must become consciousness of moral philosophy and philosophy of culture and history. That explains why a true philosopher must shoulder the moral and cultural missions of his generation.

Section 15. The Moral Nature of the Truth-Seeking Mind and Its Degeneration

In the above, we have discussed various kinds of consciousness of science and philosophy which are all based on the mind that seeks to transcend and encompass. Precisely because the activities of this mind have different kinds of expressions, there are various kinds of sciences and philosophies. We think

that this mind is fundamentally an impartial moral mind. And
our moral mind in its consciousness of moral philosophy and
cultural philosophy can have a perfect understanding of a mind
like this. Our thesis can be formulated in a very simple way.
Both science and philosophy aim at understanding the truth concerning the universe and human life, while all truths are universal and can be known by all human minds. Hence our truth-
seeking mind is one that seeks to know that which are universal
to all minds; and when we seek truth, we realize that what we
are searching for is something that connects our own mind and
other minds. Thus, our truth-seeking mind has implied the recognition and assertion of both our own mind and other minds.
Such recognition and assertion show that our truth-seeking mind
is a universal mind that transcends the individual mind and encompasses both our mind and other minds. After the expression
of this universal mind and its demand for realization, we naturally have the concrete and moral desire to convey the truths
we know to others. Furthermore, our truth-seeking mind also
demands to control and suppress our selfish desires and instinctive impulses. Surely it would refuse to confine itself to
the limited scope of existing knowledge and preconceptions in
order to avoid entrapping the mind. Thus, we have established
that the truth-seeking mind is, in its origin, a moral mind.

Although we say that the truth-seeking mind is originally a
moral mind, people may not be conscious of the fact that it is
a moral mind. For example, scientists believe that to seek empirical or mathematical knowledge is to seek knowledge for
knowledge's sake, which has nothing to do with morality. Many
philosophers also hold such a view, the reason being that the
truth-seeking mind is purely contemplative in character; its
goal is not practice or action. But this view contradicts our
praise for the moral character of scientists and philosophers.
They are open-minded, sincere and frank, do not monopolize
the truths they know, and are pleased to convey them to others.
All these virtues are based on our belief that truths are universal and should not be monopolized by individuals. Of course we
may say that scientists and philosophers are not necessarily

open-minded or sincere and frank. They may hold on to their biases or conceal the truths they know and publish them only when they bring fame or profit. Hence it seems that the truth-seeking consciousness of scientists and philosophers may or may not help to form any moral character, and that this consciousness appears to be neutral, nonmoral, or beyond morality.

Our answer is that when scientists and philosophers hold on to their biases, they have already lost their interest in seeking truth, no longer assume the attitude of a scientist or philosopher, and are no longer scientists or philosophers. When they conceal truths from others or publish them only when they bring fame or profit, they have already forgotten that truth is universal in character and should not be monopolized. If they considered truth to be universal, then they would not conceal it from others, and if they thought that truth is what connects our mind and other minds and reaches a consciousness that encompasses both, then they would have no other goal than to share truth with others and make what has universality and can be known by all become what is actually known by all. When the mind has been developed into one that equally encompasses our mind and other minds, it will no longer seek only fame and profit for the individual. Hence if someone conceals the truths he knows from others and publishes them only when it serves his selfish purposes, then he is not conscious of the fundamental character of truth and either fails to realize that the mind that grasps truth is one that encompasses our mind and other minds or fails to preserve the presence of such an encompassing mind. Thus, we may conclude that the mind that has a real interest in seeking truth and is conscious of what has made it so must be moral in character. On the contrary, the mind that sticks to its biases and monopolizes truth for selfish purposes is immoral. There is simply not a neutral mind that seeks truth but is beyond morality. And the kind of thought that considers our truth-seeking mind to be beyond morality obviously fails to understand the fundamental character of this mind and hence is invalid. Moreover, this kind of thought may stimulate the tendency to monopolize truth for selfish purposes, and hence it becomes immoral. The origin of such thought lies in the fact that we confine ourselves to certain known truths and form fixed biases, thus committing a kind of original sin in the scope of knowledge. We would like to analyze and explain the types of such sin and how they arise and then point out how to avoid them to help us realize that the truth-seeking mind is a moral mind and must preserve itself as a moral mind. From this it becomes clear that even scientists and philosophers must rely heavily on the cultivation of a moral and cultural life.

Our demand to search for truth is directed toward truth concerning definite objects. Hence we must delimit the scope of objects in order to seek truth about them. It seems as if we could go so far as to say that delimiting the scope of objects is the beginning of the self-confinement of the mind's activity which confines itself to certain known truths or sticks only to one kind of truth so as to form biases. But we need not think in such a way because then we would have to regard the beginning of all truth-seeking activities as sinful. We would rather maintain that even though the delimitation of the scope of objects is a self-confinement, this confinement is a transcendence of other objects outside of the scope. It is because of our ability to transcend the interference and stimulation of other objects that we learn to concentrate and take them to be nothing. Our concentration will enable our mind to be absorbed in the objects within the scope, study them intensively from the surface to the core, and improve our ideas about them in order to get at their truth. Under such a consciousness of doing research, we will recognize that authentic truth concerning the objects is always beyond our ideas since our ideas may not be objective truth. Thus, our mind does not really confine itself and stick to its biases.

With the above-mentioned research consciousness, even if it is possible to maintain the awareness that our ideas may not be objective truth, at each stage of our research when our ideas get confirmed, we will develop the consciousness that our ideas are objective truth at that particular moment. And hence we have the consciousness that truth is acquired by us and that our ideas do contain truth. Thus, we tend to take these ideas to be something independent and self-sufficient in themselves, and the clear consciousness of our mind is congealed in these ideas so as to form a self-confinement. It seems, however, that in our process of seeking truth, usually we are not conscious that our knowledge is the result of congealment or self-confinement of the clear consciousness of our mind. This is because, in this process, we are seeking for new knowledge and also applying old knowledge to new objects in order to find out whether they work and consequently no longer take our knowledge to be something that is independent and self-sufficient. In this way we have already transcended the limitation of such knowledge. But there is always interruption in the process of seeking truth. During such an interruption, we immediately discover that the knowledge that has been established is always limiting the activity of the mind. For example, in our daily life, we have various naive reasonings and associations. Although they are based on our ideas and knowledge acquired in the past, they can be aimless, come forth unconsciously, and are not under the control of the mind, the reason being that they form a mechanism and operate in an autonomous fashion. Since our mind cannot master them, it feels limited, and the fact that this mind becomes a limited mind shows that the mind which accumulates such ideas and knowledge is also a limited mind.

Precisely because the mind which accumulates ideas and knowledge can be a limited mind, it is then taken to be the origin of our fixed biases. But our ability to accumulate ideas and knowledge, on the other hand, originates from the mind that can transcend the limitation of sensations. When we self-consciously apply the knowledge we accumulate to objects to see whether they work, we have already broken the limitations posed on the mind by such knowledge. Thus, even if the mind that accumulates knowledge is a limited mind, it is not yet the beginning of evil. Only when we fail to consciously apply the knowledge accumulated to objects in order to transcend its limitations and subject ourselves to such limitations so as to take truths to be nothing but the knowledge we accumulate, would we use them to make dogmatic assertions about objects. Then we are truly caught by our own biases resulting from the self-confinement of knowledge.

We must realize that only when we are caught by our biases resulting from the self-confinement of knowledge would we insist that knowledge is for knowledge's sake and that our truth-seeking mind does not contain any moral values. When our mind does not confine itself to knowledge that has been established, it would apply it to objects. Its truth must be judged by the objects that are independent of our ideas and knowledge. And the truths we seek must be objective truths that transcend the ideas and knowledge that have been established. If truths are regarded as objective, then they are not just knowable to us only. And if we are conscious that we can seek them, then we realize that others can also seek them. If we assert that we should seek them, we also assert that others should seek them. Thus, after we achieve knowledge of them, we surely would hope that others would also know them, and we would do something to help others know them. In this way, the assertion of the objectivity of truths and the moral demand that truths should be known to all are inseparable. In effect, our demand to seek objective truths has included the demand to make truths known to all. Hence the demand to seek knowledge merely for knowledge's sake cannot exist all by itself. Its nature dictates that it has to develop into the moral demand to make truths known to all, showing that it includes a moral nature. The reason why such a moral nature may not be developed or may not be manifest, as if it did not exist, lies in the fact that after we know truths of objects, we then think that truths are within our ideas and knowledge and fail to assert their objectivity. When we fail to make such an assertion, we also forget that our ideas and knowledge are based on the existence of objects; thus we no longer apply our ideas and knowledge to objects and hence reflect only on the results of past searches for truth or previously established knowledge. This means that our truth-seeking activity has stopped, and we are confining ourselves to our own knowledge and consider truths to be within our knowledge, declaring that our search for knowledge is only for the sake of acquiring truths. We then fail to realize that when we start out to seek truth, there still exists the assertion of the objectivity of truth which implies a moral demand to make truth known to all, and we fail to see that the consciousness to seek truth is originally a moral consciousness. Hence the consciousness that confines itself to established knowledge is no longer the same as the original truth-seeking consciousness. When we have already confined ourselves to the former consciousness, we naturally fail to understand the moral nature of the latter consciousness because the former is a degeneration of the latter and is immoral in nature. Seen through the eyes of such an immoral consciousness, naturally the moral nature of an originally moral consciousness disappears, and the truth-seeking consciousness is considered to have a nonmoral character.

In the above we have argued that the original truth-seeking consciousness implies the moral demand to make truths known to all. It is only when we confine ourselves to a mentality dominated by knowledge already established that we consider the truth-seeking consciousness to be originally nonmoral in character. Because we often cannot avoid confining ourselves to knowledge we ourselves achieved and often feel that to seek truths is to acquire knowledge for the self, the moral nature of the truth-seeking consciousness is prevented from developing. Confining ourselves to knowledge already established is a degeneration of the truth-seeking consciousness and is an evil. And the thought that seeking truths means acquiring knowledge for the self also comes from this tendency to degenerate and is also an evil. In order to save our truth-seeking mind from degeneration, we must refute such thought and think according to the development of our truth-seeking mind. Thus, we must realize the moral nature of the truth-seeking mind in a self-conscious way, as we have suggested in the above, so that it will receive proper development and avoid falling into degeneration.

Section 16. The Implications of the Mentality That Confines
Itself to Established Knowledge and of the Mentality
That Seeks Truth in an Open-Minded Manner

The essential difference between these two mentalities lies in
the difference between the attitude that considers truth to be
within our subjective knowledge and the attitude that considers
truth to be objective and public and present in both the objects
under consideration and also in other minds. According to the
mentality that confines itself to established knowledge, the further search for truth means only to acquire another knowledge
in order to be confined to it again. The purpose is to expand
the content of knowledge within the subjective mind and to have
possession of more truths. On the contrary, according to the
mentality which seeks truths in an open-minded manner, the
knowledge of truths which is acquired is still regarded to be
something objective and public that cannot be possessed by the
self. Thus, according to the mentality which confines itself to
established knowledge, one feels that the discovery of truth is
dependent on the self to make it manifest and that the acquisition of knowledge is due to one's effort; while according to the
mentality which seeks truth in an open-minded manner, one
hopes that truth is pre-existent and feels that the reason one
is able to grasp truth and knowledge is that objects, Heavenly
spirit, others' inspiration, and the help of sages and gods allow
access to such truth and knowledge. With the former type of
mentality, one eagerly runs after truth, but once truth is acquired, he is full of a sense of pride, which could cause his
mind to be closed and to suffocate. With the latter type of mentality, before one grasps truth, he aspires toward it, and when
truth is reached, he feels a sense of ease, which shows the
openness and understanding of his mind. When the mind is
closed and suffocated, it is cut off from objective reality and
other minds, but when the mind is open and has understanding,
it feels a sense of communion with objective reality and other
minds. Actually, the mind can never be closed and suffocated
for long; it always seeks communication with other minds.

Hence even if one were confined to established knowledge, he would still like to publicize it and would wish to convey it to others. But when he pours out the truth he knows, the emphasis does not lie in helping others reach and enjoy the truth but rather in showing off to others that he has possession of truth or that it is due to his effort that truth is discovered or becomes manifest. When he publicizes the truth, he wants to make sure that others know that it is he who does it and that it is because of his effort that truth is attained. Thus, this mind is one that seeks fame in the academic world and which does not stress helping others to understand truth but rather making others recognize that it is this particular individual who publicizes the truth. Hence the mind that seeks fame looks for communication with other minds only when it is using such universal truth as a means to attract others' attention. The emphasis is on that particular individual. But, if the goal is only to attract attention from others, then before saying anything one may attempt to say something that is contrary to the truth he believes in order to please others for the sake of seeking fame, and after words are said, even if they do not contain truth, this person would appeal to sophistry and clever words to cover up faults so that he would get attention and become famous. Thus, one's love of fame would lead to the loss of interest in seeking truth. When one cares only for himself, other selfish desires easily follow suit. On the contrary, under the mentality of seeking truth in an open-minded manner, one keeps in mind that truth is objective and public. Then, even if truth is attained, it is not regarded as one's own possession; one feels that his mind has to depend on contact with truth in order to have communion with objective reality and other minds. A mind like this is open and has understanding; it is not closed and suffocated, and it does not need others' attention or praise. When a truth is put forth, a common public language is used to express this truth that belongs to the public. This implies the assertion of and respect for other minds. Our publications are nothing but a result of making use of the language used and understood by others, which is arranged and organized to express the truths that are apprehended by the individual. Thus one's own speech has implied the assertion and respect of other minds; the common basis is the human mind. And the truths set forth by us are realized to be objective and public. This means that our own speeches and publications are using something that is public to express something that is public and are helping truths that are originally public and universal to realize their public and universal nature, understood and owned by all people. Thus language and truth are not regarded as private possessions. Our only goal is to make truths universally known. And our idea is to follow universal truths in order to illuminate other individuals and in such a way as to be able to encompass them. Truths thus become the means to expand our moral selves. Hence we would be loyal to truth and never betray truth for the sake of cheating the world in order to earn fame. If our words do not contain truth, we must revise them according to truth. And when others get hold of truth through our words, we cannot only give credit to our words and our efforts to seek truth. When one is not obsessed by the self, the virtues that transcend the individual grow. Thus, the mentality that seeks truth in an open-minded manner is totally different from the mind that confines itself only to established knowledge.

The aim of our discussions of the difference between these two mentalities is to urge us to reflect on our attitude toward truth and knowledge. This would enable us to distinguish what is moral and what is immoral. When we conducted such self-reflection, we would find that our attitude toward truth and knowledge is often either moral or immoral and that our effort to carry out moral discipline must include the rectification of the immoral attitude toward truth and knowledge. Hence not a single scientist or philosopher in his process of seeking truth and knowledge can completely transcend matters concerning moral discipline. And such moral discipline not only is aware of the immoral attitude toward truth and knowledge and tries to overcome it but is also in corroboration with the cultivation of other aspects of a moral and cultural life. The reason is that not only the mind that confines itself to established knowledge would provide stimulus for other selfish desires, but matters concerning our life would in their turn also exert influence on the formation of the tendency to confine ourselves to established knowledge only. These issues may be discussed under the following three items.

1. If the self-confinement in established knowledge can give rise to the tendency to seek fame, to pay attention only to the individual, and to cause selfish desires, then, conversely, seeking fame and other selfish desires can also cause the loss of the attitude to seek truth in an open-minded manner, make us treat truth and knowledge as private possessions, and make us stick to established knowledge only. Hence if we do not have the discipline of a moral and cultural life to take control of and to transcend the mind which seeks fame and other selfish desires, then even if we want to lift ourselves from the trap of established knowledge, we will not be able to do so.

2. Although our knowledge-seeking activity is a spiritual activity, it must depend on the energy coming from our body. Truths are discovered by thought, while the objects of thought are universal principles that transcend the physical body. When we think, it seems that our thinking activity tends to exhaust the body and the brain and weaken the energy of the natural life. When we think about a principle, it is thought to be something that is beyond the individual and his physical body. The activity of the brain and the body related to thinking seems to be one that exhausts, weakens, and even destroys itself. The relation between the mind and the body will be discussed elsewhere. Regardless of what we have to say about this issue, it is a commonly known fact that it takes a lot of our energy to think. When one is young, healthy, and strong and when his energy is plentiful, it may be a pleasure to think. But when one becomes weak or old, it then becomes painful even to think. When one feels thinking to be a burden and nevertheless must think to the point of hurting his health, he then follows the natural biological instinct to keep his physical health, and there naturally emerges a desire to stop thinking. If under such a condition we are still forced to think, our natural biological instinct, without the

support of normal physical health, will penetrate into consciousness and tenaciously hold on to the ideas, terms, known truths,
and knowledge within the mind; thus our mind will be confined
to established truths and knowledge. Hence in seeking for
knowledge, we should also care for the well-being of our physical body and natural life. One method would be to make use of
material and other ways of life to give nutrition to our physical
or natural life. Another method would be to make us gradually
transcend the biological instinct to maintain our normal physical conditions. All these would involve cultivation of life and
culture besides the activity of seeking truth and knowledge.
Such cultivation must also be moral and impartial. If selfish
desires are involved, then they will still confine us to a tena-
cious holding of knowledge.

3. Although we are seeking universal truths, they must
be manifest in particular realities. When we seek knowledge,
we self-consciously abstract universal principles from particular things in reality. Hence in our activity to seek knowledge
of principles, we are trying to forget or transcend the particularity and reality of things that we contact in our life. Such an
activity tries to use universal principles to separate the relation between us and particular realities. In a sense, the activity
of abstracting principles from particular realities in order to
achieve knowledge and to be separate from reality is like the
activity of a silkworm making its cocoon. And the nature of our
activity of seeking truth and knowledge is to acquire knowledge
or even systems of knowledge in order to be indulged in them.
But we need not say that such has to be the case because, in
another sense, on the basis of our knowledge of universal principles, our mind has been able to transcend the particularity of
particular individuals and things. Moreover, after knowledge
has been acquired, it must further be used to apply to particular realities in order to break up the limitations of established
knowledge. Hence, even if in its beginning our knowledge seems
to imply that we must use universal principles to separate the
relation between us and particular realities and cause a split
of our world, in the end it turns around to use universal

principles to penetrate into particular realities and create a reunion with particular realities. Now we know that various realities are penetrated by various principles and hence are endowed with even richer meanings which would make our life also become more meaningful. Whether knowledge is good or evil for life: the key lies in whether we can apply knowledge to new realities in order to break up the limitations of old knowledge. But only when new realities emerge would we be able to apply our knowledge to them and make judgments; without the emergence of new realities, our knowledge would have no means to expand itself and hence would have to be bound by the shackles of established knowledge. The emergence of new realities, however, has to depend on our life, not on our established knowledge. It is in our life that our sensation and perception would make external physical reality stand out and that our emotion and will would make inner spiritual reality become manifest. The content of our life always has to be broader than the content of our knowledge; when it continues to appear in reality, it then becomes the context to liberate us from the limitations of knowledge. Thus, if we do not want to be confined by established knowledge and would like to keep up the mentality which seeks truth in an open-minded manner in order to transcend the limitations of established knowledge, we would have to rely on the content of life beyond knowledge in order to make reality present. Moreover, this life must be moral in character. In the above we have explained why the rectification of the immoral attitude toward truth and knowledge must depend on cultivation of a moral and cultural life beyond knowledge and truth, and in the meantime we have also shown that our attitude of seeking truth and knowledge can never be self-sufficient or become moral in an independent fashion.

17

MY OPTION BETWEEN PHILOSOPHY AND RELIGION*

From the Appendix of The Reconstruction of the Humanistic
Spirit — An Epilogue Replying to Criticism

I

I wrote this essay for three reasons. First, in proofreading
The Reconstruction of the Humanistic Spirit, I felt that this
great pile of articles contained only general discourses on the
social and cultural problems of China and the Western world
but did not mention my own philosophical position and religious
faith. Although the pattern and style of the essays in this book
might excuse this defect, I was afraid that some of my readers
would find it difficult to grasp the main themes of thought in the
book. Therefore, I wanted to write an article to compensate a
bit for this shortcoming. Second, for many years, in teaching
courses on Chinese or Western philosophy, I have been used to
following the general lecturing method of university professors
who stress the objective introduction of philosophical doctrines
to enrich students' knowledge. This does not seem to be blame-
worthy. However, those who want to learn philosophy or study

---

*T'ang Chün-i, "Wo tui-yü che-hsüeh yü tsung-chiao chih
chüeh-che." Jen-wen ching-shen chih chung-chien [The Reconstruction of the Humanistic Spirit], Vol. II (Hong Kong: New
Asia Research Institute Press, 1955), pp. 556-589. Translated by Yuk Wong.

religion have always been motivated by their search for a definite faith or an ultimate concern. In more peaceful days, one could sit in one's study for a lifetime researching, studying, and appreciating the doctrines of various philosophical schools without any fixed convictions of one's own. A pure historian of philosophy could probe into philosophers' lives or write the history of philosophical development without believing in any philosophy or religion. But this is not the original motive or primary goal of studying philosophy or religion, especially during such a time of suffering and hardship as ours. Man's primary incentive and final objective in learning these two subjects consist in resolving the problems that he keenly feels in his life and securing for this life an ultimate settlement or shelter. Genuine philosophers and religionists are quite different from the historians of philosophy and religion. The former must have their own doctrines and convictions. Achieving their own enlightenment, they would like to enlighten others. Of course, one may alter his own convictions. He may contradict the beliefs of his contemporaries or of the ancients. He hopes that he can achieve an objective understanding of others' beliefs in order to revise or substantiate his own. However, he always has some beliefs or seeks for certain beliefs. Once acquiring his beliefs, he is willing to brave the vast universe and be responsible for what he believes whether his beliefs are true or fallacious. If they are true, he is responsible for maintaining them; otherwise, he is responsible for abandoning them. In either case, he will never evade his own duty. The beliefs for which he is responsible may also be those for which others are responsible; they may be the common beliefs of a philosophical school or a religious sect or even be platitudes. Nevertheless, his own spiritual attitude of taking responsibility for his beliefs is unique for himself. And only insofar as a man is willing to be responsible for his beliefs will he become a man of independent character. Otherwise, his thought is always wavering in determination. He is no more than a wandering soul devoid of independent individuality. This makes me feel that in teaching philosophy and religion, it is necessary for the teacher to spell out his own convictions as well as objectively introducing the doctrines of various schools or sects. This is by no means a handicap to objective investigations or to people's pursuing their own beliefs. In past years when my pupils or juniors asked me about what I advocated in philosophy and religion, I did not say much and merely urged them to make their own judgment and selection after studying the ideas of great philosophers, Chinese or Western. Now I have realized that this attitude is not appropriate because I did not show them that I have been industriously pursuing my own beliefs: nor did I try to demonstrate my faith. This being the case, how could I tell people that if they try to search for a faith, they will be able to find it. Therefore, I would like to present this essay as a brief account of what I believe after choosing between philosophy and religion and as an illustration of how one reaches his own convictions. Third, recently a certain Mr. Teng Tse-min published an article in Wah Kiu Yat Po on four consecutive days criticizing my opinion on Christianity and the problem of peace as set forth in my essay, "The Fundamental Problems of Western Culture" published in The Democratic Review. Although Mr. Teng's article was not much concerned with purely theoretical issues, it sprang from his enthusiasm for defending his religion. Usually I do not overestimate the opinions of today's intellectuals because they constantly talk a great deal but seldom believe in anything. Neither do I like to argue with others. However, I respect any authentic religionists. Their beliefs are where their souls reside, and they should be respected. Many friends of mine are Christians or Buddhists. Except for scholarly discussions, I refrain from attacking their beliefs because I feel that this is what I should do according to the Confucian principle of magnanimity. Mr. Teng's article, however, might make people think I am against Christianity. In fact, I do not oppose Christianity; on the contrary, I deem it necessary for religious spirit to revive in this age. Apart from mentioning this point many a time in my writings, I am quite willing to help any religionists in publicizing their beliefs, hoping that most people will understand religions. For instance, during the last several years I have been responsible

for inviting most of the people who gave speeches at the more
than 100 cultural lectures held in the New Asia College. Christians and Buddhists lectured at least ten times. I have never
denied the good points of Christianity that Mr. Teng emphasized
in his article, but I feel unspeakable sorrow at the fact that the
different religions fail to recognize the value of other religions.
I sincerely hope that all religionists attain mutual understanding and eliminate whatever causes mutual antagonism. In my
opinion, this can be gradually achieved insofar as some ideas
of Christianity, which is most influential today, undergo a modification or evolution. Hence my comments on Christianity in
some essays. Issues concerning religious principles are bound
to be subtle and profound. To express my opinions on these may
necessitate the publication of at least one book. Because of
Mr. Teng's criticisms, I consider it necessary to elucidate my
choices among religious principles as well as my hopes for
Christianity to improve on itself. This essay is written for the
aforesaid reasons. Although I fear that I cannot write it satis-
factorily, I must try.

II

The Reconstruction of the Humanistic Spirit only concerns
the society and culture in general, not specialized issues of
philosophy and religion. But what this book opposes is very
clear from its philosophical point of view. It is opposed to all
thoughts that treat man as only a natural animal. Examples are
the Marxist view that stresses human survival from a materialistic point of view, Freud's view of the sexual drive, Nietzsche's
and Adler's views on the will to power, and Pavlov's and the behavior psychologists' views on the conditioned reflex. Although
successful in discovering something about human nature, these
doctrines fail to see the truth of human nature and are unable
to genuinely regard man as man. If people think that these
scholars have mastered the whole truth of human nature, then
I am obliged to deem this heretical and to resolutely refute it.
These thoughts may be advocated by others in a free society,

414

but it is necessary for some people to refute them. All fallacious thoughts may last for some time, but their value and
meaning will become extinct gradually after being repudiated.
Human thought cannot be free from errors; erroneous concepts
are unavoidable. The meaning and value of experiencing fallacious thoughts consist in recognizing their features and avoiding
doing the same thing in the future. The faith in freedom of
thought allows man to try on all possible forms of thought, and
finally realizes the wrong to be wrong, the heretical to be heretical, the true to be true, and the right to be right. It is certainly
not the case that no distinction should be made between right
and wrong or true and fallacious.

Why do we consider all thoughts which treat man as merely
a natural animal to be wrong and heretical? How do we truly
know that man is different from other animals? How can we
truly grasp the essential characteristics of human nature? The
answers are simple in one sense but complicated in another.
Man may be studied from the aspects of biology, psychology,
literature, religion, philosophy, etc. This problem involves our
views toward the whole universe and our metaphysical beliefs.
In the following I shall speak about the process by which I think
about these issues and my choice between various philosophical
schools and religious faiths. From this the background of my
philosophy in this book will become clear. People will understand what kind of philosophical and religious beliefs I hope to
establish in the depth of my mind in order to settle down my
life. These are what the book was not able to include, and they
concern some of my personal experiences that I have scarcely
told others.

In retrospect the root of my apathy toward all thoughts regarding man as a natural animal can be traced back to an experience when I was only six or seven years old. One day my
father told me the scientific prophecy that the light and heat of
the sun would vanish and the end of the world would come when
there was only one man with his dog. This story aroused my
boundless interest. Several days later the earth of my courtyard cracked and wrinkled in the sun after a rain. Seeing this

I could not help thinking that the earth might split and collapse. I remember the scene of the courtyard very distinctly though it occurred some forty years ago. This event has been the source of my philosophical thought and my views of human nature. Why do people think of the destruction of the world? In this are included the mystery and dignity of human nature and the differences between men and animals. Can this be interpreted in terms of the activities pursuing survival, gratifying sexual desire, the will to power, or performing conditional reflexes? This can never be. For these activities are all dependent on the existence of the world. Whenever man is thinking about the destruction of the world, the world turns into nonexistence in his mind, which implies the impossibility of all these activities. How could I imagine the havoc of the whole world and bear the existence of this catastrophe in my mind? Later I understood that man has an existence which transcends the material world. Of course I did not know this at the age of six or seven.

Besides thinking about the destruction of the world at age seven, there are many events concerning the origin of my philosophy worthy of mentioning, one of which happened when I was thirteen or fourteen. I read Liang Ch'i-ch'ao's article entitled "What Are the Objectives of Human Life?" He pointed out that all men are busy, exemplified this with more than one hundred sorts of business, and asked what people are busying themselves for. But this essay provided no answer. Having read it, I suddenly felt that I had achieved a great enlightenment and discovery, which was actually exceedingly simple: man lives for his own happiness. I realized that even sacrificing oneself for the sake of humanity is just pursuing one's own mental happiness. I fetched a giant piece of paper and intended to write a long essay. When I had written over one hundred words, nothing remained to be said. I can still remember the sight of the piece of paper ninety percent of which was blank. Why did I need a giant piece of paper when I could fill up only ten percent of it? Now I understand the reason: the range of thought in man's self-consciousness is far smaller than the scope of possible thought which he intuitively achieves. Soon afterward I began to read

Mencius and Hsün Tzu and became interested in the issue of whether human nature is good or evil. At that time I believed that there was both good and evil in human nature and I thought that both Mencius and Hsün Tzu actually taught this theory using different terminologies. I said Hsün Tzu regarded the mind as good and nature as evil, while Mencius deemed nature good and the desires evil. To clarify this I wrote an essay of several thousand words and believed in its validity for five years. I looked upon the desires of the senses as evil and the body as the meanest thing. All corporeal lusts should be banished; the aim of life was to extinguish desires. Despite being unable to get rid of eating and drinking in my practical life, I linked the theory of eliminating desires with the idea of pursuing happiness in human life to construct a doctrine which I then deemed unprecedented. Reflecting upon the fact that the state of mind of people who had satisfied their desires was characterized by the absence of desires and the presence of happiness, I inferred that if man could get rid of all desires, his state of mind would forever be boundlessly full of happiness. Now I still have to admit that there is a certain truth in such a thought. Because of my family education, the books I had read were mostly classics which rarely stirred up questions in my mind. Just at that time the debates between the so-called scientific view of life and the metaphysical view of life occurred. The debates were hot and I read articles representing both sides. Meanwhile, when I could find them and although I could not understand all of them, I also read books handed down from the May Fourth Movement of new tides of thought that criticized Chinese culture. However, they did not change my convictions. At the same time, I obtained a definitive insight into the universe and human life: the human mind can be self-conscious. This self-consciousness is different from consciousness. It can never be assimilated into those objects of which it is conscious. Hence I developed a kind of dualism which made me reject materialism from then on and idealism for some time.

When reading the writings of the heated "war," I was vehemently opposed to what metaphysicians said about freedom of

will, intuition, etc. For at least several years I believed absolutely in the necessity of causality, physical and mental, and
thus that man does not have so-called free will. Even so, he
can still make an effort to do things because such an effort is
also predetermined. At eighteen or nineteen, I had read some
books of the Buddhist School of Mere Ideation and listened to
lectures about this sect. I felt that its teaching that there are
no external objects beyond consciousness was contrary to my
dualism. One of the several refutations I worked out was that
if external objects cannot be independent of my mind, then others' bodies that my mind sees cannot be independent of my
mind; but since the existence of others' minds is inferred from
the activities of others' bodies, only my mind exists. That is
why the doctrine of mere ideation cannot but become a solipsism
in view of one's inability to affirm the existence of other minds.
I found that the reply to the issue of the existence of other minds
contained in the Confirmation of the Mere Ideation System
[Ch'eng-wei-shih lun] was unable to relieve me of my doubt.
Later I knew this refutation was a common argument used in
the West to refute idealism. However, I went two steps forward
in saying that if the external objects that I recognize do not exist independent of my mind, then when I reflect upon my past
self, this past self becomes the object of my present self and
so cannot exist independent of my present mind, and then my
past self is not a real existence. Furthermore, no sooner has
my present self been reflected upon than it becomes my past
self, and there is no present self to be spoken of if it is not reflected upon. Therefore, the consequence of idealism is inevitably that neither the existence of the self nor the existence of
the mind can be established; thus there is no mind to be accentuated. In setting up this type of argument to refute idealism, I
was trying hard to philosophize in the Western way for the first
time.

The above-mentioned desire-eliminating hedonistic view of
life, dualistic and deterministic view of the world, and realistic
epistemology formed my first options among possible answers
to philosophical problems. Despite being my immature thoughts

before I was twenty, they were my conscious beliefs. They matched my high esteem for purely intellectual and scientific methods of philosophy. I once thought that if my thinking had come to a standstill at this stage and if I had studied more science, I might have become a scientific philosopher. From that time on all progress and alterations of my thought have been achieved bit by bit through struggles against my own convictions. The erroneous beliefs that I held, once shown to be wrong, will never prevail in my mind again.

III

The first time that I felt difficulties in my philosophy was after reading an article in William James' Essays in Radical Empiricism at the age of twenty-one. The conclusion of the article entitled "Does Consciousness Exist?" is that the mind can only be a stream of consciousness which is a series of wavelike experiences. When an experience arises to succeed the experience preceding it, the previous experience immediately turns into an "object," whereas the present experience is the "subject." Thus there is not a singular consciousness or self. This differs entirely from my dualistic idea that treats consciousness and its object as two things. Having experienced such a great shock in my thought, I felt it necessary to study the philosophies of others and revise my earlier thought. As a college student, I constructed another system of thought aside from reading books. By means of two principles, namely, the law of identity and the relationships among perceptions, I explained all beings in the universe and the habits and mental activities of all kinds of humans. The application of these two principles were confined to experience. Therefore, any transcendental substance or reality was definitely incapable of existence. However, I did not continue to follow this trend of thought. Otherwise, I might have become a present-day logical positivist. It was the writings of British and American realists such as G. E. Moore, W. P. Montague, R. B. Perry, and Spaulding that made me unable to stay in empiricism and phenomenalism. Realism made me believe that there were subsistent universals capable of being experienced but not experienced yet. I took immense joy in the belief that the universe had innumerable subsistent universals capable of existence, including the infinite values of truth, beauty, and goodness. Furthermore, the philosophical love of Socrates and Plato, their aspiration to the world of ideas, and what modern minds like Russell and Santayana rested on appealed to me simultaneously.

Contemporary realists claimed to have founded their philosophy on new logic. This caused me to spend half a year reading books on new logic. However, my question concerned only its primitive concepts and basic propositions. Where did these things come from? Could they be reduced to a certain most simple thing? I attempted to take Logos as their source, but I lacked the talent to develop Logos into a logical system. Having gained only some intuitions, I was unable to formulate a philosophy of logic. It was not until I read Mr. Mou Tsung-san's Fundamental Principles of Logic (Commercial Press, 1941) that what I had intuited was verified. When my thought on this issue came to a complete rest, I no longer took interest in learning logical operations.

In attacking idealism, new realism concurred with my first attitude toward idealism. At that time I thought the idealism of the West must be fallacious because realism was the newest philosophy in vogue. But I still had my worries. If I had not read their works, how could I be sure the idealists were wrong? Only after seeking out their mistakes could I really overthrow them. The contemporary idealist whom the realists liked to attack was Bradley, the philosopher of philosophers in the eyes of British idealists. Thus I read Bradley's Appearance and Reality. The paradoxical arguments that frequently emerged in the first half of this book were almost the same as those in Buddhist classics which I had read as a child, particularly the Treatise on the Middle Doctrine [Mādhyamika śāstra or Chung Lun] and the Treatise on Twelve Gates. My interest was so keenly aroused that I wrote an essay to compare Bradley with the Three Treatise School of Buddhism and published it in the

Philosophical Review (1933). From Bradley's masterpiece I was led to study the works of great idealists like Kant and Hegel. Having read Hegel's Phenomenology of Spirit, I realized that beyond the realm of the realists' philosophy, there were higher realms of philosophy to pursue. However, even Kant and Hegel did not seem to be convincing, and in fact I did not really understand them. Since then the range of my reading has become broader and broader. Although I have read books of almost every philosophical school whenever I could get hold of them, I have never done specialized research into any school. However, I have always had to reflect on the right and wrong of all thoughts different from mine before making choices among them. If unable to make a choice, I have let the problem stay in my mind for even more than ten years. It is now unnecessary to mention these issues. At the age of about thirty my reading and thinking resulted in my fondness for Western idealism. I had not expected this before. Then, on rereading Pre-Ch'in Confucianism, Neo-Confucianism, and Buddhism, I realized that these philosophies excelled Western idealism in some respects. It was not until the last five or six years, after writing the essay entitled "The Nature of Religious Consciousness" in 1948, that I began to affirm the value of religions and recognize the religious spirit in Confucianism. Objectively speaking, the process by which I chose among Chinese and Western philosophies and religions may not have much meaning or value; but subjectively speaking, it abounds in struggles against myself and is thus the history of eradicating my prejudices to make way for my step-by-step advancement. Up until now, numerous wounds and blood stains of my thought have already been forgotten, just as the trail of a sailing ship is gradually swallowed by the ocean. However, I still want to talk about them because my experience can serve as an example for others. I hope young friends who devote themselves to learning will understand from this that man needs convictions, that he can make progress only after absorbing the good points of others' beliefs, and that in learning and thinking there are countless levels to be climbed. What one utterly opposed may become what one most ardently accepts.

At the same time, one will never commit the errors that he truly realizes to be erroneous; so long as one diligently pursues truth, his progress will be unfailing. In what follows I shall indicate several paths of philosophy and religion awaiting people's choices as well as the straight road leading to the loftiest truth of the universe and human life. It is impossible to present all the grounds and reasons for my conclusions which will be presented in a more or less dogmatic way. Those who are willing to follow this way are advised to do so; those who are reluctant may seek their own ways. The truth of the world converges through divergent speculations and avenues. Wheels of thought which are on the wrong track may return to the right one however many bends they may take.

IV

In seeking truth, the starting point for making choices among thoughts is to choose an attitude of thinking. In the final analysis, should we follow opinions formed according to our habits or customs or our authentic wisdom? In the first two cases, our minds are always in a passive state liable to be bewildered and charmed by political, religious, and social propaganda. This state is also apt to render us ready to adapt to the newest trend of thought without inquiring into its truth and falsity and to be overwhelmed by men of reputation. Thus, we are prone to become the most obedient subjects and subservient slaves under authoritarianism. For all these depend on one and the same passive mentality. As a matter of fact, most people's mentality is always fettered by opinions. It is extremely difficult to eliminate this condition. Anyway, to start making choices among thoughts we must transcend this mentality, free ourselves from habit and public opinion, and think in accordance with our real knowledge and wisdom.

The second phase of making such choices is to determine what kind of genuine wisdom is needed or wanted. At different times man may pursue true wisdom of different sorts. Because of individual dispositions, each man is probably in partial pursuit of a certain kind of true wisdom. Some will become scholars, some will become religionists. Whatever kind of true wisdom is sought, self-determined judgments are indispensable. Self-determination implies that our conclusions can contradict public opinion, so severely that we have to walk alone on the path of seeking genuine wisdom. Whoever has decided to find true wisdom should be well prepared to willingly shoulder the fate of loneliness or the destiny of solitude. He ought to cultivate the will and bearing which Mencius expressed: "I will proceed despite the hostility of thousands of people." The orientation of seeking wisdom varies with the sort of wisdom one seeks. Straightforwardly pursuing practical wisdom is one avenue, while striving for purely academic knowledge and insight is another avenue of which science, history, and philosophy are branches. One may seek true wisdom by various paths and eventually discover their concourse. However, at any rate they are different. Turning from one path to another, one must change direction in his wisdom-seeking activities. A man with great wisdom can consciously and freely modify his orientations in wisdom-pursuit with a view to approaching perfection. He never confuses these directions. One who has made up his mind to strive for a certain kind of true wisdom should always be conscious of his chosen orientation. Here I shall not speak about practical true wisdom, being content to briefly clarify the three paths leading to true wisdom in history, science, and philosophy. Seeking true wisdom in history is striving for an understanding of the flux of events; finding wisdom in science and philosophy is pursuing an understanding of principles and rules. However, in seeking knowledge and wisdom in science and history, there is a duality between the mind seeking understanding and the object of study (forms, numbers, Nature, societies, historical facts, etc.), and it is essential to distinguish this object from other objects even if only in a relative and temporary fashion. Historians have to investigate, analyze, and guess at historical objects according to literary records, relics, and other sources. Finally, they attempt to reconstruct past historical events in their minds before finding links between these events in order to reveal the clues and directions of their causes and effects. Scientists repeatedly observe, measure, calculate, describe, experiment with and conjecture about their objects of study in order to understand their nature or their causal and functional relations with other objects so that their traits, functions, and activities can be prescribed or defined by laws. Anyway, all activities of seeking knowledge in history and science commence with our concentration on, or circumspection of, a particular object. These activities are directed toward the given objects dual with and seemingly external to the mind that probes into them. In studying science and history, however, introversive reflections must also be used to test whether the conjectures and hypotheses made are possible, and whether the inferences based on these conjectures are legitimate or appropriate. Nevertheless, these activities advance through recession. Seeming to be introversive, they are still intended to understand objects. The truth and falsity of all conjectures and hypotheses made through introspections are subject to our verification through experience or intuition of the objects, e.g., historical materials, natural objects, social objects, forms, and numbers. If they are true, the authentic wisdom about them still concerns and rests on these objects. The extroversion of the wisdom-seeking activities in history and science is prescribed by the nature of these two fields, or is simply their nature. Whoever can best direct this kind of wisdom-seeking activity toward external objects and make progress through recession as mentioned above will succeed in achieving superb discoveries and inventions in history and science. Whoever can render his wisdom-seeking activities most concentrative and circumspective on a particular domain will become an excellent specialist in a certain branch of science or history. This is where the similarity between these two fields lies.

The starting point of the path of philosophy is opposite to that of science and history. Of course, this does not mean that philosophers should deny the value or conclusions of science and history, but rather that the orientation of the wisdom-seeking activities in philosophy is primarily contrary to that in science and history. In the latter, wisdom seekers know that their chosen objects differ from those which have not been chosen. This choice limits such wisdom-seeking activities. The meaning of this limitation has two levels: first, being limited to particular objects; second, being limited to extroversion. Such a limitation is indispensable to the acquisition of all knowledge concerning particular objects and to the development of the human mind. Otherwise, the human mind would remain in its chaotic, undifferentiated state. In order to break up the chaos, the duality between subject and object has to arise. The light of the subject's mind must stream into its subject so as to complete a knowledge-seeking activity which needs a particular object lest it should become suffocated and then resume its state of subsistence and potentiality. But there is originally no limitation on the mind itself or on knowledge-seeking activities themselves. Hence, we are uneasy with this confinement and desire to transcend it. Where does philosophy begin? It begins with man's yearning to transcend this limitation. (Its highest objective is to bridge the gaps between different sorts of knowledge and between subjects and objects in order to return to the root of wisdom-seeking activities and become conscious of the wholeness of the human mind.) Therefore, we must first either withdraw from or further expand our wisdom-seeking activities which concentrate on or are circumscribed by particular objects. An expert in science and history is not content to confine his research to a specialized field because of his philosophical impulse to dash outside his limited domain. If reluctant to study philosophy, he must either found his philosophy on his understanding of the flux and orientation of human history, or regard the principles and rules known in science as philosophical principles irrespective of time and space. Otherwise, he would have to take the commonsense view of the universe and life as his own philosophy. There have never been scientists or historians who were absolutely devoid of the philosophical consciousness which transcends scientific or historical knowledge. This is not because they are not historians or scientists, but because they

are also humans. There is a real internal contradiction between the limitation of their knowledge-seeking activities and
the origin of these activities. On the other hand, there have
also never been philosophers who have never confined their
knowledge-seeking activities to particular objects in order to
acquire historical or scientific knowledge. Thus, people always
have these two kinds of wisdom-seeking activities. However,
at different times, a person must choose whether he is studying
history, philosophy, or science and follow his orientation in a
self-conscious way. At the same time, he must choose one of
them as his main concern for his whole life.

V

If a person wishes to take the philosophical path for a period
or throughout his life, he must also choose between two routes.
One alternative is to start from pursuing true wisdom in practical living, and human society and history, that is, from one's
own position or status in human society and history and in one's
practical living, and to reflect and conduct verifications anywhere and at any time in order to attain philosophy. Generally
speaking, this is the path of Eastern philosophy and also the
path of philosophy of which most people are capable in any time
and space. This thoroughfare is the broadest and plainest. Whoever chooses it needs to have moral sincerity. Without it he is
liable to frailty or arrogance. A man with moral sincerity can
rise above the frontier of particular knowledge to attain an exalted and intimate realization of the origin of the universe and
human life, whether he lives and behaves according to Confucianism, Taoism, or Buddhism, or solely engages himself in
reflecting on his personal status amid human communities and
history. It is a pity that nowadays the majority of Chinese intellectuals dislike this path. For China, which needs science
and tends to worship it, cannot help worshiping the West and
comparatively despising history. No wonder that today most
Chinese intellectuals rarely treasure the living paths indicated
by Eastern sages. Not valuing history, man cannot really know

his own position and responsibility in human society and history. Only those with heroic spirit can take this path. Unless the ancient method of teaching and lecturing is revived, it would be difficult to bring people onto this track. The other alternative is to lead people from scientific knowledge to philosophy. This may be said to be the way of Western philosophy in general. Apart from being more suitable to this age, it is more substantial and steady and not prone to degenerate into fickleness and impetuousness. Nevertheless, from this path to the realization of the realm of the Eastern sages, we have to walk through an utterly winding and distant road in our thought, that is, to go beyond numerous philosophical schools of the West. Because of this hardship, man is apt to abandon his endeavor midway, remaining content with a philosophical system that is purely intellectualistic. However, if he can patiently stand the bends that his thought undergoes and can bring his intellect into full play in order to attain the realm that transcends the intellect, a man can also return to the sayings of Eastern sages with modes of understanding or comprehension that are different from those of the first alternative.

There are two ways to take the thoroughfare of Western philosophy. The first is to straightforwardly follow and stick to scientific knowledge; the second is to retrace the way that scientific knowledge is fashioned. The former way is the method of generalizing the principles of one or more sciences to form a world view and then a life view. For instance, having recognized the principle of evolution in biology, Spencer proceeded to understand the evolution of celestial bodies and human societies in order to construct a comprehensive evolutionary philosophy. In general, his method of thought was to free the application of evolutionary principles from the scope of biology, to diffuse and expand them to embrace the whole universe, and to accomplish philosophical activity that rose above the knowledge-seeking activities of specific sciences. These philosophical activities were broader in range than those of science. However, the philosophical principles thus obtained were due to the generalization of the principles directly acquired from specific sciences. The purpose of this kind of philosophical activity is to find out the most comprehensive principles. In a way it is contrary to the tendency that scientific activity seeks to define a principle in a specific way in order to explain a particular set of objects. But its contrariness lies only in this point. The truth and falsity of the principles acquired from such philosophical activity rely on the truth and falsity of the particular scientific knowledge on which they are grounded. They are bound to vary with scientific knowledge. Hence the lack of independence of this sort of philosophy in principle. However, philosophy of this kind is comparatively easy to set up. Insofar as we discover in any science a principle capable of offering an explanation of the universe, we may construct a philosophy. If there is something that the generalization of a single principle cannot embrace, we can always supplement it with subsidiary principles, and our philosophical activities can continue forever in this fashion. Thus, we may establish materialism according to the principle of the existence of matter, energetics according to the principle of the existence of energy, vitalism according to the principle of the existence of life, mechanism according to the principle of mechanical devices, teleology according to the principle of goals, monism according to the principle of unity, and dualism according to the principle of duality. Perhaps we may combine different principles to advocate a materialistic energetics, a mechanistic teleology, or an emergent evolutionism, etc. All Western philosophies which have claimed to be scientific in any age and all cosmologies of the West and modern China that are not grounded on epistemology are established in such a way. The ideas mentioned above which treat man as matter or animal are some examples of philosophy of this kind. When philosophizing in this way, the richer the scientific knowledge one possesses and the stronger the intellectual ability to abstract and generalize one has, the fewer will be his mistakes and the greater will be his achievements. But, however brilliant the achievement is, the moment that the scientific theories on which this philosophy is grounded must change, this philosophy is at once considered to be unfit or untrue. Therefore, this kind of scientific philosophy can never become an absolute necessity and always is dependent upon verifications. Man can never obtain from it his mind-settling belief. To use this path to establish absolutely necessary philosophical conviction necessitates the arrest of scientific progress. This is why the Russian dialectical materialists who relied on physics of the nineteenth century would have to oppose the theories of the new physics that contradict their philosophy.

The other way, the one which traces the formation of scientific knowledge, comprises philosophies on different planes. On the first level is the so-called critical philosophy of science which examines the established systems of scientific knowledge in order to find out whether the methods used and the correlation between theories have logical necessity at all and what the systems' fundamental postulates, principles, and concepts are. The next step is to elucidate these postulates, principles, and concepts through analysis. Philosophy of this kind does not accentuate knowledge about the entire universe, and takes it as no more than mere hypotheses. It demands knowledge concerning scientific knowledge. While scientific knowledge moves forward, this kind of philosophy goes the other way around; it watches the steps taken by science to see whether its paces are wrong or disorderly and whence its process or course starts. At most, it can tell scientists that if they start from a certain point, they will or should arrive at a certain place, and it can also tell them what they must say, and how they must perform observations and experiments. But it does not prescribe a certain starting point for science. In its purest form it demands nothing from science, merely standing aside to watch the progress of science. Its present development in the West is the so-called analytical technique of logical positivism, by means of which positivists hope to reduce systems of scientific knowledge into some primordial sentences, to frame sentence-systems according to certain laws in the transformations of syntax, and to unify these into a system of physical language. Although their ambitions are great and their undertakings heavy, this kind of philosophy, in a certain sense quite like that mentioned above, forever trails behind science. It is not until science ceases developing that this kind of philosophy becomes capable of completion, and its completion implies its death.

There is a difference between regarding logical positivism as an analytical technique of scientific knowledge and as a general philosophy. From the former viewpoint, logical positivism does not and cannot antagonize any philosophy. In fact, it does not even bother to talk about other philosophies. From the latter standpoint, logical positivism advocates something concerning epistemology, metaphysics, and the theory of value. On the one hand, it says that in epistemology such controversies as the one between realism and idealism are meaningless, that metaphysics is impossible, and that judgments about values are simply expressions of feelings and attitudes. On the other hand, positivists are in epistemology empiricists who take sensory experience as the ultimate criterion for the truth and falsehood of sentences, as well as conventionalists who deny the a priori rational foundation of logical principles; in metaphysics, phenomenalists or agnosticists; and in the theory of value, subjectivists or relativists. In philosophy this can be traced back to the old tradition from Hume to Mach, i.e., the old empiricist trend. It was Hume who condemned metaphysics and regarded value judgments as subjective expressions of approval and disapproval. However, in comparison with the philosophical task of pure scientific criticism, even an empiricist philosophy is advanced in its attempt to reflect on how scientific knowledge is formed. For the former may not question why and how the systems of scientific knowledge can be erected by man, and on what data in human aspects these systems are based; while empiricism definitely affirms that man can establish systems of scientific knowledge and that their initial point is human experience. The most primordial experiences are those of sense perceptions. This kind of philosophical activity reflects upon the activities in pursuit of scientific knowledge of all things in the world and turns back to see the starting point in experience of this activity which is most concrete and actual to anyone at any moment in his whole life. Such a conclusion necessitates

more introvert and convergent reflections because empiricism
is a philosophy contrary to the way of the sciences. One who
asserts the reality of his sensory experience acquires a starting point of self-affirmation and philosophical independence.

However, all empiricisms and all thoughts that merely ascertain an analytical intellectual ability aside from sensory experience, e.g., ideas from Hume to contemporary logical positivism, are philosophically bound to be surpassed. Thoughts of
this type affirm too little and destroy too much. According to
Hume, most books in libraries ought to be burned to ashes.
(See the last page of his Enquiry Concerning Human Understanding.) Thinkers of this type probably would burn books and
scholars alive as authoritarians did. But if we try to think more
deeply, we realize that it is impossible to explain the establishment of scientific knowledge solely through sensory experience,
habits formed by experience, conditional reflexes, and other
random conventional principles, and that it is impossible to explain the causal principle and logical necessities in terms of
the nonexistence of exception or counterexample in experience
and tautologies. It is also impossible to accept logical necessities but to reject the existence of inner or a priori reason. To
deny metaphysical principles that transcend experience and to
deem metaphysical propositions meaningless according to empiricism can be based only on an arbitrary meaning of the term
"meaning" and an equally arbitrary list of meaningful propositions. Such a convention is devoid of objective meaning. If it
has objective meaning, it can merely be a kind of dogmatism
which grounds itself neither on experience nor on reason. This
dogmatism originates from the fact that our rational activities,
having concentrated on sensory experience, firmly maintain
that sensory experience is the unique reality and deny anything
else to have primary reality. Now that anything else is regarded as beyond experience, the negative activity of reason
cannot have any objective meaning. This denial is to deny that
reason further affirms something, hence it is an expression of
reason's self-denial. Such denial does not have objective significance in ontology. Since these discussions involve special

problems in the philosophy of language and epistemology, let me stop here. (Among the books which deal with these issues from Western idealistic viewpoints similar to mine are the following: Urban, Language and Reality, 1938; and Blanshard, The Nature of Thought, 1950.)

VI

If it is impossible to deny a priori reason and metaphysical principles and propositions, the ways to philosophize transcending sensory experience are opened up. In the Western philosophical tradition, there are three such ways. The first path is rationalistic; it constructs the principles of metaphysical reality by objectifying the principles in reason, e.g., those of identity, causality, sufficient reason, continuity, the identity of indiscernibles, or rational concepts (like the identification of the perfect being's essence and existence). This is the basis of the philosophy of Descartes, Spinoza, and Leibniz. The second path is to infer from the universals or ideas recognized by reason in the empirical world the external causes or subsistents for actual existence. This is the trail from Plato and Aristotle through St. Thomas Aquinas in the medieval age, to transcendental realists and modern new realists. The third way is to reflect on the internal and external conditions for the formation of the realms of knowledge and experience and to discern which must spring from experience and so enter the mind from the outside and which must originate from a priori reason and arise from the inside. This is the trail of Kant's critical philosophy. In a sense, these three types of philosophy together resolve the problem of how scientific knowledge is constituted. According to the first type, the principles in reason emerge from reflection when man, in pursuit of knowledge, uses the activities of his mind which can know and think. In the second type, forms and universals are manifest in actual or possible objects when man acquires knowledge. In the last type, the transcendental categories and ideas are the inner patterns of arrangement for objects that can be experienced, or the ideal principles which induce us to formulate systematic knowledge when man seeks knowledge. But the first two ways admit only that man's discursive or contemplative reason can lead to both scientific knowledge and metaphysics. Whereas in view of the formation of scientific knowledge dependent both on external transcendent objects and internal transcendental categories and ideas, which are originated from the transcendental rational self, the third way recognizes that both ends of the knowledge realm are dependent on a metaphysical principle transcending both knowledge and experience. From this, it can further affirm the practical reason beyond pure, cognitive reason, and it is from this practical reason that another gate to metaphysics is opened. Hence, we find in the West moral metaphysics that transcends science and religious philosophy based on ethics. Kant's metaphysics of morals, through Fichte and Hegel, became the metaphysics of the objective spirit. This stimulated the rise of existentialism that stressed ethics and religion and personal idealism, and, more or less, positively or negatively, directly of indirectly, it also stimulated all realistic philosophies that emphasized value, e.g., the philosophy of Whitehead. Anyway, the choices involved here are too subtle to be further discussed in this essay.

Since the nature of philosophy is to reverse the activities of pursuing scientific knowledge from without and seek knowledge from within the mind, among the aforesaid three metaphysical paths, it is, of course, the last that can, by realizing the origin of the formation of scientific knowledge, be most conducive to moral and religious realms that transcend science. It is also this path that can best demarcate the range of science and ethics and religion and metaphysics. The reason why these do not blend with one another lies in their different scopes as well as in the fact that the truths they embrace pertain to different levels. Science may possess its own truth. Because of the scientific method, man can probe into outer space, penetrate the center of the earth, make conjectures about the most ancient times and have visions of the future. Macrocosms like galaxies and constellations, microcosms like nuclei, external worlds like nature and society, and internal realms like psychology and physiology can all be studied by science. Nevertheless, scientific knowledge is subordinate to our knowledge-seeking activities and is their fruit. However advanced scientific knowledge is, whatever new theories emerge inexhaustively to contradict preceding ones, they cannot go beyond the possible scope of the activities in pursuit of pure knowledge. But there are other realms beyond the domain that scientific knowledge covers. These realms are discovered through man's activities of practical reason, aesthetic taste, and religious belief. These activities, including purely cognitive ones, and the realms they discover appertain to man's transcendental self. Of course, purely intellectual activities and their harvest are valuable. But who is to accept or ascertain the value of these activities? The only answer is the very self. Without this self, these activities immediately become meaningless to me. Furthermore, they are no longer my activities. Their outcomes do not concern us. Even the entire world known becomes irrelevant to us; it submerges into nothingness and chaos before us. Thus, all scientific investigations become unnecessary and impossible. Fortunately, this self affirms not only the value of purely intellectual activities of science with their outcomes, but also that of aesthetic, practical, and religious activities with their offspring. In other words, the self transcendentally embraces and maintains these activities and their outcomes. An individual can, in principle or under particular circumstances, judge the value of these activities and their offspring before making a choice among them. This judgment needs the consciousness of value, or conscience [liang-chih] of the self. Conscience judges the value of all activities by seeing whether they accord with one's inner aspirations and standards or with the principles of conscience. What accords with the latter is affirmed; what does not is denied. Conscience likes what is good and dislikes what is evil. Thus it becomes the source of moral wisdom and moral practice and the inner supreme lord of human life. People may ask whether this conscience can be studied by psychologists and sociologists. If it can be, does it not fall into the range of science? We answer that this does not matter. When psychologists and sociologists study conscience, the latter is objectified. Anyway, there is at least one thing that cannot be totally objectified, i.e., the "psychological mode" of the psychologists and sociologists with which they investigate conscience. Is this mode itself of value? This answer has still to be judged by their own consciences. They may reflect upon the reason why they want to probe into conscience. What are they after: fame, profit, truth, or the enlightenment of others' consciences? Their consciences will tell them that the value of studying conscience for the sake of reputation and wealth is inferior to that for the sake of finding truth, while the latter is lower than that for the sake of illuminating others' consciences. Thus the scientific work of sociological and psychological research in conscience is still subject to a higher being, namely, conscience. Anyhow, this is like the situation that the monkey can never somersault beyond the palm of the Buddha. It is not until conscience admits their value that all scientific activities become possible, i.e., they are forever governed by conscience but not vice versa. All doubts and criticisms about conscience which are cast by scientists and philosophers are inevitably raised on a lower plane. To these criticisms we may reply through deeper reflection on conscience. The teaching of the conscience can never be shaken even to the slightest extent. Here I need not dwell upon this subject.

Having established that the conscience of the self is the lord of scientific activities which judges and selects the value of all cultural activities and decides whether the latter should be performed, we realize that the principles established according to anything (other than conscience) studied by science cannot exhaustively account for the essence and nature of the conscience of the self; nor can any phenomenal objects of one's purely intellectual activities become the origin of the existence and intrinsic value of conscience because they are merely the objects for purely intellectual activities which are affirmed by conscience. All philosophies based on the findings of one science or a combination of various sciences and those that merely

objectify pure reason and rely on it to recognize external universals and forms are incapable of penetrating into the source
of man and the universe. For they are ignorant of the fact that
only the conscience can be self-conscious of its intellectual activities and affirm their value and hence be the ultimate source
of these purely intellectual activities and philosophies. Since
the conscience can always assert its own value and its "ought
to be," it is the source of its own being and inherent value as
well as the origin of human activities that can affirm themselves. It is only through conscience and all the valuable activities of human life which it affirms that man can realize the
metaphysical origin of the universe and the absolute heavenly
principles.

What is the origin of the universe, anyway? We may say that
it is Heavenly Wisdom. But we should not regard Heavenly
Wisdom and conscience as two absolutely separate things. Conscience may be considered to be Heavenly Wisdom present in
us. Heavenly Wisdom is simply the maximum realization of the
conscience. Hence their identification. If we want to say that
they are still two, then their relationship must be complementary and one of mutual maintenance instead of causality, substance and attribute, or creator and created. Terms like causality and creator are suitable only to explaining nature, not to
Heaven-man relationships. From here we may enter the depths
of metaphysical, philosophical, and religious issues. (My readers who desire a precise understanding of Wang Yang-ming's
teaching of conscience may read Mr. Mou Tsung-san's book
entitled Wang Yang-ming's Teaching of Developing Conscience.)

VII

From the above, I may proceed to speak of my choices among
religions. Religionists have to mention immortality or future
life or resurrection, Paradise or the World beyond, God, Allah,
Brahman, Buddha, Bodhisattva, or immortals. These beings,
which religionists assert, can neither be verified by commonsense and science, nor be totally described by literature and

arts from an aesthetic point of view. Furthermore, they do not
directly pertain to the range of sociology, politics, and economics. Moral practices in general can also be established independently of such assertions. Thus we deem religious spirit
to be beyond human culture. This does not mean that religionists do not engage themselves in social and cultural enterprises.
On the contrary, religion is a branch of culture because all religious undertakings are related to man. However, the unique
feature of the religious spirit lies in the affirmation of the
supernatural world with superhumanistic metaphysical objects.
It is obvious that what religionists pursue is another life above
the actual life. Otherwise, how can religionists differ from
mundane people and what marks the holiness and dignity of religion? Therefore, my saying that the religious spirit is superhumanistic is by no means a depreciation of religion. What we
should be concerned with is to explain why superhumanistic religious spirit is necessary to human culture, or why man's conscience needs to ascertain the value of religion, and how we
argue for and elucidate the truthfulness of these metaphysical
objects in religion before making judgments and choices among
them. These are the very issues that roused endless controversies among various sects of religious philosophy or theology.
Here I would like to dwell on the last question.

It is not easy to answer this question since no particular
teaching of any religion can be dogmatically regarded as a criterion. Every religion considers its own doctrines to be the
criterion for judging other religions. Even the words of God
cannot serve as a criterion because God, never speaking directly to man, speaks through mouthpieces. A human criterion
is needed to discern which are truly the Words of God. But
what is this criterion? The answer still lies in the human conscience and in pure intellectual reason and experience under
the guidance of conscience.

Some religionists deny that conscience is the criterion for
judging religion on the grounds that only God can judge human
affairs, while humans cannot judge God's. In the strict sense
of judgment, what is judged must be placed below the activity

of judgment. We may say that man can never judge God's affairs because God transcends all activities of judgment. Instead of being one who is judged, God can only be one who is believed in. But as far as the strict sense of judgment is concerned, conscience, the origin of man's judgments, transcends all judgments. Since it cannot become the thing that is judged, conscience can merely verify its own enlightenment. Thus, it is impossible to say whether God can judge conscience. However, if we accept the loose sense of judgment, the acts of verifying, becoming enlightened, and believing are equivalent to judging. Hence, while God can judge man's affairs, man can also judge God's. For instance, religionists who remark that man cannot judge God may say that, refraining from judging God, man will obtain God's grace. Thus they judge God's mind. Even if we believe that man's judgment is what is judged by God, this belief itself is man's judgment. Religionists who have made this judgment affirm it according to their own judgment. Even if we admit that our actions, volitions, and ideas (including judgments) are all known to the transcendent God and that on the Day of Judgment we have to undergo the final judgment of Jesus as the incarnation of God, how can we know that this Judgment does not consist of or necessarily involve our transcendental conscience finally judging ourselves? If this judgment absolutely need not be accepted by our conscience, then can this God still be deemed benevolent? We will not dwell here on the problems concerning the correlation between God and conscience, the possibility of the Day of Judgment, or the conditions on this Day. In any case, when a man believes in these, at least his own conscience admits that this belief is good. Actually man has to ascertain the existence of conscience as the criterion for his judgment on religion. Therefore, in what follows I shall make choices concerning the value of religions according to the criterion of conscience.

1) According to the criterion of conscience, the transcendental beliefs of all great religions, we may say, arise from man's demand for supreme good, ultimate truth, perfection, infinity, and eternal life; for the eradication of all evils and sins; and for

awarding the virtuous while punishing the vicious in order to
realize everlasting justice and righteousness. Therefore, man
should have transcendental beliefs. We cannot say that man
should not possess this demand. Without it, man would also not
have his social, political, legal, or cultural enterprises of pursuing survival, rooting out evil and suffering, and, above all,
realizing justice. Although this demand is subjective on the one
hand, yet on the other hand it also affirms the objective existence of the object that can satisfy this demand. This objective
existence is metaphysical. It is also impossible to deny the
value of the religious demand and the existence of the metaphysical objects ascertained by religion solely on the basis of
man's purely intellectual activities and of the factual situation
of the natural world that they know. For, from the conscience's
point of view, the imperfect, sinful, actual world is to be negated and reconstructed through our moral practice. Such a
world should not be taken as the ultimate reality. Moreover, it
is gradually changing into nonreality. Hence the essential nature of this world is not totally real. Thus, the actual or natural world can never become a criterion for judging the unreality
of metaphysical realms accepted by religionists. Nor can the
scientific languages which are true for actual existence be used
as the criteria for deciding whether religious languages embrace truth.

2) According to the criterion of conscience, we may say that
God, Allah, or Brahman, of which the higher religions speak, in
the final analysis cannot be separated from the human conscience. If any one of them and conscience are separated to
make two, such duality has to be approved by the conscience itself. But this approval at once combines the two into one or, at
least, renders the relation between the two interpenetrative and
mutually complementary. The theories of creation in Christianity (including Catholicism) and Islam propound that man's conscience, or soul, which commits sin as soon as it is created,
becomes alienated from God, or the Heavenly Mind, and that the
Savior, or Prophet, as the incarnation of God is sent to act as
the road between man and God. These are more complicated

than Confucian doctrines. As to Buddhism, the mind of Tathāgata
Garbha, or the everlasting authentic mind, which embraces both
karuṇā [compassion] and prajñā [wisdom], actually refers to
conscience through which man and Heaven are unified. Thus,
the nature of the mind of the embryonic Tathāgata, or the Womb
of Tathagatahood, is not different from that of God of the West.
However, according to Buddhism, the mind of Tathāgata Garbha
presents itself only when our kleśa [evil passions] totally vanishes and saṃsāra [birth and death] troubles us no more; ordinarily, our mind is tainted with entanglements on account of
saṃga [attachment]. No wonder that Buddhist cultivation stresses
eliminating contamination, or attaining liberation, and Buddhist
theories accentuate śūnyatā [emptiness, or Void]. Christianity
positively links man with God by means of man's faith. Thus,
Christian cultivation emphasizes the exaltation of man's mind,
and Christian doctrines stress "being." However, deeming our
mind contaminated by original sin, Christianity, like Buddhism,
is bound to lay emphasis on purifying our mind at the present
instead of straightforwardly undertaking the good radicals of
our mind. As for Chinese Confucianism, insofar as man reflects
on himself and becomes sincere, he understands that conscience,
the supremely good human nature, does exist right in his everyday mind with all its contamination and guilt. The difference
between ordinary people and sages hinges on the fact that the
former see a beam of light from a narrow portion of the sky,
whereas the latter see the magnificent splendor from a panorama of the heavens. But the difference is not essential at all.
Recognizing that even a soft ray is still light, man can penetrate
into grand brilliance; knowing that even a tiny part of the sky is
still the heavens, man does not estrange himself from the vast
space. Having realized this principle, we may rise to the loftiest spiritual realm while practicing the Doctrine of the Mean,
eliminate the alienation between the mundane world and the
supernatural world, and, above all, affirm all values of human
life and culture. From the ability of this principle in penetration, we believe that sages over any ocean have the mind of
the same principles. Then by abandoning the diversions in

terminologies and cultivation methods, we can reach the concourse of all religions and render them compatible and co-
existent.

3) Christianity considers that man's life after ascending to
Heaven belongs to the divine mystery and is thus unspeakable.
However, Buddhism discusses the levels, or phases, of sage-
realms which transcend mundane ones. Therefore, Christianity
is inferior to Buddhism with respect to its exposition of the attainment of virtue verified through cultivation. Buddhism is inferior to Christianity in that the latter, hoping to bring the
Kingdom of God to Earth, advocates endeavor for social welfare.

4) Whether literally or metaphorically, Christianity maintains that all things were created for the sake of man and that
only man can receive salvation. This displays the spirit which
elevates the status of man in the universe. However, affirming
all sentient beings' ability to attain Buddhahood, Buddhism
shows a more magnanimous mind of compassion. The eternal
Hell in Christianity expresses the righteous principle that evils
and crimes must be punished, urging man to fear evils and refrain from committing crimes. According to Christianity, which
rejects the Buddhist doctrine of metempsychosis, people who do
not do good in this life are bound to fall into the Inferno in their
afterlife and await the Day of Judgment. This idea urges people
to perform good deeds in this life. This everlasting Hell that
God created for sinners succeeds in enhancing God's dignity
and arouses in man a greater sense of holiness. Nevertheless,
this is the efficacious value of the Christian faith. After the
Day of Judgment, sinners in the Inferno are eternally tortured
without the ability to repent and receive God's blessing. If not
expediently or metaphorically speaking, the above Christian
doctrine, once treated as factual, has to deny the principle that
man's conscience always voluntarily shows itself and works to
repent of its own sin, and the doctrine consequently renders
God's love lower than Buddha's compassion in dashing into the
Hell to rescue people.

5) There is more than one way in which man may rise above

the mundane to attain sageness. Actually God's revelation is, in reality, not essentially different from the authentic enlightenment of conscience or the emergence of Buddha's mind of great compassion. Christians can never attain magnanimity if they maintain that only those who believe in Jesus can ascend to Heaven and that everybody ought to kneel down before Jesus, Son of Mary. In the West the wars between Christians and Moslems and Catholics and Protestants, the combat between the sects of Luther and Calvin within Protestanism, and all judgments, exiles, and slaughters imposed on heretics arose from an erroneous belief in the uniqueness of the road to sainthood. This "exclusive theory of salvation" (in criticizing Christianity, Robinson employed this expression in his book Mind in the Making) is just what I call "The seed of war in Christianity."

6) If we stress the duality between (instead of the unity of) man's mind and God's mind, then there are several respects in which the latter transcends the former, and vice versa. God's mind excels man's in its pure goodness devoid of evilness and suffering, while man's mind surpasses God's in its ability to feel pain and vice and to transcend them. In Christianity, Jesus, as the incarnation of God, has the nature of both God and man to shoulder evil and suffering. Apart from showing God's love and grace for man, this demonstrates that God has to possess man's nature and experience, transcend the evil and suffering that man experiences, and become God in Trinity. What is meant by this is that God's and man's natures depend on and complement each other. (There is an excellent elaboration on the "Freedom of Spirit" in the Russian philosopher Berdyaev's book The Destiny of Man. Whitehead considers the relation between God and all things to be mutually inclusive, implicative, and complementary.) Christianity straightforwardly considers Jesus, who has the dual nature of God and man, to be the Savior (instead of God, the Holy Father). Thus, the core of this religion is still the emphasis on man. To worship Jesus is not only to worship his hypostasis of God, but also that of man. However, the Christian spirit of elevating the status of man has not been developed to its utmost extent. For, despite worshiping Jesus and observing

sacrificial rites to God as if to man, Christianity lacks the
spirit that observes sacrificial rites to man (ancestors, sages)
as if to God. In its theory of the relation between God and man,
it does not adequately esteem man's conscience. Maintaining
that man's salvation is solely due to the inspiration of the Holy
Spirit or the Grace of God, it does not value the active enlightenment of man's conscience. In a certain sense, man's enlightenment may be said to spring from God's Grace. But the re-
ception of God's Grace still relies on man's enlightenment, so
the latter may be regarded as what approves and admits God's
Grace. Only in this way can the unity of Heaven and man be revealed. The Christian accentuation of God's Grace is intended
to remove man's arrogance and cultivate his humility. But in
addition to modesty, lofty illumination is also man's virtue.
Revering Heaven while humiliating man cannot but deprive man
of his lofty illumination. Hence, my understanding that it is the
ultimate in religious morality for Chinese Confucianists to copy
the highness of Heaven and teach lofty illumination in intellect,
while copying the lowness of Earth and teaching modesty in propriety. A perfect religion needs not only to serve God as though
He had personality, but also to serve man as if he had divinity.
Only through this can we esteem and perform sacrificial rites
to great personalities among the heretics in order to achieve
the new religious spirit that affirms sacrificial rites to both
Heaven and man. This spirit can be formed by the expansion of
the inherent religious spirit of the Chinese people which stresses
sacrificial rites to Heaven and Earth and to parents and teachers. It will manage to harmonize all religions, satisfy their essential needs, forever eliminate religionists' mutual contempt,
and even nip religious wars in the bud.

7) To achieve this new religious spirit, Confucian magnanimity should be revived. It is also necessary for all religionists to get rid of their prejudice according to their own religious
conscience. Because today's Christian countries are the richest
and strongest and the strength of Christianity is also the most
abundant, I hope Christians will first develop their religious
conscience to the full.

Hoping that everybody will receive salvation, the religious conscience refrains from asserting the existence of a perennial Hell.

Knowing that God's love is omnipresent, it avoids saying that God's revelation reaches only the leader of its own religion.

Further, the religious conscience should believe that God's love will make Him willing to open the Gate of Heaven wide and reveal Himself in the mind of everybody with religious spirit among all nations and in all ages.

8) Jesus himself did not deny that God's revelation could reach heretics. Jesus was not jealous of the possible fact that God would reveal Himself in others' minds. Most historians of religion have remarked that Jesus never claimed to be God's only son. God in the New Testament, unlike God in Judaism, is not jealous of other gods worshiped by people. Therefore, it is man's fault that Christianity is not magnanimous. Jesus' disciples overesteemed their teacher, and the induction of the spirit of Judaism and Roman Law into Christianity. (Many thinkers have already dwelled on this problem.) In medieval Christianity, some people, such as Origen and Duns Scotus, advocated the idea that all people could receive salvation and repudiated the notion of the perennial Inferno on the ground that man's finite sin should not incur infinite punishment. Despite being more in accord with Jesus' spirit of willingly remitting all people's sin, this idea was judged to be heretical in the Middle Ages. However, if we follow our religious conscience and fully develop Jesus' spirit, this heretical belief should be exalted to become orthodox. In Christianity, there are some people who maintain that there should be spiritual churches as well as formal ones. These spiritual churches could embrace whoever does not formally believe in Christianity and ascertain his ability to enter Heaven. Thus the two defects that I criticize could be disposed of, while Jesus' spirit could be continued and propagated, and the Christian seed of war could be destroyed.

9) The deeper problem of religious life itself and its relation to moral life has not been expounded in this essay. This problem will require a shift from philosophy and theology to the

learning of sageliness. However, I have insisted that all religions should pursue their mutual acknowledgment of the value of other religions' beliefs and dogmas, and rectify the elements of their own religions that contradict human conscience, or else leave these elements alone and do justice to those elements which accord with man's conscience. Today the bitterest enemy of religion is materialism: If the latter controls man's thought, no religion can survive. So religions should fully exert themselves to condemn materialism instead of disdaining one another. In addition, logical positivism, sensory empiricism, and a certain kind of naturalism that denies spiritual values are all strong enough to ruin religion. Unlike materialism, these philosophies are not politically promulgated. They are against both religion and materialism. Thus, religionists should approve their value to a certain extent. Philosophies other than the above mentioned are more or less helpful toward the establishment of religious belief. They ought to be investigated by religionists, who are not to become overly conservative but to demolish evil doctrines and advocate appropriate convictions.

If unable to make choices among religions, we had better assume the attitude expressed by the Confucian saying: "to treat the known as known and the unknown as unknown." Whoever does not understand my philosophy may regard this essay as meaningless. For my words are devoid of the meaning of "meaning" in materialism, logical positivism, and sensory empiricism. Nevertheless, the meaning of "meaning" is not confined to their definition. It is against human nature to restrict the meaning of this term within a tiny scope. However, if willing to step one pace forward, people can still see a broad domain to which "meaning" refers. All men, I hope, will think and philosophize before attaining spiritual conciliation sooner or later.

18

THE FORMATION OF CONFUCIUS' POSITION IN CHINESE HISTORY AND CULTURE

I. Introduction

A popular opinion concerning the lofty position of Confucius in the history and culture of China which has circulated since the founding of the Republic of China is that Confucius was merely one of the thinkers or philosophers of the pre-Ch'in period and that he was later elevated to his lofty position through the manipulations of the various emperors and political leaders down through the centuries. Extremists have even gone so far as to say that this was done through the efforts of Emperor Wu of the Han dynasty who suppressed all other schools of philosophers and elevated only Confucius, so much so that for two thousand years Chinese culture and thought have never been able to depart from the Confucian tradition and thus have never been able to make any meaningful advancement. Such popular views seem to have some facts to substantiate their argument. For instance,

Author's note: Recently I have published the volumes of "Tracing the Origin of the Way", and "Tracing the Origin of the Teaching," which are portions of my latest book, The Original Theories and Principles of Chinese Philosophy. The book deals with the origins and developments of the principles and meanings in Chinese philosophical thoughts. The two volumes are over one million words long and consequently it can hardly be expected that everybody will have the patience to read them through. In the present article, written at the request of The China Forum, I have briefly sketched the ideas and points concerning the position of Confucius in Chinese history and culture which are scattered throughout those two volumes. Summarizations, omissions and reorganizations are inevitable. Those who would like to know more about the development of the principles discussed here are invited to read the complete book.

emperors down the history used to confer titles upon Confucius, and to have temples erected in memory of him. Governments after the T'ang and Sung dynasties administered examinations for official posts on the classics compiled by Confucius; those who passed these examinations became officials in the government and thus a scholar well versed in the Confucian classics easily became a member of the ruling class. Furthermore, Confucius insisted on the distinction and obligation between the emperor and subject. All these have been given as evidence to support their objection to Confucius. In their eyes, Confucius was merely one of the philosophers of the pre-Ch'in period, and he ascended to such a unique position only because his ideology favored the imperial rule so the emperors all elevated him. Consequently, in modern China, which has turned democratic, Confucius should no longer be worshipped because to do so could only cause history to regress. This attitude gradually consolidated during the last years of the Ch'ing dynasty and the first years of the Republic; once it came to a head it became popular all over China. When such views reached the West, they began to affect such sinologists as Max Weber, who wrote on the Chinese bureaucracy, Karl A. Wittfogel who wrote on Oriental despotism, John Fairbank who writes on modern China, and Joseph Levenson who wrote on the Confucian state. They in turn influenced the general viewpoint of the Westerners toward Chinese society and political affairs; even the foreign policy of Western countries toward China was affected. But I shall not dwell upon these matters here. As the anti-Confucian movement permeated China, it joined forces with Marxism and Leninism imported from Russia. This resulted in a distorted view of the Confucian canon as an ideology which supposedly rendered service to the ruling class in a feudalistic slave society. The recent criticism of Confucius on the mainland in order to attack political enemies and Chinese culture also stems from this short history of denigration of Confucianism. Even some modern Chinese intellectuals are of the opinion that Confucius was merely one of the thinkers of the pre-Ch'in period and that even if Confucius is overthrown there are other thinkers and other schools of thought from that period out of which a strong Chinese cultural heritage could still be constituted. However, if one cares to trace back to the heart of the matter, one can instantly see that the above-mentioned theses and attitudes only seem to be correct. Before the founding of the Republic of

China, Confucius was never regarded simply as one of the thinkers of the pre-Ch'in period or simply as the head of a school of thought called Confucianism; r.either had he been considered simply to be a philosopher. On the contrary, he had been venerated as the foremost sage and the foremost teacher of Chinese history. The formation of Confucius' position in Chinese history and culture was not at first the result of the efforts of emperors or occupants of high political positions. As a matter of fact, it was Confucius' disciples, latter-day followers of his school of thought, and the leading intellectuals of various periods who have had the most to do with elevating Confucius to his position of unique distinction. These people most of the time were harassed by poverty and troubled by tribulations in a time when the life of the Chinese race and the survival of Chinese culture were in peril and the whole country was on the verge of ruination. It was during such periods that the teachings of Confucius were found to be enlightening and encouraging, Thus these people advocated and popularized Confucius' teachings. They wished to inherit the great learning of the great sage so that they could pass it on to future generations. Consequently, for the past 2500 years, the deference of the Chinese toward Confucius was never on the decline but has continued with ever renewing strength. Confucius has been interwoven with Chinese history and culture, and no separation should be allowed between the two, for they constitute the flesh and blood of the cultural life of the Chinese people. The high regard paid to Confucius by the emperors was done in compliance with the desires of the people, and in a sense the rulers had no other choice but to do so. Thus in this matter the emperors should only be regarded as followers and imitators of the people and considered secondary in the Confucian cult. There is no ground for anyone to say that the position of Confucius owes to the promotion of the political rulers; that is to put the cart before the horse. This article intends to develop this thesis and to survey the historical facts in order to correct this mistaken concept. Only then can we begin to discuss Confucius' teachings.

II. Confucius as a fountainhead of pre-Ch'in thinkers, Confucius as an object of reverence by his disciples as well as the various thinkers, and the initial position of Confucius in Chinese learning and culture

Let me first make it clear that since the end of the Ch'ing dynasty critics who only saw Confucius as one of the pre-Ch'in thinkers or as one Confucian, or as a mere philosopher in the modern sense have missed the point. Scholars before them and their knowledgeable contemporaries never adopted such a position, and it is most likely that people in the future will not accept their line of argument either. According to Pan Ku 班固 who composed the *Han Shu I Wen Chih* 漢書藝文志 in the tradition of the *Ch'i Lueh* 七略 by Liu Hsiang, 劉向 the scholars of the nine schools "considered Yao and Shun as their spiritual ancestors, modelled upon the King Wen 文王 and King Wu 武王 of the Chou Dynasty, and all went to school to Confucius" (see the section "Chu-tzu Lueh" 諸子略); Confucius himself was not included among the scholars (or "Confucians" 儒家) though Mencius and Hsun Ts'u were. Furthermore, while discussing the nine schools, Pan Ku pointed out that each derived from or conformed to one aspect of the system of Confucius, especially Confucius' Six Disciplines 六藝 . For example, he said that the Nominalists 名家 (variously translated as "Dialecticians," "Logicians," "School of Names," "School of Forms and Names") conformed to Confucius' principle of "the rectification of names," the Legalists 法家 stressed the "justified penalty and lucid laws" of the *I Ching,* the Ying-Yang school followed the principle of "announcing with reverence the seasonal time" of the *Shu Ching,* the Diplomatists 縱橫家 repeated Confucius' emphasis on the importance of "envoys," the Agriculturalists 農家 cherished Confucius' emphasis on "sufficient provisions for the populace," the Fictionalists 小說家 echoed Confucius' utterance that "There are things to be appreciated even in the lesser ways," and the Taoists 道家 centered on the idea of "humility" preached in the *I Ching.*

But Pan Ku never said that Confucius was one of the nine schools of thinkers. The learning of Confucius received its basic tenets from the Six Disciplines, and he presided over the nine schools of thinkers. This is a recognition shared almost by all the scholars from Pan Ku to those in the later years of the Ch'ing dynasty. Furthermore, many of them revered Confucius as the foremost sage and the foremost teacher with only the famous exception of Chang Hsüeh-ch'eng 章學誠 , who called Duke Chou 周公 the foremost sage and Confucius the foremost teacher. Only in the later years of the Ch'ing dynasty and the early years of the Republic, did scholars begin to compare the culture of the pre-Ch'in period to that of ancient Greece. Thus Confucius was viewed as one of the thinkers of ancient China just as Socrates was one of the philosophers in ancient Greece. Some of them juxtaposed Confucius and Lao Tzü, regarding the former as the leader of the northern school and the latter the leader of the southern school. Others juxtaposed Confucius and Mo-tzu, regarding them respectively as leaders of two co-equal schools. Some even listed Confucianism, Mohism 墨家 , and Taoism as three co-equal schools or the Confucianism, Mohism, Taoism, and Legalism 法家 as four co-equal schools, that appeared simultaneously. But Mo Tzu 墨子 came eighty years later than Confucius, and Lao Tzu 老子 came even later than Mo Tzu according to modern research. The works entitled *Yen Tzu* 晏子 and *Kuan Tzu* 管子 were mistakenly ascribed to Yen Tzu and Kuan Tzu; but, according to qualified opinion, they are neither by Yen Tzu nor by Kuan Tzu. We have no reason to consider Yen Tzu a Mohist nor Kuan Tzu a Legalist. Therefore, from a historical perspective, the authors, whoever they were, of the books entitled *Lao Tzu* and *Kuan Tzu* and *Yen Tzu* were all later than Confucius and must not be regarded as Confucius' contemporaries, nor should they be put on an equal footing with Confucius.

Recently, I have published a book on the origins of Chinese philosophy, *The Original Theories and Principles of Chinese Philosophy* in which the main emphasis is on the principles and tenets of Chinese philosophy, and not a discussion of historical origins. But even from a purely conceptual viewpoint, I was compelled to assert the unique position of Confucius. That is to say, before Confucius there was only Duke Chou whose teachings on rites and music were inherited by Confucius. The origins of the various thinkers had to be traced back to the learning of Confucius.

During the age of Confucius, the so-called confrontation between the southern and northern schools of thought actually did not exist, much less the confrontation between the Confucians and the Mohists. However, within the system of Confucius, there were the two sides: "to practise righteousness in order to make the Way prevail" so that the country can be ruled with justice and the people can live in security on the one hand, and on the other hand, "to become a recluse in order to safeguard one's own principle" so that the self can be cultivated without being damaged by external intrusions. According to Mencius, Yi Yin 伊尹 the ancient worthy, "called upon T'ang 湯 five times and called upon Chieh 桀 five times" with the intention of making his principles pervade throughout the world, for this was the duty of the sage who wanted to see that the populace was governed well. But Po I 伯夷 wished only to keep himself free from worldly taints and to uphold his own lofty ideals, for he set his eyes on the purity of a sage's life, and his concern was solely with self-cultivation. Confucius was able to have both. When it was time to advance, he advanced in accordance with propriety; when it was time to withdraw, he withdrew on principle. Therefore, he was the sage who knew the appropriateness of timing.

The Mohists advocated their principles, with which they wished to benefit the world; they wanted to sacrifice themselves in order to bring salvation to the populace. What they advocated is pretty close to Yi Yin's duties of the sage, and is certainly an outcome of the development of the aspect of Confucius' thought of "practising righteousness in order to make the Way prevail." The Taoists avoided the affairs of the world in order to keep themselves pure and their ideals lofty so that they could plumb the way of Heaven and Earth and the origin of all things. This is certainly a result of the development of Confucius' idea "to become a recluse in order to safeguard one's own principle." And it is close to the ideal of Po I who represents the life of purity of the sage. The threads of the principles connecting the thought of Confucius, the Mohists, and the Taoists, and the historical connections of how they were passed on are not easy matters. I have given an overview of these problems in book one of my *The Original Theories and Principles of Chinese Philosophy*.

Legalism rose even later. Some of its concepts can be traced back to certain aspects of Confucianism, Mohism and Taoism. But its basic spirit lies in the use of expediency and power in order to establish an authoritarian political system. Other pre-Ch'in schools also dated long after Confucius and part of their theories also harked back to Confucianism, Taoism, Mohism, or Legalism. In short, the learning and thought of the pre-Ch'in period took Confucius as its starting point and developed step by step from there. Therefore, it is wrong to regard Confucius as merely one among the various thinkers; he was in a sense the intellectual ancestor of all the later thinkers. How could the ancestor be taken as one of his progeny? This is precisely why our forefathers did not take Confucius to be merely one of the thinkers but honored him as the patriarch of the Confucians, as the foremost teacher, the foremost sage, and the proof of the existence of the wisdom of the sages.

The reason I have had to reiterate the Chinese traditional view toward Confucius, which is to regard Confucius not as just one of the thinkers but as a sage, lies in my intention to correct the current popular view that Confucius was merely one of the Confucian philosopher. If Confucius was merely a scholar or philosopher, his position would be equivalent to that of the other philosophers. If Confucius was not a sage but only a "philosopher", then his position would not differ from that of a scientist, statesman, or educator. Equal status would be construed as relative status, not absolute status. But Confucius' position in Chinese history and culture has been absolute. Confucius' heritage comprised the Six Disciplines and the culture developed in the Shang and Chou dynasties and it was his self-assigned duty to defend this cultural heritage which centered on revering the king and repulsing the barbarians. And he made possible the historical position which the subsequent philosophers achieved. Consequently, he is unique and has no compeer, and his position is thus absolute.

Confucius of course was the patriarch of the Confucians (*ju-chia*) but he did not call himself a Confucian. Mencius regarded Confucius as the confluence of all the worthies existing before him but Mencius never said that Confucius was a Confucian. It was Hsün Tzu who first considered Confucius and Duke Chou in terms of great Confucians. However, the word "Confucian" (*ju-chia*) in Hsün Tzu's lexicon has to be explained as "one who comprehends the totality of the Way of the *sage* kings." A scholar in such a sense cannot be taken to be one of the Nine Schools or one among the thinkers. The reason that I have been elaborating this distinction is to once again confirm the unique and elevated station to which Chinese history and culture have assigned Confucius, and to point out that such a station was not gained merely through the founding of a school of thought. That Confucius occupied the position he did in Chinese history and culture was the result of the honor paid him by his disciples, by those who followed him in intellectual history such as the Taoists, the Mohists and the Legalists, and by all the distinguished figures in learning and culture of the following ages. We must recognise this before we can understand the inseparability of Confucius and all the history and culture of China. Then, we shall understand that it is not by his own merit alone but by the efforts of the people who came after him that Confucius came to occupy the position as he has been occupying in Chinese history.

The greatness of Confucius is not only a personal greatness but also a national greatness of Chinese learning and culture. In other words, whoever insults Confucius insults all those down through history who honored Confucius, and insults the intellectual and cultural life of the Chinese people. Any treason committed against Confucius becomes a treason against the life of Chinese learning and culture as a whole.

This article will not dwell upon the greatness of Confucius as a person and the greatness of his learning, the various schools of thinkers that derived from him and the similarities among their thoughts, or the confrontation that existed among them. This article will only point out the high regard in which later generations held Confucius so that it can be understood that the formation of Confucius' position in Chinese history and culture is not merely a result of his philosophical thinking and even less the result of the patronization of the emperors of the various dynasties who happened to find his ideas congenial to their politics and thus raised him to a unique position.

Of course, even during his lifetime there were people like Shu-sun Wu-shu 叔孫武叔 who reviled Confucius as recorded in the *Analects* 論語. But the *Analects* also record that the Tai Tsai 大宰 asked Tzu Kung 子貢 whether "Confucius was a sage," and there were people who looked upon Confucius as a "wooden drum from Heaven to waken the people." But the way of Confucius failed to become popular in his own time. After his middle age, Confucius became an exile and wandered in foreign lands. According to his biography in *Shih Chi* 史記, "even when he was old he had nothing to his name" and finally he returned empty-handed to his home country, the state of Lu. After his death, only Duke Ai of Lu 魯哀公 uttered a single line of condollence, "Heaven would not spare even this grand old man."

The awakening and enlightening words of Confucius had little impact in his own time except upon the hearts of a few disciples. *Shih Chi* claimed that Confucius had three thousand students, but this seems to be merely a guess. Those that can be proven by historical documents number no more than twenty to thirty people. And those who made up Confucius' constant companions were no more than ten persons. But after his demise, according to the "Teng Wen Kung" 滕文公 chapter in the *Mencius* 孟子, all his disciples maintained a vigil at his grave for three years as if he had been their parent. Upon the completion of the three years' mourning, "the disciples packed and were about to leave. They went to bow to Tzu Kung 子貢 and they looked into one another's eyes and wept and lost their voices and then they departed." But, "Tzu Kung returned to the grave and built a cabin on it and lived alone there for three more years and then departed." This description from *Mencius* concerning the vigil the disciples kept over Confucius' grave is sufficient evidence to show that the seventy disciples adored Confucius in the sincere manner; they were not just paying lip service to him. According to "Kung Tzu Shih-chia" 孔子世家 in the *Shih Chi* on the authority of Mencius, after Tzu Kung's three years of mourning at the grave, "disciples and the people of Lu went to make their homes beside the tomb, and there were more than one hundred of them. Thus the place was called the Kung Village 孔里. From generation to generation during the period of the Lu state, rituals in memory of Confucius were held at Confucius' tomb and the Confucians came to the tomb to lecture on propriety, and hold the *hsiang* archery contest 鄉射 and the big archery contest 大射. The tomb of Confucius occupied one hectre and a temple was built by his disciples to house Confucius' clothes, hat, harp, cart, and books. This continued for over two hundred years well into the Han dynasty." We should pay particular attention to this passage, which makes clear that the position of Confucius in Chinese history and culture was the accumulated effect of the admiration of his disciples and the common people who loved and adored him. It was the end result of a natural and sincere process and had nothing whatsoever to do with the patronization of political rulers.

It is recorded in "The Biography of the Confucian Scholars" in *Shih Chi* that following the death of Confucius, his seventy disciples dispersed among the various states. The greater ones became teachers to ministers, and the lesser ones became teachers to officials, and some of them avoided the affairs of the world. Tzu Lu 子路 was in the state of Wei 衛, Tzu Chang 子張 was in the state of Ch'en 陳, Tzu Yü 子羽 of Tan Tai 澹臺 was in the state of Ch'u 楚, Tzu Hsia 子夏 resided in Hsi Ho 西河, and Tzu Kung died in the state of Ch'i 齊. T'ien Tzu-fang 田子方, Tuan Yü-Mu 段于木, Wu Ch'i 吳起, and Ch'in Hua-Li 禽滑厘 all received instruction from Tzu Hsia and his fellows and all became teachers of kings." This dispersal of Confucius disciples and of their disciples throughout China to be teachers of kings, thus shows that the influence of Confucius' teachings became widespread and affected the learning, culture, society, and politics of the time. Gradually from a small beginning it became manifest. It was not accomplished just overnight.

T'ien Tzu-fang was actually a Taoist, Ch'in Hua-Li was a Mohist, and Wu Chi was a Militarist and Legalist. This again is proof of our previous assertion that the schools of Taoism, Mohism and Legalism emerged one after another only after the time of Confucius. Therefore, not only Mencius and Hsün Tzu commended and respected Confucius, but even the anti-Confucian Mo Tzu said that among the words of Confucius there were things "that are so appropriate that no change could be made." (*Mo Tzu*, "Kung Meng" 公孟). Mo Tzu objected only the propriety and the music in Confucianism and he blamed Confucius for being "ornately decked out and decorated" and for being "over-indulging in songs and dances." But Mo Tzu admired verse and essays, advocated benevolence and righteousness, all of which were inherited from Confucius. Hence, *An Outline of Huai Nan Tzu* 准南子要略, says of Mo Tzu that he first "went to school to the Confucians *(ju-chia)* and was educated in the learning of Confucius."

Chuang Tzu and his fellow Taoists gave free rein to their imagination on the ways of Heaven and Earth, and the origins of all the things in world. They certainly found uncongenial the propriety, music, benevolence and righteousness stipulated by Confucius. But they still valued much of Confucius' personality, moral conduct and teachings. In the chapters entitled "Jen chien shih 人間世," "Teh Chung fu 德充符," and "Tai tsung shih 大宗師" in the *nei-p'ien* of the Chuang Tzu 莊子, we find Chuang Tzu paying respect to Confucius and disciples such as Yen Hui 顏回 for their moral character and the elevation they had reached through spiritual self-cultivation.

There are similarities and correspondences in the viewpoints and attitudes of Chuang Tzu and Yen Hui. But of course in "Tao Chih 盜跖" and "Yü Fu 漁父" in the *Inner Volume* nei-p'ien of the Chuang Tzu there are comments denigrating Confucius. However, according to qualified opinion, these writings are not from Chuang Tzu's own hand. And in the Wai-p'ien section in chapters such as "Ch'iu Shui 秋水," "Yü Yen 寓言," "Ta Sheng 達生," "Tien Tzu-fang 田子方" words in praise of Confucius can be found in many places.

Legalists such as Han Fei Tzu 韓非子 with their emphasis on punishment and penalty in governing people went directly counter to the humanizing policy of Confucianism. But Han Fei Tzu in the "Wai Chu Shuo 外儲說 of the *Han Fei Tzu*" mentions several times that Confucius did not reject punishments and in so doing is evidently trying to make himself important by quoting Confucius. But this also serves to prove that in the eyes of Han Fei Tzu Confucius was still worthy of respect. Han Fei Tzu said in his "Wu Tu 五蠹" that "Confucius was the sage of all under Heaven.... Duke Ai of Lu, was a minor ruler.... but Confucius had nonetheless to serve him as minister." Certainly, the real meaning is that the benevolence and righteousness of Confucius were nothing compared with the worldly power wielded by Duke Ai of Lu, which Han Fei Tzu used to support his theory of the importance of political power. The fact that he castigated Duke Ai of Lu as a lesser ruler and had praised Confucius as the sage of all under heaven is sufficient proof that he recognized the worth of Confucius' tenets and revered Confucius the man. In short, while the post-Confucian schools of thinkers such as the Taoists, the Mohists, and the Legalists and thinkers of other descriptions did differ from Confucius on many ideological premises they all paid close attention to the words and actions of Confucius and they all showed him respect in various degrees. The position of Confucius in pre-Ch'in history and culture was thus established and confirmed by the praise of him in the writings of these thinkers. It was certainly not merely because of the esteem of the Confucianists that he was established. Even less was it because of the esteem of the Chou kings that he was established.

III. Confucianism in the late Chou period and in the Ch'in and Han dynasties, the classical learning and historical studies in the Han dynasty, and a further confirmation of the position of Confucius

Owing to the efforts of his disciples who went their various ways to act as teachers to the populace, Confucius won general esteem. Consequently, from the late Chou to the Ch'in dynasties, a continous line of scholars was found to embrace the learning of Confucius. Aside from the books of *Mencius* and *Hsün-tzu* which are known to have been written by Mencius and Hsün Ch'ing, the authorship of other Confucian works such as the "Ta-hsüeh" 大學 "Chung-yung" 中庸 "Yao Chi" 樂記 and "Li Yün" 禮運 , chapters of the *Li Chi, the Commentaries to the I-Ching,* and the *Hsiao-ching* 孝經 is problematic. But these books are broad in their scope, rich and grand in their style, substantial in their content, and have lustre. If people nowadays find the *Analects* 論語 too brief and plain in recording the words of Confucius and have thus missed much of Confucius' spirit, they should first read these works.

According to the Han scholars, all these books were compiled from questions his disciples addressed to Confucius and the answers he gave them which they then wrote down. According to the "Li Yün" was written by Tzu Yu 子游 , the "Yao Chi" by Tzu Hsia 子夏 , the "Ta-hsueh" and the *Hsiao Ching* by Tseng Tzu 曾子 , the "Chung yung" by Tzu Ssu 子思 , who was Confucius' grandson, and the *Commentaries to the I-Ching* by Shang Chu 商瞿 . But the research of Sung dynasty scholars and modern scholars has raised many problems concerning their authorship. Many scholars today do not believe in the claims of the Han scholars, but that is a long story. But to make a long story short, whenever the words of Confucius are quoted by these books, they are always headed by the prefix "The master says..." And this should imply that words or utterances not headed by "The master says" are not actually from the mouth of Confucius. The statements of Han Confucians that these works were from the hands of Tzu Yu, Tseng Tzu, Tzu Hsia and others were merely suppostions. But if the Han Confucians insisted that these books contained the utterances of Confucius and that these works were written down by his disciples, their reason is obvious: they wanted to settle the authorship problem once and for all and by extension venerate Confucius and his disciples.

But if we say that these works do not contain the actual words of Confucius and that these works are not written by his disciples, this should not be construed to mean that Confucius could not have said such words and that Confucius should thus suffer in reputation.

Actually, the content of all these works is of such a nature that they may well contain the words of Confucius as found in the *Analects* and these words are easily identifiable by the prefix, "The master says..." Of course, Confucius had the knowledge to have made the statements found in these works. But this argument cannot be turned round and be used as a testimonial that only Confucius and no one else could have uttered these words. Being a great master, Confucius caused his disciples and their disciples to have the ability to take the implied meaning of what Confucius said explicitly and to elucidate it and stated more explicitly. Therefore, I do not agree to the theory that these works were based on what Confucius said and were written down by his disciples. But I do not want to make an issue of it. If some one insists on this theory, I think he has that right since all these still belong to the Confucian tradition. But historical evidence favors my side that is to say the *Li Chi, Hsiao Ching,* the *Commentaries* to the *I-Ching* and the other were written by Confucius' disciples or their disciples, and that these works must have been completed during the late Chou and Ch'in and Han dynasties.

Now, to say that these works are not the words of Confucius directly recorded by his disciples means that we are unable to authenticate the authorship of these works. Consequently, it is possible that some might find this regrettable and be dissatisfied. But this situation can be looked at from another point of view. Precisely because we are unsure of the authorship of these works we feel even more admirable the spirit of these anonymous authors, whose sole concern was to elucidate the principles and tenets of Confucius, not to pass on their own names. That is why in my book *The Original Theories and Principles of Chinese Philosophy* I have said that these authors must have been those worthy Confucian scholars during the late Chou and Ch'in and Han dynasties, who "hiding themselves from the world were unknown, and yet were without regret," and also that they were the true heroes in a world of chaos and later under the despotism of the Ch'in dynasty.

Aside from these authors, those who participated in the compilation of the *Lü Shih Ch'un Ch'iu* 呂氏春秋 under the Chin and the *Huai Nan Tzu* 准南子 of the early Han dynasty included many Confucians, but they were not known to future generations through historical records. Because of their participation, these books were inevitably colored by Confucianism. These Confucians refused to reveal their own names but were single-mindedly devoted to one idea, to pass on the name and learning of Confucius and to preserve them under the Ch'in and Han dynasties. This testifies to their greatness, and they deserve our admiration. Without them it would have been next to impossible to establish Confucius in such a lofty position. They were just anonymous people among the populace, and obviously cannot be said to have had any actual political power.

Under the despotism of the Ch'in dynasty, its First Emperor Ch'in Shih Huang 秦始皇 ordered the burning of the books and the burying alive of scholars. The first man who dared to stand up and oppose the Ch'in regime was a man called Ch'en She 陳涉, who in the "Ju lin chuan 儒林傳 " of the *Shih Chi* was said to take a fancy to Confucianism. After Ch'en She crowned himself, many scholars of the state of Lu went to serve him with their ritual vessels. And Ch'en She appointed a descendant of Confucius, K'ung Chia 孔甲 , as Erudite 博士 . It is safe to say that at the time Confucian thoughts existed only among the populace.

At first, Kao-tsu, the first emperor of the Han dynasty 漢高祖 did not have a high opinion of the Confucian scholars. But when he passed through the Lu state, he nevertheless paid homage to Confucius by offering the Grand Sacrifice. After he became emperor he began to listen half-heartedly to Lu Ku 陸賈 who advocated benevolence and righteousness in governing the country. But the government of the early Han dynasty applied a mixture of Huang-Lao Taoism and Legalism, and Confucianism did not achieve influence. Tung Chung-shu 董仲舒 composed an article entitled "Hsien-liang Tui-tse" 賢良對策 in which he called upon Emperor Wu of the Han dynasty 漢武帝 "to rectify his sense of righteousness, but not scheme for his profit; to make clear the way, but not to plan for his achievements." This was a check on the desire of the emperor who wanted to get quick returns and to obtain instant results. Although the emperor adopted Tung Chung-shu's proposal and founded the system of the Erudite for the Five Classics and the Disciples of the Erudites, he did not really take any fancy to the Confucian way advocated by Tung Chung-shu. Tung Chung-shu in the "San-tai wen chih kai chih" chapter of Chun Chiu fan lu 春秋繁露 explicity proposed the theory that dynasties must change. As in the theory of the succession of the five virtues 五德

of the Ying-Yang School, when the virtue of one dynasty declined, there would be a new dynasty that would succeed it and flourish. But in origin this is rooted in the concepts of Confucius and Mencius and Hsün Tzu, who were all of the opinion that the country does not belong to any one single person. The dictates of Heaven were inconstant; only those who had the people's support were favored by Heaven. Loyalty should be paid only to those kings who had won the hearts of the populace. Hence, Confucius praised the abdiction of Emperors Yao and Shun, and Mencius and Hsün Tzu praised the revolutions led by Tang and Wu 湯武 Consequently, the ideas of the Ying-Yang School and Tung Chung-shu in this aspect originated with Confucius. Later on, Sui Hung 眭弘 , a disciple of Tung Chung-shu, claimed that in accordance with the teachings of his master "the Han emperor must seek out the sage and hand to him the crown and reduce himself to an earldom of one hundred *li* in size." (See the "Biography of Sui Hung," in *Han Shu* 漢書 . Such thoughts from Tung Chung-shu certainly were not formulated to win favor from the emperors of the Han Dynasty, nor were they devised for the sake of protecting the rule of any one single family.

Emperor Wu of the Han dynasty established a monopoly on the sale of salt and iron by government agencies thereby competing for profits with the common people. After the death of Emperor Wu of the Han dynasty and in the time of Emperor Chao 漢昭帝 and Emperor Hsüan 漢宣帝 some sixty men of letters participated in a great debate with government officials over the policy of the monopolization of salt and iron sales, which is recorded in Huan Kuang's 桓寬 *Discourses on Salt and Iron* 塩鐵論 .

The premises on which these men of letters based their arguments were the Confucian thought of Tung Chung-shu, which stressed the need to look after the interests of the people. They were opposed to the Legalist attitudes of the then chancellor and the grandee secretary who wanted only to increase the wealth of the state but not the wealth of the people. They sought to revoke the law which gave the government the monopoly of the sales of salt and iron, and finally this law was abolished at their insistence. This corroborates that the Confucian thought represented by Tung Chung-shu and the men of letters and the Legalist thought of the high government officials occupied diametrically opposite positions. The former used "reason" to combat the "power" of the high ranking officials. Considering this, how could one possibly believe the assertion of some that the philosophy of Confucianism merely served authoritarian emperors? How could it be possible to say that the reason Tung Chung-shu promoted Confucius was to please the emperors, or to say that the elevation of Confucius originated from Emperor Wu's adoption of Tung Chung-shu's suggestion to honor solely Confucius? Chi An 汲黯 said that the emperor "was greedy inside but on the outside appeared to be dispensing benevolence and justice". How could one then say that the emperor was really in favor of honoring Confucius?

Tung Chung-shu and the men of letters were all in the lower echelons of the political hierarchy and they struggled with the sole purpose of popularizing the teachings of Confucius. Owing to their efforts, the position of Confucius and the position of Confucianism in the Han dynasty rose day by day. More and more Confucian scholars appeared. Finally, Emperor Kuang-wu of the Later Han dynasty 漢光 武 was himself a student of the Imperial University. Consequently he paid even greater homage to Confucianism. In the 13th *Chüan* of the *Jih Chih Lu* 日知錄 by Ku Yen-wu 顧炎武, it is said that the refinement of the customs of the Later Han dynasty can be seen in the popularity of the lectures given by the Confucianists and the appearance of scholars of high principle. This shows the degree of the impact exerted by Confucianism on the political situation of the Han dynasty, and this is also proof that the popularity and success of Confucianism was not a result of the superficial respect Emperor Wu paid to Confucius.

Confucian thought from the time of Confucius, Mencius and Hsün Tzu to the Han dynasty certainly had a very complicated relationship with practical politics. Of course, the Confucian school did not lay the foundation for the practice of democracy nor did conditions in ancient China allow the practice of it. It was the proposal of the Confucians that during peaceful times there must be the distinction in rank between the king and his subjects so that the order and hierarchy of the body politic could thus be maintained. But the ideal of the Confucianists was for men to be ranked socially and politically according to their degree of ability and virtue. If this becomes impossible or the ruler becomes a tyrant, the Confucianists then advocate either abdication or revolution.

Thus, as far as the application of Confucian thought to actual politics is concerned, it is certainly possible that the politicians might make use of the Confucian insistence on the distinction between the ruler and the ruled in order to safeguard their privileges and to maintain the *status quo*. But the abdication theory could also be utilized by demagogues to force the ruler to give up his throne. For instance, starting with the yielding of the Han throne to Wang Mang 王莽, to the "abdication" of the last Han emperor to the Wei dynasty, the "abdication" of the Wei dynasty to the Chin dynasty, and thus on to the transfer of political power through the dynasties of the Five Dynasties, Sung, Chih, Liang, Chen, the seizure of the crown by a subject was all done in the name of abdication in the Confucian style, though in reality it was simply the overthrowing of one dynasty and the establishment of another. Furthermore, the Confucians also upheld the right of the ruled to revolt against the ruler if he fails to act in accordance with righteousness and benevolence. The *Analects* record that when Kung-Shan Fu-Jao 公山弗擾 and Pi Hsi 佛肸 revolted, Confucius wished to visit them. We are at a loss as to the real purpose of Confucius' intended visit but evidently Confucius did not completely disapprove of such political revolts. In the chapter "Anti-Confucianism" in *Mo Tzu* many episodes were recorded of Confucius' disciples revolting against the rulers they served. Ch'en She 陳涉 was a good Confucian who started a revolution.

Political revolutions down to the end of the Ch'ing dynasty were all based on the premise of Mencius' statement that people are important but the king is not. Confucianism together contains three tenets: maintenance of the distinction between the ruler and the ruled, abdication of political power, and revolution. No matter which one you wish to utilize, you can always fall back on the authority of Confucianism. Confucianism refuses to give greater value to either the king, the minister, or the common people. When the king is a good king, the king should be obeyed and when he becomes incompetent, he should give up his throne to a better candidate. If the king becomes a tyrant, the people have the right to put him to death. Confucianism insists only on the "Way" and "virtue" of mankind as the political standard and ideal. Those who wish to take advantage of Confucian concepts—the despotic king who wants to strengthen his rule, the minister who wants to usurp the throne, and the mob that wants to raise a rebellion can all go to Confucius for distorted support. But we are all aware that no matter how good a school of thought is, it is always liable to be misquoted, misused, and distorted. Consequently, the thought passed on by Confucius which has been thus utilized bears no responsibility for this, and Confucius' position is left unshaken by it.

If we really want to understand the process of the formation of Confucius' position in the history and culture of China, we shall have to examine it further from the various perspectives of religious thought, historical studies, literature, and philosophy. Actually, in the broadest sense, the "way of the teacher" in Confucianism comprises religious thought, historical studies, literature, and philosophy. For instance, in the Han dynasty the rise of the reputation of Confucius should be ascribed to the image of Confucius that was found in the *Apochrypha* 緯書. The *Apochrypha* contain a mixture of Confucian thought and the thought of the Ying-Yang School. They display the popular religious thought current among the popular intellectuals during the Han dynasty, but are simply falsely related to Confucius

According to the *Apochrypha* Confucius was a god who was the incarnation of the Dark Emperor of Heaven. When Confucius wrote his *Spring and Autumn Annals* 春秋 , "the sky rained down grains and the ghosts wept at night," and Confucius predicated that the Ch'in dynasty would perish and established the cardinal canons and laws for the benefit of the forthcoming new age. It is on the basis of this popular image that Confucius was esteemed by the Han people as a law-maker.

The apotheosis of Confucius in the *Apochrypha* resembles the apotheosis of Jesus Christ in the *New Testament,* and both occurred about two thousand years ago. But at first Jesus Christ was apotheosized as a redeemer, not a judge of sinners. Jesus Christ would become a judge of sinners only with the Second Coming. In the *Apochrypha* Confucius was deified as a sacred judge passing sentence on momentous events in history and politics; he was not a mere judge of personal sins. That Confucius was defied and was raised to a pedestal higher even than that of the worldly king resulted from the homage the common people paid to him. This resembles again the deification of Jesus Christ who was honored as the King of Kings, and this could not have been accomplished unless the common people wished it to be so.

If allowed to develop in the direction indicated in the *Apochrypha,* Confucianism could have developed into a religion. But in a spirit typical of Chinese humanism, Chinese scholars could not swallow the diefied Confucius of the *Apochrypha* which were criticized as works of superstition and devilry by scholars like Chang Heng 張衡 and Huan Tan 桓譚 , and especially in the detailed criticism of Wang Chung 王充 . But the image in the *Apochrypha* of "Confucius as a judge of history and political events" was accepted universally by the historians and the scholars specializing in the *Spring and Autumn Annals.* As a result of this the study of the three commentaries on the *Spring and Autumn Annals* flourished, Confucius became the "uncrowned king" 素王 who had the power to "castigate emperors, judge history, and reprimand grandees," and such unprecedented historians such as Ssuma Ch'ien 司馬遷 and Pan Ku 班固 appeared.

There was no scholar during the Han dynasty who would oppose to Confucius. The specialists in the classics considered the Six Classics handed down by Confucius as sacred documents. But the one who really appreciated and comprehended the spirit and personality of Confucius and paid him appropriate homage was, in my opinion, Ssu-ma Ch'ien 司馬遷 . Ssu-ma Ch'ien in his *Shih Chi* 史記 established Confucius as a "Hereditary Family" 世家 . Later scholars who criticized this were not few. Confucius' "Hereditary Family" is not the same as the other "Hereditary Families". It was a "Hereditary Family" formed from passing down a heritage of culture and learning. Confucius could not be included in the "Basic Annals" 本記 because he was not a king or an emperor, and therefore he could not be treated as one. A king or an emperor was the political leader of a certain age and he was limited to an age. To treat Confucius as a "Hereditary Family" is to imply that Confucius is a man for all ages and makes clear his enduring significance. Ssu-ma Ch'ien composed the *Shih Chi* in imitation of Confucius' *Spring and Autumn Annals,* for it was also his intention to pass sound judgements upon historical figures by means of the different styles and forms which he used to describe them. In the "Preface" to the *Shih Chi* Ssu-ma Ch'ien said, "My predecessor's (i.e. his father Ssu-ma Tan) said, "After the demise of Duke Chou five hundred years passed, at the end of which Confucius appeared. Since the demise of Confucius it has been five hundred years. Is there a period which is able to continue this illustrious heritage and rectity the *Commentaries to the I Ching,* extend the *Spring and Autumn Annals,* and make fundamental the *Book of Odes* 詩, the *Book of Documents* 書 , the *Book of Rites* 禮 , and the

Book of Music 樂 ? Here was his intention! Here was his intention ! How dare this lowly son abdicate it? " Mencius said, "Every five hundred years there emerges a great king." Ssu-ma Ch'ien argued with Emperor Wu of the Han dynasty 漢武帝 on behalf of Li Lin 李陵 and was thrown into jail and was punished with castration. His anger at Emperor Wu can be discerned in his letter addressed to Jen An任安Thus Emperor Wu did not meet Ssu-ma Ch'ien's ideal of a king. A great king did not emerge but what emerged at the time was a great work, the *Shih Chi*, which was sufficient to inherit the next five hundred year revolution after Confucius. This was the ambition of Ssu-ma Ch'ien. The *Shih Chi* became the model for all later historical works. And Ssu-ma Ch'ien realized his ambition to continue the work of Confucius and to pay homage to Confucius by writing the *Shih Chi*.

Years later, Pan Ku felt dissatisfied with the respect Ssu-ma Ch'ien had paid to hermits and knights-errant, and he focussed all his reverence upon Confucius and made use of Confucius' doctrines as a standard for evaluating the various pre-Ch'in thinkers. The position of Confucius was thus elevated even higher and further confirmed through the united forces of Ssu-ma Ch'ien and Pan Ku. Hence, all the future historians would not dare to detract from Confucius. Today while we are examining the formation of Confucius' position in Chinese history and culture, we must not neglect the contribution of these historians.

IV. Confucius as a sage to the metaphysicians in the period of the Wei and Chin dynasties, the position of Confucius in. Buddhism, and Confucius as an object of veneration to the men of letters from the period of the Wei and Chin dynasties to the period of Sui and T'ang dynasties

From the period of the Wei 魏 and Chin 晋 dynasties to the period of the Northern and Southern dynasties 南北朝 and the Sui 隋 and T'ang 唐 dynasties classical and historical learning merely took over the results of what was achieved during the Han and little new development was made. From the purely intellectual viewpoint, this was an unprecedented period for Neo-Taoism 玄學 and Buddhism. In the area of general culture, this was a period of literature, arts, and religion, the efflorescence of which again was unprecedented. Generally speaking, the Neo-Taoists engaged in pure discussions 清談 about Lao Tzu and

Chuang Tzu, while the Buddhists merely worshipped their Buddha.

We must not forget, however, that the Neo-Taoists during the Wei and Chin period such as Ho Yen 何晏 Wang Pih 王弼 , and Kuo Hsiang 郭象 , though specialists and devotees of Lao Tzu and Chuang Tzu, still venerated Confucius as the standard of a sage. Lao Tzu and Chuang Tzu only triumphed in their theory of "nothingness" 虛無 In the chapter entitled "Refined Learning" in the *Shih shuo hsin yü* 世說新語 Wang Pih says, "The sage is bodiless, but without a body it is hard to establish a model; therefore, the sage has to insist on substance. Lao Tzu and Chuang Tzu cannot help ignoring substance, and they constantly point out the insufficiency of substance." That is to say, Lao Tzu and Chuang Tzu spoke of "nothingness", but recognized "nothingness" is not enough to explain everything in the world. Kuo Hsiang admired Chuang Tzu most highly in his preface to Chuang Tzu but he also remarked that Chuang Tzu "failed to conceal his wild words." That is to say Chuang Tzu failed to reach the level where the sage, having arrived at the highest degree of wisdom, becomes speechless. Hence, one could "speak wildly" and could become "the head of the one hundred schools". But being the foremost in the one hundred schools is still being just one of the one hundred schools.

In the eyes of the Neo-Taoists of the Wei-Chin period, the concept of Confucius as a sage was naturally different from the Confucius as a sage in *Apochrypha* or in the minds of the classicists and historians in the Han dynasty. But we cannot say that Confucius' personality and spirit definitely had none of the aspects sought by the Neo-Taoists. Confucius himself had said, "Empty as empty could be." Again, "I am speechless." Again, "What could Heaven say? The four seasons rotate in order, and the hundreds of things spring and grow. What could Heaven say? " These are surely the Neo-Taois, ideal conditions of the sage of "bodilessness" and "alive, but in a state of non-being." Therefore, we cannot say that the Neo-Taoists had nothing that was compatible with Confucius' thought. The principles discussed by the Neo-Taoists were often based on Lao Tzu and Chuang Tzu. But when they discoursed on the conditions of the sage, they took Confucius as the standard. This, we should all take note of.

Certainly, the Neo-Taoism which originally discussed principles is a philosophy. The greatness of these Neo-Taoist philosophers lies in that while dwelling on philosophy and "dark learning" 玄學 they were conscious that a sage like Confucius was above their own level and the state of a sage is neither a philosophy nor "dark learning." Therefore, the Neo-Taoists, such as Fan Ning 范寧 and others, dwelled on their metaphysics and neglected state affairs by losing themselves in "pure conversation." But they still put Confucius above Lao Tzu and Chuang Tzu, we cannot say that they revolted against Confucius.

Thus, we can see that the Neo-Taoists knew the sagehood of Confucius was above all their abstruse speculations, and they nevertheless recognized that have the merit of raising Confucius to an even higher position.

After the introduction of Buddhism into China, it naturally became another stream of learning and religion. It also stirred up some conflict and turmoil with indigenous Chinese learning and religion. Conflict between Buddhism and Taoism was especially frequent. But Buddhism in its initial period in India opposed the traditional religion and culture in that country, and finally it was rejected by the people of India. When Buddhism was first introduced into China, it did not adopt an attitude of opposition and disparagement of Chinese tradition of learning and culture. This is rather like when Christianity arose in the West, it revolted against Judaism and fought against the religion and philosphy of Greece and Rome and the Muslims, but when it came to China at the end of the Ming dynasty, though it was opposed to the "Li hsüeh 理學 " or Neo-Confucian philosophy of the Sung and Ming dynasties, Christianity still attached itself to ancient Confucian orthodoxy. Upon its arrival, Indian Buddhism was gradually absorbed and assimilated by the Chinese and it became sinicized.

This is a long story and we do not have time to dwell on it. In short, the first man who was able to comprehend and absorb the true essence of Buddhism and was able to express what he knew in native Chinese in systematic discourse was Seng-chao 僧肇 . In the eyes of Seng-chao there was no difference in the saintly states of Confucius, Lao Tzu, Chuang Tzu, and the Buddha. Therefore, in his books, he constantly made use of the remarks of Confucius, Lao Tzu, and Chuang Tzu to explicate and expound the concepts of Buddhism. It was only later that Chi-tsang 吉藏 and Chih-i 智顗 began to disparage Lao Tzu and Chuang Tzu. But with regard to the five basic human relations designated by Confucianism, Chih-i pointed out in the sixth volume of Mo-ko chih-kuan 摩訶止觀 that these resembled the five abstinences of the Buddhists. Later on, in the *Family Instructions of the Yen Clan* 顏氏家訓 Yen Chih-t'ui 顏之推 said the same thing. In the first volume of *Wei mo chieh ching (Vimalakirti-sutra) hsüan-shu* 維摩 詰經玄疏 and in the Ching-chin fa-hsing-ching 清淨法行經 Chih-i said that Confucius was the incarnation of the Mahayana Bodhisattva 大乘菩薩 and that he was sent by Buddha to China to prepare the way for Buddhism by the introduction of propriety and righteousness. Later, in the Hua Yen School's 華嚴宗 *Hua yen shu ch'ao* 華嚴疏抄 and in Kuei Feng's 圭峯 *Yuan chio ching shu ch'ao* 圓覺經疏抄 remarks from the Confucian classics were frequently quoted to expound the Buddhist tenets. For example, *Cheng-kuang Shu Ch'ao* 澄觀疏抄 used the Way of Heaven of the *I Ching* to illustrate the "right awakening," used the Way of Man to illustrate "having feelings," and used the Way of the Earth to illustrate "the human world." The preface of Kuei Feng's *Yüan chio ching shu ch'ao* quoted from the *I ching,* "The great, the penetrating, the advantageous and the correct constitute the virtue of *Chien (乾)* to provide an illustrative parellel to "Constant joy and purity of the self constitute the virtue of the Buddha."

In the Sung dynasty, the monk Chih yüan 智圓 of the Tien-t'ai sect 天台宗 called himself "the man of the golden mean" and he advocated equal propagation for Confucianism and Buddhism. And the monk Chi-sung 契嵩 wrote systematic works about Confucianism. Tsung-kao 宗杲 of the Zen sect 禪宗 in the Sung dynasty regretted the decline of Confucianism and hoped that the Buddhists would do what they could to revitalize Confucianism. Teh-ch'ing 德淸 and Chih-hsü 智旭 also two monks, at the end of the Ming dynasty annotated *The Doctrine of the Mean* ("chung-yung") and *I Ching* in order to show that Buddhism and Confucianism originated from the same source, and this harked back to the ideas of Seng-chao.

Of course in the mind of the Buddhists the first place went to Buddha while the second place was reserved for Confucius, the same as with the Taoists, who gave the first place to Lao Tzu and the second place to Confucius.

After Christianity was introduced into China during the period between the end of the Ming dynasty and the beginning of the Ch'ing dynasty, the Christians gave the first place to Jesus Christ and again the second place to Confucius. The Confucianists might look askance at this kind of ranking, but they should accept it and enjoy it. Certainly, it is only natural that Buddhists should regard Buddha as the foremost, Taoists should regard Lao Tzu as the foremost, and Christians should regard Christ as the foremost. To them, of course, Confucius was but a guest, and the guest naturally has to be given the second place. But Buddhists and Taoists mutually excluded each other and refused to coexist. After its arrival in the Ming-Ch'ing period, Christianity excluded both Buddhism and Taoism. Buddhism and Taoism considered Christianity to be heretical. To put Christianity in the position of a heresy is not the same as to place it in a secondary position. Only Confucius always occupies the second place in any religion in China, next only to the lord of that religion.

In Confucius' given name, Chung-ni 仲尼 , Chung means in Chinese "the second". Some of today's superficial and vulgar men of letters used the term "K'ung lao-erh" 孔老二 (the second brother K'ung) to insult Confucius, but this actually cannot insult Confucius. This second place that Confucius occupies is to be found throughout Chinese religion, and this allows all these religions to co-exist in Chinese culture. Thus Confucius in Chinese culture and history still occupies the first place. Therefore, the second place they assigned to Confucius in their own religions, a place second only to the place they assigned to the lords of their own religion, helps to confirm the central position that Confucius occupies in Chinese history and culture. Taking it in such a perspective, a Confucian should not regret the second place assigned to Confucius in Taoism and Buddhism ever since the rise of these religions in China during the Wei-Chin period, the Southern and Northern dynasties and the Sui-T'ang period.

This should not be construed as a downgrading of Confucius. The followers of Confucius should have this magnanimity and tolerance so that whenever they are in the temple of Buddhism, the shrine of Taoism, or the church of Christianity, Confucians should regard themselves as guests and let the Taoists, the monks, and the priests and ministers to act as masters. It is also in consonance with Confucian propriety to take the second place in somebody else's house. This is the way to exhibit one aspect of Confucianism which stresses that "different ways could proceed in parallel and would not collide" and that "nothing is not contained." Furthermore, we must know that it is exactly because of this magnanimity and tolerance that Confucius has been able to rank the first in Chinese history and culture. Followers of Confucius should be grateful to the Buddhists, Taoists, and Christians who give Confucius the place of the guest of honor, second only to their own masters.

The fame and brilliance of the Wei-Chin, Southern and Northern dynasties and the Sui-T'ang period is found in its Neo-Taoism and Buddhism. The traditional study of classics and Confucianism in this period had substance but no brilliance, and nothing was contributed to raising the historical position of Confucius. During this long period, the emperors and kings did not particularly favor or honor Confucianism, and the T'ang emperors especially honored Taoism and Buddhism. Meanwhile, there were men of letters—writers and critics—who showed profound deference to Confucius. An example is the great critic and author of *The Literary Mind and the Carving of Dragons* 文心雕龍 , *Liu Hsieh* 劉勰

, Liu Hsieh left home (he lived with a monk) to become a Confucian and worte *The Literary Mind and the Carving of Dragons.* This work occupies the same position in Chinese literary criticism as *Shih Chi* by Ssu-ma Ch'ien does in history. Ssu-ma Ch'ien was five hundred years later than Confucius and he intended to continue the tradition of Confucius by writing a great historical work. Liu Hsieh came five hundred years after Ssu-ma Ch'ien, and it was his ambition to develop the heritage of Confucius by writing this great piece of literary criticism. Of course, some of his literary ideas were taken from Taoism and Buddhism. However, the first chapters in the book, "Yuan Tao 原道 ," "Chêng Sheng 徵聖 ," "Tsung Ching 宗經 ," and the concluding chapter "Shu Chih 述志 " and the main contents of the entire book convince us that the book was intended as a continuation of the teachings on poetry and music. Therefore, in the chapter "Shu Chih" Liu Hsieh said of himself, "When over thirty years of age, I dreamed I had in my hand the painted and lacquered ceremonial vessels and was following Confucius and travelling toward the south." Again, he said, "As a matter of fact, the function of "wen chang", or literary writing, is an offshoot of the function of the Classics" (Dr. Vincent Shih's translation). Thus, Liu Hsieh exerted himself to the utmost in the writing of this book for his ambition was to inherit the tradition first established by Confucius.

Poets and essayists who paid homage to Confucius include such great writers as T'ao Yuan-ming 陶淵明 , Ch'en Tzu-ang 陳子昂 , Li

Po 李白 , Tu Fu 杜甫 , and Han Yü 韓愈 , In the poetry of Li Po and T'ao Yuan-ming, sentiments and thoughts of Taoism abound. And Li Po wrote, "I was originally a wild man from Ch'u and I sang wildly and laughed at Confucius." But the following lines are from T'ao Yuan-ming: "In the wilderness human affairs are scarce, good chance for me to wander and explore in the Six Classics"; "The ancient master has instructed us to worry about the way but not about poverty." The ancient master referred here is Confucius. In another poem, T'ao Yuan-ming wrote,

> Fu-hsi and Shen-nung left us long ago,
> In the entire world few have restored their truth.
> Anxiously, anxiously that venerable man of Lu
> Filled and patched to make it pure.
> Though no phoenix came,
> Briefly the rites and music were renewed.
> Between the Chu and Ssu streams his subtle teachings ended,
> Drifting until the reckless Ch'in.
> What crime had the *Odes* and *Documents*
> That in one morning they should be turned to ashes?

This proves that the man he admired most was Confucius and he greatly lamented the burning of the *Book of Odes and Book of Documents* by the harsh Ch'in dynasty. Therefore, T'ao Yuan-ming also has a poem about Ching K'o regretting that he did not succeed in assasinating the First Emperor of Ch'in, "Although the man is long dead after a thousand years he moves us still."

Li Po in his old-styled poetry intended to revive the style and mode of *Shih Ching* 詩經 and *Li Sao* 離騷 , and the first poem goes like this:

> The great *ya* 雅 has laid in dust for a long time,
> And to whom should I complain about its decline?
> The pattern of the kingly rule is cluttered in the weeds,
> And the warring states are now but thorns and bushes.
> The dragon and the tiger eat each other up,
> And warfare continued until the reckless Ch'in.

The line expressing his hatred for the Ch'in dynasty was derived from T'ao Yuan-ming. At the end of the same poem Li Po writes.

> My ambition is to delete and to express,
> To pass down brightness for a thousand springs.
> If the desire for the sage can become a reality,
> I shall relinquish my pen upon the obtaining of the sacred beast

Here we can see that his intention to renew the style of *Shih Ching* and *Li Sao* lies in his wish to become an heir of Confucius.

Then came Ch'en Tzu-ang of whom Yao Hsüan 姚鉉 said in the *T'ang Wen Ts'ui* 唐文粹 "The T'ang dynasty ruled the country for three hundred years by means of humanistic principles, but only upon the rise of Ch'en Tzu-ang, did the styles of the *Feng* 風 and the *Ya* 雅 in *Shih Ching* become revitalized." He wrote 38 poems commonly entitled "On Times and Opportunities 感遇詩 ", which expressed his yearning and ambition, the last poem of which begins, "Confucius sent his voice into the very beginnings and the source of transformation, and the dark and shadowy are in harmony with the sunny and peaceful," which reveals where his intentions lay. Tu Fu who came later, was generally recognized as a sage of poetry, and his poetry expresses the sentiments of a Confucian scholar. He clearly and explicitly asserted that "the dandy will not die of starvation, but the cap of the scholar will often ruin one's person." Tu Fu called himself, "a worthless scholar between Heaven and Earth." When he wrote poetry, "he only knew how to sing loudly to make the ghosts and spirits weep, how could he knew starving to death and leaving his body in the gutter? " "His ambition was to follow the steps of Confucius in order to bring about a ruler who surpassed Yao and Shun, so that the customs will become pure again." Han Yü's essay revitalized a prose writing tradition which had gone flaccid in the previous eight generations. He wrote a prose work, "Tracing the Origin 原道 ," in order to criticize Buddhism and Taoism so that the doctrines of Confucius could be extended.

T'ao Yüan-ming, Ch'en Tzu-ang, Li Po, and Tu Fu differ from Mencius', Hsun Tzu's and Tung Chung-shu's use of philosophy and classical learning, and from Ssu-ma Ch'ien's use of history, and from Liu Hsieh's use of literary criticism in continuing the tradition of Confucius. T'ao Yüan-ming and Tu Fu became heirs to Confucius because they found congenial the pure and honest nature of Confucius. Ch'en Tzu-ang and Li Po were attracted by Confucius' work in re-establishing the style of the *feng* and *ya Odes* so that they also tried to be his heirs.

Han Yü's criticism of Buddhism and Taoism did not attain in intellectual substance to any impressive level. But the monks, nuns, and Taoists were so numerous in those days and they all lived upon the fat of the land without doing anything constructive or productive, so the people throughout the empire became impoverished. In face of such a situation, he had the courage, in the midst of universal adulation for Buddhism and Taoism, to request the Hsien Tsung Emperor of the T'ang dynasty 唐憲宗 not to greet a relic bone of the Buddha, but he was sent into exile because of this. Han Yü wrote a letter to the Minister Meng 孟尚書, saying about his opposition to Buddhism, "Even if I were to be killed ten thousand times, I would not go back on my conviction." Thus, since "Confucius succeeded to the way of Yao, Shun, Yu, T'ang, Wen and Wu," Han Yü looked upon him as the successor to the same tradition and as a propagator of the same heritage.

We may say that the philosophers, classicists, and others of the Confucian school failed to make the way of Confucius shine and prevail from the Wei-Chin period to the Sui and T'ang dynasties. But the "literati" or men of letters displayed a profound intuition into the personality and spirit of Confucius and they used their literary works to express their memory of and honor for Confucius in order to maintain Confucius's traditional position.

V. The rise of the Confucians from the populace in order to maintain world order and the confirmation of Confucius' position as the foremost sage and the foremost teacher in the Sung and Ming dynasties

Confucianism passed through the Sui and T'ang dynasties and the Five Dynasties without much fanfare, but it underwent its first renaissance in the Sung and Ming dynasties. This renaissance was not completely due to the efforts of the Emperor T'ai Tsu 太祖 and Emperor T'ai Tsung 太宗 of the Sung dynasty who decreed certain political measures to promote the cult of Confucius. The renaissance of Confucianism during the Sung dynasty has to be ascribed, as the scholarly records from the Sung and Yuan dynasties indicate, to the enthusiasts who rose from the masses. These Confucian enthusiasts such as Sun Ming-fu 孫明復, Shih Chieh 石介, and Hu An-ting 胡安定 lectured constantly on the learning and teachings of Confucius. These scholars came some 1500 years after Confucius and had no political prospects or positions; they were only poor scholars who lectured upon Confucianism among the common people.

Later on, Confucianists such as Fan Chung-yen 范仲淹 and Ou-Yang Hsiu 歐陽修 rose from the peasantry to become ministers at

court and they are to be given the credit of providing encouragement
to the Confucianists. But we should all know that in the first years
of the Northern Sung dynasty, a majority of high ranking officials
such as Yang I 楊億, Lü Yi-chien 呂夷簡 , and Han Ch'ih-kuo 韓持國
believed in Buddhism. Ou-Yang Hsiu composed an article entitled
"On the Origin 本論 " and said that "Buddhism is popular and strong,
and it is difficult to combat it. All we can do is first make our principles
clear. Once our principles are established it will be unnecessary to
combat it..." From then on, scholars like Chou Lien-hsi 周濂溪 ,
Chang Hêng-chü 張橫渠 , Ch'eng Ming-tao 程明道 and Ch'eng Yi-
ch'uan 程伊川 were spurred to elucidate Confucianism. Chou .Lien-
hsi was a hermit who lived in the mountains and was unknown to
the world. It was in Chu Hsi's 朱熹 *Lien-hsi hsien-sheng hsiang tsan*
濂溪先生像贊 that he was then honored as the "first prophet" after
the "way of Confucianism had been lost for over one thousand years."
And now he was revered as the dean of Sang and Ming Neo-Confucianism. Chang Heng-chü said in his essay "Cheng meng chien ch'eng" 正蒙
乾稱 , "A learning which was born one thousand and five hundred years
ago is now in the shadow of the rampant Buddhism....unless the man is
dedicated and self-confident and has super-human talent, how could
he stand in their midst and compare with them the right and wrong,
the strengths and failings [of that learning and Buddhism.]"

Erh-ch'eng i-shu 二程遺書 records Ch'eng Ming-tao as saying,
"The meeting yesterday talked nothing but Buddhism and this made
one feel pretty unhappy. After returning home, I was disappointed
about it for a long time. Buddhism has become the most popular
topic in the world nowadays. How can one turn back this trend? .....
I myself have little talent and am poor in virtue, and there is nothing
I can do about it. But the present situation has become so bad that even
if we had several Menciuses we could hardly make any headway."
Ch'eng Ming-tao again complained in the same work, "The way of
man has been abandoned .....Between Heaven and Earth human beings
are completely isolated." These remarks render very clear the mood
of Ch'eng Ming-tao at the time. After his death, Ch'eng Yi-ch'uan
wrote on his epitaph, "Mister Ch'eng Ming-tao after 1,400 years
obtained the untransmitted learning [of Confucius] from the surviving
classics. He is the only one in the past one thousand years." This
is not an intentional exaggeration of the importance of Ch'eng Ming-
tao. It is Ch'eng Yi-ch'uan's lamenting the Buddhists who "claim

that they have exhausted the ultimate and comprehended the mystery of changes, while in fact they do not have the ability to explore the material world in order to achieve great enterprises. They say that they are comprehensive and nothing goes beyond their grasp, but they put themselves outside of human ethical relations." Again he said, "if the way of the sage fails to prevail, a hundred generations will not witness a good government. If the learning of the sage is not transmitted, then for a thousand year's there will be no true scholar." All these can serve as evidence for the herculean job Chang, the Ch'engs, and others had on their hands in reviving Confuciansim. Agaiñ we can also see that their restoration of Confucianism was a heroic action they undertook when no one else would.

Chang Heng-chü lectured only in Kuan Chung 關中 . The two Ch'engs were court officials but they were pushed out by Wang An-shih 王安石 . Later on, Chu Hsi 朱熹 inherited the scholarship of Chou Lien-hsi, Chang Heng-chü, Ch'eng Ming-tao, and Ch'eng Yi-ch'uan, but his scholarship was rejected by Han T'o-chou 韓侂冑 as false. The two Ch'engs and Chu Hsi were all unsuccessful in political careers, and as teachers at first they had very few students. This line of scholarship passed from one generation of scholars to another through the Yüan dynasty to the founding of the Ming dynasty when the first emperor, Chu Yuan-chang 朱元璋 , made the works of Chu Hsi the texts on which examinations to select government officials were formulated. But of course once Chu Hsi's books were made examination materials, his school became the door to fame and fortune, which was unfortunate for Chu Hsi. Consequently, during the Ming dynasty the vital and active Confucianism had to be found in such scholars as Ch'en Pai-sha 陳白沙 and Wang Yang-ming 王陽明 , who were closer to the school of Lu Hsiang-shan 陸象山.

Ch'en Pai-sha's master was Wu Kang-chai 吳康齋 , who just like the three scholars at the beginning of the Sung Dynasty, Sun Ming-fu, Shih Chieh and Hu An-ting, was a poor scholar living among the masses without any official affiliation Ch'en Pai-sha while a student at Wu's house had to go with his master to the paddy fields to till and to plant, and there is a story that Ch'en cut his hand while reaping. The teacher of Wang Yang-ming's early years, Lou Liang 婁諒 , was also educated by Wu Kang-chai. Wang Yang-ming was able to attain high official position, but he became aware of the principle of intuitive to knowledge earlier white he was in exile at Lung ch'ang 龍場 and his life was precarious. The school of Confucianism in the Ming dynasty ended with the Tung-lin school 東林學派 , of which scholars like Ku Hsien-ch'en 顧憲成, Kao Pan-lung 高攀龍 , Liu Chi-shan 劉蕺山 , Fang I-chih 方以智 , Huang Tao-chou 黃道周 , and Chang Huang-yen 張煌言 all died as martyrs for their moral principles. That Sung and Ming Confucianism could become the main stream for hundreds of years of Chinese learning and culture has to be credited to the struggles and sacrifices of these Confucians. The emperors of the Sung and Ming dynasties mostly believed in Taoism, and the high ranking officials mostly believed in Buddhism. Hence, it is evident that the position Confucianism was able to achieve during that period has to be ascribed to the efforts of those scholars who lived as common people and who lectured among common people. All this is supported by history.

The Confucius of the Sung and Ming Confucians was not the "uncrowned king" of Han dynasty, nor the "bodiless sage" of Ho Yen 何晏 , Wang Pi 王弼, and Kuo Hsiang 郭象. He was even less the incarnation of Buddha of the early Chinese Buddhists in the Wei-Chin period, and he was not the same as the Confucius of T'ao Yuan-ming, Li Po, and Tu Fu. In the eyes of Sung and Ming Confucians, Confucius was a sage who taught mankind to emulate great men and sages. It was because of the efforts of the Sung and Ming scholars that Confucius' position as the foremost sage and grand teacher in Chinese history was recognized and established. Thus, the emperors of Ming and Ching dynasties followed suit and would no longer give Confucius the title of "king of letters" but canonized him as the "foremost sage and grand teacher." As for those martyrs at the end of the Sung and the Ming dynasties, Wen T'ien-hsiang 文天祥 and the scholars of the Tung-lin school, Confucius was not only the foremost sage and the foremost teacher but a resolute man of principle who would rather die than compromise.

The image of Confucius in the Sung and Ming dynasties as the foremost sage and the grand teacher focussed on his function as a teacher of mankind and his establishment of a complete program of ethical education. This is different from the image of Confucius in the eyes of the Confucians during the Ch'in and Han dynasties who looked upon Confucius as the "uncrowned king" who composed the *Spring and Autumn Annals* to pass judgments on villainous officials and tyrannical kings or who laid down laws for the benefit of the people. This is also different from the Confucius in the *Apochrypha* 緯書 and in the eyes of the scholars in the Han dynasty, who took Confucius as a sage sent down by Heaven and was beyond the imitation of ordinary people. The Sung and Ming scholars revered Confucius as a great personality whose learning and virtues were still within the reach of the common people who, if they exerted themselves, would be able to imitate him. For instance, Chou Lien-hsi said "The scholar emulates the virtuous person, the virtuous person emulates the sage, and the sage emulates Heaven." The two Ch'eng's strongly believed that "It is truly possible to learn to become a sage." Confucius the sage to the scholars was a teacher, and the student's learning may someday ascend to the level of his teacher. Therefore, all learners in the world can become sages and resemble Confucius. This is also why Mencius said that "everybody can become either a Yao 堯 or a Shun 舜," and Hsün Tzu 荀子 said, "The man on the road can become a Yü 禹." On what grounds were they able to make such assertions? Because, according to the Sung and Ming scholars, any common person or any common scholar shared with Confucius the same heart, the same mind, the same nature, and the same reason.

From the renaissance of Confucianism in the first years of Sung dynasty, five hundred years elapsed until the appearance of Wang Yang-ming, who again preceded us by five hundred years. It was the popular belief that everybody had the inborn conscience and shared with the sage the same heart and the same human nature. Thus, it was only reasonable to conclude that everybody had the potential to turn himself into another Confucius. We can say that in the depth of every human heart there is the embryo of a Confucius. Wang Yang-ming had a line of verse, "Every heart cherishes Confucius." The reason that he said this is not difficult to find, for he pointed out clearly that the innate knowledge and the heart and nature of any common person were equal to and as precious as those of Confucius.

On the other hand, by saying this he also anchored the position of Confucius deep in every human heart. We do not have to think that Confucius was a born sage and that he was a sage in the remote past. All we should think is that Confucius lives at this very moment in the intuition, heart, and nature of every human being. If we look into ourselves, we shall find him there. It was due to such a recognition and a faith in Confucius that disciples of Wang Yang-ming in the last years of the Ming dynasty were able to display great heroism and sublimity. Finally, the members of the Tung-lin school such as Liu Chi-shen, etc., had iron shoulders to carry the Way and the principles of Confucius, and they were not afraid to die for their principles.

VI. The position of Confucius in learning and culture in the Ch'ing dynasty, the flood of theories denigrating Confucius in the last years of the Ch'ing and the fallacies of these theories.

The cultural position of Confucius in the Ch'ing dynasty was again different from that in the Sung and Ming dynasties. The scholars of Ch'ing dynasty frowned upon the practice of the Ming dynasty scholars who tended to indulge in discourses on human heart and human nature and who disliked scholastic studies; as a result, the Ch'ing dynasty scholars laid strong emphasis on research in classics and historical documents, and in their scholarly efforts, they went back to the classicists in the Han dynasty for models. Confucius said that he himself loved the past and was diligent in examining it; so, when we study Confucius we also ought to love the past and be diligent in examining it. Moreover, we ought not overlook the fruits of the textual and critical studies of the classics and histories. For these are also the transmitters of the spirit of Confucius' love for the past and examination of it. This, in sum, is the position Confucius occupied in Ch'ing learning.

Now, if we were to express this somewhat differently, Confucius occupied a position in the culture of Ch'ing dynasty that was unprecedented in the history of China. First, the K'ang Hsi 康熙, Yung Chen 雍正 and Ch'ien Lung 乾隆, emperors of the Ch'ing were perhaps the most scholarly of all the emperors of China, and they surpassed their predecessors in appreciating the value of Confucius and in honoring him, whom they placed above Buddha and Lao Tzu. At the beginning K'ang Hsi was very much interested in the natural science introduced by the Catholic priests from the West; however, he adamantly expelled those priests when Rome prohibited Catholic converts from paying homage to their ancestors and to Confucius. This is admirable. The emperors in the early period of the Ch'ing dynasty honored Confucius as their teacher and called themselves Confucius' students. This certainly helped in raising the position of Confucius. But the emperors of Ch'ing were Manchus and in their rule of the Han people, they did not want Han Chinese talking about nationalism. As a result, more than once they put men of letters in prison thereby doing harm to the world of learning. The Yung Chen emperor of the Ch'ing dynasty wrote *Ta i chio mi lu* 大義覺迷錄 as a retort to Tseng Ching's 曾靜 concept, inherited from his master Lu Liu-liang 呂留良 , of "distinguishing between the Han people and the barbarians." Yung Chen chose to stress the Confucian cultural concept that "when the barbarian lives in China, he is a Chinese". But he tried deliberately to suppress the national sentiment of Confucius, "The Han peoples are the inner races while the barbarians are the outer races."

The Yung Chen emperor centralized all political and religious power in himself and where his power prevailed, his "principles" prevailed. And with his power, his "principles" gagged the mouths of the empire. This was the greatest wrong any generation of Confucian scholars had ever suffered and the Chinese intellectuals no longer dared to stick out their necks to determine the correctness or falsity of real "principles." Consequently, the scholars during this period had no choice but to bury themselves in historical research and philological studies. The Way of Confucius was to be found now only in the objective and detached documents, which required lifelong work from the scholars. Thus, scholars no longer dared to assume his Way as their own, and even less did they dare believe as had the scholars of the Sung and Ming dynasties that everybody had the potential to imitate and to become a sage like Confucius, or that "Confucius was in the heart of everyone. The Way of Confucius existed only in detached and objective historical documents, and he was merely a sage who lived and taught two thousand years ago. Unless the study of the records was complete, Confucius' Way could be admired, but not approached and Confucius' personality could be admired at a distance but was impossible to reach. Confucius belonged to the remote past, and thus did not exist in the human heart but was far away on the horizon.

After the middle period of the Ch'ing dynasty, the Taiping Rebellion led by Hung Hsiu-chüan 洪秀全 and Yang Hsiu-ch'ing 楊秀清 occurred. Yang and Hung's impetus to revolt was based on the racial consciousness of the Han Chinese. However, unable to attach themselves to traditional Chinese culture, Hung and Yang turned

to Christianity for inspiration. They denied Confucius in the name
of the Christian God and considered the Six Classics to be books of
wickedness which they burned together with the temples of Confucius.
At the time, such scholars as Tseng Kuo-fan 曾國藩 and Lo Tse-nan
羅澤南 all versed in the classics and believers in Confucianism, trained
troops in the countryside which they used against Hung and Yang. It
should be noted, however, that Tseng Kuo-fan in his call to attack Hung
and Yang did not mention loyalty to the Ch'ing dynasty. He only said
that the rebellion raised by Hung and Yang "had swept away all the
ethical practices from China. This is not only a drastic change in our
great Ch'ing dynasty, but is also the greatest displacement of the
teachings of the sages since the beginning of this country. This certainly
would make our Confucius and Mencius weep in their graves. How can
any literate man put his hands in his sleeves and look on without
thinking of taking some action to rectify this situation....."

No matter what criticism might subsequently be directed at Tseng
Kuo-fan, at least it is clear that he and his comrades on their own trained
troops in the countryside in order to chastise Hung and Yang. He did this
solely for the sake of protecting the cultural heritage of ethics and
education established by Confucius, and he emerged from the populace
and courageously took up in his hands the destiny of the country.
The Confucius in this atmosphere was utterly different from the Confucius in the eyes of the historical researchers in the early years of
the Ch'ing dynasty. The Confucius who "would weep bitterly in the
grave" was the Confucius who lived in the heart of Tseng Kou-fan.
Only such a Confucius could move educated men and cause them to
unite and take up arms to suppress the revolt of Hung and Yang.

During the reign of the Ch'ien Lung and Chia Ching 嘉慶
emperors, the great historian Chang Hsüeh-ch'êng 章學誠 , was of the
opinion that it was Duke Chou 周公 who embodied the total learning
of antiquity. Therefore, in his opinion Duke Chou was the foremost
sage, and Confucius was only the grand teacher, for he merely
transmitted the Six Classics which constituted the laws and policies
of the former kings. His main interest was in teaching and education
and he himself left nothing in writing to posterity. During the period
of the Tao Kuang 道光 and Hsien Feng 咸豐 emperors, the Old Text
School 古文學家 was replaced by the New Text School 今文學家 .
Members of the New Text School stressed the application of statecraft
經世 and in their eyes Confucius was a law-giver. Those who specialized
in "Kung-yang School 公羊家 ," such as Liao Ping 廖平 and K'ang
Yu-wei 康有為 , during the last period of Ch'ing dynasty laid great

emphasis on Confucius' political thought in order to introduce plans for a utopia. Dr. Sun Yat-sen also emphasized Confucius' political thoughts which centered upon the motto "The world belongs to all people" in the "Ta Tung 大同" section of the "Li Yün 禮運."

Chang T'ai-yen 章太炎 in the final years of Ch'ing dynasty considered Confucius as only a historiographer whose contribution lay in compiling and classifying ancient texts and documents, and whom Chang compared to Liu Hsin 劉歆 of the Han dynasty. Liao Ping and K'ang Yu-wei exaggerated the importance of Confucius in his ability to bring about a utopia. Furthermore, they opined that the *Six Classics* were written by Confucius who attributed them to the work of ancient reformers, and that they reveal only Confucius' own thought. This would make Confucius' learning on the contrary "what former generations had not inherited." Chang T'ai-yen in his early years, using Buddhism as a basis, attacked the *Mencius,* the *Hsün Tzu,* the *"Chung Yung"* and the *Commentaries* to the *I Ching* and denigrated the Confucian studies of the Sung and Ming periods. Since Chang T'ai-yen looked upon Confucius as only a historiographer who compiled and classified ancient texts, that meant Confucius' learning seemed to be "what later generations did not initiate." Chang T'ai-yen and Liang Ch'i-ch'ao, a student of K'ang Yu-wei, even considered Confucius to be no more than one of the pre-Ch'in thinkers, and to them Confucius' position might even be lower than that of Lao Tzu and Mo Tzu.

The founding of the Republic of China at the beginning of this century was done in accordance with the Confucian concept of distinguishing between the Han people and the barbarians, and the guiding principle was "drive away the Tartars and restore the reign of the Chinese people," the final goal being to establish a great federation of the five races of China. This is no less than the greatest experiment in Chinese history—putting into practice on a grand scale the national and cultural thought of Confucius.

However, in the early years of the Republic the intelligentsia could not cut itself free from the tradition of the late Ch'ing period. They continued to accept the arguments of K'ang Yu-wei and Liao Ping that the Six Classics were written by Confucius himself but were ascribed to ancient authorities—this is no less than saying that Confucius committed forgery—and invariably doubted anything from antiquity and refused to believe in whatever ancient culture was inherited by

Confucius. Since Chang T'ai-yen would only give Confucius credit for compiling and classifying the ancient texts and documents, and he replaced the Confucius spirit and the Chinese cultural essence with "ordering the nation's antiquity" which was added to the theory of Confucius' taking advantage of the transmission of antiquity. This is mirrored again in those early years of great political turmoil in the Republic. Yüan Shih-k'ai 袁世凱 wanted to be emperor; since the Ch'ing emperors all paid homage to Confucius and so did most of the high ranking officials and ministers of the Ch'ing court, Yüan Shih-k'ai felt it necessary to continue to uphold Confucius in order to consolidate his own political position. He said that from the very beginning Confucius existed only for the support of the imperial reign in China and the position Confucius had enjoyed was the result of the promotion of the various emperors down through history. This of course only evoked much ridicule and resentment. Furthermore, since China for the past one hundred years had been subject to continual foreign humiliation, intellectuals blamed everything on the traditional culture of China. They lost faith in themselves and they wanted to overthrow the traditional symbol of Chinese culture, Confucius. "Overthrow the K'ung family shop 打倒孔家店 " was their popular slogan. This trend later on joined forces with the imported Marxism and Leninism, and then the communists and their fellow-travellers downgraded Confucius to the position of an idea-fabricator in the service of feudalistic landlords and slave masters, and they even more said he should be overthrown. This is a brief history of the growth of the anti-Confucian movement.

But, fortunately, such a view of Confucius was short-lived. These views could not at all explain why Confucius came to occupy such a venerable position in Chinese history and culture. Scholars before them had never held any similar opinion regarding Confucius. Now if we want to get to the heart of the matter, we should know that from the Kung-yang School in the middle period of the Ch'ing dynasty to the present, those who look at Confucius from the point of view of social and political organization and legislation have laid emphasis on the "outwardly being a king" aspect of Confucius. But in the eyes of Tseng Kuo-fan and Lo Tse-nan, the teachings of Confucius that should be preserved were in the ethical and cultural teachings Confucius passed on. Chang Hsüeh-ch'eng was not wrong in regarding Confucius as the foremost teacher, but he was wrong in saying further that only Duke Chou was the foremost sage and that the Six Classics were all historical records of the policies and laws of the ancient emperors. According to the opinions of the Sung and Ming Confucians, the Six Classics and the principles of Chinese learning and the teachings of rites and music originally were not merely the policies and laws of a certain period. Confucius was the foremost teacher and he was also the foremost sage. In the eyes of his disciples, Confucius was simultaneously sage and teacher, and in the eyes of the Neo-Taoists and Buddhists of the Wei-Chin period, Confucius was a sage. In the apochrypal texts 緯書 Confucius was the incarnation of a god from heaven. To the Han scholars, Confucius was the "uncrowned king." which to Ssu-Ma Ch'ien, Liu Hsieh and the literati of the Chin-T'ang period, Confucius was the fountainhead of all historiography and literature.

If we want to ascertain objectively the historical position of Confucius in Chinese culture, we have to put together all the images of Confucius through the various periods of Chinese history, and consider the contributions of Confucius to philosophy, literature, historiography, religion, and ethics, and to understand last but not least his central concept of "inwardly a sage and outwardly a king 內聖外王 " before we can come to a more truthful appreciation of Confucius. Then, we shall know that the formation of the position of Confucius was the result of the deference and homage paid to him by the Chinese over the past two to three thousand years. This process was slow and arduous but it was embodied in the growth of Chinese culture and history. The whole of Chinese history and culture is comprised of multitudinous strands which combine to form a single body. Could such a position be destroyed by radicals in a short period? Moreover, we have sufficient reason to reject the idea popular since the May Fourth Movement that "The learning of Confucius from the very beginning existed solely for the support of the ruling class and his position was the result of the emperors' promotion" as a false statement and contrary to historical fact. Now, on the basis of what has been said in this paper, let me raise a few more objections, which will further expose the fallacy of this position.

I said at the beginning of this paper that the position of Confucius began to take shape when his disciples revered and obeyed him from the bottom of their hearts, and when after his death they all went to keep vigil over his grave for a period of three years. The people of the state of Lu made their homes in the vicinity of Confucius' grave. The pre-Ch'in thinkers all demonstrated a degree of respect for Confucius, and during the late Chou period and under the tyranny of the Ch'in dynasty many anonymous scholars continued to spread his ideas. I would like to ask: did any of these activities have anything to do with the political leaders and rulers of the time?

I have also pointed out in this paper that Tung Chung-shu 董仲舒 wanted the emperors to abdicate one after another, and his disciple Sui Hung 眭弘 asked the Han emperor to yield his throne. The talented and worthy literati according to their teachings were opposed to the government's competition with the people for profits and they staged a protest in opposition to the officials and ministers in the court. Ssu-Ma Ch'ien, who admired Confucius most and followed his steps, protested to the emperor on behalf of the wronged Li Ling and was thus punished by castration. We have to ask, what did these activities have to do with the autocracy of the ruling emperors? We are all aware that intellectuals and the Neo-Taoists in the Wei-Chin period were often persecuted and even executed by order of the political rulers, because in politics they proposed that a good king should practise "non-action" 無為 . They honored Confucius as the foremost sage because they found in Confucius the same idea of "do nothing in order to rule well." If Confucius was really a supporter of the interests of the emperors and imperial tyranny, how could these people come to regard him as a sage?

I have also pointed out in this paper that Liu Hsieh was simply a Buddhist monk, T'ao Yüan-ming and Tu Fu were only impoverished poets, Ch'en Tzu-ang was merely a poor scholar although he was a minor official for a short while, yet they all honored and believed in Confucius. Did they do this for any political reason or for any political gain? Did they honor Confucius because they expected the Confucian system to maintain the *states quo* of the imperial tyranny? Confucianism was given a boost through the endeavors of Sung and Ming Confucians such as Sun Ming-fu 孫明復 , Shih Chieh 石介 , and Hu An-ting 胡安定 and Wu K'ang-tsai 吳康齋 who gave lectures among the populace, and their intention was to oppose the popular Buddhism in order to renovate Confucianism and to teach people that "the scholar should wish to become the worthy and the worthy would wish to become the sage." Again did this have anything to do with

484

the interests of the emperors? I have also said that the Buddhists, the Taoists, and the Christians all regarded Confucius as a sage. Did this have anything to do with the emperors?

But looking back through the history, we know that the position of Confucius was truly established gradually based on the respect paid to him by these people. The various emperors and the political leaders down through the history of China in compliance with the opinions of the people have bestowed titles upon Confucius, and made use of the Confucian classics to select officials in order to help them to govern the country. Can we put the cart before the horse and say that Confucius was elevated to his present position by the emperors? Only sychophants would reverse the order of cause and effect to say that only the emperors had the power to make anybody important in history, and thus only the emperors had the power to raise Confucius' historical position. Even if we are willing to make numerous concessions, we can only say that elevation by the emperors was an auxiliary cause in the formation of Confucius' position. If you want to say anything more than this, you must be an elitest and you know only the power of the emperors but do not know the strength of the common people.

VII. Conclusion and epilogue—the unity of Confucius and the vitality of Chinese Culture

Now let me conclude what I have said in this paper. My purpose in writing this article is to explain why Confucius occupied an elevated position in Chinese history and culture. We must not accept the idea current since the May Fourth Movement that Confucius was merely one of the thinkers of the Nine Schools of philosophy, and that his position was made possible because the Emperor Wu 漢武帝 of the Han dynasty suppressed all the schools of philosophy with the exception of Confucianism, which he raised to the highest position, because Confucius was honored by the emperors throughout Chinese history, and because the Confucian classics were assigned as texts on which examinations were administered to select government officials. According to what I have presented here, the formation of Confucius' elevated position was a result of his inheriting the Six Classics and his opening up the ways for the advent of the various pre-Ch'in thinkers, and the moral impact his personality exercised upon his disciples. Thus, from generation to generation, the homage to Confucius accumulated and turned him into a "great hereditary family" 世家 in Chinese learning and culture. I have also made clear that admirers of Confucius were not limited only to the Confucian school; the Mohists, the Taoists, and the Legalists in the pre-Ch'in period all exhibited a measure of respect for Confucius, and in later ages admirers of Confucius were not limited to students of the pre-Ch'in thinkers or to philosophers. Confucius and his thought have been woven into the texture of Chinese culture, and he can be traced through Chinese philosophy, literature, history, religion, and in short, throughout the whole body of Chinese culture. One cannot be separated from the other.

Why is this so? On the one hand, this is due to the greatness of Confucius' thought, learning and personality, which have elicited admiration and adulation from the Chinese people. Yen Yüan 顏淵 the most distinguished disciple of Confucius, said of his master: "When I look at his teachings, they seem to become higher. When I penetrate into it, it seems to become firmer. When I look for him in the front, he is in the back. The master mildly and methodically attracts people to go onto his Way. He enlarges me with literature and restrains me with propriety. Though I wish to stop, I cannot. I have exhausted all my ability. If anything can be established, it is established loftily and nobly. Though I wish to follow him, there seems to be no clearcut path." Tzu Kung 子貢, another disciple, said, "Ever since the birth of human kind, there has never been anybody who has surpassed Confucius." Again, "The master is unreachable just as the Heaven is unreachable by ascending a ladder." The partisan of Ta Hsiang 達巷黨人 said, "Great is Confucius, his knowledge is comprehensive and he does not want only to make a name for himself."

We must remember that before Confucius Chinese culture had had a history of two to three thousand years. In those two to three thousand years countless people were born and died, and out of those countless people a single Confucius was produced and regarded as a sage; that is not too many and that is not too strange. Confucius praised only the ancient emperors Yao, Shun, Yu, and T'ang, contemporary worthies Kuan Tzu 管子 and Yen Tzu 晏子, and his own disciple Yen Yuan 顏淵. With regard to himself he said only that he was assiduous in learning. He looked upon himself only as a common person. He said, "As to being considered a sage and benevolent, I dare not presume to be." Moderns may have only looked at the words left by Confucius himself and jumped to the conclusion that Confucius was nothing much since he had said so himself, and then they started to find fault with him and even to revile him. But how would you compare in talent, wisdom, and virtue with Mencius, Hsün Tzu, Ssu-Ma Ch'ien, Liu Hsieh, Li Po, Tu Fu, Han Yu, Ch'en Ming-tao, Chu Hsi, Lu Hsiang-shan and Wang Yang-ming? If you feel that you cannot compare with them, you should be humble and ponder why so many men of great genius have honored Confucius throughout history. There must be some reason for it. If you say that Confucius is not great and is not a sage, granted. For Confucius never called himself great nor considered himself a sage. Perhaps Confucius himself would agree to what you say, but all the people who honored Confucius down through history for thousands of years would not agree to what you say. If you want to turn the tables on all these people, you should consider your moral strength and knowledge and wisdom, and you must also first consider the reasons that made them honor Confucius. It is not enough to pass judgement on Confucius on the basis of what you yourself know about Confucius. Schopenhauer once said that a great book is a mirror, and you see in the mirror your own image. Confucius' words and actions also constitute a mirror. If you are a great man, you see a great man in the mirror; if you are a dwarf, you see therein only a dwarf. If you see nothing meaningful and valuable in Confucius' words and actions, that only goes to prove that your yourself are ignorant. You must reserve your own judgment and examine first the image of Confucius in the eyes of all those historical figure and then you may begin to judge Confucius.

Looking at the matter from another angle, we can say that the elevation of Confucius' position results not only from the personal greatness of Confucius himself but also from the greatness of all these historical figures who have paid homage to Confucius. We can say that Confucius' position in our intellectual history has been established by such Confucian philosophers as Mencius, Hsün Tzu, Tung Chung-shu, the Confucians of the Sung, Ming, and Ch'ing dynasties, historians such as Ssu-ma Ch'ien and Pan Ku, and by poets such as T'ao Yüan-ming and Tu Fu. Confucius' religious position has been established by the deification of him in the *Apochrypha* and the recognition of Confucius as a sage by the Taoists, the Buddhists, and the Christians. Confucius' position in political thought has been established by the Han Confucians who honored him as the "uncrowned king" and then by the emperors of T'ang and Sung dynasties who canonized him "the king of letters." Confucius' position as the foremost sage and grand teacher has been established by Confucius' disciples and the scholars in the Sung and Ming dynasties who revered Confucius as their teacher. Confucius was great, and those who honored Confucius were also great. If these people were not great themselves, how could they have the capability to recognize the greatness of Confucius?

Of course, people will say that men throughout the history of China have endowed Confucius with the greatness they had in their own hearts so that Confucius was made to appear to be ever greater. One can say this, but by the same token, we can also say that Christ and Buddha are not great of themselves; only through the homage paid to them by their numerous followers and believers that they become as great as they are. Hence, it is not necessary for us to belittle those historical figures who honored Confucius in order to pay homage to him, but by honoring Confucius we also honor those historical personges who also honored him. Furthermore, if we really understand and honor Confucius and all those great historical personages who honored and understood him, we shall not run the danger of belittling ourselves but on the contrary we can become great ourselves, for as Wang Yang-ming has said, "There is a Confucius in each and every human heart." Essentially we are all equal to Confucius. We do not have to downgrade ourselves in order to honor the ancients. We should be aware that only when we ourselves are small, have no respect for ourselves, and do not know our own values, then do we begin to lose sight of the greatness of historical figures and especially the greatness of Confucius. Then do we frivolously malign them. But the fact is that in so doing we are only betraying our own smallness and meaness as if we were but dwarves three feet tall standing in front of a great mirror.

Here, people will certainly want to ask me whether the greatness of Confucius belongs to Confucius himself or his greatness is conferred upon him by the homage paid to him by the historical figures? This is a question which can be posed, but which has no definite answer. This answer depends upon the intellectual predilection of each individual. Actually it is a question that should not occur, for such a question would not have occured either to Confucius himself or to those who

honored him   The homage paid to Confucius in the later generations
has been accumulating year by year just as mud accumulates to
create a mountain. Thus was Confucius' position raised year by year
to its present height. This is a historical accumulation and the total
effect is beyond argument. All we need to say is that the greatness of
Confucius is a combination of Confucius' own greatness and the
greatness of all the historical figures who respected him. Of course, we
cannot say that the greatness of Confucius was merely created out of
nothing by those who venerated him. But even if we allow this
possibility for the sake of argument, we can go a step further and ask,
Why did they not fabricate something about somebody else? Why
did they not pay homage to somebody else as they did to Confucius?
Nobody in his right mind could argue that Confucius had some
mysterious power with which to hypnotize people, or that the emperors
elevated Confucius because they wished to make use of him and as a
result for two to three thousand years all the Chinese were compelled
to honor and worship Confucius.

    As I have said in this article, all the men who honored Confucius
down through history arose from among the common people, and they
honored Confucius out of their free will. The only reasonable thing to
say is that Confucius and his admirers attracted and echoed one another
in thought, spirit, and personality, and that out of this emerged
universal homage to Confucius and his unique position in Chinese
history and culture. If we understand that the position of Confucius
is the result of a long process in which Confucius and his admirers
attracted and echoed each other in thought, spirit and personality, we
can say that Confucius assumed different forms to different people
throughout history. For instance, Mencius' image of Confucius does
not have to be the same as Hsün Tzu's and as a historian, Ssu-ma Ch'ien's
image of Confucius does not have to be the same as the poets, T'ao
Yuan-ming, Li Po, and Tu Fu. To the Han, Sung, Ming, and Ch'ing
Confucians, Confucius again assumed different images. Consequently,
some people advocate the idea of returning the Confucius of the Han
Confucians to the Han Confucians, the Confucius of Sung Confucians
to the Sung Confucians, etc., and this is not a bad idea. Students can
work on the image of Confucius to Mencius, to Hsün Tzu, and so on,
and write a doctoral dissertation on it. Because each individual's image
of Confucius belongs of course to that individual.

But this is obviously not enough. For if each individual holds onto his own image, the historical Confucius would be broken up into countless Confuciuses, and there would not be a complete and total and true Confucius. We must realize that each individual's image of Confucius, though not complete in itself, has to be a part of the total Confucius. If Confucius did not possess the aspect which Mencius had in mind, Mencius would not have honored Confucius. If Confucius did not possess the aspect which Hsün Tzu had in mind, Hsün Tzu would not have honored Confucius. Now everyone of these aspects of Confucius combines to form the total and complete thought, spirit, and personality of Confucius. Therefore, we should not say there are as many Confuciuses as there are admirers, in whose minds he has found a place and in whose vision he has constituted an image. We should say there was a historical Confucius who lived in the pre-Ch'in period and he had a totality in thought and spirit and personality, but in the various periods in history aspects of his thought and spirit and personality emerged one by one in relation to the emphasis each age placed upon him. Thus he was admired and honored for the different aspects that appealed to them and only those aspects became important and valuable to those admirers.

According to what has been stated here, we cannot say Confucius lived only for those 73 years which were his lifespan in the pre-Ch'in period, but that Confucius lives in thought, spirit and personality of all those people who know him and appreciate him and honor him. It is wrong to say that Confucius or his thought were limited to his age. If Confucius did not exist today, no one would bother to try to overthrow him. It is also wrong to say that Confucius' thought is limited to the society and the political system in which he found himself. For people since him living in a different society and a different political system still felt attracted to his thought and spirit and personality. We may compare the thought, spirit, and personality of Confucius, and the thought, spirit and personality of those people who honored Confucius to a beacon. Confucius' beacon shines backward through many centuries on Duke Chou 周公 who lived five hundred years before him and shines forward on all the generations that live after him. Five hundred years after Confucius came Ssu-ma Ch'ien, who succeeded to Confucius with his historiography. Five hundred years later came Liu Hsieh, who carried on Confucianism with his literary work. In yet another five hundred years there were the three masters (Sun Ming-fu, Shih Chieh, and Hu Ting-an) in the early years of the Sung dynasty who started a renaissance of Confucianism. And in still another five hundred years Wang Yang-ming claimed that "there is a Confucius in every human heart," which anchored the position of Confucius in every person's heart.

The spiritual light of all these people also shines across the chasm of two thousand and five hundreds years of history and shines backward on Confucius. Two thousand and five hundred years can be compared to a single day, and during this one single day the impact of Confucius' thought, spirit and personality upon the world and the honor the world pays to Confucius all take place and become commingled, ensuring the position of Confucius in Chinese history and culture. This reciprocal influence and impact can be compared to the mutual illumination and heightening of light of many bodies of light. We are not here to say that the light of Confucianism comes only from Confucius nor can we say that the light comes only from his admirers. The light of Confucianism is the confluence of all the light that emits from Confucius and all his admirers, and this light becomes thus the light and life of Chinese culture as a whole. The brilliance of Confucius' spirit and the brilliance of the spirit of all those who admire and honor Confucius combine to create the cultural brilliance of the Chinese race, the greatness and loftiness of Confucius becomes the greatness and loftiness of Chinese culture, and the formation of the position of Confucius becomes the process in which the cultural life of the Chinese as a whole gradually takes shape. This is the most proper and suitable way to regard the formation of the position of Confucius.

According to this view, in the cultural context of the Chinese race there are many things aside from Confucianism. People have the right not to talk about Confucius or they can just talk about a specific aspect of Confucius and cast doubt upon other aspects. But no one has the right or the justification to throw mud upon Confucius as a whole. And it is even worse if one makes use of Confucius as a foil in order to attack somebody who has nothing in common with Confucius. "Confucius" is a person's name, not the "x" in an algebraic formula; to look upon Confucius as an "x" is also an insult to Confucius. Anybody who insults Confucius insults anyone who has admired and honored Confucius throughout Chinese history and insults the cultural life of the Chinese and the Chinese people as a whole. This is what

Confucius meant when he said, "There are things that can be tolerated and there are things that cannot be tolerated." The trend since the May Fourth Movement has been to undermine Confucius's historical position and to belittle his learning. But it is a trend which represents only an eddy in the mainstream of Chinese intellectual history, and this eddy will eventually flow into a stagnant pond and eveporate into nothingness.

If we are able to really recognize the factors upon which the position of Confucius has been formed in Chinese history and culture, we then have only contempt for those people in mainland China who willingly turn themselves into slaves of Marxism and Leninism and vilify and denigrate Confucius in every way imaginable. These people have no conscience, no intellectual integrity, and no sense of morality whatsoever. It seems that since Confucius can not defend himself, they can do whatever they want with his name. This is cowardly and mean. It is agonizing to watch some Chinese fall into such a state of shame and villainy. It is beneath one's dignity to argue with whatever they have to say about Confucius. Whatever comes out of the latrine will return to the latrine. Whatever they have said about Confucius will play no part in the mainstream of Chinese culture; that is to say their mental and emotional effusions have no roots and will have no fruits. We can quote Mencius with confidence that "whatever has no roots will dry up in the twinkling of an eye."

Appendix I

A Manifesto on
the Reappraisal of Chinese Culture

By *Carson Chang, Hsieh Yu-wei, Hsu Foo-kwan,*
Mou Chung-san and Tang Chun-i

Our Joint Understanding of the Sinological Study Relating
to World Cultural Outlook

Editor: The motive in writing this manifesto originated with Dr. Carson
Chang when, in a talk with Prof. Tang Chun-i in the spring of 1957, he
showed much concern over the many short-comings with which some Westerners approach the study of Chinese academic works, while their basic
understanding of Chinese culture and political outlook was also variously in
adequate. Thereupon, Dr. Chang wrote both Prof. Mou Tsung-san and
Prof. Hsu Fu-kwan, asking for their consent to jointly publish an article to
express their corrective views.

With the agreement and suggestions of Professors Mou and Hsu, Prof
Tang drew up the first sketch of this treatise while still on tour in the
United States and sent it to Prof. Hsieh Yu-wei in Taiwan for consultation
After several revision this booklet took its final shape.

The purpose of this article is primarily to benefit Western intellectua
in aiding them to appreciate Chinese culture. It took considerable time fo
translation from Chinese into English. This, together with conviction tha
any attempt to modify Westerner' prejudices toward our culture should k
based first on our own true evaluation and self-examination, prompted us 1
publish it earlier in Chinese in the "Democratic Critique" and "Nation
Renaissance."

This treatise is divided into two parts under the following twelve topic

1. Preamble, our reasons for issuing this manifesto;

2. Three best-known motives of Westerners who pursue Chinese studi
   and their shortcomings;

3. Affirmation of the spiritual life of Chinese history and culture;

492

4. Chinese philosophy and its relation to Chinese culture as differing from Western systems;

5. The ethical, moral and religious spirit of Chinese culture;

6. The import of the Chinese "Doctrine of Transcendental Mind" in moral practice;

7. Reasons governing durability of Chinese history and culture;

8. Development of Chinese culture in the natural sciences;

9. Development of Chinese culture in national democratic reconstruction;

10. Our understanding of China's current political history;

11. Our expectation from Western culture and what the West should learn from Oriental wisdom;

12. What we hope for from the formation of a new world of academic thought.

PART I

Chapter I. Preamble, Our Reasons for Issuing this Manifesto

Prior to the presentation of their formal views on this subject, the writers wish to make known that the publication of this manifesto has been a matter of repeated consideration among them. First of all, we believed that if what we undertake to present is true, then its intrinsic value would remain the same regardless of whether it was signed by one or by several authors. Next, the ideology of the five writers is not completely identical in all of its aspects. In addition, the number of Oriental and Occidental intellectuals who generally embrace the same ideology can not be limited to us five.

Furthermore, we also believed that formation of any one authentic, ideological or cultural movement must depend chiefly on several independent emissions along more or less the same lines of thought after reciprocal situations and responses were taken up by thinkers in their natural course of action. Should only a few thinkers of a certain school publicize their ideology along certain pattern, the joint action as such might, by making others feel that ideology has nothing to do with them, create stumbling-blocks to the spreading of such an ideology.

On the other hand, the authors also have taken into consideration the fact that we at least hold the same general view and convictions toward Chinese culture. Should we be shy to publicize what we hold as common convictions, portions in them which might be conducive to the formation of truth would be unwittingly hidden from notice. The result of this would be a halt in further verifications of theories and attainment of truth.

As for many other intellectuals, both at home and abroad, who might have held generally the same ideology ourselves, the authors regret that they cannot approach each one of them for confirmation of this manifesto. We believe that many among them would readily express views in accord with our own. Therefore, we shall not look upon this ideology as an exclusive personal possession. This point we should like to stress before launching our treatise.

In this declaration we shall discuss our basic understanding of Chinese culture in the past and present, together with its outlook for the future. We will also give directions for the study of Chinese culture and academic works and the tackling of Chinese problems by all intellectuals, both at home and abroad, together with our expectations for the future development of world civilization.

Although we have paid close attention, as did numerous others scholars or statesmen both at home and abroad, to the aforesaid topics in the past years, we might not have attained such a lucid discernment of them, were it not for the fact that about eight years ago China suffered from an unprecedented cataclysm which forced us to take shelter abroad. The feeling of sadness and loneliness in turn urged us to contemplate reflectively many fundamental problems. We thus believe that genuine wisdom is born off suffering. Only through afflictions may our spirit be set free from fixed life patterns to produce an exalted and broad mind which may tackle any and all problems in a philosophic way.

Others who have not suffered as we have, may not be able to appreciate what we comprehend. The authors are determined to present to the whole world the essence of our thought, with a request for all intellectuals to give their impressions and reflections.

We make the announcement because we sincerely believe that some crucial issues on Chinese Culture bear a world-wide significance. We mention this because China is one of the very few nations in the world whose cultural history of several thousand years had not been completely disrupted, because Chinese culture had won ample praise from Europeans before the 18th century, and this because it had made considerable contributions to mankind as a whole.

China possesses nearly one-fourths of the world population. The problem of how to arrange or to settle the life and spirit of this vast number of people may have been in fact a common concern of all humanity. In other words, China's problem has long transformed itself into a world problem. If the conscience of mankind will not tolerate the use of atomic bombs to wipe out China's more than 500,000,000 people, than the destiny of this sum of about one-fourths of the world population will forever be a common burden on human conscience as a whole. This knotty problem is closely bound up with genuine understanding of Chinese culture in its past and present, and in its future development.

If Chinese culture is grossly misunderstood, then the life and spirit of the vast number of Chinese people will possibly be deranged without proper settlement in sight. This will not only result in a common disaster for mankind but will also blast the common hopes of the entire humanrace.

Chapter II. Three Best-known Motives of Westerners who Pursue Chinese Studies and Their Shortcomings

For several hundred years Chinese academic studies and Chinese culture in general have been made an object of research throughout the world. In the last hundred years China as an international issue and Chinese culture as a world problem have also attracted the world-wide attention of scholars. And yet most students of China living in the midst of their own cultural patterns, may still be unable to answer such question as these:

Where is the center of the Chinese cultural spirit?

What will be the direction of its development?

Where is the weakness of Chinese culture located?

What will be its course of development if the leading spirit of Chinese culture is left intact?

Since this is so, it would be harder still for many foreign scholars to acquire a true understanding of Chinese culture. This may be so on account of constrained viewpoints motives. Such restricted viewpoints hinder research and appreciation of Chinese culture in its breadth and depth.

Generally speaking, there are three well known motives entertained by most foreign sinologists in their pursuit of Chinese studies. Weighing these three motives, we can readily understand why Chinese culture has not been really understood by most foreigners, and why, consequently, it has not been correctly appraised by them. These three motives may be described as follows:

1. Many Chinese academic works were first introduced to the Western world about three hundred years ago by Jesuit missionaries. They came to China avowedly to preach Christianity in the Far East while their sideline was also to bring to China some sort of scientific knowledge and skill. Having later returned to Europe, they then introduced some ancient Chinese classics and the orthodox Confucian study of the Sung (960-1278 A.D.) and Ming (1368-1644 A.D.) Dynasties to the West. Of course, the merits of those Jusuit missionaries in pioneering the West-East cultural interflow are enormous.

However, since the primary motive of those missionaries was the spreading of Christianity in China, their focus of attention toward Chinese learning and ideology was centered around those Chinese classics related to the legends of God, together with those ancient a savant who showed reverence toward Heaven, at the same time they expressed strong objections to the Sung-Ming Confucian school that emphasized rationalism and idealism. Those diversionary or divergent works of the latter category may well be represented by the "Authentic Meaning of Catholicism" of Matteo Ricci and the "Commentary on Chinese Rationalism" of J. C. Anderson. Their sinological presentations of Sung-Ming Confucianism to the European world, while more less informative might have been inadequate on crucial points. They had, as a matter of fact, treated the Sung-Ming Confucian principle as identical with the current Western rationalism, naturalism or even materialism. Thus it happened that misrepresented Sung-Ming ideology was often quoted in Europe by the atheist and materialist as concurring with their own ideas.

According to our view, Sung-Ming Confucianism was more in line with the idealism of Immanuel Kant and his followers. However, most Western idealists would not treat Sung-Ming Confucian scholars as their fellow-travellers. This type of discord was due chiefly to the misrepresentation of the Chinese ideology by those early Jesuit missionaries whose chief motive was to spread Christianity in China while their ideological technique, as though striving for supremacy, was to take up the Chinese six Classics and orthodox Confucianism as allies in their fight against the Sung-Ming school, Buddhism and Taoism. Therefore, their introduction of the Sung-Ming doctrine was inadequate while their comprehension of it was based on the missionary standpoint.

2. During the past century the Westerner's study of China was reacti-

vated by the Chinese "Open Door Policy" following the Opium War and the Boxer Incident. Occidental sinologists were motivated by curiosity aroused by art works exported to the West or else discovered on Chinese territory. For instance, in the latter category we find Sir Aurel Stein and Dr. Paul Pelliot, well known in the "Tun Huang" study for their discovery of Buddhist sculptures in Tun Huang Grottoes. Starting from the motive of curiosty, they extended their studies to include Chinese fine arts, archaeology, Chinese geography of the Northwest region, Chinese history of frontier development including Sinkiang and Mongolia, the history of West-East communications, and from there to the history of Liao, Khin and Yuan regimes, while the ancient Chinese language written on metals, stones, turtle shells or animal bones was lined up with their study of Chinese dialects as well as the characteristics of Chinese written and oral languages.

In this category, the studies of both Chinese savants and European sinologists have in the past several decades yielded valuable results. Nevertheless, we can not deny that the intensive effort of most Western sinologists in unearthing, collecting and transporting various sorts of Chinese antiques as source materials for their research, was not directly concerned with the study of China as a living nation or of Chinese culture in its changing mood; nor did it probe into the Chinese cultural life and spirit, with their true sources and directions of development carefully taken consideration. Their keen interest, derived mainly from curiosity, may be analogous with the study of ancient Egyptian civilization or the cultural relics of Asia Minor and Persia.

Meanwhile, most of the Chinese scholars in the Ch'ing Dynasty (16440-1911 A.D.) indulged in brain-cudgeling over the so-called "Han School of Learning", which stressed verification of Principles or annotation and connotation of ancient classical works by proof of source materials, with archeological research, as the main theme. Later in the early years of the Republic of China, the vogue of "Rearranging Ancient Cultural Works" in the midst of "New Cultural Movement" also adopted the academic method of the Ch'ing regime for its pattern. The coincidence of approach toward Chinese studies by both Western and Eastern sinologists appeared as though it were orthodox sinology.

3. In the last ten or twenty years, a new, glamorous direction of sinological research seemed to have developed through interest in modern Chinese history. Such an interest may have been derived from the Sino-Japanese war and the Communist invasion of the China mainland.

Since the Sino-Japanese war, many Western advisers to the Chinese government and foreign diplomats in China have been posing as leading figures in the study of modern Chinese history. Their motive has been primarily derived from actual contact with Chinese political or social institutions related to the international situation. This sort of realistic motive is just the opposite of the aforementioned one of curiosity. It seems more inclined to study the Chinese nation as a living being, and view its problems in an atmosphere of change. From this realistic standpoint, most Chinese studies seek to know the present by tracing threads leading to the past.

Present day politics are in reality always changing just as the attitude of observers varies in different periods. In cases where the motive of a research worker is aroused by a certain political phenomenon, what he formulates as the main issue of study, what he treats as the relevant facts for testimony, what he uses as his hypothesis to explain the facts finally the conclusions he draws—all these may be inevitably influenced by his individual emotions when confronting certain political actualities. He may even be swayed by his subjective attitude toward the issue though in name he is pursuing an objective or scientific study. Therefore, in this regard, he is liable to be swaged by individual prejudice.

To correct the aforesaid mistake, a political student must follow the order of development of Chinese cultural history, tackling the subject at its historic source, and thus move from cause to effect. Furthermore, he must grasp the true nature of Chinese culture and its historical changes, sinuous or fluctuating though it be, in order to appreciate the real meaning of modern Chinese history in order to forecast the future development of Chinese culture.

With such a method the researcher of current history must first transcend his own subjective attitude toward the issue and be wary lest incidental trifles or transient phenomena deceive him; he must become aware of abnormal conditions in the stream of Chinese culture. Subsequently, the main object of his research, facts, hypotheses, and conclusions must all be based upon his knowledge of Chinese cultural history in its entire process of development.

However, as most sinologists entertain only fragmentary knowledge of Chinese culture while their interests are aroused chiefly by transient contacts with the Chinese political situation, or else by attention to Chinese politics in its relation to the international situation, the aforesaid pitfalls appear to be the hardest for them to avoid.

What we have related above does not deny the objective value of these efforts of Westerners dedicated to the study of Chinese cultural history. Such objective value may have even overcome drawbacks derived from the subjective motive of the original research. Or else, in the process of study, the worker's motives make become progressively purified

Nevertheless, we cannot refrain from asserting that most sinologists may, in fact, have often steered their course of study along some biased viewpoint in the study of Chinese culture. Such studies easily result in numerous misunderstandings or misrepresentations of Chinese culture in its past and present stages together with possible lines of future development. Hence, we would like to propose another method for the study of Chinese culture in general and for the study of certain academic works in particular. At the same time, we present to our readers what has been gathered in our study of Chinese culture in its past and present and likely future development in accordance with the proper motive and attitude.

Chapter III. Affirmation of the Spiritual Life of Chinese History and Culture

Chinese culture is a thing very much alive. We cannot deny that in the eyes of numerous Chinese as well as Westerners, Chinese culture has been looked upon as a museum piece.

As Oswald Spengler saw it, Chinese culture was already dead during the Han Dynasty (204 B. C.-220 A. D.). Later in the campaign of "Re-arranging the ancient Works" following the "May 4th. Movement" of 1919, most Chinese scholars engaged in this field may also have treated such cultural relics as fitted only for the waste-paper basket, even though they had been rearranged and shelved···for good! As for further proof, the repeated failure of China's struggle for national, democratic reconstruction seemed most convincing. Even as we write these lines, ninety percent of her people have been bludgeoned into silence under the images of Lenin and Stalin, while less than ten per cent of them are exiled to Taiwan and overseas countries. These two phenomena tend to substantiate the charge that Chinese culture is a corpse. Thus scholarly studies nearly all emit an air of reverence reserved only for ancient relics. Our advise is that this sort of thinking is gravely erroneous and vitiates the entire study of Chinese culture.

Of course, we cannot deny that the repeated setback China's national democratic reconstruction in the past hundred years has frequently disappointed many foreign friends as well as Chinese patriots. Nor can we deny that Chinese culture is afflicted by an illness, its original shape terribly marred by enormous ugly moles and warts. Neverthless, the Oriental Sickman is still alive. Before we attempt to cure his diseases, we must from the outset affirm the existence of his life. We should not presume that he is already dead, a cadaver fit only for the anatomic study of medical students.

But where and what is the evidence to prove that Chinese culture has not been claimed by rigor mortis?

Some objective proofs may be postponed to later chapters, but there is one proof right before our eyes. The authors of this article are in self-consciousness very much alive. Should our readers happen to be students of Chinese learning, we trust that you too are still very much alive. As both you and we are sprightly in existence and all of us recognize the exitence of Chinese culture, then this culture could not have died or perished. Anything once cherished by the human heart, though it may have perished once, may still be revived by the living soul. Hence, ancient Chinese history and culture continue to live in human consciousness, especially in the mind and soul of research scholars. This observation is self evident common sense. No archaeologist would deny his life or vital functions, nor his written work permeated with so much sweat and blood. Wherever the living heart or soul prevails, all that was past may yet vividly appear before the eyes.

Some absent-minded prefessors may have in practice ignored the fact that the traditional culture of any nation is the accumulation or crystallization of the mental and spiritual products of living souls, although the object of their study and source materials may be mute or even fossilized. They may easily have forgotten that such cultural relics still embody human blood, sweat, tear and smiles and thus preserve and transmit human ideals and spirits. By foregetting or ignoring this fact, many cultural students might be unable to treat the ancient culture as an objective expression of the spiritual life of mankind. Hence, their studys lack sympathy and respect and preclude any prospect that such spiritual qualities could endure for future development. Nor do they realize that in the main current of historical world cultures, there are still living souls trying to prolong the life of what seems to them nothing but a corpse. Hence, the former group of researchers may also lack sympathy and respect toward the latter. The former group might treat such matter as one involving emotional commitments, thus hamstringing objective research. They may also take it to be the concern only of literary men, political propagandists or suave philosophers who would try to give the semblance of life to ancient relics.

Here often lies the basic mistake of cultural research workers. By separating emotion and intellect, they are lead astray and could now easily overlook the most significant elements in their study of the spiritual life of a nation. They seem likewise to have ignored the fact that the history and culture of mankind must be differentiated from mere external, inanimate, and natural phenomena. When they apply the method of natural science study to the research of human history and culture, they may thus unwitting identify the latter with a mere fossilized relic. Such an attitude is surely unscientific.

Since history and culture originally expressed the spiritual vitality of mankind, even in much later ages, they deserve objective study and appraisal. It should be obvious that cultural students, basically devoid of sympathy and respect toward human affairs, past and present, cannot actually understand them in their essential reality. Most human affairs are mere passing phenomena, the meaning of which can be truly grasped only when they are illuminated by the light of our own spiritual force with its sympathetic attitude towward people and nations which gave birth to and nurtured such mental or spiritual activities. To achieve this goal, we must first pay affirmative respects to the objective spiritual life, we are studying and go beyond the limit of our own individual, subjective views or mental activities. This sort of transcendentalism is not derived from experience, but rather the necessary conditions for the extention of human experience and human knowledge. It is a ray of light guiding the activity of our wisdom so as to penetrate and understand the inner spiritual or mental life of others. This guiding light alone, unless wisdom also aids our research, cannot insure the necessary understanding of the subject. Devoid of this sympathy we are apt to explain at random all the surrounding phenomena from our subjective point of view, habitual bias, or even accidental whimsies. Such an undertaking certainly will produce numerous misunderstandings in research work without promoting objective comprehension.

To secure the aforesaid comprehension in its trustworthy mood, we must be guided by appropriate respect toward the intended object. The greater the respect, the greater will be the application of wisdom toward the matter, and the more profound our understanding of it. Where respect is deficient at a certain point, the activity of wisdom or the application of mental or spiritual forces will also be wanting. The external evolution of the subject matter as a human affair is thus stopped at the point as appeared in the consciousness of the observer, or else as inanimate, spiritless, inorganic matter. Furthermore, it may even exist as an object of free-for-all subjective interpretation, with varying degrees of misunderstanding.

Thus, our view is that the history and culture of China willl appear to be only a heap of dead, fossilized bones if the observer cannot sincerely recognize them as the living product of numerous generations of Chinese as an objective expression of their spiritual life. That could be the case in one who is lacking in sympathy and respect. Any inference that Chinese culture as dead would therefore be a great blunder. To dead eyes, all things are dead!

Neverthless, we readily acknowledge that those who have trained their paralysed eyes toward Chinese culture to study it with keen interest, may have kept their spiritual functions still alive; their academic publications also bear witness to their vivacious spirit and mental vigor. Our earnest request in this regard is that all of us extend our self-consciousness to the realm of Chinese culture, thus affirmatively recognizing it as a living reality, as the flowing stream of a nation's perennial spiritual life, still very much alive. Our studies would bear great fruit with such a supposition. Without such an affirmative position, or if such recognition is precarious and inconstant, then all studies of Chinese history and culture, no matter how calm and objective they might appear, might still in fact be colored by subjectivity and capriciousness, conjectures and interpretation totally unjustified by objective truth.

It is therefore essential that all academic scholars in this field examine their motives reflectively, for this is the important hinge upon which the success or failure of their research depends.

Chapter IV. Chinese Philosophy and Its Relation to Chinese Culture as Differing from Western Systems

As stated above, Chinese history and culture with all of its academic branches should be treated as an objective expression of the spiritual life of the Chinese nation. Now, we may ask: where is the nucleus of this spiritual life? Our answer: It lies within the general thought or philosophy of the Chinese people.

This does not mean that prevailing Chinese thought or philosophy determines the reality of China's culture and history. It means only that our research must begin with Chinese thought and philosophy if we are to attain an understanding of the spiritual life of Chinese culture in its historical aspect.

Hence, the main road to travel in studying Chinese culture is necessarily a philosophical one, developing outward layer upon layer. In other words, we are not justified in picking up at random various topics of Chinese culture for study and then drawing generalized conclusions. Such a method feasible only if the scattered leaves and branches of a tree are related to the trunk and roots which give them life and meaning.

However, we should also realize that scattered leaves and branches sometimes conceal the trunk and roots from immediate and clear observation. Leaves can be fascinating in themselves, and the collecting of them can dissipate all our energy if we are not prudent. If we care to find the trunk and roots, we must work our way beneath the complicate foliage.

To do the job correctly, we must inquire deeply into cultural matters and thus distill their philosophic essence for study in our laboratory. Having first examined the trunk and roots, we must extend our research to its branches and myriad leaves in order to appreciate its spiritual vigor and potential vitality.

The metaphor of trunk and leaves aptly expresses the relationship between Chinese philosophy and various phases of China's history and culture, and the spiritual quality of that culture. This figure of speech explains on the one hand the characteristics of Chinese culture, and on the other hand, points out that to understand Chinese philosophy, we cannot adopt the same method as these used for studying some Western pholosophical doctrine.

What we mean here by the characteristic of Chinese culture is its "unitary system." Such unity means that by origin Chinese culture is of a single system. Its singularity, however, does not deny a plurality of roots. In ancient China there were also various cultural sources which jointly constituted one traditional, main current. For instance, the Yin Regime (1751-1122 B.C.) succeeded by revolution to the Hsia (2183-1752 B. C.) and accepted its cultural heritage, which later Chou (1112-256 B. C.) did the same to the Yin Dynasty, accepting also its cultural heritage. Hence, the civilization formed one lineage of three dynasties. Since then the Chin regime (255-206 B. C.) succeeded Chou; the Han dynasty (204 B.C.-220 A.D.) followed Chin; with later T'ang (618-906 A.D.) Sung (960-1279 A.D.), Yuan (1280-1368 A.D.) Ming (1368-1644 A.D.) and Ch'ing (1644-1911 A.D.), following in proper order. All of them showed that even though in political affairs China had suffered from various dynastic changes, yet her cultural flow generally has followed the line of a great unity. Her political split or solidarity had never affected the general tend toward one center of the Chinese cultural system. This is what we called the succession of cultural essence in one great lineage.

The so-called "orthodox cultural lineage" in Chinese history may not have won undisputed approval of modern Chinese and Western scholars. Regardless of such dissension, the existence of such a lineage is an historical reality. This observation has been derived from the unitary system of Chinese culture.

The Chinese concept of "Orthodox cultural lineage," aside from the theoretical explanation now pending presentation, has its factural grounds. For one thing, cultural origins on the China mainland were very different from those on the European continent. In the ancient Greek city state, there was no unified Greek empire as its diversified cultural forces were scattering over Greece proper and its overseas colonies.

Aside from its Greek source, modern Western culture also has for its fountain-heads Roman, Hebrew, German and Moslem patterns. On the contrary, Chinese culture about one hundred years ago unquestionally formed a unitary system at its root, even granting that fact that various fragments were imported from India and Arab countries together with the socalled "Four Barbarian Frontiers", while still other portions were indirectly transmitted from Greece and Rome.

Due to the actual complexity of sources, Western culture can hardly set up any orthdoxy as its exclusive lineage. For some time westerners had adopted a religious belief in God, a supernatural being, and this gave unity to a spiritual worship consolidated from the Hebrew, Greek, and Roman sources. Thus we find in the Middle Ages the temporary existence of the Holy Roman Empire, a quasi unitary system of Western culture. However, such unity did not last long. Now, should the Western countries attempt to have their diverse cultural heritages assimilated under one roof, it could be achieved probably only when all mankind in living harmoniously under the principle of "one world as one family."

One the other hand, Chinese culture has enjoyed from its origin a unitary orthodoxy. Such is a basic difference between the Oriental and Occidental cultural patterns worthy of our attention.

As Western culture had various independent sources which made its contents especially complicated and also highly enriched, such a condition developed the land-marks of schools and subjects, with many cultural realms keeping relative independence among themselves. Generally speaking, western science and philosophy originated from Greece, the legal system from Rome, and religion from Hebrew sources. As their fountain-heads were diverse, their research methods, attitudes and objectives were not necessarily the same. Each of them set up its own sphere of knowledge, influence, action, etc., with boundaries well defined and fixed. Taking philosophy as an example, we find that ever since the Greek era, the "Love of Wisdom" or the seeking for it long occupied the speculations of a few scholars in this particular field. Hence, the world of Western philosophers usually is a world of extraordinary men. Within that secluded universe, every dedicated savant attempts to create is his own independent system, striving hard to express his own thought in written works with the motto of "Dum spiro spero." They study merely for the sake of philosophical study. Only a few of them mean to put their own lofty thoughts into actual practice in daily life. Their written works are as a rule endowed with strict definitions, coupled with enormous proofs of their theories and complicated explanations with detailed analysis of essential points. Hence, by use of such an academic viewpoint in examining the philosophic works of Chinese scholars, any reviewer may feel, at least at the out-set, disappointed by their appearance of simplicity and crudeness. This may be at least one reason why most western sinologists are unwilling to invest much of their time and energy in the study of Chinese philosophical works.

Nevertheless, it should be no cause for wonder that most Chinese philosophical works are found lacking in definitions and the establishment of elaborate proofs for theories, for they had as their ideal presentation one simple rule: "Essential teachings are never cumbersomely worded." Furthermore, if we have from the start recognized the "unitary system" of Chinese culture, we should appreciate also that philosophy, science and religion, together with political thoughts, law or jurisprudence, ethics and moral principles, have all been derived from the one and unique source while in the past no single individual boldly assumed to establish an independent universe of his own. No single Chinese philosopher strove to create an idependent system by himself, urged on by the lofty nation "one system for each philosopher."

Most Chinese philosophers have tried to put their own high ideals into practice in public as well as in private life. Should we desire to understand any one of them thoroughly, we must begin by examining his personality, living conditions, significant conversations with his mentors and friends, as well as his analects. Even the intimte contacts of daily life have their significance, for they are reflections of much deeper realities. Our task would be extremely difficult, but necessity demands it. Approaching a Chinese philosopher in this way, one would accept the possibility that even though his written works appeared simple and crude, yet the spiritual, cultural and historical meanings underlying them might be extremely rich, subtle and profound. It is just like our tree: the trunk, though rough and unbecoming, may still nourish innumerable branches lavish in foliage, which in turn gvie evidence to the magnificent vitality and wealth of the whole.

This metaphor helps us to understand that to appreciate Chinese culture, we must trace its vitality to a philosophical core; likewise, any attempt to understand Chinese philosophy must take into account its cultural significance. Since Chinese culture has its unitary personality, there is also authoritative lineage or sovereignty in politics, and academic lineage in its philosophy.

On the other hand, if we ignore the unitary tradition of Chinese culture, if we cannot clearly discern the position of any Chinese philosopher or the main ideological current of Oriental culture, (as different from that of Western philosophers and Western thought in Occidental culture) then we might be unable to view properly the relationship between Chinese philosophy and Oriental culture in various phases of transition. Besides, we might not even know where to look for his historical core of Chinese philosophy. Thus obsessed by the Western point of view, the simple and crude outward appearance of most Chinese philosophical works deceive us into believing they are not deserving of our study. Hence, when appraising Chinese philosophical works from the Western point of view, we are liable to be blinded by Western cultural patterns and so be unable to recognize the independent nature of Chinese culture with the unitary system as its fountain-head.

We now arrive at one definite conclusion: Since Chinese culture traces its source to a unitary system, the formula for expressing its spiritual life must be different from that expressing Western cultural life, which latter has its roots in diverse soils.

Chapter V. The Ethical, Moral and Religious Spirit in Chinese Culture

Glancing at Chinese culture as a whole, one prevailing notion has been pinpointed by Chinese and Western sinologists; that is, Chinese culture emphasizes ethical and moral principles in human relationships, but not religious faith of man towards the supernatural being of God. Such a notion may not be wrong in principle.

If this is interpreted to mean that Chinese ethico-moral principles are merely for adjusting relations among men in order to maintain their social and political order, such regulations governing only the external conduct of the human world and entirely devoid of supernatural emotion for the control of one's internal spiritual life, such an idea would be grossly inadequate.

Such an opinion is explained by the fact that most Westerners who visited China in the early stages were Christian missionaries, merchants, military servicemen and diplomats. Their prime objective was not to understand China, for they did not enjoyed opportunities to make close contacts with Chinese who could represent her cultural spirit. Hence, what impressed them most was merely the outward fórm of Chinese living conditions and customs, together with the ethical norms and social rites which regulated social and political activities. They then ignored the fundamental principle of ethico-moral precepts involving the internal spiritual life of the Chinese people, together with transcendental religious-like emotions. Especially in the view-point of most Western missionaries whose ultimate mission was to spread Christianity, there was an inclination to find fault with Chinese culture in its obvious lack of religious spirit. Besides, since missionaries in the early stages of their China crusade kept in touch with people of lower status, their attention was absorbed by prevailing religious superstitions of the general masses. Among such superstitions, there was hardly discernible any lofty religious spirit.

Moreover, as happened during the last hundred years, Western merchants, followed by missionaries, pioneered their works with gun-boats to open Ghina's doors, and were not welcomed at the out-set. Traditional Chinese culture has been deeply opposed to military force and merchants; therefore, those missionaries trailing after the gun-boats and merchant ship's were soon look-ed upon as symbols of a Western cultural invasion. No wonder then that the Chinese intelligentsia, since the last stage of the Ch'ing dynasty till the well-known "May Fourth" enlightenment movement of 1919, were generally indifferent to the western religion while they in turn slighted the religious element in Chinese culture.

Furthermore, those leaders of the May Fourth movement were more or less inclined to admire "science and democracy" while in their philosophical resort believed rather in pragmatism, utilitarinism, materialism and natural-ism. Hence, their interpretation of Chinese culture was chiefly set in the light of lacking religious faith. Levelling against the ancient moral princi-ples, they attempted to wipe them out as social evils which appeared in the form of decadent rituals and harmful customs. They likewise treated Chi-nese ethico-moral patterns as sheer formalities of external behavior without any intrinsic, spiritual worth.

More recent still, the Communists, atheistic by prenatal obsession and crazy in their pursuit of material efficiency, have been even more hostile to the religious-like element in Chinese culture. Hence, they have been stone blind toward the internal spiritual life which serves as a foundation for Chi-nese ethico-moral principles.

All of the aforesaid views found a place in the thoughts of some Western missionaries during their early visits to China, and so resulted in the same fallacious conclusion.

According to our viewpoint, it is unquestionable that China lacked the Western-type Church system and religious wars. Christianity since the Middle Ages, with its diversified practices and acute conflicts, has been developing an independent religious culture from its Hebrew heritage. Later it coalesced with Greek philosophy, Roman civilization and German national characteristics to form a unity, after religion split into the Greek Church, the Roman Catholic Church and the Protestant Churches, several centuries of terrible religious wars followed.

On the contrary, there were in China no indepnedent religious heritage comparable to that of the Hebrew tradition and no such solid organization of priests as that of Christendom. Therefore, no such religious system is found in China as in the West. However, this does not mean that the Chinese nation locked a religious spirit, with only ethical or moral principles emphasized in daily life. It is very plain that since the religious faith and moral principles of the Chinese people had roots in the same unitary culture, they were merged into one even during later stages of development.

It is regrettable that many Western sinologists by applying their own narrow viewpoints while appraising Chinese culture, frequently overlooked the above mentioned fact. According to our own observation, it is very obvious that China's ancient Classics emit a profound sense of reverence toward God and true faith in Heaven.

In this regard, some Jesuit missionaries who visited China three hundred years ago, noticed this in the solemn rites paying tributes to Heaven and Earth held to be of ultimate significance by later Confucian scholars. Rituals such as these were reverently observed by all Chinese rulers through out various dynasties, even till the early years of the new Republic. Meanwhile, in some Chinese households we still find the symbolic, combined worship of Heaven, Earth, ruler, ancestors and tutors, as a remnant of the traditional culture. It cannot be denied that in such religious worship, we find genuine sentiments of profound reverence toword God and true belief in Heaven.

Of course, in ancient China only the Emperor could rightly perform the offering of sacrifices to Heaven. This rigid ceremonial precept might palpably have diluted popular religious sentiment. On the other hand, official worship of Heaven by the ruler may yet be a perfunctory matter for the purpose of consolidating his sovereign rights at that point, the Emperor's worship of Heaven was tainted by merging politics and religion into one system which is drastically reproved by both modern Chinese and Westerners alike.

Certainly, the ancient Chinese practice of reserving to the Emperor the exclusive right of Heaven-worship had some justification. It treated the sovereign as a unique representative of the people in performing this ritual, just as the Pope of Roman Catholicism may pray to God in the name of his people. The unification of politics and religion under one soverignty has been severely rebuked by Westerners, chiefly because the papacy and the historical government system had different cultural backgrounds and origins. No matter whether it was the Church ruling over the State, or vice versa, one of them would suffer one way or another. Therefore, their separation was predestined. Objectively speaking, separation might have brought to each of them the respective value of suitably domains. This arrangement also is recognized favorably by us Chinese in principle. And yet due to the traditional difference between the Chinese and Western cultural systems, the unification of politics and religion, which is condemned in the West, may not have been decried so frequently as a monstrous sin in Chinese history.

In summing up, it is obvious that just as in the West, where religion is separated from government, social, ethical or moral practices, and the status of religious worship thus distinctly emerges, so also in China we find the existence of religion, though it has been blended in certain respects with politics and ethicomoral precepts. This point might still deserve the attention of all those who pursue the study of Chinese culture.

Besides, while investigating China's practice of moral or ethical principles, we will also discover the religiously transcendental feeling embedded within them. In Chinese Humanism, there can be no denial or negligence of the concept of "Conformity of Virtue between Heaven and Man" or "Unity of Heaven and Man". This may be interpreted as "Nature and human nature are two in one," or "Heaven and Man are in comprehensive harmony." "Heaven" so-called may, of course, portray various meanings. In one sense, it is the visible sky. However, the concept of Heaven in ancient China plainly refers to God as having human personality. Although a variety of interpretation appeared in the thoughts of Confucius, Mencius, Lao Tzu and Chuang Tzu, they all attributed to the concept of Heaven a transcendental meaning as distinguished from the realistic man himself or from the realistic relation between man and man.

Now, the real problem for all true students of Chinese culture is to inquire into the process by which ancient Chinese religious faith in Heaven was transformed in later periods into the concept of "Unity of Heaven and Man," and how the theological notion in ancient Chinese culture later blended with the ethical teachings or other academic studies in Chinese culture.

In pursuing such a course of study we should not tackle the problem whether Chinese ideology admits the existence of God and true religion. The answers we seek should go beyond the mere existence of God, or religion itself and proceed to examine how Chinese cultural developments gave life to "Reciprocal Conformity between Heaven and Man," with Heaven descending to infuse itself as an intrinsic element of Man, while Man ascended upward to diffuse himself with Heaven. This theory may not be clearly understood by direct analogical interpretation from the Western point of view.

Furthermore, in learning the practical side of Chinese Humanism, the field belongs to the so-called "Yi-Li" study, the study of "righteousness in terms of reason." It is the discernment of right or wrong along the course of moral reason in self-consciousness to shape or regulate one's own intention and behavior. Such a process obviously is not limited to the superficial adjustment of relations between man and man so as to maintain the political or social order; its objective is the actual perfection of man's moral personality. The perfection of such a noble personality consists in observing everywhere the natural course of righteousness in terms of reason, regardless of personal benefit or harm, welfare or disaster, gain or loss, life or death. The objective adherence to a course of righteousness through reason, even in spite of contemptible living conditions, has long been stressed by Confucian studies.

Those who pay allegiance only to the tangible values of life, such as Machiavellian utilitarians, naturalists and materialists, cannot face death unperturbedly. For death is the nonexistence of their all, it is thus made an object of metaphysical, religious study.

On the other hand, the Confucian school of thought has been stressing the necessity of taking a correct view of both life and death. The so-called "Sacrifice of Life for Attainment of Humanity," or that "for Securing Righteousness," with other sayings of like meanings all tend to urge the human being to set the value of humanity and righteousness shiningly above that of his individual life when faced with death. Upright Chinese scholars in various periods have thus proved themselves ready and capable of sacrificing their lives for attaining humanity or justice.

Most Westerners recognized in the religious martyrs, the embodiment of transcendental religious faith. By analogy, can transcendental faith in a religious-like creed such as that evolved in Confucian teachings or sterling intention, or will power be wanting to such devoted scholars? The "vital spirit" or "moral integrity" stressed by Confucian scholars might have been placed with "the choice of martyrdom by contemplation" as its highest ideal, for it means the sacrifice of life to attain righteousness by self-conscious consideration.

How can it be achieved if absolute faith in terms of righteousness is lacking? Such faith may be looked upon as discernible in terms of humanity and justice itself, or in terms of Tao itself. It might also be interpreted as an act to "preserve the Righteousness of the universe." It may also be called an action just to "comfort one's own conscience" without necessarily committing one's self to observance of God's commandment. Nevertheless, where conscience could find peace, or the "way of life" called Tao find its right course, there the Righteousness of the universe is located, with which man might make himself indifferent to his own fate of life or death. Therefore, the Tao in which the conscience finds its comfort is on the one hand embedded within the Mind, and on the other transcending his individual realistic life. Is not human faith in this Tao exactly the same as the religious belief in a supernatural order?

After all, we hope that Western sinologists would pay due attention not only to Chinese realistic norms for the regulation of conduct among men for upholding their social or political order, but also to the ideology in the norms involving the application of "unity of Heaven and Man," with which the moral practice is endowed also with the religious-like faith in Tao. This is another point to which we hope the Westerners would pay also due attention.

Chapter VI. The Import of the Chinese "Doctrine of Transcendental Mind" in Moral Practice

From the discussion of Chinese religious-like faith in "Tao", we may proceed to talk about Chinese Rationalism or the learning of "Moral Mind and Moral Reason." This was another phase of the so-called "Yi-Li" study or the study of "Righteousness in terms of Reason." It may be treated as a discourse on the origin or the fundamental principle of "What ought to be."

This study of "Moral Mind and Moral Reason" or "Hsin and Hsing" (心性之學) has been greatly neglected or misunderstood by some Western sinologists. And yet in reality this course of learning forms the very nucleus of Chinese academic study. It is in this rationalism that we can find an explanation for the formula of "Conformity of Virtue between Heaven and Man."

Chinese rationalism held sway in the Celetial Empire during the Sung and Ming dynasties. Sung-Ming Neo-Confucianism may be looked upon as the second crest of Chinese thought in its development after the pre-Chin (the Warring-State) era. In that earlier period, Confucian and Taoist philosophies had already treated the cognizance of "Hsin" (Mind or Conscience) and "Hsing" as the nucleus of wisdom and thought. (About this subject, we have already talked at length elsewhere.)

The Ku-Wen-Shang-Shu" (Ancient Edition of Cultural History) recorded the so-called sixteen word traditional secret handed down from the Empire (2183-1752 B.C.). This book is proved beyond all doubt to be a forgery by some scribes of a later period. The fact that later scribes should be guilty of such counterfeiting, and the fact that Sung-Ming Confucian scholars liked to defend it as the sourse of Chinese culture indicates that they believed this "Hsin-Hsing" doctrine must be the origin of Chinese orthodox culture. However, most Chinese and Western scholars now cannot appreciate this point of view. One main reason is that most Chinese savants in the Ch'ing dynasty, for a period of about 300 years, devoted themselves chiefly to archaeological matters and annotating works of ancient cultural value. Reacting to the Sung-Ming Confucian School, they detested the discussion of Conscience and Human Nature. In some respects, they were half induced and half compelled to do so, for under the Manchu regime they enjoyed no freedom of thought and no freedom of speech.

At the closing stage of the Manchu rule, Western studies were imported gradually into China. What the Chinese admired in occidental culture was at first its warships and firearms, and later also its science and technology, as well as its political and judicial systems. Even later in the May 4th Enlightenment Movement around 1919, as the Chinese intellectuals clamored for the promotion of "Science and Democracy", they also propagated the pragmatism of Yen yuan and Tai Chen of the Ch'ing dynasty, in contrast to Sung-Ming Confucianism. It was chiefly because they conceived that in the archaeological study there was some sort of scientific methods.

Still later, imported Communism taught some Chinese scribes to talk about materialism, that existence determines Consciousness. Its followers also disliked the Sung-Ming school of thought.

Generally speaking, religious notions imported from the West urged man to confess the embodiment of original sin in his own nature, but the traditional Humanism of China rather treated human nature as essentially good. Between those two, there was disagreement at least in appearance.

Besides, the Sung-Ming Confucianists indulged in the metaphysical study of "Reason and Vital Spirit," which differed from the ancient classics on discourse of Heaven or God. Hence, Christian missionaries in China have disliked Chinese rationalism from the days of the early jesuits.

From the end of the Ch'ing dynasty up to the present, only the Buddhist followers. Meanwhile, "Antiquarian Scribes" such as Chang Tai-yen and "Savants" such as K'ung Tin-haum and Kang yu-wei together with disciples such as Tan Shih-tung, also took pride in having dipped into Buddhist scriptures.

However, the Buddhist doctrine of "Hsin and Hsing", with emphasis on Nirvana and future generations of the soul, is decidedly different from Confucian rationalism. With spiritual trance any mystic meditation as their tools of study, Buddhist monks may have deep and subtle penetration in their research; yet they also fail to appreciate the general characteristics of Sung-Ming Humanism. Therefore, as in the Ch'ing dynasty the traditional rationalism of China, called what you may as the study of Conscience and Human Nature in terms of Heaven, yet with humanism for its nucleus, has been for several hundred years generally neglected even by the Chinese intellectual circle in successive generations.

As related above also, while the Jesuit missionaries introduced Sung-Ming Confucianism and ancient Chinese classics to the West, they misrepresented the former as merely one type of Western rationalism or as naturalism and materialism. Hence, Chinese rationalism won a sympathetic hearing only among Western rationalism such as G. W. Leibniz and materialists such as Holbach. Later, although some sinologists translated the Doctrine of Human Nature from "Chu Tzu's Analects" and other fragments of Sung-Ming Confucianists, none of them seem really bent on deligent study of Chinese rationalism.

As the analects of some Sung-Ming Confucianists were in appearance even more fragmentary than those of the pre-Chin savants, with their philosophical systems usually hidden between the lines or scattered through several chapters, they hardly appeal to Western scholars of philosophy. Therefore, Chinese rationalism has been neglected by both Chinese and Western scholars even in the present age.

One of the main causes still persisting today in misinterpreting Chinese Rationalism is that some philosophers constantly identified this learning with the Western traditional theory of Rational Soul, or a doctrine involving some sort of epistemology and metaphysics, or a sect of psychology. The Western religious viewpoint, handed down by the Jesuit missionaries who had from the start treated the Sung-Ming rationalism as atheistic naturalism, insists in its fanciful interpretation of Hsin and Hsing as identical with the human heart and nature in their natural status or condition. From that time to the present, the Chinese word Hsing has always been translated by Western scholars as Nature.

The meaning of Nature as found in Greek Stoicism, in modern Romantic literature and in the philosophy of Baruch Spinoza, bears as a rule some profound imports which may be analogous with the Chinese word "Hsing".

However, since Christian teaching adopted the epithet "Super-nature" in contrast to "Nature," the latter has been gradually degraded to the meaning of common usage. As modern Western naturalism and materialism have come into vogue, we talk about Human Nature, generally relating it to human psychological factors such as instincts and desires in their natural projection, according to plain and trite meanings. Then and there, Chinese Rationalism usually is interpreted in the light of common and even superficial usage instead of the original Western viewpoint that may tend to probe the inner state or activity of Man's spiritual life.

Hence, according to our comprehension, it is fundamentally inaccurate to identify Chinese Rationalism with Western psychology or the Doctrine of a Rational Soul and with Epistemology or metaphysics. It would be completely wrong to treat the Chinese Hsin-Hsing principles in terms of Western naturalism as contrast to the supernatural, while interpreting Oriental Rationtalism only according to common and superficial usage.

So-called "scientific psychology" in the modern Western world is used to treat Man's natural behavior as an object of experimental scientific study. It is a purely factual research without the evaluating process of psychological activities. On the other hand, the Doctrine of a Rational Soul in traditional Western philosoply treats the human mind as an entity, stressing its formal qualities of unity, immortality, and self-existence. Meanwhile, Western Epistemology is the study of pure intellectual cognition; the question is how do we know external objects, thus rendering intellectual knowledge possible. The common school of Western metaphysics has set for its first aim to penetrate ultimate reality and the general construction of all beings in their abstract or objective senses.

On the other hand, the Chinese teachings of Hsin-Hsing handed down from Confucius and Mencius to the Sung-Ming savants might be interpreted as the learing of "transcendental mind" (as more or less preached by Kant) in a moral sense with metaphysical implications. Nevertheless, it emphasizes this learning chiefly as the foundation of moral practices in our daily life, individually as well as collectively in human society. Meanwhile, the depth of this learning varies in accordance with the depth of actual practice of the moral life. Therefore, differing from western metaphysics, it does not first of all definitely set up a psychological standard or spiritual entity as its objective for exterior abstract investigation. Nor will it seek to analyze the possibilty and acquisition of knowledge.

This Chinese Rationalism contained in itself also one type of metaphysics, but this metaphysics is bordering on Kant's "moral metaphysics." It serves as the basis for moral practices in daily life, and also it is (a metaphysics which must be) testified by our moral practices. It is nor like abstract metaphysics which by inference based on experience and reasoning, leads one to conclude that there exists an objective Supreme Being.

Since Chinese Rationalism has its peculiar characteristics any one who is not devoted to moral practice, (or even though so dedicated, but only to some fragmentary moral principles of a certain society, or else to canons of a certain church as contained in the Old and New Testaments,) would not be really able to understand the learning of Hsin-Hsing in its full significance. In other words, this subject of study does not permit the student to take up any one object for cool research and then adjust his attitude of behavior to the object only when it is well understood. Such a manner of study might be employed in the study of external natural science or external social conditions, or even of faith in a transcendent God. However, it cannot be used with satisfection in the pursuit of our own moral practices and the "transcendental mind" conceived or revealed through such practice. In it practice must arise out of consciousness of one's moral tenets, and in turn such consciousness might also be increased through regular pratice. Consciousness and practice thus make parallel progress.

This state of being conscious may be expressed in words which, however, will not be fully or truly understood by other persons unless they too have caught the same consciousness through like practice. In case practice is weakened one degree, consciousness and actual understanding will also decrease proportionately. In their interdependence, practice or moral principles may be directed definitely toward some body or something outside oneself. and yet consciousness of them is purely within one's own mind.

Hence each step forward in the practice of moral teaching finds a corresponding advance in inner consciousness.

Similarly, when man's morly application covers the family, its inner consciousness may also permeated the household; when it extends to the country, the consciousness of it may extend to the nation; and when reaching out to the realm of the universe or the historical domain, and all good or evil factors, together with their circumstances, then man's inner feelings may also approach the vast span of the cosmos with all the related factors concerned in it.

Therefore, all moral practices in human life for the accomplishment of material affairs might "boomerang" as factors for the formation of its own inner virtue toward the achieving of its own self-perfection. As viewed from outside, the moral practice may have been merely an act following the social ritual or legal regulation, the Order of Heaven. But as viewed from inner consciousness by introspection, all that is accomplished is a mere exertion of one's own "transcendental mind." Human will in the practice of moral principles may have no limit in its involvements. Accordingly, the transcendental mind may have no bounds for its exertion. However, in the limitless domain of the Chinese Hsin-Hsing, there should be no purely abstract speculation. It may be displayed without bounds in the perspective and thus attract our attention when our moral practice itself is boundless so as to attest to the hypothesis that man and the universe, together with all the myriad things involved, are in essence "one harmonius whole." By this attestation, it is evident that the "Innate Mind (Hsin)" and "Human Nature (Hsing) "are at the same time and in the same artery joining Heaven in the course of action.

Therefore, by exerting the Moral mind (Hsin) to understand the moral reason (Hsing), one might be able to understand Heaven or the Heavenly Way; by cherishing well the Mind and nourishing the Moral reason he might thereby "attend to Heaven." It is said that Human Moral reason is precisely Heavenly Reason, and human virtues coincide with the celestial virtues; all human events performed for the full development of Moral Reason with the accomplishment of virtuous deeds, can assist the transforming and fourishing influence of Heaven and Earth.

Hence, Sung-Ming Confucian scholars inferred from "The Doctrine of the Mean" their doctrine that the Moral Reason of man is the Celestial or Divine Reason; the Innate moral mind, Heart, is the Cosmic Mind; the lucidity of human conscience is the lucidity of the universe together with all things in it; human conscience and innate ability manifest, therefore, the principle of "omniscience of Heaven and omnipotence of Earth." This is the the so-called theory of "Unity of Heaven and Man."

The subtlety and sagacity of Chinese Rationalism cannot be discussed here in detail. Nevertheless, as it has been conceived by Confucius and Mencius and later developed by Sung and Ming scholars, there is obviously one common understanding among them. They invariably believed that actual moral practice and the enlightening or enlightened knowledge make reciprocal progress by mutual reliance, and that all moral practice toward the external world is generated by the internal drive on self-exertion of Conscience and Moral Reason, -which cannot by themselves stop the urgent demand of action. They likewise jointly recognized that when man develops or exerts his internal "transcendental mind" in its plenitude, he eventually approaches Celestial Virtue, Heavenly Reason and the Cosmic Mind, so as to achieve the "Conformity of Virtue between the Universe and Man," or the "Formation of a Trio (Ternion) with Heaven and Earth." This is the traditional essence of Chinese Rationalism.

If we can appreciate such Rationalism as the essence of Chinese culture, we should definitely rule out the misunderstanding that the main current of Chinese culture has limited itself to external realistic adjustment of relationships among human beings at the expense of internal, spiritual activities and religious or metaphysical transcendental feelings, Rather by the learning of Moral Mind and Moral Reason man's outward actions are all referred to, and directed toward the achievement of internal, spiritual activities. They are all likewise directed toward the celestial virtues in assisting the transformation and nourishment of the powers of Heaven and Earth.

Chinese Rationalism, therefore, is an ideological hinge upon which the man's internal life is his outward life and the universe. It holds the communication line in the systematical conveying of social, ethical, ritual and legal activities, in their internal transformation or cultivation, in connection with the religious spirit and the metaphysical conception, so as to make them combined into a unity.

On the other hand, the Western culture follows generally a different pattern. Its metaphysics or philosophy and science are treated only as a pure intellectual study of the objective world and has nothing to do with moral practice. This is the traditional culture of Greek origin. Concerning religion, it has had set up a supreme being with fixed attributes and ordinances of God. This is the Hebrew tradition, And concerning law, politics, rituals and ethics, it fears the premise that all of them are external norms for the regulation of human behaviors. This principally is the tradition originating from Roman jurisprudence and ethics.

Chinese Rationalism, however, differs from all these three traditions of Western Culture. It is liable, therefore, to be slighted over by modern Western scholars and Chinese savants who are accustomed to the Occidental academic points of view, or else even misinterpreted by those with some partial knowledge. In the absence of a true conception of the Chinese learning about the transcendental mind, no one can really understand Chinese culture in its essential meaning.

Chapter VII. Reasons Governing Durability of Chinese History and Culture

If we cauld understand the important meaning of Chinese Rationalism, we could proceed to discuss the problem concerning how Chinese history and culture could have lasts several thousands of years without any interruption.

In the matter of the duration of a cultural history, only India may compare with China. However, as the East Indians have long persistently reposed their minds in the religious faith of eternity they have lacked the temporal, or historical perspective. Even though their cultural history has been long in terms of years, they may not be actually conscious of this duration. On the other hand, China preserves the long perspective of her cultural history in such a way that she is the only ancient country that is still conscious of its longevity.

But, then, how could Chinese culture and history have lasted such a hony long time? It cannot be explained away by a hypothesis such as Spengler's that since the Han Dynasty (204 B.C.-220 A.D.) Chinese cultural progress has been bogged down in stagnation. In fact, it has not been bogged down all this time, for, otherwise, it may have disintegrated or simply wiped out.

Some one has said, that the durability of Chinese culture and history wa chiefly due to the Chinese people's emphasis on the maintenance of a realistic life, as different from the Western culture which was devoted more t the pursuit of idealism or a Christian paradise.

Others said, that the long duration of Chinese culture was due to it conservatism, with which all the human activities were confined to habitua

processes without waste of much energy. Hence, the Chinese national vitality could preserve its continuity on account of its frugality.

Some others have said, that the reason may be more simple still, namely,
the Chinese foundness of having numerous offsoring; their marvelous repoduc-
tivity had been able to offset frequent losses of the population through natural calamities and national disasters.

Besides, these, there are also many other explanations. It may not be
possible for us to brush them aside as entirely devoid of same valid grounds.
However, none of these reasons can solve our problem, so we have to resort
to Chinese ideological factors for the answer. According to our viewpoint,
the culture of any one nation is the expression of its spritual life and has
for its nucleus its ideology pure and simple. Therefore, the answer to the
problem must be found in Chinese ideology.

For academic discussion, we may rather affirm our conviction that the
Chinese ideology in genaral has ever since ancient times demanded for
co-ordination of the Chinese realistic life by use or cultivation of sort of
transcendental mind. This view may well dispose of the former hypothesis
that Chinese culture laid more emphasis on the maintenance of a realistic life
at the expense of the necessary pursuit of transcendental activities.

Next, it may be more correct to say that Chinese ideology has, ever from
the beginning, urged the people not to exhaust its energy by outward exer-
tion, but to reserve it for the appreciation and cultivation of its reproductive
vitality. This theory is to rectify the former hypothesis that Chinese culturae
had merely over-emphasized conservatism, that the Chinese people had thus
led only some sort of habitual life without much waste of their energy.

Furthermore, from earliest times in Chinese history, Chinese ideology laid
emphasis on the value of human life, and thus highly praised its everlasting
continuation with the pride vested in the possession of enormous offspring as
a mere corollary.

In summing up, the duration of Chinese culture and history was rooted
in Chinese ideology and its philosophy of human life, in other words, it was
not due to any mere external causes that the national culture enjoyed longevity without interruption.

One of the eminent conceptions of human life according to the Chinese
transcendental mind is, as objective evidence shows, the aspiration for "eterni-

ty" which took shape in earliest Chinese thought. In ancient religious tenets, there was the notion "the Decree of Heaven may not stay permanent on certain people," It means that Heaven or God is no respecter of persons, be they kings or subjects. That is, the decree of heaven rests with the virtuous: Godness obtains it while the want of godness loses it. The Duke of Chow was deeply impressed by the fact that the Ordinance of Heaven had been changed in accordance with the possession of virtue as exemplified in the two previous dynasties, Hsia (2183-1752 B.C.) and Yin (1751-1111 B.C.). And so the Chinese sage earnestly cautioned the then newly established government of Chow, together with the people, through specific messages, how to keep the Heavenly blessing in order to prolong its sociopolitical heritage. This was the doctrine bent on seeking the blessing of "eternity" on the national culture.

With it, the Chow dynasty did last for about 800 years as the longest of all past Chinese ruling houses. Thereupon, the reflective teaching of the Duke as its first prime minister Cannot be denied of its merits.

Later, the philosphical concept of eternity was formally presented by the Confucian classics in the Book of Changes and the Doctrine of the Mean. In them there were the notions of "the possibility of achieving magnificence and permanency;" and thus, by "reaching far and continuing long," the possibility of "perfecting all things." Meanwhile, Lao-tze also urged the people to model themselves after the Tao of Heaven and Earth in "attaining immortality" with "deep-rooting and firm calyptra as similitude for achieving long life and perspective."

The Book of Changes, the Doctrine of the Mean and the work of Lao-tze were all written around the era of Chinese "Warring, states." That epoch was in ancient China was one of many critical changes, hence, all social and political conditions could not last long. It was exactly in that era that the the theory of eternity was emphasized by both Confucian and Taoist schools or thought. This may help clarify that the seeking for eternity was first embedded in the ancient Chinese thought by their self-consciousness.

Later, each of the ruling houses such as the Han, Tang and Sung, etc., each of which held the governmental reins respectively for several hundred years, might have been benefited by the political and cultural plannings assigned for the pursuit of durability. As in the masses of the Chinese people, the longevity of their national culture might also be ascribed to their continuous flow of thoughts striving for permanency. This variety of teachings, as recorded by ancient historiographers, together with political mandates and other exhortations, while later the causes of accomplishments or collapese of the ruling houses in China in different periods as related by historians, and then the diverse principles governing the ways and means to attain permanency or other-wise as deduced and expounded by philosophers are very complicated and rich in there contents when apreading all over the vast nation.

Briefly speaking, the eternity principle as expressed under the cloak of Taoism is a sort of utilitarianism taking pride in tactical the strategy of "retreating only for advancing further" in its path. As Laotze put it: "Heaven and Earth are long-lasting. The reason why Heaven and Earth can last long is that they live not for themselves, and thus they are able to endure" He preached that "Life will proceed forward to perfection by leaving behind its animal instincts, and it can persist in existence by abandoing all of its outside entanglements. This principle exactly preaches the necessity of subordinating the realistic prejudices of mankind to Reason; and, therefore, of refraining from overexertion of his energy by reserving it internally so as to attain well being and longevity. This attitude urges man to abate selfish-ness and selfish desires, to "return to the state of a plain child," to attain the state of a mental vacuum and tranquillity, and to concentrate the vital spirit on sobriety so as to make life "return to its origin." The application of this principle is aimed at making the mortal man reach to the fountain of his natural vitality and thus preserve his natural energy for a long time.

On the Confucain side, a more or less similar principle was presented in a somewhat different style. Many Confucian scholars also advised man under certain circumstances, to reserve his natural vitality for the inner man with a view of perfecting the ritual relationship among men. For instance, by following as closely as possible the Ritual Regulations of the Chow Dynasty in both public and private life, the Confucian school identified the virtues of the superior man with the qualities of jade, the characteristics of which are gentle in appearance but firm and strong inside. With material firm-ness and moral strength kept within, humn life might tend to accumulate all of its vitality as time went on. The difference of strength between the peo-ple of Northern regions and those of Southern regions as described by the Doctrine of the Mean, lies in the fact that the former emphasied the exer-tion of forces outward whereas the latter stressed "for bearance and gentleness in teaching others with such self-control as not even to revenge an unreasona-ble trespass." Thus reserving the strength inward, with gentleness shown without and firmness kept within, the Southerners could constantly build up their morality even under trying conditions. Hence, Confucius taught it with the remark that the superior man should make it his study.

It is also worth mentioning that such a virtue as we have describe above would enable a man, after he had reserved and accumulated his inward vitality, to release more effectively both his abundant energy, and moral strength at the right moment, when some righteous cause calls for action. By keeping regular hours the built-up morality within would also express itself through the human body by enriching or illuminating a man's natural course of life. That was what Confucian teaching about the "person made lustrous by his virtue." In other words, "a broad mind may also beget a healthy physique."

In Western ethical studies, the discussian of morality usually is devoted to a discussion of regulations for human behavior and the social value of moral codes in their relation to religious worship; yet very few of the scholars who have treated this topic have particulaily stressed this point that moral practices should thoroughly transform the behaviour of our natural life so as to make its attitude and manners show the reorientation of its inners virtues. In the meantime, there is the value of such internal virtue which can illuminate and enrich life. On the other hand, the traditional Confucian studies have been emphasizing just this point with much emphasis.

As we have discussed before, all Chinese virtues in the Confucian conception have their roots in human nature or in the mind in its transcendental sense. This nature is identical with the highest universal reason, the Heavenly ordained principle, and this mind, is also communicated with Heaven's mind, cosmic mind. Therefore, human nature and mind, in communicating with those of Heaven, are the inexhaustible fountain of man's virtues. While these virtues can emollient and enrich our physical beings, the existence of which is then under the control of the transcendental mind in conjunction with the permeation of Celestial Reason and Heaven's Mind. In this way man gets adjusted, gets protection and nourishment in realistic existence in the universe.

In regard to the long conservation of Chinese national life, the Chinese obsession of having offspring should not be interpreted merely as a biological instinct to preserve the race or tribe. Ever since the Chou dynasty, such a custom has been followed in a selfconcsious way for the purpose of perpetuating ancestral lineage. It has an ensemble of religious, moral and political meanings. Usually, the natural instinct of mankind is limited to the love between man and woman or between husband and wife, together with the parental love of their own children. This instinctive desire for continuation of their lives is flowing forward and downward. However, it requires some sort of transcendental concept over the aforesaid tendency in order that it could accentuate filial piety toward parents and ancestors who gave births to their own lives. By this keen filial piety, they could also be cautioned with fear that their ancestors may be cut out from receiving ceremonial worship should they have no children of their own. This concept is exactly a transcendental mind over the realistic life as to comfort their parents' anxiety and their ancestors' spirit. By this principle it was emphasized, "There are three things which are unfilial, while the lack of posterity is the greatest of them." And then, the desire to perpetuate one's realistic life down to thousands of generations may also be looked upon as a transcendental ideal which must not be interpreted as a mere animal instinct for preservation of its race. It should be viewed through the prevailing Chinese conception that, as man's mind ought to reach back to epochs thousands of the in the past epoch and ahead to myriad generations in the future, the Mind manifests its unfathomable vastness.

By analogy, we might come to recognize that neither should the Chinese desire to perpetuate their civilization to endless ages be interpreted as a mere habit of conservatism.

The desire to perpetuate ancestral lineage and the desire to prolong cultural heritage have the same objective evidence for their transcendental mood. That is, in ancient Confucian scholastic thought, it clearly denounced the act of destroying others' state or annihilating others' ancestral lineage as one devoid of righteousness. Accordingly, the Confucian notion of justice and nobility was extended over an attempt not only to keep intact the culture handed down by the Duke of Chou but also to restore the varied traditions of the Hsia and Yin dynasties, with descents reinstituted to prolong their ancestral worship. What the "Annals of Spring and Autum" had championed as a great virtue in "reviving the perished state and restoring the broken family," was then an objective and universal principle prvailing not merely in the state of Lu, the native land of Confucius.

While the sage was making tedious trips to several countries, he obviously intended to propagate his politicomoral principles in the entire Chinese empire and apply them if he could find the opportunity. His courageous yet hazardous crusade, with many disciples in the entourage, might have well explained that the Confucian school had no sympathy for racialism or narrow nationalism. Nor has it followed any conservative habit in its motive to perpetuate the Chinese race and culture.

Regarding Confucius' advocation of sovereignty for Chou over the Empire in renunciation of all barbarian tribes, it has been true that later all his followers throughout Chinese history have also pursued more or less the same line of discrimination. And yet we find also the broder view "to treat barbarians as Chinese should they adopt the Chinese way of life." In accordance with Chinese Rationalism, which formed the nucleus of Chinese culture, the volume of Mind is so vast as to be without limit, whole that of Nature (Reason) is also unfathomable. Therefore, alien cultural elements acceptable to the Chinese transcendental mind, would also be tolerated by the Confucian school. This is what the Doctrine of the Mean stressed as "appropriate ways of life, like the courses of sun and moon, which be getting along well without colliding." By this concept of the universe, Chinese culture has been endowed with the nature of magnanimity which is the root of its longevity. Hence, the Chinese nation has been famed as the most tolerant toward religious faith. All the persecution of Buddhists in Chinese history and the Boxer Uprising against Christianity were in fact fomented by political agitation rathor than cultural factors. This point needs no futher discussion.

Therefore, it is plain that we can never accept the view that the endearment of Chinese cultural life in its durability and the longevity of Chinese history were interpreted as chiefly due to Chinese racial instinct and conservative habits. To explain why the ancient Chinese so discriminated against the barbarians on their borders, the crucial reason probably lies in the objective value of Chinese culture which was actually higher than that of the barbarians. Hence, it was not advisable to change the Chinese way of life by adopting on inferior one from abroad. On the other hand, many Chinese had absorbed the best elements of other cultural patterns and handed them on after assimilation.

By the same process of cultural interflow, even though all Marxist followers had doggedly renounced the value of Buddhism, Christiantity, and Western culture, most of the real Chinese people are still willing to fight for their preservation. How long will that act of conservation last? It many be millions of years. What will this sort of obsession follow? It will follow the course and magnitude of the Chinese Heart, which is always traceable baek thousands of years transmittable to thousands of generations in the future. This is the core of reasnoing in Chinese self-consciousness for endearing the preservation of Chinese culture and history. And it also is the core of reasoning that explains why Chinese history and culture have been able to attain substantial preservation in their traditional transmission lineage in the past several thousand years.

The foregoing statement is made as a clarification of some prevalent yet inaccurate view-points held by both Western and Chinese scholar on Chinese culture, especially regarding some of its basic characteristics. These characteristics are significant, for in them lies the obverse or the positive value of Chinese culture.

Of course, we also acknowledge the many shortcomings in the idealistic phase of Chinnse culture and we admit defects in its realistic application. These points will be discussed later in our treatise. Nevertheless, we must recognize this fact: Any type of culture, if actually treated as an expression of the objective spiritual life of mankind, should be considered in terms of its positive value as provided by its original idealism. We may well understand that any defect in its idealism can only be reflected when it is extended to higher or greater ideals. Its shortcomings or errors in actual implementation might be reflected when its application is limited, obstructed or interrupted by other unfavorable entanglements. Such as observation is of secondary importance.

Toward an individual person, if we can first ascertain the merits of his ideas, then we may also extend to him due respect. Later when we discover shortcomings in his ideas or defects in their practice, we might still offer remedial measures to show our kind regards toward him. This same treatment should apply also to any cultural system which is an expression of the spiritual life of mankind in its objective phases.

PART 2

Chapter VIII. Development of Chinese Culture in the Natural Sciences.

As we have just related, the shortcomings in Chinese culture in its idealistic phase may only be detected through reflective processes when its ideal is extended to a higher or greater state. In other words, we cannot calculate the value of Chinese culture or direct its future course by the exclusive use of external standards. In an attempt to discuss its ideological defects, we must first conceive what should be the direction of its development in order to achieve any higher or greater status, by which the shortcomings of its former state might then be discovered through timely reflection.

In an attempt to extend the ideal of Chinese culture to a higher or greater position, a common proposal may make it best to include the ideal pattern of other cultural domains with that of the indigenous product. However, such a project may tend to expand the ideals by mere addition without regard for the direction which the native culture may be best developed to its ideal perfection. By such addition, Chinese culture should try to absorb the best elements of other civilizations, for this process could also mean expansion of its idealogical domain. For instance, China has the Rationalism which unifies philosophy, morality and religion into one school of the transcendental mind, yet lacks an independent system of philosophy and religion which we are also willing to embrace in order to enrich Chinese heritage.

However, in the ideal state of Chinese traditional culture, we should recognized that it is not a serious defect for China to lack an independent system of religion and philosophy. On the other hand, because of the separation of philosophy, religion and moral teachings in the West, Chinese Rationlism would probably meet defeat in Western civilization. This point will be discussed later. In any case, we should set side the addition method in a projected expansion of our cultrual domain for its ideal attainment. And we might proceed only to point out what should be the ideal goal for extention of present Chinese culture in accordance with the demand for a desirable course by itself.

We thus advocate that in accordance with its own demand for development, Chinese culture must develop a full-fledged ideal of culture in a way that the Chinese people not only realize themselves to be a moral subject (moral being) through their Rationalism but also a political subject (political being) with regard to politic matters, and an epistemological self (epistemological being) in dealing with the world of knowledge, and a technolological, practical subject (technoIogical, practical being) in controlling their social and natural enviroment. This means also that China needs real democratic reconstruction and science education together with practical skills. Chinese culture also needs to absorb the good features of the Western and its contributions to genuine culture. Chinese thought, following the lead of Western cultures must recognized itself to be not only a moral subject, but also a political subject, an epistemological self and a technological, practical self. Such procedures will then enable the Chinese perionality to attain a much higher plane of perfection; moreover, the objective spiritual life of the Chinese race will attain a higher state of development. On closer scrutiny, we discover that just such a higher plane of perfection and higher state of development is precisely what the Chinese people demand when they consciously strive to make themselves to be moral subject; and it also meets the original demand of the Chinese race in the developing process of its objective spiritual life.

We acknowledge that historical Chinese culture lacked the modern Western democratic system, Western scientific study, and the current practical skills in technology. As a result, China has been unable to attain real modernization and industrialization. However, we still cannot acquiesce in the charge that in the Chinese ideal state the notion of democracy was lacking. or that the internal aspiration of Chinese political development did not urge the establishing of a democratic system. Nor can we acknowledge that Chinese culture is anti-scientfic, radically contemptuous of technical skills. Its democratic spirit will be discussed in a later chapter.

Concerning science study and its application, we might well have observed that the culture of ancient China placed definite emphasis on practical knowledge and skill. This is proved by the fact that all the sage-rulers, according to tradition, were inventors of one or more appliances. The Confucian school also held the notion that the "Tao of metaphysical import might be expressed through substantial appliance." It stressed the need of "establishing virtues," "exploiting utilities," and "enriching lively hood." Hence, in ancient China, knowledge of astronomy, mathematics and medicine early flourished with remarkable success. Before the 18th century, China also surpassed the West, as is generally recognized, in such items as handicraft and agricultural skills. Nevertheless, we still concede that Chinese culture lacked Western-type science because the fundamental spirit of the latter was set above the motive of daily application for short-term profits.

This Western science spirit, orginating from the Greek theory of "seeking knowledge for the sake of knowledge," tended to set up from the start an objective or ideal realm for its pursuit. It reserved, at least temporarily, all of its practical activities and moral purposes. It surpassed all consideration of profit or loss and even bypassed the criterion of its moral evaluation. It makes our cognitive mind possible on the one hand to observe the objective reality as such (and every phenomenon which is presented to this mind), and on the other hand, it is able to engage in pure theoretical deduction according to logical reason, by means of which both the laws of objective reality and the categories of thought and logical rules (which are manifested in this procedure of reasoning) may also become clear and be explicitly and unmistakably contempleted and discovered by this pure cognitive mind of ours. Such a scientific spirit was found wanting in ancient Chinese studies which were, therefore, limited in the development of theoretical science. For this reason, Chinese knowledge in applied arts and technology was also limited in its progress. Such a handicap in turn restrained the extension of such activities in the realm of technical skill to exploit nature for the enrichment of the nation.

A basic reason why China lacked the Western scientific spirit is that ancient Chinese thought over-emphasized the combined teaching and practice of moral principles. It thus cannot persistently reserve its adjudgement on the value of world affairs in their objective realm. It was for such a short-term, if not exactly short-sighted, adjudication that most pursuits of knowledge directly transfered themselves to internal moral cultivation and external practical usage. It was a process by which the act of "establishing virtues" was directly brought over to that of "exploiting utilities for enriching livelihood." Then and there, due to the lack of an intermediary in the expanding field of theoretical science, the act for establishing virtues cannot reach to the broad or positive act of exploitation of nature and economic advancement. Worse still, it may even retreat to the state of internal moral cultivation for the sake of mere individual complacency.

Even though retreating may make an individual better realize the dignity of internal moral subjectivity with his moral mind and moral reason reaching up and joining those of the universe--(this was exactly the accomplishment of the Sung-Ming Rationalist School), nevertheless, such an achievement may at the same time block the way of this moral subjectivity in its exit for outward expansion, resulting in isolation and withering death.

It was not until such Confucian scholar as Wang Fu-chih, Ku Yen-wu and Huang Chung-hsi sounded the alarm at the end of the Ming dynasty that China apprehended the shortcomings of "inward shrinkage" of morality. The necessity of finding an out-let became apparent.

As China lacked the tradition of theoretical science, many scholars in the subsequent Ch'ing dynasty, although striving to expand their moral strength outward, still were attracted chiefly to ancient cultural matters; proudly they undertook archaeological studies and annotations. Eventually, their mental forces atrophied like the antiquities they contemplated. Internally, they neglected or missed the enlightement of moral subjectivity of Sung-Ming scholars, whereas externally they could not exploit utilities for enriching livelihood through establishing of their virtues. Such an academic drawback thus unfortunately brought about greater seclusion and a stagnancy of the Chinese cultural spirit.

There was, nonetheless, one minor stream of academic thought striving to reach the original goal of national economic reconstruction by use of scientific knowledge thus far gathered by Confucian scholars at the end of the Ming dynasty and handed down to those in the Manchu regime. This minority group stressed utilitarianism in water conservation and the irrigation system, agricultural development, medical research, calendar study, and astronomical observation. It was then led by such savants as Yen Yuan and

Tai-Cheng and followed up by those who championed the "Wealth and Power" movement till the end of the Ch'ing dynasty. Their common short-coming was rooted in the lack of Western-typed theoretical science together with the technical methods for intermediaries. Their traditional ways and means therefore, could hardly approach the desired goal. When an attempt is made to grasp Western theoretical science and put its spirit to work, the Chinese people must at least temporarily withhold their practical obsession, and ban the moral objective embedded in it. Unfortunately, this keynote was never comprehended by Chinese thinkers during that crucial period in the last three or four decades of the 19th century.

In case the significant point is to be recognized, the Chinese must not only through self-consciousness treat themselves as a moral subject by which they can utilize theoretical knowledge directly through desirable economic application as a technological, practical subject; but they must also self-consciously set themselves up as a pure epistemological subject. And when attaining the latter form of subjectivity, the Chinese should also temporarily forget that they exist merely for accomplishment of some moral engagement. They must also abandon the obsession that all knowledge had its worth merely in its practical value. Such an exalted stage of "seeking knowledge for the sake of knowledge" was hardest to attain for those who were well-learned in China's traditional culture.

Actually, when the Chinese cannot treat themselves through self-consciousness as an epistemological subject they can neither fully assume the role of a moral and technological subject. In other words, if the Chinese really want to set themselves up as a moral subject they must try also to set themselves up as an epistemological subject. In that subtle process, the former should temporarily suspend its role or at least temporarily retreat behind the latter as its supporting character. That must be done till the latter has accomplished its mission and resolved knotty problems. Till then, the moral subject might step forward, evaluating, guiding and promoting its pragmatic activities. By this process, our moral subject might elevate itself to the mastership of controlling its forward or backward action while, at the same time, controlling the "to-and-fro" movement of the expistemological subject, with the former even better facilitated in its attainment of moral aubject.

We might reach the conclusion here that the human moral subject must elevate itself to such a status of controlling its own forward or backward actions together with the advancement or retreat of its epistemological activities. In that exalted status the moral subject may attain its supreme role. This is what we call the greatest benevolence of mankind which necessarily consists of Benevolence and Wisdom or intellect. Wisdom or intellect employed should be free to speak its mind with calm discernment of its object, free to carry itself to the world-wide action at its best, while Benevolence is kept in the background. On the contrary, when Wisdom is not employed in certain circumstances, it should be "rolled up and kept in secrecy," whereas Benevolence must prevail with its moral evaluation. The dominant theme is how to employ available wisdom or intellect solely for the purpose of establishing one's self and related matters.

By use of the aforesaid formula to guide the future development of the Chinese culture, it is necessary to establish in the culture a purely theoretical science realm or an independent scientific cultural domain. In other words, it will be imperative that along with the Chinese traditional moral principles and their practices, a new academic system, for the continuous rerearch of scientific knowledge, must be established. Just such an undertaking is what the traditional spirit of Chinese culture should have demanded for the perfection and elevation of itself.

Consequently, the application of theoretical science for the promotion of practical skills to facilitate the industrialization of China, is in conformity with the ancient Chinese cultural spirit; of several thousand years standing and may be expressed in the formula: to establish virtue, exploit for use and enrich the standard of life. It goes without saying that the Chinese people must strive for the realization of these goals as a matter of course.

Chapter IX. Development of Chinese Culture in National Democratic Reconstruction

Regarding the issue of national democratic reconstruction, we have stated above that in Chinese cultural history there was a lack of a modern Western democratic system. In its earliest stage, China had an aristocratic feudalism in vogue; and later, since the Chin·dyuasty (221-206 B. C.), monarchy prevailed till 1911. Under the monarchical system, the supreme sovereignty was vested in the ruler, not in the people. By this basic political concept, the Chinese system of government presented numerous knotty problems. Such problems as the order of succession to the throne, the change of the ruling house, and the arrangement of the exact status of the prime minister, were usually not resolved with reasonable satisfaction. Especially during the inevitable change of a ruling house, these were many heroes fighting for the throne, fighting with all of their spiritual and armed might at the expense of the people, till a new dynasty was born again in the name of a Heavenl; Decree, and the empire was once again unified under one man's rule.

Under the monarchical hereditary system, if the ruler happened to be good and capable, there was political stability for the time being. Should the ruler be capable, yet wicked in behavior, he might most likely get into trouble with his prime minister and would also oppress the people with despotic taxation and conscription for military or labor services. In case the monarch was neither capable nor good, then some royal relatives, powerful ministers, and even tricky eunuchs in the court would tend to fight over the crumbling throne, with subsequent chaos throughout the nation. As the reign of a good and capable ruler was not a matter of course, any dynasty thus set up was bound to get decline if no new bracing up was possible. Hence, the Chinese political history has been one studded with peace and chaos in an alternative pattern.

Now, the only way to break up such an unfortunate political rotation depends upon the establishing of a modern democratic system. Hence, about 48 yeaas ago there was the inauguration of the Chinese Republic. The present problem pending adequate solution is how to tackle the task of actually achieving the national democratic reconstruction.

Even though China is still unable to accomplish her democratic reconstruction, we cannot say that in the internal aspiration for the Chinese political development there is the centrifugal tendency against democracy. Nor should we assert that Chinese culture lacks the seed of democratic thought.

First of all, we must understand that even though the monarchical system had long prevailed in China, yet it did not correspond exactly with the Western monarchical system. One basic difference was that from the beginning according to Chinese political thought, popular will was identical with a Heavenly Decree. Hence, the ruler who proclaimed himself the recipient of the celestial blessings must act theoretically in faithful response to the people's will, and must be able to pass the popular trial. Accordingly, in ancient Chinese court regulations, the emperor "should take into consideration the poems offered by his ministers and scholars, ... the persuasions of many of the lower officials, the petitions of the common people, the advice of courtiers, the supplementary observation of royal relatives and also the cautions of historio-graphers," thus making the government one capable of exchanging opinions between the governing and the governed. In the meantime, the historio-grapher's impartial keeping of court records and the right of officials, to make the posthumous title for the ruler, had some restraining influeme upon the behavior of the monarch. There was some sort of spiritual shackles put upon the ruler's actions.

Subsequently, ancient China's political development produced a more or

532

less definite form of a cabinet system which represented the then intellectual elements in the nation. There was the censorial system with cenors to watch the ruler's as well as the common official's behavior and actions against any malfeasance. There were also the royal invitation system, selection system and official examination system, etc., to promote intellectual personnel to government posts. All these systems might tend to curb the monarchical power in a moral, if not exactly in a political, sense and also keep the bridge open between the central government and the masses of the People. The establishment of all such systems showed the Chinese cultural influence as represented by the intellectual class. The only deplorable phenomenon was in that whether these systems were honored by the ruler depended upon his individual integrity. - Should he think fit to ignore or violate them, there was no fundamental law of the land—a constitution which must be mutually observed by the ruler and the ruled—to put a definite check upon malfeasance. Hence, the intellectuals might still be subjected to the subservient employment of the monarch and his courtiers, or to his oppression, banishment or even be given the death sentence. In such circumstances, the Chinese intellectuals could behave only as upright scholars or martyrs.

In the righteous spirit of those Chinese scholars, has usually shown in their protests or resistance to the ruler's and his courtiers's arbitrary power and despotic will. In case such a resistance still could not save the government from corruption and the country from perishing, owing to monarchical despotic power, the situation might then call into action of the people's emergency power which was to put a decisive brake on the governing machine. Then and there, the former political system which was subjected to the monarchical mandate had to transform itself into a new system set up by the people under a constitutional system. The old political authority which might only have changed hands through a conp d'etat, or war, had to be transformed into one liable to get changed through a peaceful succession of political parties. This is what we call the natural development of the Chinese monarchy and the Chinese cultural resistance to, and demand of, the monarchy: the new political system is bound to replace the old and inclined toward establishing a modern democracy.

Meanwhile, as we have related, it is unjustifiable to assert that there was no democratic seed latent in Chineae culture, because both Confuciar and Taoist political thought had confirmed that the ruler should never abuse his power. Instead, they advised him to "reign by non-action" or to "reign by means of virtue." This was in principle putting a check upon, or a controlling force over, the monarchical authority. Ordinarily, it was but a moral design on the monarchy. However, the Confucian school had also paid high tribute to succession to the throne on account of moral strength as practised by the Emperors Yao and Shun, or else through armed revolution by King Tang of Shang and King Wu of Chow. It signified the conviction that "the empire belonged to no single individual but to the people as a whole," and also that "the throne is liable to change hands;" and that an ideal government should be bent on satisfying the people's desire while extirpating aversion. This is one systematic principle handed down by Confucius and Mencius and later expounded by Huang Li-chow (1610-1695 A. D.) at the end of the Ming dynasty.

Formerly, two obvious shortcomings in the Confucian political thought were its ambiguity about legal provisions governing the right of succession to the throne, and its vagueness as how to formulate effective policies in response to the people's general feelings. The highly praised act of "harmonious relinquishing and accepting of the throne" as practiced by the emperors Yao and Shun; if pursued merely in accordance with the sovereign's personal whims, is still but a private and not a legal instrument. The Confucian view of "harmonious abdication and succession" was later abused by some usurpers to camouflage a coup D'etat. By the same token some sort of continuous revolutionary campaigns could not establish a durable state of peace. The revolution of the King of Shang or that of the King of Chow, as championed by the Confucian school, was also evoked by later ambitious figures to fight for the possession of the Celestial Empire when fishing in troubled waters seemed opportune or justifiable.

Nevertheless, many Confucian principles are noteworthy such as "the empire belongs to no one individual alone; "that in the matter of moral advancement, "all human beings are eligible to be Yao and Shun or other types of sage and superior men;" and that "the sovereign should follow the people's sentiments of their likings or dislikes." All these principles signify the Chinese noble concept that "the empire is jointly shared by the general public and should be maintained impartially in the public interests," with equality of personality of the people duly stressed. This concept definitely might be treated as the fountainhead of the Chinese democratic ideology, or at least the seed of it.

We make the aforesaid observation with a corollary that the ancient Confucian political philocophy eventually must develop to be the modern democratic principle and its materialization, because its develoment inevitably was contrary to the monarchical system. As an absolute ruler treated the empire as his own household, it was in every respect treated as private property. At the same time, while the political status of the people cannot be equal to that of the monarch, under the fiction that "the emperor can do no wrong but hie subjects are guilty of any and every charge," then, even their moral status and personality were degraded for below those of the ruler.

On the contrary, as the Confucian principle revealed, both the ruler and the people were actually on the same moral and human level. Then, in political matters the people might also claim the right to carry out the doctrine of reciprocity in that "while the people can do no wrong, the emperor must be answerable for his guilt." In attempting to make such a notion realizable, the Confucian doctrine eventually tended to transform the monarchy into a democracy. Hence, the teaching of "the empire is for the public" and "men are born equal in personality" certainly could develop into on affirmation of a democratic system.

Besides, there is one more profound reason to account for the certain development of a democratic system in China. Under the Oriental monarchy, the ruler may of course claim the noble idea of "government by morality", while the people may accordingly enjoy the blessings of moralization and attain the peace of the nation. However, this was not the right course for the people, because, when they were merely subjected to a moralizing rule from above, their own moral Consciousness could never be established. It was only the monarch that was entitled to set himself up as a responsible moral agent. If this is the case, even though the ruler may be a sage, then his exclusive claim to being a sage might mean his selfishness in usurping the "Sage" role. With that sort of selfishness plaguing him, he could neither really attain the magnnificent role of a sage nor actualy set himself up as a real moral subject.

If the ruler virtually can behave as a responsible moral subject, he should not only be able to moralize for the masses of the people but also be so selfless as to reveal as public knowledge the secret art of government or any other qualificatious suitable for the noble job in order that the people themselves might learn to moralize about the art of government among themselves.

Meanwhile, the sage-ruler must be able also to complacently hand over his political position to the general public that within the state all those qualsfied to hold high office may have on equal opportunity to run for it. By this it is affirmed that every citizen may enjoy equal political rights and every citizen be on an equal political footing. Accordingly, it is quite natural that the fundamental law of the land should be formulated on the strength of the popular will as shown by a consensus of opinion of popular plelrscite. It is quite natural that such a constitution of the country might serve as the common platform by which the people as a whole could exercise their political rights. It thus prescribes the government as one democratic, constitutional set-up of the people, by the people and for the people.

In accordance with the aforesaid observation, we might well infer from the Chinese historical culture, which stressed the need of setting one's self up as a moral politoial paragon, that such a cultural pattern would inevitably develop into a democratic system in politics, for only in this may could the citizens set themselves up as subjects.

A democratic government should provide that any and all public functionaries be promoted to, or retired from, their positions according to law. On the contrary, under the monarchical system, though the ruler may be a sage, he seldom could, by his own free will, retire from office once he had ascended to the throne. And even though there might be one or many sages in government service, they never can peaceably get hold of the scepter. They could only retire from, but not advance in political life of their own free choice.

Nevertheless, the moral subjectivity in its control over the human body certainly will demand in its political activities the freedom of action in both ways. There was in it a basic contradiction between the moral spirit of the Chinese culture and the monarchical absolutism. Such a contradiction might only be solved by application of democratic constitutionalism which confirms that all citizens are equal as masters of the political organization. This democratic constitutionalism is the requirement borne with the development of the moral spirit in the Chinese culture.

The democratic reconstruction of China in the present era, therefore, is a great event resulting from the evalution of Chinese history and cultural development. This is the foremost reason for tho achievement of the said reconstruction.

Chadter X. Our Understanding of China's Current Political History

In the foregoing chapter we have discussed the development of Chinese history and its cultural spirit up to the present stage which certainly will demand the realization of a democratic reconstruction. This subject has touched upon the current history of China. Hence, we should proceed to relate our basic apprehension about Chinese (current) political development.

Those who have entertained doubts whether China can achieve democratic reconstruction have ofter derived some evidence from the history of the Chinese Republic. From its early stage, the Chinese democratic reconstruction suffered many setbacks. Yuan Shih-kai had once proclaimed himself an "emperor", later, Peiyang warlord Chang Hsuan also put up a brief restoration of the Manchu regime; then the political disturbance was closely followed by many Peiyang warlords' armed struggle for supremacy until the unification of China by the Nationalist revolutionary force in 1926; and still later, the Nationalist Political Tutelage started for a period of twenty years. At the end of the political tutelage, a Constitution was adopted by the National Assembly on December 25, 1946, and put into effect in 1947. Soon afterwards, the Chinese Communists staged the unprecedented military coup and have occupied the mainland since 1949 with their totalitarian despotism. All such episodes may possibly be aduced as proof that China can never proceed on the road of democratic constitutionalism. And some one may have doubted whether the Chinese people actually want to have a democratic political regime.

According to our viewpoint, it is self evident that the Chinese people want democratic rule. As Yuan Shin-kai's monarchical interlude lasted only a few months, he even had to fabricate some sort of "popular will" to support his wild action. The restoration of the Manchu regime by Chang Hsuan was more transient. The Period of Political Tutelage was from the beginning, as revealed by Dr. Sun Yat-sen's teachings, a mere preparatory step toward the Period of Constitutional Administration.

It is only Marx-Leninism, as championed by the Communists, that is theoretically opposed to Western democracy. Even so, they hypocritically had to label their dictatorship a "people's democracy" and preceded under the smoke-screen of the "new democracy". All such gestures indicate that the Chinese Communists could not really denounce democracy. And all these fictions tend to prove that the Chinese people are fond of democracy beyond any doubt.

The present burning question is: As the Chinese people have been aspiring for democracy, why is it that democratic constitutionalism connot yet be realized in the past several decades of Chinese history? The answer may be found in the social reality and also in the academic thinking of the Chinese people.

Regarding the early stage of the Republic of China, the success of the 1911 revolution was derived from the failure of the political reform movement of the Manchu regime. With the rousing of nationalism propagated by the Kuomintang, the revolution easily wiped out the monarchical rule although the old reform movement had also clamored for the adoption of a constitution. Its objective was centered around "employment of new talents to attain national wealth and strength." Meanwhile, the flourishing of the nationalistic sentiment among the Han people (who form the grestest bulk of the Chinese) was armed at purging the humiliation under the 300-year old domination of the Manchu regime. Although there were some vague notions of people's rights and democracy in the revolutionary campaign, the actual import of such notions was not clear to most of the Chinese people of the era who might have mistaken the founding of a new republic as a mere change of dynasty as had happened so often before in Chinese history.

The Chinese social institutions of the time lacked such solid organizations as religious, economic, or cultural bodies. These was absent a tradition of local self-government and the social hierarchy of different classes. Hence, most of the Congressmen in the early days of the Chinese Republic were all drawn from intellectual circles without any objectively concrete social institution for their background, and they could hardly represent the interest of a certain organization or a certain class of people.

On the other hand, the source of Western democracy was the struggle of various civic organizations or different classes of people for their respective interests. And then their representatives usually have also some social force in objective sense as the effective basis of their voices.

It is no wonder that the Chinese congressmen in the early period of the republic could neither stop Yuan Shih-kai from his imperial adventure nor oppose Tsao Kun in his corruptive practices in the presidential election. It was chiefly due to the fact that China had been all along putting the intellectual elements in the social center while they held themselves aloof from the industrial and commercial circles. Furthermore, they lacked a cohesive religious faith. The congress, then, was nothing but an assembly of drifting intellectuals.

Of course, a considerable current of democratic thought prevailed in the early stage of the Chinese republic. The Principle of Democracy propagated by Dr. Sun Yat-sen, the general theory of representative government, and the high-sounding catchword of "Science and Democracy", spread by such figures as Ch'en Tu-hsiu in the "New Youth" weekly, were all democratic by nature.

However, a minor exception should be allowed in the case of Ch'en

Tu-hsiu, who proclaimed as his objective the promotion of "Science and Democracy," because at the same time, he was opposed to the ancient Chinese culture, with his slogan of "knock out the Confucian store." In his case, the notion of democracy was a pure importation from the West, without any roots in Chinese culture.

By employing the catchword of "Science and Democracy," to fight against the old Chinese culture, the clique of Ch'en Tu-hsiu might have inflicted some serious damage on the traditional culture, but the redical view of democracy still could not take root in the Chinese soil. Nor could it win many supporters for long and thus turn itself into system. Hence, Ch,en Tu-hsiu turned his attention to the social and economic phases, paying attention to Western imperialism and capitalism and their invasion of China; he there upon, plunged himself into the snare of Marxism, in contrast with what he called the "bourgeois" or "capitalistic democracy."

Such men as Ch'en Tu-hsiu, who had particularly clamored for the promotion of democracy, eventually ended up by denouncing it summarily. This is a glaring example that at the early stage of the Chinese republic, many intellectuals denied the very principle of democracy. By such a vacillating trend, they then gradually, if, albeit, unwittingly, lined themselves up under the Marxist banner. Some of them did register themselves as Communists. Even some ardent followers of Dr. Sun, such as Hu Han-ming and Liao Chung-kai, were said to have posed once as converts to the materialistic interpretation of history. In 1924, the Nationalist Party also stayed a dramatic show, which resulted in the adoption of the policy of "allying with Soviet Russia and absorbing the Communist elements." To be sure, it stressed the need of setting up a joint revolutionary front in preparation for the Northern Expedition against the Peiyang warlords, with a veiw to implement democratic ideals.

From the begininng, Dr. Sun Yat-sen, as opposed to Ch'en Tu-hsiu, was firm in holding on to one complete set of democratic ideals which were to to be realized in the three distinct stages of "military operation, political tutelage and constitutional administration." Later, in the actual process of the Nationalist Revolution, these three stages became rather vogue; the concept of democratic constitutionalism was not sharp or clear-cut enough to invite the attention of the people sufficiently. Even in the twenty-year period of political tutelage, the lofty concept was almost replaced by that of a "gevernment of the party, by the party, yet for the people."

Then again the 20-years long peried of Political Tutelage by the Kuomintang may be explained on two counts. First, it was due to the subjective view that the Nationalists were not willing to give up the political mandate in a hurry without the due process of legal provisions. Secondly, the objective necessity of the Chinese nation to centralize its will power and material forces for resistance against the Japanese invasion ever since 1930, when Japanese warlords occupied Manchuria and threatened China with-all out aggression. This resistence also sharply aroused the Chinese nationalistic fervor which tended to entrust the political mandate to the party in power against foreign invasion. By then, in Europe, there were even popular sentiments favoring centralization of power as witness the governments under Hitler or Mussolini. Later, when the war of resistance against Japan broke out in 1937 and lasted till 1945, there could be no change of government without some justifiable cause.

Nevertheless, it is still never justifiable for any publicist to infer from the foregoing phenomena that the Chinese people were willing to be forever governed under the "political tutelage" of the nationalists. "Therefore, any maneuvering schemes apart from strenuous efforts to realize democracy shall be void or ineffective for solving China's problems properly.

Now, the Communist dictitorship on the mainland may seem to offer the most glaring evidence that the people are not craving for democracy. When one considers this fact in the light of Chen Tu-hsiu's conversion from democracy to Marxism, and the deviation of some Nationalists' with their thoughts or deeds colored by Communism and Fascism, one is liable to see even further evidence that the Chinese intellectusls from 1922 on did not pay much attention to democratic principles.

Against the above argument, onr answer is: that the fountain of Communism basically was not indigenous in China. It could secure a transient foothold for spreading rampant on the mainland chiefly due to the fact that ever since the 19th. century China actually had suffered from an invasion of Western capitalism and, in due course, became the victim of foreign imperialism. Then, some intellectuals who were cornered in some attics in the Settlements of Shanghai became keenly conscious of the injustice of capitalistic-imperialism and resorted to Communism as their weapon for a counter-attack. It is plain that such a fetish, as it was introduced into China, was imported chiefly due to the fact that when the original Chinese culture and the people were obstructed in their straight course of development, they had to find some way out with some outside help. Communism itself was not accepted in its positive aspect because it ran counter to the proper or objective demand of the spiritual life of the Chinese people.

Later, two other important factors helped to catapult the Chinese communists onto the pinnacle of power over the China mainland. First, the Reds were curried favor through their false trumpeting about a "united front" to resist the Japanese invasion. These "united front" slogans appealed to the Chinese people's nationalistic sentiment. Secondly, the Chinese Communists could displace the Nationalist government, primarily by hypocritically lining up with some native "democratic" parties or cliques in urging the Kuomintang to "restore the political power to the people, thus plunging the KMT's party-rule into spiritual debilitation. This plot was effectually carried out even beyond their own expectation. But the Communists succeeded in scheme precisely because of the democratic aspiration of the Chinese people, which had tended to baffle the spirit of the Nationalist Party.

These two factors prove that even though the Chinese Communists are obsessed in clinging to Soviet Russia one-sidedly, and actually the practice a weird form of proletarian totalitarianism, their superficial success on the Chinese mainland really depends, as from the beginning, on the dimocratic aspirations of the people, together with their nationalistic sentiment, and not upon of the Marxist-Leninist ideology which plagues the people. Therefore, the Leninist dictatorship definitely cannot last long positive aspect on the Chinese mainland as the supreme guiding principle of Chinese culture and political philosophy.

There are five basic reasons available to prove that the Red dictatorship cannot last long as the guiding principle of Chinese cultural and political institutions on the mainland.

First, the Communist fetish has violated the general principle followed by all of the highly civilized world, especially the Chinese traditional culture which is deeply rooted in the moral concept which has the "Moral Mind" and "Moral reason" for its basis. The Marxist-Leninist doctrine recognizes only that sort of human nature which has been crucified by the class struggle and denies the existence of a universal human nature. Hence, by its tendency to jealousy, suspicion and hatred, with its perpetual impulse to fight for supremacy over others, it attempts to wipe out all those cultural institutions which have been founded upon universal human nature, such a religion, philosophy, literature, the fine arts and morality. All these are held to be "deviating" from the Communist dogmas. When thoroughl obsessed with the fetish of class-struggle, the Leninist followers have ventured to disrupt the heritage of Chinese history and culture by brutal force

Secondly, the Marxist-Leninist principle has absolutely violated the huma rights of individuals under the pretex of practising proletarian dictatorship. It attempts to regiment all individuals under a few privileged class leaders, and thus puts the masses of the people at the mercy of their devilish jugglings.

Thirdly, the historical development of Chinese culture has, on the contrary, pointed in the direction that every individual must be endowed with rights, not merely as a moral being, but also as an independent political being, an epistemological being and a technological being. Then, as an epistemological being, any innocent person must enjoy unconditionally the freedom of thought and freedom of academic pursuit without the bondage of dogmatic tenets.

Fourthly, in striving to preserve the status of political being, the Chinese people have been opposed already to the existence of a one-man rule, and they will not tolerate any more one party hegemony, with all others, not affiliated with the dictatorial clique, classed as the governed.

Fifthly, even though the old Chinese tradition made no adequate provision to settle such controversial issues as a change of dynasty or the right of succession nevertheless, there was the customary practice of priority whereby the eldest son succeeded to the throne. On the contrary, in the Communist totalitarian system, the succession to the Red leadership lacks any fixed rule even though an "heir apparent" may have been governed. The aspirants for the office of head man in Soviet Russia, will have to fight it out by an incessant life-and-death struggle among themselves as happened after the death of Lenin or of Stalin. The danger of mutual slaughter or purge is forever present as a matter of course, because in the Communist world every one and all of them treat each other as a potential enemy while any expression of non-conformity of opinion might signify the necessity of a power struggle between different cliques. The fatal dogma which dictates as a rule the impossilibity of the coexistence of non-conformists is always burning in the Communist hearts, for it is a psychological pattern shaped by the Communist system. By the same token, the perpetual power-struggle among the Communist leaders always arouses the same fear in their blind followers. Their destinies are always subject to a haphazard "purge." Such a beastly practice is an innate product of the Communist party dictatorship. In order to avoid the mutual slaughter that takes place in the Communist world, there is only one remedy, namely, that a free and popular election system. should be adopted in accordance with a fundamental law of the land, set up by the people themselves. By it the transfer of political power should be made possible by peaceful processes.

For the aforesaid reasons, even if we admit that in a short span of time,

542

certain collective, practical, technological enterprises which have been carried out under the absolute dictatorship of the Chinese communist totalitarian government may happen to achieve certain results temporarily yet, we can still absolutely assure ourselves that, in the long run, its destiny must be fore doomed to failure owing to its sharp break with the whole development of Chinese culture, its supression of the human rights of individuals, its in human nature, not to mention its break away from world humanism and human civilization as a whole. Therefore, the Communist dictatorship cannot last long, and is bound, in fact, to condemn itself to death, in virtue of its own folly coupled with its brutality.

After all, one crucial point that presages a short duration for the Communist dictatorship on the China mainland lies in the fact, as we have re lated above, that the Marxis-Leninist principle never gained such a positive response in the psychology of the Chinese as would seem to be postulated by the objective demands of Communism. Some Chinese accepted Marxism voluntarily for a time, but this fact was due, chiefly to the agitation that the doctrine was being adopted as an instrument for the avowed, purpose of fighting against directly the aggression of Western imperialism and capitalsm It was this facet of Communism that shone in brighter than that of any other system of Chinese thought or Western principles. Communism with its ample dynamic force seemed capable of meeting China's demand of the moment. It was thus that it had sailed with the wind in some parts of the mainland around 1923-24.

However, the anti-imperialism movement of the Chinese people wa stirred up chiefly on the premise of fighting for their own national inde pendence and survival, with the perspective of continuously propagating thei own culture in the modern world. This positive demand has been embedded in the spiritual life of the Chinese nation all along. When put into a dial ectic formula, the positive demand is a "thesis" while the fact that it had been denied or else oppressed by the imperialist-capitalistic force in the pas hundred years is an "anti-thesis," and yet Marxism, which was temporarily adopted by the Chinese, was treated only as another evil in opposition to the "anti-thesis" without the possibility of achieving a "synthesis."

In other words, Marxism at its root, was a mere temporary tool employ ed possibly for meeting the positive demand of the Chinese people. Hence it should never be substituted in place of the Chinese original positive de mand. Nor should it be tolerated when committing some sort of a blight on the original demand.

If the practice of Marxism in China is hamstringing the aforesaid "posi

:ive demand" of the people, the indomitable demand might in the same way ıbandon Marxism for its tool which was employed sheerly to meet the ex-:ernal invasion or oppression, for it was contradictory to the original purpose.

In summing up, it may be said that the spiritural life of the Chinese ›eople will certainly up-surge once again and press forward along the course ɔf democratic reconstruction no matter how zigzag a course beyond our im-ıgination the Chinese political development may choose to follow. Most ıssuredly, Marxist-Leninism itself will eventually be discarded by the Chi-nese people as a whole.

Chapter XI. Our Expectation from Western Culture and What the West Should Learn from the Oriental Wisdom

Western culture is one that has been dominating the modern world since the early 19th century. This is a fact which we cannot deny. Since the begining of the past centnry, various types of culture in different countries throughout the world have all been exposed to the influence of Occidental culture. They have been trying hard to adopt western religion, science, phi-losophy, literature, law and technology. This is also a fact which no one could refute.

But there is a series of questions which beg adequate answer: Eventual-ly, is the Western culture itself alone sufficient in potency to lead the civi-lizations of mankind as a whole?? Aside from the Easterners taking lessons from the West, is there any need for Westerners also to learn something from the East? And what do we expect Westerners to learn from Eastern culture? By the process of the reciprocal exchange of West-East cultural workers, what do we anticipate to achieve by way of a world-scale academic and ideologi-cal good? On such a momentous questionnaire, we deem it apropos to present our views.

According to our survey over the Western culture, we recognize that the best expression of its spirit lies chiefly in its having achieved absorption of the Greek scientific and philosophical system together with the Hebrew reli-gious spirit. The latter has made possible the Westerner's "Mind" directly communicating with God. The fomer has also helped them to study and to understand with clear and meticulous minds the mathematical order of the universe. They are able to formulate the general principle of all things in existence, and many logical principles governing the processes of human re-flective thinking. Hence, they are enabled to behave as an epistemological

544

subject while presiding over the natural world and living in the general domain of reason.

Modern Westerners are descended from the aboriginal northern European tribesmen, whose primitive, naive souls absorbed the Greek and Hebrew cultural heritages and then assimilated them. Hence, the mind of modern Westerners have been accustomed to, on the one hand, communicating with the alleged unique, unlimited holiness of God, while, on the other, also following the general principle of reason that enabled them to probe and understand the natural world. Having been educated in the Renaissance peried of the 14th. to 16th. centuries, the Westerners had then better self-consciousness of their own personality. It was then that both the religious and the scientific spirit joined hands so as to produce the self-consciousness of the dignity of individual personality with the demand for spiritual freedom. From then on, there were movements for religious reformation, gradually for establishment of the national state, and furthermore for the free employment of reasoning power, thus formulating the Enlightenment Campaign. There was also the intellectual advancement aiming at comprehension of natural phenomena and human activities in different phases while attempting also to use the knowledge concerned to remodel the natural world and the human world. Thereupon the political principle of liberty and democracy, the economic tenet of freedom and justice, and the sociological doctrine of fraternity and equality took shape in a consecutive order. With them, the American Revolution, French Revolution, and such movements as that for Negro liberation, colonial independence and the Socialist upheaval were also surging forth in succession.

By applying the theory of scientific progress to reconstruction of the natural world and to reformation of social, political and economic ills, their reciprocal utilitarian practices resulted in mutual achievements of greater feats. Hence, Western culture in the past one or two hundred years has surged forward, greatly surpassing and leaving behind all other traditional cultures in the world. This Western cultural advancement has universal and perpetual academic value which deserves the respect, acclamation, study and imitation of all other peoples over the globe. They are taught to react thusly in order to keep equal strides in progress.

On the other hand, modern Western culture in its surging forward process has also exposed various conflicts and many burning problems. For instance, by the religious reform movement, hot religious wars were brought about; by establishing national states, there international wars; were incessent by the industrial revolution, antagonism developed between the employee and the employer in the capitalist society; for the purpose of acquiring natural resources abroad, colonialism took root accompanied by imperialistic oppression of weak or minority races; the seizure of colonial territories brought numerous conflicts and armed clashes among the imperialist countries; communism was smuggled in on the pretext of achieving economic equality, and with it a totalitarian regime of Soviet Russia, the deadly enemy of Western democracy. Furthermore, since the beginning of the 20th century, the upsurge of nationalism in Asia and Africa already pitted itself against the vested interests of Western countries, while (by comparison with the wealth and strength of the West), the whole of Asia and Africa look like a mere mammoth proletariat class. Therefore, the Afro-Asian bloc, resenting the West for its previous political and economic invasion, now exposed many weak spots which Communist agitators exploited for subversive purposes. The marriage between Afro-Asian nationalism and Communism in order to oppose the Western democracies may also facilitate Soviet Russia's aggressive plots. In the present era, as nuclear weapons are powerful enough to annihilate mankind in a total war, all human beings are subjected to constant fear. These are only some of the bitter fruits brought about by the rapid growth of Western culture.

What now should be our reappraisal of Western culture? What shall we expect from it? These two problems must be carefully considered by us.

From the optimistic point of view, several grave issues brought along by modern Western cultural progress have been solved one by one by the Westerners themselves. For instance, by the firm establishment of the principle of freedom of worship, the religious wars then subsided. By better adjustment through various political, economic and social channels, the Western democracies have also considerably mitigated conflicts between the employer and the employee. By setting-up the League of Nations and the United Nations Organization, it is now possible that narrow-minded nationalism among states may gradually dissolve. Ever since the United States of America won freedom and independence from Britain, the conscience of mankind, especially in the 20th century, has moved in one direction, the setting free of all other colonial territories.

The most serious problem remaining now and demanding urgent solution is the antagonism of Commmunist totalitarian against the democratic world, while Afro-Asian nationalism may possibly be exploited and ensnared by Communism. This knotty issue also occupies the thoughts of Westerners.

According to our viewpoint, even though a greater part of the aforementioned problems have been solved, yet those which are deeply rooted in defects of western culture itself still remain stubbornly threatening world peace and security. In appearance, the seriously antagonistic situation which exists might be analyzed as one between the Soviet totalitarian bloc and the Western democratic front.

In the contest for supremacy between the Soviet bloc and the democratic camp, a third force that might tip the scale in either direction is the Afro-Asian clique. Ordinarily, the Chinese, Indian and Moslem cultures in this area are in their parental state non-materialistic, and so in principle they should have been readily coalesced with the Western democratic culture; and yet, up to the present moment, they are still set at loggerheads with each other. Such an unfortunate situation really deserves penetrating reflections by Westerners.

The primary step of Westerners in a self-examination of their own behavior, is the fact that since the 19th century they have been busy with aggression against Asia and Africa, and even at the present time remnant colonies still remain on these two big continents. The second step in such a self-examination may be as Bertrand Russell and Oswald Spengler have remaked. The Westerners, in expanding their cultural force over the world, exerted at the same time their strong will to power and will of conquest, thus prodding unfavorable reactions of the conquered.

And yet according to our view, the will to power involved is superficial, One real defect in the Western spirit lies in a straight-for-ward attempt to spread their culture uniformly over the entire globe, despite conflicts with traditional characteristics of other cultures. Hence, Westerners lacked respect and sympathetic understanding for other peoples' cultures They usually ignored the latter's genuine demand for self-development, and thus neglected also the value assessment of Western culture toward other We have made this observation above in a previous discussion on Chinese culture but without fuller explanation.

Ordinarily, the method of employing straightforward reasoning in a attempt to spread uniformly fixed concepts all over the world, has been common pattern of mankind. Due to the Western adoption of Hebrew an Greek cultural heritages, together with their emphasis on practical technology, westerners are particularly prone in this direction. Greek cultural tradition has taught man to reflect self consciously on universal truths that might be presented to the human vision, while the Hebrew religious tradition ha taught man to believe that God has pre-determind the course of the world from above (false). By applying the technological spirit of the modern era man in reformation of nature and society is bent on materializing our universal ideals shaped by our reason in accordance with fixed ways and means.

Hence Westerners who believe in God with universal ideals shaped by reason in their possession, coupled with a technological spirit, have adopted self-consciously or otherwise a difinite way of acting. By proclaiming the observance of God's decree they try to force their ideals, shaped by the reason, down to lower strata of cultural patterns. Such procedure might not produce serious consequence if it occurs in an individual. However, when it takes place in a group of people to shape religious, social, political or economic reforms, such activities surge forward like an uncontrollable tidal wave clashing with other groups of people with different ideals. This theme shows why in the religious wars, the conflict of nationalism class struggle in economic affairs, and the feud among followers of different political principles in the modern era, acute intensity resulted without possibility of solution or compromise. It reveals also why the political, economic or cultural forces of Western countries must find an outlet by diverting their course of expansion toward Asia and Africa so as to slow down their own internal conflicts. That sort of outward expansion has repeatedly brought invasion and pressure upon weak and minority peoples, thus bringing war for possession of colonies abroad. This theme also explains why most Westerners, though conscientiously denouncing colonialism and willing to treat the Afro-Asian peoples on the same plane, still fail to comprehend asiatic cultural characteristics, while their mutual assistance is often limited to superficial readjustment.

Again, according to our oriental perception, most individuals from the West who came to the East to tackle diplomatic or political affairs, or to preach religion, or to manage cultural institutions, while studying things Oriental, may constantly have had about them a manner unbearable to Orientals yet not easily described in written words. This is manifest in an attitude which proclaims the superiority of their coolly analytic scientific methods, a heritage of Greece, and behind the attitude there lies a predetermined ideals or plan pending execution after study.

Under such circumstances, the oriental may have self-consciously realized himself as the object of cool Western research on the one hand, while on the other he might also feel that the Occidental is threatening to carry out premeditated plans as a force from above to permeate the former's body and soul. In the apprehending of one's own body and soul as an object of the Westerner's icy study, the former may even feel that he is repulsed by the latter with a delicate touch of harshness. In apprehending the Westerner's premeditated scheme of clamping down upon him, the Easterner might also sense a sort of spiritual oppression. Such feeling may have further made direct contact between them only superficial in appearance.

Hence, if the Westerner believes that his ideals are universal and also good for Orientals, he would encounter only the latter's facial cooperation without spiritual coordination because of the Oriental's misunderstanding of his good will, or else of the Oriental's feeling of remotness or inferiority, his hatred, or his narrow nationalism or his obstinate cultural consciousness. Such unfavorable elements blocking East-West coordination may exist in different forms and in various degrees, or even prevail more in certain localities. All such variations of response depend chiefly upon the attitude of the Westerner himself. At its root this attitude is a direct product of the Western inheritance of the Greek cultural mood, the Hebrew tradition and the modern technological spirit. The merits of Occidental culture are thus not easily differentiated from those of the Westerners set on the same footing of human beings.

If we understand the pluriform cultural background of this Western attitude, we should also understand or forgive the Westerner. If on the other hand, the Westetner genuinely wishes to renovate his attitude and to gain intimate contact with the East in order to better secure world peace by which Western culture itself might enjoy permanent existence in the temporal world, it must progress beyond its own heritage limits and learn something of Oriental wisdom. In this regard, we present the following five points for common discussion:

I. The spirit of "Accepting the Present with Contentment" without constantly striving for change and progress is a noted Oriental virture. It is true that one outstanding merit of Western culture is its impulse for unlimited progress. However, in the very process of such a relentless pursuit, even though the Westerner may resort to religious faith in God for his last shelter yet in his temporal life he will always find himself devoid of substantial ground for personal security. Hence, either in the case of an individual or that of a nation, the poor creature must always strive forward in the pursuit of progress in order to fill up the deep senes of "vacuum." As soon as his energy is exhausted or frustrated by outside obstructious, his individual life, or the natural life concerned, may seem to collapse at the same moment. Hence, old persons in the West usually are lonely people, whereas in Western history many strong countries may have suffered collapse once and for all because of overexertion.

On the other hand, as the Chinese have taken up the notion of transcendental mind as the basis of all temporal value, the learned Oriental may be contented with the self-sufficient and full-presentation of the human value in conjunction with the cosmic value simply by a flash of his self-consciousness of "transcendental mind" in its enlightening mood. Human life then finds shelter in such an illuminating flash. It is called the human domain of "accepting the present status without much ado." The Chinese consider it to be a crisis in life when one burns with a sense of progress without the counter-balance of retreat. The lack of a complementing sense of retreat, or retirement from active life, is another characteristic of Western culture. It takes shape in the incessant urge to rush forward, leaving no place for the spirit or soul to find complacent rest.

Chinese wisdom, in accepting the status quo with contentment, might provide the Westerner with a foothold as he sees fit to use it. This adoption in its wider sense might also increase the feeling of security and elasticity of Western culture as a whole.

Next, strongly influenced by the intellectual activity and methods of Greece, Western culture expresses itself as a rule of certainty in the formation of concepts. This is an indispensable condition for the acquiring of knowledge. However, Westerners who have indulged themselves in the accumulation of conceptual knowledge may unwittingly evaluate human life by examining the quantity of fixed concepts thus accumulated. This might have certain merits, yet all concepts in themselves are distinct from the substance of human life, and because of their limitations create obstacles to one another. If human life is constantly burdened with such the human heart would be unable to expand. This deficiency is the main obstacle to achieving authentic communication between peoples of the East and West. For authentic communication occurs only when the hearts of both parties expand, when the rays of their lives directly radiate to each other. But fixed concepts on either side may work a difference. Favorable concepts may, of course, be also a means of establishing communication between one another, especially when they can find an echoing response in others. But many fixed concepts can likewise ultimately block authentic communication between one another.

These fixed concepts consist of our premediated plans and objectives, our abstract ideals for human relationship, and our abstract standards for evaluating human conduct, together with our prejudices or habitual notions, etc. When attempting to secure authentic contacts between one another, they must first abandon all the pre-occupying concepts. Such abandonment may secure authentic understanding between men through the mutual radiation of their lives with direct affirmation of their worth.

The aforesaid matter seems easy, but in reality is quite difficult, become only with a very profound cultivation of wisdom and virtures. For attainment of the authentic understanding, there are several strate of cherishing works to be employed in regular intervals. Only thus may we secure genuine contact with others and gain the necessary, true understanding even at emergency moments. This prerequisite, ordinary cultivation of wisdom and virtues, is embedded in our daily life, with self-consciousness always kept alert in surpassing any object presented to it and then in trying to release it from undesirable entanglement.

This wisdom of "release from everything" is called in Indian philosophy "wisdom of the void" or "of liberation." In Chinese Taoism it is called the "wisdom of emptiness or of non-being", in Confucianism, "the state of vacuum", which may well be interpreted as "without a foregone conclusion, without arbitrary judgement, without obstinacy and without selfishness", as in a "broad mind of impartiality". By use of such high and vast wisdom, man might then see through everything in daily life and every ideal subject matter as though they were transparent. He may still possess ordinary knowledge with concepts and ideals at work, but he should? must? may? also detach himself from any entanglement with them. This wisdom of a detachment exalts man above the actual state of being or non-being, with seeming existence of either of them. For instance, the wisdom of detachment might make a millionaire feel penniless, and a great statement feel "even his exalted political deeds are like buoyant clouds fleeting over the sky," It would also make all great scientists and philosophers feel like their months are "hanging helplessly on the cold wall." It also makes renowned preachers feel that "all their sermons are void without benefiting any one." It makes diplomats feel their role "vain as that of some transient visitors."

The wisdom of detachment as shown in Indian theology and Chinese Confucianism, Taoism and Buddhism, together with China's literature and fine arts, is really worthy of study by Westerners, provided they detach themselves from their traditional cultural concepts. Only then will they learn to appreciate, understand, and enjoy the boundless flavor of this Oriental wisdom. The root of this learning is still embedded in the vision of "right here without the need of much ado", and that of "all things being equal in the fleeting course of human life." This is the first point that Westerners should learn from Oriental culture.

2. Next comes the Oriental "wisdom of being round and spiritual.'

While the aforesaid wisdom of detachment is negative in action, the wisdom of getting roundness and spiritualization is positive. This term is adopted from the Chinese classic "The Book of Changes" as contrasted with the figurative phrase "square and wise."

We may say that in Western science and philosophy, all universal ideas and principles grasped by intellectual reason are straight in symbolism. Lines connecting one with the other might be said to form a square. Because Western thinking proceeds from the abstract, it will always neglect or suppress something of concrete reality when applied in actual practice to concrete matters. It cannot do justice to the speciality and individuality of matters concerned with flexible application. Here our wisdom is needed, the wisdom of flexibility following winding paths of the specific and concrete in their changing conditions; and not wisdom which starts from the universal and lead rigidly to the specific.

The application of such flexible or round wisdom from the outset does not uphold any universal rule, but rather merges the universal into the specific to examine the specific in order that the latter should prescribe the universal in its application. Nevertheless, the universal or general principle which is here determined or differentiated by the specific becomes a general principle again through man's consciousness. Then it must be merged again into the specific so as not to make of itself a static, abstract universal. Thus progressing, man's mind can be elevated to a lively dynamic state which is not limited by any particular instances, nor is it limited by any cold abstract universal, but always keeps contact with immediate reality. It is like a projected straight line following on direction and instantly moving round and round till it has become a circle surrounding the central motion of concrete matters. This is the wisdom of being round and spiritual. It is what Chuang Tzu calls "spiritual release" and "meeting an object with the spirit" (instead of looking at it with naked eyes). Or, as Mencius said, "Wherever a superior man passes, there is transformation; wherever he abides, there is spiritual influence; his spiritual life is all-pervading reciprocally through Heaven and Earth."

The word "Shen"(神) here does not mean God as the divinity, but rather spiritualization in action. In other words, it possesses the connotation of "development." In case a man observes things from the viewpoint of abstract general ideas, he may be partly in agreement with objective things and partly not. Where there is no harmony (agreement), there is stagnation. Where there is stagnation, the inner spirit cannot fully deploy itself. Hence, the wisdom of changing the abstract and general in accordance with the concrete and specific is necessary to achieve "roundness," thus resulting in development of the inner spirit without obstruction. That is what we called "round and spiritualized wisdom."

This is not merely dialetic wisdom, because dialectic wisdom remains within the sphere of rational intellect; it is close to what Henri Bergson called "Intuition." The wisdom as prescribed by dialetics is employ some universals to determine the concrete and specific matters. With the limitation or determination examined, there emerges another more concrete universal to describe the subject matter. The so-called "universal" in this process still are emerging one by one before the human consciousness.

On the other hand, the wisdom of being round and spiritual might tend to reconcile all the universals concerned within the mind without letting them emerge as distinct ideas. Hence, before human consciousness there is only one round and spiritualized wisdom briskly following the winding course of the subject matter in its changing conditions. Hence, it is more or less close to what Bergson called the Intuition."

However, as Bergson's "Intuition" is but his personal philosophical concept, a Chinese with his "round and all pervasive" wisdom may everywhere understand the life of nature, observe the transforming symptom of the universe, rejoice in the vivacious personality of man, and thus base himself on such wisdom for examining and forecasting the change of time and tide, together with that of national destiny. He may even base himself on this wisdom for furthering his discussions of studies which might meet all challenges with eloquent responses and roam as far and high as the natural sounds of Heaven. Such wisdom prevails in all our literature and fine arts and the "Confucian Analects," "The Works of Mencius," the "New Maxims in Chinese Folklores," the "Buddhist Analects," the "Analects in Sung-Ming Confucianism," and many other academic correspondences by ancient Confucian scholars. Only after deep immersion in Chinese culture can men correctly and profoundly understand them.

Westerners also need this "round and spiritual (all-pervasive) wisdom" if they really wish to meet other peoples and cultures unreservedly in an atmosphere of sympathy and respect, and also if they wish to recognize the communication of all true, concrete life beyond the provincialism of their own traditional culture in rational patterns, knowledge, religions, technical industries and departmental humanities. Only in this way will Western scholars attain authentic conversations with reciprocal appreciation among themselves over and above their own independent bulwarks of academic research and publications.

3. The third point which Westerners should learn from Oriental culture is a feeling of mildness and commiseration or compassion. It is true that many Westerners often surpass Orientals in loyalty to ideals, a spirit of social service, and enthusiasm and love toward others in their practical aspects. Such a virtue is indeed very precious. But the highest feelings between or among human beings are not limited to enthusiasm and love. Their will to power and possessive desire may also pervade enthusiasm and love with evil influence. To prevent these uncalled-for intrusions, many Westerners rely mainly on humility molded by religious faith, considering all of one's own merits as bestowed by God's grace to serve towards the glory and service of God.

However, the Westerner's concept of service to God may also be distorted to serve his own selfish purposes. Man's will to power can also employ the name of God as a subterfuge in the belief that his own activities are sanctioned by God and thus push forward undue expansionism. Man can also selfishly wish to possess God such as to implore his help to gain victory in battle. In such cases, God's way and the devil in man's heart may alao interfuse in development. Hence, in trying to avoid this evil, Christianity also teaches forgiveness towards one's enemies. When carried to the extremity, such a virtue of forgiveness may tend to complete denunciation of the world in an effort to obtain individual blessings. To counter this unworldly inversion, again the principle of humanity and enthusiasm are needed.

Thus we have a vicious circle without any definite resolution while love and enthusiasm still are mixing with the will to power and selfish possession. An ultimate solution can only derive from removing the roots of the will to power and of the possessive urge at the starting point where man extends enthusiasm and love toward others. To achieve this, love must truly be joined to respect. The most significant feature of this fusion of love and respect is the feeling that, since love toward others is based on God's unlimited love, my respect towards others should also be boundless. It means that my respect toward others must parallel my veneration of God. This is what is meant in China by the Confucian teaching that the "good man serves his parents like serving Heaven," and "governing the people is like performing a great worshipping ceremony." There should be no room here for any reflection on the presumption that "I myself alone believe in God with the understanding of his love, but the oppnent does not." Such an attitude places the other person on a lower level, and then my respect toward others would remain unfulfilled.

True respect towards others must be unconditional and absolute, directly treating them in the objective sense that "all men are created equal." Then human love, expressed in some form of etiquette, preserves its inner worth and becomes mellow and mild. Thus, the deepest human love is transformed into the noble feeling of commiseration and humanity. This is identical with the Buddhist notion of "great compassion."

Commiseration and compassion differ from ordinary love, because in love there is only the feeling that one's own life or spirit is directed toward others on the premise of "considering others as himself." But here, the "possessive impulse over others" may make an appearance as dregs. On the other hand, commiseration and compassion mean communication or mutually internal vibration of mine and the other's real life-spirit. Here, there is also a natural interflowing of true-sympathy and fellowship between each other or among the human beings concerred. And yet this interflow of sympathy or any other sort of kind feeling may be outwardly partly directed and partly absorbed by self. Thus it produces an emotion returning to self. This emotional force may then expurgate the ordinrily mixed dregs of possessive impulse or other soiling sentimenal impurities. There is great truth in this statement.

More philosophically interpreted, if the fraternity stressed by Westerners is to be actually transformed into compassion, it is then necessary that God, the source of this ardent love, should be looked upon not merely as the one who transcends the human spirit, and not merely the unifier and the object of man's prayer. It is necessary that God be regarded as the One who is living within the man's innermost heart, the one who manifests through our bodies his direct interflow of all the spirit and life in actual existence. A detailed discussion on this problem is not feasible in this treatise.

4. The fourth wisdom that Westerners should learn from the East is how to perpetuate their culture. As we have related above, Chinese culture is the only one in the world that is historically durable with self-consciousness as being so in the Chinese mind. It is true that modern Western culture is very glitteringly pompous. And yet many observers are already worried by the perspective of how to avert its course from withering and perishing as those of ancient Greece and Rome.

We believe that culture is the expression of the spiritual life of each people. According to natural laws, all expressions of vigor drain the energy of life. There is no force in natural existence that can escape withering by over-exertion. This is also true of man's spiritual energy. If it is not to diminish, man must possess a transcendental mind which is formed by historical consciousness in communicating with past history and future generations; moreover, he must with this exalted mind, be able to encounter the life-giving source which underlies the heart of men and the principle of all things in their perpetual development. In the West, this cosmic life-giving source is called God. By means of a religious life, many Westerners can more or less approach this cosmic life-giving source. But if the usual religious life is a rendezvous with God merely through prayer and faith, then God can only be transcendent as an external force while man can only think of God's eternity. Thus he can't yet directly acquire a lofty mind which is formed by historical consciousness linking up the past with future generations.

Moreover, approaching this God as the cosmic life-giving source through prayer and faith, means that we encounter Him only through man's transcending or striving mind; it does not yet mean meeting Him directly with one's own existing self.

To achieve the aforesaid state of mind, it requires further painstaking labor. The starting point of such a great task is to see to it that all outwardly directed expression in our life does not merely follow a natural course, but that from time to time it must fight against nature in order to return to this cosmic life-giving source and from that only to fulfill the natural evolution of life again. This is precisely what we have earlier called the wisdom whereby Chinese history and culture could prolong themselves in evolutionary development.

This is not simply a theory of Chinese philosophy, but it is something which permeates the whole of Chinese literature, art and etiquette. With this wisdom, the Chinese people have in all their cultural life striven to find never-ending resources. This is the conservatory way to store up man's life energy, so that it will not be drained up or strained excessively; by going against all natural ways by which man seeks to expend his energy, it will tend to divert the energy into communicating with the cosmic life-giving sources.

Judging modern Western culture from the foregoing viewpoint, its quest for speed-up efficiency constitutes a great problem. Of course, the easy-going attitude of the Chinese is in many aspects not suitable to meet the present world situation. Yet, this hustling tendency in the Western hemisphere, which necessitates a like scurrying about of the rest of mankind, will ultimately immerge into a greater void in space even if each human being could sent to separate star by space-ships. And yet this is not the proper way for human cultures, including that of the West, to achieve everlasting life. There will come a day when Westerners must also realized that God alone is eternal without continuity of human history and culture, and that if men cannot live together peacefully on this earth, they cannot expect to do so on other planets. Westerners should develop this exalted wisdom for the prolongation of their own culture, with a broad mind formed by historical consciousness. Linking up past and future generations, they may make use of such a vast and transcendental mind, thus approaching the cosmic life-giving resources while in their daily life they look for the value of preserving their life-energy. By so doing, they also come to a true appreciation of the meaning of filial piety, of the desire for posterity in order to prolong the culture and history of their ancestors. This problem cannot be discussed in detail in this treatise.

5. The fifth point which Westerners should learn from the Orientals is the feeling of "one world one family." We admit that at present there are still many countries which must first bring themselves to national democratic reconstruction. Beyond this stage, all of mankind will have to attain the goal of merging into one family of nations. Hence, modern human beings, as citizens of any one country, should also entertain the feeling of world brotherhood. Only in this way can the world eventually attain the unity of a single family.

Viewed from this point of view, most Orientals are richly endowed with a feeling of world brotherhood. The Chinese have been traditionally fond of talking about the empire as one world and one family. All Chinese schools of thought and religion have contributed their share to foster this sentiment. Mo-tzu advocated the principle of equal fraternity to the extreme; the Taoists urged man to get along with others by forgetting their differences; Buddhism advised mankind to show commiseration with love toward all living things; Confucianism taught man to extend universal kindness to all the empire with its "one world, one family." Hence, all Chinese people must be treated as one man. By expanding this human sense or goodness, Confucinism also believed that "all men may make themselves as Yaos or Shuns (by striving for lofty attainment)." Similarly, Confucianism believed that "within the borders of the four seas, for a thousand generations back and a thousand generations yet to come, all sages are endowed with the same mind and adhere to the same principles of truth and righteousness." The concept of human goodness in Confucianism is clearly aimed at this high ideal in its ultimate and universal implications, and thus it is close to the universality of Christian love.

While Christianity insists that all men are inflicted with original sin;

the Christian bases himself upon God's will, that is, something imposed from above for the salvation of mankind. Confucianism, on the contrary, rather believes in the goodness of human nature, in man's own possibility to attain sage-hood by personal striving as to be in harmony with the virtue or the good influence of Heaven. There is between the two a sharp contrast in the fundamental creeds.

Nevertheless, differences in doctrines might still be circulating along parallel tracks each with beneficial influence bestowed upon mankind and its cultural progress since their aims are not in direct conflict. In fostering the noble feeling of world brotherhood, we think it better to rely on a combination of Christian and Confucian doctrines rather than on Christian thought alone. It is chiefly because Christianity is a systematic religion with many organized sects not readily harmonized. Christianity also has the dual concept of Heaven and hell. All heretics and non-believers may be doomad to be relegated to hell. There is therefore never equality or unanimous stand even among various Christians, and one main distinction is marked between those who do and those who do not belong to the same denomination. Those who belong to a certain sect may as alleged go to Heaven while all others may go to hell. Hence, although Christian love is unconditional as preached by the Gospel, there is in practice one condition that to attain it the man must "believe my doctrine." On this point there is a stupendous problem pending resolution.

According to the Confucian school, the only condition for being able to to attain sagehood and to be in harmony with the good influence of Heaven, is to be a good human being on his own birth right, there is no church organization discriminating against any one. Nor is it necessary for everyone to worship Confucius, because basically every body can become a sage like Confucius. This is why the Coufucian teachings are not inimical to any contemporary religion. Confucianism was a concept of Heaven and Earth, but not of hell; nor will it have a hell to accomodate non-believers. One of its guiding principles is: "All things may be nurtured without harming each others; many ways might be followed without hindering others" provided they are directed eventually toward the same goal of goodness.

In the event that all of mankind wants to embrace the exalted feeling of world brotherhood, the Confucian spirit is really a worthy-subject for all peoples to learn as a preparatory step for the noble crusade. Besides, the same attitude might also be found in Buddhism and Brahmanism, which alike teach that "All men are eligible to the Buddhisthood," and "all men are able to merge as one with the great Brahman. This variety of Oriental related to Eastern types of literature, fine arts and rituals in which Westerners may find something worthy of diligent study.

The five points presented above do not exhaust the list which we deem the Occidentals should learn from the Orient should they endeavor to promote Western culture to a completely satisfactory role of world cultural leadership, or at least to the upward trend of its own development with perpetuity definitely assured. It does not mean that these five essentials are totally absent from Western civilization, and do not exist there even as seeds. We simply hope that these seeds will germinate, grow and flourish with fruition for the benefit of world culture as well as for Western culture itself.

Chapter XII. What We Hope for from the Formation of a New World of Academic Thought

Since we believe that Western cultural also has something to learn from the East, we may as well present three main points of view concerning the future course or direction of both Chinese and world academic development.

First of all, due to the fact that expansion of Occidental culture has done much to foster contact between all the peoples on earth, while at the same time unfortunately causing heavy damages in headlong collision, we must do something now to apply a remedy. For a desirable remedy, we consider the main direction of modern academic progress should be readjusted so as to convince all peoples to examine the defects of their won cultures, and to acquire a broader and far reaching perspective of problems as a single, overall issue, to be solved in the most friendly spirit possible.

Aside from the multiplicity of Western cultural sources which produced departmentalism of specialized studies in science and philosophy, all of mankind must develop some sort of magnanimous feeling so as to jointly search for solutions of their overall problems. Such a magnanimous feeling must consist in mutual respect and sympathy toward each other's culture, though it may be of different patterns as adopted by different people, with genuine commiseration and compassion toward the adversity of mankind as a whole. By this feeling we might recognize that all of the national patterns are expressions of human spiritual-lives, in each of which there is the crystallization of human blood, sweat and tears. Hence, all of mankind must learn to adopt the Confucian spirit of "reviving the perished state and restoring the broken family" so that in mutually influenced co-existence, all nations can work together toword the goal of the brotherhood of man; and thereupon they can come to have a common concern for their respective problems

That is a preparatory step for realization, through concerted efforts, of the "one world one family ideal".

Secondly, in the cultivation of the aforesaid grand feeling. it is evident that the cool, objective or scientific study of nature and society is only one-sided. It is inevitable that another kind of study is needed, which treats mankind itself as an existential subject and there tries to elevate it gradually to "lofty sagehood," with its heart expanding and wisdom purifying day by day so as to reach the stage of mental roundness of spiritual perfection. This study is, in other words, aiming at the daily aggrandizement of that human feeling of kindness, with the heart overflowing with commiseration and compassion.

Such a study is not theology; nor is it the study of outward ethical codes or of mental hygiene. It is a type of scholarship which connects knowledge and action by which man can transcend his own being and attain higher spiritual enlightenment, This is what Confucianists call the "Study of moral mind (Hsin)and Moral Reason (Hsing). It is otherwise called the "Study of Ultimate, Righteous Principles" or the "Study of Sagehood."

The same type of study also exists in Western religious devotion to spiritual ascendency and the Indian practice of Yoga. Likewise, the emphasis on how to become a true Christian by self-cultivation instead of attending church service, as first preached by Danish Kierkegaard on Existentialism, is aimed at securing a way by which man transcends his existence to attain a higher spiritual realm. Yet because of the different cultural origins of the West, which were split into the rational pursuit of science (from the Greek heritage), the religious cherishment with faith in God's revelation (as handed down by Hebrew culture), and in the social, legal and political research (as stressed by the Roman tradition), this type of study has not attained the ideal stage as the core of Western thinking.

If man cannot transcend his own actual being so as to attain the higher spiritual realm, then his existing body cannot embrace God while his religious faith may be shaken as a result. Meanwhile, nor can he embrace and control with complacency his own scientific and technological achievements. There is subsequent danger of having atomic or nuclear bombs slipping out of his control to annihilate the human race. Nor can man regulate his own invented political, social and juridical institutions so as to avert their oppression of individual liberty. Such oppression is manifested in modern totalitarian countries, while certain industrialized civic organizations also suffer from this same type of collective hardship. The chief trouble is that man tries to understand the world objective and, with knowledge thus obtained, tries to form ideals which he again continuously objectives in the natural and social world. Hence, the whole structure of external culture and material riches thus continuously accumulated with its accelerating preponderance, automatically fetters human life in such a mechanical manner beyond, it seems, the control of human forces.

On the other hand, the great learning, as related above in attempting to "turn the Heaven and Earth around" for human benefit, means the planting of self-dominance of the true subjectivity of man's subjective existence. Such a planting of the self-dominance of true subjectivity depends upon the transcendental development of the human being in its present shape. This is what we call in China the "Learning of Setting up the Human Ultimate (立人極)". Human being as a pole between the Heaven-Pole and the earth-Pole. Blessed with the accomplishment of such "human ultimacy," can man then embrace what he believes and put all of his inventions under strict control. This is a great learning our contemporaries must study with adequate appreciation.

Finally, human existence as formed or manifested by the "study of the Human Ultimate" is a moral subject, but at the same time it transcends itself toward a higher spiritual enlightenment, so that it can also truly embrace God in the Chinese version of "becoming harmonious with Heavenly virtue." "Therefore, the man's secular existence is at the same time "merged into moral and religious existence." By virtue of its being a moral subject, man in the political sense is an authentic citizen in a democratic state, setting himself up as a political subject. And when proceeding into the "one world" stage of mankind, he will become what Mencius called "Heaven's subject," while still behaving as a "political subject of the Heavenly Empire."

Meanwhile, in the realm of knowledge, the same man becomes also an "epistemological being." As an "epistemological subject" or an "intellectual being," he does not remain bogged down in the objective world, but rather stands above it; at the same time, his concepts or ideas are not limited or fixed by any particular instances, so that his conceptual knowledge will not be contradicted with the "round and all-pervasive wisdom" which in the whole of cultural history makes him a "subject living in a lasting and boundless historical culture linking up the past and future." From this view point, human life becomes integrated with the cosmos. In this orderly universe, he will witness the "Eternal Way," or, as is said in the West, "God's Direct Revelation." This is the direction which we think, a new learning must take for all the peoples of the world.

As for the final goal, "Learning of Setting up the Human Ultimate," by following the aforesaid direction, we attain the goal for uniting in its development all the diverse cultural heritages of the West and the religious and moral wisdom of the East.

We do not know when this ideal will be realized. But if we want to implement such an ideal, we can begin right now. For us Chinese, it is necessary that we begin with our realistic position of carrying out a more dynamic cultural program in order to help accomplish the national, democratic reconstruction dating back several scores years, thus bringing scientific industrialization to China. That is, in fulfilling the demand for self-development of Chinese culture, the aforesaid dynamic program is aimed at setting-up the Chinese people's existence as a political subject and also an epistemological subject.

For Westerners, there is need for self-examining their own cultural weaknesses so as to learn something valuable from the East, with better understanding of other cultural traditions. That being the case, Western democracies, in their position of world leadership, will have to champion also the enlightened development of other people's cultures together with their aspiration for national democratic reconstruction. It should be done by demonstrating their noble spirit of "reviving the perished and restoring the broken." This magnificent task, if well done, will make all peoples first attain the status of true citizens in their respective countries, and later will promote them all into the position of "Heaven's People" in the "one world, One Family" utopia. To attain this the attitude of Westerners in studying Oriental scholarship, cultural pattern and history, should also be modified as we have related above.

We can well recall that before the 18th century many learned Westerners had particularly admired Chinese culture. Later in the early 19th century, China assumed world leadership by treating the Westerners, rightly or wrongly, as barbarians. But from the latter half of the 19th century up to the present, most Westerners have been looking down upon some Eastern nations, including China, as "under-developed" peoples. Meanwhile, most Chinese after self-examination considered themselves inferior to others in many, if not all, respects. Past history has thus shown a succession of reciprocal admiration and depreciation between China and the West, as though the "Heavenly Way of Rotation," or The Buddhist version of "Karma," were at work.

But now, the time has come for a meeting of minds between the East and the West in the light of true equality for mutual benefaction. Apparently, Chinese culture is now chaotic despite its past imcomparable brilliancy. At present, although Western culture is overwhelmingly glittering, its future will be a hard nut to crack. Time and tide are calling all the peoples of the world to mutually understanding in the mood of "like mind, like comprehension," and the rotating "wheel of the Cosmic Law," so that by jointly carrying the common burdens of hardships, maladies, deladies, defects and mistakes of mankind, a new road may be opened up for all humanity.

Appendix II

Contemporary Chinese Philosophy
Outside Mainland China

Joseph S. Wu

I. INTRODUCTION

TO MANY of our readers, the title of this article appears insignificant, if not self-contradictory. How can there be any Chinese philosophy outside China? Even if there is Chinese philosophy outside China, how can one justify the value of writing on such a theme? Some American scholars who have taught and published in Chinese philosophy proclaimed, manifestly or suggestively, that Mao Tse-tung was the major or even an exclusive representative philosopher of contemporary China, and Maoism was the only Chinese philosophy of our age.[1] To the belief of this author, Maoism is merely an elaborate ideological device of an unusually ambitious politician to realize his political goal. It is far from being a spontaneous product growing out of the Chinese philosophic tradition.[2] In the light of this consideration, whether Mao can be taken as a major representative of contemporary Chinese philosophy is highly questionable. I do not mean to dismiss the significance of the study of the thought of Mao, but I do not want to see that his place in Chinese philosophy is improperly exaggerated so as to undermine the genuine contributions of contemporary Chinese philosophers. Mao's thought is important for Westerners in understanding the impact of Marxism and Leninism on contemporary China. It is also significant for Westerners if they want to know how Mao has modified the original Marxism and Leninism in order to facilitate his totalitarian ruling of the Chinese people. But to consider Mao's thought as an outgrowth of the Chinese philosophic tradition is to commit the fallacy of

---

[1] A notable example is H.G.Creel's popular book *Chinese Thought: from Confucius to Mao Tse-tung* (New York: New American Library, 1953). A relatively recent one is John Koller's *Oriental Philosophies* (New York: Scribner, 1970), in which Mao occupies the entire last chapter, and no treatment is given to Chinese philosophy outside the mainland at all.

[2] Cf. Joseph S. Wu, "Understanding Maoism: A Chinese Philosopher's Critique," *Studies in Soviet Thought*, 15 (1975), 99-118. This paper has been anthologised into *Clarification and Enlightenment: Essays in Comparative Philosophy* (Washington: Univ. Press of America, 1978), by the same author.

564

what this author has called "misconceived continuity.''[3] In fact, the continuity between the Chinese philosophic tradition and contemporary Chinese thought is found outside the Chinese mainland rather than in the thought of Mao. The reasons for some scholars' taking Mao as the representative for contemporary Chinese philosophy might be very complicated, but a most important one is the lack of information about the genuine contributions of the Chinese philosophers outside mainland·China. The chief purpose of this article is to fulfill a need for information, giving a descriptive account of contemporary Chinese philosophy outside the Chinese mainland.

Contemporary Chinese philosophy outside mainland China is a panoramic scene of extraordinary multiplicity. In giving an account of this scene, we need to set a geographic limit. Hence the geographical scope of my account will be limited to three places: Hong Kong, Taiwan (Republic of China), and the United States. The development of Chinese philosophy in other countries such as Japan, France and Germany will not be included. The two islands outside the Chinese mainland are the most important bases for the continuous development of Chinese culture without violent suppression, persecution, or governmental - distortion. In addition, in these two islands we find many original thinkers and accomplished scholars who fled from the mainland for free intellectual development. So I do not need to justify my choice of these two places. In fact, many of my readers could not think of places other than these two islands for representing Chinese philosophy outside mainland China. But what is the justification for my inclusion of the United States which is neither a nation of Chinese-speaking people nor a colony of Chinese culture?

It is a demonstrable fact that the United States is a great melting pot of ideas and values of our age. In this country, one can find varieties of cultural specialties from every corner of the world. Regarding Chinese philosophy, the United States is probably the only non-Chinese speaking country which has fostered so many college teachers in this field.[4] This is probably due to the political reason that many Chinese philosophy students, after getting their doctoral degree, remain permanent members of the American academic world. As a result, the effort devoted to the promotion of Chinese philosophy has become strikingly phenomenal. Within a short period of the last three years, *The Journal of Chinese Philosophy* was established and the International Society for Chinese Philosophy was founded.[5]

In the academic year of 1976-77, this author was given an opportunity to have direct contacts with the philosophy circles of both Hong Kong and Taiwan. He

'*Studies in Soviet Thought, art. cit.*, pp. 102-104.

'I have gone through the *Directory of American Philosophers* (edited by Archie J. Bahm), 1976-77, and discovered that there had been over 200 philosophy scholars claiming a specialty in Oriental philosophy, and over twenty of them specifically in "Chinese philosophy."

'*The Journal of Chinese Philosophy* was founded by Chung-ying Cheng of the University of Hawaii. In spite of its very recent origin, hence not yet fully established academic prestige, it is the only journal devoted to Chinese 'philosophy in the English-publishing world. The International Society for Chinese Philosophy had its first annual meeting at Fairfield University from May 30 to June 4, 1978, with the theme "Being and Nothingness in Chinese and Western Thought."

spent the entire academic year in doing research work and lecturing there, where he was a student in his youth under some prominent philosophers. As a visitor from the United States, he was welcomed by the Catholics as well as the Buddhists, the liberals as well as the conservatives, the Confucianists and the followers of Dr. Sun Yat-sen. So this article is in a way a report of his direct experience of his Sabbatical leave. Nevertheless, his observation had been prepared by his continuous attention to the development of Chinese philosophy in these two places and his tireless study of the important philosophical works written by prominent Chinese thinkers.

In spite of the multiplicity and diversity in the panorama of contemporary Chinese philosophy, this report will be divided into the following four sections: Chinese Buddhism, Chinese Scholasticism, Neo-Sunism, and Contemporary Confucianism. This author is quite aware of the unclassifiable nature of some individual thinkers, and this will be briefly supplemented in the last section.

II. CHINESE BUDDHISM

During the early period of the founding of the Republic of China, long before the communists took over the Chinese mainland, Buddhism in China had an exuberant revival in which Au-yang Ching-wu and Master T'ai-hsu were the central figures. Since 1949, it has continued its gradual development in Taiwan and Hong Kong. The main representative in Taiwan is Master Yin Hsun, a very learned scholarly monk who was a graduate from Wu Chiang Buddhist Academy and earned a doctoral degree from a Japanese university. Nearly eighty years old, he is still active in lecturing and writing, with a chair in philosophy at the College of Chinese Culture. Master Yin Hsun wrote volumes on Buddhism and his most recent work *The History of Ch'an Buddhism in China*[6] exhibits much more substantial scholarship than other works of the same kind. Following Master T'ai-hsu, Yin Hsun advocates Buddhism as a means to the creation of a new world culture. From his viewpoint, Brahmanism was a local product of the Hindu people, and Judaism, a local product of the Jewish people. Although Hinduism and Christianity attempted to break the local limits, yet they still exhibit a very strong attitude of intolerance and exclusiveness. Buddhism is the only religion in the world which is all-tolerant and all-inclusive. A convert does not need to abandon his previous religious beliefs since Buddhism recognizes the genuine values of other religions. Therefore, the promotion of Buddhism can lead to the creation of a new world culture which features genuine love, freedom, and equality.[7]

[6] Yin Hsun, *Chung Kuo Ch'an Chung Shih* or *History of Chinese Ch'an Buddhism* (Taipei, 1971 first printing; 1975 second printing).

[7] Yin Hsun, "Promotion of Buddhism as Means to Create New World Culture," *Che Hsueh Lun Chi* or *Collected Essays in Philosophy*, edited by Yi Wu (Taipei: Hua Kang Publishing Company, 1976). This collection of essays consists of fifty essays written by contemporary Chinese thinkers representing all trends in contemporary Chinese philosophy except Maoism. Most of the essays were written by invitation and a few of them were selected from published works.

A very unique Buddhist personality is a female scholar, an artist-nun with the religious name Shig Hiu Wan (Cantonese pronunciation—Mandarin should be "Shih Shao-yun").[1] Instead of being trained in a monastery in her youth, she was a graduate of two art institutes of South China, including one in Hong Kong. After her college years in Canton, she went to India to study art. Having been a visiting professor of art in India, she is now the director of the Institute for the Study of Buddhist Culture of the China Academy and a professor of the College of Chinese Culture. Her academic field in Buddhist studies is T'ien T'ai school, but her genuine and unique contribution lies in her blending the Buddhist culture with the artistic spirit of the Chinese tradition. In recent years, she advocates the philosophy of "field and garden" *(t'ien-yuan hsu hsiang)* which was originated in naturalist poets like T'ao Yuan-ming. This type of philosophy could not have been produced by a Buddhist without in-depth cultivation in Chinese culture. Shig Hiu Wan herself is an excellent painter and a writer, as well as a nun of very high religious level. Nevertheless, being a female herself, her influence on her disciples or laymen awaits for the future when her position is more appreciated and recognized by the intellectual world which has been male-dominant.

Another scholar who synthesizes Buddhism and Chinese culture together is Professor Hu-t'ien Pa who has been a professor of National Taiwan Normal University, National Taiwan University, and Tung Hai University. While Shig Hiu Wan has blended Chinese painting and T'ien T'ai Buddhism, Pa in himself has synthesized Ch'an Buddhism and Chinese poetry. Although he never published huge volumes, his short papers were written with a high degree of clarity and penetration, so his readers and students recognize him as a top authority in Ch'an Buddhism. His writings were anthologized by himself into a volume called *I Hai Wei Lan (Mild Waves in the Ocean of Literature)* with a subtitle "Ch'an and Poetry."[9] As far as this author knows, the greatest contribution to Ch'an by Professor Pa is his interpretation of *kung-ans* (koans). Unlike Japanese scholars (e.g. D. T. Suzuki) who mystified and obscured the specific meanings in a *kung-an* with general remarks about the irrational nature of Ch'an, Professor Pa is able to render each *kung-an* in a clear and intelligible manner with his solid scholarship in Buddhism and his sharp awareness of the poetic ways of using language. After his retirement from university teaching in Taiwan, he became an immigrant of the United States residing in Las Vegas which to him is the same as an old temple amid the mountains.[10]

[1] I met Rev. Shig Hiu Wan at the temporary residence of Professor T'ang Chun-i, who was recovering from his lung surgery. Subsequently I was invited by her to give a lecture on Buddhism to her group of students at Hua Kang, Yang Ming Shan.

[9] Hu-t'ien Pa, *I Hai Wei Lan* or *Mild Waves in the Ocean of Literature* (Taipei: Kwang Wen Book Company, 1971).

[10] I received a letter from Professor Pa about Christmas time of 1977, in which was included one of his recent poems, indicating that the renowned casino city is, to him, no different from an old temple among the mountains. This is, of course, a result of a life-long cultivation of Ch'an philosophy.

In Hong Kong, the most influential and reputed scholar in Buddhism is Professor Lo Shih-hsien, a student of the late Master T'ai-hsu and follower of Au-yang Ching-wu. In addition to his writings promoting *Wei-shih* Buddhism (Yogacara School), Lo tirelessly gave lectures on the celebrated classic *Cheng Wei Shih Lun* every Monday for a continuous period of over ten years. His student, the late Professor Wai Tat, after attending his lectures, rendered the entirety of this important classic into English. Lo and his students seventeen years ago founded the Society for Fa Hsiang Buddhism which is probably the only academic society for Buddhism in the British Colony of Hong Kong. Now in his sixties, Lo is still actively engaging himself in a very ambitious publishing project, an extended commentary on the Shu Chi of Kwei Chi. This is a ten-volume project, and the first volume has been out for just a year.[11] Lo's most brilliant and learned student (also a student of T'ang Chun-i who will be reported under contemporary Confucianism), Tu-hui Fok, a lecturer at New Asia College of the Chinese University of Hong Kong, has been very active in the academic field of Buddhist philosophy, and published many articles which contributed tremendously to Buddhist studies.

Is there any movement of Chinese Buddhism in the United States? Buddhism in the United States seems to have been dominated by the Japanese, yet we find a very important exception. This is Master Hsuan Hua, the head monk of the Gold Mountain Monastery of San Francisco. Hsuan Hua, who was known as Tu-lun in Northern China, went to Hong Kong after the Maoists captured mainland China. Being at odds with the Hong Kong environment, he came to the United States to educate American people with Buddhist philosophy. As a result of his pedagogic effort, a number of American young scholars became his disciples, among whom Ronald Epstein, who holds a Ph.D. from University of California, Berkeley, is probably the most prominent one. Two years ago, together with the effort of his American disciple Heng Kuan and others, Hsuan Hua started an ambitious project of founding the first Buddhist University in the Western world. This is Dharma Realm University located two-miles east of Ukiah, California. While this author was on sabbatical in Taiwan, he met Heng Kuan, the Vice-president of Dharma Realm, who went to Asia for fund-raising and faculty recruitment. As a result of his recruitment effort, Professor Yi Wu, a prominent scholar in Chinese philosophy teaching at the College of Chinese Culture, accepted the position of chairman of the Department of Chinese Philosophy and Religion.

III. CHINESE SCHOLASTICISM

Another movement of religious philosophy in contemporary Chinese philosophy is "Chinese Scholasticism." I deliberately use this term for two reasons. First, the major representatives in this movement have a great respect for, and a good understanding of, the Chinese cultural traditions. Secondly, the

---

[11]"Shih-hsien Lo, *Cheng Wei Shih Lun Shu Chi Shuan Chu,* Vol. 1 (Hong Kong: Fa Hsiang Academic Society, 1977).

effort is not a mere promotion of Catholicism or Scholasticism in China. Rather, it is an effort to fuse the basic spirit of Scholasticism with the traditional values of Chinese culture, particularly those of the Confucian tradition. This philosophic movement has its institutional basis at the Catholic Fu Jen University and a journal of its own—*Universitas: Monthly Review of Philosophy and Culture.*

The chief exponent of this philosophic trend is Dr. S. Lokuang, the publisher of *Universitas* and the archbishop of Taipei. Bishop Lokuang is a very well-learned scholar in both Eastern and Western philosophy and has published many volumes of philosophic treatises. His most recent work *The Future of Chinese Philosophy (Chung Kuo Che Hsueh te Chien Wang* published by Hsueh Sheng Shu Chu of Taipei) suggests an attempt to synthesize the East and the West through blending together Confucianism and Christianity.

Other active exponents include John C. Wu, director of the doctoral program in philosophy at the College of Chinese Culture, Albert Chao and Thaddeus Hang of National Cheng-chi University, Cheng-tung Chang and Chih-tsun of Catholic Fu Jen University. There are still many others in this group. Wu was a professor of international law at Seton Hall University until his retirement. In addition to his publications in his major field, he has devoted the rest of his academic energy to philosophy, introducing Taoism and Ch'an to the West, Christian philosophy to China. Albert Chao has written extensively virtually on every topic of philosophy. His philosophic position is quite humanistic in spite of his position of being a Catholic priest. He regards religion as an important part of humanity, and the concept of humanism should be broadened to include religion which is an expression of the humanistic spirit.

Now, the question is, what do they propose as philosophic guideline for a synthesis of scholasticism and traditional Chinese philosophy? Each exponent has his suggested ideas. The most systematic and all-encompassing suggestion is found in a recent article "Chinese Thought and the Christian Religion" *(Chung Kuo Hsi Hsiang yu Chi Tu Tsung Chiao).*[12] The author is Pei-yung Fu, the former editor of *Universitas*, currently instructor in philosophy at National Taiwan University. In this article, Fu suggested ten points for consideration:[13]

1) *Problem of Human Nature:* Confucianism maintains that human nature is originally good, while Christian philosophy believes in original sin. This appears a serious incompatibility between the two. Fu suggests that since the theory of original sin has been reinterpreted through the centuries, the Christian theory of human nature can be modified to emphasize the idea of man as created after the image of God. This will be more acceptable by the Confucians yet this idea is originally a part of the Christian doctrines.

2) *Self-Reliance and Reliance on God:* Recognizing the innate goodness of

[12]Pei-yung Fu, "Chinese Thought and the Christian Religion," *Universitas*, 4 (July, 1977); reprinted in *Fu Jen Ta Hsueh Shen Hsueh Lun Chi* or *Theological Essays of Catholic Fu Jen University*. Quotations will be from the latter.

[13]*Fu Jen Ta Hsueh Shen Hsueh Lun Chi*, pp. 214-216.

human nature, Confucianism emphasizes self-reliance in self-realization while Christianity emphasizes the reliance on God. But a careful reading of Jesus' sayings in the *New Testament* will reveal that self-reliance is equally important in Christianity. The common saying "God helps those who help themselves" reveals this point aptly.

3) *Immanence and Transcendence:* Christianity features transcendence, while traditional Chinese thought as influenced by Confucian humanism and Mahayana Buddhism emphasizes immanence. Nevertheless, the difficult situation of contemporary philosophy tends to compel Chinese thinkers to seek the path of transcendence. This means that the two are hopefully getting closer.

4) *T'ien-Jen as One and God-Man as One:* One of the main themes of traditional Chinese thought is that *T'ien* (Heaven, Sky, Nature, or Supernature, no exact English equivalent) and Man are not separate from each other. The ultimate moral purpose of man is to attain all the virtues of T'ien. Being with God through Jesus Christ is a fundamental belief for all Christians. Therefore, this is a good meeting ground for Christianity and Confucianism.

5) *Harmony in the One and Being One with God:* Both represent a form of mystical experience. Although Confucian philosophers de-emphasize experience of this kind, yet it is quite fundamental in Taoism. Being one with God as mystical union is very fundamental to the Christian mystics.

6) *The Problem of Creation:* In traditional Chinese cosmology, man is the co-creator (together with T'ien and Ti) of the universe. In Christianity man is a creature of God rather than a creator. These two philosophies appear conflicting each other. But Fu maintains that it was only the same process viewed from different angles.

7) *Confucius and Jesus Christ:* Confucius is the greatest sage of the Chinese tradition, but he never claimed himself as a divine being. We can say, suggests Fu, the birth of Confucius in China was indeed God's gift to the Chinese people. This means God sent Confucius to educate the Chinese people.

8) *The Confucian Jen and Christian Love:* On the one hand, Jen represents the never-ceasing process of life; on the other hand, love is the ever-existing process of creativity. The two in fact bear striking similarities. This is again a very good meeting ground for Christianity and Confucianism.

9) *Religion as Based on Morality and Morality as Based on Religion:* The former is the way of Christianity, and the latter, Confucianism. They appear very different from each other, yet a good balance and compromise between the two will create a more ideal morality as well as a more healthy religion.

10) *The Unity of Knowledge and Action and the Unity of Belief and Deed:* Both Confucianism and Christianity emphasize philosophy lived rather than philosophy theorized. This also features the religious nature of Confucianism.

These ten points are, according to Fu, suggested for speculation or theorization. Any fruit generated from this suggestion awaits the efforts of both the Catholic thinkers and scholars in the Confucian tradition. But, in order that Christianity can become a part of Chinese culture, a meeting between Christianity and Confucianism is not enough. Therefore, a meeting

570

between Christianity and Buddhism is a necessary step before Christianity can become a part of the Chinese tradition. Unfortunately, as Fu pointed out correctly, most of the exponents (possibly all) of Chinese Scholasticism do not know Buddhist philosophy well.[14] What is more, since most of the Chinese Catholic thinkers got their doctoral degree from Europe, they seem well satisfied with what they got from European philosophy. Consequently they have developed an attitude of ignoring the philosophic panorama of the United States, for they mistakenly think that the only philosophy in the United States is analytic philosophy accompanied by some declining trends of pragmatism.

IV. NEO-SUNISM

I have coined the term "Sunism" to name the thought of Dr. Sun Yat-sen, the founder of the Republic of China. Unlike Mao Tse-tung, who had to draw heavily upon Marxism-Leninism, Sun was a thinker with originality, and his *San Min Chi I* (The Three People's Principles) is a comprehensive synthesis of diverse cultural values, both Western and Chinese. It had become the official ideology of the Republic of China before the Maoists took over the mainland.

Dr. Sun's doctrines were originally delivered in very plain language. They were intended as ideological instruments for the Nationalist revolution. Nevertheless, after the Nationalist government moved to Taiwan, his thought has become the subject-matter of academic studies. *San Min Chu I* is now a required course for every college student in order to get a bachelor's degree. In recent years, universities established graduate programs leading toward master and doctoral degrees in this field.

There are many representative scholars in this school of thought. They are mostly high-ranking officials in the government, members of the Nationalist party, or professors teaching *San Min Chu I* or related subjects in a college or university. Among them Professor Jen Cho-hsuan is the most prominent and productive. His systematic interpretation of Sun's thought was first published in 1942,[15] and was revised and published under the title of *Sun Chung San Che Hsueh Yuan Li (The Philosophical Theory of Sun Yat-sen).*[16] In 1976, Jen wrote an article "The Philosophy of *San Min Chu I*"[17] summarizing the main points of his major work. In what follows, I shall present a summary of his own summary, which provides an interpretation of Sun's thought in accordance with the following six points:

1) *Hsin Wu Ho I Lun, or "Mind and Matter in One"*: Sun rejects materialism and idealism as extreme positions, resulting from selective emphasis on one aspect of reality at the cost of the other. If we examine the

[14]*Ibid.*, p. 202.
[15]Cho-hsuan Jen, *San Min Chu I te Che Hsueh Chi Chu*, or *The Philosophic Foundation of San Min Chu I* (Taipei: Tai Ho Shih Tai Hsu Chao She, 1942).
[16]Cho-hsuan Jen, *Sun Chung San Che Hsueh Yuan Li* or *The Philosophical Theory of Sun Yat-sen* (Taipei, Po Mi Erh Book Co., 1960).
[17]Cho-hsuan Jen, "The Philosophy of San Min Chu I," *Che Hsueh Lun Chi*, pp. 19-33.

fundamental existence of a person, we shall realize that Mind and Matter require each other, supplement each other, and complete each other. But Sun tends to place more weight on the role of the mind or spiritual power by calling our attention to some historical battles where the more spirited side (but less armed side) had the eventual victory.

2) *Yu Chou Chin Hua Lun, or "Evolutionary View of the Universe"*: Sun maintains the universe is an evolutionary process which can be conceived in three stages. The first stage is the evolution of pure matter or inorganic existence. Inorganic activities consist in interaction of atoms with one another. The second stage is the evolution of organic matter or biological existence. The emergence of life is the feature of this stage. The third stage is the evolution of man. This is marked by the emergence of spirituality. Sun's theory might have been influenced by Charles Darwin, Samuel Alexander, and Lloyd Morgan, with the emphasis on spirituality as the essence of man.

3) *Jen Lei Sheng Tsun Lun, or "Theory of Human Survival"*: Rejecting the Marxist theory of historical materialism, Sun maintains that the problem of human survival occupies the center of history. Human survival, Sun holds, plays a very important role in economics, politics, and social progress. Nevertheless, human activities, energized by the urge to survive, are not merely physical. Instead, both the physical and the mental (or the spiritual) are involved in the survival process.

4) *Jen Lei Hsing Wei Lun, or "Theory of Human Action"*: In order to motivate his followers to participate in revolutionary activities, Sun elaborated his theory of action which has been known as *Chih Nan Hsing I Shuo*—the theory that action is easy but knowledge is difficult. He has worked out ten arguments to support this thesis, calling our attention to the fact that many people develop the habit of doing something without being aware of doing it. Due to some logical difficulties, the late president Chiang Kai-shek has modified this into a more pragmatic and vitalistic theory called *Li Hsing Che Hsueh,* or "Philosophy of Effortful Action."

5) *Jen Lei Hu Tso Lun, or "Theory of Cooperation"*: Sun conceives human survival as a social problem rather than an individual problem. It is an iron fact that human beings need to rely on one another in order to survive. This logically leads to the thesis that we need to cooperate in order to attain survival. This concept automatically rejects any theory which advocates hatred, struggle, or violence. Once Sun rejects Karl Marx saying that "class struggle" is only a symptom of a sick society, but not the normal course of social progress. It follows that Marx can only be a pathologist rather than a physiologist of human society.

6) *Shih Chien Jen Shih Lun, or "Pragmatic Theory of Knowledge"*: Sun speculates that primitive people lived the life of doing without knowing. Later, with further development and progress, people gained knowledge from doing. This means that knowledge is gained through inductive generalization. After the rise and development of science, we can have knowledge before we proceed

to do anything. A modern man, suggests Sun, should fully utilize his knowledge to guide his action.

Being a follower of Sun in both theory and action, Chiang Kai-shek has developed Sun's philosophy much further. For brevity's sake, I am going to mention only two points of importance: First, in theory of reality, Chiang has substantiated Sun's evolutionary view of the universe with the renowned Chinese classic, the *I Ching* or *The Book of Changes*. In his theory of knowing, Chiang goes back to the celebrated Chinese philosopher Wang Yang-ming for a stronger theory of knowledge and action. In addition, Chiang has contributed a great deal in his promotion of Confucianism, particularly the Confucian theory as contained in the two classical essays *Ta Hsueh* (Great Learning) and *Chung Yung* (Doctrine of the Mean).[18] After his death, there have appeared in Taiwan a number of scholarly articles devoted to the exposition and interpretation of his thought.

V. CONTEMPORARY CONFUCIANISM

I use the term "contemporary Confucianism" deliberately in order to make a contradistinction between Confucianism today and the kind of Confucianism developed by Sung and Ming philosophers. Since the term "Neo-Confucianism" has been conventionally used for Sung-Ming Confucian policy *(Sung-Ming Li Hsueh)*, its unqualified use for Confucianism of the twentieth century would result in linguistic confusion. So, I will use "contemporary Confucianism" to indicate the Confucian philosophy of our age.

Contemporary Confucianism is probably the most influential and widely spread trend of thought outside mainland China. In addition to its large number of exponents and adherents, it has maintained its prominent and prestigious status through the educational system of Taiwan, and with certain limits, the curriculum of the schools in Hong Kong. *The Four Books, the Confucian Analects, Mencius, The Great Learning,* and *the Doctrine of the Mean* constitute a three-year course (in fact three different one-year courses) required of all the students in the National Taiwan Normal University, which has been the major cradle of high school teachers.[19] The National Taiwan University, which is characterized by a more liberal spirit, perhaps inherited from the May Fourth Movement, still requires Mencius as a text for freshman Chinese. Confucian doctrines are also taught at the high school level both in Taiwan and in Hong Kong. A Hong Kong high school even required that *Hsiao Ching (The Book of Filial Piety)* be taught as a part of the course on Chinese Literature.[20] From all these we can observe that, in spite of the Maoists'

[18]Chang, Tsai-yu wrote an article on Chiang's contribution to *Ta Hsueh* and *Chung Yung;* it is included in *Che Hsueh Lun Chi*, pp. 93-108.

[19]I myself am a graduate of this university and went through all the courses in which students are required to memorize all the *Four Books* by heart and comprehend all the philosophical subtleties thoroughly.

[20]This is Tak Ming Secondary School (called Tak Ming College) in Kowloon, Hong Kong, where this author taught for one year. The *Hsiao Ching* requirement was instituted by the former

demotion of Confucius, the Chinese people still respect and honor their sage wherever they get freedom of thought and action.

There are too many accomplished scholars in this trend of thought to be treated in this brief account. So in this short section I will present only five very prominent individuals: Professors Chen Ta-chi and Hsieh Yu-wei of Taiwan, Professors Mau tsung-san and T'ang Chun-i of Hong Kong, and Professor Wing-tsit Chan of the United States.

Professor Chen Ta-chi, being well-trained in logic in both Western and Hindu traditions, is probably the most clear and fluent writer among contemporary Chinese thinkers. Being very well educated in classical Chinese culture, he is able to clarify the subtle problems in classical writings. After publishing numerous articles elucidating major concepts and problems in classical Confucian philosophy, he published a systematic exposition of Confucius' philosophy.[21] Unlike some other Confucian scholars who try to fit Confucius into some ready-made schemes, Chen tries his best to disclose the original ideas of Confucius without westernizing or modernizing the sage. It is not surprising that when the Society for Confucius and Mencius was founded, he was elected the first president.

The late Professor Hsieh Yu-wei, having been once a student of Alfred North Whitehead at Harvard, contributed to the Chinese academic world through his tireless introduction of Western thinkers to Chinese readers. Nevertheless his philosophic position was a Confucian one. He gained his reputation as a Confucianist by his persistent promotion of the philosophy of filial piety. According to Hsieh himself, he got the idea of promoting "filial piety" in 1934 when he wrote on the philosophy of loyalty advocated by Josiah Royce. He published his first article on "Filial Piety and Chinese Culture" in *Hsi Hsiang Yu Shih Tai (Thought and Time)* in 1943. His second article was written in English and was presented to the third East-West Conference at the University of Hawaii in 1959.[22] This article aroused considerable controversy in the conference and since then Hsieh has become a confirmed advocate of filial piety. Later in Hong Kong, Hsieh published a third article (in Chinese) explaining the compatible nature between filial piety and democracy. After his retirement from the Chinese University of Hong Kong in 1969, he continued his teaching at the College of Chinese Culture in Taiwan until his death. In Taiwan, he continued his philosophizing in the hope that he would write a book on this concept some day. Unfortunately he was unable to fulfill this wish for he died in 1976 at the age of seventy-three. His last article on filial piety

---

principal Mr. Shu-woon Chan who later immigrated to the United States and became a professor in some college in the Bay Area. Chan is a person of deep piety with intense pedagogic zest and strong respect for traditional Chinese culture.

[21]Chen Ta-ch'i, *Kung Tzu Hsueh Shuo,* or *The Theory of Confucius* (Taipei: Cheng Chung Publishing Company, 1964).

[22]Hsieh Yu-wei, "Filial Piety and Chinese Society," in *Chinese Mind,* edited by Charles A. Moore, (Honolulu: East-West Center Press, 1967), pp. 167-187. This article has its Chinese version published in *Hsin Ya Hsueh Pao,* 4 (August, 1958).

574

was "The Nature of Filial Piety and the Need of It" *(Hsiao Chih Hsing Chih chi ch'i Ssu Yao)*, published shortly before his death.[23]

Professor Mou-Tsung-san is a very talented original thinker. He is well-trained in logic, like Professor Chen Ta-ch'i. But unlike Chen, who tries to disclose the original meanings of ancient philosophical classics, Mou is more inclined to conceptualize previous philosophers in order to reconstruct their philosophy according to his own insights. In his college days, he studied mathematical logic with tremendous effort. But he found the logic of the Whitehead-Russell tradition not very rewarding, because it fails to account for the knowing subject. Then he turned to the study of Kant and has since been deeply involved in the philosophy of subjectivity. Being a student of Hsiung Shih-li, who reconstructed Confucianism with the concepts and methods of Yogacara *(Wei-shih)* Buddhism, Mou attempted to reconstruct Confucianism with Kant's method and some Kantian modes of thinking. His main contribution is the affirmation of the validity of moral knowledge attainable by intuition. His representative works are the three-volume work *Hsin-Ti yu Hsing-Ti* and *Chih te Chih Chueh yu Chung Kuo Che Hsueh*.[24]

Professor T'ang Chün-i, who died on February 2, 1978, is probably the greatest Confucian philosopher China has produced since Chu Hsi and Wang Yang-ming. Differing from Mou who took a shortcut through Kant, T'ang developed his version of Confucian philosophy through very careful and judicial assessment of each philosophic position of both Eastern and Western philosophy. His mode of philosophizing has been influenced by Hegel, but his ideas are so existentially and culturally grounded that in his philosophy we find an unprecedentedly comprehensive synthesis of the East and the West. In addition to a systematic re-interpretation of the entire Chinese philosophic tradition in his six-volume work *Chung Kuo Che Hsueh Yuan Lun*,[25] he has developed a comprehensive theory of culture through which the reconstruction of Chinese culture is possible. His masterpiece, a two-volume work entitled *The Existence of Life and the World of Spirituality (Sheng Ming Tsun Tsai yu Hsin Ning Ching Chieh)*, was published several months before his death.[26] This is a rare product of high originality with persistent effort in moral cultivation, philosophic discipline, and ultimate concern for the destiny of man. It is a piece of work which should be placed among Plato's *Republic*, Kant's *Critique of Pure Reason*, Heidegger's *Being and Time*, and Whitehead's *Process and Reality*. Some selections from T'ang's writings were translated into English and

[23]Hsieh Yu-wei, "The Nature of Filial Piety and the Need of It," in *Che Hsueh Lun Chi*, pp. 425-439.

[24]Mou Tsung-san, *Hsin Ti yu Hsing Ti* or *Mind and Nature*, 3 volumes, (Taipei: Cheng Chung Book Company, 1968-69). Also, *Chih te Chih Chueh yu Chung Kuo Che Hsueh* (Taipei: Commercial Press, 1971).

[25]T'ang Chün-i, *Chung Kuo Che Hsueh Yuan Lun*, or *The Origin and Development of the Basic Concepts in Chinese Philosophy*, 6 volumes, 1966-1973, initially published by New Asia Research Institute of Hong Kong. Since 1976, copyright goes to Hsueh Sheng Shu Chu of Taipei.

[26]T'ang Chün-i, *Sheng Ming Tsun Tsai yu Hsin Ning Ching* or *The Existence of Life and the World of Spirituality* (Taipei: Hsueh Sheng Shu Chu, 1977).

were published in 1973 and 1974 in *Chinese Studies of Philosophy*.[27] In spite of his difficult writing style, his influence has been far-reaching because his written works cover the entire range of human culture and experience, ranging through philosophy, history, art, literature, education, morality, law, politics, international relations, and even architecture and landscaping. It is a great pity that none of his works has been translated in entirety for the English-speaking world.

Professor Wing-tsit Chan of Chatham College, Pennsylvania, is a very important figure in the contemporary scene of Chinese philosophy. He has added a new but significant dimension to the development of Chinese philosophy outside mainland China. His selection, compilation, and translation of Chinese classical writings from Confucius to twentieth century has laid down the foundation for the development of Chinese philosophy in the English-speaking world, particularly the United States. With solid discipline in the English language and the study of history of ideas, Chan's translation (most of the time with annotations and comments) demonstrates admirable scholarship and a high degree of accuracy. Without his *Source Book in Chinese Philosophy*,[28] the teaching of Chinese philosophy in the English-speaking world would be limited to early Confucianism in scope, and Arthur Waley or James Legge in texts. Besides his contribution in source introduction, Chan's articles elucidating problematic facets of historical figures and important concepts in Chinese philosophy have demonstrated an unprecedented reservoir of cultural information and scholarship in the history of Chinese thought.[29] In addition, he has written extensively in order to provide truthful descriptive accounts of Chinese philosophers and philosophical movements, and has compiled extensive bibliographies which greatly facilitate research on Chinese philosophy in the English publishing world.[30] In spite of his historical knowledge of Buddhism and Taoism, his own position is Confucianist. In one of his recent poems, he even confessed that the figures who often appeared in his dream were Chou

---

[27]*Chinese Studies of Philosophy: A Journal of Translation*, 5 No. 1 (Fall, 1973) and No. 4 (Summer, 1974), were entirely devoted to the publication of the translation of selections from Professor T'ang's writings.

[28]Wing-tsit Chan, *Source Book in Chinese Philosophy* (Princeton: Princeton Univ. Press, 1963).

[29]Professor Chan's scholarship as exhibited in his English articles is well-known to scholars in the English-speaking world. Here I would like to emphasize that Professor Chan's articles written in Chinese exhibit even more solid scholarship. Thus his recent Chinese article "Confucianism in the Early Period" in *The Bulletin of the Institute of History of Philology*, Vol. XLVII, Part 4, pp. 707-782, published in 1976 by Academic Sinica, demonstrated unprecedented scholarship in the history of Chinese philosophy. This article is a result of using 148 published items, with 683 footnotes of documentation.

[30]Professor Chan has contributed many articles to Encyclopedias, chapters to books providing accurate accounts of Chinese philosophic activities and movements. Besides, his compilation of bibliographies on Chinese philosophy is admirable. The following two items are particularly important: *An Outline and Annotated Bibliography of Chinese Philosophy*, rev. ed., 1969, by the Far Eastern Publication of Yale University, and *Chinese Philosophy 1949-1963*, (Honolulu: East-West Center Press, 1967).

576

tun-i, the Ch'eng brothers, Chu Hsi, Lu Chiu-yuan, and Wang Yang-ming.[11]

It is an obvious fact that Confucianism still plays a very significant role in contemporary Chinese philosophy. Even the adherents of Chinese Buddhism, Sunism, and Chinese Scholasticism are Confucian to a certain extent. The influence of Confucianism in the West today cannot be directly measured. But as far as this author experiences, American philosophers and scholars are quite capable of understanding Confucian philosophy even without knowing the Chinese language. When the author was a teaching assistant to an American professor teaching Chinese philosophy, he was surprised that this professor represented and spoke for Confucius in so accurate, vivid, and moving a manner that one might imagine that Confucius has been re-incarnated in the English-speaking world. What is more surprising is that this professor did not have any knowledge of the Chinese language.[12] This indicates the universal appeal of Confucian philosophy. As a conclusive statement in this section, this author would venture to say that provided the Chinese people in the mainland had the freedom to make their choice, they would still choose the path of Confucius.

VI. CONCLUSION

To present a full account of contemporary Chinese philosophy besides Maoism would require an extensive volume. This paper has provided only a very rough sketch. It is inevitable that some names of accomplished scholars which deserve at least mentioning have been omitted. In conclusion, I shall make a couple of points in order to make up, at least partly, for what has been left out. First of all, I feel uneasy for having left out a few unclassifiable thinkers who should have been included, had they belonged to any of the categories. Secondly, the effort in comparative philosophy has been a striking phenomenon together with the developmental trends mentioned above. Both will be mentioned briefly in this conclusion.

The first unclassifiable thinker is the late Professor Thomé H. Fang of National Taiwan University. He had a Confucian family tradition, a personally preferred Taoist way of life, a Buddhist religion, and a Western philosophic discipline. In spite of the fact that his published works are not comparable in quantity to most of the individuals mentioned in this paper, he has exercised tremendous influence through his classroom teaching. For over thirty years, he taught at National Taiwan University, which was the only university having a philosophy department until recently. Therefore many of the younger scholars teaching Chinese philosophy today were once his students and are still his admirers or followers. Although he did not publish many volumes, his

---

[11] In 1977, Professor Chan wrote three short Chinese poems a copy of which was sent to this author. In one of them he expressed his deep love for Confucianism as exemplified in his usual dreaming of the Neo-Confucian philosophers.

[12] This American philosopher is Professor William H. Forthman, now the chairman of the Department of Philosophy of California State University at Northridge.

published works like *Che Hsueh San Hui (Three Sources of Philosophic Wisdom)*[13] and *The Chinese View of Life*[14] demonstrate his originality and comprehensive knowledge in the philosophic traditions of both East and West. Besides, his presence in the East-West Conferences has impressed his fellow participants with his eloquence, humor, and philosophic sharpness, together with his enthusiastic defense of Chinese philosophy. Immediately after his death in July 1977, his students, headed by Professor Chen-hua Huang, the renowned Kantian-Confucian scholar and chairman of the Department of Philosophy at National Taiwan University, started gathering all his tape-recorded lectures, letters, fragmentary notes, published or unpublished, in order to compile *The Complete Work of Thomé H. Fang*. So, Fang's position in contemporary Chinese philosophy may still be too early to assess.

The second unclassifiable individual thinker is Professor Constant C. C. Chang of National Taiwan Normal University. Chang started earning his academic reputation as a scholar in the philosophy of Lao Tzu, although his personality is far from being Taoistic. Later, as co-author with his student Yi Wu (mentioned under Chinese Buddhism), he published a well-written book called *A Story of Chinese Philosophy*, which has become one of the best-sellers in the intellectual world of Taiwan.[15] In recent years, he has developed his ideas of *Ta T'ung* (Great Commonness) Society. In 1972, he was invited to give a series of television talks on his own theory, and since then he has become a popular social philosopher among the younger generation. Chang at the same time founded The Academic Society for *Ta T'ung* in February of 1974. Participants included Confucianists, Buddhists, Neo-Sunists, and Catholics. The archbishop Yu-pin was elected the chairman of the executive committee, and Chang himself was chosen as secretary. In one of his published articles, Chang has outlined his fundamental principles and a program for further research and action.[16] With his continuous effort, with the support and cooperation from other Chinese thinkers, particularly thinkers of the younger generation, Chang's philosophical movement can become a strong anti-Maoist intellectual force in our age.

The third and last unclassifiable thinker to be mentioned is Professor Hsu Fu-kuan of the New Asia Research Institute of Advanced Chinese Studies in Hong Kong, founded by Professor T'ang Chün-i. He is generally known as a scholar in the Confucian tradition. But, as this author observes, he is much more than a Confucian scholar. Unlike most of the Confucian scholars who concentrate on ethics and metaphysics of morals, Hsu has contributed significantly to art theory and Chinese esthetics. I still remember reading

[13]Fang Tung-mei (Thomé H. Fang), *Che Hsueh San Hui*, or *Three Sources of Philosophic Wisdom* (Taipei: Hsin Chung Kuo Ch'u Pan She, 1968).

[14]Thomé H. Fang, *The Chinese View of Life* (Hong Kong: The Union Press, 1957).

[15]Chang Ch'i-chun (Constant C. C. Chang) and Wu Yi, *Chung Kuo Che Hsueh Shih Hua*, or *The Story of Chinese Philosophy* (Taipei: Hsin T'ien Ti Ch'u Pan She, 1964 first printing, 1973 fifth printing).

[16]Chang Ch'i-chun, "Toward a Ta Tung World," in *Che Hsueh Lun Chi*, pp. 307-325.

578

Professor Hsu's *The Spirit of Chinese Art (Chung Kuo I Shu Ching Shen)* and found his interpretation of the principle of *Chi Yun Sheng Tung* interesting, refreshing, and penetrating, with a high degree of originality. Besides, Hsu is an excellent writer of editorial comment on current events, public affairs, and international situations. He has attracted many admirers, partly because of his originality and partly because of his sharpness in rhetoric. Although Hsu is not readily classifiable, he is nonetheless a valuable asset of the Chinese intellectual world today.

The second point which has to be mentioned in this concluding section is the continuous effort in comparative philosophy. Comparative studies of philosophy and culture started very early in the Chinese academic world, due to the need of re-evaluation of traditional values and importation of new values from the West. Several distinguished works were published before the Maoists took over the mainland. Thereafter, being inspired by the East-West Conferences taking place at the University of Hawaii, Chinese scholars have continued their effort in comparative studies. The Society for Asian and Comparative Society in the United States was founded in the academic year of 1968-69; quite a few Chinese younger scholars, including the present author, became a member, actively participating in the annual workshops for presentation and discussion. At the same time, there have appeared papers of comparative study by Chinese scholars in journals like *Philosophy East and West, International Philosophical Quarterly,* and the recently founded *Journal of Chinese Philosophy. Inquiry,* a celebrated international journal with its headquarters in Europe, in the academic year of 1968-69 approached this author for editing a special issue devoted to Chinese philosophy. In addition to nominating possible contributors, I wrote the introductory article on "The Paradoxical Situation of Western Philosophy and the Search for Chinese Wisdom," which was primarily a piece of work in comparative philosophy.[17]

Scholars and students in Taiwan have also been fascinated by the comparative approach. The journal *Universitas* has selected articles in this area. Suggestions have been made to institute a course in comparative philosophy. As a result, the present author was offered a visiting professorship to start the teaching of a course in *Pi Chiao Che Hsueh* (Comparative Philosophy) for the graduate program of National Taiwan University. In addition, I have been approached by several Chinese publishers to contribute book manuscripts in this area. As a result, my recent work *Pi Chiao Che Hsueh yu Wen Hua (Comparative Philosophy and Culture)* was published.[18] It was perhaps the first book with such a title in the Chinese publishing world.

From the viewpoint of this author, comparative philosophy is more a method of approach than a branch of philosophy. This method can apply to any

---

[17]Joseph S. Wu, "The Paradoxical Situation of Western Philosophy and the Search for Chinese Wisdom," *Inquiry,* 14 (1971), 1-18. Also the same author's *Clarification and Enlightenment: Essays in Comparative Philosophy* (Washington: Univ. Press of America, 1978), pp. 47-71.

[18]Wu Sen (Joseph S. Wu), *Pi Chiao Che Hsueh yu Wen Hua,* or *Comparative Philosophy and Culture* (Taipei: Tung Ta Publishing Company, 1978).

branch of philosophic inquiry and is not restricted to the comparison between the East and the West. With proper use of it as a method, together with a judicious and tolerant attitude it may bear substantive fruit in research. But, if it is employed improperly, comparative philosophy can become a mere battle-field for cultural chauvinists, or the gymnasium for the intellectual gymnasts with "academic vanity" as the hidden motive. Hence, the assessment of the results of this approach still wait for the future.

In spite of the diversified philosophic trends in Chinese philosophy outside the Chinese mainland, there is one thing in common—Anti-Communism. The contemporary Confucian philosophers reject Communism because the Chinese communists destroy traditional Chinese values. Buddhism and Scholasticism do not accept Communism because under communist rule there is no room for spirituality. Dr. Sun's followers reject Communism for multiple reasons of which the political element is probably the most weighty one. None of the scholars mentioned in this article would heartily recognize Mao Tse-tung as a philosopher. Nor would they approve calling Maoism a philosophy (unless they were forced under political threat, as happened to Fung Yu-lan on the mainland). It is quite conceivable that if the Chinese people inside mainland China were given the kind of freedom of thinking that is enjoyed by the Chinese outside the mainland, they would reject or abandon Marxism, Leninism, and Maoism. It is a fact, that after the death of Mao, his wife was put in prison, and his thought is no longer sacredly believed as it was before. This author would venture to predict that in the forseeable future, Maoism will become simply a chapter in the Chinese history, unlike Confucian philosophy which has offered the world something of permanent value, and appeals universally to all mankind.

英文論著彙編

著　作　者　唐君毅
出　版　者　臺灣學生書局有限公司
發　行　人　楊雲龍
發　行　所　臺灣學生書局有限公司
地　　　址　臺北市和平東路一段 75 巷 11 號
劃　撥　帳　號　00024668
電　　　話　(02)23928185
傳　　　眞　(02)23928105
E - m a i l　student.book@msa.hinet.net
網　　　址　www.studentbook.com.tw
登 記 證 字 號　行政院新聞局局版北市業字第玖捌壹號
定　　　價　新臺幣七二〇元

一 九 八 八 年 十 二 月 全 集 校 訂 版
二 〇 二 二 年 六 月 全 集 校 訂 版 二 刷